PLAYS AND PLAYWRIGHTS

2007

edited and with an introduction by

Martin Denton

18 February 2007

Dearest Jewel –

Thank you for the passion,
the pressure,
and
the praise .

Your ex-boyfriend, forever friend, and
endless admirer,

Stanly .

Published by The New York Theatre Experience, Inc.
P.O. Box 1606, Murray Hill Station, New York, NY 10156
www.nyte.org
email: info@nyte.org

ISBN 978-0-9670234-9-6
ISSN 1546-1319

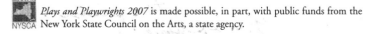

Plays and Playwrights 2007 is made possible, in part, with public funds from the New York State Council on the Arts, a state agency.

NYCULTURE *Plays and Playwrights 2007* is also made possible, in part, with public funds from the New York City Department of Cultural Affairs.

Plays and Playwrights 2007 is also made possible, in part, by support from the Peg Santvoord Foundation.

Book and cover designed by Nita Congress

PERMISSIONS

TABLE OF CONTENTS

FOREWORD

John Clancy

When I first met Martin Denton years ago in an auto-repair-shop-turned-performance space on the Lower East Side where I used to work, I didn't realize I was meeting a patron saint.

See, Martin looks more like an accountant. Which makes sense, since that's exactly what he was up until about ten years ago. And not just a guy in an office somewhere running numbers, Martin was some kind of big-shot major accountant for the Marriott Corporation, ran their whole payroll or something. And then one day he saw that they were offering classes on this "Internet" thing that the kids were getting into and he signs up and one of the assignments is to put together a website and presto-chango "Martin's Guide to New York Theatre" appears on the web. A few years later, Martin's Guide becomes www.nytheatre.com, Martin quits Marriott and with his mom Rochelle moves up to New York and we all end up standing around an auto-repair-shop-turned-performance space talking about some crazy-ass play we just saw.

I've had the privilege and the pleasure of talking with Martin about innumerable crazy-ass plays since. You have to understand that Martin sees *everything*. It's like there are nine of him. And then he writes about them, beautifully, and talks about them with passion and honesty and insight and every year he publishes a collection of them. And this is what makes him the patron saint of the unpublished playwright, of the unknown theatre company, of the next generation of American theatre artists.

So the next time you're on the road and you end up at a Marriott and something's wrong with the bill, you might consider letting it slide. After all, they lost one of their best guys. But we got Martin.

ACKNOWLEDGMENTS

It has been a great pleasure to bring the scripts in *Plays and Playwrights 2007* from eleven different New York City stages to these 400-plus pages. And that's largely because it has enabled me to work with the many talented people who made this book possible. I am proud and privileged to acknowledge their contributions here.

First and foremost are the playwrights themselves, who have graciously agreed to include their works in this volume; in alphabetical order: Brendon Bates, Chad Beckim, bluemouth inc. (Stephen O'Donnell, Sabrina Reeves, Lucy Simic, and Richard Windeyer), Andy Chmelko, James Comtois, Ashlin Halfnight, Boo Killebrew, Taylor Mac, Bryn Manion, Stan Richardson, and Tom Rowan. Thank you all for your talent and generosity.

Second, the friends, donors, and colleagues who provide unwavering support for The New York Theatre Experience, Inc.'s publication program: the New York State Council for the Arts, the New York City Department of Cultural Affairs, the Peg Santvoord Foundation, and Bev Willey, to whom we are grateful for financial support; and Gyda Arber, Arthur Aulisi, Michael Baron, Janine Barris, P. Seth Bauer, Doug Brandt, Steve Caporaletti, Barnaby Carpenter, Hamilton Clancy, John Clancy, Nita Congress, Calder Corey, Cary Curran, Kevin Doyle, Alec Duffy, Christopher Eaves, Ginger Eckert, Philip Emeott, Tim Errickson, John C. Fitzmaurice, Josh Fox and International WOW Company, Chris Gentile, Christine Goodman, Steven Gridley, Christian Haines, Jack Halpin, David Hanbury, Jack Hanley, Vanessa Hidary, Richard Hinojosa, Allen Hubby and the staff of Drama Book Shop, Scott Hudson, Catherine Jhung, Jack Judson, Erich Jungwirth, Aida Lembo, Michael Lew, Robert Lyons, Kelly McAllister, Maria McConville, Timothy McCracken, Eric McNaughton, Nina Mehta, Scott Miller, Arian Moayed, Paul Newport, Sean O'Hagan, Adele Pichon, Alix Price, Deepa Purohit and Sanjit DeSilva, Michael Puzzo, Stan Richardson, Eugene Rohrer, Carmen Roman, Trav S.D., Ragini Shah, Thom Sibbitt, Alyssa Simon, Saviana Stanescu, Margie Stokley, Sara Thigpen, Jessica Warner, Amy Laird Webb, Sidney Williams, Sam Younis, and the late Glyn O'Malley, all of whom made possible two amazing public events celebrating *Plays and Playwrights 2006.*

Third, the people who helped me find this year's plays: Pete Boisvert, Tim Errickson, Roi "Bubi" Escudero, Matt Freeman, David Fuller, Elena K. Holy, James David Jackson, Judith Jarosz, Morgan Jenness, Ron Lasko, Robin Reed, John Gould Rubin, Josh Sherman, Melanie Sylvan, and the members of CollaborationTown. Thanks for guiding me to these remarkable plays and/or playwrights, thus making this book happen.

Fourth, Michael Criscuolo, who contributed the bios and assisted in compiling the appendix, among many other invaluable tasks (with more to come): I am very grateful to have you on the *Plays and Playwrights* team.

Fifth, two very special people without whom these anthologies would not exist: my mother, Rochelle Denton, whose tireless efforts, sage advice, and wise perspective keep NYTE and me afloat; and my sister, Nita Congress, who gives so fully of her time and talent to edit and design this book—the only person who could possibly do justice, year after year, to the artists and impulses represented here.

Sixth, perhaps whimsically (but perhaps not): Logan and Briscoe, who watched over the editing process with the concentration and stillness that can only be achieved by Siamese cats.

Beginning with *Plays and Playwrights for the New Millennium* back in 2000, we've published nineteen plays that appeared in the New York International Fringe Festival, making that high-energy annual affair far and away the most prolific source of scripts for this series. By happy coincidence, FringeNYC and nytheatre.com, the website I founded and edit, both celebrated their tenth anniversaries this year. We are grateful for the terrific theatre that FringeNYC brings us every year, and the smart and talented artists it introduces us to. *Plays and Playwrights 2007* is dedicated to all the folks who make FringeNYC happen, and especially to Elena K. Holy, the festival's producing artistic director, for fellowship and support that seem to strengthen and deepen every year.

INTRODUCTION

Martin Denton

Plays and Playwrights 2007, the eighth volume in our annual series of new works from the ever-burgeoning and expanding indie
theatre scene, contains eleven plays that couldn't be more different
from one another. Yet they have a great deal in common. Most
obviously, they all premiered in New York City between September 2005 and September 2006 (though a couple of them actually
had world premieres before that, one of them in Canada back in
2000). They're all dazzlingly contemporary, addressing significant
issues such as the war in Iraq and the scary booming world trade
in child sex slaves, and tracking social attitudes about topics as
up-to-the-minute as the alienating effects of the Internet and other
high-tech "connectivity" and our accelerating cultural obsession
with celebrity and fame. And of course they're really good; these
plays all work brilliantly in performance and deserve to be seen
again and again on stages around the world.

These eleven plays also reflect the evolving landscape of indie theatre
in the way they were developed. Three of the pieces in *Plays and
Playwrights 2007* came out of the New York International Fringe
Festival: *Kiss and Cry* by Tom Rowan originated in the 2004 Fringe-
NYC and then went on to a full-blown engagement at Theater Ten
Ten a year and a half later; Brendon Bates's *Corps Values* and Ashlin
Halfnight's *Diving Normal* both debuted at the 2006 festival. Bates
and Halfnight are both winners (for earlier works) of FringeNYC's
playwriting award; they've smartly utilized the Fringe as a nurturing
environment to hone their craft, with the results apparent later in this
volume. The HOT! Festival, the long-running summertime celebration of queer performance at Dixon Place, is the source of the fourth
of this year's plays, Stan Richardson's *Another Brief Encounter*.

1

Six of the remaining seven plays of *Plays and Playwrights 2007* come from theatre companies—tight, close-knit collectives of artists who collaborate using various structures and formats to create new work that is uniquely their own. This is exemplified by the Canadian-American hybrid bluemouth inc., who made a sensational New York debut with *LENZ*; the Long Island City-based troupe Aisling Arts, whose co-founder Bryn Manion is the author of *Convergence*; CollaborationTown, the energetic group of Boston University grads who gave us Boo Killebrew's *They're Just Like Us*; and Partial Comfort Productions, a young company now based in Midtown's Theatre Row and represented here by Chad Beckim's *'nami*. James Comtois is the artistic director of Nosedive Productions and worked with his longtime collaborators in that company to create *The Adventures of Nervous-Boy*. And Andy Chmelko, who is an associate producer at Bubi Escudero's ETdC Projects' Performance Art and New Media Theatre Experimental Creative Lab, joined forces with rising young Impetuous Theater Group for *Office Sonata*, a most fortuitous collaboration.

Rounding out this year's collection is the singular Taylor Mac, whose *Red Tide Blooming* premiered at P.S. 122, where it was commissioned under the auspices of the first-ever Ethyl Eichelberger Award. Mac's work bridges musical theatre and performance art in a dizzyingly direct fashion: call it, maybe, NeoRidiculous—at once a nod backward to the origins of off-off-Broadway and a leap forward acknowledging new styles of individual and collaborative indie theatre-making.

This book celebrates the ways, both traditional and innovative, that playwrights and other artists are working together to make theatre that's resonant and relevant, timely, and in and of the here and now. Read on and meet 2007's plays and playwrights.

In September 2005, I got an email inviting me to see the New York debut of a company from Toronto called bluemouth. What really piqued my interest was the fact that this show, *LENZ*, was to be staged in three rooms of a small hotel called Ye Olde Carlton Arms, located on East 25th Street in Manhattan.

When audience members arrived, they were told to select a random key from a big bowl. Attached to each key was a tag listing three rooms in sequence, like this: "Room 9D – Room 14B – Room 1D." This list designated the order you would see the three components of *LENZ*. There are three possible sequences, each of which yields a different experience: *LENZ* is a mystery, and the fact that each of the members of your party may be gathering the clues in a different order makes the overall happening all the more intriguing.

At the heart of *LENZ* is the story of Jacob Lenz (a character in a story by George Buchner that is the inspiration for this piece). His sister Iris, whom we meet in Room 9D, tells us this about him:

> I am my brother's keeper. *(Lies on the floor, gestures toward the fan.)* A man walks into a police station and confesses to a murder committed prior to his birth. *(Walks over to the dresser and takes a photo out of the top drawer. She turns on a small bedside lamp and looks at the photo under the light.)* How would I know this person I was looking for, my brother? I now had the vague description of a bearded homeless man hanging around Times Square panhandling for change.

LENZ hooks you in each of its three remarkable scenes, which are a monologue delivered by Iris, a film whose dialogue is mostly in French, and an environmentally staged one-man show featuring Lenz himself. The four versatile artists who comprise bluemouth—Stephen O'Connell, Sabrina Reeves, Lucy Simic, and Richard Windeyer—combine consummate acting with multimedia wizardry to make their play a completely immersive event. The experience of *LENZ* is dramatic in the traditional sense, but what's genuinely thrilling about it is actually *doing* it: *LENZ* exists in the intersection between the active observer and the actively observed.

bluemouth followed *LENZ* with *What the Thunder Said* (July 2006), staged in a big empty room on the ground floor of a downtown Manhattan office building. Itself part of an epic trilogy called *Something About a River*, this work continued bluemouth's exploration of theatre as a fully participatory (though not necessarily interactive) event, requiring its audiences to be entirely present in ways that most plays and musicals only aspire to.

A few years ago, I saw a short play called *The Zaks Complex*, by a young man named Andy Chmelko. It depicted a battle between two high-powered corporate executives whose egos won't allow them to give way and walk past one another in a corridor.

Chmelko took this delicious idea and combined it with a number of other sharply observed details of modern corporate life to create *Office Sonata*, a very funny play that will resonate with anyone who's ever worked in one of the ubiquitous, cubicle-laden offices of a large American company. Set in a mega-corporation called

Empie Advertising Agency, *Office Sonata* tells the story of an ordinary fellow named Kyle who just wants to do his job right and get ahead. Surrounding him are a bunch of outsized characters who nevertheless ring precisely true: Meghan, an actress who works at Empie to subsidize her career; Martin, a prototypical slacker; Marisa and Lester, the aforementioned two executives with Zaks Complex; and many others.

What makes *Office Sonata* special is the keen satiric eye Chmelko turns to the everyday: all of us have surfed the Internet on company time, but we hope and pray to never cause the outlandish ruckus that Martin does here when he pays what he thinks is a harmless visit to a porn site. The institutionalization of corporate soullessness seems particularly irksome to the playwright, as demonstrated here:

> MEGHAN: You're right Kyle, I don't! But that doesn't mean these people can treat me like a second-class citizen and then expect me to believe that it's helping me in some twisted way! God, between the finger-flippers and the human centrifuges...and there's even a rumor going around that they're bringing the Blame Lottery back.
>
> KYLE: The Blame Lottery?
>
> MEGHAN: Something they discontinued not long after I started here. If one of the really big execs made any kind of huge mistake that could ruin their lives...they put the names of everyone beneath them into one of those lottery machines...the ones that spit the balls out? And whoever's name came up took the blame for the executive, no matter what they did.

Chmelko's director Jason Zimbler thought outside the box (to use a bit of trendy corporate-speak) to stage *Office Sonata* as a high-energy circus of a play, with Internet sites literally brought to life on stage (and Chmelko has a few tricks up his sleeve to make office technology much more vivid than usual). This is as contemporary as comedy got this season; I expect theatres all over the country will want to mount this delicious paean to corporate culture.

Long before Douglas Carter Beane's *The Little Dog Laughed* took its satiric swipe at the so-called "taboo" of gay movie stars, Tom Rowan's *Kiss and Cry* weighed in on the same topic with much more serious sense of purpose. *Kiss and Cry* tells the story of Stacy and Fiona—respectively, a young world champion figure skater on his way to the Olympics and a rising movie actress—and how they become America's sweethearts. They meet, in the play's first scene, at a party where they instantly hit it off. A photographer snaps a picture of them as they get into Fiona's waiting limousine, and immediately the rumor mill gets to work. Soon—with the active participation of both parties, especially the ambitious Fiona—the country has fallen in love with this glamorous young couple. What we know, but the rest of the country doesn't, is that both Fiona and Stacy are gay, and their so-called romance is a huge publicity stunt.

Rowan doesn't treat this story satirically, but finds the truth in it instead. He also doesn't sensationalize it, taking his play in an unexpected direction in its second act so that instead of merely being a thought piece about cultural homophobia, it becomes ultimately a meditation on what it costs artists to make art they can be proud of—and what it costs an individual to be the person he or she can be proud of.

Kiss and Cry was beautifully staged by Kevin Newbury and featured an excellent ensemble, led by Julie Leedes and David Lavine as Fiona and Stacy and, in a breakout performance, Nell Gwynn as Lauren, Fiona's partner and the play's conscience:

> LAUREN: Why should I go see a movie designed expressly to get teenaged suburban heterosexuals to spend more money in shopping malls?
>
> FIONA: Oh I don't know. Because you love me?
>
> LAUREN: And therefore I don't need to see you merchandised.
>
> FIONA: *(Munching on her breakfast.)* And yet you're going to go spend an evening nibbling cheese and avoiding wine and looking at "installations" Dina put together out of old broken toys?
>
> LAUREN: The difference being that that's her lifeblood. Your movie you did for the money. Which yes, we all have to do. But I don't ask you to come down to the bookstore and watch me run a cash register.

The social pressures that drove, say, Representative Mark Foley to live deeply in the closet are the same ones Rowan explores so incisively in *Kiss and Cry*. These are timely issues that merit serious, as opposed to merely flippant or parodic, treatment in the drama.

They're Just Like Us is one of two plays in this book to confront head-on the increasingly alienated high-tech culture of young urban adults. The Internet, cell phones, iPods, PDAs, and so on—devices all designed to make communication easier—seem instead to make connection more and more impossible. At the same time, blogs and reality TV allow any of us to become stars, if only momentarily, as the world moves closer and closer to Andy Warhol's famous prediction. The four twentysomethings at the heart of this very funny, very moving play—Jen, Frank, Gene, and Ann—exemplify the paradox. Their craving for company manifests itself in an obsessive desire for attention; significantly, they never stop long enough to actually find what they need:

ANN: Hey, Frank!

FRANK: Ann, where you off to?

ANN: I have this thing—but I saw you from across the street and thought I'd say "hey" real quick!

FRANK: I gotta go, too, but I just saw Gene.

ANN: Where has he been?

FRANK: I don't know, he didn't say.

ANN: What?

…

ANN: He's always been a bit of a mystery.

FRANK: You think?

ANN: Oh, yeah.

FRANK: Yeah, I guess he is.

ANN: Shit, I gotta go!

FRANK: *(Looks at his watch.)* Me too—I'll call you!

ANN: Definitely call me!

The rhythms of these characters' existences are perfectly captured by playwright Boo Killebrew, who shrewdly never shows us these people anywhere other than in public places, and always in passing. Their ambitious but empty lives are contrasted in *They're Just Like Us* with a pair of people who actually are famous—a hip-hop star named Biz and a TV/film actress named Beth—and another pair, who aren't—Beth's boyfriend Richard and a teenager named Marty. Together, the inhabitants of this play's high-stakes, high-energy urban environment paint a telling portrait of the transformations taking place in America right under our noses.

They're Just Like Us was presented by CollaborationTown, one of the New York indie theatre scene's smartest young companies. In just three years, beginning with *This Is a Newspaper* at the 2003 New York International Fringe Festival and continuing with such works as *The Trading Floor* (2004) and *The Astronomer's Triangle* (2005), they've demonstrated that their highly collaborative approach—group members variously write, direct, produce, act, design, and work behind the scenes, depending on the project—can be astonishingly fruitful. Killebrew and her comrades in CTown are just at the beginning of very promising careers. It will be exciting to see what they do next.

The same can absolutely be said for Aisling Arts, the company behind *Convergence*. Founded by Bryn Manion and Wendy Remington, this emerging troupe is based in Long Island City, Queens (and thus *Convergence* has the distinction of being the first play in the *Plays and Playwrights* series to have debuted in that borough, which is becoming a nexus for indie theatre). 2006 was a banner year for Aisling Arts; in addition to *Convergence*, they presented a fine revival of Synge's *The Playboy of the Western World* as well as Manion's new twist on *The Beggar's Opera*, *Imminent, Indeed*, which made a splash at FringeNYC.

Convergence is the final play in a trilogy, collectively titled *Force*, that also includes *Wanderlust* and *Threshold*. While the three pieces definitely work together, each is intended to be an independent evening of theatre. *Convergence* contains a number of interwoven stories: a war correspondent named Jack Kavanagh temporarily leaves his wife to search for an old contact he knew when he was covering the conflict in Kosovo; Jack's wife, Ann, visits her family home in Vermont and encounters an old flame; Ann's brother, Rob, forms an attachment to a young woman named Sara who is obsessed by tornadoes; a man named Hal loses his wife, Lotte, who one day simply picks up his wallet and car keys and disappears.

Linkages beyond the obvious ones pop in and out of these disparate stories, demonstrating the inextricable (and inexplicable) ways that human connections ebb and flow. Characters in one part of the play share dreams or realities with characters they've never met from other sections; as the title portends, lives and ideas and themes flow together and cohere as this epic-within-an-epic (*Convergence* spans five acts) progresses. One of the things I particularly love about this play is that, even when it's all over, many questions remain unanswered. That's like life; it marks Manion as a mature playwright, well in command of her craft.

Manion directed a startlingly spare, fluid production of *Convergence* at the New York Irish Center in what looked very much like a converted apartment. The bare bones elements of theatre—words and actors—accomplish everything in this play, taking us on unexpected journeys and introducing us to a remarkable array of characters:

BRIAN: What is she doing? Why is she holding her breath?

JACK: *(To KATARINA'S SISTER.)* Why does she do this?

KATARINA'S SISTER: Oooooooh, American.

(She moves to KATARINA and whispers into her ear.)

JACK: My brother would like to know why she does this?

KATARINA'S SISTER: Why not?

Postmodern musicals have become a pervasive part of the landscape in the past decade or so, from *Urinetown* to this season's Canadian import, *The Drowsy Chaperone*. But nothing has really jolted the musical out of its complacency the way that, say, *Hair* or *Company* did thirty-five years ago—nothing, that is, until Taylor Mac's envelope-pushing *Red Tide Blooming*. Here, at long last, is a musical that's authentically subversive and enormously entertaining and that includes some incisive political and social commentary to boot.

Following the Ridiculous Theater model of Charles Ludlam and others (including Ethyl Eichelberger, in whose honor Mac was commissioned to write the show in the first place), iconic forms are fitted out with as transgressively inappropriate content as possible: a vaguely *Wizard of Oz*-type journey is undertaken by a green-skinned hermaphrodite named Olukon, who encounters a bizarre coterie of self-described freaks and other characters, including Vice President Cheney's wife and an all-powerful construct/being called The Collective Conscious that is portrayed by a green sweater. Musical numbers are burlesques of every valid description. Theatrical tricks, from puppetry to masks to Brechtian fourth-wall-bashing songs, are employed, constantly keeping the audience on its toes. There are moments in *Red Tide Blooming* that are actually shocking and even one or two that are scary. That's how powerful this piece is.

Consider for example, this song, which introduces one of the play's key "Establishment" figures, compromised golden boy weatherman Collin Clement:

I HAVE EVERYTHING ANYONE COULD EVER WANT

FAME AND FORTUNE, BEAUTIFUL GOLDEN LOCKS

I AM THE WEATHERMAN FOR THE LOCAL ISLAND NEWS

I HAVE MUSCLES, I HAVE SMOOTH SKIN

I CAN AFFORD THE VEGETABLE TANNING SPRAY

I'M THE STATE HERO, I PROVIDE THE PEOPLE WITH THE OBVIOUS

This number comes in the middle of the show's pièce de résistance, a dark, vitriolic sequence set in Clubland, an apocalyptic vision of mainstreamed outré culture so dark that it makes Sam Mendes's version of *Cabaret* feel like Disneyland.

Mac, who directed and starred in *Red Tide Blooming*, proves incontrovertibly here that theatre can still shake up an audience: this show was designed to make people feel a little bit uncomfortable. The nudity, profanity, and other forms of vulgarity in this show are presented with such forthright naïveté that they actually begin to mean something again.

Mac also proved himself a theatrical force to be reckoned with. He was seemingly everywhere in 2006, touring his one-man show, *The Be(a)st of Taylor Mac* (including engagements at the Public Theater in New York), bringing his unique gender-bending performance art persona to audiences around the world.

James Comtois's *The Adventures of Nervous-Boy*, like *They're Just Like Us*, explores the contemporary urban landscape, where hyperconnectivity seems to yield noise and alienation rather than meaningful communication. The eponymous hero of this horror show-cum-modern-day-comedy-of-manners is a young man who finds himself not quite able to click with the people and things around him in the Big City. His anomie alarms him, but he's not quite sure what to do to reignite his fuse. He fears that something terrible may happen and that it may just be his own doing when it does.

The characters who parade through this dizzying joyride of a one-act rival *Red Tide Blooming*'s over-the-top denizens in their eccentricity. Yet they're all undeniably recognizable and familiar (which is one of the reasons that *Nervous-Boy* may be said to cross the line from satire to a kind of horror tale: the world really is pretty much the way Comtois presents it to us). Right at the outset, the playwright demonstrates his talent for capturing the pulse of interactions in today's America:

> *(He [NERVOUS-BOY] is now in line at a food stand manned by a SERVER. A GUY ON A CELL PHONE is in front of him.)*
>
> GUY ON CELL PHONE: *(To the person on the phone.)* Hold on. *(To SERVER.)* Uh…hold on. *(To the phone.)* Hold on a sec. *(To SERVER.)* Hold…hold on. *(To phone.)* Uhhhhhh…hold on. *(To SERVER.)* Hold on. *(Etc. Keeps going like that.)*

As the play progresses, we meet office dweebs, weird people in bars, performance artists, a stripper, a skank, a very scary dude named Asmodeus, and three inarticulate acquaintances of Nervous-Boy's whom Comtois has christened Grog, Phht, and Hrmph. There's also a vague ray of hope in the person of Nervous-Boy's sort-of-girlfriend Emily; will she be able to put down her cell phone long enough to have a real conversation with him?

The Adventures of Nervous-Boy, presented by Comtois's company Nosedive Productions with expert direction by his longtime collaborator Pete Boisvert, was something of a sleeper hit in the summer of 2006, extending its run a couple of times and generating a bit of positive buzz for this talented young playwright. It deserved to: the design and staging were superb, as was the cast, which included Comtois himself in a smallish role and was headed by another playwright, Mac Rogers, who was delightfully ingratiating as the tense title character.

Stan Richardson had plays presented in two of New York's major theatre festivals in the summer of 2006: *The Children*, a musical he cowrote with composer Hal Goldberg, was part of the New York Musical Theatre Festival, while *And/Or*, a program of four short plays, was featured in the HOT! Festival at Dixon Place. *Another Brief Encounter* was part of *And/Or*, and offers firm evidence that a major playwriting talent I've been watching develop for several years now has reached maturity.

This, the shortest of the plays in this volume (it runs perhaps thirty to thirty-five minutes), is among the most complex. Richardson does two things here: he parodies the famous Noel Coward-David Lean film *Brief Encounter*, and, by setting it in contemporary Chelsea on Gay Pride Day, he also scrutinizes and/or satirizes aspects of a gay/youth culture that may sometimes feel too centered around Starbucks and self.

Actually, Richardson accomplishes a third thing in *Another Brief Encounter* as well, something he may be less conscious of: he places himself, or at least a stand-in for his own artistic temperament, in a supporting role in the play, with the result that the piece can be viewed both as a clever and brittle observation from without and as a more heartfelt, emotional observation from within.

The story line itself is fairly simple: a young man, called 1, has a chance encounter with a romantic stranger (2) and possibly jeopardizes his long-term relationship with his partner (6). Richardson intends for 2 and 6 to be played by the same actor, suggesting that one "moral" of the story may be that each of us has one and only one soulmate; I leave that for you to decide when you read the play.

Richardson fills the piece with colorful characters and quirky details, the most notable of which is a proper English lady reminiscent (not at all coincidentally) of Celia Johnson in the Coward film, who speaks 1's innermost thoughts. And almost in passing, he packs in, with deft economy, some fairly profound musings on some big themes, such as this, spoken by 5, the writer character in the play:

> I know it's not very political, but I think that for people to actually *be* political, they have to determine first how or *IF* they want to interact in the world...Politics are about what we fight for, right? But if you feel unlovable, why bother fighting?...People who feel unlovable don't need newspapers. We need *fairy tales.*

Few American plays in 2006 addressed the issue of the war in Iraq, and almost none did so with the raw honesty of Brendon Bates's powerful drama *Corps Values*. This tight, emotional play is rooted in the conflict between a father and son, one of the mainstays of American drama from O'Neill forward. And in its recognition that all acts are inherently political, it hearkens to the socially conscious work of Arthur Miller.

Corps Values takes place in the kitchen of a remote house in western Pennsylvania, where Wade Taylor, a Vietnam vet with a drinking problem, lives by himself. His wife was just killed in an auto accident, and his son, Casey, has returned home on leave from a tour of duty in Iraq; like his father, Casey is a U.S. Marine.

As the play begins, we learn that Casey has disappeared, apparently having gone AWOL. One of Wade's comrades from Vietnam, a career Marine named Kyle Adamson, has arrived at the house to investigate. In flashbacks that are skillfully interwoven with the forward action, Bates reveals what happened to Casey and, in particular, what transpired when father and son had a fateful confrontation. For Casey had told his dad that he intended to go AWOL:

> CASEY:...I'm not going back.
>
> WADE: Pardon?
>
> CASEY: I'm not returning to duty.
>
> *(Pause. WADE laughs.)*

WADE: You have to go back. You got six months left.

CASEY: I know.

WADE: You got an entire Company counting on you.

CASEY: Half my Company has been wiped out.

WADE: Well, the *other half* is counting on you.

CASEY: I'm writing a letter to each member of my platoon, explaining myself, asking for their forgiveness…

WADE: What?

CASEY: Encouraging them to do the same.

WADE: Encouraging them to do what?

CASEY: To walk away from the war.

WADE: Have you lost your mind?

CASEY: I'd rather rot in jail than…

WADE: *(Interrupting him.)* What are you saying?

CASEY: I'm saying I'm done with this war.

Part tantalizing mystery story, part gripping family drama, part searing indictment of a culture and seemingly ceaseless cycle of war, *Corps Values* explodes in one of the most harrowing and exciting climaxes seen on any stage last season. I leave it to you to discover on these pages; it's a play that demands to be seen and heard, and Bates is a playwright who is going to leave his mark on American drama.

If *Corps Values* is the most overtly political play in this collection, *Diving Normal* is perhaps the most blisteringly intimate. It's about a young man named Fulton Ditmer, a reasonably successful graphic novelist, single and living alone in New York. When we meet him, he's just had a chance encounter with Dana, a girl he had a crush on in high school. Now, about a decade later, she barely remembers him, but he's in seventh heaven, certain that he can ignite the romance that never was.

And he does: Dana, whose life has gotten more and more out of control following a car accident in which her mother was seriously injured, likes the stability, security, and, yes, sentimentality that Fulton provides. She also likes, against the odds and probably her better judgment, Fulton's quirky neighbor Gordon, a librarian whom Fulton describes as "harmless": he's endearing but odd, not very good in social situations. Gordon falls in love with Dana at first sight, and complications ensue.

The author of *Diving Normal*, Ashlin Halfnight, distinguishes himself by constantly surprising us and constantly keeping things real. Gordon, for example, could easily turn into a Kramer sort of character (from *Seinfeld*), but Halfnight never lets us lose sight of the ache that's underneath an admittedly comical surface:

> GORDON: I go every Sunday to the YMCA to take my diving lessons. I used to go to church, but now I go to the pool. *(Beat.)* Today is Sunday.
>
> DANA: Yes. It is.
>
> GORDON: Yes. I go *every* Sunday, except in April when the pool is closed for cleaning.
>
> DANA: You—um—what kind of dives do you do?
>
> GORDON: Head first. *(Beat.)* And other kinds. *(Beat.)* I have green swimming trunks.

Halfnight has remarkable control over his characters, and he gives them each singular, distinctive voices These beautifully written characters are roles that actors will want to play; designed economically for just three people and a single set, *Diving Normal* should have a long and healthy life in theatres, where the tangled web that evolves among Fulton, Dana, and Gordon can be spun and respun. I should mention that the original players, Josh Heine, Eliza Baldi, and Jayd McCarty, set a very high standard for subsequent performances of this play, under the thoughtful direction of Mary Catherine Burke; they helped make *Diving Normal* one of the breakout hits of FringeNYC 2006.

The genesis of *'nami* is in the devastating tsunami that hit Indonesia and other Indian Ocean nations in late 2004. Subsequently, a trade in human beings began to flourish: orphans were being kidnapped and sold as sex slaves to Westerners in record numbers.

From this awful circumstance, playwright Chad Beckim created a compelling tragedy about two married couples who are neighbors in a low-rent apartment house in Queens. Harry and Lil have been together a long time and have been through a lot, including a recent episode involving her fragile mental health. He's a cabbie struggling to make ends meet. She desperately wants a baby. Next door are Keesha, a young black woman who works at a nearby McDonald's, and Roachie, whom the playwright indicates is black or Latino, a one-time hoodlum Keesha is trying to rehabilitate as best she can.

What none of these people realize, as *'nami* begins, is that their landlord Donovan has gotten hold of an Indonesian girl and he is about to sell her for a great deal of money. No one emerges unscathed from this terrible act.

Beckim's play is superbly plotted, his characters artfully drawn, and the various themes he weaves through the piece well articulated and important. Lil becomes convinced that she's hearing a baby crying in the apartment next door; we know that Harry knows that she's mentally unstable and obsessive about her childlessness. Is she crazy? What is she supposed to be do when the person closest to her in the world won't—can't—believe her?

> LIL: I could hear her, Harry. I could hear her crying. All night. She wouldn't stop. I could hear her through the wall. She was crying so hard, Harry. She wouldn't stop—
>
> HARRY: I don't—Who—What—What happened—
>
> LIL: But then she did stop! Like someone made her. She just stopped. But when I went to pee, I could hear them talking through the hole from where you hung the picture so I made it a little bigger—just a little bit—and it crumbled a little so I pulled at it a little more and it got bigger and bigger and before I knew it the whole wall was broken but I could hear them, perfectly, Harry! I could hear them talking—Oh God!
>
> HARRY: What are you talking about? Look at me! LIL! *Look at me! (Rises.)* I have to call the doctor.

Beckim imbues the play's other primary relationship, between Roachie and Keesha, with equal urgency. Thanks to the tight script, a superlative cast, and exquisitely economical direction by John Gould Rubin, the original production of *'nami* proved to be a taut, resonant thriller that gripped the audience until its end.

'nami is the kind of script that deserves to be done over and over again; so are the other ten pieces printed on these pages. One of our main objectives in putting this collection together is to encourage producers and theatre artists all over the world to mount these plays, not only because their playwrights are worthy, but because they're smart, viable, eminently producible works of theatre. As you will discover when you read *Plays and Playwrights 2007*, American drama is as vibrant and vital as it was in the so-called "golden ages" of the 1920s or '40s. Please spread the word about these extraordinary plays. I hope you enjoy reading them!

LENZ

bluemouth inc.

BLUEMOUTH INC. creates original and exciting site-specific interdisciplinary performances that engage both audience and artists into new forms of play. Founded in Montreal, Canada, in 1998 by Lucy Simic and Sabrina Reeves, the origins of the collective's aesthetic can also be traced back to Radix Theatre in Vancouver, another site-specific collective that Simic, Richard Windeyer, and Stephen O'Connell worked with in the early 1990s. Bluemouth draws its inspiration from such companies as Les Ballets C de la B in Belgium, De La Guarda in Argentina, The Wooster Group in New York, DV8 in London, and Pina Bausch in Germany. The company won a 2004 Dora Mavor Moore Award for Outstanding Production for *Something About a River*, a five-hour journey across downtown Toronto along the buried Garrison Creek. In May 2007, bluemouth will premiere their newest piece, *How Soon Is Now*, in Toronto as part of The Theatre Centre's site-specific spring season. They have also started working on a new project inspired by the 1930s Depression-era dance marathons.

STEPHEN O'CONNELL was raised in New Jersey. He has a BFA in modern dance from Rutgers University and an MFA in interdisciplinary art from Simon Fraser University, Vancouver. From 1990 to 1997, he was co-artistic director of Radix Theatre in Vancouver. His collaborations include experimental films which have been screened at the Vancouver International Film Festival, the American Dance Festival, and the Moving Pictures Festival in Toronto. He is also a co-curator of FREE FALL, a pan-Canadian festival of experimental performance hosted by The Theatre Centre in Toronto, and the co-artistic director of bluemouth inc. He lives in the East Village in New York City and waits tables.

SABRINA REEVES grew up in Massachusetts and graduated from Carnegie Mellon with a BFA in drama. Upon graduation she moved to New York, where she worked as an actor in film and theatre from 1990 to 1997 (some credits: *Big Night*, *The Misanthrope*, *My Children! My Africa!*, *Soul Food*). In 1997, she moved to Montreal, where she co-founded bluemouth inc. with Lucy Simic. Reeves is also a professional photographer/videographer who contributed to the War Child documentary *Musicians in the War Zone* and directed the David Usher video "My Way Out." She lives in New York City's East Village, with her husband and her daughter, Coco Aranya.

LUCY SIMIC grew up in Vancouver. She holds a BA in French literature with an extended minor in mathematics and modern dance from Simon Fraser University, Vancouver, and an MFA in playwriting from York University, Toronto. Her particular area of interest is the integration of text and movement. She has been creating performance pieces for close to ten years; in Vancouver as co-artistic director of Radix Theatre; as an independent artist in Montreal, where she co-founded bluemouth inc. before moving to Toronto; in London, England, in collaboration with Woodenhead Works and Sirius Productions; and most recently in New York City. Simic lives in the East Village and waits tables.

RICHARD WINDEYER was raised in Peterborough, Ontario. He has a BFA in music composition from Wilfred Laurier University and an MFA in interdisciplinary art from Simon Fraser University, Vancouver. He creates music, sound, and visuals for experimental theatre, radio, film, and integrated media projects. When not working with bluemouth inc., he collaborates with laptop trio Finger and the Open Ears Music Festival, and does the occasional solo project. His work has been heard across Canada, in Europe and the U.K., and on the Internet. Windeyer lives in Toronto, and teaches music composition at Wilfred Laurier University.

The U.S. premiere of *LENZ* was presented by bluemouth inc. on September 29, 2005, at Ye Olde Carlton Arms Hotel, New York City, with the following cast and credits:

Lenz .... Stephen O'Connell
Iris ....Sabrina Reeves

Crew: Eric Pelletier, Jean Jacques Quinsac, Lucy Simic, Robert Tremblay, Richard Windeyer, Christopher Taylor-Wright, Francoise Noury

Previous productions of *LENZ* were presented as follows:

Theatre La Chapelle, Montreal, Quebec, February 2000
Cast and crew: Elijah Brown, Stephen O'Connell, Eric Pelletier, Sabrina Reeves, Lucy Simic, Richard Windeyer

The Gladstone Hotel, Toronto, Ontario, May 2001
Cast and crew: Stephen O'Connell, Eric Pelletier, Sabrina Reeves, Lucy Simic, Richard Windeyer, Christopher Taylor-Wright

The Gladstone Hotel, Toronto, Ontario, October 2002
Cast and crew: Stephen O'Connell, Eric Pelletier, Jean Jacques Quinsac, Sabrina Reeves, Lucy Simic, Robert Tremblay, Richard Windeyer, Christopher Taylor-Wright, Francoise Noury

Some of the text written on the wall in Room 14B is from Brian Massumi, *A User's Guide to Capitalism and Schizophrenia: Deviations from Deleuze and Guattari* (Cambridge, MA: MIT Press, 1992).

Pierre Rivière's confession is from the original 1835 manuscript, as quoted by Michel Foucault in *I, Pierre Rivière, Having Slaughtered My Mother, My Sister, and My Brother…: A Case of Parricide in the 19th Century,* translated by Frank Jellinek (New York: Pantheon, 1975).

INTRODUCTION

LENZ was initially commissioned by Theatre La Chapelle in Montreal as part of the Mois Multi, a month-long program of inter-disciplinary performance in February 2000. This initial workshop of LENZ was created for a proscenium stage with a large scrim situated downstage separating the audience and performers. The scrim allowed for the super-imposition of film projections onto the performance area. The original text was inspired by the Georg Buchner short story, also entitled "LENZ," and was a response to the feelings of alienation experienced by a monolingual Anglo-phone living in French-speaking Canada.

Two years later, in the spring of 2001, *LENZ* was resurrected, and a second workshop was presented at the Gladstone Hotel in Toronto. Two new characters were added, and the piece moved from a stage performance to a performance installation in three separate rooms of a turn-of-the-century hotel. The audience was asked to randomly select keys from a container located in the lobby of the hotel. At-tached to the keychain was a list of numbers that determined the order in which individuals would see the rooms.

Each section ran twenty minutes in length and took place simul-taneously on different floors of the hotel. Couples were separated by chance and would cross paths during the course of the piece, leaving with a significantly different reading of the fractured nar-rative depending on the particular order they experienced.

Each room was able to accommodate a maximum of fifteen people for a total of forty-five people per performance. Two of the rooms contained live performances, and the third room housed a film installation that was projected onto a table covered with salt as the audience stood around the table listening to the binaural soundtrack from individual headphones.

LENZ had its premiere in fall 2002 as part of FREE FALL hosted by The Theatre Centre.

In fall 2005, *LENZ* was produced in New York City at Ye Olde Carlton Arms, a one-hundred-year-old hotel located on 25th Street in Gramercy Park.

ROOM 9D

One performer: IRIS. IRIS sits in an open window, looking out past the fire escape onto the city below. She sings "Country Roads," ending with the line "Driving down the road I get a feeling that I should have been home/Yesterday." She faces into the room.

I haven't spoken to Lenz for a couple of years. It's not intentional. In fact I had planned on coming to the city a number of times recently, it's just that time has that way of sneaking up on you. When my parents finally called I think it was out of desperation.

(IRIS goes into the bathroom and turns on the water to draw a bath.)

They had lost touch with Jacob, that's his full name, Jacob Michael, but most people just call him Lenz, they hadn't heard from him in almost a year and they were worried.

(As the water runs, IRIS goes over and closes one window and then the other.)

At this point he had already been living on the street for almost six years. But my parents, well my folks aren't as young as they used to be and I think they just couldn't handle the stress anymore.

Anyway, last week a friend of our family spotted Jacob outside the Port Authority bus terminal panhandling for change. He was dirty, barefoot, the whole scene. This friend said he "looked bad." I'm not sure what relative scale he was speaking from, why last week's "bad" was any worse than last year's "bad" or five years ago or ten years ago's "bad" but…my parents were worried and that meant something.

(Physical gesture.)

I am my brother's keeper.

(Lies on the floor, gestures toward the fan.)

A man walks into a police station and confesses to a murder committed prior to his birth.

(Walks over to the dresser and takes a photo out of the top drawer. She turns on a small bedside lamp and looks at the photo under the light.)

How would I know this person I was looking for, my brother? I now had the vague description of a bearded homeless man hanging around Times Square panhandling for change.

(She shows the photo to an audience member, allowing him or her to hold it. She then takes it back and places it carefully on the edge of the rug and proceeds to roll up the rug around it, walk over to the door, and toss the rug out of the room, slamming the door behind it.)

When it comes to impending disaster there are always signs, you just have to look…to listen. I think some people are just better at denial than others. In this case, that would be my mother. She had it mastered, the fine art of, "Oh no dear, everything's fine, don't worry about us. Your father and I are super." So when I say they didn't know how to respond to Jacob what I'm saying is that it literally wasn't in their programming. They had no vocabulary for it. Do any of us? I don't know.

Whenever I think about it, though, I have to laugh. I mean okay, if he wets his bed or he doesn't come home or he shits on the kitchen floor, you can "straighten that boy right out!" But what could they possibly do at the sight of their only son dancing naked in Lincoln Center waving his red boots and singing "I'm the queen of rubies"?

And they were with their brand spanking new neighbors to top it off. On their way home from an evening of dinner at Elaine's and the latest John Guare play. Their friends thought this crazy guy was hysterical, and I'm sure they were right. Oh my God, picture it!…picture it? I've seen it, for Christ's sake!! Well, for them it saved an otherwise predictable evening. A tedious first act only to become moderately more engaging after the intermission. Mom and Dad, well they had no real opinion per se. But they did have these new neighbors who seemed to be very much "in the know" about all things cultural on the New York scene. And Mom and Dad certainly didn't want to give any indication that perhaps they didn't fit quite so neatly into this new neighborhood that they had pinched and saved to buy into. Of course they would love to go to Elaine's, it was their favorite! And a show, the perfect way to round out an evening. Mom always managed to slip into those facades a bit more comfortably than Dad.

Strangely though, they didn't seem to find the humor in the naked man under the fountain, even when the neighbor pointed to him during his grand finale when he pisses out of the fountain in a perfect arc, "Now *that's* a performance!"

(She screams abruptly, loudly, and reaches for her legs. And just as quickly as she began, she stops. Looking to the person next to her:)

The ride back to Jersey must have been unusually quiet.

Some people believe the day we're born and the day we die mark the beginning and the end of our one lifetime. They believe that we choose our lives and survive our fabrications. Through the haze we glimpse countless lives within this one,

label our deaths nostalgia, and a cheap lie threads the edges of our own design.

(Throughout the following: a physical vocabulary that grows out of the simple gesture of writing.)

When I first arrived I thought about taking a room at a boarding house or at the Chelsea Hotel or something classically down-and-out like that, Tom Waits-ish…I suppose some perverse inclination towards authenticity. I couldn't bear what I knew to be my borders: "good," "nice," and all the deadly four-letter words you never want to be called, the "make your parents proud" crisp starched "I stole a pack of Big Red from Woolworths when I was eight does that count for something?" kind of good girl.

That something fine that we're all given as an ante at the start of the game had been gradually whittled away by the crushing sameness, the predictability of my moves until I seemed to hold not even a few last tokens of a life. I think I'm in some interim purgatory; not without hope, not with hope, and not lucky enough to be numb. I know that I am guilty of imagining Jacob's life on the street to be thrilling and somehow glamorous. I'm jealous, I suppose that somewhere inside I had fantasized that when I got around to it, when it fit my schedule I would come for him and it would be just in the nick of time and he would see me and the milky clouds over his eyes would break and there would be my beautiful brother and he would say, "I miss you, you have saved me from my nightmare. I was taken by the wrong tribe, let's go together, you and me we'll start our own."

Infinitely, immeasurably, indescribably far from what I was to find in this, the city of dreams.

(She stands on the window ledge looking out at the city.)

Rivulets, trickling down the pane by my bed.

Reluctantly the neighborhood starts to wake.

My building houses five apartments. I don't know if they're all two-bedrooms, but ours is.

The couple in the apartment next to us works nine to five and drives a Camry.

When they leave I look at her stockinged legs and tightly pulled-back hair...we're in the stairs. I'm in my pajama bottoms and a windbreaker on my way to get milk. Her whole face smiles wide as if there's an "on" switch behind her head.

"Morning!" she says.

"Hi," I manage to muster.

She starts down the stairs. I can see from her profile as she rounds the landing that there's also an "off" switch. We neither one of us are liking the rain this morning.

They have a car but they take the bus to work. It's more practical.

(She goes directly to a woman near the door and explains:)

We were to be taken to our new tribe. He was absolutely sure of it, he would say, "I hear them coming, I hear them. Listen, Iris—you'll hear them too."

I never heard them, but they did come. They only wanted the first born. They only wanted the son.

(She goes toward the bathroom and then collapses on the floor.)

I read because I have no thoughts, because I have no feelings. Why try so hard and

get nowhere? Use force in situations that require tact? Retreat in defense? The fight-or-flight wires have gotten crossed, scaring away help and coddling the enemy. Who is the enemy? My ally? The friend to my foe? Make yourself happy. My, my. My head is crowded with talk, thinking, speaking fast that is incomprehensible. Wanting to speak so hard that he—I run out of breath. I'm terrible. Wandering familiar territory again and again, creating a deep rut. Back and forth back and forth turning the earth to shit. The towering shit closing in and touching the top of the trench until it all collapses and I have to spend the rest of the day digging my way back out. But it's the digging, the expending of vast amounts of energy that makes me happy! From this moment on my body will conform to such activity. Certain muscles will develop beyond proportion while others atrophy. Isn't that the nature of freedom? Dance is a released activity. It just takes so much effort to move effortlessly. It's not in my nature, I guess. I relax and the enemy within will have won. I may remain assured of my unhappiness. This is a comforting thought. Amongst this pattern of thoughts strung together to form this fabric, this piece of soul, a little of this, a little of that. Willy-nilly. Uncle Bill happy and round died of cancer while his car remained covered on the lake and Aunt Helen never spoke to us again after that, poor woman. Poor men, immigrating to a better strife on the opposite side of the coin. How sad. Sad for who? Sad for her or sad for me? I mourn myself, so save the effort for the dance.

(She opens the door to the room and leaves it ajar.)

I'm so mad and I don't know why. I'm mad because my shoes won't get a grip on the ground. I'm mad because the wind won't stop blowing in my face.

(She goes into the bathroom and closes the door behind her.)

ROOM 14B

One performer: LENZ. The audience enters, and LENZ is seated on the floor writing on the near wall with a penlight. Once the audience members have all arrived and the door has been closed, he turns the light out. He flashes the light at the opposite wall and then shuts it off immediately. In the darkness, he crosses the room and proceeds to write on the opposite wall with the penlight, while standing.

Words, words, words, books I chew. Right through. Dad said eating too fast wasn't good for you. It didn't allow you time to realize that you were full. Full of words.

(He turns out the penlight. He turns the light back on and traces a line down his head and torso with his glowing red thumb held over the tip of the penlight.)

The initial blow. The blow to her head. The joy of a prize as the treasured contents spill onto the floor. A moment cheated by the anticipation of its closure even before the joy has ended.

(He turns the penlight off, goes to the wall, and begins writing again.)

Beneath this rock you will find the solitary mole busy at work. Tunneling, mining, undermining. Designing to corrupt all that is good. He may appear strange, as would any creature deprived of light or a proper sleep. Ah, to sleep. Gently moving. Slowly moving ahead. Led by a conviction. Convinced of eventual daybreak.

(He pauses from his frantic writing. Briefly he falls off to sleep, and as he slowly drops to the floor, the light once again goes out. The light comes back on and he is seated on the floor with the penlight directed onto his torso.)

I could have chosen a different mode of transport to arrive at who I am. Gone a different direction to settle where I ought. But I did not. Over the course of this day, I have made decisions, been impacted by circumstance, exercised my will, moved, stalled, changed over and again in this normal, quote abnormal, abominable, abdominal world. You know what I mean? Today alone I changed my mind seven times in ten. I stayed in bed and in that decision alone changed the course of my entire life. As if I had a choice. This is the part where I usually like to sleep.

(He lies down on the floor, placing his head upon someone's lap.)

Earth. Day one. The plan. The plan of getting back to being a man. I haven't had what you would call a good week. Drooling at the kitchen table, falling fast asleep. This is a fluffy story. Or would you rather a horror story? There's a short circuit, so to speak, between what I feel and what you think. These are my boots, that are filled with the lead I call my feet, that prevent me from flying. Through the airways people can read my mind. Like a television wired for sound from a master control room out there with the plan, the plan to drive me crazy. This is the part where I definitely need some sleep. Day done. Nothing will ever be the same.

(He performs a bound arm movement, silhouetted by the penlight, that steadily moves up through his torso. He flicks the switch on the wall, illuminating a muted overhead light. From floor to ceiling, the walls are covered with the following text.)

I am the dying nomad, the model of absurdity, presenting to you my scrambled interior, as a resident of this state of bedlam. Rather than linger in the reflections of this world, I hold out to you a brick, a symbol of what has been used to erect monuments to reason and thrown through the windows of justice. What is the subject of this brick? The arm that throws it? The body connected to the arm? The brain encrusted in the body? A situation which brought the brain and body to such a juncture? All and none of the above. What is the object? The window? Your head? The institution? No? Ah, yes. A belief. The laws that shelter that belief? The class and power encrusted in that law? All and none of the above. What interests me is that the brick in its inherent usage is nothing but a set of circumstances at a volatile juncture. A vector. A point in time. A force moving through space at a given velocity in any given direction. An opportunity. An invitation. It is an action. Careful. Force is not to be confused with power. Power is merely the domestication of force. Force in its wild state arrives from nothingness to break restraint and open new vistas. Power on the other hand builds walls, while force creates revolution. I am the anti-Christ who has come down to you from the mountains to obliterate meaning. I am the savior destined to free us all from these illusions of truth.

(He is standing by the door and facing into the room with his arms stretched out in front of him.)

I met two birds circling in my teacup. One just below the other in perfect formation. Moving a course across the glazed surface. As I drink from the cup the tip of her wing sweetly touches the crack in my lower lip.

(We hear the amplified voice of Pierre Rivière coming from down the hall. LENZ stands silhouetted in the door frame, then steps out into the hallway and begins a flicking movement with his back to the audience.)

La Bête s'est éveillée*
Même si la nuit persiste
Ma faim, s'évapore
Un souvenir ou une prémonition
Un thème qui revient souvent
Qui vole mon souffle et se refuge dans mes
    poumons. Qui tente de refaire surface

---

*The beast has awoken
Yet the flight of night persists
I, hunger, evaporate
A memory or a premonition
A recurring dream that steals my breath and
    seeks shelter within my lungs
Trying to find its way back to
An event so painful
That it needs witnesses to exist
He is sent to me in my sleep
My portal was open and the pain searching
    for a container to rest
My shame is buried within a box
Stacked upon shelves of like boxes
Like a trembling child wrapped in white
    tissue paper
It somehow finds no place to hide
Separated, disoriented, continually shifting
    barriers turn and circle me
I have been imprisoned countless times in
    my sleep
And in my travels an empty vessel waiting
    to be filled
Every night by the senseless blows of hu-
    manity
I witness the truth in the eyes of the dying
So I perish every night and wake every
    morning
Closer to their pain and somehow further
    from my tenuous reality

un événement tellement douloureux
qui ne peux ressurgir sans témoins
Il m'est envoyé dans mon sommeil
Mon portail était ouvert à la douleur qui
    cherchait refuge
Ma honte est enterrée dans une boite,
    empilée sur des tablettes de boites
    semblables
Telle un enfant enveloppé dans du papier
    mouchoir et ne trouve aucune place
    pour se cacher
Séparé, désorienté, avec des barrières chan-
    geantes qui tourne et m'encercle
Je me suis fait emprisonné, poursuivi à
    maintes reprises dans mon sommeille
    et dans mes voyages
Il y a toujours un vaisseau en attente de
    se faire remplir par l'insensibilité de
    la race humaine
Je vois la vérité dans la face de la mor-
    talité
Donc je meurt a chaque nuit pour
    m'éveiller chaque matin
Plus proche de la douleur et en même
    temps, plus éloigné de ma triste
    réalité

*(He continues the flicking movement down
the hallway, gradually building in intensity. When he arrives at the end of the hall,
he reaches up and turns out the hall light.
He addresses the audience.)*

Oh what a pity. My sister beauty in
search of her beloved brother depravity.
What is she really after?

I moved into this room in the spring-
time, when this place looked a little
bit nicer than it does right now. In my
sickness and in my health, this building
which was once home to romance, filled
to capacity with lovers and poets, is now
prison to my misfortune. Night and day
I have knocked upon the doors that line
this hallway and my neighbors who I

hear about me day and night, nobody
would receive my call. Pierre Rivière
knocked upon my door one sleepless
night and I, desiring some diversion,
well I invited him in. We spoke casually
of many things and he, being well educated in the ways of men at their best and
worst, he began to show me that pain is
a very powerful place.

My sweet little sister. I pretend not to
notice her because it enables her to feel
special when I'm crazy. It enables her to
continue to ignore that what she's really
afraid of is her own mind. Skillfully she
calculates every single step, all the while
telling herself that it is me who needs
to be saved. Then she steps on a nerve
sending both of our lives tumbling into
a tailspin. And for what end? So I can be
dragged back to Jersey to wear the house,
the smile, and the suit? Oh how nice and
tidy that world would be where I would
take my medicine and sleep. And you
and I are beneficiaries of his violence.
Twins separated at birth born of events
greater than ourselves. I offer myself up
humbly. Eternally returning to the same
point in the circle of time where I lift
hammer and arm descending upon her
skull in crushing blows again and again
and again. A single act willed by me. A
copper coin soaked beneath my tongue.

*(He gradually makes his way down the hall
and through the audience.)*

I don't know what has come over me.
Something brighter and more alive than
anything I have felt in my entire life. And
when the flush passes. And believe me it
always does. The guilt that consumes me
is unbearable. I have done an unspeak-
able thing and I am sorry.

*(He ducks into a small passageway midway
down the long narrow hall and unscrews*

*all the light bulbs to create complete dark-
ness. He then begins manipulating three
individual headlights attached to various
parts of his body. A video projection of
multiple-layered time code is frantically
counting down from 3:00:00 minutes to
0:00:00 with amplified music filling both
ends of the hallway.)*

Wake up, wake up, the day is done. Lay
down the pick and pick up the gun.

This roof of rotten and roughing decay,
lot dealt.

Enough, enough, the time has come, lay
down you prick or pick up and run.

This roof of mud. My hole, my soul, my
testament to containment.

I am dying. Steal tummy fat and cold,
distended drum dragging upon the
belly yellow.

Wake up. The siren screams, crying for
the lost life. Death. Confront the life of
shame. Inhale. Digest. Then shit. Next
question. I've listened to what you have
to say and I disagree with your progno-
sis. There I sat at your side, listening to
every word. Hung upon syllable, swung
from vowel. Studied, stayed up night
after night, slept when you rest, woke
before you rose. There I sat at your feet
quietly waiting, watching, patience my
ally, pride my drug. Day passes to year,
year to generation, epoch, time infinite
and in this moment, I have a thought. A
rare insight when all that was presently
foreign becomes awash in clarity new.
The illusion no longer suiting this disfig-
ured frame drops from hip revealing the
essence of my humility. If I am unreason-
able then the world be my alibi. I invite
you to board this ship of fools floating
far adrift from these shores of reason. In
my head I hold the key to man's fate. My

hand, the instrument of torture. This is
the price of purchase, the sail with no
wind. This is the final solution, the end
to the day's torment and the morning to
freedom's lament.

*(He crawls over and past the clustered
audience and collapses by a window frame
with his back to the audience. He is lit from
the side and speaking very closely into a
microphone.)*

It is beginning. The end of six days of
woe. Last night was the first time that I
managed sleep in weeks. Moments ago
the music was slow and peaceful in time
with the color and temperature of my
room and the rhythm of the falling snow.
I am not entirely myself today. Right
now I am on the edge of an episode.
Over the past six months I have come
up for air on occasion only to submerge
myself once again in doubt. This evening
I experienced a fit of dizziness so severe
that I had to put down my bag for fear
of falling.

*(The light fades to black. He eases his way
back into his room and gently closes the
door behind him.)*

ROOM 1D

*A twenty-minute 16mm film projected
onto the surface of a bed with the audience
seated around listening to the soundtrack
on individual headphones.*

1. Exterior day overhead / B&W /
   Pierre Rivière sitting in the woods
   smirking.

2. Title scrawled across the image
   as if it is being written by hand /
   accompanied by scratching noise /
   the text reads: **"Moi, Pierre Rivière
   ayant égorgé ma mère, ma soeur
   et mon frère…"**

3. Wide exterior day/ B&W / A country farm on a foggy fall morning.

4. Medium exterior day/ B&W / Silhouette of Pierre standing in a field on a foggy morning.

5. Close up exterior day / B&W / Horse's head.

6. Close up exterior day/ B&W / Pierre's head silhouetted by trees.

7. Wide exterior day / B&W / Pierre walking through the forest with a knife in his hand.

8. Wide exterior day / B&W / Pierre tosses the knife and lies down by the edge of the river.

9. Interior night / B&W / Ghostly image of a woman seated in front of a fireplace.

10. POV Close-up interior barn day / Color / Looking up at Pierre's arm stabbing through the air. / Accompanied by the sound of heavy breathing and the sounds of a horse-drawn carriage passing in the distance.

11. Voiceover in French with English subtitles: **"Details and explanation of the events which occurred in June at Aunay in the village of Fauctrie written by the perpetrator of these events."**

12. Wide exterior day / B&W / Overhead shot of Pierre lying on the forest bed with the camera slowly zooming in to a tight close-up. / Voiceover in French with the English subtitles superimposed across the center of the image. / **"I, Pierre Rivière having slaughtered my mother, my sister and my brother and wishing to** make known the motives which led to this deed, have written down the whole of the life which my father and mother have led together since their marriage. I was witness of the greater part of the facts and they are written at the end of this history. As regards the beginning I heard it recounted by my father when he talked of it with his friends and with his mother, with me and with those who had knowledge of it. I shall then tell how I resolved to commit this crime, what my thoughts were at the time and what was my intention. I shall also describe the life I led among the people, what went on in my mind after doing this deed. The life I led and the places I was in after the crime up to my arrest and what were the resolutions I took. All this work will be very crudely styled for I know how to only read and write, but all I ask is that what I mean shall be understood and I have written it all down as best as I can remember."

13. Montage sequence / Sound of a sudden knocking at the door. / Color / Pierre stabbing in the air. Lenz washing his bloody hands in the sink. Iris lying unconscious on the tiled bathroom floor. / B&W / Pierre stabbing with knife. / Color / Iris and Lenz dancing in a circle, shot from above.

14. Interior elevator shaft / B&W / Pierre hiding in an elevator shaft shot from above with a slow panning away from the subject. / Accompanied by the sound of approaching footsteps.

15. Sudden sound of a camera shutter / Oversaturated and cross-processed color / Montage of a pregnant Iris lying unconscious on the bathroom floor with a French voiceover and large English subtitles superimposed over the center of the image. / **"Death Certificate By The Doctor. Having entered and found the body in the following. The first victim, a woman who we were told was a certain sister of the said Rivière, lying on her back her feet slightly inclined, the right hand at her side, left hand clenched to the breast. A cotton cap spread under the corpse's head a huge pool of blood extended around. Parietal bone on the right side was completely crushed. The blow extended toward the crown appeared as reduced to a mere pulp. Since the woman was with child, we proceeded at the request of the authorities."**

16. Interior / Color / The camera slowly pans across the surface of the wood floor in the old hotel. / Accompanied by the sounds of a struggle and a woman choking for air.

17. Interior close-up / Color / Slow motion of Iris and Lenz dancing in a circle with the movement occasionally changing direction. / Accompanied by the voice of Pierre in French repeating his confession.

18. Cut to interior bathroom / Lenz washing his blood-stained hands in the sink. / Sudden voiceover, **"DONE."**

19. Exterior day close-up / B&W / Pierre running through the forest frantically with the camera pointed up toward his face with the tree tops silhouetted in the background. / The percussive rhythm gradually builds to a grating crescendo of metallic humming. Cut to silence.

20. Interior night / B&W / Ghostly image of a woman in front of a fireplace with a dark figure looming behind her. / Accompanied by horse and carriage sounds.

21. Interior bathroom / Color / The camera slowly panning over the various surfaces of the black and white tiled bathroom. / Accompanied by the sound of a woman breathing deeply.

22. Exterior / Color / As the camera pans across the interior of the porcelain bathtub it fades to white, and Iris in nineteenth century French clothing throwing a shawl across her shoulders with Pierre lurking behind her. / Deep slow stabbing sounds.

23. Interior bathroom / Color / Fade from white back to the camera panning the surface of the bathtub; arrives at Iris lying unconscious on the floor.

24. Exterior day close-up / B&W / Pierre smirking and looking up at the camera while seated on the ground in the forest.

25. Interior hotel / B&W / Sequence of still photographs of Lenz twitching in the long hallway of the hotel. / Accompanied by the sounds of a horse-drawn carriage, getting louder and punctuated by a woman gasping for her last breath.

26. Interior bathroom / B&W / Close-up of Iris gasping for air from beneath the water while lying in

her bathtub. / Punctuated by the sound of one last gasp.

27. Exterior day / B&W / Cut to the camera panning across the roof-tops of buildings in a large city. / French voiceover with English subtitles superimposed across the image. **"The beast has awoken yet the flight of night persists. I, hunger, evaporate. A memory or a premonition. A recurring dream that steals my breath and seeks shelter in my lungs. Trying to find his way back to an event so painful that it needs witnesses to exist."**

28. Interior bathroom / B&W / Cut to an image of Iris in the bathtub underwater with the camera panning across her body. / The voiceover and subtitles continue, **"Pierre was sent to me in my sleep. My portal was open to the pain searching for a container to rest. My shame is buried within a box stacked upon shelves of like boxes. Like a trembling child it somehow finds no place to hide. Separated, disoriented…"**

29. Interior day / B&W / Cut to the camera panning down a radiator and its plumbing toward the wood floor. / The voiceover in French with English subtitles continues, **"Continually shifting barriers turn and circle me…"**

30. Interior day / B&W / Cut to camera panning across Pierre sleeping in his bed. / **"I have been imprisoned countless times in my sleep and in my travels an empty vessel waiting to be filled…"**

31. Interior day / B&W / Cut to the camera panning across a handrail in a stairwell and then over the radiator and across the floor. / **"…every night by the blows of inhumanity. I witness the truth in the eyes of the dying. So I perish every night and wake every morning closer to their pain and somehow further from my tenuous reality."**

32. Interior day / B&W / The camera pans across Lenz lying in bed with his eyes open.

33. Exterior day / B&W / Cut to a statue of a gargoyle outside a building.

34. Exterior day / B&W / Looking through the window at Iris asleep in her bed.

35. Exterior day / B&W / Cut to close-up of Iris sleeping in her bed. / Accompanied by a scratching noise and a high light echo of a cymbal.

36. Exterior day / B&W / Cut to city shot of a bridge spanning across a river.

37. Exterior day / B&W / Close-up of Lenz. Superimposed image of Iris on the image of Lenz. Iris is looking in the opposite direction from Lenz, then turns to look the same way.

38. Exterior day / B&W / Cut to overhead shot of Lenz lying at the bottom of a shaft crouched in fetal position.

39. Exterior day / B&W / Panning shot over the rooftops of city buildings. / Silence.

40. Cut to black with white titles, **"Please remove your headset now and quietly proceed."**

41. Cut to black.

OFFICE SONATA

Andy Chmelko

ANDY CHMELKO is an actor and a playwright. He was born on March 19, 1977, in Buffalo, New York, and grew up in Scotia, New York. He received a BA in theatre from Oswego State University, where he studied acting with Shannon Penrod, Mark Cole, and Ron Medici and playwriting with Brad Korbesmeyer. His short plays *Quicksand* (1996), *This'll Only Hurt* (1997), and *Sexaholic* (1999) were all selected for staged readings in Oswego State University's Annual New Voices Playwriting Competition. His plays *The Zax Complex* and *kindlovetalent...* were included in Brass Tacks Theatre's 2nd Annual Rosetta Festival of New Works (2003), and his plays *Buh* (cowritten with Brian Smallwood) and *Speaking as a Child of the 90's* (cowritten with Luis Miguel Echegaray) were part of Impetuous Theater Group's 47:59 Annual Play Festival (2005). Chmelko's acting credits include *Swim Shorts*, an evening of theatre presented entirely in or around the swimming pool on the roof of the Midtown Holiday Inn (Word of Mouth, 2002–03). He has also appeared in *After Charlie* (2004), *La Playa (The Beach)* (2005), and *what@trip!* (2006), all of which were created, written, and directed by Roi "Bubi" Escudero through ETdC Projects' Performance Art and New Media Theatre Experimental Creative Lab, where Chmelko studies acting and serves as associate producer. His next stage appearance will be in Bubi's upcoming production, *Antonin...Mon Artaud*. Chmelko lives in Long Island City, Queens.

Office Sonata was first presented by Impetuous Theater Group
(James David Jackson, Artistic Director; Josh Sherman, Managing
Director) on December 2, 2005, at the Irish Arts Center, New York
City, with the following cast and credits:

McCormick/Prisoner 1 .... Brendan Bradley
Martin/Pedro .... Bryce T. Gill
Prisoner 2/Tina/Jill .... Beth Jastroch
Lester/Vance/Straight Arrow .... D.H. Johnson
The Computer/Pleasant Voice/Female Understudy .... Shashanah
        Newman
Meghan/Monica .... Heidi Niedermeyer
Marisa/Prisoner 3 .... Rose O'Hara
The Intercom/Male Understudy .... Brian Smallwood
Kyle/Super Porno Blowout .... Justin Swain
Elias Empie .... Steve Lavner [cut from final production]

Directed by: Jason Zimbler
Assistant Director: Jamie Klassel
Set Design: Rachel Gordon
Costume Design: Kara Harmon
Lighting Design: George Gountas
Sound Design: Ryan Dowd
Script Consultant: James Carter
Fight Director: Qui Nguyen
Assistant Set Design: Janene Husband
Video Editing: Andrew Gaines
Technical Director: Sam Narrison
Stage Manager: Nancy Valladares
Assistant Stage Manager: Mana Fujikatsu
Props Mistress: Amanda Haley
Production Manager: Joe Powell

www.impetuoustheater.com

Special thanks to:

Martin, Rochelle, Michael, and everyone involved in the publication of this book; Josh Sherman, David Jackson, all of the members
of Impetuous Theater Group, and anyone who's ever been involved
in any of their productions; Mom, Dad, Jill, Jason, all my aunts,
all my uncles and cousins for their never-ending love and support; all of my wonderful friends; Roi "Bubi" Escudero and Seth
Kramer for helping me grow as an artist and a person; Jen Daum
for her constant encouragement; and very special thanks to Justin
Lambert, who helped nurture my sense of humor long ago when
I needed it the most.

CHARACTERS

MARTIN: a disgruntled, smart-aleck low man on the corporate totem pole with a promising future he's not even aware of.

KYLE: a young man just getting his foot in the door.

MEGHAN: an aspiring actress forced to rely upon Empie Advertising by day to pay her bills.

LESTER: an Executive Vice President. And an Excessively Vicious Prick.

MARISA: another suit with a slight ego problem.

PRISONERS ONE, TWO, and THREE: three people in a whole lot of trouble.

STRAIGHT ARROW: the deliverer of said trouble.

McCORMICK: the right-hand man of the enigmatic CEO of Empie Advertising.

VANCE: a friendly but annoying mailroom worker.

TINA and PEDRO: two specialists.

JILL and MONICA: two different kinds of specialists.

SUPER PORNO BLOWOUT: the voice of the greatest website ever created.

ASSORTED P.A. VOICES and OFFSTAGE VOICES

NOTE

Many of the stage directions in *Office Sonata* are kept to a minimum so as to allow different interpretations. For example, the original production used videos projected on the back wall for the opening segment and Lester's "This could be you." This is of course not mandatory if you are unable to create videos for your own production, as both scenes can certainly be staged. Also, the setup of the area that holds the "prisoners" is open to any kind of interpretation, as is the "Super Porno Blowout" scene (in the original production the S.P.B. "voice" was not merely a voice but a live actor sharing the stage with the unfortunate Martin). By all means, use your imagination and have fun molding the bizarre world of Empie Advertising into whatever you envision.

SCENE 1

We hear a PLEASANT VOICE accompanied by cheesy music.

PLEASANT VOICE: Founded in 1985 by Elias Empie, the Empie Advertising Agency is one of the most respected forces in the world of advertising and marketing. Our diverse list of clients includes Gorden and Douglas, Inc., the world-renowned corporation responsible for, among many other products, Fruity Fruit Munchies, Elizabeth Anthony Cosmetics, and the popular prescription antidepressant Comatrin. Here at Empie we apply the most cutting-edge motivational techniques to ensure that all of our employees are doing the best job that they are capable of. These top-secret techniques were created by Elias Empie himself and are guaranteed to eliminate all but the strongest from the herd. Just remember that disclosure of these methods outside the walls of the agency is punishable to the fullest extent of the law. All of us here at Empie would like to wish all of our new employees the best of luck!

(Lights up: two desks with PCs and a never-ending sea of paperwork. The unfortunate homes of MARTIN ARMSTRONG and MEGHAN ALTMAN, just two more faces in Corporate America who had other plans for their lives but are now saddled with go-nowhere jobs. The two are going about their routines of banging away at their computers when there comes an unpleasant shout not far from MEGHAN.)

LESTER: *(Offstage.)* Meghan!

MEGHAN: Yes, Mr. Skollar?

(LESTER enters from his office. He is a smug, incredibly sharply dressed executive VP, and unfortunately MEGHAN's supervisor.)

LESTER: Oh you missed it Meghan, I was just having one of the most satisfying belly laughs anyone has ever had. For a minute I really thought I might hyperventilate or soil my suit. Care to hear why?

MEGHAN: Um…sure…

LESTER: You see I noticed a little something that a certain someone left on my desk. Well, left on my chair actually. I *have* discussed with you how much I hate that, haven't I?

MEGHAN: Yes sir, I'm really sor…

LESTER: Mm-hmm, just checking. Anyway my anger was quickly washed away by the side-splitting piece of literature left there. Are you ready for this, Meghan?

MEGHAN: *(Sadly, knows what's coming.)* Yes.

LESTER: I found…on my very chair…a request…from you…for two weeks off! *(Begins laughing very loudly and very fake.)* Starting tomorrow! *(More laughing.)* And here's the best part…I honestly believe you're serious! *(Busts a gut fake laughing. Slowly he collects himself. Then, angrily…)* TWO WEEKS, MEGHAN?!

MEGHAN: It's an audition, sir. A very important one that I literally just found out about. I have to fly to LA and stay for two weeks in case I get called back. I'm so sorry for the inconvenience but this isn't something that I can just pass up.

LESTER: Meghan…unfortunately due to the fact that we discussed your…acting aspirations before I agreed to take you on as a temporary assistant, I'm going to give you your two weeks.

MEGHAN: Oh sir, thank you so m...

LESTER: But the whole time that you're chasing your little daydreams in LA, I want you to know that I will be doing everything to ensure that an ungodly amount of work is waiting for you when you get back. Maybe you can use that little mental picture as motivation in case they ask if you can cry on command.

(LESTER exits to his office. MEGHAN looks furious. Meanwhile, MARTIN appears to be trying to say something to her to lighten the mood. Finally he gets up the courage.)

MARTIN: Hey. Why did Helen Keller's dog jump off a cliff? *(Beat.)* Wouldn't you if your name was "Auughguhguhugguuuuuh"?

(Beat. No reaction from MEGHAN.)

MARTIN: Uh-oh, was that a smile? I think I see a smile! I think...oh, oh yeah, yeah we've definitely got smileage goin' on here!

(MEGHAN's face has not changed one bit throughout the above lines despite MARTIN's claims otherwise. MARTIN tries to play one more card.)

MARTIN: Why did Helen Keller masturbate with—

MEGHAN: My sister's deaf, you asshole.

MARTIN: Oh...

MEGHAN: You sit there gawking at me for weeks without saying a word and *this* is how you break the ice? Helen Keller jokes?!

MARTIN: I...

MEGHAN: Last time I checked, the sign out front said "Empie Advertising" not "Junior High." *(Goes back to work.)*

MARTIN: Jeez, just trying to cheer you up. *(Tries to think of something else to say. Finally he's got it.)* How do you know when it's bedtime at Michael Jackson's house?

(MARTIN is cut off by a wailing offstage.)

MARISA: *(Offstage.)* MARTIN ARMSTRONG!!!

MARTIN: *(Freezes up.)* What the...

(MARISA SANBORN, MARTIN's less-than-pleasant boss, storms onstage holding a videotape.)

MARISA: What is this?! *What is this?!?*

MARTIN: Oh God no...

MARISA: You have *ruined* me, Martin! You should have seen the look on the Fruit Munchies people's faces! I can't believe you couldn't hear the *screams* from here!!

MARTIN: Marisa, I can totally explain...

MARISA: I don't even want to know, Martin! I am getting on the phone right now and you are going to pay dearly for this tomorrow!!! *(Runs into her office and slams the door.)*

MARTIN: Oh man...this can't be happening...I am so completely screwed.

(MEGHAN finally smiles. Lights down. Lights up on a MAN seated in a chair in an empty waiting room.)

PRISONER ONE: Could use a little company here... *(Beat.)* Hello? *(Beat.*

He gets up and starts to pace around.) I know you can hear me...

(Lights down.)

SCENE 2

The next day. A nervous, unsure YOUNG FELLA approaches MARTIN's desk as he types something on his computer. MEGHAN has gone on her audition.

KYLE: Excuse me? Is this, uh... *(Consults a Post-it Note in his hand.)*...Marisa Sanborn's office?

MARTIN: I wouldn't go in there now, she's in one of her moods.

KYLE: Oh, I just have to return these expense reports to her.

MARTIN: Trust me. Come back in...a week? Yeah, a week ought to do it. I hope.

KYLE: But we won't be able to pay these until she fixes this mistake.

MARTIN: You new here?

KYLE: Started Tuesday.

MARTIN: Right. Well, the first thing you need to learn is never give Marisa Sanborn bad news unless you got skin like concrete.

KYLE: If you say so.

MARTIN: I know so. That woman's got mental problems that haven't even been invented yet.

(He takes the expense reports from KYLE.)

MARTIN: I'll give 'em to her tomorrow.

KYLE: Thanks.

MARTIN: I'm Martin, by the way. *(Offers KYLE his hand.)*

KYLE: Kyle.

(MARTIN shakes with him.)

MARTIN: They ain't kickin' your ass too hard yet, are they?

KYLE: It doesn't seem all that different from anywhere else I've worked.

MARTIN: And a crazy person doesn't seem all that different from a guy with his shit together until he opens his mouth. This place just hasn't opened its mouth yet. Give it a while.

(Beat.)

KYLE: Are you a writer?

MARTIN: What gave me away?

KYLE: Well for starters there's the long sad poem on your computer...

MARTIN: *(Dives for his mouse.)* That's a work in progress.

KYLE: "Meghan Hates Me?" Who's Meghan?

MARTIN: "Meghan" is in the recycle bin now; she's none of your concern.

KYLE: Sorry.

MARTIN: You should be. I'm trying to help... *(Suddenly looking off in the distance.)*

KYLE: Martin?

MARTIN: Oh *shit.*

KYLE: What?

MARTIN: He's coming.

KYLE: *Who's* coming?

MARTIN: See, if you make a big mistake here they don't necessarily fire you. And they don't necessarily demote you or give you a lecture.

(A GRAVE-LOOKING MAN approaches MARTIN's desk with his hand in his coat.)

MARTIN: Instead you get a visit from a guy who...

(The GUY stops to MARTIN's left and shoots his middle finger out from his coat right into MARTIN's face. He leaves it there for the remainder of the scene. MARTIN tries desperately not to look at the finger.)

MARTIN: Bet you're glad you sent your resume here now, right?

KYLE: I...how can...what... *(Talking to FINGER MAN.)* C'mon, man, stop giving him the...

MARTIN: Kyle. Kyle. Kyle. Don't talk to him, it's useless.

KYLE: How long will he be here?

MARTIN: Five hours.

KYLE: No way!

MARTIN: Unless I gotta pull overtime, then he stays until my work is done. Depends on what you did wrong. I heard one time he stayed up all night with a guy who sexually harassed a receptionist.

KYLE: Wow.

MARTIN: Mm-hmm. Followed him home, too. They say he drove up alongside him with his finger out the window the whole time. And the guy had a three-hour commute.

KYLE: What did *you* do?

(MARTIN lets out a pained groan and puts his head down on the desk. FINGER MAN immediately lifts MARTIN's head up by the hair.)

MARTIN: Sorry-sorry-sorry.

KYLE: That's not allowed?

MARTIN: You don't have to look directly *at* the finger but you can't purposely shield your eyes from it. So anyway, I put together a promotional reel for Marisa this week. Then yesterday when she needs it a buddy of mine upstairs loans me this really sick porno as a gag. He says, "Martin you gotta see this to believe it." He gives it to me on an unmarked cassette. Just like the unmarked cassette Marisa's reel is on. Do I even have to tell you where this is going?

KYLE: Oh man...

MARTIN: Cued up to the nastiest part of the movie, too.

KYLE: What part was that?

MARTIN: There were...she-males...in a barnyard...

KYLE: Got it.

MARTIN:...midgets...

KYLE: I got it, thanks.

(Long beat.)

MARTIN: Is he still there?

KYLE: He's still there. I thought he had to stay for five hours.

MARTIN: He does, I was just hoping maybe he took a bathroom break or something. *(Directs his attention to FINGER MAN without looking directly at him or his finger.)* Hope you went before you got here, buddy. Man, what if you dropped a deuce in front of Marisa's office? *(Beat.) Would* you drop a deuce in front of Marisa's office? 'Cause I'd *really* appreciate it. *(Beat. To KYLE.)* Still there?

KYLE: He's not budging, man.

MARTIN: *(Slowly, reluctantly turns to face the finger directly in front of his eyes.)* That's great. That's…your wife must be so proud. Especially if you can keep other things up for this long. Yeah. *(Gives him a thumbs-up.)* See? I can stick up a finger too, maybe you guys should hire me on. Huh? Aren't I great?

KYLE: Thumb's not a finger, man.

MARTIN: I know a thumb's… *(Looks away again.)* They're probably wondering where you are upstairs.

KYLE: Right. Well…good luck?

MARTIN: I'm sure I'll survive.

(KYLE leaves. MARTIN sits for a second and then reaches across the desk for his phone. FINGER MAN is in the way.

MARTIN: Could you…maybe just…scootch…over…there…

(FINGER MAN doesn't move.)

MARTIN: Or not. Fine. Wonderful. *(Sighs.)* Oh how I love my job. *(Painstakingly reaches around FINGER MAN, picks up the phone, and dials.)* Yeah hi, this is Martin Armstrong, Marisa Sanborn's assistant?…Yeah that's right, me again…I know, but Marisa should have gotten a discount on this flight and for some reason…listen I'm *extremely* short on time here, so I'm only going to say this once more: Marisa has a huge cell phone payment to make this week and it will be very hard for her to do that unless she receives the money she should have saved from…

(FINGER MAN suddenly pulls the phone from MARTIN's hand and hangs it up.)

MARTIN: Are you KIDDING me?! You can *not* be allowed to do that!

(Silence from FINGER MAN, as usual.)

MARTIN: How are you authorized to interfere with my work?!

(Nothing. MARTIN can't take any more.)

MARTIN: SAY SOMETHING!!!

(We hear a VOICE from the office next to MARTIN's.)

MARISA: Martin?

MARTIN: Oh wonderful, see what you've done now?

(MARISA enters.)

MARISA: Are we having problems out here?

MARTIN: Marisa, I was just trying to get you your discount on your trip to Puerto Rico and before I could do anyth…

MARISA: I need that money *today*, Martin.

MARTIN: I understand that, but I wasn't able to finish negotiating with the travel agent because this guy hung the phone up on me!

MARISA: Martin, I refuse to stand here and listen to you whine and sling blame like some kindergarten tattletale. He hung up the phone on you?

MARTIN: Yes.

MARISA: And would he even be around to do that if we hadn't had our little misadventure with the videotape?

MARTIN: But what does that have to…

MARISA: Martin, if you hadn't handed me that transsexual/farm animal/midget nightmare instead of my reel, there would be no one at your desk right now to hang up the phone on you. And that money could be in my hands right now.

Your fault, Martin. All your fault. Do you understand me?

MARTIN: But... *(Beat.)* Yes.

MARISA: I really hope that you're learning something from all this, Martin. Did I ever tell you about my assistant from a few months ago who also couldn't seem to do anything right? *(Beat.)* Martin?!

MARTIN: No. You didn't.

MARISA: First offense someone gave him the finger. Second offense two people gave him the finger. Third offense five people gave him the finger. The fourth offense resulted in his termination which if I remember correctly went something like this. Fifty people gave him the finger while they made two phone calls: one to his parents expressing the company's disappointment in them for raising him wrong, and another to his girlfriend to tell her that he'd been seen in a bar kissing his old high school sweetheart. Then they took turns flicking his ears, kicking his shins, and urinating into his thermos. Next they styled his hair in a ridiculously outdated fashion and forced him to wear a T-shirt that said "Hitler Is My Homeboy." When it came time for him to leave they shot at him with beanbag bazookas to chase him to the elevators. Then when he got downstairs two rather large gentlemen grabbed him by the arms, led him out of a special door...and no one's seen him since. You are closely hovering around the two-finger range, Martin. I suggest you do something about it. You walk yourself downstairs to that travel agency and don't even *think* about leaving until you've gotten my discount. Understood?

MARTIN: Yes.

MARISA: It's twelve already, I'm leaving at two today. Get going.

(She storms back into her office. MARTIN dejectedly rises from his seat. He looks over at FINGER MAN, who is smirking.)

MARTIN: Why don't ya go easy on that smirk, you cocky prick?

(He doesn't.)

MARTIN: C'mon, we're headed down to the seventh floor. But I gotta hit the men's room first. And this time, I don't care if you have to stick the finger under the door. You wait *outside* the stall.

(FINGER MAN shakes his head no.)

MARTIN: Thought so. Let's go.

(They exit. In the darkness, we hear a VOICE over the intercom.)

INTERCOM: May I have your attention please? We have recently discovered that a certain employee, Mr. Christopher Murray, has been using his floor's copy machine for personal reasons. As a result, all copy machines in the building will immediately be shut down and remain that way for the next twenty weeks. Anyone needing to make copies during that time must go to the Kinko's across the street and pay all expenses out of their own pocket. Anyone dissatisfied with this policy is free to discuss it with Mr. Christopher Murray in office 462 on the fourth floor. If you cannot see Mr. Murray at this time, feel free to call him at home at 212-555-7425 or try his cell phone at 917-555-5166. Thank you.

(Lights up on PRISONER ONE sitting in his chair, looking down at a BODY on the floor. There is also another chair beside him now. PRISONER TWO, the body on the floor, comes to with a startled yell. She looks at PRISONER ONE.)

PRISONER TWO: Why did you bring me here?

ONE: Whoa, wait, I didn't…

TWO: There's been a mistake, you've got the wrong person…

ONE: I didn't bring you here.

TWO: You don't work here?

ONE: No. I mean I work…here, for this company but…I don't work for this place. I'm stuck here same as you.

TWO: Stuck? I'm not stuck anywhere. *(Begins walking around the room, calling out to anybody.)* Excuse me? Hello? Whoever's out there, I have to get back to work. You have no idea what you just interrupted. Do you hear me? Let me out!

ONE: *(Very quietly.)* Nobody's listening…

(TWO ignores ONE and continues.)

TWO: Let me OUT! You do not just sneak up on people while they're working on something very important and throw them in a…hole!

ONE: What were you working on?

TWO: I'll tell you what I was working on. Something that people were going to remember for a long time. Something that had *passion*. Want to hear it?

ONE: Look, maybe you shouldn't…

TWO: You'll love it, I guarantee you'll love it. *(Takes a deep breath and…gets a horribly confused look on her face.)* Wait a minute…wait just a minute here…

ONE: Can't remember it, can you?

TWO: Oh my God…they drugged me.

ONE: I don't think so…

TWO: They had to have! I knew it backwards and forwards out there!

(Yelling to whomever and occasionally banging on the walls.) Whoever you are, when I get out I am going to make sure that this place gets shut down and that you end up…tarred and…feathered and…hanging upside down by your toes while…buzzards and…ants…LET ME OUT OF HERE!!!

ONE: Wow. No one in here's ever been so…animated.

TWO: There are others here?

ONE: Well…not anymore.

TWO: Why not? Where are they?

ONE: *(Pauses for a moment.)* They're…somewhere else. Another room maybe. But they were all so boring. When they were brought here they just sat here like lumps. It was like pulling teeth trying to get any of them to talk. But you…you're different. And I like that.

TWO: Thank you.

ONE: So I'm uh…I'm an accountant.

TWO: I'm an artist. A damn good one.

ONE: I'm…sure you are. *(Holds out his hand.)* It's very nice to meet you.

(TWO pauses for a moment and then shakes his hand.)

TWO: It's nice to meet you too.

(Lights down.)

SCENE 3

MARTIN sits happily working at his computer. He takes a second to check his watch.

MARTIN: Twelve o'clock and all's well.

(He smiles and returns to his work. VANCE, a rather odd mailroom worker, drops off his mail.)

VANCE: Hey Martin.

MARTIN: *(Almost hiding his displeasure.)* Vance.

VANCE: Where's um…where's the birdman today?

MARTIN: Out of my life as of today.

VANCE: That's good. Hey, you like that? How I called him birdman? 'Cause you know, a middle finger is called a "bird" in some cultures, you know?

MARTIN: Yeah that's a good one. You ought to write that one down, Vance.

VANCE: Sure, sure, I will. *(Actually writes it down using MARTIN's office supplies.)* Thanks Martin.

MARTIN: Well listen, I got a ton of w…

VANCE: We got one following one of our guys around too.

MARTIN: Really? That's terrible.

(MARTIN tries in vain to get back to work as VANCE rambles on.)

VANCE: I know. See he opened someone else's mail. I mean that's a federal offense. That's what I told him, I said, "Eddie that's a federal offense." Eddie doesn't listen to me though. He does lots of bad stuff. This one time he goes, "Hey Vance, wanna come to my party this weekend? There's gonna be beer and weed!" Can you believe it? So I said, "As long as by 'beer' you mean 'milk' and by 'weed' you mean 'Jesus.'" He laughed. He laughs a lot when I'm around, I don't know why. Boy, were they mad when they found out what he did with

the mail. But they said they'd drop the charges if he let one of those birdmen follow him nonstop for one whole month. I'd almost rather go to jail. I mean he's gonna get followed *everywhere*. On dates, in the shower, the bedroom, probably the bathroom, too…can you imagine one of those guys in the bathroom with you while you're tryin' to…

MARTIN: No Vance, that certainly must be horrible.

VANCE: He told me he's got a family reunion next weekend in Philadelphia. And he had to buy two train tickets if you know what I mean.

(Beat.)

VANCE: If you know what I mean.

(Beat.)

VANCE: See 'cause the guy's gonna be…

MARTIN: I get it Vance, I get it. Look man I got so much work to do here…

VANCE: Oh sure, sure. Sure. All right Martin, you have a good day.

MARTIN: You too, Vance.

VANCE: *(Begins to leave. He looks at someone offstage.)* Hey Mr. Newman.

VOICE: *(Offstage. Sounding much like MARTIN did earlier.)* Heyyyy…Vance…

(VANCE exits. MARTIN goes back to work. Soon MARISA calls to him from her office.)

MARISA: Martin?

MARTIN: Yeah?

MARISA: I gotta head off to the shoot now. Did you get that tape made up for me?

MARTIN: *(Holding up a videotape.)* Right here.

(MARISA enters from her office and takes the cassette from MARTIN. She looks at it and gives MARTIN a reproachful look.)

MARTIN: It's the right one, I swear.

MARISA: Did you watch it?

MARTIN: Four times. And I never took my eyes off it from the second it left the VCR until right now. It's definitely the right one.

MARISA: If it isn't...

MARTIN: If it isn't may God inflict so much pain on me that Job'll look down and say, "Whoa dude, sucks to be you." See, nothing happened, it's the right one.

(Beat. MARISA can't help but be skeptical.)

MARISA: How about those expense reports?

(MARTIN points to his outbox.)

MARISA: Did you do my taxes?

(MARTIN hands her a folder.)

MARISA: Make my lunch?

(MARTIN hands her a brown bag.)

MARISA: Call my kids and tell them I love them?

MARTIN: Yup. They love you too.

MARISA: Behave yourself, Martin.

(She leaves. MARTIN is now completely alone. He looks around deviously.)

MARTIN: What would Marty like tonight? *(Types something into a search engine and clicks his mouse.)* Hmm...

"Super Porno Blowout. Best porn site on the planet (yeah, never heard that one before), one-hundred-percent free (okay, that I can handle), impervious to any and all corporate monitoring software, look up any nude celebrity photo ever"...oooh, maybe they got Condoleezza Rice... *(Clicks his mouse. Beat.)* C'mon, any day now. Some of us are on a schedule here. *(Beat.)* Frozen...it figures. Guess a little satisfaction after the week I've had is too much to a...oh here we go.

(And then a VOICE comes booming from MARTIN's computer.)

VOICE: Welcome to the SUPER ...**PORNO...BLOWOUT!!!**

MARTIN: Oh crap.

(Ridiculously loud, driving rock music comes blaring from the computer along with the moans of women having orgasms and a ROBOTIC VOICE that constantly, rhythmically drones "ASS AND TITTIES, ASS AND TITTIES, ASS AND TITTIES." MARTIN tries desperately to turn his speakers down: nothing happens. He frantically clicks his mouse to exit the website: nothing happens. Finally he dives under his desk and unplugs his computer: and yet the sounds continue.)

MARTIN: WHAT THE HELL?!?

VOICE: THE SUPER PORNO BLOW-OUT IS PART PORNOGRAPHY WEBSITE PART COMPUTER VIRUS! WE ABSOLUTELY WILL NOT SHUT DOWN UNTIL WE'VE DELIVERED TO YOU ALL THE ASS AND TITTIES YOU CAN HANDLE!

MARTIN: *Nooooooo!!!*

VOICE: AND HEY THERE, MARTIN, WHILE YOU'RE AT IT...

MARTIN: *How do you know my name?!?*

VOICE: WELL SINCE YOU DIDN'T LOG OUT OF YOUR EMAIL ACCOUNT BEFORE YOU PAID ME A VISIT, WE KNOW PRETTY MUCH EVERYTHING ABOUT YOU! SO ANYWAY, WHY NOT SHARE YOUR DISCOVERY OF THIS FANTASTIC WEBSITE WITH ALL OF YOUR COWORKERS THERE AT EMPIE ADVERTISING?

MARTIN: Don't you dare…

(Instantly VOICES are heard offstage.)

MAN #1: What's going on here?

WOMAN #1: Mr. Newman, there's *porno* on my computer!

WOMAN #2: That is dis*gusting!!!*

MAN #2: It won't STOP!!!

MAN #3: Aw man, this ROCKS!!!

WOMAN #3: Is that a HORSE?!

MARTIN: *(Picks up his chair and holds it over his head.)* I'll smash you to pieces you son of a bitch!

VOICE: OH I DON'T THINK THAT'S SUCH A GOOD IDEA MARTIN. IF YOU SMASH YOUR PC NOT ONLY WILL WE ERASE EVERY HARD DRIVE IN THE BUILDING, BUT A BOLT OF ELECTRICITY WILL COME FLYING OUT OF WHAT'S LEFT OF YOUR SCREEN AND STRIKE YOU DEAD ON THE SPOT! AND AS EMBARRASSED AS YOU ARE RIGHT NOW, I REALLY DON'T THINK YOU WANT THAT TO HAPPEN!

MARTIN: Bullshit! You're bluffing!!

VOICE: AM I? WHY DON'T YOU GO AHEAD AND TOUCH YOUR SCREEN RIGHT NOW, MARTIN?

(MARTIN slowly reaches out and touches his screen. An electric shock sound is heard, and MARTIN quickly lets go.)

MARTIN: OW!!!

VOICE: MAY AS WELL GET USED TO IT MARTIN! **HEY THERE, EMPIE ADVERTISING AGENCY! ENJOYING YOUR AFTERNOON DELIGHTS? WHY STOP THERE? WE HERE AT THE SUPER PORNO BLOWOUT HAVE JUST SENT EACH OF YOU A SPECIAL "CARE PACKAGE"…CONSISTING OF THE LOOSEST, SKANKIEST HOOKERS IN THE CITY!!!**

(We hear VOICES offstage again.)

MAN #1: Get away from me lady!

WOMAN #1: How did you get past security?!

WOMAN #2: Excuse me, we do NOT smoke crack in this building!

MAN #2: Eww, this one's got WARTS!

MAN #3: Hey baby, how much?

WOMAN #3: Is that a *HORSE?!?!?!?*

(At this point, MARTIN has gone fetal under his desk.)

VOICE: **THAT'S RIGHT EMPIE ADVERTISING AGENCY, JUST ENJOY THE RIDE. AND HEY, WHILE YOU'RE AT IT, WHY NOT EXTEND A HEARTY THANK YOU TO MARTIN RONALD ARMSTRONG IN CUBICLE 975 FOR PROVIDING YOU WITH ALL OF THIS. YOU'RE**

OUR KIND OF PERV, MARTY, AND TO SHOW OUR APPRECIATION ANOTHER CARE PACKAGE IS ON ITS WAY TO YOUR MOM AND DAD IN LARGO, FLORIDA, AS WE SPEAK! OH BOY ARE WE GLAD THEY HAD YOU! AND MAYBE, WITH THE HELP OF THE SUPER PORNO BLOWOUT, THEY'LL BE INSPIRED TO TRY FOR ANOTHER JUST LIKE YOU!!! That's Martin Ronald Armstrong in 975.

(VOICE laughs maniacally, and the ROBOTIC VOICE begins to drone MARTIN's name as MARTIN begins to sob. Lights down. Lights up on PRISONER ONE and PRISONER TWO.)

TWO: It'd be nice if they'd turn the lights on once in a while.

ONE: Yeah, they only do that...every now and then.

TWO: And no windows anywhere? What's that about?

ONE: I know. I never thought I'd miss windows so much.

TWO: I watched the sun come up for the first time before they put me in here. It really is beautiful. Did you ever...?

ONE: Sure. Quite a few times. But...this is my home now I guess.

(Beat.)

TWO: What was it like for you out there? I mean, I know that accounting couldn't have been all that thrilling but...

ONE: Actually sometimes I really enjoyed playing with facts and figures. I wasn't as passionate about it as you are about your work but...I feel like it's what I was meant to do. But yes, it was nice to get away now and then.

TWO: *(Smiles mischievously.)* You went wild when you weren't working, didn't you?

ONE: Well I...wouldn't exactly say...*wild*, but...

TWO: Oh come on. I could see you being one of those quiet types who totally lets loose when work's over. What kind of stuff would you do when no one was looking?

ONE: Um let's see...well, I like music. In fact I'd usually wind up at more than a few concerts out there.

TWO: Oooh, that's exciting!

ONE: Yeah, all kinds. Metal, rap, jazz, classic rock, even some country once in a while. I'd just drop in wherever my feet would take me.

TWO: I never made it to a concert, but there was a time when I was interested in traveling. Took a trip to the islands not too long ago.

ONE: Cool. How was that?

TWO: *So* beautiful. I got to go swimming, clubbing, hit the day spas...definitely going back someday.

ONE: Well when you do I'm definitely stowing away in your luggage.

TWO: You got it.

ONE: Let's see what else...I did most of the fun stuff on late nights when I got swamped with work and needed a break.

TWO: Oh yeah, you gotta pry your eyes away from the work now and then before they fall out of your head.

ONE: Yup. That's when I'd sneak away and watch a movie, check out a game, even hit a strip club every now and then!

TWO: Excuse me?

ONE: I said…wait a minute…I didn't just say what I think I did, did I?

TWO: If you think you said "hit a strip club" then…yes, yes you did.

ONE: Um…it just kinda…happened, ya know? It was pretty hard to walk away when it was sitting right in front of me…sometimes a, a guy's gotta…oh God you must think I'm such a pig.

TWO: *(Laughs.)* You don't have to apologize to me! Wanna know a little secret? *(Very quietly.)* I've been to those places before myself.

ONE: Really?

TWO: Sure! I guess just about everybody does it at least once in their lives.

ONE: I wouldn't doubt it. Hell, I've even seen Straight Arrow in there before! He didn't stay long, but…

TWO: Who's Straight Arrow?

ONE: He's… *(His face contorts to a mask of horror as he realizes what he just said.)*

TWO: What's wrong?

ONE: Nothing.

TWO: Why do you look so scared all of a sudden?

ONE: I'm not scared…

TWO: I knew you were hiding something!

ONE: Please…

TWO: What happened to the others?

ONE: I don't know.

TWO: Yes you do!

(TWO jumps on his lap. She grabs him by his collar and shakes him.)

TWO: Now you tell me the truth! *What happened to the others?!*

(ONE says nothing.)

TWO: Is Straight Arrow the jailer?

(ONE does not respond.)

TWO: Is Straight Arrow the executioner?

(ONE closes his eyes.)

TWO: Are we going to die?! *(Beat.)* ANSWER ME!

ONE: No!

(TWO lets him go and backs away slowly.)

ONE: We're going to be killed.

(Lights down.)

INTERCOM: May I have your attention please? May I have your attention please? This morning our security cameras captured footage of one Abigail Vera from the Elizabeth Anthony account coming to work in an obviously inebriated state. Ms. Vera, please report to the Human Centrifuge for Hangover Amplification immediately. And then return to your desk and prepare for a sixteen-hour work day. Anyone wishing to further accentuate Ms. Vera's hangover may pick up air horns in the lobby and visit her in office 319 at their leisure. Thank you. Hope it was worth it, Ms. Vera.

SCENE 4

The next day. MARTIN sits at his desk staring straight ahead dejectedly. There are now TWO PEOPLE giving him the finger, one on each side of him. Both are very angry and professional-looking women. MARISA enters from her office. She stands behind MARTIN and looks down at him angrily. MARTIN cannot bring himself to look her in the eye.

MARISA: *(Barely able to contain her anger.)* Everyone's computers are finally back up and running.

(MARTIN stays quiet.)

MARISA: All of the…prostitutes…have been rounded up and taken to jail.

(Beat.)

MARISA: The one employee who actually took them up on their offer is responding well to his…antibiotics.

(Beat.)

MARISA: And I will be approving a *great* deal of overtime for you this week so that you can get to know your two new female companions better.

(Beat.)

MARISA: Oh and by the way, my kids told me that you never called and told them I love them yesterday. But now I'm glad…because if you ever speak to my kids again I will see to it that you spend the next few years in prison giving killers and rapists their *own* little "Super Porno Blowout." Understood?

(MARTIN nods.)

MARISA: Moping will not make them go away. Get to work, Martin. *(Retreats to her office and slams the door.)*

MARTIN: *(Sighs deeply and picks up a stack of paperwork.)* Look girls…

(GIRLS wordlessly put their fingers closer to MARTIN's face.)

MARTIN: This whole thing is just a big…

(GIRL ON LEFT gives MARTIN a short slap in the head.)

MARTIN: Since when is that allowed?!

(GIRL ON RIGHT does the same.)

MARTIN: Knock it off!

(GIRL ON LEFT gives another quick smack; GIRL ON RIGHT immediately does the same.)

MARTIN: Fine fine fine, I'm shutting up now.

(GIRLS ease up a bit.)

MARTIN: *(Mutters under his breath.)* Excuse me for being a man.

(GIRL ON LEFT pushes all of MARTIN's paperwork off of his desk.)

MARTIN: Oh that's…

(Slap from the left.)

MARTIN:…that is just…

(Slap from the right.)

MARTIN: A woman's place is in the home!

(MARTIN instantly ducks under the two subsequent slaps.)

MARTIN: Ha!

(GIRL ON RIGHT immediately digs her high heel into MARTIN's foot. He winces and grits his teeth but keeps from crying out.)

MARTIN: I'll just…pick up my papers now…*ladies*…

(He limps over to his piles of papers, and GIRLS follow him. As he begins picking up the papers, we hear a VOICE offstage right.)

McCORMICK: *(Offstage.)* Jill, Monica, take a break for a bit.

(GIRLS quickly drop the fingers and exit from the direction the VOICE has come from. MARTIN looks in that direction and is shocked.)

MARTIN: What the hell do *you* want?

(The owner of the voice enters: it is FINGER MAN from the beginning of the play.)

McCORMICK: Martin Armstrong.

MARTIN: You took time out of your rigorous schedule to learn my name, how sweet.

McCORMICK: I have something to discuss with you.

MARTIN: Something to discuss with me? After you've found a permanent home in my nightmares for the last seven days?

McCORMICK: Look, what do you want me to say? "I'm sorry"? When it comes to what puts food on my table I'm as unapologetic as you get. Besides, I heard what you did to deserve it. Pretty stupid if you ask me.

MARTIN: I don't *remember* asking you.

McCORMICK: Save it.

MARTIN: I suppose you're the guy in charge of this little flipping-off operation?

McCORMICK: Well...I *do* supervise all of the Termination Alternative Artists, but I myself...

MARTIN: "Termination Alternative Artists"?! YOU GIVE PEOPLE THE FINGER FOR A LIVING!

McCORMICK: You know, based on the stuff you've done this week it's the general consensus of most of the higher-ups around here that you're a pig.

MARTIN: Oh I care, trust me.

McCORMICK: All of them except one: the man I answer directly to. You might have heard of him...Elias Empie.

(Beat.)

MARTIN: You're full of shit.

McCORMICK: Never have been, never will be.

MARTIN: Hardly anyone's ever even seen the man!

McCORMICK: Very true. In fact that's not even his real name. He's on the run from a lot of people...for a lot of reasons.

MARTIN: And he doesn't think I'm a pig?

McCORMICK: Not at all. In fact...he wants to offer you a new job.

(Beat.)

MARTIN: Is this some sort of new punishment you guys have invented...?

McCORMICK: No...

MARTIN:...some kind of practical joke...

McCORMICK:...no...

MARTIN:...offer me an imaginary job and...

McCORMICK:...if you don't shut up for two seconds I'm calling Jill and Monica back and telling them to start twisting some scroat! Ya dig?

(MARTIN goes silent as McCORMICK calms himself down.)

McCORMICK: That's better. Now…you may feel that this past week has been one of the worst ever, but it's really been one of the luckiest. You see, the "Super Porno Blowout" was Elias Empie's version of a Golden Ticket. He's had that little doozy floating around every employee's Internet for months now just waiting for someone to click on it.

MARTIN: A website that wrecked everyone's computer and sent a gang of hookers to the building is supposed to be some kind of *reward?*

McCORMICK: Martin, those hookers were just actresses.

MARTIN: What about that guy that got the clap?

McCORMICK: Um…look the important thing is that he planned to monitor whoever finally opened the website to see what their reaction was. And at the end of the day you stayed in the building, owned up to your mistake, and took your punishment like a man. He respects that.

MARTIN: Okay, I'll admit I'm intrigued, Mr.…

McCORMICK: Oh jeez I'm sorry, my name's McCormick. Dan McCormick.

MARTIN: Right.

McCORMICK: I think you're gonna like this new position, Martin. There *are* late hours from time to time but the pay is fantastic and the benefits can't be beat. And best of all…no more kowtowing to Ms. Marisa Sanborn. I have a feeling you could go pretty far with this.

MARTIN: And why is that?

McCORMICK: My first day on the job Elias sensed I was nervous, so he gave me a little pep talk. He told me something I never forgot. "If you're able to combine business with a spoonful of crazy, you'll find that the world is more or less yours for the taking." We work on your business sense and you could be unstoppable. And your first lesson is that when opportunity falls into your lap you pick it up before that slippery son of a bitch goes flying into someone else's lap. *(Beat.)* So Martin… *(Offers his hand.)*…do we have a deal?

MARTIN: *(Looks down at McCORMICK's hand.)* What's the job?

(Lights down.)

SCENE 5

One week later. We are at the same setting, but now it's KYLE sitting at MARTIN's desk. Like MARTIN, he is laden down with paperwork and highly stressed. He is on the phone.

KYLE: Okay, I understand all that, but Ms. Sanborn *has* to have that conference room at noon tomorrow. We've got a…I'm not the one who waited 'til the last minute! Her last assistant was supposed to…give me a break, I haven't even been here a week! I am not shouting at you I am…will you listen I am not SHOUTING AT YOU! Hello? Hello? Oh for Christ's sake…

(MARTIN enters stage right.)

KYLE:…what the hell am I gonna do? She's gonna have my… *(Notices MARTIN.)* Martin?

MARTIN: How's it going, Kyle?

KYLE: I didn't know you were still here!

MARTIN: Got me a little promotion.

KYLE: Wait, a *promotion?* I figured you got fired after you downloaded that…

MARTIN: Ancient history, my man.

KYLE: Ancient history? At least five people a day still come here to yell at me thinking I'm you!

MARTIN: Yeah hopefully that'll pass. So you've been doing my old gig for what, a week now?

(KYLE nods.)

MARTIN: And…?

KYLE: Well…I had kind of a rough first day…

MARTIN: I heard. Ordered the wrong lunch for a violently lactose-intolerant client?

KYLE: Yeah he was, um, a little mad at me for causing him to stink up the conference room. And the elevator. And the cab home. At least they finally reopened the men's room this morning.

MARTIN: Wow, that's too bad. But that's also why I'm here.

KYLE: What do you mean?

MARTIN: That little promotion I told you about?

KYLE: What about it?

(Beat. MARTIN gives KYLE a "think about it" look. Suddenly KYLE is horrified.)

KYLE: No. But…you…this can't be…*you* can't be…!

(Instantly MARTIN sticks the bird directly in KYLE's face.)

KYLE: You…you…you sellout! You of all people! How could you do this?!

(Silence from MARTIN.)

KYLE: I asked you a question, Martin!

(Silence.)

KYLE: Oh this is…I mean…the one thing close to a friend I make in this company…

MARTIN: *(Looks around to make sure no one's looking and then talks under his breath.)* Stay strong, man.

KYLE: What?

MARTIN: I hate having to do this to you, but they tripled my salary and got me the best medical and dental on the market. All because I was a good sport when the shit hit the fan. Take my advice, just stay tough and maybe…

(MARTIN notices someone coming and immediately goes silent again. VANCE enters and drops mail on KYLE's desk.)

VANCE: Hey Kyle.

KYLE: Vance.

(VANCE looks at MARTIN, then back at KYLE.)

VANCE: Tough break.

KYLE: Yeah.

VANCE: *(To MARTIN.)* Wait a minute…aren't you…(gasp)…*you*…

MARTIN: Go about your business, Vance.

VANCE: You put the boobs on everybody's computer!

MARTIN: I strongly suggest that you go…about…your business…Vance.

VANCE: I didn't wanna see boobs until I got married. Oh God, I've cheated on my wife!

MARTIN: Oh for…you don't have a…you know what Vance? I never liked you. Tomorrow you get a finger just for pissin' me off.

VANCE: Hey hold on now, you can't…

KYLE: Vance, just go!

VANCE: Well this isn't right. This isn't right at all. *(Leaves.)*

MARTIN: Don't listen to him. This is *so* right. Maybe there'll be an opening for you someday.

(MARTIN goes silent again. KYLE picks up the phone and dials.)

KYLE: Yes hi, this is Kyle Matranga I just spoke to you five minutes ago about the conference room…hello? Hello? *(Slams down the phone.)* Shit! I'm never gonna get that room!

(He puts his head down on the desk. MARTIN immediately lifts his head up by the hair.)

KYLE: Sorry-sorry-sorry. *(Beat. KYLE sighs.)* Oh how I love my job.

(Lights down. Time for another message…)

PLEASANT VOICE: Everyone comes to this city dreaming of making a better life for themselves. And no one provides better opportunities for advancement than Empie Advertising. Employees who stay motivated and do what's expected of them find themselves advancing up the ladder so rapidly, they soon become the wealthy, persuasive dynamos that deep down we all wish to be. Just listen to this testimonial.

(LESTER appears.)

LESTER: I was fresh out of business school when I started here, a pimply little nobody that even the losers in the mailroom used to laugh at. But in time I honed my attitude to the point where I was offered a position as a Termination Alternative Artist due to my abrasiveness. After putting lazy failures in their place for a few years I was ready to rejoin the regular workforce with my newfound confidence. Today I'm an executive vice president. I've got a sexy wife, a summer home in the Hamptons, access to the best restaurants and clubs in the city, and best of all…complete superiority over ninety-nine percent of the people I pass every day. Take a long hard look. This could be you.

SCENE 6

Lights up on the PRISONERS. ONE is sitting in his chair; TWO is standing facing away from him.

ONE: I've been here…a few months now. There have been times when I've had this whole place to myself, and other times when it's been packed wall to wall. All the people that were here before you…they were all kind of like me. Boring jobs…not much to say. Now…a few of them got let out. I don't know why, but for some reason they were pardoned. A few were repeat offenders. They got let out and then ended up right back here. But most of them…Straight Arrow killed them instantly while I watched.

TWO: How?

ONE: He…well it's kinda hard to explain. But at least it seems to be painless.

TWO: Why didn't you tell me?

ONE: I know I should have, but I couldn't. It was so wonderful to have company again that I didn't want to ruin anything.

TWO: This can't be happening. You don't get a death sentence just for expressing yourself.

ONE: It happens a lot more than you'd think. I'm sure more people in this world have died from expressing themselves than from certain fatal diseases. Here though…it only seems to happen if you do it wrong.

TWO: I did *not* do it wrong! I didn't even get a chance to finish! They can't do this! (*Crumbles into a corner and sits in shock.*)

ONE: Listen, you're not like me. My kinds of mistakes are usually the ones that end up being fatal. You might still have a chance.

(*TWO seems to snap back to reality.*)

ONE: What is it?

TWO: I have an idea.

(*Lights down.*)

INTERCOM: May I have your attention please? I am happy to announce that this past weekend our brave volunteers from Empie Advertising were victorious in the barbed wire cage/exploding ring/chainsaw battle royal against the representatives of AOL Time Warner. As a result the hostile takeover of Empie Advertising will not take place. We strongly encourage all employees to take time to visit the three surviving members of our team at the ICU of St. Vincent's Hospital. And now, please join us in a moment of silence for the twelve other team members who weren't so lucky.

(*A sappy song plays for a moment.*)

INTERCOM: Thank you.

SCENE 7

Lights up. KYLE sits at his desk working away as usual. After a moment, LESTER comes out of his office, looking off in the distance. He begins to clap sarcastically. After a bit of this, we see whom he's clapping for: the returning MEGHAN. She walks slowly, embarrassed, back to her desk.

LESTER: Ladies and gentlemen the internationally renowned superstar Meghan Altman has returned! Please, please, no autographs folks, give the young lady some room to breathe here! Now Ms. Altman I won't waste too much of your time, Lord knows you're busy enough as it is with all of your glamorous world premieres to attend and your smorgasbord of offers from huge producers, so I'm just going to ask you the question that's on EVERYbody's mind today…you didn't get the part did you?

(*Beat.*)

LESTER: C'mon Ms. Altman, everybody's dying with anticipation here, you didn't get the part did you?

(*Beat.*)

MEGHAN: No sir.

LESTER: Beg pardon?

MEGHAN: No sir.

LESTER: One more time Ms. Altman, with feeling!

MEGHAN:…No…sir.

LESTER: You heard it here first everybody…MEGHAN ALTMAN BLEW ANOTHER AUDITION!!! I mean really, I am shocked and appalled, I was so sure that unlike your last…what are we up to now, ten auditions? Twenty? A hundred? Well, I was SURE you'd get this one right. So anyway now that we've covered that topic I'd love for you to direct your attention back to the man responsible for paying your bills, okay? I was very generous and gave you two weeks off, and now we have clients coming in from France in a matter of days…FRANCE! And if you were…and no one else is going to have the guts to tell you this so you should be thankful for me…if you were a good actress at all you would have no reason to be working here. Someone would've discovered you a long time ago, honey. And deep down you know that and that's why you keep coming back here and doing what I tell you to. And I am telling you now to screw your head on straight the way it belongs, and join us here in the REAL WORLD! I spent an obscene amount of overtime while you were gone preparing for this client meeting, and now it's your turn to roll up your sleeves and pitch in. And God help you if I ever hear the word "audition" out of your mouth again!

(He goes into his office. MEGHAN slowly sits at her desk. KYLE looks at her sympathetically, not knowing what to say. He's just about to open his mouth when LESTER returns from his office holding enough paperwork to burn for a hundred winters. He drops it on MEGHAN's desk.)

LESTER: I need all of this in Power Point.

(LESTER heads back to his office. MEGHAN begins pitifully leafing through the stack of paper. Before LESTER goes in, he turns to MEGHAN.)

LESTER: And in French.

(He slams the door. After a few moments, MEGHAN lays her head down on her desk.)

KYLE: Hey, um…Meghan?

MEGHAN: *(Lifts her head up.)* What?!

KYLE:…You okay?

MEGHAN: Do I *look* okay? Would *you* be okay after all that?

KYLE: I'm sorry, I…

MEGHAN: *Please* just get back to work.

KYLE: I just thought…hey, I know how you feel.

MEGHAN: You know how I feel, huh? How? Are you an actor too?

KYLE: Oh no, no. I just meant that, working for Marisa I know how it feels to be talked down to all the time. Man, I wish I could do what you do. To get involved in a field that's so competitive…to get up there night after night in front of total strangers…I respect actors. I think you're a lot tougher than you give yourself credit for, Meghan.

(Beat. MEGHAN is genuinely touched.)

MEGHAN: Thank you.

KYLE: Is it fun? Being on stage?

MEGHAN: When you can actually find work? There's nothing like it.

KYLE: Well, I got a degree in business. So…I'll probably be in places like this all my life. But I really want to make my way up the ladder here. That's why once I heard this position was open I requested to be moved here.

MEGHAN: You *asked* for this?

KYLE: It's like my dad always taught me, "Kyle, take the jobs no one wants and do 'em better than anyone's ever done 'em before and sooner or later you'll catch someone's attention."

MEGHAN: And you believed him?

KYLE: Well he also said, "Kyle, your mom walked out on me because I was too good for her and she knew it. But when she gets remarried watch me act all happy instead of wringin' her freakin' neck…" and that's usually when he'd pass out.

MEGHAN: Interesting…

KYLE: Yeah, having a dad like that's not without a certain…entertainment value.

(MARTIN enters listening to an iPod and singing or humming to himself. He could also be carrying a bottle of water, a bag of snacks, or a book. He looks like he's enjoying himself to no end. He passes KYLE's and MEGHAN's desks. MEGHAN tries not to look at him.)

MARTIN: Kyle. Meg.

KYLE: Look man, neither one of us has done anyth…

MARTIN: Relax, relax, relaaaaaaaaaax. I'm not here for you guys.

(He puts his arm around KYLE and points out toward the audience.)

MARTIN: See that guy [woman] over there? Parked in Dan McCormick's space yesterday. He [She] thinks we don't know about it. *(Chuckles mischievously.)* We do. See you 'round. *(Exits into the audience.)*

MEGHAN: God I hope not.

KYLE: But see this is what my dad was talking about.

(MARTIN picks SOMEONE out of the audience and flips them off for the remainder of KYLE and MEGHAN's conversation. As he does, he can continue to sing along with his iPod, drink his water, have a snack, read his book, whatever…as long as he doesn't drop the finger.)

KYLE: That guy started out working right here, and he was just as stressed as we are. And now look at him. At first I called him a sellout. But the more I see him work and the happier I see him get every day…he's got the right idea. You just have to eat a little shit here and there and sooner or later you'll get what you actually deserve.

(Beat.)

MEGHAN: We have *so* got to get out of here.

KYLE: Hey I chose this, I'm willing to…

MEGHAN: *This?* You chose to work for heartless bastards that live to belittle people until they're so broken that they become what they hate? *That's* what you chose? Because that's definitely what you got.

KYLE: I know it's hard for you because this isn't what you want to do for the rest of your life, but…

MEGHAN: You're right Kyle, I don't! But that doesn't mean these people can treat me like a second-class citizen and then expect me to believe that it's helping me in some twisted way! God, between the finger-flippers and the human centrifuges…and there's even a rumor going around that they're bringing the Blame Lottery back.

KYLE: The Blame Lottery?

MEGHAN: Something they discontinued not long after I started here. If one of the really big execs made any kind of huge mistake that could ruin their lives…they put the names of everyone beneath them into one of those lottery machines…the ones that spit the balls out? And whoever's name came up took the blame for the executive, no matter what they did.

KYLE: That can't be true.

MEGHAN: Not only is it true, it's why my friend who got me the job doesn't work here anymore! A senior vice president got busted for insider trading, so he drew her name and they carried her out in cuffs! She worked in the art studio, she had never even met this jerk, and to this day I still don't know what happened to her!

KYLE: Well…as long as they're not doing that anymore…I mean it's not like I've never worked for real hardasses before.

MEGHAN: You've worked for Marisa how long now?

KYLE: A week.

MEGHAN: Give it time, Kyle. Just give it time.

(MARTIN leaves. From here the lights change, and the scene turns into a montage representing a few weeks in the lives of KYLE and MEGHAN. We hear the sound of a timekeeper's bell. Then MARISA runs in and yells at KYLE in a very animated fashion. The bell rings again and she leaves. KYLE rolls his chair over to MEGHAN's desk. She takes a spit-bucket from under her desk and works on KYLE the way a trainer would work on a boxer who's being pum-

meled. The bell rings again. KYLE goes back to his desk, and this time MARISA drops stack after stack of paper on his desk. KYLE winces each time she drops a stack as though he's being punched. The bell rings again, MARISA leaves, and KYLE rolls back over to MEGHAN's desk, wearier this time. MEGHAN works on him again. The bell rings and MEGHAN motions for him to return to his desk. KYLE shakes his head no and pleads with MEGHAN not to make him go back. She tries to pull his chair back to his desk but KYLE clutches her desk with a death grip. Finally she pries him loose and wheels him back to the desk. As soon as KYLE turns to face MARISA's office, she runs out and decks him in the face, knocking him out cold to the floor. MEGHAN rapidly counts to ten and the bell rings for the final time. All of the above is done silently over music of the director's choice. KYLE crawls back into his chair as if he has no idea where he is. Lights return to normal. KYLE looks half dead.)

MEGHAN: So…how do you feel now?

KYLE: I…I…

MEGHAN: Yeah?

KYLE: I feel… *(Drops to the floor, out cold.)*

(Lights down.)

SCENE 8

Lights up on the PRISONERS. PRISONER TWO is crouched down beside her chair as though she's ready to pounce. PRISONER ONE looks as though he was trying to do the same, but now is nodding off. After a moment TWO notices this, approaches him, and backhands him across the face.

TWO: Wake up!

ONE: *(Snaps to attention.)* Huh? Wha?

TWO: *(Returns to her position.)* You were falling asleep again. Make up your mind, are you with me on this or not?

ONE: He's not coming.

TWO: He's got to come back sometime.

ONE: Maybe he forgot about us.

TWO: Maybe that's just what he wants us to think.

ONE: Listen…I don't think we can do this.

TWO: Of course we can! There's two of us and one of him.

ONE: We both know how strong he is.

TWO: Okay fine, he's strong. But he's never going to see this coming. Now let's go over it one more time. Straight Arrow comes in, I start begging him not to kill me. While I'm doing that, what are you doing?

ONE: *(Completely without enthusiasm.)* I sneak around behind him and get on all fours. You push him over me and we both hold him down, beat the hell out of him, and force him to let us go.

TWO: Exactly.

ONE: And what if he won't?

(Beat.)

TWO: I think we're gonna have to torture him.

ONE: Torture him? With what?

TWO: With…well, there are parts of him we can step on, parts we can twist, parts we can bite…

ONE: Okay, now you're starting to scare me.

TWO: Our lives are depending on this! This is not the time— *(Starts to yawn.)* This is not— *(The yawn becomes enormous. She tries to say "This is not the time to have second thoughts" but it's completely drowned out by the yawn.)*

ONE: Listen to yourself. You're every bit as exhausted as I am. I'm telling you, we can't do this. Remember what I said about the…

TWO: The magnetism. Yes you covered that several times. But maybe we can fight it!

ONE: Listen…

TWO: I'm not going to die in here!

ONE: Please…

TWO: We are going to— *(The yawn comes again. She tries to say "We are going to make it out of here alive" but of course it just doesn't happen.)*

ONE: Let it go.

TWO: No.

ONE: Once there were twelve of us in here. I stood by and watched while he killed all eleven of the others one by one. He's gonna do whatever he wants with us.

TWO: You said you wanted to do this.

ONE: I know I went along with it. I guess a part of me was even hoping it would really work. But…

TWO: But what?

ONE: Not too long ago we were actually somewhat happy in here. We were talking, getting to know each other, having a few laughs…I loved it. Now look at us. We haven't slept in forever, we're afraid all the time, we never talk about anything but Straight Arrow anymore. I…I want things to be the way they were when you first got here.

TWO: But what if we…

ONE: I want to tell you something. I meant it when I said I'd never met anyone like you before. You came here and you saw another side of me. For once you didn't see me as just another boring accounting guy. You were genuinely interested in me. And you made me feel…like it was okay being alive even if I was trapped in here. I don't care about Straight Arrow. I don't care about what might happen to me. I care about you. Whatever happens to us, however little time we might have left in here…I want to spend it with you. As you really are. Not like this.

(Beat.)

TWO: I don't want to die.

ONE: I know you don't. But why fight to stay alive when you're only going to be living in fear the whole time? It's time to stop. All we can do is enjoy each other for as long as we've got. And know that whatever Straight Arrow does to us…at least we died unafraid. *(Touches TWO's face.)* Trust me?

(After a moment he lifts her head up so her eyes meet his. They look at each other for a moment and…lights down.)

SCENE 9

Neither MEGHAN nor KYLE are at their desks. LESTER comes out of his office holding a document. He crosses to the shredder stage left. As he does, MARISA comes out of her office and puts piles of paperwork on KYLE's desk. She drops some, stoops down to pick it up, and stands up directly

in the way of LESTER, who by this time is returning from the shredder. They look at each other for a moment and then…

LESTER: Don't even tell me…

MARISA: Oh you've gotta be kidding me!

LESTER: Okay, I have no time for this.

MARISA: Uh, me neither?

LESTER: Move.

MARISA: You move.

LESTER: You move.

MARISA: I'm not budging.

LESTER: I'm not budging.

MARISA: Get out of my way.

LESTER: Get out of my…

(MARISA suddenly screams and points somewhere behind LESTER as if to scare him into moving. LESTER looks at her as if to say, "what the hell was that?")

MARISA: I got another plan… *(Turns and looks behind her.)* KYLE!

(A bedraggled KYLE emerges from MARISA's office.)

MARISA: Hey, listen to me. You can put the expense report down for now. I have a much more important job for you. Are you listening? Okay, I want you to come on over here, grab this nitwit around the waist…

LESTER: Don't you…

MARISA:…and throw him out of my way as hard as you possibly can!

(KYLE begins to approach.)

LESTER: Oh for God's sake…KYLE! Kyle, don't you come anywhere near me…

(KYLE retreats slightly.)

MARISA: Don't tell my assistant what to do!

(KYLE approaches again.)

LESTER: Shut up! Kyle, stay right where you are…

(KYLE shrinks away again.)

MARISA: Don't tell me to shut up!

LESTER: Shut up shut up shut up! Kyle, if you touch me I will send you rocketing to the unemployment line so fast…

(KYLE shrinks away further.)

MARISA: Who the HELL gave you the authority to fire my assistant?!

LESTER: I'm sorry, what is your name?

MARISA: Marisa Sanborn!

(KYLE has begun to approach again.)

LESTER: What is it you do here exactly?

MARISA: A.S. for F.F.M.

LESTER: And in English that would be…?

MARISA: Account Supervisor for Fruity Fruit Munchies, genius!

LESTER: Right, those shriveled lumps of sugar that taste like sweaty socks.

MARISA: And how do you know what sweaty socks taste like?

LESTER: I…listen, I'm Lester Skollar, and I'm Executive VP of marketing, KYLE do NOT move!

(KYLE stops in his tracks. At this time, MEGHAN has entered behind LESTER.)

MARISA: You aren't the Executive VP of me, you pompous, arrogant… *(Suddenly gets an idea. She calls out over LESTER's shoulder.)* Excuse me, miss? Yes you, hi. What is your name sweetheart?

LESTER: Oh no you don't, MEGHAN IGNORE HER!

MARISA: Meghan honey, your boss and I are in a little predicament here; could you possibly maybe lend us a little hand?

LESTER: I am warning you Meghan…

(KYLE approaches again. LESTER gets into an exaggerated martial arts stance.)

LESTER: Don't even think about it!

KYLE: It's okay. I'm not going to touch you, sir.

MARISA: KYLE!

KYLE: Well I'm sorry, but he said…

MARISA: What he said should be of no relevance to you, Kyle!

KYLE: Um…he is an Executive VP…

MARISA: Kyle I swear to God I am that close to smacking you in the mouth right now!

LESTER: Would you please? Just step right over to him there…

MARISA: You'd love that, wouldn't you! Consider yourself very lucky, Kyle!

(MEGHAN approaches. KYLE talks quietly to her.)

KYLE: What is going on here?

MEGHAN: Zack's Complex.

LESTER: Hey!

MARISA: Meghan, did you just call me crazy?

MEGHAN: I'm not calling you anything, just stating a fact.

KYLE: What do you mean, "Zack's Complex?"

MEGHAN: It's a...slight...mental disorder that usually afflicts the rich and/or powerful. They first discovered it in this oil tycoon named Zack...something or other. If two people with Zack's Complex run into each other they won't move out of each other's way unless either they die or there's...force involved.

KYLE: I've never heard of that.

MEGHAN: It's kinda rare. I read all about it on the Internet.

LESTER: Wow...Meghan neglected her work to surf the Internet, now there's a shocker.

KYLE: So what can we do?

LESTER: I think it's obvious what you two can do, Kyle. Go over there, move that woman out of my way...

MARISA: Either one of you touches me and you will be hit full force by Hurricane Fucking Marisa! It's him that needs to be moved.

LESTER: Meghan, am I or am I not a black belt in jiu-jitsu?

MEGHAN: Double black belt.

LESTER: Soon to be a triple. Move me at your own risk.

KYLE: Can I make a suggestion here?

MARISA: As long as it's somewhat intelligent.

KYLE: Why don't, like, you jump to your left, and you jump to your left at the same time, then you won't be in each other's way anymore and no one had to move first?

(LESTER and MARISA both laugh.)

MARISA: That's your idea of intelligent, Kyle? Jump out of Mr. Big Bad EVP with the Big Bad Not-Quite-Triple-Black-Belt's way?

LESTER: Oh I'm not jumping anywhere!

MARISA: I would rather stand here until I starve to death!

(Beat.)

MARISA: Kyle, go downstairs and buy me a bag of chips.

LESTER: Meghan, go downstairs and grab me a bottle of water.

KYLE: Yeah, uh...let's go get their stuff, Meghan. Maybe they'll have worked something out by the time we get back.

(MEGHAN and KYLE exit upstage left.)

LESTER: Thousands of employees at this company and they stick me down the hall from the one person in the building that also has Zack's Complex.

MARISA: I know! You'd think they'd know better than to put us so close together. Maybe it was someone's sick idea of a joke...

LESTER: I'm going to miss that entire meeting.

MARISA: Well then sooner or later...you're just going to have to move.

LESTER: Don't you worry, I'll move...as soon as you've passed out from exhaustion.

MARISA: Oh yeah?

LESTER: Yeah. How many of these have you ever been mixed up in?

MARISA: Six.

LESTER: Ha! Fourteen.

MARISA: What was the longest you ever went?

LESTER: Four hours.

MARISA: Pfft. Eleven.

LESTER: I once made a three-hundred-pound bouncer move first.

MARISA: I once made a truck driver move first.

LESTER: So?

MARISA: He was still in his truck!

LESTER: Liar.

MARISA: You wanna see the newspaper article? It's right in my office… *(Almost moves as if to go get it.)* …damn it!

LESTER: You want to move so bad you can taste it.

MARISA: In your dreams, buster.

LESTER: I give you one hour.

MARISA: I give you a half hour, tops.

LESTER and MARISA: You're on.

(The lights change, and from here the scene becomes a montage like KYLE and MEGHAN's earlier. The two stare each other down intensely for a bit and then KYLE and MEGHAN enter, KYLE with MARISA's chips and MEGHAN with LESTER's water. Lights down. LESTER and MARISA both screaming at each other. Soon KYLE and MEGHAN enter. KYLE applies deodorant to MARISA and MEGHAN brushes LESTER's teeth. Lights down. Lights up and LESTER and MARISA are still staring each other down but now are doing what appears to be the pee-pee dance. KYLE and MEGHAN enter with coffee cans and some kind of

screens. They hand LESTER and MARISA the cans, completely cover them with the screens, and look the other way. After a moment LESTER's and MARISA's hands come from behind the screens, handing MEGHAN and KYLE their respective cans. KYLE and MEGHAN take them disgustedly and exit. Lights down. Lights up on LESTER and MARISA sleeping standing up with KYLE and MEGHAN holding them up by the shoulders. Sadly, when one of them tries to move their boss out of the way, they immediately wake up. Lights down. LESTER and MARISA are now both on their cell phones. KYLE and MEGHAN are gone. Lights up full.)

LESTER: Hi sweetpea!

MARISA: Hi baby!

LESTER: Yes I'm still here…

MARISA: Still at the office unfortunately…

LESTER: No I've been eating, got plenty of water…

MARISA: I've even been getting some sleep…

LESTER: Listen sweetie, I'm so sorry our plans three nights ago got ruined…

MARISA: I feel so terrible that we never got to have our date…

LESTER and MARISA: Could you hang on a second? Thanks. *(They cover their receivers.)* Excuse me, I'm on the god-damn phone! SHUT UP! *(They uncover the receivers.)* Sorry about that.

LESTER: Honey, I just want you to know that you've been so good to me through all this…

MARISA: Thank you so much for not walking out on me because of this…

LESTER: And I promise…

MARISA: And I swear…

LESTER: We'll pick up where we left off as soon as I'm home.

MARISA: I'm so going to make it up to you when this is over.

LESTER and MARISA: Okay? Love you too. Bye. *(They hang up.)* FOR GOD'S SAKE MOOOOOOOOOOOOOOOVE!!!

(KYLE and MEGHAN enter. KYLE holds a container of Chinese food, MEGHAN a bottle of Zima.)

MEGHAN: Everything okay up here?

LESTER: I am not even going to dignify that with an answer, Meghan.

KYLE: Got your lo mein.

MEGHAN: Got your… Zima.

LESTER: Did you let it breathe?

MEGHAN: Yes… yes I did.

LESTER: Good girl.

MARISA: Kyle. Lo mein. Now.

KYLE: You got it.

(KYLE opens the box, removes some noodles, and pelts them at MARISA's head.)

MARISA: KYLE!

KYLE: Oh I'm sorry, did you want more?

(He removes more noodles and again wings them at her head.)

MARISA: What in the hell do you think you're doing?!

KYLE: It's called staging a revolt. Meghan?

MEGHAN: *(Brandishes the Zima bottle.)* Have a little drink, sir!

(She splashes some of the Zima in LESTER's face.)

LESTER: MEGHAN!

MARISA: You two are so dead when we get out of this!

(KYLE continues throwing noodles at MARISA.)

KYLE: Um, I kinda doubt it. By the time you wake up Meghan and I will be long gone.

LESTER: By the time we wake up?!

KYLE: Oh did I forget to mention? Meghan actually knows a lot more about this Complex you two have… it's SO fascinating.

MEGHAN: See, there are these guys that call themselves "Separation Specialists"?

MARISA: Oh no…

LESTER: Separation Specialists are an urban myth, Meghan!

MEGHAN: 'Fraid not, Les. We happened to find a little agency right down the block from here. They said they'd be around in a matter of minutes.

MARISA: Kyle…

(KYLE pegs more noodles at MARISA. She ducks, and the noodles hit LESTER.)

LESTER: Marisa will you kindly tell your assistant to stop throwing that garbage?

KYLE: I don't answer to Marisa anymore, pal. You know I actually used to admire people like you. But if climbing up the corporate ladder means that some day I'm gonna be so arrogant that I can't even move out of somebody's way when they approach me in the hall...I would hope that when I get to the top of that ladder there's a guy up there with a shotgun ready to go Old Yeller on me! I would rather move back in with my dad...and...well...maybe not...no, no, I would rather move back in with...Dad...than put up with this for one more day!

MARISA: You and I both know that you don't have one ounce of the guts to...

KYLE: Yeah, I think that's quite enough.

(KYLE pours the remaining noodles over MARISA's head. She screams.)

KYLE: Meghan?

MEGHAN: Well, I really hope you've enjoyed the time you've spent ridiculing me for my blown auditions, Lester. I deserved it for wasting so much time here in the office and not spending enough time studying my craft. Well not anymore. And when I finally do catch my break, and believe me Lester I will, I can't wait to do my first big television interview where I completely run your name into the fucking ground! And even if that doesn't happen...I would rather live off of credit cards or even food stamps for the rest of my life than spend one more minute in your presence. And I can't believe you wet your pants, Lester.

LESTER: What?

(MEGHAN immediately splashes the rest of the Zima directly on LESTER's crotch and tosses the bottle over her shoulder.)

MEGHAN: C'mon Kyle let's go.

(They start to exit. MEGHAN turns.)

MEGHAN: And for the record, Lester is not an expert in jiu-jitsu...his wife is. If you need a good laugh, Marisa, have

him tell the story of what she did to his kneecaps after he hit on her sister.

(They exit. There is a moment of extremely uncomfortable silence as LESTER and MARISA try to figure out how the hell to react to what just happened.)

MARISA: I thought you had a bit of a limp.

(Lights down on MARISA and LESTER. MEGHAN and KYLE are leaving when they run straight into MARTIN.)

MARTIN: Hey guys! Leaving a little early today, aren't we?

KYLE: Just...get out of the way, Martin.

MARTIN: Sounded like you two had a pretty interesting conversation with your bosses.

KYLE: Martin...

MARTIN: Forgot about that little talk we had, Kyle?

MEGHAN: Don't listen to him.

MARTIN: I'll be making six figures this time next year. I've got my eye on this swank apartment on the Upper East Side. My luck with the ladies these days? Indescribable. I went through everything you guys did and just look at how well they're taking care of me.

(An announcement comes over the IN-TERCOM.)

INTERCOM: May I have your attention please? We would like you all to know that as of this afternoon the Empie Advertising Blame Lottery has been reinstated. Thank you.

MEGHAN: I knew it. Kyle, we gotta go.

MARTIN: Kyle, I'm not gonna let you wimp out like this!

KYLE: I don't want this anymore Martin! I don't care about the money, I don't care about the benefits, I don't care about the…women…well…no! Not this way! Not ever again!

(INTERCOM comes to life again.)

INTERCOM: May I have your attention please? We would like to announce that **Martin Armstrong** has been selected to accept the blame for **Chief Operating Officer Bennett Rosenbloom** for **embezzling from the company.** We would like to ask that **Martin Armstrong** please report to **the menacing black van out front** at this time. Thank you.

(Beat.)

MARTIN: Did you guys just hear that?

KYLE: Oh yeah.

MARTIN: But they can't be serious…

(McCORMICK appears with a pair of handcuffs. KYLE and MEGHAN back up and watch.)

McCORMICK: Martin…I think you'd better come with me.

MARTIN: Dan, come on man! It's *Marty!*

McCORMICK: Martin please… *(Produces a can of mace.)* Let's do this the easy way.

MARTIN: Okay. Okay. You win, Dan. I'll go quietly, and take my punishment like a…

(MARTIN instantly runs off screaming. McCORMICK takes out a walkie-talkie.)

McCORMICK: It's McCormick. He'll be running directly into you guys in

about five seconds. Let the new guy take him down. Tell him to use that thing I showed him.

(We hear a taser-like sound and MARTIN howling in pain and then falling on the floor…followed by VANCE chuckling like a kid in front of an anthill with a magnifying glass. McCORMICK starts to exit in the direction that MARTIN fled, calling out to the "NEW GUY.")

McCORMICK: Good work, Vance!

(He exits. KYLE and MEGHAN look at each other like "what the fuck just happened?" Lights up on MARISA and LESTER. During their dialogue, KYLE and MEGHAN are looking off in the opposite direction at SOMEONE approaching.)

LESTER: Well I hope you're satisfied. We no longer have assistants because of you.

MARISA: Don't even try to blame this on me! Why didn't you see me? I was right in front of you!

LESTER: I was shredding!

MARISA: Ah-HA! So you admit that it's all your fault!

LESTER: Lady I like to think that I can shred or fax or do whatever the hell I please without running into some psycho!

MARISA: *(Mimes talking on the phone.)* Hi, kettle? This is the pot. Just calling to say you're black!

LESTER: That is it. I'm through screwing around here! I was hoping it wouldn't come to this, but I'm moving you by force mys…

MARISA: COME AND GET IT!!!

(*MARISA leaps at LESTER, and the two begin wrestling around on the floor. Soon KYLE and MEGHAN lead two Separation Specialists, PEDRO and TINA, over to where their former bosses are. After a moment, PEDRO produces a small blowgun-like weapon, holds it up to his mouth, and rapidly fires twice. LESTER and MARISA instantly go limp.*)

TINA: Nice shootin' Pedro!

PEDRO: Damn, that was a tricky one!

TINA: I hear that. I mean I've seen some chronic Zack's Complexes before but these two were unreal! Look at that! The guy even pissed his pants!

PEDRO: Hey Tina? These things always end in violence?

TINA: Pretty much whenever it's two guys, but this is the first time I've ever seen a man and a woman start throwin' hands. These two got it bad.

PEDRO: Where we takin' 'em?

TINA: Just sit 'em back in their chairs until the car gets here. (*Turns to MEGHAN.*) Whose office is whose here, lady?

MEGHAN: Lester's is back there, Marisa's is over there.

PEDRO: Got it.

(*TINA lifts up MARISA while PEDRO scoops up LESTER. They carry them off their separate ways.*)

PEDRO: This, uh, "Zack's Complex"? It's some scary shit, man.

TINA: (*Offstage.*) That's why we use the triple-strength tranquilizers.

PEDRO: Do they really know for sure who's most at risk for it?

(*PEDRO walks back onstage with his back turned, as if checking to make sure MARISA will be okay in her chair.*)

TINA: Jeez Pedro, we gonna do this every day? It's JUST the RICH and POWERFUL!!

PEDRO: All right, all right! Dios mío.

(*TINA also comes on stage backwards.*)

TINA: Of course just like everything else, I'm sure there are a few unlucky ones who come down with it when they least expect it.

(*TINA and PEDRO back into each other. They turn around and face each other, eyeing each other suspiciously for a second. TINA starts to say something, but PEDRO immediately shoots her with a dart, rendering her unconscious. He scoops her up and looks at KYLE and MEGHAN.*)

PEDRO: Can't be too careful. (*Exits.*)

MEGHAN: Kyle…I don't know about you but I don't feel like sticking around to see what they do to people who quit.

KYLE: I know, I know. There's just a couple of things I wanna do first.

MEGHAN: Like what?

KYLE: Need to make a little change to my answering machine message. And save a few things onto a disk.

MEGHAN: All right, just make it quick. I'll keep an eye out for anything weird…er.

KYLE: (*Checks his computer.*) Oh hey Meg…I've been meaning to tell you this…when I first came up here and met Martin? He was writing a really sad, pathetic poem…about you!

MEGHAN: Okay, I can feel my lunch crawling up my throat.

KYLE: But get this…it's still here in the recycle bin! Want to read it before we head out?

MEGHAN: Oh God no, just get rid of that crap.

KYLE: You got it. *(Moves his mouse.)*

SCENE 10

Lights up on the PRISONERS. They are asleep in each other's arms. After a moment, TWO stirs. She looks at ONE, smiles, and strokes his hair until he awakes.

TWO: Hey you.

ONE: Morning.

(He kisses her.)

TWO: Chilly this morning.

ONE: Want me to go fix the thermostat?

TWO: Sure. And while you're doing that I'll whip us up some breakfast.

(They laugh. He kisses her again.)

ONE: So what are we having?

TWO: Mmm, I could go for some…French toast. Two inches thick. Dripping with syrup. Scrambled eggs…a little sausage…

ONE: And a Bloody Mary.

TWO: Yes. Several Bloody Marys.

(Immediately all stage lights come up. The PRISONERS jump up and sit back in their chairs as though they've been pulled into them.)

TWO: Oh no.

ONE: Just relax…

TWO: It's him.

ONE: It's gonna be okay…

TWO: No, we gotta stop him!

ONE: There's nothing we can do.

TWO: HELP! PLEASE SOMEBODY HELP!

(STRAIGHT ARROW, a seven-foot computer screen arrow, enters)

TWO: STAY AWAY FROM US!

(STRAIGHT ARROW crosses rapidly to PRISONER TWO.)

ONE: Leave her alone!!

TWO: DON'T TOUCH ME!!!

(STRAIGHT ARROW touches PRISONER TWO and looks straight ahead.)

STRAIGHT ARROW: Delete.

VOICE: Are you sure you want to delete the document "Meghan Hates Me"?

STRAIGHT ARROW: Yes.

(PRISONER TWO falls to the floor, dead.)

ONE: NO!

(STRAIGHT ARROW picks up TWO's body.)

ONE: You can't do this! LET ME UP YOU BASTARD!!!

(STRAIGHT ARROW exits. Lights come back down, and PRISONER ONE stands.)

ONE: You can't take her…I won't let you…bring her back… *(Falls to his knees.)* Please just bring her back…

(Lights up on KYLE. MEGHAN enters.)

MEGHAN: Kyle!

KYLE: *(Turns suddenly and blocks his computer screen.)* Okay, I think I'm all set here.

MEGHAN: *(Playfully.)* You sure? I mean, you weren't writing any love poems about me on that thing, were you?

KYLE: Pfffft. Poetry. That's only for people too afraid to reach out and take what they want. And as of this day... *(Faces MEGHAN.)*...that's never going to be me again.

(He kisses her very weakly. She looks at him for a moment and then:)

MEGHAN: Oh Kyle, no. No, no, no, no, no.

(As KYLE looks down embarrassed, she lifts his chin and kisses him fervently.)

MEGHAN: See you at the elevator. HURRY! *(Exits.)*

KYLE: *(Giddy, goes to his computer.)* Guess I won't be needing you anymore. *(Fiddles with the mouse.)*

SCENE 11

PRISONER THREE stands beside KYLE's computer and recites a poem as STRAIGHT ARROW slowly sneaks up behind her.

PRISONER THREE: I'd hold you with every ounce of love I could muster
Stroking your hair with the confidence of a thousand generals
Letting your eyes hold my soul captive in your blissful embrace of understanding
Electrifying your every curve with my...

(STRAIGHT ARROW grabs PRISONER THREE from behind and stares straight ahead.)

STRAIGHT ARROW: Delete.

VOICE: Are you sure you want to send "Meghan Would Be Mine If I Wasn't Such a Pussy" to the recycle bin?

STRAIGHT ARROW: Yes.

(STRAIGHT ARROW picks up PRISONER THREE and drops her on the floor near PRISONER ONE, who is sitting in his chair not looking at her. After a moment, PRISONER THREE rises the same way PRISONER TWO did in Scene 2 and approaches ONE.)

THREE: Mister? What is this place?

ONE: Hell. And the devil's coming for you any minute. Now leave me alone.

THREE: What are you talking abo—

(All lights up as STRAIGHT ARROW enters. PRISONER THREE falls into the chair as he touches her.)

STRAIGHT ARROW: Delete.

VOICE: Are you sure you want to delete—

STRAIGHT ARROW: Yes.

(PRISONER THREE falls dead. STRAIGHT ARROW picks her up and leaves. Lights down again as PRISONER ONE stands.)

ONE: I hate you!!! You think it's all right to just kill us because we made a few mistakes?! You think it's all right to take someone I care about from me and just leave me here to rot? DO YOU THINK THIS IS FUNNY?! WHY DON'T YOU COME BACK HERE AND LAUGH IN MY FACE YOU SON OF A BITCH?! COME ON!!! COME AND GET ME, STRAIGHT ARROW, I'VE FUCKING HAD ENOUGH!!!

(Lights up on KYLE.)

MEGHAN: *(Offstage.)* Kyle? Someone could be coming for us any minute!

KYLE: Just gimme two more seconds, Meg!

MEGHAN: *(Offstage.)* Hurry up!

KYLE: *(Pauses.)* Yeah...screw this place. May as well get rid of everything.

(Lights up on PRISONER ONE. The door opens and STRAIGHT ARROW comes in. He touches PRISONER ONE.)

STRAIGHT ARROW: Delete.

VOICE: Are you sure you want to delete the workbook "Third Quarter Totals version 1"?

(With great effort and a huge scream, PRISONER ONE runs at STRAIGHT ARROW and the two begin to wrestle. Lights up on KYLE.)

KYLE: The hell's the matter with this thing?

(KYLE fiddles with the mouse as ONE and STRAIGHT ARROW fight. KYLE taps the hard drive.)

KYLE: C'mon...

(He shakes the hard drive. The fight continues. Finally KYLE gives the hard drive a gigantic kick. A short circuit or explosion sound is heard. PRISONER ONE and STRAIGHT ARROW both fall to the floor dead. KYLE gets a shocked look on his face. He then starts laughing and runs out the door, victorious. Lights down. Sound of an answering machine beeping.)

KYLE: *(Voiceover.)* Hi you've reached Kyle Matranga. I'll be out of the office until they're building snow forts in hell because I fucking quit, along with the beautiful and talented Meghan Altman. Remember that name because she's going to be huge someday. If you need immediate assistance please contact one of the many assholes that still work here. Thank you, have a great day.

(The End.)

KISS AND CRY

Tom Rowan

TOM ROWAN is a director and playwright. He was born in New York City, and grew up mainly in Boulder, Colorado. He has a BA in drama from Trinity University, and an MFA in directing from the University of Washington School of Drama. He is the author of the one-act *Chamber Ensemble*. As a director, Rowan's credits include the premieres of Craig Lucas's *Grief* (2001) and Deborah Grimberg's *The Honey Makers* (2003) in the Ensemble Studio Theatre Marathon; *Slight Alterations* by Ron E. Edens (Abingdon Theatre Company, 2002); and *Twelfth Night*, *The Winter's Tale*, and *The Two Gentlemen of Verona*, all for Theater Ten Ten. For the Princeton Rep Shakespeare Festival, he directed *The Comedy of Errors* and *Romeo and Juliet*. As artistic director of The Mirror Players in Denver, Rowan directed *As You Like It*, *Hamlet*, *A Midsummer Night's Dream*, *Romeo and Juliet*, and *Love's Labour's Lost*. He also directed the regional premieres of Steven Dietz's *Trust* and Nicky Silver's *Raised in Captivity* for the Avenue Theatre in Denver, as well as *Orpheus Descending* and *The Road to Mecca* at the Denver Civic Theatre. He is the recipient of a 1998 Drama League Directing Fellowship and of the 1992 Denver Drama Critics Circle Award for Best Director (for *A Midsummer Night's Dream*). He has served as literary manager at the Ensemble Studio Theatre, literary assistant at the Denver Center Theatre Company, and new play consultant at Queens Theatre in the Park. He also works as an acting coach and script consultant. He is working on two new plays: *David's Play*, and *The Second Tosca*. Rowan currently lives in Midtown Manhattan. Learn more at www.tomrowan.net.

Kiss and Cry was first presented by Jorelle Aronovitch as part of the New York International Fringe Festival (Elena K. Holy, Producing Artistic Director) on August 15, 2004, at the Black Box Theatre at 440 Studios, New York City, with the following cast and credits:

Fiona.. Julie Leedes
Stacy ....David Lavine
Lauren... Nell Gwynn
Trent .... Gregory Marcel
Ethan .... Paul Siemens
Brittany.. Elizabeth Cooke

Directed by: Kevin Newbury
Set Designer: Robert Monaco
Costume Designer: Joanne Haas
Lighting Designer: Greg Emetaz
Sound Designer: Robert Gould
Production Stage Manager: Taylor Hansen
Music Consultant: Robert Korwek

Kiss and Cry was subsequently presented by Theater Ten Ten (Judith Jarosz, Producing Artistic Director) on February 13, 2006, at Theater Ten Ten, New York City, with the following cast and credits:

Fiona.. Julie Leedes
Stacy ....David Lavine
Lauren... Nell Gwynn
Trent ....Timothy Dunn
Ethan ....Reed Prescott
Brittany.. Elizabeth Cooke

Directed by: Kevin Newbury
Set Designer: Robert Monaco
Costume Designer: Joanne Haas
Lighting Designer: Diana Kesselschmidt
Sound Designer: Robert Gould
Production Stage Manager: Taylor Hansen
Assistant Stage Manager: Jessica Fisher
Skating Consultant: Emrah Polatoglu
Press Representative: Ron Lasko, Spin Cycle
Recorded Voices: Joe Fellman, Adam Gordon, Rachel Lillis, Ross Maxwell

Special thanks (for development and production support): The Theatre On Broadway (Nick Sugar); *Show Business Weekly*; The Producers Club; Ensemble Studio Theatre (Curt Dempster); Jorelle Aronovitch; Kevin Newbury; Brandon Fradd; the New York International Fringe Festival (Elena K. Holy); Theater Ten Ten (Judith Jarosz).

CHARACTERS

FIONA, twenty-five, an actress. Gorgeous and charismatic, with an irresistible energy and zest for life.

STACY, twenty-two, a champion figure skater. A beautiful young man with a gentle, boyish charm; moves like a dancer. Not as naïve as he sometimes seems.

LAUREN, thirty-five, a playwright/director. Fiercely intelligent, driven, and committed to her art and her politics.

TRENT, twenty-one, a college student. Cute and sexy, with a hip style and a wicked sense of humor.

ETHAN, twenty-seven, a figure skater. Bigger and sturdier than Stacy, with a big heart and a great smile. Could use a boost in self-esteem.

BRITTANY, sixteen, Stacy's pairs partner. Adorable and talented. Her upbringing has been rigidly conservative, but she is developing a mind of her own.

TIME

The late 1990s.

SETTING

The play moves swiftly back and forth between Los Angeles, New York, Denver, Las Vegas, and Seattle. Numerous locations are suggested, each by one or two furniture pieces. Scene changes are accomplished during the music cues and voiceovers (prerecorded excerpts from TV and radio broadcasts, etc.) that are played during the blackouts.

ACT ONE
ONE.

Three a.m. in Los Angeles: the terrace of a huge house in the Hollywood Hills. An ornate balustrade hung with vines. FIONA is by herself, taking in the view, when STACY enters from inside the house, carrying a mug.

FIONA: Oh!

STACY: What?!

FIONA: You scared me.

STACY: I'm sorry.

FIONA: Not your fault. I'm jumpy.

STACY: I'm Stacy.

FIONA: *(Laughs.)* Fiona, actually.

STACY: I know.

FIONA: Can I help you with something?

STACY: No thank you. I mean…sorry, I just wasn't expecting to see you out here. Everyone left at the party is wondering where you are.

FIONA: Woops. I'm being bad. I just had to get away from all the…you know. All of it.

STACY: I think I can relate to that. *(Pause.)* Jeepers.

FIONA: Excuse me?

STACY: I've never…Well, never mind.

FIONA: No, what?

STACY: Well I was going to say I've never met a movie star before. But then I remembered I met two earlier tonight. Anyway, it's an honor to meet you. Sorry to disturb you. The movie was great! I'll leave you to…

FIONA: No, stay. It's nice out here. If you look over that way, you can see the Hollywood sign.

STACY: *(Looking.)* Cool.

FIONA: Yeah. *(Pause.)* Forgive me. I believe I'm suffering from slight inebriation.

STACY: I'm sorry. *(Beat.)* Would you like some of my coffee?

FIONA: You have *coffee* in there?!

STACY: You were expecting?

FIONA: I don't know what I was *expecting*. Yes! I will have some. What time is it anyway? *(Takes the mug and drinks.)*

STACY: Almost three a.m.

FIONA: I should—should I not?—go back in. I don't want to get a reputation for…antisocial…ism? *(Beat.)* How is it in there?

STACY: It's fine. I mean…it's different. From what I'm used to at least.

FIONA: *(Whispers.)* To tell the truth, me too. *(Beat.)* I have to admit I'm not really in my element here.

STACY: Well, I guess that's not surprising.

FIONA: I mean, I've done New York parties. I *am* New York parties. But L.A…—What do you mean that's not surprising? I wanted you to be surprised.

STACY: Well this is your first big studio movie, right?

FIONA: Correct. Three years out of acting school. I've been waitressing in Manhattan. Waitressing and doing no-budget plays in basement theatres off-off-off-off. Then my agent sent me in for…well, you saw it.

STACY: *(Overlapping.)* The rest is history.

FIONA: *Maybe.* Or maybe I'll be a sauce in the pan.

STACY: Do you mean a flash—

FIONA: Fifteen minutes of Warhol! Here today, gone by Labor Day!

STACY: I don't think so. Tonight's premiere was, as they say, really well received. I think they all loved you.

FIONA: Potentially. There's a *potentiality* of love. But this was friends. Family. Industry people, studio yes-men. Paid escorts. Not critics. Critics could trash me unmercifully. *(Beat.)* Of course, there were like twenty guys at the party that like wanted my ass. That's one reason I'm out here now.

STACY: I understand.

FIONA: Do you? You didn't come out here to hit on me, did you?

STACY: No.

FIONA: I didn't think so. Who are you, anyway?

STACY: My name's Stacy.

FIONA: But I mean, where do I know you from?

STACY: No place. *(Smiles.)* We've never met.

FIONA: But I mean, your face—or, well, actually your *butt*—looks familiar. Haven't I seen you on TV or something?

STACY: Maybe.

FIONA: One of the soaps? Orrr…a sitcom?

STACY: No. I'm not an actor. I'm just a fan. Of yours. Especially after seeing the movie tonight.

FIONA: Oh please! Don't be nice to me! "Vampire Campus" is like the dumbest movie of the year!

STACY: *(Trying not to laugh.)* Shhh! The producer and director are still here.

FIONA: *(Exaggerated whisper.)* Sooorry. *But.* It is dumb.

STACY: But entertaining. And *you* are terrific in it. A lot of the people at the party were saying your career is going to really go places.

FIONA: Yeah, right. Now that they know I can scream and grow fangs.

STACY: No, you can act. You made me…believe that you believed in those vampires.

FIONA: You're cute.

(He looks away.)

FIONA: I'm sorry! I bet you've been hearing that all night, right? From women, men…But I mean it. And not cute in a superficial way, like a Beanie Baby or something. In a good way! And I'm not saying that because I want anything from you. I'm just…responding to your truly genuine, *inner* cuteness.

STACY: I don't know what to say.

FIONA: Oh! That is so cute.

STACY: I think I'd better be…

FIONA: No! Wait don't. I mean…really. I want to tell you something. C'mere.

(Pause. STACY slowly moves over to her.)

FIONA: I'm a lesbian. Truly.

STACY: Oh.

FIONA: Are you shocked?

STACY: No. Surprised, a little.

FIONA: That's okay. People tend to be. I don't fit whatever their, you know, narrow little stereotype of a dyke is. I've got long hair, I like makeup and clothes, blah blah blah.

STACY: Sure.

FIONA: Did I make you uncomfortable? I just wanted to…clear the air of any, how shall we say, misunderstanding. About my motives in befriending you.

STACY: No, that's cool. *(Pause. He is interested.)* Do you have a…girlfriend?

FIONA: A life partner, we call it. Yes, I do. Her name's Lauren and we live together in a one-bedroom basement apartment in the Village.

STACY: What village?

FIONA: Greenwich. In New York.

STACY: I've never been.

FIONA: Sweetheart, you should go there. Believe me.

STACY: What's she like?

FIONA: Lauren? She's brilliant. She's…on her own path, let's put it that way. We met at U-Mass Amherst. I was a drama major and she was in the grad directing program, but now she writes, too. After school we moved to New York together to start our own theatre company.

STACY: Wow. What's it called?

FIONA: It's called "Women for the New Millennium." Isn't that unprepossessing?

STACY: Totally.

FIONA: You're a sweetie. So what about you?

STACY: What about me?

FIONA: Do you have a…girlfriend?

STACY: No. (Smiles.) Actually, I have a "partner" too.

FIONA: Aha.

STACY: A skating partner. Her name's Brittany, and she's sixteen.

FIONA: Ice skating! On TV! That's where I recognize you from.

STACY: Guilty as charged.

FIONA: I'm a fan. I mean, not enough to remember the names or anything. But I remember you were great. And that's why I recognized your butt!

STACY: I thought you said you were a—

FIONA: Oh please. That doesn't mean I can't appreciate the male bun on like a purely artistic basis. You and that girl are like…ballet dancers.

STACY: Thanks.

FIONA: I've seen you skate in Nationals. And like, Internationals.

STACY: Worlds.

FIONA: Them too! And the Olympics.

STACY: I wish. That's the dream. But we've got another year and a half.

FIONA: You'll make it! You're the best. What I love is when you do that triple lutz/triple bypass combination.

STACY: You mean triple lutz/triple loop? A triple bypass is like…heart surgery.

FIONA: Come on, I'm sure it's not that hard for *you*; you're the champ. Oh look!

STACY: (Alarmed.) What?

FIONA: Over there!

STACY: The Hollywood sign? You showed me.

FIONA: No no no. Higher! You can actually see two stars.

STACY: (Looking.) Who?

FIONA: Not movie stars, dummy. There's a hole in the smog! Two actual heavenly bodies.

STACY: Oh yeah. I see them.

FIONA: Let's make wishes!

STACY: (Smiling.) What?

FIONA: Pick one of the stars and make a wish on it. I'll do the other!

STACY: That's silly.

FIONA: Oh no no. I totally believe in this. Which star do you want?

STACY: Couldn't we share?

FIONA: I don't know, I wouldn't recommend it. I make big wishes.

STACY: Okay. You choose.

FIONA: The one on the left. Are you ready?

STACY: Yes.

(They close their eyes and wish.)

FIONA: Are you done?

STACY: Uh-huh.

FIONA: Okay. What'd you wish?

STACY: Well if I tell you it won't come true, right?

FIONA: *(Exasperated.)* Now *don't* tell me you're superstitious! I can't stand that.

STACY: *(Laughs.)* What'd you wish?

FIONA: That I one day win an Academy Award. Is that tacky? I mean, be honest.

STACY: You wished for an Oscar?

(She nods.)

STACY: For "Vampire Campus"?

FIONA: *(Hitting him.)* No no no! For some...great movie I do. A great American film I make at the height of my career. For which I will be...remembered.

STACY: That's cool.

FIONA: Thank you. I think if I told Lauren that she'd leave me. Or at least laugh at me.

STACY: Well I think you should wish for what *you* want.

FIONA: Thank you. I like that. So what'd you wish?

STACY: Nothing.

FIONA: Oh yes you did. I could feel you wishing for something hard. *(Beat.)* Come on, Stacy, no fair. *I* told. What'd you wish for?

STACY: Guess.

FIONA: An Olympic gold medal!

STACY: No.

FIONA: *(Gently.)* What, then?

STACY: Okay. *(Quietly.)* I wished for...that special person.

FIONA: Who?

STACY: You know. What I always wish. For a special somebody. The person I could trust with anything and they'd always be there.

FIONA: Go on.

STACY: Well, that's it. You know, don't you? I want to be...the most important person in somebody's life. Forever. And have them be that for me. *(Shrugs.)*

FIONA: "Them," huh?

STACY: What?

FIONA: Nothin'. *(Smiles.)* That's very lovely. I hope your wish comes true.

STACY: I hope yours does.

FIONA: Let's make a deal.

STACY: Okay.

FIONA: Careful! You have to find out what it is first. Don't *ever* agree to anything in advance—or you're never gonna make it in this town.

STACY: I live in Denver.

FIONA: True. Well sports is just as bad.

STACY: Sometimes. So what's the deal?

FIONA: Whoever's wish comes true first promises to call the other one and tell!

STACY: Deal.

FIONA: Although I guess if yours comes true you might not know at first. I mean about the "forever" part.

STACY: I think I'll know. *(Beat.)* But you won't have to call me to tell me about your Oscar. I'll be watching on TV!

FIONA: I'll call anyway.

STACY: All right. Do.

(Pause. They smile.)

FIONA: Do you think you could do me one little favor?

STACY: Absolutely.

FIONA: *(Hitting him.)* You did it again! We're going to have to work on this.

STACY: Sorry! *(Fake deep voice.)* Depends on what it is.

FIONA: Get me outta here.

STACY: What do you mean?

FIONA: Just…hold my hand and walk me downstairs past whatever…drunks and hangers-on and wannabes and piranhas are still in there.

STACY: No problem. So how're you getting home?

FIONA: There's a limo waiting for me in the driveway, actually. Don't laugh! It's a perk. I'll have the chauffeur drop you off first.

STACY: Deal. After you?

FIONA: Wait! *(Finishes the coffee.)* I said holding hands, remember?

STACY: Holding hands.

(They do. Blackout.)

VOICEOVER

Music.

WOMAN ANNOUNCER: Welcome back to *Entertainment Tonight.* Last night we checked out the premiere of the summer horror flick "Vampire Campus"— and the all-night party afterwards, which was a bona fide who's who of who's hot in today's young Hollywood. Our cameraman caught this footage of the movie's glamorous co-star, Fiona Blake, leaving the party hand in hand with—can you tell who that is?—Stacy Clifford, the figure skating champ who's considered one of the U.S.'s best hopes for a medal at the next Winter Olympics. We can't say for sure they're a couple, but don't they kind of look like a winning pair? Count on us to keep you posted on the latest developments. For *Entertainment Tonight,* I'm Julie Patterson.

TWO.

The stage is divided in half. Stage right is TRENT's apartment in Denver, represented by a rumpled bed, with TRENT barely visible under the covers. Stage left is the Greenwich Village apartment FIONA shares with LAUREN; we see a table with two ladderback chairs. LAUREN is sitting in one of them, working on her laptop computer. We hear a key in a lock offstage, followed by the sound of a door closing. FIONA, a bit bedraggled, enters with a duffle bag.

FIONA: *(Ironically.)* Hi honey, I'm home.

LAUREN: *(Holding up an intense hand.)* Just a sec!

(Not looking up, she continues to type. FIONA stands by and watches.)

LAUREN: Just one…more…wait!—two…more…sentences. Got it! *(Looks up.)* Hey you! *(Stands.)* Welcome home!

FIONA: *(Kissing her.)* Hey. That was a…different kind of greeting.

LAUREN: Sorry sorry. I had a good idea and you know me; it takes over.

FIONA: How's everything been?

LAUREN: Good. The new play is coming along. Slowly but…hesitantly. In bursts, I should say. Of something or other, we'll see. I saw Annie's piece at the EstroFest. *Raw.* In the good sense and the bad. Mostly good, I think, but she's gotta clear out the family stuff and hone in on the regenerative. I talked to her. And *tonight.* We've got Dina's opening. Nine sharp.

FIONA: Oh jeez. A play?

LAUREN: No, babe. Her large installations. The Chelsea space.

FIONA: I may beg off; I'm beat. That's the last time I'm taking the redeye from LA.

LAUREN: You can't beg off. Dina's one of our sister artists, and she has agreed to do the set for our next show sight unseen. I don't know how you expect people to work with us if we don't support the work they're doing. *Capiche?*

FIONA: Like, whatever. *(Beat.)* So! Did you miss me a little?

(Lights down on them, up on stage right. STACY, shirtless, comes in from "the bathroom," and TRENT stirs in the bed.)

TRENT: What are you looking for?

STACY: My shirt. *(Beat.)* I didn't know you were awake.

TRENT: I hate it when they leave without saying goodbye.

STACY: I didn't want to wake you. It's after six o'clock.

TRENT: Don't tell me you have a paper route.

STACY: If I'm in my room at home before Brittany and her parents get up for church, they won't know I was out all night.

TRENT: You weren't. Saturday night doesn't end until at least one o'clock Sunday afternoon; do I have to teach you everything?

(Pause.)

STACY: Was I that bad?

TRENT: That's not what I mea—

STACY: I warned you I'm not that experienced.

TRENT: Experience is overrated. You have the…raw materials.

STACY: I didn't mean to put you in the position—

TRENT: Honey, put me in any position you want. Just don't leave me alone in the middle of the night, okay?

(Lights fade on them. Up on stage left. FIONA is sitting alone at the table.)

FIONA: What are you doing in there, babe?

LAUREN: *(Calling from offstage.)* Making you some breakfast.

FIONA: I ate on the...never mind. Thanks. Aren't you gonna ask me about how it was?

LAUREN: *(Offstage.)* How what was?

FIONA: LA. The premiere.

LAUREN: *(Offstage.)* Well I would, hon, but I assume LA was LA and the premiere was a teenage vampire movie.

FIONA: Featuring *me*.

LAUREN: *(Offstage.)* Uh-huh.

FIONA: *(Peering warily at a newspaper left on the table.)* So you haven't...heard anything?

LAUREN: *(Offstage.)* About what?

FIONA: Well, the premiere was like all over *Entertainment Tonight* last night.

LAUREN: *(Offstage; deadpan.)* And you just know I watch that all the time. *(Enters with cereal.)* Here ya go. Put your feet up; I can't believe you took the redeye.

FIONA: Couldn't wait to see you.

LAUREN: I'm glad you're back home where you belong.

FIONA: The New York opening is Friday.

LAUREN: Of what? *(Thinks.)* Nora's show at HERE?

FIONA: "Vampire Campus."

LAUREN: Oh yeah. *(Looks at her computer screen.)*

FIONA: Wanna go?

LAUREN: Why should I go see a movie designed expressly to get teenaged suburban heterosexuals to spend more money in shopping malls?

FIONA: Oh I don't know. Because you love me?

LAUREN: And therefore I don't need to see you merchandised.

FIONA: *(Munching on her breakfast.)* And yet you're going to go spend an evening nibbling cheese and avoiding wine and looking at "installations" Dina put together out of old broken toys?

LAUREN: The difference being that that's her lifeblood. Your movie you did for the money. Which yes, we all have to do. But I don't ask you to come down to the bookstore and watch me run a cash register.

FIONA: I do, though.

LAUREN: Only since we put in the coffee bar. *(Beat.)* So let me think what else. *(Consults calendar.)* You missed my anniversary.

FIONA: What? Our anniversary's in November.

LAUREN: No, *my* anniversary. Last Thursday. Two years of sobriety.

FIONA: Right! Congratulations. I'm so proud of you.

LAUREN: And then Sunday night there's an Artists Against AIDS meeting, I said we'd be there.

FIONA: Sunday?!

LAUREN: Problem?

FIONA: Don't you want to watch the Tony Awards?

LAUREN: Um—hello? I picketed that last year, remember?

FIONA: *(Whining.)* Lauren, you should love the Tonys! It's the one night of the year when all America gets to see what's going on in New York theatre!

LAUREN: Correction. What's going on on *Broadway*. Which you of all people should know by now is not the same thing. Speaking of which! I think I finally got the last scene solved in "Journey of the Daughter."

FIONA: Well I can't wait to read it.

LAUREN: No need to wait. *(Starts offstage.)* I printed it up yesterday. Have a seat.

FIONA: *(Under her breath.)* Maybe later? I just got in the—

LAUREN: *(Reentering with manuscript.)* What, babe?

(Beat.)

FIONA: Lay it on me!

(LAUREN hands her the script as the lights fade on them, and come up on stage right, where TRENT is kneeling on the bed, kissing STACY.)

TRENT: Why are you so beautiful?

(Pause.)

STACY: *(Laughs a little.)* Sorry; I thought that was the beginning of a poem.

TRENT: I'm an English major; I just talk like that.

STACY: I like it. *(Starts looking for his shirt again.)*

TRENT: And yet you're leaving.

STACY: It's not 'cause I want to. I just don't want to deal with their questions. Can't, actually. *(Beat.)* It's a very complicated situation.

TRENT: Sounds like something out of a Victorian novel. Not that I mind; I

read them. Will you have to sneak in a window when you get home?

STACY: Not if I make it on time.

(They both laugh.)

STACY: I know it sounds ridiculous. *(Beat.)* The bus comes in five minutes, and I can't find my shirt.

TRENT: If you go like that you could probably get someone to give you a ride. *(Beat.)* Stay another few minutes, and *I'll* drive you.

STACY: That's nice of you, but it's so early. Don't you want to go back to bed?

TRENT: That's the point I've been trying to make! Sit.

(He pulls STACY back down on the bed.)

TRENT: So was this a one-night thing, or will I get to see you again?

STACY: I'd love to see you again, are you kidding? I can't believe you'd want to.

TRENT: Considering how many medals you've won, your self-esteem is surprisingly fucked up.

STACY: I guess.

TRENT: Thank you. For a lovely night.

STACY: Thank you for writing the letter.

TRENT: Oh jeez.

STACY: I'm embarrassing you; sorry.

TRENT: Hey, I don't embarrass. I'm just glad it worked. Guess it pays to go with a good photographer.

STACY: No, that's not what I'm talking about. I mean, the picture was nice, of course. But the letter. It got to me.

TRENT: Never underestimate the U.S. Postal Service!

(He pulls STACY's shirt out from under the covers and hands it to him. STACY starts putting it on.)

STACY: No, I mean it. I'd never have the guts to do something like that.

TRENT: *(Picking his own clothes off the floor and starting to get dressed.)* Oh no, definitely not. You just…jump up in the air, spin around three times, and land on one foot in front of millions of people. Or twirl some chick around your head like a lasso!

STACY: *(Laughs.)* Okay. But I'd be more scared to do what you did. I mean, what if I had been mean and rude and wrote back something cruel to embarrass you?

TRENT: Like I said, I don't embarrass.

STACY: Right.

TRENT: *(Beat.)* I knew you wouldn't do that.

STACY: How?

TRENT: You can tell a lot about a guy by watching him skate.

(The lights shift back to stage left, where FIONA is sitting alone at the table, reading the last page of the manuscript.)

FIONA: Wow.

LAUREN: *(Entering from kitchen.)* You're done?

FIONA: Yeah. I mean, I've got to read it again, there's so much in there. But yeah. Wow.

LAUREN: Works for you?

FIONA: I love your anger. Always have.

LAUREN: Now that you've read it, I can let you in on the…thing.

FIONA: Which is?

LAUREN: Sharon wants to co-produce. And she thinks she can get one of two Theatre Row theatres for a late fall run.

FIONA: Late fall this year?

LAUREN: This very. *(Smiles.)*

FIONA: Okay okay. It should be fine, but don't sign anything until I've talked to Lex.

LAUREN: About?

FIONA: Well, there's a couple film projects that have…expressed interest, as they so carefully put it. And I really have to be available when "Vampire Campus 2: Sophomore Year" starts shooting. It's not nailed down, timewise.

LAUREN: I wrote this for you. It's what we've been working toward for five years.

FIONA: Right right right. All doable. It's just a matter of workin' the dates. *(Gesturing with the script.)* The script is just…wow. You are the best. You are *important*. You speak to a culture.

LAUREN: We think the same way. Always have.

FIONA: Are you sure you want to direct it too?

LAUREN: Absolutely.

FIONA: Because I was thinking—you know me—just an idea!—file it, stow it, chuck it—but for whatever it's worth, I met a guy in LA who directs and might have just the *eye*—

LAUREN: A *guy?*

FIONA: Oh, probably gay.

LAUREN: *Probably?!*

FIONA: He did a short film that *rocked* at Sundance! Could be the ticket.

LAUREN: Ticket?

FIONA: To get...where we wanna be.

LAUREN: This *is* where we want to be. Theatre Row. New York. Women. *Us.*

FIONA: The magazine?!

LAUREN: You and me!

FIONA: Oh that! Okay, yeah. I was just thinking, and like I said, it's your call, but a lot of people—women!—think it's good for the playwright to not also direct. Like another creative mind can bring in a certain, you know, objectivity.

LAUREN: I'm *opposed* to objectivity. On principle.

FIONA: Which is valid.

LAUREN: What is this about?

FIONA: *(Grinning.)* Well. Okay. I was thinking that if we got somebody like this guy on board now, the whole project *might*—just dreaming here at this point, but that's what we do, right?—be able to be *developed* as a *film.*

LAUREN: It *is* a *play.*

FIONA: Absolutely.

LAUREN: The movie industry has been trying to kill off the live theatre for fifty years. It's not gonna get me.

FIONA: *(Beat.)* You know who you are; I've got to give you that.

LAUREN: I thought we both felt that way.

FIONA: Well, yeah, whatever. Absolutely. *(Beat.)* Although I happen to like

film acting. In some ways I think it suits my temperament better than the stage.

LAUREN: Wonderful.

FIONA: Like in stage acting there's no second chances. You mess up, the scene's history, at least till the next night. Film you can always do another take; there's like, less pressure, you know?

LAUREN: Are you just doing this to infuriate me?

FIONA: *(Grins.)* You are sexy when you're mad.

(She runs into the bedroom, LAUREN following. Blackout.)

Voiceover

Spectacular music.

MAN'S VOICE: Chris Burlington! Michelle Kwan! Todd Eldredge! Oleg Gorchakov! Brittany Bell and Stacy Clifford! See all your favorite Olympic, U.S., and World Figure Skating Champions, on tour, this summer, at an arena near you! Available now from Ticketmaster—or call our toll-free number, 1-800-SKA-TING. The best seats will go fast—call now!

Three.

The men's locker room at the training rink in Denver. TRENT is sitting on a bench. STACY clumps in, wearing his skates with skate guards and warmups.

TRENT: You skate so sexy.

STACY: *(Surprised to see him.)* Trent. *(Beat.)* Thanks. You watched practice?

TRENT: Just the end.

(Beat.)

STACY: How did you get in?

TRENT: It's open to the public, apparently. *(Picks up a dance belt.)* Is this yours?

STACY: No. *(Starts dialing his locker combination.)* I don't leave my stuff lying around.

TRENT: Too bad, it smells good.

STACY: Trent.

TRENT: I thought you wanted to see me again.

STACY: I did—I *do*. But this is where I work. *(Starts taking off his skates.)* I'm sorry.

TRENT: *(Looking around.)* I don't know, it has possibilities. I haven't done it in a locker room since high school. There was this guy on the swim team—

STACY: Trent!

TRENT: Oh jeez, they're making ice skates out of plastic now? Whatever happened to quality?

STACY: They're called skate guards. So I don't blunt the edges walking around off the ice.

TRENT: This warm welcome is blunting *my* edge. Don't I even get a kiss?

STACY: What if someone comes in?

TRENT: Don't worry; I'll behave.

(ETHAN barges in, his skates slung over his shoulder, and violently flings open a locker.)

ETHAN: Fuck!

TRENT: I sincerely hope you're not addressing me.

ETHAN: Six years of skating with the same girl—excuse me: woman!—and we can't even do a side-by-side camel spin without getting off unison.

STACY: Sure you can, I've seen you. A hundred times.

ETHAN: Not this week. She's speeding up. Every time. And of course Geoffrey's blaming me.

STACY: It'll be better tomorrow. Every pair has bad days.

ETHAN: Three months running? *(Puts his skates down.)*

TRENT: Hey, he has those plastic thingies, too!

ETHAN: *(Looks at him.)* Who are you?

TRENT: *(Before STACY can say anything.)* Bo Hendrickson. I'm a male model. We're doing a shoot here at the rink when you boys are done practicing. A new line of winter sportswear.

ETHAN: *(Frowns. To STACY.)* Do you know him?

TRENT: We just now met. But he wasn't very convivial. You athletes are another whole...ball game.

(TRENT hands dance belt to ETHAN.)

TRENT: You shouldn't leave these things lying around. It could trip someone. *(Exits.)*

(STACY takes off his sweatshirt.)

ETHAN: What a character.

STACY: Yeah.

ETHAN: Think he's queer?

STACY: Could be. A lot of male models are.

ETHAN: How do you know?

STACY: I've heard. *(Untaping his knee.)*

ETHAN: Need any help with that, buddy?

STACY: No thanks.

ETHAN: Knee acting up again?

STACY: Always. To some extent.

ETHAN: Shit. *(Starts taking off his practice clothes and hanging them in his locker.)*

STACY: You said it. Doc Jensen doesn't think Brittany and I should do the tour this summer. Thinks I should stay in therapy and a carefully monitored practice schedule.

ETHAN: Sounds like good advice. Not that I'm the authority. An asteroid would have to wipe out the world championships before anybody would ask me and Roberta to do a tour.

(A loud banging on the door.)

ETHAN: Go away!

BRITTANY: *(Offstage.)* Are you boys decent?

STACY: What is it, Brit?

BRITTANY: *(Offstage.)* There's a reporter here who would like to talk to you.

STACY: Really? Well, okay. Send him in I guess.

BRITTANY: *(Offstage.)* It's a *her.*

(ETHAN wraps a towel around his waist.)

ETHAN: Have a blast. I'll be in the shower. They wouldn't want pictures of me anyway, even naked. *(Exiting.)* They only want to talk to the contenders.

(He's gone. STACY hastily pulls on a T-shirt—as FIONA walks in. She's wearing sunglasses and has her long hair piled up under a 1940s man's hat with a white card bearing the word "PRESS" attached to the front of it.)

STACY: How can I help you?

FIONA: *(Faking an exaggerated New York accent.)* I'm from "Figyuh Skating Monthly." Got an hour tuh tawk?

(STACY looks bemused. FIONA pulls down her sunglasses and peers at him over the tops.)

FIONA: It's me, silly.

STACY: Fiona? What are you doing here?

FIONA: I was in the neighborhood and thought I'd…don a disguise and drop by to say hi. Hi, Sesame Seed.

STACY: In the neighborhood of Denver? I knew you were bicoastal, but—

FIONA: Watch your language, young man. The walls have ears.

STACY: How long are you in town for?

FIONA: *(Consulting her watch.)* About…two hours. I scheduled a layover on the way back to LA.

STACY: Really? *(Beat.)* Why?

FIONA: Actually it was just an excuse to get into a men's locker room. I've seen those reporters on TV do it.

STACY: Why would you be interested in that? *(Beat.)* And who would believe that get-up?

FIONA: Sixteen-year-old girls are easy to fool. But of course, you knew that.

STACY: You look like something out of *The Front Page.*

FIONA: *(Taking off the hat and looking at it.)* Actually I think that *is* where this came from. Lauren has a whole closet full of stuff like this, left over from her summer stock days. *(Shakes out her long, curly hair.)* Were you afraid I cut it off? I never would. Lauren calls this my Pre-Raphaelite look.

STACY: So why are you really here? I mean I know you think I'm cute and everything...

FIONA: ...but there are already enough rumors about us floating around out there.

STACY: *(Laughs.)* Did you see that?

FIONA: *(Pulling the newspaper out of her purse.)* Got it right here. *(Pause.)* I'm actually here to ask you a favor.

STACY: Sure, anything.

FIONA: *(Hitting him on the arm.)* I thought I told you not to do that! Find out what it is first.

STACY: What is it first?

FIONA: It's...well, it's not really a favor, really. Because it could be so...mutually beneficial. To you as well as I. Let's call it a...a business proposition.

STACY: A what?

FIONA: I was talking to my manager yesterday and he had an idea. About that article. And the thing on *Entertainment Tonight.*

STACY: Ohmygosh, I didn't even see that one.

FIONA: More of the same.

STACY: So you want me to call the editors and tell them it's not true?

FIONA: *(Pretending to think it over.)* Ummm...no thank you.

STACY: What then? Your friend Laura? Is she jealous?

FIONA: Lauren. No, she reads a different class of newspaper.

STACY: Then what? Clue me in.

FIONA: My manager, Lex—his name is actually Lex, can you believe it?—thinks it would be a good idea for us to um...play along.

STACY: Play along with what?

FIONA: The rumor.

STACY: I don't get it.

FIONA: Meaning...don't deny it. Meaning act like it might be true.

STACY: What? Why?

FIONA: Think about it. I'm the new Hollywood cover girl. Have you seen the reviews of "Vampire Campus"? Hate the movie; love me. I'm gonna be in teenage boys' lockers all over the fuckin' country!—I mean my *picture* will, of course. The scripts are gonna be, like, rolling in. *If* I play my cards right. And keep certain ones very close to the vest.

STACY: I'm still a little lost here.

FIONA: Do you think anybody's gonna hire me for leading love interest-type roles if they even suspect I like women? This is Hollywood we're talkin'. Everything would be much easier if the world thought I had a boyfriend. Especially a very cute, world-class figure skater.

STACY: *(Laughing.)* Oh yeah? And what's in it for me?

FIONA: Great PR, buddy. Sports figures need it just as much. Don't you want to snag all those *lucrative* endorsements once you've got your medal? A little financial security for the Canadian orphan. Don't tell me you wouldn't love a chance to get out from under the Born-Again Christian wing of Mr. and Mrs. Bell, who discovered you in a cold, lonely rink in Calgary and basically *adopted* you so their precious baby daughter could have a pairs partner?

STACY: Hey, how do you know so much about me all of a sudden? Last weekend all you had was some vague memory of seeing my butt on TV.

FIONA: *(Putting the press hat back on.)* I never show up for a performance unprepared. I spent last night on the Net reading up on you. I'd say the Bells made a pretty good investment if you ask me, since there's so many more American girls than boys going into figure skating. You know, the whole gay stigma thing. *(Pause.)* It would hardly take any effort on our part, Stacy. Just let them take our picture once in a while—they'll make up the rest. You have a great look—they'll put you on all the covers.

STACY: But *lying?* I don't know, it feels sordid. Why encourage an untrue rumor?

FIONA: *(Loud whisper.)* To shut down the *true* ones. *(Pause.)* I might not know a lutz from a camel, but I do know the figure skating community's as notoriously homophobic as the movies. Maybe more so.

STACY: *(Beat.)* And what does that have to do with us?

(FIONA gives him a look. Another loud knocking on the door.)

STACY: *(Relieved.)* Yes?

BRITTANY: *(Offstage.)* Can I come in?

STACY: What's the problem?

(BRITTANY enters.)

STACY: *(Gently.)* This is the men's locker room, sport. You know better.

BRITTANY: I thought you must be decent because I knew there was already a lady in here.

FIONA: *(Back with the New York accent.)* I haven't been cawled dat in a while.

BRITTANY: Are you doing an interview?

FIONA: You could cawl it dat.

BRITTANY: Can I help? *(Beat.)* Sorry to intrude, but I like to do interviews.

STACY: Actually, Fiona was just leaving.

BRITTANY: *(To FIONA.)* Did you get everything you needed?

FIONA: *(No accent, with a glance at STACY.)* Hard to say. Looks like maybe not.

BRITTANY: Ask me some stuff! I know all about this character.

(FIONA looks at her, and raises an eyebrow.)

BRITTANY: You look familiar. Have I met you before?

FIONA: I don't think so, dear. *(Pause.)* Have you seen "Vampire Campus"?

BRITTANY: Yes! I mean no. But I've seen the commercial like six times. You're a great screamer.

FIONA: Actually, I've been getting more discreet.

STACY: As I said, Fiona was just leaving.

FIONA: Toodaloo! *(Ducks out.)*

BRITTANY: Wow. Is she your girl-friend?

STACY: Whoa. What? No.

BRITTANY: Why is she here?

STACY: That's a good question. To say hi, I guess. I met her last week when I was in California to see that knee specialist.

BRITTANY: So then you're…friends?

STACY: I don't know, actually. *(Laughs.)* Certainly nothing more than friends. She's weird.

BRITTANY: Would you tell me if you had a girlfriend?

STACY: Uh, yes. If that ever happened, you can be sure I would tell you.

BRITTANY: We tell each other everything, right?

STACY: *(Looking down.)* Something like that.

BRITTANY: *(Carefully.)* Could I ask you a question?

STACY: Okay.

BRITTANY: Promise you won't be mad.

STACY: At you? Never.

BRITTANY: Why didn't you come to church with us on Sunday?

STACY: What? I don't know, I was tired. Sometimes I stay up late on Saturday nights.

BRITTANY: I know. Momsy said you once didn't come in till like three twenty-six in the morning.

STACY: Wow, good thing my car didn't turn into a pumpkin.

(Pause. She is not looking at him.)

BRITTANY: Stacy…Could I ask you something else?

STACY: Sure I guess.

BRITTANY: Are you a faggot?

STACY: What?! No! Brittany, what are you asking me?

BRITTANY: Dadsy says he worries sometimes that you might be a faggot. And when you don't come home at night, he says if he ever found out you were out fagging around he'd ship you back north faster than you can do a flying camel.

STACY: Brittany, you shouldn't talk like that.

BRITTANY: Like what?

STACY: The word "faggot." It's not nice. Nobody wants to be called that. It's a bad word. It's like using the "N" word to mean an African American person.

BRITTANY: But Momsy and Dadsy say faggot all the time, and they hate bad words. Momsy said people like that make God cry. *(Beat.)* And if they ever thought you were…funny…they wouldn't let us skate together anymore.

STACY: I'll never let that happen, sport. You can trust me.

BRITTANY: But you said you're not, so it's fine. Anyway, it'll be easier to deal with in the book.

STACY: What book?

BRITTANY: My autobiography. "Champion Spirit: The Brittany Bell Story."

STACY: Kinda early for that, sport.

BRITTANY: Late you mean. Horton and Murphy have promised me a fifteen-thousand-dollar advance for the hardcover rights, but only if I get it done by September.

STACY: You're kidding.

BRITTANY: *(Heads for the door.)* On the contrary. I'm meeting with my editor over hot cocoa in thirty minutes; I've got to change. Don't be late for afternoon practice!

STACY: Am I ever?

BRITTANY: *(Turns back.)* No. But that's because I keep you in line.

(She is gone. STACY, shaken, sits on the bench for a moment. Suddenly, FIONA pops back in.)

FIONA: You're right of course; you'd have nothing to gain from the arrangement. You'd just be doing me a huge favor, and you don't even know me all that well.

STACY: I thought you were gone.

FIONA: I am. Gone head over heels over a cute young figure skater.

STACY: You are a good actress.

FIONA: That I am.

STACY: And a good eavesdropper, apparently?

FIONA: The walls have ears in this place, Sesame Seed.

STACY: That's for sure.

FIONA: A business agreement, Mr. Clifford. And after it's served its purpose, no strings.

(Beat.)

STACY: I'm not comfortable talking about this anymore *here.*

FIONA: Great. Let's go out for lunch someplace. On me.

STACY: What kind of place would you like?

FIONA: Someplace where gossip columnists and photographers hang out!

STACY: You're awful.

FIONA: I know. Don't you love me?

(Blackout.)

VOICEOVER

Music: lush and romantic.

WOMAN'S VOICE: This is one of Stacy and Brittany's most special routines, based on the idea of Cinderella and Prince Charming at the ball.

MAN'S VOICE: Opening with a spectacular star lift—oh! That's just terrific. She looks like she's really flying there, doesn't she?

WOMAN'S VOICE: And loving every minute of it. Here come the side-by-side triple toe loops…Beautiful!

MAN'S VOICE: His back positions are just splendid; he's got a balletic discipline and delicacy in his skating that you usually only see in the Russians. They really may have a shot at a medal next Olympics.

WOMAN'S VOICE: They sure do. It may turn out to be a modern-day Cinderella story for her. And whose parents wouldn't want a Prince Charming like Stacy for their daughter?

MAN'S VOICE: I guess Fiona Blake's mom and dad must be counting their blessings then, don't you think?

WOMAN's VOICE: *(Laughs.)* Now now, let's not bring the gossip columns into it. Look at this death spiral!

MAN'S VOICE: And wasn't that breathtaking? Just breathtaking!

(Music out.)

FOUR.

Lights up on stage right: TRENT's apartment, with TRENT and STACY sitting on the bed watching a TV in the fourth wall. They are listening to the last couple lines of the preceding voiceover.

TRENT: Unfuckingbelievable.

STACY: Silly, isn't it?

TRENT: You *left* a party with the woman at three in the morning—*one* party, *one* night over a month ago—and they're still making up stories about the two of you?

STACY: *(Shaking his head.)* Imagine.

TRENT: *(Turns off the TV.)* Okay, what's the deal here, Stace? The two of you are even in *Time* magazine this week. Is there more to this than meets the eye?

STACY: Less, actually.

TRENT: You are such a shitty liar.

STACY: What do you mean?

TRENT: The eyes, lover. Those puppy dog eyes. Adorable, but incapable of concealing a falsehood.

STACY: *(Uncomfortable.)* Trent…

TRENT: You're not secretly bi, are you? You're not boffing this starlet behind my back?

STACY: No, of course not.

TRENT: So what do you two…talk about?

STACY: Lots of things. We've gotten to be friends. She's really fun. *(Beat.)* She calls me Sesame Seed.

TRENT: Why, do you get stuck between her teeth?

STACY: She says it's because of my nice buns. Get it?

TRENT: Hmm. Sounds like it's time we got to…how shall we say? The "bottom" of this.

STACY: Cute. *(Pause.)* All right. I guess. Can I trust you?

TRENT: Sure. *(Beat.)* I'm waiting.

STACY: Jeepers, where to start? Okay. Here goes nothing.

(STACY begins to tell TRENT the whole story, but the audience can't hear him; the two of them are just seen conversing silently in very dim light while the full stage lights come up on LAUREN and FIONA's New York apartment, stage left. LAUREN is packing a suitcase.)

LAUREN: It's not too late to change your mind and come with me. It would do you a lot of good.

FIONA: I wish I could. I so wish that. You know how much I wish that. But this is gonna be a dream come true for you anyway.

LAUREN: My dream of Edinburgh always included you. I wrote this play for you.

FIONA: Gina will be brilliant.

LAUREN: Not the point.

FIONA: I'd give anything to be there, but the schedule just…

LAUREN: I know.

FIONA: And actually, we should be glad they moved up the filming of "Vampire Campus 2: Sophomore Year." Now it'll be all over by the time we go into rehearsal for our off-Broadway gig—which is our main event, right? Edinburgh is just a one-act. This one's gonna be your masterpiece.

LAUREN: Yeah, but who knows when it's finally gonna happen? Sharon said she might not be able to get the theatre we really want until after the holidays, and it still depends on—

FIONA: *(Worried.)* Just make sure we're done by mid-March.

LAUREN: Excuse me? What if we're a hit? It's open ended.

FIONA: Nothing's open ended in the movie business.

LAUREN: I'm not *in* the movie business.

FIONA: Well I am. And I have to keep that March-April time free. They're already talking contracts for "Vampire Campus 3: Junior Prom."

LAUREN: I sure hope you don't think I'm gonna wait around for you to finish vampire graduate school.

FIONA: Touché.

LAUREN: Is that the kind of career you want?

FIONA: No, you know it isn't. That's why I'm trying to get Lex to delay the contract on that one. I haven't said anything because I don't want to jinx it, but…he thinks he can maybe get me a screen test for "Moonlight on a Ranch."

LAUREN: A movie of the book by Seth Brown?

FIONA: Exactly. *(Grins.)* Prestige Project! It's been a *New York Times* best seller for seven months!

LAUREN: I know, I work in a bookstore, remember? I think it took me forty-five minutes to read that novel. Counting my barf break.

FIONA: You're awful. I thought it was lovely.

LAUREN: Then you must have a secret life as a suburban housewife.

FIONA: How come you have to belittle my projects all the time? Aren't you a little bit proud of me? I could win an Oscar and you'd still be looking down your alternative culture snob nose at me, wouldn't you? I'm close to being a movie star, Lauren. And it's building. They're predicting "Vampire Campus" will end up as the biggest money-maker of the summer. And if I get "Moonlight on a Ranch," it could be *huge*.

LAUREN: Since when is it about money? I thought we understood that *reaching people* is the most important thing.

FIONA: Exactly. So what do you have lined up in Edinburgh? Four performances in a fifty-seat theatre? "Vampire Campus" played to two and a half million *opening weekend*.

LAUREN: And I'll bet it really changed their lives.

FIONA: Well maybe their lives didn't *want* to be changed. Ever think of that? What the fuck's wrong with *entertaining* people? You're always talking about like, *connections*, right? Movies connect! People are *talking* about "Vampire Campus" all over the country! The *world* soon. Scotland, even! Did you know that movies are one of the main topics of social conversation? Almost as big as sports, and certainly ahead of politics—only the weather has a clear advantage. I'm being discussed around water coolers and in bars all across the nation! Don't tell me that's nothing. You can't do that from a converted garage in the East Village.

LAUREN: I'd rather touch twelve people's souls in a basement theatre than drown twelve million in inane, violent, sexist bullshit.

FIONA: So if it's not post-lesbian radical...whatever!—then it's automatically garbage, right? I used to buy into that, but you know what? I don't feel like an outcast from society! I'm connecting with the world! I'm making waves! I'm rocking the boat! I'm—

(Lights down on them and back up to full on STACY and TRENT.)

STACY: "Selling out"? Is that what it sounds like to you?

TRENT: Well gee, I don't know. A gay male and a lesbian pretend to be a straight couple so they can make more money. Sounds like more of a personal statement to me.

STACY: Am I gonna be sorry I trusted you with this? *(Beat.)* I didn't want to have any secrets from you.

TRENT: Well I guess I should feel pretty special then, since your whole *life* is a secret from everybody else.

STACY: Just please don't tell anyone. Especially about Fiona. She trusted me.

TRENT: As I've told you before, I don't believe in outing people. I think they should come out on their own when they're good and ready. If not sooner.

STACY: Thank you.

TRENT: Incredible story, doll.

STACY: Come on. It's not that weird. It's probably not all that uncommon.

TRENT: That's a scary thought. No, it's just crazy enough to be true.

STACY: Of course it's true! Why would I lie about lying? I mean, say I was lying if I wasn't lying? I mean...you know what I mean.

TRENT: You wouldn't. Plus, if you were I'd be able to tell, right? I mean, we've got that established.

STACY: Are you mad?

TRENT: Why should I be mad? I've got great blackmail material!

STACY: What's your price?

TRENT: *(Tickling him.)* Sexual favors.

STACY: You're cheap.

(They roll over on the bed. Lights down on them and up on stage left, where LAUREN is looking for something.)

LAUREN: Damn. Have you seen my Doc Martens?

FIONA: Under the bed.

LAUREN: *(Exiting to bedroom.)* I've gotta get to the airport. It's almost three already.

(FIONA spots something in LAUREN's open suitcase and quickly pulls it out.)

FIONA: *(Calling offstage.)* Uh, Lauren?

LAUREN: *(From off.)* What is it?

FIONA: You're not taking this *Time* magazine to Scotland, are you?

LAUREN: *(From off.)* I was going to read it on the plane. Why?

FIONA: There's an article in here that I really...want to read.

LAUREN: *(From off.)* What's it about?

FIONA: Figure skaters. I mean! *(Improvising.)* Uhhm...Lesbianism. You know, politics? Gay rights and shit?

LAUREN: *(From off.)* Really? I'd like to see it.

FIONA: *(Quickly shutting the magazine.)* I thought you were in a hurry...And anyway, oh shit. *(Puts the magazine down on the table.)*

LAUREN: *(From off.)* What's the matter?

FIONA: I just spilled coffee all over it. *(Does so.)* I'm so sorry.

LAUREN: *(Reentering, with shoes and a sweater.)* Fiona, what is with you today?

FIONA: I'm just upset that you're leaving! I'm gonna miss you so much!

LAUREN: *(Touched.)* Well I'm gonna miss you too. A month is a long time.

FIONA: A month in Scotland. No American newspapers or magazines! No American TV! You'll feel like you're in another world!

LAUREN: Well I guess that's one way of looking at it.

(FIONA hugs her.)

FIONA: Have a wonderful time!!

(Music. Blackout.)

FIVE.

The weight room at the rink in Denver. A bench, a suspended punching bag, and a rack of free weights. STACY and ETHAN are working out.

ETHAN: You know what I hate about you?

STACY: Fifteen, sixteen—no, what do you hate about me?—seventeen, eighteen...

ETHAN: That you're a natural.

STACY: How dare you say such a thing.

ETHAN: It's just so damn easy for you.

STACY: It's very hard work and you know it.

ETHAN: But it's *natural* work. When you and Brittany get out there on the ice it's obvious that's where you were meant to be, by whoever...means us to do whatever we're...meant to do. You know, God or like that? When you're skating you're totally...who you are. When I'm skating it's like, okay, analyze it, force it down, learn it, analyze it again, make it better—a *little* better—and then! if I'm lucky!—work with the sports psychologist.

STACY: *(Laughs good naturedly.)* Are you done with this barbell?

ETHAN: Sure.

STACY: *(Lifting it.)* Hey, you put a lot of weight on this. Are you lifting heavier these days?

ETHAN: Got to. You'd better hope Brittany doesn't get a growth spurt. Roberta's not sticking to the training diet, and it makes a big difference.

STACY: She looks the same as always.

ETHAN: Yeah, you don't spend six hours a day skating with her. Four pounds on the hips since last month. I know every inch of that woman's body.

STACY: You two working things through?

ETHAN: Not like you mean. The relationship part was a mistake, I think we both know that; simpler this way. *(Beat.)* Actually, I think you and Blake have the right kind of deal.

STACY: How do you mean?

ETHAN: Long-distance relationship. Her in LA or New York, you here in Denver. See her once a month or so. Sounds about right. Any more than that you drive each other crazy.

(STACY laughs.)

ETHAN: Are you two getting as serious as they're saying?

STACY: That depends. How serious are they saying?

ETHAN: Let's just say I'm always running into the two of you at the grocery store. On the checkout line.

STACY: Very funny. *(Beat.)* You know those things are half made up.

ETHAN: Which half?

STACY: I don't know; I don't even read them.

ETHAN: So is she as hot as she looks?

STACY: Ethan.

ETHAN: Come on. We're buds.

STACY: I don't know what to say. I like her. It's…an adventure. She's fun to be with.

(They work out in silence for a moment.)

ETHAN: Stacy?

STACY: *(Out of breath.)* Yeah?

ETHAN: Could I ask you something personal?

STACY: You have been.

ETHAN: I mean…*(Beat.)* Can I?

STACY: *(Not looking at him.)* I don't know. I guess.

(BRITTANY comes in with a magazine.)

ETHAN: Never mind.

BRITTANY: Am I interrupting something?

STACY: No, sport. What's up?

BRITTANY: Well…I just stopped by King Soopers to pick up the new "Teen Dream," 'cause I wanted to read the article about the Backstreet Boys, and look who's on the cover.

ETHAN: Oh yummy. Give me! *(Grabs the magazine.)* Lookit, Stacy, it's you. In a Speedo!

STACY: What? Ohmygosh. That was the day I met Fiona at the beach after her publicity shoot. I didn't even know they shot any of me.

BRITTANY: Tell him what the headline says.

ETHAN: *(Reading.)* "Meet Stacy! Find out all about the Dream Boat on Skates!"

STACY: You're making that up.

ETHAN: Nuh-uh! See for yourself.

(ETHAN hands STACY the magazine.)

STACY: Holy mackerel. Well, it'll all be made up. The article, I mean. 'Cause I never did an interview with them.

BRITTANY: Someone did.

STACY: What?

ETHAN: *(Takes back the article and reads.)* "Ask Fiona! Fiona Blake, the new actress on every girl's Wanna-Look-Like List, tells what it's like to date the world's cutest figure skating champ!"

STACY: Jeepers. She didn't tell me she was gonna do that.

ETHAN: Maybe she didn't. *(Reads, and laughs.)* On second thought, it looks pretty authentic.

STACY: Don't.

ETHAN: *(Reads.)* "Teen Dream: So what attracted you to Stacy Clifford first? Fiona: Probably his charming wholesomeness. He was the first person I've ever met who actually uses words like 'jeepers' and 'holy mackerel.'"

STACY: It does not say that!

ETHAN: Right here! I'm gonna go hit the rowing machine. *(Exits.)*

STACY: *(Looking at the article.)* Jeep—I mean, "drats."

BRITTANY: I have an idea.

STACY: Let's hear it.

BRITTANY: Maybe it would be good…if you didn't call me "sport" anymore.

STACY: Really?

BRITTANY: Yes. I'm getting too old for that.

STACY: Well, okay, spo—I mean, Brittany. *(Laughs.)* Jeepers. I mean…!

BRITTANY: Thanks, Stacy.

STACY: You are welcome. *(Pause.)* Something else?

BRITTANY: Uh—yeah. Elise showed us sketches for the new short program costumes. With swatches.

STACY: Cool.

BRITTANY: Momsy and I both thought they were really exquisite. Do you want to take a look?

STACY: I trust you guys on costumes.

BRITTANY: Dadsy and Momsy want us to look just right this year. Because this year is so special.

STACY: It is?

BRITTANY: Yes!

STACY: How so?

BRITTANY: Our year to win Nationals, dork! You're a silly.

STACY: Oh that.

BRITTANY: *(Laughs.)* Stop it. *(Beat.)* And Dick Button said on TV the other day that we have a better chance of taking gold at the Olympics than any other U.S. pair since the seventies.

STACY: That's the rumor.

BRITTANY: Do you believe it?

STACY: Sure I do. We can do anything we set our minds to.

BRITTANY: My mind is set.

STACY: I can tell it is. You're gonna be a *star* out there one of these days, Brittany. Hey, maybe that's what I'll call you now instead of sport: "Star." How's that for a nickname?

BRITTANY: I could get used to it.

(They laugh. She looks down.)

BRITTANY: And you're already one.

STACY: One what?

BRITTANY: A star.

STACY: Nuh-uh.

BRITTANY: Uh-huh! How many magazine articles does it take?

STACY: No amount. That's not what makes somebody a star.

BRITTANY: I'm not so sure.

STACY: Well it's all pretty silly, Brittany. Just between you and me, it doesn't really mean anything.

BRITTANY: It could, though.

STACY: How?

BRITTANY: Well, I was talking to Geoffrey about it. And Miss Danelli. And that sports agent man.

STACY: *(Winks.)* You take a meeting? Or do lunch?

BRITTANY: *(Serious.)* No, Stacy. Everybody really is talking about it. Because if we're celebrities—if *you're* a celebrity—going into the big competitions, it could actually affect the judging.

STACY: The judging's based on how we *skate.*

BRITTANY: Well, yes. But maybe no. It's not all totally scientific. Geoffrey said judges tend to mark you based on their expectations of how you'll do. So if you're in the news all the time and people are always saying how great you are and stuff, then you might be more apt to win because people are thinking of you as the best already.

STACY: So that's good, right?

BRITTANY: *Maybe.* But if we don't skate perfect, they might mark us down even more because they were expecting so much. Does that make sense?

STACY: No. You'll drive yourself crazy if you try to analyze all that stuff. All we can do is skate our best.

BRITTANY: You always make it sound so simple.

STACY: Well it is.

BRITTANY: Miss Danelli says it isn't. She was talking to Dadsy in the pro shop. She says it's all about image. She said your image is changing every day and we need to control it. We need to spin it our way.

STACY: Jeepers, where are you getting this vocabulary?

BRITTANY: Plus, Fiona's a little sleazy and everything, she's from New York and she does those kind of slightly kinky movies? So that whole wholesome, Christian kid appeal we had working for us is shot out of the water.

STACY: I'm having trouble keeping up here.

BRITTANY: So if it's not true then I think you should say so. Tell the reporters that it's just a rumor that got out of hand and you're just casual friends with her. Unless…

STACY: Unless what?

BRITTANY: Unless it's true and you really are in love with Fiona Blake. Which it doesn't seem like you are, Stacy. You don't talk about her that much. You hardly ever see her. *(Beat.)* But as your partner, I would like for you to level with me.

STACY: Well, that's understandable.

BRITTANY: We used to tell each other everything, didn't we?

STACY: More or less.

BRITTANY: You're my best friend.

STACY: You're mine.

(Beat. She waits.)

STACY: All I can tell you, star, is that I like being with Fiona. I'm learning a lot from her. She makes me laugh. She's…excited about life, and it's contagious.

BRITTANY: So is that being in love?

STACY: Love is a big word.

BRITTANY: Four letters. *(Grins.)* I forgot you didn't finish high school.

STACY: You're so mean to me.

(ETHAN reenters, and picks up two dumbbells.)

BRITTANY: Gotta go. I've got Bible study. *(Exits.)*

ETHAN: *(Counting reps.)* Four, five, six…

STACY: You're gonna pull something if you don't lighten up.

ETHAN: *(Pushing even harder.)* Yeah right. Gotta get my body fat down to four percent.

STACY: That's suicidal.

ETHAN: Well if I kill myself working up to the Olympics, maybe I won't have to after.

STACY: What kind of talk is that?

ETHAN: Realistic. Me and Roberta have to move up three places from where we were last year to even make the team. And if I have to torture myself—and her—to make that happen… *(Smiles grimly.)*

STACY: Is it worth it?

ETHAN: That's easy for you to say. Not everybody's subsidized by the Rich Christian Nuclear Family That Ate Colorado.

STACY: That has its drawbacks.

ETHAN: So does going home to your middle-class parents and saying "Hey, thanks for not taking a vacation for the past ten years. Thanks for giving up the possibility of ever being able to retire! Oh, and by the way, the investment didn't pay off—I came in fifth again."

STACY: Maybe they weren't investing in gold options. It sounds like they love you.

ETHAN: Well it's fuckin' time I gave something back. And I don't know how I'm gonna do that when my pretty partner and I can't even agree on music.

STACY: *(Laughs.)* That's never easy.

ETHAN: I can't believe you let Brit talk you into that Muzak you're using for the long.

STACY: It's an Oscar-winning song.

ETHAN: "Love Theme from Little Red Riding Hood"?! Spare me. How can you make yourself skate to that shit?

STACY: Brittany loves it.

ETHAN: And your opinion doesn't count?

STACY: Not really. *(Beat.)* But that's what pairs skating is about, you know? The girl is the jewel. We're like the setting. We set them off.

ETHAN: Uh, sorry to break it to you, champ, but you're the one in the magazines. When you skate half the women in the audience, and at least ten percent of the men, wish they were skating with you.

(STACY laughs, embarrassed.)

ETHAN: Roberta and me just don't make magic like that.

STACY: Maybe you could go back to singles?

ETHAN: And learn a quad at my age? Nope, this is it for me. The Moment of Reckoning. Then real life kicks in.

STACY: "Real life"? What does that mean?

ETHAN: You, my good friend, have asked the million-dollar question.

(Pause.)

STACY: *(Trying to be helpful.)* It comes around every four years.

ETHAN: Yeah, uh-huh. And I'm gonna make the Olympic team when I'm thirty-two and Roberta weighs two hundred pounds.

STACY: *(Laughs.)* You're terrible.

ETHAN: That's exactly what I've been saying.

STACY: Not at *skating.*

ETHAN: You know where Geoffrey's taking Roberta and me tomorrow?

STACY: I'm afraid to ask.

ETHAN: A hypnotist.

STACY: Yikes. Do you believe in that?

ETHAN: Sure, why not? All he has to do is psych us into thinking we can be the best. Or at least beat everybody else one time, when it counts. I mean it should be that simple, right?

STACY: I never thought about it that way.

ETHAN: *(Needing to know.)* How do you think about it?

STACY: I don't know.

ETHAN: Well we gotta know, right? So we can prove we're better than anybody else out there.

STACY: Who else is out there? *(Beat.)* It's just you and her for four and a half minutes.

ETHAN: Great, so what do I do with that?

STACY: Just make it beautiful.

(Pause, as ETHAN considers this. STACY towels himself off and gets ready to leave.)

STACY: I've got to go change for afternoon practice. See you there? *(Starts out.)*

ETHAN: Stacy, can I ask you something?

STACY: *(Turning back.)* What?

(Long pause. ETHAN can't find the words.)

STACY: Are you okay?

ETHAN: Yeah! I'm fine! Talking really helps. *Thank you.* Very much.

STACY: No biggie.

(STACY exits quickly. ETHAN watches him go, then attacks the punching bag furiously.)

ETHAN: Damn!

(Music. Blackout.)

Six.

New York. LAUREN and FIONA's apartment, full stage. LAUREN is sitting alone, reading an old, wrinkled manuscript by candlelight. We hear the front door open and close, then FIONA enters.

FIONA: Hi honey, I'm home! *(Looks around.)* Lauren? *(No response.)* Why are you sitting in the dark? Did we blow a fuse or something? *(Heads for the light switch.)*

LAUREN: Leave it off.

(FIONA stops and looks at her.)

LAUREN: I'm making a new rule in my life. No artificial light. Just the real thing.

FIONA: *(Puzzled.)* Okey-dokey, I guess. *(Sits beside her.)* It's kinda romantic anyway, huh? Whatcha readin' there?

(LAUREN shows her the manuscript.)

FIONA: "Susan and the Witch"! Ohmygod! I haven't read this in years. I love this! *(Flips through the script affectionately.)* Wasn't this the first one-act play you wrote for me? I always thought it deserved to be done again. Are you going to submit it to the EST Marathon or something?

LAUREN: Hardly. Blank verse I wrote in grad school? Nobody deserves to be subjected to that.

(LAUREN hands FIONA the candle.)

LAUREN: Burn it.

FIONA: *(Laughs uncomfortably.)* Are you kidding? *(Beat.)* Lauren, are you okay?

LAUREN: Just hold it to the flame and set it on fire. Don't you want to?

FIONA: Of course I don't. Can I turn a light on? *(Stands.)* You're weirding me out a little. Let's get out of here and go get some dinner or something.

LAUREN: Sit back down.

FIONA: What?

LAUREN: Leave the light off and sit back down.

(FIONA complies.)

LAUREN: Do you even remember what it was about?

FIONA: What what was about? *(Looks down at the manuscript in her hand.)* Susan and the Witch? Well, yeah, it was like your lesbian version of *The Crucible*.

(She laughs a little and looks at LAUREN, who is silent.)

FIONA: Okay, it's about this girl named Susan—played by me!—during the Salem witch trials who falls in love with this older black woman named Isabel who claims to have healing powers.

LAUREN: Go on.

FIONA: You wrote it, don't you remember what it's about?

LAUREN: *(With a weak smile.)* I thought I did.

FIONA: Okay... Well okay. Then Susan's brother James sees the two of us making love in the woods, so we get arrested and tried as witches. And then the preacher comes to me in prison and says I'll be set free if I denounce Isabel as a witch and sign a paper that says she corrupted me. And I'm like, no! I'd rather burn at the stake than betray the woman I love. *(Flips through the script to find a line.)* This was my favorite line: "If magic 'tis, a woman to adore, Then brand me as a witch forevermore!" So they burn us. *(Laughs.)* Guess we weren't too subtle back in those days, huh? *(Kisses LAUREN.)* But its heart was in the right place.

LAUREN: Was it? *(Beat.)* What I'm trying to get my brain around is that I wrote that play for you. You inspired it.

FIONA: Great. *(Gets up.)* And now I'm going to inspire you to stop sitting in the dark and being morbid and creepy. *(She switches on a light, then turns back to LAUREN and sees a pile of magazines and tabloids on the floor at her feet. Cautiously.)* Sooo…what else have you been reading lately?

LAUREN: Just a few articles Mark and Steven saved for me when I was in Edinburgh.

FIONA: Those bitches.

LAUREN: About you "dating" some teenaged figure skater.

FIONA: He's twenty-two.

LAUREN: What?

FIONA: Uhhh—I said "There's plenty…too."

LAUREN: Of what?

FIONA: Untrue rumors floating around out there! I mean, you know, it comes with the territory. That's Hollywood! This kind of thing happens when you get to…a certain level. At least they didn't say I'm carrying an alien baby or losing my hair or something like that.

LAUREN: So I guess these photos of you making out with him on Malibu Beach are computer generated? Or how about this *New York Times* picture of you posing with him after a skating competition in Montreal?

FIONA: All right all right. I really did give some of those interviews. But none of it's true, don't worry! We made it all up.

LAUREN: Is this one of your "get into a role by playing it in public" kind of character studies?

FIONA: No way! I outgrew that junior year!

LAUREN: Then *what*, Fiona?

FIONA: I think I can make it in the movies! I already *am* making it. But how many movie stars do you know who are lesbians? Wait! Don't answer that. How many that are *open* lesbians?

LAUREN: Oh God.

FIONA: See, you always do this. That's why I kept putting off telling you, because I knew you'd get up on your Militant High Horse and preach at me! Just give me two minutes to explain before you—

LAUREN: *Explain?!*

FIONA: All right, it's a fucked-up system! You know that and I know that. So why not manipulate it for a little while till I get where I want to go? Right? I can't change the world all by myself.

LAUREN: I thought we were going to change it together.

FIONA: That was college, Lauren. "Susan and the Witch." This is real life. *(Beat.)* You didn't really think I was in love with him, did you?

LAUREN: I'd rather you were! Anything would be better than this. Fall in love with a man if that's what floats your boat! Fuck a baboon for all I care, but write a song about it! It's the dishonesty that you're killing me with. To hide who we are from the world in order to…*coddle* somebody else's idea of…*(Picks up the script of "Susan and the Witch.")* Every play we've ever done has been…*(Shakes her head.)* Damn. *(Looks at FIONA.)* Did you *ever* get it? I'm thirty-five years old. Where did I put the last five years? *(Beat.)* I'm going to spend the night at Dina's. I expect your stuff to be gone by the time I get home from the bookstore tomorrow night. Don't bother leaving your key; I'm gonna get the lock changed.

FIONA: Lauren. Can we back up here a minute?

LAUREN: This isn't a movie, Fiona. We're over. You had one take only, and you blew it.

(LAUREN exits quickly, slamming the door behind her. FIONA, shaken, sits down on the couch for a moment, unsure for once what to do. Music. Blackout.)

SEVEN.

STACY and TRENT are sitting in a restaurant in Denver. Menus and water glasses, but no food.

TRENT: So, last week I was in a toy store in Cherry Creek and guess what I found?

STACY: *(Embarrassed.)* Uh-oh. Those things are ridiculous.

TRENT: "Sports Heroes for Tomorrow!" The all new Stacy Clifford and Brittany Bell dolls!

STACY: They call them action figures.

TRENT: Cutest fuckin' thing I've ever seen. Of course I had to get one. Took him home and put him on my bedside table.

STACY: The clothes are an exact replica of our long program costumes from last season.

TRENT: And they come off.

STACY: I think the Brittany one looks more like her.

TRENT: I threw that one out. Kept you.

STACY: You're awful.

TRENT: Needed something to remind me of what you look like.

STACY: It hasn't been that long. You know I miss you. But they have me scheduled twenty-five hours a day at the rink.

TRENT: I'm just teasing. The real thing's way cuter.

(TRENT tries to take STACY's hand.)

STACY: *(Pulls his hand away and looks around nervously.)* Careful. That's for later.

TRENT: Sorry, I forgot about your armoire for a minute.

STACY: My what?

TRENT: The word closet is so over-used.

STACY: *(Laughs.)* I *have* missed you. *(Beat.)* Maybe we could get a booth. This table is…

TRENT: Too "out" for you? Don't worry, I'll play it real butch. I can convincingly pull off the preppy frat boy thing. Until they notice the piercings. *(Fake deep voice.)* So, bud, let's talk sports. How's practice goin'?

STACY: Slow but okay. It's taking a while for my knee to bounce back from the tour. But I like our programs this year. Brittany's parents hired a new choreographer for the long.

TRENT: Will I ever get to see it?

STACY: Of course. I don't know about all these side-by-side triples though. Every year there's more jumps you've gotta do to stay competitive.

TRENT: Like jumping through hoops with your paper doll sweetheart? Making kissy for the photographers?

STACY: Something like that. We've been going to these crazy parties; she's filming a movie up near Breckenridge: "Moonlight on a Ranch"? And she said something mysterious to me on the phone. Some video project idea she wants me to work on with her or something.

TRENT: The money'd better be good. In fact, she should have been paying you all along for taking part in this promotional relationship.

STACY: It's not really work. She's fun to be with.

TRENT: Doesn't mean you shouldn't get a cut of all the dough she's raking in.

STACY: It's not like I'm doing it all as a favor to her. It's…mutually beneficial.

TRENT: So far anyway.

STACY: What's that supposed to mean?

TRENT: Lies come back to haunt you. That's why I stopped.

STACY: I wish I could afford to be as honest as you are.

TRENT: Someday. (Sings.) "Somehow. Somewhere…"

STACY: (Trying to stay polite.) Please keep your voice down.

TRENT: Oh, sorry! Momentary lapse. (Looking offstage.) Hey Lady Hot Tits! Got a sister for my friend here?

STACY: You are awful.

TRENT: Make a choice, buster. You're calling the shots.

STACY: I'm sorry. Fiona just has me paranoid. When we're out together she acts like there are microphones hidden all over the place.

TRENT: Maybe that's a clue that you should spend less time with your pretend lover and more with your real one. (Smiles.)

STACY: I promise I'll have more time after Worlds. Maybe you and I could go someplace in April. Up to Vail or someplace?

TRENT: Actually, Switzerland has always been on my wanna visit list. Heidi was my favorite book as a kid.

STACY: (Sighs.) Sorry. That wouldn't…

TRENT: Whatever you say, boss.

STACY: I mean, I would love it if you could come to the Olympics with me.

TRENT: Honey, I'm unemployed and my mom works for an airline. I want to sit with you on that poofy couch where you wait for the scores—what's it called?

STACY: The "Kiss and Cry" area? That's for coaches…

TRENT: (Overlapping after "area.") Yes! I love that name. You can tell them I'm your Kissing Cousin from Canada!

STACY: I think we should talk about something else.

TRENT: Let's! I do have a trip coming up. New York City.

STACY: That sounds fun. What are you gonna do there?

TRENT: I'm auditioning for a job as a veejay on the Cable Music Channel.

STACY: *(Laughs.)* Seriously.

TRENT: I am serious. They're doing a national search. I sent in a video of myself with orange hair, talking about the Squirrel Nut Zippers in an outrageously opinionated manner. Now I'm a finalist.

STACY: Well good for you! That's really fantastic, Trent. I hope you get it.

TRENT: Then we'll both be media personalities.

STACY: But if you move to New York I'll hardly ever get to see you.

TRENT: *Plus ça change, plus c'est le même chose.*

STACY: Sounds good whatever it means. *(Beat.)* I'm hungry. Doesn't anybody work here? I feel like we're invisible or something.

TRENT: You get what you wish for.

STACY: I'm serious. We haven't even ordered. *(Looking around the room.)* What's going on around here, anyway?

TRENT: Actually, I believe that comely young man over there is our waiter. He's been giving me dirty looks ever since he noticed I was sitting here with you.

STACY: See?—I asked you not to talk so loud. I thought you said this place was gay-friendly.

TRENT: Oh it is. All the waiters are gay, including Todd himself.

STACY: I'm confused.

TRENT: This is news? He's not avoiding us because he disapproves of our lifestyle. He's actually jealous.

STACY: Oh no. One of your exes?

TRENT: Could put it that way.

STACY: Shoot. Do you think he recognizes me?

TRENT: Change the channel please.

STACY: I'm sorry. *(Beat.)* So. Let's go someplace else then. There's plenty of restaurants in this town.

TRENT: Fine with me.

STACY: That poor guy must have really cared about you.

TRENT: Apparently I'm irresistible.

STACY: Yes you are. How long ago was it?

TRENT: Uh, let's see…Tonight's Thursday? *(Counts on his fingers.)* Four days.

STACY: Excuse me?

TRENT: We met at the club Friday night and spent much of the weekend at my place.

STACY: Not funny.

TRENT: Not joking. You were…busy practicing. Sleeping? Whatever.

STACY: I trusted you, Trent.

TRENT: To do what? Wait by the phone and play with my Stacy doll? Till we can finally go out and pretend not to be seeing each other?

STACY: I thought you…

TRENT: Cared for you? I did. I mean do.

STACY: I meant…well, that, yes. And, I thought you said you were fine with the arrangement.

TRENT: Do I not look fine to you? The arrangement works great. Gives me plenty of flexibility. *(Pause.)*

STACY: Gosh. I'm almost scared to ask this, but...

TRENT: Was he the only one? Stacy, I've been "seeing you," if the word even applies, for almost six months. And I'm not even allowed to tell my friends!

STACY: If you weren't happy you could have talked to me about it.

TRENT: Who says I'm not happy? *(Beat.)* Look, I'm twenty-two and I'm never gonna be this pretty again. If anyone has a problem with the "arrangements," it would appear to be you. *(Waves delicately to an offstage person.)* And Todd, I guess.

STACY: I don't know what to say.

TRENT: Might try "golly" or "jeepers."

STACY: Screw you.

TRENT: *(Shrugs.)* If you don't, somebody will.

STACY: At least you're honest. I'll give you that.

TRENT: Oh, I never lie. It comes back to haunt you.

(Blackout.)

VOICEOVER

Peppy pop rock music.

MAN'S VOICE: Welcome to Stacy and Fiona's Home Workout for Couples Home Video! Here are your favorites: movie star Fiona Blake and figure skating champ Stacy Clifford!

(Music crescendos. Applause and cheers.)

FIONA'S VOICE: Hey, Sesame Seed, you look hot in that tank!

STACY'S VOICE: Hiya, Fi! You look beautiful in that leotard!

FIONA'S VOICE: And the reason we do...

STACY'S VOICE:...is because we work out!

FIONA'S VOICE: Together!

STACY'S VOICE: At home! And now you can work out with us. We'll start with some of the warm-up stretches I do at the rink.

FIONA'S VOICE: And then we'll do some of the aerobic exercises I do on the set! And you can follow along at home! But remember, Stacy and I are very athletic. If you're over twenty-eight, you should check with a doctor before starting this or any strenuous exercise program. Are you ready, Stace?

STACY'S VOICE: Ready as I'll ever be!

FIONA'S VOICE: Great!

BOTH: Let's work out!

EIGHT.

STACY's new apartment in Denver. No furniture, just a couple of large cardboard boxes. STACY enters with FIONA, who's carrying a picnic basket.

FIONA: Oh, I like. Hardwood floors are *so* retro. You done good.

STACY: Thanks. I think I'm gonna like it. It's just sort of quiet so far. I've never lived alone.

FIONA: Well the timing works, right? You've got your own place: No more making up stories to appease the Born-Again Nazis. Welcome to being a grownup!

STACY: Thanks. *(Beat.)* I'm glad you're here. Sorry there's no furniture yet.

FIONA: I noticed. When are you gonna finish moving in?

STACY: I sort of am finished. I don't really have any furniture. Never have.

FIONA: You shittin' me?

STACY: No. Since I've never had my own place…

FIONA: I'm seeing a window of opportunity here. Because I, myself, have a keen eye for design. And I am also a shopper of rare brilliance. I could take you in hand and we could have a blast making this place totally funky-artsy cool.

STACY: That sounds fun.

FIONA: In fact, maybe we could get a reporter and photographer from "Interior Design Monthly" to go with us. They could do a cover story.

STACY: Sure, I guess.

FIONA: *(With a touch of bitterness.)* I mean now that I'm *single*, I have a lot more time for playing house. *(Thinking about sitting.)* Is this floor clean?

STACY: I don't know. Well, probably not. How could it be?

FIONA: Well then we're just gonna have to get our pants dirty, are we not? Because I have here a gourmet picnic dinner to celebrate your housewarming, complete with champagne!

STACY: Sounds good to me. *(Opens one of the boxes.)* I've got a quilt in one of these cartons…Here it is.

FIONA: Presto! A picnic for two. I can't wait till you taste these delicacies I picked out at Alfalfa's.

STACY: Good. I'm real hungry.

FIONA: *(Unpacking the picnic basket.)* I got only the most wholesome, veggie-oriented entrees for my athlete in training.

STACY: Looks really good. I love this curry stuff.

FIONA: Have you stocked your fridge? Are you gonna have to learn to cook for the first time too?

STACY: Yes, and no. My grandma was pretty sick a lot of the time when I was growing up. I sort of had to learn early.

FIONA: Well then maybe you can cook me dinner one night when I get off the set. Give me a break from the location caterer.

STACY: That'd be really fun. How's "Moonlight on a Ranch" going?

FIONA: I think okay. Steve Remington is really nice to work with. I was surprised—he's like totally laid-back, a genuinely nice human. But he looks really old in person. I'm telling you they do a lot with lighting and choosing just the right camera lenses. You look pale, by the way.

STACY: Really?

FIONA: Really. And even thinner than usual. You're not losing weight are you?

STACY: A little. They weigh us every day at the rink. The new schedule's a killer.

FIONA: How much have you lost?

STACY: About five pounds.

FIONA: Five pounds? *(Feeling his rib cage.)* Honey, that's a lot on you! I'll bet you're not eating right.

STACY: Maybe not. It's hard to eat since…

FIONA: What? *(Pause.)* Come to Fiona.

STACY: Trent left me.

FIONA: He did *what*?!

STACY: Well, not exactly that. He seemed willing to keep it going, but he was seeing other guys the whole time. I never even suspected.

FIONA: You are so trusting. He, however, is a royal jerk. Doesn't he know how lucky he was?

STACY: Yeah right. I'm not much of a prize these days.

FIONA: Excuse me. *You?* You are like the kindest, most gentle, sweetest…in fact, can I tell you? If I were a guy, I'd probably fall for you myself.

STACY: I could hardly get any time away from the rink to see him, and if we did go out I'd get all paranoid that somebody was gonna see us together and blow my cover. That's not exactly a turn-on.

FIONA: Well he must have known you weren't out when he first got involved with you.

STACY: Sure, but things were different then. I could be seen with a guy in public and not get recognized. Now that you and I are these big media figures…I don't know. In a way I don't blame him.

FIONA: Oh shit, Sesame Seed. Things have gotten out of hand, haven't they?

STACY: What? I don't know.

FIONA: Are you starting to hate me?

STACY: Am I what? No! Why would I hate you?

FIONA: I never expected it would last this long.

STACY: What would?

FIONA: Our little game, silly. Here you are still playing my boyfriend, what? Over six months later?

STACY: Yeah, I guess it has been that long. Doesn't feel like it!

FIONA: So talk to me, Sesame Seed. You have needs too. If our little…arrangement isn't working for you anymore, maybe it's time to make a change.

STACY: What? I didn't mean—

FIONA: Lord knows it's been successful! Our little "run." I mean, look at us! Me starring in the biggest *prestige* movie of the year—look Ma, no fangs!—and you the heartthrob of the skating world. But it's time to move on. I mean, what's the point of carrying on this huge plot to keep our personal lives secret if it keeps us from even *having* personal lives, right?

STACY: Yeah well. I guess that sounds kind of true.

FIONA: It's served its purpose. The whole world thinks we're as hetero as we could possibly be. We could stage a much-publicized breakup—just to remind them—and call it a wrap. Here's a thought!—come to LA next weekend and I'll throw my drink in your face at Spago.

STACY: You make it sound so tempting.

FIONA: We'll get some mileage out of the split, then go our separate ways.

STACY: What do you mean—"separate ways"?

FIONA: I mean get back to our *lives*. Get *real*. Find *love*. You deserve that.

STACY: But not...Not not *see* each other anymore?

FIONA: Well hey, I don't know about you, but I could like totally stand to save the airfare!

STACY: But I like you. I mean, it's not *all* a put-on. Is it? I really love...being with you. We've gotten to be best friends. Don't you think? And that's a good—

(Sound of a phone ringing.)

FIONA: That's me. *(Rummaging in her large purse for the cell phone, which rings again.)* Hold that thought, Sesame Seed. This'll just take me a minute. *(Into phone.)* Fiona Blake. Hey, Lex. No, it's not a bad time. In fact, I was just thinking about calling you. Stacy and I—Lex, what? Slow down. *(To STACY, covering the receiver.)* He sounds all spazzy. *(Into phone.)* Calm down, Lex, I can't even understand what you're— *(Pause.)* Uh-huh...uh-huh...shit. Uh-huh...uh-huh...uh-huh...Shit!!! *(Pause.)* Okay. I need to take this all in. Yeah you're right—the timing absolutely sucks. Listen, I'll call you back in a bit, okay? We'll get on this. Bye, Lex. *(Hangs up phone.)* Wow. *(Looks at STACY.)* That was Lex.

STACY: That much I got. Bad news?

FIONA: Lauren wrote a new play. Got a good review in the *Times*.

STACY: Great.

FIONA: Uh, you could say so. In fact, the buzz is so good they're already talking about possibly moving it to Broadway.

STACY: Well cool. I mean, you're happy for her, right? Even though?

FIONA: I'm delirious. Stace, it's a play about a lesbian writer.

STACY: Uh-huh. "Write what you know," right?

FIONA: Who's involved with an actress. And the actress starts to have like this really big movie career. So she hooks up with this gay athlete guy and they concoct a whole harebrained scheme to pretend to...

STACY: Uh-oh. *(Beat.)* Who'd ever believe a crazy story like that?

FIONA: Very funny. Sounds like she changed a few details, but...

STACY: Well...maybe it's nothing to worry about. Nobody in LA knows you were involved with her, right? If she changed the names—

FIONA: Would you grow up?! A *lot* of people in the New York theatre know about me and Lauren. And if this play's a success...yikes. The *shit* will *hit*. Will you marry me?

STACY: What?

FIONA: *(On one knee.)* Will you marry me, Stacy Clifford?

STACY: *Marry* you?

FIONA: Exactly.

STACY: I'm confused.

FIONA: It's our only choice. I mean, nobody gets *married* as a joke.

STACY: Well...there's reasons for that!

FIONA: Just! *Calm down.*

STACY: I am calm.

FIONA: I'm not! *(Beat.)* Stacy, this is the *worst possible timing* for us. For *both* of us! You have Nationals coming up. I have the biggest movie of the year! My best chance for the elusive Mr. O.

STACY: Mr. O?

FIONA: You know! The gold naked man.

STACY: Your Oscar.

FIONA: Fuck you, don't say it! You'll jinx it!

STACY: Jeepers, Fiona.

FIONA: I am in control here! I am not freaking on any level. Marriage is the obvious solution.

STACY: But when are we going to have time to plan a wedding? I'm in practice all day. It sounds so complicated. Your parents'll want to be involved. All our friends…

FIONA: You're right. *(Beat.)* So let's elope then!

STACY: Say what?

FIONA: It would be a blast. We could leave tonight. Drive till midnight and sleep under the stars on the western slope, then get an early start and see the sun come up over Utah. We'll stop for black coffee and steak and eggs at some truck stop diner in the desert, then head on to Vegas. *(Beat.)* And since we're never gonna have sex or anything, we can get it annulled once the coast is clear.

STACY: Can you get out of filming?

FIONA: I'll tell them I'm on the rag. What about practice?

STACY: My knee hurts. *(Beat.)* I could stand to get out of Denver for a few days. A road trip sounds exciting.

FIONA: Thank you thank you thank you!!

(She kisses STACY on the mouth, then stands up.)

FIONA: I'll make it all up to you someday, Stacy, I promise. Anyway, I've got to make some calls and get a change of clothes—sorry I kissed you. Throw some stuff in a duffle bag and I'll pick you up in an hour.

STACY: No prob. *(Beat.)* Gosh. What if somebody recognizes us?

FIONA: That's the point, you dork!

(She hurries out as the lights fade.)

ACT TWO
ONE.

An empty frame is hanging downstage center. Behind it stands FIONA, dressed in a simple sheath gown and jewelry, framed as if on television. She holds an Academy Award.

FIONA: *(Emotionally overwhelmed, but smiling graciously.)* First I'd like to thank the Academy for this great honor, so early in my career. I hope I can continue to live up to it for years to come. And I want to thank the director, Jason Bailey, for having faith in me; my manager Lex, who first thought of me as Maureen and got the ball rolling; Steve Remington and the wonderfully talented cast of "Moonlight on a Ranch"—I learned so much working with you guys!—for creating an environment where I could truly, truly blossom. And most of all I want to thank my best friend, my husband Stacy Clifford, for putting up with me and believing in me—and for being there that special night in the Hollywood Hills, when we wished on a star. Thank you all very much.

(STACY enters behind her in a tuxedo shirt, socks, and undershorts, combing his hair.)

STACY: Bravo. But shouldn't you wait till you at least finish the movie?

FIONA: Of course. (*A little embarrassed, she fusses with her hair; the frame is a mirror in their hotel room.*) I didn't know you were through in the bathroom. But if somebody gives you an Oscar, you have to respond in a certain way.

STACY: Even if it's a plastic one from the hotel gift shop?

FIONA: Especially then.

STACY: It's the thought that counts. (*Taps the statuette.*) Hollow.

FIONA: But almost life-sized!

STACY: Have you ever seen one that was alive?

FIONA: Touché.

STACY: (*Gently.*) Why do you want it so bad?

FIONA: 'Cuz. (*Beat.*) I've always wanted to be the best actress I can be, right? And when you win a major award, it means…

STACY: (*Dubiously.*) Uh-huh.

FIONA: Oh, Stacy. Acceptance. Love! The ratification of who I am, right? After years of being on the outside, on purpose or not. It's like the ultimate expression of "You like me!"—which is a cliché but so true. All America finally makes it up to me for junior high!

STACY: But does it count if you have to pretend to get married to me to get there?

FIONA: Who's pretending? We *are* getting married.

STACY: Then do you think you could help me tie this bow tie?

FIONA: (*Deftly complying.*) Absolutely no problem. Lauren used to wear these to openings.

STACY: (*Laughs.*) Trent was more casual—he wanted to be a cable veejay. The torn T-shirt look.

(*FIONA tickles him.*)

FIONA: That can be sexy if the tears are strategically placed.

STACY: They were. (*Beat.*) Now all we have left is each other.

FIONA: What makes you think I tell you everything?

STACY: Oh. I just…

FIONA: No, you're right. (*Beat.*) But never fear—true love is just around the corner for each of us. I can feel it. You have yet to meet the great love of your life, Mr. Stacy Clifford. And when you do, I want to be the first person you call.

STACY: Likewise.

FIONA: Deal. (*Beat.*) A stranger vow was never made by two people about to get married.

STACY: Perhaps not.

(*FIONA adjusts his tie.*)

FIONA: You're gorgeous.

(*She kisses him.*)

FIONA: Put your pants on.

STACY: Do you think it's bad luck for me to see you before the wedding?

FIONA: Too late now.

STACY: I don't think those kind of rules hold in Las Vegas, anyway.

FIONA: Are you kidding? This town is the capital of good luck charms! Let's go find somebody to give me away.

(Blackout.)

VOICEOVER

Music, grand and inspiring.

ANNOUNCER'S VOICE: From majestic Seattle, Washington, ABC Sports is proud to present the annual United States National Figure Skating Championships. Tonight, we bring you the men's short programs, taped this afternoon, and live coverage of the pairs technical programs!

TWO.

Seattle; behind the scenes at the Nationals. A curtain and a bench. FIONA has her makeup kit open and is deftly brushing colors onto the face of BRITTANY—who is wearing a velvet-and-lace skating dress under her warm-up jacket. She has sneakers on, but her skates are visible in the corner. Muffled music, a dramatic movie theme, can be heard in the background.

FIONA: And then if you add just a touch of highlight *above* this line, your cheekbones will look wonderfully high and classy.

BRITTANY: That is so cool.

FIONA: Now blend…like this… *(Holds up mirror.)* What do you think?

BRITTANY: Wow. Too much?

FIONA: Just right. We're talkin' TV lights.

BRITTANY: Thanks for helping me, Fiona.

FIONA: It was fun. I can't wait to see you skate.

BRITTANY: That makes two of us. I hate drawing last. It's so much harder to stay warmed up. *(Slides to the floor in a split.)*

FIONA: Where's your partner?

BRITTANY: Didn't he tell you? He's out in the stands watching Ethan and Roberta. I never watch anyone else skate before I go on. But Stacy's weird that way. He says it's 'cause Ethan's his friend, but he even watches people he doesn't know. For some reason it doesn't make him nervous.

FIONA: I should—should I not?—go away and let you concentrate.

BRITTANY: On what? It's probably better to have someone around to distract me, actually. I've practiced all I'm going to practice.

FIONA: *(Looking around.)* Isn't your coach supposed to be with you for this?

BRITTANY: Geoffrey will be around. He coaches Ethan and Roberta too, don't forget. He has to watch them from the boards and then be there for them to wait for their scores in Kiss and Cry. Or in their case we should probably call it Sulk and Whine.

FIONA: That's not very nice. I think I'm starting to like you.

BRITTANY: I'm just calling it like it is. They have talent, but they usually crack at big competitions. They just can't take the pressure.

FIONA: Why do you think that is?

BRITTANY: It's difficult to say. Everybody's different. In their case I think it's probably a lack of scriptural grounding and personal commitment to the Lord.

FIONA: Okey-dokey.

(Uncomfortable pause.)

FIONA: So...when will you put your skates on?

BRITTANY: Soon. Stacy and I are the sixth and last pair in this group. So I will probably put them on when the fourth pair begins their program; that's my usual routine. Stacy used to wait till the last minute, but he switched because it made me nervous. If you wait till the pair right before you, there might not be time to correct an unforeseen problem with your laces or something.

FIONA: Oh yeah. Isn't that what happened to that Tonya what's-her-name?

BRITTANY: Precisely.

(The offstage music ends. Sound of a large arena audience applauding and cheering.)

BRITTANY: That means Roberta and Ethan are finished. We'll hear their marks in a minute.

FIONA: Sounds like the audience liked them.

BRITTANY: They're an attractive couple on the ice. And they have a sort of desperate quality that can be quite appealing.

ANNOUNCER'S VOICE: And the marks for Roberta Mallory and Ethan Holder. For required elements: 5.2, 5.3, 5.0, 5.1, 5.2, 5.2, 5.2, 5.1, 5.2. For presentation: 5.3, 5.2, 5.4, 5.1, 5.1, 5.3, 5.0, 5.2, 5.3.

(STACY has entered upstage, unseen by the women. His costume is made of the same fabrics as BRITTANY's.)

BRITTANY: *(Overlapping the scores.)* That's pretty good for them. They

must have only made a couple of major mistakes.

STACY: They did well. The star lift was gorgeous. And *fantastic* speed. They did get totally off unison on their sit spins. And the throw double axel was...yikes. But they were good.

(ETHAN enters, wearing a sequined skating costume and his skates with guards. He's very sweaty and has a towel over his shoulder, and he's carrying several bouquets of flowers and a large, pink stuffed dog.)

FIONA: *(Taking the toy dog.)* How absolutely...garish.

ETHAN: *(Sitting to take off his skates.)* Roberta thinks it's cute. I was afraid they were gonna start throwing those Stacy and Brittany dolls. That would have hurt.

STACY: You did good, my friend. It was an exciting program.

ETHAN: Yeah. Wondering if somebody's gonna fall on their tailbone can really get the blood going.

STACY: You're too hard on yourself.

ETHAN: If Roberta gains any more weight she's gonna need two partners.

FIONA: Oooh—ménage skating! I like. It's a concept.

ETHAN: *(To STACY.)* Who said she could be back here? *(Putting on his team warm-up jacket.)* I'm serious, Roberta has no sense of inner rhythm. Get in a competition and she goes twice as fast, especially on the spins. I'm like, "This music is still playing at thirty-three, you're going forty-five." And she's like, "Don't talk to me when we're skating, you fucker."

BRITTANY: Thirty-three? Forty-five?

FIONA: It's a grown-up thing, honey.

STACY: *(To ETHAN.)* It really was better than that.

FIONA: Yeah, Eth. Look on the bright side. At least you didn't drop her on her head.

ETHAN: That's the bright side? *(To STACY.)* Later, dude—you guys rock out there. Winner buys. *(Exits.)*

BRITTANY: No wonder Roberta cries all the time. I can't imagine what it would be like to have a partner who talked about me like that behind my back.

STACY: Aw, he's just frustrated.

FIONA: Sexually.

STACY: What?!

BRITTANY: Not in front of the child.

FIONA: Sorry, Brit.

BRITTANY: I was referring to Stacy.

FIONA: My cue to leave—and become an audience member. I'll see you in Kiss and Cry. Break a leg, you two.

BRITTANY: What?!!

FIONA: That's how actors wish each other luck.

STACY: Might not be the best choice for skaters though, hon.

FIONA: I didn't think of that! I take it all back. *(Thinks.)* Okay, then. *Merde!* *(Exits.)*

BRITTANY: What does that mean?

STACY: I don't know. I think it might be French.

(Music. Blackout.)

MAN'S VOICE: Welcome back to the U.S. Figure Skating Championships in Seattle, Washington, where the judges will be choosing not just the National champs but the Olympic team.

WOMAN'S VOICE: And hasn't it been an exciting week of skating so far, Dick?

MAN'S VOICE: Oh my yes. The pairs short programs last night were terrific, just terrific.

WOMAN'S VOICE: Brittany Bell and Stacy Clifford skated the best short I've ever seen them do—they're going into the long program Thursday night with a lot of confidence and solid first place scores.

MAN'S VOICE: Join us later this evening for the ice dance finals and exclusive network coverage of the men's long programs!

THREE.

Seattle: the stands in the arena. Soft music plays, sounding far away. STACY enters with FIONA, who is wearing STACY's team jacket. Both of them are drinking Cokes.

FIONA: *(Surveying the arena.)* Looks like the men's singles don't attract as much of a crowd as the pairs.

STACY: They will. It doesn't start for over an hour.

FIONA: You dork! Why'd you drag me up here an hour early?

STACY: To watch the warm-ups. *(Sits.)*

FIONA: Um…okay. *(Sits beside him, peering down at the rink.)* Thanks for letting me wear your team jacket.

STACY: No problem, honey.

FIONA: It makes me feel so…I don't know, *American*, or something. *(Looks at him.)* I was so proud of you last night.

STACY: *(Blushing a little.)* Thanks. That was just the short program; tomorrow night's the make or break.

FIONA: I'm envious.

STACY: No reason to be.

FIONA: *(Pointing down toward the ice.)* I mean it's like, see that guy trying to spin?

STACY: Adam Robinson. I like him.

FIONA: He can't skate for shit compared to you.

STACY: Adam's great.

FIONA: Oh please, he's skidding around like a toy top, trying to look like he knows which end is up. When you spin you've got like this, this very centered stillness inside you, no matter how fast you're moving, it's like a thread connecting your heart to the center of the earth and nobody can break that. *(Beat.)* It's art, what you do out there.

STACY: Thanks.

FIONA: Lauren always told me it's impossible to do art until you're honest with yourself about who you are. And, well…not just yourself. "Honest with the universe!"

STACY: Do you think she's right?

FIONA: I don't know; I guess I'd better hope not, right?

(Beat; STACY doesn't laugh.)

FIONA: Like, she said to me once at a rehearsal, "Acting isn't putting on a

disguise, it's stripping away the layers that cover your soul."

STACY: Wow.

FIONA: *(Cheerfully.)* But watching you got me thinking maybe none of that's true. I found it encouraging.

STACY: Gee thanks. I think.

FIONA: I'm really glad I came. *(Looks offstage left.)* Hey, photo op!

(She suddenly grabs STACY's face in both her hands and plants a major kiss on his mouth. A flashbulb goes off, catching them in mid-kiss, then ETHAN enters, carrying a camera.)

STACY: Ethan, I can't believe you just did that. I'm sorry, Fiona.

FIONA: No worries. *(To ETHAN.)* Just make sure to sell it to one of the better magazines. Toodaloo, I'm off to study my lines. *(Exits.)*

ETHAN: I knew I'd find you here. *(Sits down beside him.)* Haven't had your fill of skating this week?

STACY: *(Smiles.)* Never.

ETHAN: I just don't understand why skaters find it necessary to watch each other practice.

STACY: *(Simply.)* I love it. *(Beat.)* Wow! Did you see that? Chris Burlington just did a perfect quad toe loop!

ETHAN: Missed it. I was looking at you.

STACY: Look, Adam's gonna try it now. He'll never let himself be outdone by Chris, even at practice.

ETHAN: Think he'll have the guts to try it in competition, though?

STACY: Depends on who skates first tonight. If Chris lands his, Adam will want—

ETHAN: Fuckin' hotshot jerks.

STACY: Pardon?

ETHAN: Nothin'. Mr. Sixth Place Going Into the Long is just a little bit down on himself and his sport.

STACY: I guess that's understandable.

ETHAN: Skip the pity.

STACY: I wasn't—

ETHAN: Oh jeez, listen to that!

(A new piece of music has started, romantic and haunting.)

STACY: *(Laughs.)* Oh well. What can you do?

ETHAN: Adam's using the same fucking music you and Brittany used for your short!

STACY: There's no rule against it.

ETHAN: There should be.

(Pause. STACY is watching the ice with interest. ETHAN sits very still, with his head in his hands.)

STACY: Fantastic triple axel. *(Looks at ETHAN.)* Hey, you okay?

ETHAN: I just can't stand to watch him skate to this. *(Short pause as he listens.)* Here's where you guys do the star lift!

STACY: *(Surprised.)* That's right…

ETHAN: *(Eyes closed.)* Moving into the side-by-side double toe…Jesus.

STACY: You know it?

ETHAN: *(Quietly.)* Uh-huh. How could I not?

STACY: You've only watched us skate it a few times…

ETHAN: Sure, but I could run through the whole thing right now if I had to. It would look like shit, of course, me skating it instead of you. But I know the choreography inside out.

STACY: Wow. You're a quicker study than I am, I guess.

ETHAN: Nothing to do with that. It just…stayed in my mind because it makes so much sense, you know? Everything follows everything else. It's like God choreographed it, and I'm not even religious!

STACY: Morgan does good work.

ETHAN: It's not about her. It's you. The way you and Brit skate together it's like you're one person. Your hearts are even beating in unison.

STACY: How can you tell *that*?

ETHAN: I don't know, I just can. The way you lift her and just…*place* her back on the ice like she's made of glass. It's so gentle it hurts to watch. *(Pause. Eyes closed.)* Here's the camel spins.

STACY: *(A little taken aback.)* Right again.

ETHAN: It would take an earthquake to get you off unison. What's that like?

STACY: What's what like?

ETHAN: Being that in sync with somebody. Trusting somebody that much. Till your bodies are all one beautiful line and you can't even tell where one of you ends and the other one starts. You know what I mean.

STACY: Yeah.

ETHAN: So I need to know. What's that like?

(Pause.)

STACY: Kinda lonely.

ETHAN: *(After a beat.)* Shit.

STACY: Yeah.

ETHAN: You know what I want to do right now?

STACY: What?

ETHAN: *(Not looking at him.)* Touch you.

STACY: Say what?

ETHAN: Even just touch…your hand for a minute. That little vein in the back of your hand.

STACY: *(Weakly.)* Why?

ETHAN: Because I have to see you every day. At the rink. The god damn locker room. Even here, they make us roommates for God's sake. I have to look at you every damn day. And I'm not allowed to touch you.

STACY: Ethan, what are you saying?

ETHAN: I'm telling you who I am, Stacy. Finally. You were the one who helped me figure it out! And after that, it only took me about two more years to get up the courage to tell you.

STACY: Would you be careful? This is a public place.

ETHAN: There are two girl skaters from Lake Placid sitting with their mothers fourteen rows down from here. Nobody behind us. And the acoustics in here suck. *(Pause.)* Hear me out. Please?

STACY: I'm married.

ETHAN: You think I don't know that? *(Beat.)* But for some reason…Even if there's just a chance in a million, I have to find out. You move me very much. Everything about you.

STACY: *(Standing.)* I have to go, I'm sorry.

ETHAN: Stacy!

STACY: Your timing…! This is Nationals, Ethan. I have to skate a long program tomorrow night and hopefully get Brittany on the Olympic team. Some of us still have something at stake here.

ETHAN: I have everything at stake! Believe me, I didn't plan this. I just need to know if you care about me at all.

STACY: Of course I care about you. But not.…Jeepers. Why are you doing this to me right now?

ETHAN: I don't know. *(Pause. Sadly.)* I guess because it's Olympic year, right? Go for broke.

(BRITTANY enters, with yogurt.)

BRITTANY: Found ya! You boys really like to sit in the back don't you? Want some yogurt? I got a good workout just walking up here. *(Sits down between them.)* I love to watch the men practice, don't you? Isn't Adam a cutie? I like his new haircut so much. But it sucks that he's using our music. Momsy told his coach she thought it was uncomradely. Is that even a word?

(Music. Blackout.)

Four.

LAUREN's apartment in New York. FIONA is seated on the couch, reading the final pages of a manuscript. LAUREN enters with two cups of tea.

LAUREN: Finished?

FIONA: Yeah. I just finished it.

LAUREN: And?

FIONA: What can I say? *(Looks at her.)* You've still got it.

LAUREN: You liked it?

FIONA: Do you care?

LAUREN: A little. *(Beat.)* Old habits die hard.

FIONA: What can I say, it's well written. I can relate to it.

LAUREN: That's priceless.

FIONA: But…

LAUREN: Here it comes.

FIONA: Why'd you put *me* in it?

LAUREN: Should I answer that without a lawyer present?

FIONA: Oh please, I'm the one with the money, remember? *(Beat.)* Plus I forgot to copyright my life. Don't worry, you're safe.

LAUREN: I don't think I've ever quite felt safe.

FIONA: Really?

LAUREN: Well, maybe that one weekend you and I drove up to Vermont. See how wrong I was?

FIONA: You *were* safe with me.

LAUREN: "Were" being the operative word. Safe with someone means she's not going to leave you.

FIONA: Uh…hold on a sec here. *You* kicked *me* out.

LAUREN: You changed.

FIONA: Well when you love someone you're supposed to want her to grow.

LAUREN: I did want you to grow. You *shrank.*

FIONA: Well for someone who's shrinking, I've gotten very, very big.

LAUREN: So you have. Let's not do that argument again; I'm over it.

FIONA: Then why this play?

LAUREN: I wrote that months ago. I'm on to whole new vistas now.

FIONA: I'm happy for you. And yet this one is sticking around to ruin my career. Transferring to Broadway?!

LAUREN: That may not happen.

FIONA: Well it's already generating enough buzz to scare the studios. Not to mention the god damn, fucked-up Oscar-nominating committee.

LAUREN: Hey, if my little play can ruin your big career, it wasn't a career worth having.

FIONA: You never thought it was! You just did this out of jealousy, didn't you? To tear me down.

LAUREN: If I'd wanted to do that, there were less agonizing and less time-consuming ways than writing a play. One afternoon on talk TV would have done the job. Besides, I thought you said you read it. I changed all the givens. My lead character is an African American TV star from Chicago.

FIONA: Yeah yeah yeah. And she marries a figure skater!

LAUREN: Excuse me, you and What's-his-Name didn't get *married* until *after* I wrote the play, remember? *I* should sue *you.*

FIONA: Touché. *(Beat.)* But you know how hard the press is watching me.

I still think it was inconsiderate and irresponsible of you to—

LAUREN: My responsibility is to Truth and Growth. I'm a writer, so the way I grow is by taking the crap life throws at me and trying to shape it into something. Find the irony, use the absurdity, sculpt the pain until it *means* something. And thank the Goddess I can still do that! You didn't take *that* away from me. I don't care what the media do with this play. They can love it or hate it. They can shut it down or move it to Broadway. They can think it's about you or know it's about me. But if just a few of the people who see it get something from it—feel something real or think something new about how messed up the world is—then the play's done its job. Which was to take the shit you put me through and... *burn* it into some kind of positive energy. And *if* it pays the bills for a few months, so much the better—because that gives me time to write the next one! So there.

(Pause.)

FIONA: God I've missed you!

LAUREN: I've missed you too.

FIONA: Do you want me back?

LAUREN: Hell no.

FIONA: Well that's fine. *(Beat.)* I've missed New York, too.

LAUREN: Congratulations. So do you want to go see it?

FIONA: "See it"?

LAUREN: The play. There's a performance at eight.

FIONA: Lauren, I just finished *reading* the damn thing. You're asking me if I want to *see* it? *Tonight*? *(Beat.)* You bet I do.

(Blackout. Music.)

FIVE.

Split stage. On stage right, STACY's apartment in Denver. Just a phone on the floor; he still doesn't have any furniture. On stage left, a hotel room in New York City, represented by an armchair. FIONA enters, wearing only an oversized "I Love New York" T-shirt, and plops down in the chair. She dials a number on her cell phone. The phone on stage right rings, and STACY enters sleepily, rubbing his eyes. He picks it up.

STACY: Hello?

FIONA: Hey, Sesame Seed, it's me.

STACY: Fiona, hi!

FIONA: I'm not waking you up am I?

STACY: That's okay; I'm glad you called. Hey—I'm sorry about the Oscar nomina—

FIONA: Oh, please, I'm totally over that. I'm having the most incredible weekend in New York! Stacy, I saw Lauren's play.

STACY: *(Worried.)* And?

FIONA: It's fantastic. Totally deserves to go to Broadway. I think her writing's actually grown.

STACY: Um, okay. I mean is it really obviously about us? Because the Olympics—

FIONA: Oh, no, she changed everything. She made me black! And the guy, I mean, the script says he's from Texas and you're Canadian, so...

STACY: Great.

FIONA: But you know what the scary part was? They *sounded* like us. I mean, seeing this play was like a perspective-altering experience for me. Because those two characters...they were really kind of ridiculous, you know? Cooking up that whole crazy scheme just to—well, *you* know. You'd think Lauren had bugged our apartments or something—which she didn't!—but I mean she's just so fucking *perceptive*. And you know what? It was kind of embarrassing.

STACY: Great.

FIONA: It *is* great, Stace. I'm glad you feel it too. 'Cause I haven't even told you the most important part. I met the director of the play—her name's Sara—we went out for drinks after the show...

STACY: You and she and Lauren?

FIONA: No, just me and Sara. She is so intense. Really a brilliant woman, she like went to Yale and shit. She's already directed four off-Broadway plays and she's like twenty-seven. Her opinions are eye opening. Anyway, she saw "Moonlight on a Ranch" and she said she thinks my presence is like way too big for the camera—

STACY: I'm sorry. But what does she know?

FIONA: No it's great. She said the stage is where I belong.

STACY: Well didn't that used to be your dream?

FIONA: It still is, totally. And Sara's workshopping this new play called "Out Loud"—it's about this lesbian congresswoman who—well anyway, it's fantastic and she's already got major interest from Lincoln Center Theatre and the Public, both. She thinks I would be perfect for the role of the congresswoman's quirky young poet slash acupuncturist lover.

Tomorrow we're meeting the playwright for a late brunch.

STACY: A lesbian character? I thought you were trying to stay away from all that. The Hollywood image thing?

FIONA: That's what I wanted to talk to you about, Stace. A lot of things are coming together in my mind finally; talking to Sara really helped me figure some stuff out. She thinks it would be really, really powerful if I came out publicly. A lot of people loved me in the Vamp Camp movies, and in "Moonlight." And too many of them are probably homophobes, right? If I set the record straight, it could *really*...they'd have to...I mean, somebody they believe in—somebody they *like*—is a lesbian! I could get a lot of people to think about some shit, you know? *(Beat.)* And you could too.

STACY: Me?

FIONA: Sure! A gay sports hero? What a role model you could be! Think of all those teenaged fans who love you so much. Sara and I think it would be utterly courageous and inspiring if you—

STACY: *(Alarmed.)* Fiona, we're going to the Olympics next month!

FIONA: So the timing's perfect, right? You've got a platform, and how! It'll be wild.

STACY: "Wild" is not what I need right now. Brittany's parents—

FIONA: Are gonna fire you right before the Olympics? They need you to get their daughter a medal! That's the beauty of it.

STACY: No.

FIONA: You're living in the past, Stacy; we're gonna be more marketable than ever. It's *hip* to be gay right now— it's so nineties! Ellen's out, Melissa's out. Rudy Galindo, for heaven's sakes! —look around *you*. It's a whole different climate. You'll be the only skater left in the closet.

STACY: Hardly.

FIONA: Well take your time then, no prob. I'll keep you out of it. We could say the divorce is like totally my fault. Like I came out and you were like, shocked.

STACY: Wait a minute. What "divorce"?

FIONA: Well hey, that's the great part, Stace. I'm finally giving you that divorce I've been promising you for…how long now?

STACY: I never said I wanted a divorce from you.

FIONA: I know, you've been a fantastic sport about the whole thing…

STACY: Don't leave me alone right now.

FIONA: *(Pause.)* Stacy, what do you think we've been doing here?

STACY: I've never known what we were doing! But I need it to not end right now.

FIONA: You're not saying you're falling in love with me for real, are you?

STACY: No. But I…I like being married to you.

FIONA: Stacy, we've never even slept together.

STACY: Well maybe that's not what it's all about. *(Beat.)* You're the most important person in my life. The person I feel like I could trust with anything. That was the wish, remember? The big dream?

FIONA: Oh shit. *(Beat.)* Stacy, you can have that for real! Don't settle for me. *(Pause.)* Are you there? *(Pause.)* Damn it. *(Realizing.)* I've really done a job on you, haven't I? Oh *shit!* I was afraid I was talking too loud. Now Sara's waking up. I'll talk to you tomorrow, okay? *(Beat.)* Stace?

STACY: *(Pause.)* Good night, Fiona.

FIONA: Night, sweetie.

(FIONA hangs up her phone, and the light on her side of the stage goes to black. STACY sits still for a moment, staring at his phone, then hangs it up. He takes a deep breath, shudders, and then impulsively picks up the phone again and punches in a number.)

STACY: Ethan? Hi, this is Stacy. Sorry to call so late. *(Beat.)* I've been thinking a lot about what you said to me at Nationals. Is there someplace we could talk?

(Blackout.)

VOICEOVER

Loud dance music.

DJ'S VOICE: Okay, for a free copy of Madonna's latest CD, here's a trivia question for you. Who's the male half of the U.S. champion pairs figure skating team this year? That too easy for you guys? Okay, here's a real tough one: who's the male half of the fifth-ranked pair? And don't look now, but they dance as good as they skate! Party on, boys. The weekend's young!

SIX

A dark street in Denver in the middle of the night. STACY and ETHAN, sweaty and a bit disheveled, are waiting for a cab.

STACY: I can't believe your car got towed at two in the morning.

ETHAN: I can't believe I've spent the last couple hours dancing with you.

STACY: And kissing me.

ETHAN: And kissing you! Pinch me and tell me I'm awake.

STACY: When is this cab coming? I'm cold. And sweaty! *(Laughs.)* Sweaty cold!

ETHAN: I don't know, it should be here soon I guess. Here, take my jacket.

STACY: Nonono. I'm fine.

(ETHAN bundles STACY up.)

ETHAN: I insist. You're the one going to the Olympics. We can't have you getting sick. *(Looks around.)* Denver's really not a nightlife kind of town, is it? Look how deserted the streets are.

STACY: I like being a yone with Lou. I mean alone with you.

ETHAN: Me too. *(Quietly.)* Though actually there's a couple guys over there by the pizza place.

STACY: I like pizza but I can't eat it because I'm in training for the Winter Olympus in Shitzerland. Uh-oh I said a bad word. I can't talk good. *(Amazed.)* I, Clacy Stifford, am like majorly tipsy.

ETHAN: I know you are, and I'm sorry. I mean, I knew you were not a drinker. I never should have let you have that second beer.

STACY: This is true, I am not a drinker. I was raised in a fundamentalist Christian hellhole. I mean househole!

(ETHAN laughs.)

STACY: House*hold!*

(They both laugh.)

STACY: But do you know what? Drinking is good! It is very excellent. In fact, I'm gonna go back in there and ordering another!

ETHAN: *(Pulling him back.)* Stace— don't. It's closed, remember? We danced the last dance and they turned the lights on.

STACY: Oh yeah! Duh! Gosh, did you see how many gay guys there were in there?

ETHAN: *(Touching him.)* I didn't notice.

STACY: But you were the most handsomest. I love dancing with you.

ETHAN: *(Quietly.)* I've dreamed for years about dancing with you...

STACY: Dreams come true.

ETHAN: ...and skating with you.

STACY: Skating with me?

ETHAN: Sure. People say there's no chemistry when Roberta and me skate together.

STACY: Can't imagine why.

ETHAN: *(Laughs.)* But you and I would burn up the ice. I mean, were we in sync in there or what? Win the Olympics with Brittany and then cut her loose and skate with me!

STACY: Um, I think it's supposed to be boy-girl?

ETHAN: We'll rewrite the book. It's all about romance, right? Passion? That's you and me.

STACY: In case you haven't noticed, I'm a little bigger than Roberta?

ETHAN: Not for long.

(STACY laughs.)

ETHAN: So I'll pump a little more iron. I'll lift you to the *sky*.

STACY: *(Laughs.)* You are too crazy sometimes.

ETHAN: No, picture us. Side-by-side quads!

(STACY laughs.)

ETHAN: Jumps and throws a mile high! Who could say no if we skate that much better than everybody else?

STACY: There's rules, Ethan.

ETHAN: Unconstitutional rules. Sex discrimination! We'll take it to the Supreme Court if we have to. You and I could revolutionize the world of figure skating, my friend.

STACY: Gee. Wow!

ETHAN: Sounds good?

STACY: Sounds fantastic! I could kiss you right here. Hold still.

ETHAN: Shh. Watch it; those guys are still over there. I think they're looking at us.

STACY: Don't worry, sweetheart. I'm with *you*.

ETHAN: That's not what I meant. Shit, they're walking this way. Just act normal.

STACY: Normal? What's "normal," anyways? I'm so friggin' tired of "acting normal" all the gosh-darned time!

ETHAN: *(Chuckles.)* You can't even cuss when you're drunk. *(Looks over his shoulder uneasily.)* Let's just walk down to the end of the block. There's more light down there.

STACY: You are such a paradroid. I bet those guys were in the club too. Everybody's gay anymore!

ETHAN: *(Overlapping.)* Stacy, please. Not those guys. Let's just *walk*. Slowly. *(Beat.)* Damn it, they're following us!

STACY: Let 'em. It's a free country! It's a *new climate*.

ETHAN: *(Hushed.)* Shut up.

STACY: Will not. I'm so sick of *shutting up* every time I see somebody who might not *approve*. Screw 'em! There's dozens of us! Live and let love!

FIRST MAN: *(Offstage.)* Hey pretty boys, what're you whinin' about? Somebody oughtta get your kind off the streets.

ETHAN: Don't turn around.

SECOND MAN: *(Offstage.)* Hey cutie, are you a fag?

STACY: *(Turning to face them.)* No I am not a "fag"! I am a gay man and this is my boyfriend and we're gonna skate together in the Olympics some day and win a gold medal!

ETHAN: *(Overlapping.)* Stacy! Stacy!

STACY: *(Without stopping.)* And if you jerks don't like it, you can just gosh-darned well…change the channel or something!

FIRST MAN: *(Offstage.)* I've had enough of this crap.

SECOND MAN: *(Offstage.)* Let's take 'em.

ETHAN: *Shit.*

(Quick blackout.)

VOICEOVER

Hot dance music.

ANNOUNCER'S VOICE: You're watching Trent-A-Video, a weekly program of hot music videos and celebrity interviews starring the Cable Music Channel's first openly gay veejay, Trent Weathers!

SEVEN.

Lights up on a TV studio. Banks of bright lights and a large video camera. A big overstuffed couch with huge, super-colorful cushions constitutes the set of the interview show. On it sit TRENT and FIONA. Yes, it is the same TRENT. But now he has greenish hair and a trendy new wardrobe. FIONA looks different too. She wears a baggy shirt, no makeup, and slightly dorky glasses.

TRENT: I'm sitting here chattin' and laughin' with Fiona Blake, and she's one hot, happenin' movie queen slash party girl. So Fiona, tell us, what kinds of music videos are you into these days?

FIONA: Oh you know me, Trent. I like almost everything.

TRENT: Cool. That's very discerning. Any artists of the moment that rock your world specifically?

FIONA: Sure. *(Thinking.)* I really dig the Indigo Girls. Melissa Etheridge, kd lang. Ellen DeGeneres.

TRENT: Uh—she doesn't sing.

FIONA: Well, you know, Trent. Women who write the poetry of my life.

TRENT: That is so empowering. Can you illuminate our viewers—and remember, this is live TV here, which is pretty retro in itself—can you shed

some rays on your overnight—was it overnight?—transformation from hyper-hetero, way glam vampire chick to what we see before us?

FIONA: Well Trent, it wasn't so much a transformation as a...I don't know. A recognition and embraceage of who I had always on some level been *heretofore.* Know what I'm saying?

TRENT: "Embraceage," huh? Keep comin' at me with those coinages. No, I don't know what you mean.

FIONA: Meeting Sara had a lot to do with it, I know that. Just being back in New York and feeling that urgency of people who do their work because it's who they are. I'd been trying to play a Hollywood game that wasn't me for too long. I'd lost sight of what was real.

TRENT: That can happen.

FIONA: I felt that if I was to self-actualize as a creative spirit, I needed to be honest about who I was inside.

TRENT: Good answer, sister. *(To camera.)* Major league power surge! She rocks! *(To FIONA.)* So what about this play "Kiss and Cry"? 'Zat you?

FIONA: Excuse me?

TRENT: You know, Lauren Hadley's play. Wasn't she an ex of yours?

FIONA: *(Uncomfortable.)* I haven't really kept up with Lauren's projects.

TRENT: *(Feigning great patience.)* It's got like this hot young actress...

FIONA: Black.

TRENT: Who marries this pro figure skater...

FIONA: Texan.

TRENT: To conceal the fact that they're both gay.

FIONA: Wow. Is it any good?

TRENT: Art imitates life, *n'est-ce pas?*

FIONA: Or the other way around. Okay, so yes, I knew Lauren in college. And there may be one or two superficial similarities between me and the character of Suzanne. But you know, Lauren wrote that play before I married Stacy. So it couldn't be about him in any way. I mean, they've never even met. So you see.

TRENT: Wow, twisted. That is Byzantine to the nth. *(To camera.)* Well, folks at home, it looks like my guest might need a potty break. So speaking of people being themselves, let's take a look at RuPaul's video "Snapshot."

(Music in.)

TECHNICIAN'S VOICE: We're out, Trent.

TRENT: Thanks. *(To FIONA.)* So you've got a couple minutes to regroup. *(Beat.)* Sorry if I threw ya there.

FIONA: You little prick. We agreed we wouldn't talk about Stacy.

TRENT: Excuse me…I thought I heard *you* bring up his name?

FIONA: You started telling the *story* of "Kiss and Cry"!

TRENT: Oh, well…that's about some guy from Texas and a black chick.

FIONA: I don't know what Stacy ever saw in you.

TRENT: So you know. *(Beat.)* I didn't think he'd ever told anybody about me. Except his teddy bear.

FIONA: We were close.

TRENT: To what?

FIONA: If you wanted to out Stacy, you could have done that a year ago. What do you need me for?

TRENT: I'm not trying to "out" anybody. Try to look at this from my POV, baby. Every gossip columnist on both coasts has been trying to find out if that play's about you for weeks. How could I do a live interview with you and not mention it? I could lose my fuckin' *job.*

FIONA: *(Grabbing her purse and getting ready to leave.)* Stacy's going to the Olympics next month. I thought you of all people would have enough respect for him not to want to mess that up.

TECHNICIAN'S VOICE: Trent, can I see you for a sec? Something just came in over the AP.

TRENT: Sure, dude. *(To FIONA.)* Don't go anyplace. We'll figure something out.

(TRENT leaves the set and FIONA fidgets, listening to the music and trying to calm down. TRENT returns, reading a printout.)

TRENT: Holy shit.

FIONA: What now? Oh, good. Some late-breaking news story and I'm off the hook.

TRENT: This is bad, baby. *(Looks at her.)* It's about Stacy.

FIONA: What? Let me see that. *(Takes the paper and reads.)* Oh my God. *(Looks up.)* I'm outta here. I've got to get a flight to Denver.

TRENT: Wait! Hold it a sec.

FIONA: What?!

TRENT: Can you…? We're gonna be back on live in a minute. Could you— what if I give this to you again on the air? Let the nation see your reaction.

FIONA: You've got to be joking. I don't care about your stupid show, Trent.

TRENT: It's so not about that! It's about…this is a hate crime, right? People need to know. I mean, I love the guy, right? People have to see the damage this kind of thing does in our society. We could—*you* can make a huge difference right here. Blow this thing wide open. You're an actress, right? That look in your eyes was, hey. It's powerful human stuff.

FIONA: You're hopeless.

TRENT: All I need is *five minutes*. I'll call the studio limo—we'll get you to the airport in record time.

FIONA: You want to see powerful stuff?! I'll show you powerful stuff.

(To TRENT's horror, FIONA grabs the TV camera and, with a great burst of strength, knocks it to the floor. Amidst a shower of sparks, the stage plunges to blackness.)

VOICEOVER

NEWSCASTER'S VOICE: The figure skating community was rocked today by a shocking story. Stacy Clifford, who with partner Brittany Bell was a medal favorite heading into the Switzerland Olympics, was injured late last night in a random attack in Denver. Clifford and a fellow skater, Ethan Holder, were assaulted by two unidentified men before a passing police officer broke up the fight; Clifford's injuries were serious enough to remove all possibility of his and Bell's

competing in the Olympics. The assault took place not far from the entrance to Club Proteus, a popular gay dance club. No motive has been determined.

EIGHT.

A private room in a hospital in Denver. STACY is lying on the bed, staring straight ahead. ETHAN enters; a flashbulb can be seen going off behind him and a hubbub of voices is heard before he closes the door. His right hand is bandaged.

ETHAN: I keep telling the reporters you're not up to talking, but most of them are sticking around. Assholes.

(Pause; STACY is silent.)

ETHAN: Carol Danelli's out there bullshitting, and Geoffrey'll be here soon. But they just want to talk to you. *(Pause.)* I say we tell them the truth.

STACY: Go ahead I guess. I don't care.

ETHAN: You sure?

STACY: No. *(Beat.)* I've already ruined Brittany's career. I don't want to ruin her life too.

ETHAN: She's here.

STACY: Oh my God, why didn't you tell me? I thought she was still in Colorado Springs.

ETHAN: You said you didn't want to see anybody. Should I send her away?

STACY: No! Let her come in.

ETHAN: Seriously?

STACY: Yeah. I need to talk to her alone.

ETHAN: Okay. *(Beat.)* It's not your fault, you know. I'll be right outside if you need me.

(He exits. A moment later, BRITTANY enters, in her coat. She has been crying. STACY can't look at her at first.)

BRITTANY: Tell me it isn't true. Please. *(Beat.)* We have two weeks. I know your knee's messed up pretty bad, but look how fast Nancy Kerrigan got back on the ice. They're all saying we can't do it. But we can do anything we set our minds to, right?

(Pause.)

STACY: I'm sorry, Brit.

BRITTANY: Don't say that. It's not over yet.

STACY: Yeah it is, star. It's over. I'm so sorry. It's not just my knee. I have two cracked ribs. And my shoulder's a total mess. The doctor said I can't even try to lift you for at least a month.

BRITTANY: How could you do this? A dark street at two in the morning?! And Dadsy said you'd been drinking. It's two weeks till the Olympics! *(Beat.)* I'm sorry. I know it wasn't your fault. I mean it wasn't, right? *(Pause.)*

STACY: I don't know. I think it sort of was.

BRITTANY: No, Stacy. *(Beat.)* Tell me what happened.

STACY: Fiona called me last night from New York and told me she wants a divorce. *(Beat.)* I was pretty upset, for a lot of reasons. I called Ethan, and we...we talked and then we ended up going out dancing. Together. To a place where men dance together. *(Beat.)* And when we left the club...I was acting like a jerk, I guess, I was pretty drunk and I was fooling around and acting all obnoxious and trying to kiss Ethan and stuff. I guess those two guys didn't like it.

BRITTANY: So they beat you up.

STACY: No, actually. *(Beat.)* One of them did hit me in the face. But they were pretty drunk. Even drunker than we were. Well, maybe not drunker than me, but definitely drunker than Ethan. And Ethan went crazy. It was kind of great, actually. After the one guy hit me, Ethan just went ballistic and let them have it. That's how he hurt his hand. It was a major mess by the time the policeman got there; that's why he took us all in to the station. So we called Geoffrey to come down and bail us out, but he didn't have the cash so he called your dad...who was pretty upset. The sergeant told him enough that I kind of felt like I had to fill in the missing pieces. So we drove to your house. Your father made coffee and we talked in the kitchen.

(Pause.)

BRITTANY: About?

STACY: My marriage to Fiona for starters, which was a...well, we really are married. But it started out as a...I guess it was always...

BRITTANY: A lie. *(Beat.)* So nobody would know you were a homo.

STACY: That we both are.

BRITTANY: You and Ethan?

STACY: Me and Fiona. *(Beat.)* You don't seem very surprised.

BRITTANY: I am. About her. And about Ethan. You knew.

STACY: Seriously? For how long?

BRITTANY: About a year and a half. Since that day when I asked you, actually.

STACY: But I said...

BRITTANY: You're not a very good liar, Stacy. Something about the eyes.

STACY: Jeez.

BRITTANY: *(Steeling herself.)* Go on.

(Pause.)

STACY: Okay. Well, Jim...your dad was pretty angry. Understandably, I guess... and the phone was already ringing off the hook—reporters, somebody from the Olympic Committee... *(Chokes off.)*

BRITTANY: Stacy, what is it?

STACY: When I told your dad about me and Fiona, and about me and Ethan being together...he kind of lost it for a minute.

BRITTANY: What do you mean "lost it"?

STACY: Started calling me names. And I guess I was still kind of out of it, so I yelled right back. We were standing beside the kitchen table. So when your dad got real mad, and pushed me...I went right through the swinging door and fell down the basement stairs.

(Pause. BRITTANY is silent.)

STACY: It was just one of those split-second things you can't take back. He was really, really sorry, Brit. He apologized like ten times and started crying—

BRITTANY: *(Interrupting him.)* You're lying.

STACY: Not anymore.

BRITTANY: Then why does everybody think it was those two guys who hurt you?

STACY: You've got a good support team. "Spin," right? I am so, so sorry, star.

BRITTANY: Don't call me that.

STACY: I always will.

BRITTANY: *(Sits on the foot of the bed.)* I think I want to run away. Maybe I could join one of those cheesy European tours. Disco on Ice.

STACY: You've got a family here.

BRITTANY: I wish I could just stay here with you.

STACY: In the hospital?

BRITTANY: You know what I mean.

STACY: Yeah I do. *(Pause.)*

BRITTANY: I have to go talk to him, don't I?

STACY: Yeah, you do.

(BRITTANY rises, and heads for the door, then turns back to STACY.)

BRITTANY: When will I see you?

(He doesn't have an answer for this. They look at each other for a moment, then she comes back to the bed and starts to embrace him, but stops herself.)

BRITTANY: I'm afraid to hurt you worse.

(She kisses him carefully on the cheek, then quickly goes out. STACY lies back against the pillow and cries quietly. ETHAN enters.)

ETHAN: One of the punks from last night just made a statement on CNN. Got all tearful and apologized for ruining your career.

STACY: Was he too drunk to remember what really happened?

ETHAN: Or he saw a chance to get on TV and jumped on it. The doctor said you're ready to be discharged.

STACY: I don't think I want to go home. It's lonely and there's no furniture.

ETHAN: Of course there is. I've got a dumb old comfy couch, a queen-sized bed, my grandparents' dining room table, a beanbag chair…

STACY: I'm talking about *my* home.

ETHAN: Me too.

(Beat. STACY looks at him.)

ETHAN: We'll go over to your apartment and pack a bag, and then I'm gonna take you home, tuck you in, and wait on you hand and foot until you're feeling better. Then we'll take it from there.

STACY: Wow.

ETHAN: I want to take care of you.

STACY: Wow.

ETHAN: In fact, I wish we could get away from all the Olympic hoopla *totally*. In fact why don't we. I'll take you down to Mexico or someplace. We'll get a little cabin on the beach with no TV. Lie in the sun till it's over.

STACY: That sounds nice. But you owe it to yourself to go.

ETHAN: "Go" where?

STACY: Switzerland, numbskull.

ETHAN: Fuck that. I would've gone to watch you. But now I couldn't care less about it.

STACY: Have you talked that over with Roberta?

ETHAN: What does she have to do with anything? *(Beat.)* I know you've had a rough night, Stacy, but only the top three American pairs make the Olympic team,

remember? Me and Roberta came in *fifth* at Nationals.

STACY: Uh…in case you missed it, first place just opened up.

ETHAN: Tina and Mark Crawford are the alternates. That brother-sister team from Lake Arrowhead? They came in fourth.

STACY: But you have to be at least fifteen years old to compete in the Olympics.

ETHAN: Says who?

STACY: Says the new rules. Tina Crawford's only thirteen.

(Pause.)

ETHAN: Holy shit.

STACY: Better check your messages.

ETHAN: I hadn't even *thought* about that.

STACY: You're kidding.

ETHAN: I've been so worried about you I just…Wow.

STACY: What?

ETHAN: This may be the first time in my adult life I've actually thought of somebody else before my dumb self.

STACY: Congratulations.

ETHAN: So, no, I don't think I'll be going. We'll take our trip to Mexico.

STACY: You think Roberta will agree?

ETHAN: Please, I'll be saving her the embarrassment of falling on her ass in front of a billion people.

STACY: What about…?

ETHAN: What about what?

STACY: Nothing. *(Gets up and goes to get his coat.)* It's just that now that you've taken up selflessness, I thought you might want to think about that middle-class couple you're always whining about, who've worked ten years without a vacation so their little boy can go to the Olympics someday.

(Pause.)

ETHAN: You know we wouldn't have a chance for a medal.

STACY: Look me in the eye and say that again.

(Pause. ETHAN gets the point.)

ETHAN: This is going to be crazy. Roberta and I have hardly practiced since Nationals.

STACY: Well life's a fuckin' bitch sometimes.

ETHAN: Are you sure you're okay with it? That's the most important thing to me.

STACY: The last thing I want to do right now is keep one more person from skating in the Olympics.

(ETHAN gently helps STACY put on his coat. Over ETHAN's shoulder, STACY sees FIONA, who has entered from the hall a bit tentatively.)

FIONA: Hey, Sesame Seed.

ETHAN: How did *you* get in here? I specifically told the desk nurse that Stacy didn't want any visitors.

FIONA: Apparently the *wife* has special privileges.

ETHAN: Oh jeez!

STACY: It's okay, Ethan. *(To FIONA.)* I'm glad you're here.

FIONA: Honey, of course I'm here! I jumped on a plane the minute I heard! Canceled out on two important auditions.

ETHAN: But who's counting?

FIONA: Nobody!

(STACY looks at ETHAN.)

ETHAN: Take your time. *(Kisses STACY.)* I'm gonna call the rink and then pull the car around to the front.

STACY: Thanks.

(ETHAN exits.)

FIONA: So you and Ethan, huh?

STACY: Me and Ethan.

FIONA: I knew something was up with that guy. *(Beat; lightly.)* Actually, I think you could do better.

STACY: And when have you ever steered me wrong? *(Beat. STACY sits back down on the foot of the bed.)* He's an Olympic skater, in case you hadn't heard.

FIONA: I did hear that. *(Beat.)* So you could still go, right? To Switzerland? If you wanted to. Cheer for your guy?

STACY: *(Beat.)* Maybe I'll watch it on TV.

(FIONA looks at him and sits down carefully on the corner of the bed.)

FIONA: I can't believe this, Stacy. I am so, so sorry. This is all my fault, isn't it?

STACY: Must be. Everything's always completely about you, right?

FIONA: *(Tries to smile.)* Touché.

(She takes his hand.)

FIONA: God, Stacy. I wish… *(Pause.)* I just wish…!

STACY: Me too.

(Fadeout.)

VOICEOVER

ACTRESS'S VOICE: And the Tony nominees for Best Play are: "An Unlikely Friendship," by Jason Goldman, "Kiss and Cry," by Lauren Hadley, "Skeletons in the Closet," by Seamus Nigel O'Malley, and "Sag Harbor Sunset," by Peter Logan Wells. And the winner of this year's Tony Award is… "Kiss and Cry," by Lauren Hadley!

(Grand music and applause.)

NINE.

The stage of Radio City Music Hall; an elegant glass podium holds a Tony Award. Behind it stands LAUREN, wearing a black pantsuit with a purple silk shirt and necktie. She looks out at the audience.

LAUREN: Whoa, this really is a big theatre. Traditionally, the producers come up onstage with the playwright to accept the Best Play Tony but… *(Looks around.)* I think mine are in LA negotiating the film deal or something. Plus they're pretty mad at me. Anyway… I don't have a speech. In fact I'm pretty drunk. I wasn't planning on winning so I got pretty drunk before I came here just to get through the damn ceremony and now… here I am. So let's see. I thought about turning it down, sending some Indian woman to say something about

how competition kills creativity… but that would be tacky. I mean, you guys invited me and everything. *(Pause.)* People got hurt because of this play, which was not my intention. Nor was it intended to be some kind of scandal thing that capitalized on other people's private crap, and yet…. *(Shakes her head.)* And yet. It's still my play. It's really only about me, my journey. Stuff I was thinking about at the time. Not that I still think it now, but that's not the point, right? And here I am holding a Tony Award. Which is just… so fucked. Which says that a lot of people thought it was the best play of the year. Which really only means the best play *on Broadway*, which bears no relationship to all the great stuff being written out there, right? You bet your ass. But where was I?

(The orchestra starts playing.)

LAUREN: Woops, that's my cue to leave, right? So… *(Looks at the award.)* What's it gonna be? I guess I could take her home and put her on the shelf in the closet with my high school tennis trophy or something. Or give her to my parents to make up for… all that other stuff. But it wouldn't feel right. No, it wouldn't really feel right. I don't know…

(She turns and walks off the stage, a bit unsteadily. The lights iris down to a tight spot on the award, left alone on the podium, shimmering delicately. Then it's dark.)

(END OF PLAY)

THEY'RE JUST LIKE US

Boo Killebrew

BOO KILLEBREW is an actor-playwright-choreographer, and a co-founder of CollaborationTown, a theatre company. She was born in Jackson, Mississippi on August 5, 1980, and grew up in Gulfport, Mississippi. She studied theatre at North Carolina School of the Arts, and received a BFA in theatre arts from Boston University, where she received the Bette Davis Institution Award for Excellence in Acting and Professional Promise. Her plays include *Exes Meeting Exes*, cowritten with Jordan Seavey (HERE, 2000), *The Trading Floor* (Access Theatre, 2004), and *The Astronomer's Triangle* (Studio 5, 2005), both cowritten with CollaborationTown. Her acting credits include *This Is a Newspaper* (New York International Fringe Festival, 2003), *The Astronomer's Triangle*, and *The Deepest Play Ever* (New York International Fringe Festival, 2006). For her performance in *This Is a Newspaper*, Killebrew won a 2003 FringeNYC Excellence Award for Performance. She received a New York Innovative Theatre Award nomination for Outstanding Actress in a Lead Role for *The Astronomer's Triangle*, and NYITA nominations for Outstanding Full-Length Script for both *The Astronomer's Triangle* and *They're Just Like Us*. She lives in Manhattan.

They're Just Like Us was first presented by CollaborationTown on March 29, 2006, at The Red Room Theater, New York City, with the following cast and credits:

Ann .... Carly Cioffi
Gene .... Geoffrey Decas
Jen .... Boo Killebrew
Frank .... Jordan Seavey
Beth .... Jesica Avellone
Richard .... Phillip Taratula
Biz .... Ryan Purcell
Marty .... TJ Witham
Liz .... Hana Roth Seavey

Directed by: Mike Doyle
Set by: Ann Bartek
Costumes by: Meredith Neal
Lighting by: Ryan Trupp
Sound by: Brandon Wolcott
Dramaturg: Jill Rafson
Stage Manager: Andrea Berkey
Assistant Director/Vocal Coach: Terri Gabriel
Assistant Director: Matthew Hopkins

www.collaborationtown.org

CHARACTERS

ANN: twenties
GENE: twenties
FRANK: twenties
JEN: twenties
MARTY: a childlike teen (may be played by a boy or a girl)
BIZ: a hip-hop celebrity
RICHARD: late twenties/early thirties
BETH: late twenties/early thirties
LIZ: an elderly woman

TIME

The present.

PLACE

New York City.

PRELUDE

The play begins with an upbeat dance, which involves the characters "vogue-ing" etc. The dance sort of introduces everyone (cheesy sitcom, models on a catwalk are things to play with) and ends with the sound of glass breaking.

BIZ: Look at my big ol' smile, bitch.

ANN: Do you think I could be famous?

JEN: Do you think if I lost fifteen pounds, I would look good in a magazine?

GENE: Do you think if I was more reclusive that people would start to wonder about me?

FRANK: Do you think if I got a boy-friend—

GENE: Would I be a mystery?

MARTY: This year is for me.

FRANK: And we walked down the street with our hands held and sunglasses on, and one was leading the other, do you think we would look famous?

ANN: Do you think that if I really looked I could find opportunities—

GENE: Would anyone miss me?

BIZ: You see me.

ANN: If I looked I could really find open doors?

JEN: If I grew my hair out long?

ANN: The right moment at the right time?

GENE: Look at my window and wonder what I am doing.

FRANK: Look that way, I'll look this way.

JEN: I could look like that.

FRANK: No, don't look at me, look that way.

GENE: Look up and wonder if I'm up there all alone.

MARTY: Everyone for me.

ANN: I wonder if I did something drastic…something big…would they look?

BIZ: Look at me. You better believe I'm smilin'.

1.

RICHARD: I keep looking at you and you keep looking out.

BETH: Something wrong with looking out?

RICHARD: You don't always have to.

BETH: Mmm.

RICHARD: You don't always have to.

BETH: I know that. Would you rather me be looking at you all the time?

RICHARD: Not all the time.

BETH: But more than I do, right?

RICHARD: You just are always looking out.

BETH: Fine, I'll look at you more. (Stares at him for while.)

RICHARD: Stop it.

BETH: Well, then I'm just going to have to look out.

RICHARD: You know what I mean.

BETH: I just don't know which way to look.

RICHARD: Then I guess we have a problem.

BETH: Because I don't know which way to look?

RICHARD: Because you are even considering that you have to make a choice! I have no choice. It is not possible for me

to decide when you come into my head, because you are always there. I can't help but to always look at you.

BETH: Don't you think that part of the reason why you always look at me is because I am always looking out?

RICHARD: What?

BETH: How would you feel if I was always looking at you?

RICHARD: What?

BETH: It would scare the shit out of you. You would run if I needed you.

RICHARD: You've got some serious issues.

BETH: I know, and they don't have to be yours. I'm not looking at you, making them yours. I'm looking out. I'm giving little bits of my issues out to a million different things—I am spreading them out all over this city, and each piece is so tiny that no one will even have to notice. I am not staring you down, staring at you with my issues.

RICHARD: I don't think that's why you look out.

BETH: Then why?

RICHARD: I think there is another reason.

BETH: There is.

RICHARD: I know.

BETH: What if I spend all of my time looking at you? I look at you and I look at you and I look at you and I stop looking out. I look at you waking. I look at you reading. I look at you laughing. I stop looking out. I look at you folding up your paper. I look at you slipping your shoes on your feet. I look at you standing up. I stop looking out. I look at you leaving. I look at you not coming back. I look at you looking somewhere new. I don't move. I forgot how to look out.

(Pause.)

RICHARD: I don't believe that that's the reason.

BETH: Excuse me?

RICHARD: I think you know that the real reason that you always look out is too scary to admit.

BETH: Please inform me of this reason. I am dying to know how I feel.

RICHARD: You are looking out because you are always looking for something better. You don't have time or energy to really look at me, because you're too busy wondering how it's gonna happen, when is it gonna happen for me—

BETH: When is what going to happen?

RICHARD: Fame.

BETH: Fame?

RICHARD: The only thing you really have ever truly wanted.

BETH: You think that little of me?

RICHARD: I think very highly of you, actually—it's not an insult. Some people want money, some people want love…you want what you want.

BETH: You think that being famous is the only thing that I want?

RICHARD: I mean there are other little things here and there, but essentially, yes.

BETH: Fame.

RICHARD: Fame.

BETH: Wow.

RICHARD: I want you, you want all of them.

BETH: I love you.

RICHARD: I know.

BETH: I love you.

RICHARD: I know you do, but I think we love each other differently.

BETH: You think that?

RICHARD: Yes, I do. I do.

2.

FRANK runs on and catches up with GENE.

FRANK: Hey.

GENE: Oh, hey.

FRANK: Gene, I was just waving at you from across the street.

GENE: Yeah?

FRANK: Did you not see me?

GENE: I must have been looking the other way.

FRANK: Oh…I mean, I was right in front of you.

GENE: Sorry, Frank.

FRANK: No, it's okay. *(Pause.)* Where you been hiding?

GENE: What?

FRANK: We haven't seen you in weeks.

GENE: I've just been laying low…you know.

FRANK: What you got going on?

GENE: What do you mean?

FRANK: You got something going on?

GENE: I don't know what you mean.

FRANK: Well, no one's seen you or talked to you in weeks, so we were all talking about where you might be and what's going on and someone said that you—

GENE: You were all talking about me?

FRANK: Yeah, we've been wondering about you.

GENE: Really?

FRANK: Yeah. So, what's going on? You seeing somebody or something?

GENE: No, I mean, no. You know.

FRANK: No, I don't.

GENE: Yeah. Look, I gotta go.

FRANK: Where?

GENE: I gotta go do this thing I have to do.

FRANK: What thing?

GENE: Just this thing…I'll try and tell you about it sometime.

(GENE leaves. ANN walks in and stands next to FRANK.)

ANN: Hey, Frank!

FRANK: Ann, where you off to?

ANN: I have this thing—but I saw you from across the street and thought I'd say "hey" real quick!

FRANK: I gotta go, too, but I just saw Gene.

ANN: Where has he been?

FRANK: I don't know, he didn't say.

ANN: What?

FRANK: He was dodging all my questions and then he said he had to go.

ANN: Where?

FRANK: He didn't say.

ANN: What?

FRANK: He didn't say, he just said he had to go and wouldn't tell me why or where.

ANN: What do you think he's doing?

FRANK: I don't know.

ANN: What does he have going on?

FRANK: I don't know.

ANN: He's always been a bit of a mystery.

FRANK: You think?

ANN: Oh, yeah.

FRANK: Yeah, I guess he is.

ANN: Shit, I gotta go!

FRANK: *(Looks at his watch.)* Me too—I'll call you!

ANN: Definitely call me!

(They run out in opposite directions.)

3.

LIZ runs onstage. She has a stack of pictures in her hands.

LIZ: I'm worried. I'm worried that I am going to fall flat on my face. If I hid pictures around your house, in drawers and under bricks and in the ceiling, do you think that your grandchildren would find them while they were exploring? Would they find the pictures I have hidden and would they wonder about me? About me and you? Would they wonder if I was a lady that you could not keep? That I was an impossible woman and a woman that was worth taking pictures of? I'm worried.

4.

RICHARD: What are you doing?

BETH: Oh, you know, hiding from the paparazzi.

RICHARD: Don't do this.

BETH: Do what?

RICHARD: Stop it.

BETH: Stop what?

RICHARD: This.

BETH: Hiding from the paparazzi? Okay, if you're fine with being on the front page of every tabloid then I guess it is okay with me too. I'll open the blinds.

RICHARD: Stop it.

BETH: Do you wanna change? Ooh, or are you wanting to look sort of sloppy for the tabloids? Should I change into some big sweatpants and a wife beater? We can be sloppy!

RICHARD: You don't even have any sweatpants.

BETH: I'll wear yours, that'll be cute.

RICHARD: I don't even know where mine are.

BETH: Then I'll wear some basketball shorts or something.

RICHARD: This is ridiculous, why are you doing this?

BETH: I am being the person you think I am. Oh my God, do you think that the tabloids are gonna get word that

we are fighting? That would be really bad…ooh, or it could be really good for us! It would certainly make me more famous and it would get your face out there a little more. Let's keep fighting!

RICHARD: Why don't we just break up?

(Pause.)

BETH: What?

RICHARD: Why don't we just break up?

(Pause.)

BETH: Do you think that would make us more famous?

RICHARD: I think it's definitely worth looking into.

5.

Lights dark. Cool music. The spotlight hits BIZ. He is sitting and still.

BIZ: Why is Biz smilin'? Clothing line. Hotels in three countries. Cologne. Records. Film. A reality TV show. A magazine. Four production companies. A label. Shoes. Lingerie. Two clubs—one in New York, one in Miami. Construction equipment rentals. Cosmetics. Two girls. Sports gear. Cigars and champagne. That's why I'm smiling.

6.

JEN runs up to ANN.

JEN: Ann, hey!

ANN: Hey.

JEN: I spotted you way ahead of me and have been running after you for, like, five blocks.

ANN: Really?

JEN: Yeah, I was screaming your name.

ANN: Oh, well you know, it's so loud around here. So.

JEN: Yeah.

ANN: Yeah.

JEN: 'S up?

ANN: Not much. 'S up with you?

JEN: Not a whole lot.

ANN: What are you doing?

JEN: Nothing. What are you doing?

ANN: Not a whole lot.

JEN: Cool.

ANN: Yeah.

JEN: Hey, I heard Frank saw Gene the other night.

ANN: Yeah.

JEN: 'S up with him?

ANN: I don't know. Frank said he was being really strange. He had to go somewhere and he wouldn't tell Frank where he was going.

JEN: Oh my God, where was he going?

ANN: He wouldn't tell Frank where he was going.

JEN: Weird.

ANN: Yeah.

JEN: Gene has always been sort of a mystery, though.

ANN: That's what I said. You know you've lost some serious weight.

JEN: No!

ANN: Yes! Really, you look so skinny!

JEN: Oh my God, thank you!

ANN: What have you been doing?

JEN: Nothing, really. You really think I lost weight?

ANN: Oh yeah, you look great.

JEN: Thank you.

ANN: Have you been dieting?

JEN: Well, just no carbs.

ANN: Yeah, I did that for a while.

JEN: Really?

ANN: Yeah, but you know it didn't really do anything.

JEN: Were you vomiting at all?

ANN: No, I wasn't. Are you vomiting?

JEN: No.

ANN: Have you been exercising a lot?

JEN: Yeah, I've been doing some spin classes and I've just been really busy with a lot of stuff.

ANN: Yeah. Well, you look great.

JEN: Thank you.

ANN: Yeah.

JEN: Well, I gotta go.

ANN: *(Looks at her watch.)* Oh, shit, I gotta go, too!

JEN: We should get together soon.

ANN: We should have brunch or something, call me.

JEN: I'll definitely call you.

7.

LIZ runs on with her pictures. She checks her watch.

LIZ: How can I make you remember me? A tin box! I could hide an old tin box in the hole of a tree and I could put pictures and little toys and letters and poems in the box and a young explorer would find it and wonder who I was. Someone would say that you knew me. That if they wanted to know about me, they could ask you. You would be old. You would be old and they would ring your doorbell and you would open the door. You invite the explorer in. You sit him down. He hands you the box. You put on your old man glasses. You are old. You open the box and you are excited again. You open the box and you see a picture of me. I am smiling with my lips shut. My eyes are bright. I am laughing at something in my head. You are back with me. I was a great mystery. You remember how you couldn't keep me and you smile. The explorer sees that you remember and he begins to ask you questions about me. You answer. You say you can't remember why it didn't work out, but that I was a beautiful creature who needed to float. That's all you can remember. And you loved that about me. It broke your heart, but you loved that about me.

8.

BETH and RICHARD are standing face to face. He has a suitcase in his hand.

BETH: Where are you going to go?

RICHARD: I don't know. I was thinking about going down south.

BETH: What's there?

RICHARD: Space and roads and soft people.

BETH: You don't think there are any soft people here?

RICHARD: Maybe I don't have the space and the roads to really see if there are.

BETH: Space and roads are gonna make you see something in people?

RICHARD: Maybe.

BETH: Well, you tell that space and those roads that I said good fucking luck.

RICHARD: I will. It will be nice to be in a place where they don't know you.

BETH: What?

RICHARD: A place that you haven't given pieces of yourself to.

BETH: Yeah, I don't know if they've heard of me down there just yet.

RICHARD: Yeah.

BETH: Just wait.

(They sort of laugh. There is a pause. They are sad.)

RICHARD: You've given all of your pieces out and there is nothing left for me.

(Pause.)

RICHARD: I'll call.

BETH: I have to give you my new number.

RICHARD: You have a new number?

BETH: I had to get a new number. I'll give it to you.

RICHARD: Okay.

(She writes down her number on a piece of paper and hands it to him. They look at one another for a while.)

BETH: Richard?

RICHARD: Yes?

BETH: Please don't give it out to anyone.

RICHARD: Okay.

BETH: Okay.

RICHARD: Goodbye.

BETH: Please text me.

(He leaves. She gets up and goes to the window and opens up the blinds.)

BETH: *(Yelling out the window to the pretend paparazzi.)* Leave me alone!

9.

MARTY comes running onstage.

MARTY: I'm worried. My birthday is on November fifth. I am having an Outer Space Birthday Party. It will be in my backyard, but my backyard is going to turn into outer space. Pretend outer space. I am going to have a space walk and moon pies and my aunt is going to dress up as a martian. I hope everybody comes to my Outer Space Birthday Party. I hope I can get everybody in my school at my Outer Space Birthday Party. Marcy Shelton is having her birthday party on that same day and she told me that she is going to have a water slide party and I think that sounds really fun and I think everyone is going to go to her party. This year, I want people at my Outer Space Birthday Party. *(Thinks for a while.)* Biz! I'll get Biz to my Outer Space Birthday Party. Biz is my friend! Biz is my friend and he will come to my Outer Space Birthday Party. He will come to my Outer Space Birthday Party and then everyone will come to my outer space backyard and Marcy Shelton will be all alone on her water slide. All alone on her water slide!!! Everyone for me!!! I'll ask Biz to come to my Outer Space Birthday Party.

10.

ANN: Frank!

FRANK: Hey!

ANN: Whatcha doin?

FRANK: Nothing.

ANN: Yeah, I'm on my way to this thing.

FRANK: Cool.

ANN: Yeah. I saw Jen the other day.

FRANK: Yeah?

ANN: Yeah.

FRANK: How's she?

ANN: She's great. She's lost so much weight—she looks great.

FRANK: Really? Is she so skinny?

ANN: She is so skinny.

FRANK: Really?

ANN: Yeah.

FRANK: Well, good for her.

ANN: Yeah.

FRANK: What is she doing?

ANN: No carbs.

FRANK: That's all.

ANN: Well, she said she's doing a little exercise, but I think she's puking.

FRANK: Really?

ANN: Yeah.

FRANK: Is she okay?

ANN: I hope so.

FRANK: Well, you know Jen, she always has been a really passionate person.

ANN: You think?

FRANK: Oh yeah.

ANN: I never thought of her that way.

FRANK: Yeah, she may seem calm and laid back, but she really does have some sort of fire going on inside of her.

ANN: Hmmm.

FRANK: Yeah. I gotta go.

ANN: Where you going?

FRANK: I'm gonna see if Gene's home. His light has been on in his window, but when I buzz, there's no answer.

ANN: What is he up to?

FRANK: I have no idea, but I really want to know.

ANN: Well, we'll both try and figure it out and report back to each other.

FRANK: Yeah, I mean what the Hell is he doing?

ANN: I have no idea.

FRANK: Alright, I'm gonna go and try to make some progress.

ANN: Good fucking luck.

FRANK: Thanks, I'll call you.

ANN: Yeah, I might not be able to answer, but just leave a message.

FRANK: Okay.

ANN: Bye.

11.

BETH is sitting in a chair pretending to give an interview to Barbara Walters.

BETH: Well, you know it's difficult, absolutely. He is now in the land of roads and space and I suppose his world is good for him and my world is good for me. It's very hard to be in this business and have a relationship. I mean, you know this—we all know this. Some people make it. A lot of people do not. *(Pauses to listen.)* You know, Barbara, sometimes I do wonder if it is worth it. I do miss him. I guess I am a woman who needs to float. I do miss him, though. I miss getting a beer with him in the early evening. *(Begins to lose focus and sort of begins a rant.)* I miss his tired eyes. I miss his pretty hands, he had such pretty hands. I miss feeling like I could actually have a beautiful, deep relationship. *(Snaps out of it.)* Whoa…looks like the romantic in me got carried away there for a second! No, I was sick of apologizing for my choices and for my success every single day. *(Listens.)* Barbara, there are days when I think you are right. Days when I think that I will find someone who will be comfortable with my life…other days I think maybe it's just fine that I am going to be by myself. I've got it pretty good. Men may come and go, but I will always be standing right by my side. And I think that me is not such a bad thing. *(Listens.)* Yes, it was his decision, but I guess I sort of silently made it as well. *(Listens.)* I do wonder if I could have gone back and taken a different route, would I be happier? *(Loses focus again.)* Would I be able to think of the day I die without panicking that I might be the only one with me? Would I be able to slow down? And then I think, "No. I wouldn't change a thing. Honestly, I really love my life and I wouldn't change a thing." *(She is quiet.)* I do miss him, though. *(She is quiet. She stops the interview.)* This is stupid. I am so stupid.

12.

GENE: Jen!

JEN: Hey stranger!

GENE: I was on my way to this thing, and spotted you and thought I'd say "hi" real quick!

JEN: Yeah, I'm running to this thing, too.

GENE: Wow, you look different.

JEN: You just haven't seen me in a while.

GENE: No, you look different. You look great, have you lost weight?

JEN: You know everyone has been asking me that.

GENE: Yeah, Frank and Ann came over the other day for a surprise visit and they said that you were looking really great these days.

JEN: They said that?

GENE: Yeah.

JEN: What brought it up... I mean, were you guys talking about me?

GENE: No, not really, they just mentioned that you had lost a lot of weight.

JEN: Really?

GENE: Yeah, you really look so skinny, you look great.

JEN: Thanks, maybe I've lost a little.

GENE: What have you been doing?

JEN: Just exercising more and cutting out carbs.

GENE: I meant, like, what have you been up to?

JEN: Oh. Sorry. Well, nothing really. Just exercising and cutting out carbs.

(They laugh a bit.)

JEN: What about you? I hear you're keeping a little secret these days.

GENE: What?

JEN: Oh, you know, that you're up to something and no one really knows what it is. What's going on?

GENE: Who said that?

JEN: Oh, we've just been talking.

GENE: You guys are talking about me?

JEN: Well, not like talking bad about you, someone just mentioned how we hadn't seen you in a while and that you've sort of been acting mysterious these days.

GENE: Really?

JEN: Yeah. So, what's going on? You seeing somebody or doing some big project or something?

GENE: Well, I've got a few things going on here and there.

JEN: Like what?

GENE: Just little things, I'll tell you about them when they're further along in development.

JEN: What are you doing?

GENE: I can't really talk about it right now.

JEN: Why not?

GENE: I just can't.

JEN: Oh, come on, it's just me.

GENE: I can't.

JEN: Please, I won't tell anybody else, I promise.

GENE: Jen, I'm sorry, I can't.

JEN: I'm dying to know.

GENE: I wanna tell you, but I really can't.

JEN: Are you dating someone?

GENE: I really can't say.

JEN: Are you working on something?

GENE: I can't, Jen.

JEN: Oh my God, are you in danger?

GENE: No. I don't think so.

JEN: You don't think so?!

GENE: No! No Jen, I'm not in danger.

JEN: Gene, you're being weird.

GENE: Nothing too extreme Jen, I promise.

JEN: Well, okay. I'll take your word for it.

GENE: What about you?

JEN: What about me?

GENE: Are you being healthy?

(Pause.)

JEN: Yeah.

GENE: You sure?

JEN: Yeah. I mean, yeah.

GENE: Okay. You know if you ever need to talk…

JEN: Yeah, yeah…you too.

GENE: Okay.

JEN: Okay.

GENE: So, really, what have you been up to?

JEN: Nothing, really. Just exercising and cutting out carbs. What about you?

GENE: Nothing really. Just, you know…

JEN: The stuff you can't talk about.

(Pause.)

GENE: We should go get a drink sometime.

JEN: Text me, we'll set a date.

GENE: You have the same number?

JEN: Yeah, text me. Bye!

GENE: Bye!

13.

LIZ runs in with a stack of books. She is a little more panicked than she was in her last speech.

LIZ: It's going to get quiet. It's going to get quiet and I'm worried. I could write notes to you on the inside of book covers. I would choose the classics, the ones that you would never throw out, the ones that you would pass on to your children and then your children would pass them on to their children and their children would pass it on to their children and say, "Look, this book was your great-great-grandfather's. My father gave it to me, and when you have a child, you will pass it on them." Your great-great-grandchild will take the book very carefully and he will smell it and try to know you. He will open the cover. His heart will start racing when he begins to read the note I have left for you. He will try to know this story. He will read the note two times over and then he will ask his father,

"Who is this note from?" And his father will answer, "No one really knows. We think it is a lady whom your great-great-grandfather loved deeply. Would you like to see a picture of her? There is one hidden beneath the floorboard."

14.

BIZ is sitting in his chair. MARTY is walking around him, nervous. BIZ is smoking a cigar.

BIZ: See, it's not my business to know how you gonna make it happen. It's my business just to know that you are gonna make it happen.

MARTY: What do I do?

BIZ: You do what you need to do, but you make it happen. Look at me, Marty. Look at my smile. I did what I had to do, and I made things happen.

MARTY: I know, Biz. You really made things happen. I wanna make things happen, too.

BIZ: You wanna be smilin', don't you Marty?

MARTY: I do, Biz. Please, please come to my Outer Space Birthday Party. Please, please—

BIZ: Do not beg, Marty. Don't beg nobody for nothin'. You understand?

(MARTY shakes his head yes.)

BIZ: I gotta lot of people wanting a lot of things from me. You know who I have time to respond to?

MARTY: Who?

BIZ: The people who got their shit in check. You get your shit straight, Marty. You get your shit straight and I will come to your Outer Space Birthday Party.

MARTY: Biz, thank you so—

BIZ: Let me finish, bitch. I will show up to your muthafuckin' Outer Space Birthday Party for approximately twenty minutes. I will take pictures with your guests. I will bring my security team. I will pull up in a big car. I will give your party some serious hype. I will come to your Outer Space Birthday Party, Marty. I will do this at a special rate because we grew up together.

MARTY: We're friends, Biz.

BIZ: You're my boy, Marty. And for you, my boy, I will only charge you five hundred dollars.

MARTY: Five hundred dollars?

BIZ: It is ludicrous that I am making an appearance for this low of a rate. But you are my friend. You are my boy. And I feel sorry for you because you are kind of retarded.

MARTY: Thank you, Biz.

BIZ: Get your shit straight, Marty. Get your shit in check and I will be there.

MARTY: Okay.

BIZ: Okay.

(They sit for a bit.)

BIZ: Now get the fuck out of my house.

(MARTY runs out.)

15.

RICHARD walks into his house. BETH is in there, pacing. He is surprised to see her.

RICHARD: How did you get into my house?

BETH: I broke your window.

RICHARD: You broke the window?

BETH: I am a passionate person.

RICHARD: What are you doing here?

BETH: I wanted to see you.

RICHARD: So you just show up and break my window?

BETH: I am an impulsive and passionate woman. Don't worry, the paparazzi don't know I'm here.

RICHARD: Okay.

(She goes to kiss him and he pushes her away. It is awkward.)

BETH: It's really good to see you.

RICHARD: Yeah?

BETH: You know I really missed you.

RICHARD: Yeah?

BETH: Of course. It's nice to see your face.

RICHARD: Thank you.

BETH: How are you?

RICHARD: Peaceful and quiet and easy and good.

BETH: Good, are you—

RICHARD: Not a lot of buzz, buzz, buzzing going on around here, it's not loud here. I can slow down and sit still.

BETH: Yeah, I've been trying to go a little slower myself these days. I'm walking slower, leaving my cell phone at home, sitting in the park, petting dogs, calling my mom. I really have slowed down and it feels really good.

RICHARD: Yeah?

BETH: Yeah.

RICHARD: Really?

BETH: You don't believe me?

RICHARD: No, I believe you. I'm glad you're doing whatever you need to do to make yourself happy.

BETH: Thanks.

(Pause.)

RICHARD: How's the career?

BETH: Fine, I'm not really worried with it these days, like I said, I'm just trying to take it one day at a time.

RICHARD: Right.

BETH: I did get a new agent.

RICHARD: Yeah?

BETH: He really believes that I am a character actress, which is what I've known for years, so it's good that we are on the same page.

RICHARD: Great.

BETH: Oh, I did an eight-episode arc on that show "Divine Justice."

RICHARD: Great show.

BETH: Yeah, I was the head of an Internet pedophile sex slave ring while that actor—the one who is sort of cross-eyed—talked about evidence and all that.

RICHARD: Great.

(Pause.)

BETH: I'm thinking about taking a break.

RICHARD: Really?

BETH: Yeah—just taking off and going somewhere quiet and resting and swimming and driving and all that.

RICHARD: You think you'd like that?

BETH: You know I would like that.

RICHARD: Where would you go?

BETH: Oh, I don't know. *(Gives him a little smile.)* Somewhere with space and roads and soft people.

RICHARD: Where would that be?

BETH: Why are you being such an asshole?

RICHARD: What?

BETH: You know exactly how you're behaving and don't act like you don't.

RICHARD: I don't know what—

BETH: I came all the way down here! I flew down here to see you. To tell you I'm sorry! That I will stop living my life the way I was living it if that will make you happy. I want to be with you. You know that's why I'm here. You know that's why I'm here and you're just standing there with your one-word sentences—making me swim around in my own stupid words. You're just standing there thinking of how stupid I am.

RICHARD: I am not—

BETH: I'll do anything you want. Happily, I will give myself to you. I want to be slow and I want to be soft and I want to be with you.

RICHARD: I don't want you to change who you are, that's not what I want. I love who you are.

BETH: But you can't be with who I are!

RICHARD: I can't, but I would never want you to change for me.

BETH: What do you want? Please tell me what you want!

RICHARD: I want you to be happy.

BETH: I'm happy with you.

RICHARD: You would be for a while. Then you would start looking out again.

BETH: No, I won't. I won't look out anymore.

RICHARD: Yes, you will.

BETH: You love me, but you don't want to be with me?

RICHARD: I love you so much. I do love you.

BETH: But you don't want to be with me?

(He is quiet.)

BETH: You don't ever want to be with me?

(He doesn't answer. She cries. They are standing at opposite ends of the room.)

RICHARD: Look at all that passion.

(She looks at him.)

RICHARD: You're really good.

(She runs out.)

16.

ANN: Hey stranger!

FRANK: Hey Ann!

ANN: Where are you headed?

FRANK: *(Gives a little smile.)* Oh, nowhere, really.

ANN: What's going on?

FRANK: *(Very happy and sneaky.)* Nooooothing.

ANN: Come on, what is it?

(FRANK shrugs.)

ANN: What the Hell is going on?

FRANK: I met someone.

ANN: You did not!

FRANK: I did too, it's so wild!

ANN: Who is it?

FRANK: A boy.

ANN: Who?

FRANK: This amazing boy.

ANN: I'm not gay, but I can relate. Keep going!

FRANK: Have you ever seen that show "Divine Justice"?

ANN: Yeah, the one with that angel who holds court or something?

FRANK: Yeah, it actually is a really good show.

ANN: Yeah, I've just never seen it, but I know what you're talking about.

FRANK: Oh, you should watch it sometime.

ANN: Well, I'm never home when it's on.

FRANK: Well, I'll TiVo it for you.

ANN: Oh, I'd love that.

FRANK: Sure.

ANN: So?

FRANK: So, the boy is one of the production assistants for that show!

ANN: No way!

FRANK: Yes, he's so talented.

ANN: Yeah, sounds like it.

FRANK: He's just amazing.

ANN: What's his name?

FRANK: Mickey.

ANN: Cute name.

FRANK: He's so hot and amazing.

ANN: How did you meet?

FRANK: It's sort of some drama.

ANN: Oooh, what?

FRANK: He was dating my friend Jacques.

ANN: Jacques, the dancer?

FRANK: Exactly. A big group of us went to go see Jacques in *Romeo and Juliet* last month and Mickey and I looked at each other and it was just—boom! You know?

ANN: Yeah.

FRANK: We keep glancing at each other, trying not to let the other one notice that we are staring and then there was a moment where we just locked eyes and just stared at each other for like twenty-seven seconds.

ANN: Oh my God.

FRANK: I know.

ANN: Then what?

FRANK: Then we all saw Jacques after the show and I realized that they were a thing, and my heart sank, I almost started to cry.

ANN: Awww.

FRANK: Then we were all sort of standing on the corner, talking and all, and I said I had to get going and Mickey said he had to go to, because he had to get up early for "Divine Justice." We realized that we had to take the same train and so we left the group.

ANN: Oh my God.

FRANK: We just talked and talked and talked on the way home and it just felt so right.

ANN: Right.

FRANK: Then we were walking and we were at my doorstep and he said, "I can't stop talking to you."

ANN: No way.

FRANK: I said, "Can you stop long enough to kiss me?"

ANN: You did not!

FRANK: I did! And then he said, "I can try."

ANN: Oh my God.

FRANK: And we kissed and kissed and it was so beautiful and then we went upstairs and just got down and dirty.

ANN: Oh.

FRANK: Yeah, just dirty.

ANN: Wow.

FRANK: Yeah, like really kinky.

ANN: Oh.

FRANK: And since then we have been inseparable.

ANN: Awww.

FRANK: It's created this big drama among the little group because of Jacques and all, but you know, the heart wants what it wants.

ANN: Yeah.

FRANK: I really just wish that everyone would stop paying so much attention to us. I mean, get a life!

ANN: Yeah.

FRANK: I feel like we can't go anywhere without someone whispering about the drama.

ANN: Really?

FRANK: Yeah, like we're the topic of all the new gossip.

ANN: That must be tough.

FRANK: It really is. I'm just ready for someone else to cause some drama so everyone will quit talking about Mickey and I.

ANN: Yeah.

FRANK: Hey, I can't worry about it. People are gonna say what they wanna say and think what they wanna think.

ANN: Exactly.

FRANK: Well, I gotta go. I'm gonna go watch them shoot a scene for "Divine Justice."

ANN: Ooh, can I come?

FRANK: Oh, I'm sorry, it's a closed set. I'll try to get you in one day though, I promise.

ANN: Look at you with all the connections!

FRANK: Just one of the many perks of having a boyfriend that's in the business!

ANN: I bet.

FRANK: I'll text you. Same number?

ANN: Yeah!

FRANK: Bye.

ANN: Bye.

17.

MARTY: I don't have much time. I have one hundred and seven dollars from my allowance that I have been saving. I am going to sell my pink Huffy bike and my baby bracelet. I will ask my mom if we can sell our couch. That should give me most of the money. I will ask my mom for the rest. I will ask my mom and I will ask every single person I know. I will get five hundred dollars and Biz will come to my Outer Space Birthday Party and everyone will say, "You know what birthday party was the best birthday party in the world, ever? Marty's Outer Space Birthday Party. Biz was there. Can you believe that? Biz was there, because he and Marty are friends." That is what they will say. I will sell our couch for two hundred dollars.

18.

BETH is doing a press conference. She is not pretending.

BETH: Tim saw me doing that play and decided to call me in. I was told that this movie was a vehicle for Biz and that they needed a really strong character actress to play his mother in the flashback scenes. The audition went really well, I told them I didn't mind gaining the weight for the part, and the rest is history. *(Listens to the reporters.)* I gained one hundred and seven pounds. *(Listens.)* Lots of donuts! *(Laughs. Listens.)* Well, thank you very much. Yeah, it just came right off, I have a very high metabolism. *(Listens.)* Yes, it was very tough from time to time. It was a pretty intense role, and

I tend to really dive into characters and sometimes it can be really difficult to go there. I wouldn't have it any other way, though. You know, in order for me to really explore a character, I have to explore some areas of myself that have been neglected or are unknown and that can be scary. *(Listens.)* Oh, you had to squeeze that one in didn't you? I know everyone is talking about us, so it's okay. Yes, we are officially over. *(Listens.)* I did take my experience in my relationships into account when exploring this role. That was very hard, yes. *(Listens.)* I do not keep in touch with him, no. He doesn't talk to me anymore. I tried, but after a while, you have to hold onto your dignity. I don't ever want to beg anyone, and it got to that point. I was begging. And then you think, begging for what? *(Loses focus.)* Begging to be silently judged by this person every minute of every day? Begging to feel guilty about caring about yourself and your career? Begging to feel like you are secretly hated by him? To feel a lump in your throat every time you sit down to eat? To wake up at five a.m., sweaty and sticky and panicked that this could be the day that he leaves you? To know that that person will leave you one day? To know that this person will leave you? They will leave you and they will not remember you. *(Snaps out of it.)* I'm sorry, I just get passionate—sorry. So, I stopped trying. This is life, you have to move on and be thankful for what you have. My career is just getting started and I have a very full life. I do wish him well, though. I will always wish him nothing but happiness. *(Listens.)* Thank you. That's very nice of you. Thank you very much.

(A lot of flashbulbs go off. Then they get slower and slower. They stop.)

19.

GENE: Hey stranger!

FRANK: Hey. I don't have much time, I'm running a little—

GENE: Yeah, I have to go too—I just saw you and thought I'd say "hi."

FRANK: Hey.

GENE: Where you been?

FRANK: Oh, you know.

GENE: What's going on?

FRANK: Oh, nothing.

GENE: Don't give me that.

FRANK: Give you what?

GENE: Ann told me you were seeing someone.

FRANK: Since when do you care?

GENE: What?

FRANK: I figured you didn't really care what was going on with me, you know being so involved in your top-secret whatever.

GENE: Of course I care. It's not top secret it's just some stuff that I need to take care of.

FRANK: Like dead bodies?

GENE: I'll tell you everything soon, I promise. What's going on?

FRANK: Nothing, I'm just seeing this guy.

GENE: It doesn't sound like nothing, Ann told me it's quite the scandal.

FRANK: What, it's like front page news or something?

GENE: It would seem so.

FRANK: It's really nothing, just a little drama, but I think it's calming down.

GENE: Tell me!

FRANK: Gene, if I talk about it that will just fuel the fire. I don't want to talk about it anymore, I just want everything to calm down.

GENE: I heard he stars on "Divine Justice."

FRANK: He doesn't star in it, he is heavily involved, though.

GENE: Wow.

FRANK: We're actually going to the season's wrap party this evening.

GENE: So you guys are public?

FRANK: Well, I guess this is our first official public outing, but everyone already knows we're a thing.

GENE: Do you think that a public outing will cause even more drama?

FRANK: Probably, but I can't live my life worried that people are always talking about what I do. I just can't.

GENE: I thought you wanted people to stop talking about the whole thing.

FRANK: I do.

GENE: Then why are you giving them something to talk about?

FRANK: What do you mean?

GENE: By going to a very public event together, you are giving them something to talk about.

FRANK: I don't see it that way. I think that by going to this public event, we are telling everyone that there are no secrets, and they can stop gossiping.

GENE: Maybe.

FRANK: Oh my God, do you think people are gonna talk about it?

GENE: You guys might want to arrive separately and be discreet during the party.

FRANK: Really?

GENE: Do whatever you want to do, whatever you think will attract the least amount of attention.

FRANK: I am so tired of having to think about this stuff. Can't we just be together without worrying about what people are going to think?

GENE: Not when you're in a high-profile relationship. He's involved in TV, it can never be easy. Trust me.

FRANK: What?

GENE: Take my word for it.

FRANK: What are you talking about?

GENE: Being involved with someone in the business is difficult, trust me.

FRANK: Gene, what the Hell is going on with you?

GENE: I can't talk about it, Frank. If there's anyone who can respect that, it's you. I think you know where I'm coming from.

FRANK: Okay, okay. You got it. I understand.

GENE: I gotta go.

FRANK: Where are you going?

GENE: Frank.

FRANK: I'm sorry.

GENE: I'll see you.

FRANK: Okay.

(GENE goes to leave.)

FRANK: Hey Gene!

GENE: Yeah?

FRANK: Are you gonna go to Marty's Outer Space Birthday Party?

GENE: Marty's Outer Space Birthday Party?

FRANK: Yeah.

GENE: No, I stopped caring about Marty when my mom stopped caring about me and how it would be a good thing for her son to befriend the retarded kid down the street.

FRANK: Oh.

GENE: Are you going?

FRANK: Well, I feel guilty, like I should go.

GENE: You should go, take your boyfriend. All the 'tards will be really impressed with your boyfriend who's in television.

FRANK: You think?

GENE: Oh yeah. I gotta go.

FRANK: Text me!

20.

BIZ: Marty, what the fuck is this?

MARTY: My bike.

BIZ: I have no use for a hot pink Huffy bicycle with a motherfuckin' daisy-decorated basket on the handle bars.

MARTY: I have a couch.

BIZ: I do not want your mom's couch. I do not want your Huffy bicycle and I do not want your mother's couch. I want five hundred dollars.

MARTY: I only have two hundred and thirteen dollars.

BIZ: I do not care that you have only two hundred and thirteen dollars. Two hundred and thirteen dollars, a Huffy bicycle, and your mother's couch will not cut it. What did I tell you, Marty?

MARTY: About my shit?

BIZ: Yes, about your shit.

MARTY: That I needed to get it together.

BIZ: That's right, Marty. I only deal with people who have their shit together. I think you know that you ain't even close to havin' your shit, much less havin' your shit together. I want five hundred dollars, Marty. I ain't askin' for much. Five hundred dollars ain't shit. I'm giving you this offer, because I am your friend. I am your friend and I feel sorry for you. Five hundred dollars, Marty. You give me five hundred dollars and I will come to your muthafuckin' Outer Space Birthday Party.

MARTY: Biz?

BIZ: What?

MARTY: Have you ever seen "Divine Justice"?

BIZ: Fuck yeah, I love that show.

MARTY: All the stars of that show are gonna be at my Outer Space Birthday Party.

BIZ: Shut the fuck up.

MARTY: My best friend Frank's boyfriend stars on that show and he told me that all of them are coming.

BIZ: You don't have any friends, Marty.

MARTY: Uh-huh. Frank's been my best friend since I was little and he is coming and bringing all of the stars from "Divine Justice."

BIZ: Are you fucking with me, Marty?

MARTY: What?

BIZ: You lying to me?

MARTY: No, Biz. I promise.

BIZ: You promise?

MARTY: Uh-huh.

BIZ: Alright, Marty. Alright, you get the cast of "Divine Justice" there and then I'll only ask for four hundred dollars.

MARTY: Really?

BIZ: I'm a nice person, Marty. I am a giver.

MARTY: Biz, you're the best! I'll go to Frank's house and make sure they are all coming!

BIZ: Yeah, you do that. You get that for me in writing and you get me my four hundred dollars.

MARTY: Okay, Biz! *(Begins to leave with the bike.)*

BIZ: Marty, what the fuck are you doing?

MARTY: I'm going to Frank's.

BIZ: You ain't going nowhere with my Huffy bicycle, muthafucka.

MARTY: But—

BIZ: Give me my bike, bitch.

(MARTY gives the bike to BIZ.)

MARTY: Bye, Biz!

BIZ: Bye, Marty!

21.

FRANK: Hey!

JEN: Hey stranger.

FRANK: I saw you from over there and I've been calling your name over and over again.

JEN: Oh, you know me, I'm always listening to some song in my head.

FRANK: Oh.

JEN: The volume's pretty high up there. It's loud.

FRANK: Okay. How are you?

JEN: I'm good, I'm really good.

FRANK: Wow, you look great. You look so skinny! Have you lost more weight?

JEN: Maybe, a little.

FRANK: It is just falling off, huh?

JEN: Well, I've been exercising a lot.

FRANK: Are you still dieting?

JEN: Well, for the past couple of days I've been doing this cranberry-flush thing.

FRANK: What's that?

JEN: It's just sort of giving yourself a detox, flushing things out of your body.

FRANK: How do you do it?

JEN: For six days you put nothing in your body except water, cranberry juice, and almonds.

FRANK: Wow, that's intense.

JEN: You know that actress, Beth Foster?

FRANK: Oh, that character actress who played the trailer trash mom in that movie with the Biz?

JEN: Yeah.

FRANK: Yeah, I know her.

JEN: I heard she did this flush to lose the weight she put on for that role.

FRANK: Wow.

JEN: I bet she gets an Oscar for that role.

FRANK: She's a really passionate actress. And such a sweetie.

JEN: Yeah.

FRANK: Do you feel okay?

JEN: It's really hard, but after the third day, you really feel great…kind of high, you know? I'm on my fifth day and I don't want it to end. I really love it.

FRANK: Good for you.

JEN: Thanks.

FRANK: Your hair looks great too, it's gotten longer.

JEN: I've been using horse shampoo.

FRANK: That works?

JEN: Works for me, I guess.

FRANK: It would seem so, your hair looks really great and long.

JEN: Thanks. So I hear you're in love?

FRANK: Yeah.

JEN: I heard it was quite the scandal.

FRANK: Really? People are still talking about that?

JEN: Oh, yeah. It was a hot topic for some time, but I haven't heard much lately. I think everyone has calmed down a bit.

FRANK: Yeah, I've been trying to keep a low profile.

JEN: That's what I heard.

FRANK: Yeah, it's been sort of tough.

JEN: Well, I can imagine. I bet it's hard keeping a low profile with somebody in the business, especially when the relationship had so much drama surrounding it in the first place.

FRANK: Exactly.

JEN: Well, I would love to meet him…what's his name?

FRANK: Mickey.

JEN: Right, Mickey…I knew it started with an "M." He's on "Divine Justice," right?

FRANK: He's not on it, he's heavily involved with it, though.

JEN: Oh. I really love that show.

FRANK: You watch it?

JEN: I've seen it a couple of times, I really like it. Which one is he?

FRANK: No, he's not on the show.

JEN: Oh.

FRANK: He's heavily involved with it, though.

JEN: Oh.

FRANK: I should take you to the set sometime.

JEN: You could do that?

FRANK: Yeah, no problem.

JEN: That would be great.

FRANK: I'll ask him and see when I can get you in.

JEN: Great!

FRANK: Are you going to Marty's Outer Space Birthday Party?

JEN: Marty the retard?

FRANK: Yeah.

JEN: No. Are you?

FRANK: Yeah, I feel like I should go.

JEN: Oh.

FRANK: I'm gonna take Mickey and probably some other cast members of "Divine Justice" are gonna come with me.

JEN: Really?

FRANK: Yeah, you know, do a good deed.

JEN: Well, I'll go if that's the case.

FRANK: Yeah?

JEN: Yeah, not everyday do I go to a party where I can rub elbows with celebrities!

FRANK: Okay, cool!

JEN: I'll have to get an outfit.

FRANK: Me too. Hey, do you know if Ann leaves today?

JEN: What?

FRANK: You didn't hear about Ann?

JEN: No, I've been really busy, I haven't heard much about anything, except for your affair, of course…it was pretty much impossible to not hear about that.

FRANK: Yeah, tell me about it.

JEN: Where's Ann going?

FRANK: Africa.

JEN: Africa?

FRANK: Yes. You'll never guess why.

JEN: Oh my God, why?

FRANK: She's going to adopt a baby.

JEN: No way.

FRANK: No joke.

JEN: She's going to adopt a baby?

FRANK: She's said she's always wanted to do it.

JEN: I've never heard her say that.

FRANK: I knew she felt very connected to that part of the world, but I had no idea she wanted to adopt an African baby.

JEN: Since when has she felt connected to that part of the world?

FRANK: You never knew that about Ann?

JEN: No.

FRANK: Yeah, she loves Africa.

JEN: Really?

FRANK: Oh yeah.

JEN: Has she ever been to Africa?

FRANK: No, but she's always felt really connected to it.

JEN: Wow.

FRANK: I know.

JEN: That's pretty—

FRANK: —Impulsive. I know.

JEN: Wow.

FRANK: She said that she was at a point in her life where she needed to do something huge. She's never wanted to have children of her own, she's always wanted to adopt, and you know she feels very connected to that part of the world, so she decided to go for it.

JEN: So there is a baby in Africa waiting for her?

FRANK: Yeah, they approved her and she's leaving, I don't know—she might be leaving today, to go pick it up.

JEN: Ann is really adopting an African baby?

FRANK: Yeah.

JEN: Where is she going to keep it?

FRANK: I guess in her apartment.

JEN: Girl or boy?

FRANK: I think they're going to give her a girl.

JEN: What is she going to name it?

FRANK: I don't know, probably something African.

JEN: Oh my God.

FRANK: I know.

JEN: I never knew Ann was so—

FRANK: —Passionate. I know.

JEN: Wow.

FRANK: Yeah.

JEN: I should call her.

FRANK: Yeah, call and see when she's leaving.

JEN: Does she still have the same number?

FRANK: I think so, yeah.

JEN: I'm gonna go call her.

FRANK: Yeah, find out what she's going to name it.

JEN: Okay. I'll email you.

FRANK: Email me!

22.

BETH is in the park. RICHARD walks up to her. It's been a while since they have seen one another.

RICHARD: Hey stranger.

BETH: Oh my God…hey.

RICHARD: I saw you from across the park, I was calling your name. You didn't hear me?

BETH: No.

RICHARD: It's good to see your face.

BETH: Thank you. What are you doing here?

RICHARD: I was in the city for a couple of days, visiting my nephew.

BETH: Marty?

RICHARD: Yeah, wow, you remember his name?

BETH: Of course I do. I'm going to his Outer Space Birthday Party next week. It's going to be quite the event.

RICHARD: Oh, wow. That's why I'm here, actually. You're going?

BETH: I was gonna make an appearance. It's a big deal, Richard.

RICHARD: Oh, I had no idea. I thought it was going to just be a little Outer Space Birthday Party in the backyard.

BETH: No. Word has gotten out, I even heard that your sister was going to dress up like a martian.

RICHARD: Yeah, I think she is.

BETH: That's great.

RICHARD: Yeah.

BETH: How long are you in town?

RICHARD: I go back on Thursday.

BETH: Have you had a good visit?

RICHARD: Yeah, it's been great. It's weird to be back.

BETH: Do you miss it?

RICHARD: A little, yeah, but I'm really glad I left it. It's a bit too loud for me, you know?

BETH: Yeah. I think you told me that once.

(They laugh a little.)

RICHARD: You're good?

BETH: Great.

RICHARD: You look great.

BETH: Thanks.

RICHARD: You've lost a lot of weight, huh?

BETH: A little, yeah.

RICHARD: Your hair has gotten longer.

BETH: Yeah. You like it?

RICHARD: It looks great.

BETH: I'm thinking of cutting it all off.

RICHARD: Yeah?

BETH: Yeah…I'm getting sick of it.

RICHARD: It looks good.

BETH: Thanks.

RICHARD: How is everything?

BETH: Good, I'm really good.

RICHARD: I saw your movie.

BETH: Yeah?

RICHARD: You were great.

BETH: I looked pretty ugly in it, huh?

RICHARD: Yeah.

BETH: I wanted to get into the character.

RICHARD: Yeah. What are you doing now?

BETH: I'm in a show.

RICHARD: Oh, I knew that. It's supposed to move to Broadway, right?

BETH: It's looking that way now, but who knows.

RICHARD: And the guy who plays the angel-judge from that show—

BETH: "Divine Justice."

RICHARD: Yeah, he's in it, right?

BETH: Yeah. He'll probably be at Marty's Outer Space Birthday Party.

RICHARD: Wow. I read a review in the *Times*. It said you were great.

BETH: Yeah, so then you knew I was doing a play.

RICHARD: I just remembered, just now.

BETH: Okay.

RICHARD: I also hear that there is some Oscar buzz about you.

BETH: Buzz, buzz, buzz.

RICHARD: Congratulations. You're famous.

BETH: You're not.

RICHARD: Thank God.

(They laugh a little.)

BETH: How are you?

RICHARD: Good, really good. I bought a house.

BETH: Really?

RICHARD: Yeah, and a dog.

BETH: What kind?

RICHARD: Golden retriever.

BETH: Not a lab?

RICHARD: No, I saw this dog and had to have him.

BETH: That's great.

RICHARD: Yeah.

BETH: What are you doing?

RICHARD: I'm teaching, actually.

BETH: No way.

RICHARD: Yeah, I'm teaching drama at the high school.

BETH: Really?

RICHARD: Well, drama and oral communications.

BETH: You're a teacher?

RICHARD: I love it.

BETH: That's great.

(It is quiet for a bit.)

BETH: Do you have a sweetheart?

RICHARD: I do.

BETH: Of course you do.

RICHARD: A nice, normal girl.

BETH: Wow.

RICHARD: I didn't mean—

BETH: I know. How's it going?

RICHARD: Great.

BETH: Good. Well, I'm sort of seeing someone, but it's very hush-hush.

RICHARD: Oh.

BETH: Yes.

RICHARD: You wanna go grab a beer or something?

BETH: I have to go to the theatre.

RICHARD: Oh, you're performing tonight?

BETH: Yeah. You should come. Do you wanna come?

RICHARD: I would love to, but I can't. I'm meeting Gene later.

BETH: Oh?

RICHARD: He's doing some secret project or something. You should call him sometime. I know he would love to hear from you.

BETH: I'll do that.

RICHARD: Yeah, his number's still the same…do you still have his number?

BETH: I'm sure I do somewhere.

RICHARD: Call him.

BETH: I definitely will. *(Looks at her watch.)* Shit, I'm sorry—I have to go.

RICHARD: Oh, don't let me keep you.

BETH: I'm sorry.

RICHARD: No worries…the actress can't be late to the theatre.

BETH: Shut up.

RICHARD: I'm kidding.

BETH: I wish I could stay.

RICHARD: No worries. Break a leg tonight.

BETH: Thanks.

RICHARD: I wish I could be there.

BETH: Well, next time.

RICHARD: Yeah, I'll come when it's on Broadway.

BETH: Keep your fingers crossed.

RICHARD: Sure.

BETH: It was really great to see you.

RICHARD: You too, I guess I'll see you at Marty's big Outer Space Birthday Party.

BETH: Oh, yeah.

(They hug. She walks away. He calls after her.)

RICHARD: Beth!

(She is gone.)

RICHARD: I love you.

23.

LIZ runs on and is in the height of her panic. She has a huge pile of pictures and books in her hands.

LIZ: I had nothing left. I've hidden pictures. I've buried boxes. I've written notes. I've carved things out. I had nothing left for you. You will remember me when they bring you the tin box that I have hidden in the tree. You will remember me when you give your children your favorite books. You will remember me on those days. I was a woman you could not keep. I was a passionate and impulsive woman. It's getting quiet. You will remember me and you will tell your children about me. You will tell someone about me. Someone will remember me. I'm worried.

24.

MARTY comes running in.

MARTY: I'm worried. I can't get four hundred dollars. My mom won't give me any money and she got mad when she found out that I was trying to sell her couch. I couldn't sell my baby bracelets. I stole forty-two dollars out of my mom's purse, but that still doesn't give me enough. One guy in the street that I asked for money said that he would give me one hundred and fifty dollars if I came over and played with his kids. But I don't really like playing with other kids, especially older kids, and when I asked him how old his kids were he just laughed at me. So, I'm just guessing that they're older. Playing with older kids is scary. I really want Biz to come to my Outer Space Birthday Party. Everyone is going to go Marcy Shelton's water slide party if I don't get Biz. Frank told me that the stars of "Divine Justice" won't come if Biz isn't coming and Biz is only making me pay four hundred dollars because he thinks the stars of "Divine Justice" are gonna be there. I'm worried. Four hundred dollars. Four hundred dollars. I wonder how much older that man's kids are. Maybe they're not too much older. My mom always says that I should face my fear. I should face my fear and go play with those older kids. I'll play with his older kids and get one hundred and fifty dollars. I'll play with his kids and get my shit together.

25.

JEN: Hey Gene.

GENE: Hey Jen, long time no see.

JEN: Yeah, I've been really busy.

GENE: Yeah, me too. I'm actually on my way to this thing—

JEN: —Yeah, I'm on my way, too. You still keeping yourself a mystery?

GENE: Well, all that stuff is sort of dying down. I think it will be over soon.

JEN: And then will you finally be able to tell us what it's all about?

GENE: I promise, as soon as it's over.

JEN: Thank God, we miss you.

GENE: Me? It seems like you've been MIA for a while, too.

JEN: Yeah.

GENE: Have you been away?

JEN: I was in the hospital for a while, actually.

GENE: Oh my God, are you okay?

JEN: I am now, yeah.

GENE: What happened?

JEN: I was hospitalized for exhaustion.

GENE: Oh my God.

JEN: I'm okay now.

GENE: I had no idea you were in the hospital.

JEN: Really? A lot of people knew about it, I'm surprised you didn't hear.

GENE: Really?

JEN: Yeah, I think it was a hot topic of gossip for a while.

GENE: I didn't hear.

JEN: Really?

GENE: Well, you know I have really been out of the loop for a while.

JEN: Right.

GENE: I had heard that Frank was bringing the cast of "Divine Justice" to Marty's Outer Space Birthday Party and that Ann was in Africa adopting a baby, but I never heard that you were hospitalized for exhaustion.

JEN: Yeah, well, maybe the person you've been hearing all the scoop from was trying to be sensitive to my situation.

GENE: I'm sure that's it.

JEN: Otherwise, you definitely would have heard, it was a really big deal.

GENE: I'm so sorry. Are you okay?

JEN: Yeah, I'm fine now. The hardest part was everyone talking about it. You know?

GENE: I can imagine.

JEN: It's very personal. It was a very personal problem and everyone was talking about it like it was front page news or something.

GENE: Maybe they were just talking about it out of concern?

JEN: Maybe. I just wish everyone would mind their own business.

GENE: I hear that. It can be very hard to keep health problems a secret, I know.

JEN: What?

GENE: Health problems…trust me, I know.

JEN: Okay. So you heard that Frank is bringing the stars of "Divine Justice" to Marty's Outer Space Birthday Party?

GENE: Yeah. It's the big scoop.

JEN: Yeah, I am definitely going.

GENE: Really?

JEN: Yeah, I am definitely going to a party where the cast of "Divine Justice" and Biz will be.

GENE: Wait, Biz is gonna be at Marty's Outer Space Birthday Party?

JEN: Oh yeah.

GENE: *The* Biz?

JEN: Yep, that's the word on the street.

GENE: How did Marty get the stars of "Divine Justice" and *the* Biz to his Outer Space Birthday Party?

JEN: I don't know, maybe retards are in these days.

GENE: Wow.

JEN: Yeah.

GENE: Well, I'm definitely going.

JEN: Yeah, I have to buy an outfit.

GENE: Me too.

JEN: Do you know if Ann is back from Africa yet?

GENE: No, I don't know when she is getting back.

JEN: Can you believe that she is adopting an African baby?

GENE: I know! Well, she has always felt really connected to that part of the world.

JEN: I had no idea.

GENE: Yeah, she loves Africa.

JEN: I never knew.

GENE: Yeah, I guess there is a lot more to Ann than any of us knew.

JEN: I guess.

GENE: I really admire her.

JEN: Me too.

GENE: I'll let you know if I hear anything about her and the baby.

JEN: It's a girl, right?

GENE: I think so.

JEN: I wonder what she's going to name it.

GENE: Probably something African.

JEN: That's what I heard.

JEN: I'm gonna go. I'll see you at Marty's Outer Space Birthday Party?

GENE: Okay, I'll keep you up to date on Ann.

JEN: Great.

GENE: Jen, are you resting yourself now?

JEN: Yeah, there's really nothing to be worried about.

GENE: Okay. Are you eating?

JEN: I'm okay.

GENE: You sure?

JEN: Yes.

GENE: Okay.

JEN: Okay.

GENE: Bye.

JEN: Bye.

26.

BIZ is sitting in his chair. MARTY is standing next to him. BIZ is holding a wad of money and a giant contract that he gives to MARTY.

BIZ: Marty, I am very pleased to see this. I am very happy with you today, Marty. Now, in order for me to attend your Outer Space Birthday Party, I will need your signature agreeing to all my needs and stipulations concerning my appearance. You will see these needs and stipulations in the "Needs and Stipulations" section of the contract. Do you understand, Marty?

MARTY: Yes, Biz.

BIZ: You will sign the contract and I will make an appearance at your muthafuckin' Outer Space Birthday Party.

MARTY: Biz, guess who else is coming to my Outer Space Birthday Party?

BIZ: Who?

MARTY: Beth Foster.

BIZ: She is a very talented character actress. That's my girl! *(Thinks for a minute—remembering.)* That was an intense couple of days on the set. She just dove right into that character. Damn. Don't you worry, Marty, with me, Beth, and the cast of "Divine Justice" at your birthday party, ain't nobody gonna give a fuck about Marcy Shelton and her muthafuckin' water slide birthday bullshit.

MARTY: Yeah!

BIZ: Sign the contract, Marty. Sign the contract and you gonna have the Outer Space Birthday Party of the year.

27.

LIZ is in a chair. This is the first time she is still in the whole show. She doesn't have anything in her hands, and her voice is steady for the first time.

LIZ: I gave everything to this city and had nothing left for you. I should have taken you out in the rain. It would start pouring and I would make you take a walk with me and you would agree and then we would go outside in the pouring rain. We would walk to the end of your street, to the pier by the pond. I would take your hands and put them around my waist and you would dance with me. My hair would be down and wet and I would have dark makeup running down my face and you would think how you have never seen anything so imperfect and beautiful. I would laugh at you staring at me and you would hold my face and kiss my lips and taste the rain. You would think, "Who is this passionate and impulsive creature?" Then I would take off my dress and jump into the pond. I would beg you to come swimming with me, telling you that the water was warm. You would nod your head "no." It would be at that moment that you realized you were in love with me. You would know that you could never keep a woman like me. I should have taken you out in the rain. I should have taken you out in the rain and that way, every time there was a storm, or even a light shower, you would be reminded of the day that a girl took you out to a pier and made you dance with her. Every drop would be my fingers, touching you. I would be raining all over you. You would tell someone the story of that day in the rain. That person would tell someone else. That person would tell the next person the story of the wild woman who took her sweetheart out dancing in the rain. That is how people would know me. The story of how when the man watched the woman in the water, he knew he was in love. He knew he was in love and that he was in trouble. Every time it rained

someone would tell that famous story. Every time it rained someone would think of us. Every time it rained you would remember me. It's quiet. It's quiet and you have forgotten.

28.

MARTY is standing onstage next to a projector. Throughout this speech, he flashes pictures of BIZ on the projector. The pictures are from his Outer Space Birthday Party.

MARTY: I had the very best Outer Space Birthday Party in the whole world. I had an Outer Space Birthday Party on November fifth and everyone came and people are still talking about how fun it was and everyone will remember it forever and ever. I didn't even have to face my fears about playing with older kids, either. The man who said he would give me one hundred and fifty dollars to play with his kids didn't even have any kids! He gave me one hundred and fifty dollars to just sit there while he did some weird stuff. I didn't have to even be around any older kids. I gave Biz four hundred dollars and he made me sign a contract and he came to my Outer Space Birthday Party. I got Biz to my party and I got this really amazing character actress to my party and I got all of the stars of "Divine Justice" to my party! Nobody could believe that I got all of them to my Outer Space Birthday Party! Everyone asked me how I got them there, and I said "They are my friends." Everyone will remember my Outer Space Birthday Party forever and ever. *(Shows the pictures on the projector.)* Here's Biz arriving. Here's me and Biz and the angel-judge from "Divine Justice" on the moonwalk. Here's Biz with his bodyguards, Big Mo and Captain Jay. Here's Biz with my teacher, Mrs. Lyle. Here's Biz with my aunt who was dressed up as a martian. Here's Biz blowing out my birthday candles. Here's my uncle with the really amazing character actress. Here is my friend, Frank; my friend, Gene; and my friend, Jen eating moon pies with the stars from "Divine Justice." Here's a picture of my friend Jen vomiting. She ate a lot of moon pies really, really fast. Here's Biz with Marcy Shelton. Marcy Shelton cancelled her water slide party. *(Smiles.)* Here's Biz hugging me. That's why I'm smiling.

29.

GENE: Hey.

FRANK: Hey.

GENE: You going somewhere?

FRANK: No. You?

GENE: No.

FRANK: You've been around a lot more lately.

GENE: Yeah.

FRANK: It was really great to see you at the Outer Space Birthday Party.

GENE: Yeah.

FRANK: Are you finished with all of your secret stuff?

GENE: Oh, all that stuff I was doing?

FRANK: Yeah.

GENE: Yeah, that's done.

FRANK: What was it?

GENE: I really don't want to get into it.

FRANK: Gene!

GENE: I'm sorry, Frank, it's a long story and it's weird and complicated.

FRANK: You said that once it was done you would tell us about it.

GENE: I know and I will one of these days. I just need some time away from it. I need some time to think about it before I really start talking about it.

FRANK: Gene.

GENE: I'm sorry, Frank. Please understand I just need some time to let it rest.

FRANK: Are you okay?

GENE: I will be. Are you okay?

FRANK: Yeah.

GENE: I mean, are you okay about the big breakup?

FRANK: Oh. You heard about that?

GENE: Yeah, it was impossible not to. I mean, I was at Marty's party when it happened.

FRANK: Yeah.

GENE: You caught him with that cross-eyed actor from "Divine Justice" in the moonwalk, right?

FRANK: Yeah, I did, Gene. I'm okay and I'm actually ready for the whole thing to be over.

GENE: I thought it was over.

FRANK: Well, Mickey and I are completely over, I'm just ready for everyone to stop talking about it.

GENE: Yeah.

FRANK: It was just such a huge drama, the whole thing. I'm done with it.

GENE: Yeah.

FRANK: I'm going to do whatever it takes so that in the future, people aren't paying so much attention to me and my relationships. It's impossible to function like that.

GENE: It's very hard.

FRANK: It's very, very hard.

GENE: Trust me, I know.

FRANK: What?

GENE: I know. *(Looks at FRANK.)* Trust me.

FRANK: Okay.

GENE: Yep.

FRANK: I just couldn't take it anymore. I need to be with someone where there is no drama, no scandal. I need to be with a nice, normal someone who lives in the country and has a dog or something.

GENE: Yeah.

FRANK: I can't even watch "Divine Justice" without feeling sick to my stomach.

GENE: I'm so sorry.

FRANK: Thanks.

(Pause.)

GENE: So did you hear about Jen?

FRANK: How she was hospitalized for exhaustion?

GENE: Yeah.

FRANK: Yeah. Did you know she's in rehab now?

GENE: No way!

FRANK: Isn't that terrible?

GENE: Yeah, what for?

FRANK: Well, everyone says it's because of an eating disorder, but I think she also is probably in because of her tendency to take a little beak lunch every now and then.

GENE: Jen does coke?

FRANK: And then some.

GENE: Wow, I never knew Jen was such a—

FRANK: Rebellious soul?

GENE: Yeah.

FRANK: Yeah. I think she does all this because she is hiding some deep hurt that she has within her.

GENE: Wow, I guess there is a lot more to Jen than I thought.

FRANK: Yeah.

GENE: You talked to her?

FRANK: Yeah, she said she was okay and that she wanted everyone to stop talking about it.

GENE: I don't really think anyone is talking about it.

FRANK: Really?

GENE: Well, with your breakup and Marty's big party and Ann in Africa—I don't know, no one is really talking about Jen and her little stint at rehab.

FRANK: Well, that's good. I'll let her know, she'll be happy to hear that.

GENE: Yeah. She's doing okay now?

FRANK: I think so. Jen has tons of people that love her and will take good care of her.

FRANK: Okay.

(Pause.)

FRANK: Do you know if Ann is back from Africa? I heard she might be getting back today.

GENE: I don't know.

FRANK: Yeah, no one has really said anything to me about it.

GENE: I should email her.

FRANK: I should too. Maybe she is back and she's been too busy with the baby to update her MySpace blog.

GENE: Yeah, I feel bad, spending time in impoverished African countries can really haunt a person for the rest of their life.

FRANK: What?

GENE: Impoverished African countries. Trust me, I know.

FRANK: I hear that.

FRANK: *(Looks at his watch.)* I gotta run, but I'll email Ann and I'll let you know if she's back and what the deal is with the baby.

GENE: If I get a chance, I'm gonna try to email too.

FRANK: I'll text you and let you know what I find out.

GENE: I'll do the same.

FRANK: Bye.

GENE: Bye!

30.

RICHARD is pretending to give an interview, maybe looking in a mirror.

RICHARD: No, I don't really like to do interviews. I figure, you're Barbara Walters, so if I ever am going to do an interview, this would be the one to do. *(Listens.)* Yes, people do still ask me about her. A lot, actually—photographers everywhere, calling my mother, following me into the public bathroom—all that stuff. *(Listens.)* I'm great actually. I teach drama to high school students and I'm married to a wonderful woman and I have a backyard and a dog and lots of wide open space. *(Listens.)* Yes, I hear she's doing that. I'm sure it will be absolutely wonderful, she's really a very talented character actress. *(Listens.)* I called it off, yes. I just couldn't really stand that kind of lifestyle any longer. It's not me. *(Listens.)* We don't really talk anymore, no. *(Listens.)* I do miss her, Barbara. We used to have a really good time together. I miss her feet, she had great feet. *(Loses focus.)* I miss sitting in the audience, watching her onstage, and knowing that she would go home with me that night. I miss the way she would smile with her lips closed. I miss how quiet she would get every time it would rain. I miss her trying to hide pictures of herself in my sock drawer. I miss her blinking. *(Snaps out of it.)* Yes, I would say that there are times when I wonder if I made the right decision, but then I remember how she was one of those woman that you just can't keep. I was always looking at her and she was always looking out. *(Stops the interview.)* This is stupid. I am so stupid.

31.

ANN walks in, JEN runs in after her.

JEN: Oh my God!

ANN: Oh my God, hey!

JEN: Wow, welcome back.

ANN: Thanks.

JEN: I was calling your name back there.

ANN: Oh.

JEN: When did you get back?

ANN: Oh, like a month ago.

JEN: Wow, I can't believe that. Where you been hiding?

ANN: Well, I'm pretty busy these days. With the baby.

JEN: Oh my God! How's the baby?

ANN: Good, really good.

JEN: I'm so sorry, I totally forgot that you have a baby now!

ANN: Yeah, from Africa.

JEN: Oh my God! How's the African baby?

ANN: Great, really great.

JEN: Girl or boy?

ANN: You didn't hear?

JEN: No.

ANN: It's a girl.

JEN: What did you name her?

ANN: You didn't hear about any of this?

JEN: Well, a lot has been going on, Ann. I knew you were adopting an African baby, but I didn't hear any details.

ANN: You didn't get the christening FaxBlast?

JEN: I'm not getting anyone's FaxBlasts these days.

ANN: I gave her an African name.

JEN: How sweet!

ANN: Her name is—

JEN: —Is she so cute?

ANN: Yes, she's wonderful.

JEN: Do you feel weird?

ANN: A little.

JEN: I felt really weird after I was hospitalized for exhaustion.

ANN: You were hospitalized for exhaustion?

JEN: Yeah, I guess you missed that.

ANN: Yeah, I was probably in Africa adopting my baby at that time.

JEN: I'm okay now, please don't worry about me. I just want everyone to forget about that and the rehab.

ANN: Rehab?

JEN: Yes, Ann, but please don't worry. I'm fine now.

ANN: Okay.

JEN: I'm fine.

ANN: Okay.

JEN: Really.

ANN: Okay.

(Pause.)

ANN: Have you seen Gene and Frank lately?

JEN: Oh yeah, I saw them at Marty's big Outer Space Birthday Party.

ANN: Marty the retard?

JEN: He's not retarded, Ann. He's slow.

ANN: Oh.

JEN: He's a beautiful soul.

ANN: Oh.

JEN: His party was slammin'. The Biz, Beth Foster—

ANN: Neither Frank nor Gene has called me since I've been back from Africa.

JEN: You know how it is, everyone is so busy these days, Ann.

ANN: I know, I'm busy too, but you would think that they at least would have called or texted.

JEN: Have you tried calling them?

ANN: Yes, but every time I call either one of them it says their number has been changed.

JEN: Oh yeah, you weren't here for that.

ANN: What happened?

JEN: Frank's crazy ex-boyfriend, Mickey—have you seen "Divine Justice" lately?

ANN: I've been in Africa.

(JEN looks at her blankly.)

ANN: No, I haven't seen "Divine Justice" lately.

JEN: Frank's ex-boyfriend Mickey is now an actor on that show, you know the one with dark skin and curly brown hair?

ANN: I don't know.

JEN: Anyway, Mickey was calling Frank all the time, begging for him to take him back, so Frank had to change his number. Gene said he had to change his number, but wouldn't tell anyone why.

ANN: Really? Is Gene still a mystery?

JEN: I think Gene will always be a mystery.

ANN: Yeah.

JEN: But look, we should all get together and have a drink or something. You can bring your baby.

ANN: I don't really know if a bar is the best place for me to bring—

JEN: —Brunch! We'll do a brunch!

ANN: Okay.

JEN: When I see Gene and Frank online tonight we'll set the whole thing up.

ANN: Well, if you see Gene and Frank online, could you please tell them to call, text, or email me. I'd really like to talk to them.

JEN: Of course.

ANN: I'll call you.

JEN: Just text! This is my new number.

ANN: Okay.

JEN: Ann—

ANN: Yeah?

(A soft moment.)

JEN: Please do not give it out.

ANN: Okay.

JEN: It was really great to see you.

ANN: You too, I'm really sorry to hear that you were in the hospital and in rehab.

JEN: Thank you. Try not to talk about it with anyone, okay?

ANN: I really just talk to my African baby these days.

JEN: Well, don't tell your baby, okay?

ANN: Okay. I'll call you!

JEN: Just text! It's easier. Bye!

ANN: Bye!

32.

BETH is practicing a speech for the Academy Awards in front of her mirror. Upbeat music is playing.

BETH: I want to thank everyone who was involved in this project. I couldn't have done anything without such a talented and supportive group of artists. I want to thank everyone who believed in this project from the very beginning. I want to thank Biz for his incomparable talent. I thank you so much, Biz. I would like to thank my high school drama teacher, Larry Hart. He taught me so many important lessons about acting and life. I would like to thank every single person that I have ever met in my entire life. I could not have done this alone. *(Pause.)* I would like to thank you, especially. I don't even know if you remember me. Thank you for letting me miss you, because that keeps me full.

(LIZ appears on the stage with an old trophy.)

LIZ: I should have looked at you more.

BETH: Thank you for making me truly aware about what is most important to me. God, I hope you can remember me.

(A light shines on ANN with her baby.)

ANN: Shhh, baby, shhh.

BETH: Thank you for not letting me have everything. Maybe you have forgotten about me and now you are watching this and you are able to remember.

(A light comes up on FRANK, on the cell phone.)

FRANK: Yes, Mickey knows who I am, please let me speak to him.

BETH: I want to thank you for giving me a time in my life where every now and then, I was able to move slowly. I hope that you see this and you remember me.

(A light comes up on Gene and Jen. Jen vomits loudly.)

GENE: I need thirty-six squirrels by midnight on Thursday.

BETH: Thank you for loving me for a while. I hope you are watching this right now and that you remember me.

(A light comes up on MARTY with a picture.)

MARTY: This is a picture of Biz opening my presents.

BETH: I had nothing left for you.

(A light comes up on BIZ.)

BIZ: *(On his cell phone.)* I'll be there. I fuckin' love cowboys and Indians.

(RICHARD walks in with LIZ's tin box. He opens it and takes out a note. He reads it.)

BETH: I hope you can remember how you loved me. That's why I have done this. That's what all this is for.

LIZ: Remember that you loved me.

BETH: Thank you.

(She finishes her speech. The sound of monstrous applause. RICHARD closes the box.)

(END OF PLAY.)

SOME NOTES

- For the Richard and Beth scenes: I believe these two do love each other. I think that nothing they say should be flippant or insincere. They quip back and forth and are hurtful to one another, but there is deep love there. Beth starts out pretending to be famous with the interviews and paparazzi and during the play actually does become famous.

- I believe that Liz is Beth as an old woman. However, this is open for the director to decide.

- The pace of the play is really important...everything should be quick, to an exaggerated point. Everyone is on a mission and stakes are high.

- The set should be bare and props minimal. Using large metal frames in scenes really added to the original production. These frames were used to distinguish where these people were: For example, we made a tree house for Marty, a television for Beth, and a store window for Ann and Jen, etc.

- I believe that the particular location of each scene can be left up to the director. I do think that whenever the four friends meet up, they should always be en route, they should never be meeting up for coffee or at an apartment. They meet on street corners, subway stops, outside the gym, etc. In the original production, these scenes were done as a series of explosive blackouts, with actors moving on and off for individual reasons. We had the Biz and Marty scenes taking place in Biz's house; for Marty's monologues, we placed him in a tree house; and I like the idea of Liz being on a stage in an empty auditorium. There is room to play with these locales, but there should never be too much setup—people come on and off quickly, distinguish a setting, and then go, go, go.

- We had a great sound designer, who really brought so much to the piece. Brandon underscored all of Liz's monologues with really haunting music. During Liz's rain monologue, he started off with music, then the sound of applause, the sound of the applause then turned into the sound of a thunderstorm...it was great. He also started all the Biz and Marty scenes with music, played really upbeat music during Marty's slideshow, and underscored Beth's last speech with some upbeat bluegrass music that then turned into monstrous applause and that ended the play on such a strange and wonderful note.

- The last scene should not be slow and sentimental. The characters are still on a mission—I will not give up.

CONVERGENCE

Bryn Manion

BRYN MANION is a writer/director, and sometimes still an actor. She was born on August 8, 1975, in Concord, Massachusetts, and grew up in Springfield, Massachusetts. She attended the University of Massachusetts in Amherst, and graduated as a Commonwealth Scholar with magna cum laude honors with a BA in theater and English. Manion is the co-founder of Aisling Arts, a New York-based theatre ensemble for which she directs and writes, and sometimes acts. Along with her creative partner, Wendy Remington, she has produced over twenty productions for Aisling Arts in the past five years. She was also the co-producer of Free Shakespeare Project, which performed and toured free performances of Shakespeare's plays throughout New England from 1999 to 2003. Manion's plays include *Eleanor*; *Apocalypse Not Now (I Have a Headache)*; *A Few Hallelujahs; Dispersal; Imminent, Indeed (or Polly Peachum's Peculiar Penchant for Plosives)*; and the *Force Trilogy (Wanderlust, Threshold, Convergence)*. Her directing credits include *A Beggar's Opera*, *Macbeth*, *Love's Labour's Lost*, *Twelfth Night*, and *The Playboy of the Western World*. As an actress, Manion has appeared in *A Midsummer Night's Dream* (Helena), *Much Ado About Nothing* (Beatrice), *The Taming of the Shrew* (Kate), and *Life Is a Dream* (Rosaura). She works in publishing and lives in Long Island City, Queens, with Sam David and their two cats, Buddhasaurus Rex and Pachuka.

Convergence was first presented by Aisling Arts (Bryn Manion and Wendy Remington, Artistic Directors) on March 30, 2006, at the New York Irish Center, with the following cast and credits:

Jack .... Berto Colón
Anne .... Wendy Remington
Rob ....Shawn Mahoney
Sara .... Liza Pross
Brian ....Aaron Mathias
Cassie ....,..Elizabeth Sugarman
Hal... Randy Harmon
Lotte ....Karen Grenke
Eva... Sarah Stephens
Charlie ....Benjamin Beckley
Chairman David Kubrecski ....Benjamin Beckley
Katarina ....Elizabeth Sugarman
Katarina's Sister .... Sarah Stephens
Stewardess... Sarah Stephens
Drago...Benjamin Beckley
Lime Lady... Sarah Stephens
Ice Cream Man ....Benjamin Beckley

Directed by: Bryn Manion

The character of Claire, which appears in the script, was added after this production.

www.aislingarts.com

CAST OF CHARACTERS

London/Belgrade

JACK KAVANAGH: A former war-journalist, now teacher

BRIAN KAVANAGH: Jack's younger brother

EVA: A translator living in Belgrade

KATARINA: A Serbian girl who can hold her breath for a very long time

KATARINA'S SISTER: Katarina's breathing coach

DRAGO: A man in a café

Vermont

ANNE BYRNES KAVANAGH: An artist, married to Jack

ROB BYRNES: Anne's brother, a mechanic with a slight memory problem

SARA: A woman from Kansas, Rob's girlfriend

CLAIRE BYRNES: Anne's sister

CHARLIE: Anne's old flame

Any Smallish Town in Middle America

HAL: An ordinary kinda guy

CHARLOTTE (LOTTE): Hal's wife, a science teacher

ICE CREAM MAN: An ice cream vendor in America

London

CASSANDRA (CASSIE): A friend of the Kavanagh brothers

CHAIRMAN DAVID KUBRECSKI: A young Communist

LIME LADY: A British woman in a park carrying a lime

STEWARDESS: A stewardess in the Heathrow Airport

Ensemble

Various members of the cast who assist in filling out public scenes; they operate like extras in a film.

ACT ONE
Scene One

Many places simultaneously. The stage is set with two large tables. One table has two open suitcases on it with clothes surrounding them. An umbrella is set in between the suitcases. The other table is set with tulle, scissors, and the makings of wedding favors. There are also chairs, a trash can, and small tables with objects on them placed randomly throughout the space. LOTTE enters. HAL enters.

HAL: Bad dream?

(LOTTE shakes her head no.)

HAL: Insomnia?

(LOTTE shakes her head no.)

HAL: Newborn?

(LOTTE half smiles and nods.)

HAL: I wish I didn't have to work. But wishful thinking's not going to pay the mortgage. You want Mom to come by so you can take a nap?

(LOTTE shakes her head no.)

HAL: You sure?

(LOTTE nods her head yes.)

HAL: You cold? You look frozen.

(LOTTE nods her head yes.)

HAL: Take my flannel.

(HAL exits to get ready in the bathroom. During the course of his monologue, LOTTE moves to a small table with a flannel shirt, a set of keys, and a wallet on it. She puts on the flannel shirt.)

HAL: (Offstage.) Did I tell you about softball? Jimmy's starting up a team this spring. They need a catcher. I was

thinking about doing it. You know. In the spring. He was surprised I was interested. Never guessed I was all-state. Kind of embarrassing. To be old enough for softball. I can just see my sixteen-year-old self sneering at me. Snickering. You could play, too, you know. What do you think? *(Pops his head out of the bathroom.)* Think about it. You'd look cute in a cap. Hey. We're almost out of milk. You want I should pick some up on the way home tonight? Or do you want to wake Evie up and drop me off at work, take the car today?

(LOTTE offers no response; HAL goes back into the bathroom. LOTTE eyes the keys and wallet.)

HAL: Best part about softball is Dad used to play. Bring us to practice with him. Long Sundays outside. Gets me excited about Evie. All the time we have. All we get to show her. All the firsts. Hotdogs. Ice cream cones. Blowing the seeds off dead dandelions. First balloon. Hate to think of her face when it pops or blows away. Guess everyone has to lose a balloon sometime.

(LOTTE takes the keys and wallet. She walks out the door.)

HAL: Listen, babe. You sure you sure you don't want me to call my mom and have her come over? All she wants is to feel useful. I hate to be a dictator, but you could really use some sleep. Lotte?

(HAL reenters.)

HAL: Honey? Lotte? *(Realizes LOTTE has left the house. He runs outside.)*

(Music. ANNE and JACK enter and stand opposite each other at the table with the two suitcases. ANNE unpacks while JACK packs. They are not in the same

place. When he is done packing, JACK takes the umbrella, opens it, and crosses to a vacant chair and sits. SARA rushes onstage. She takes several sharp breaths as if she is having a panic attack. ROB enters behind her. He takes her hand, kisses her. They wander off. ANNE crawls under the table. CLAIRE enters. She and ANNE are in the same place. CLAIRE takes ANNE's suitcase and brings it to the other large table. CLAIRE exits. STEWARDESS enters and sits on her suitcase, adjusting her pantyhose. BRIAN enters with luggage. STEWARDESS and BRIAN are in the same place. JACK opens his phone and dials. BRIAN answers.)

BRIAN: Hello.

JACK: Brian. It's your brother.

BRIAN: I know who it is.

JACK: Are you in London?

BRIAN: Yeah. I just got of a plane. Literally.

JACK: I'm flying into London tonight. I thought maybe we could have lunch tomorrow.

BRIAN: Jack? I can't hear you.

JACK: I'm coming to London.

BRIAN: You're in London?

JACK: No. Tomorrow.

BRIAN: Jack? Man, I can't hear what you're saying.

(Music. JACK hangs up the phone and exits. CASSIE enters with luggage; she is about to board a plane. ENSEMBLE enters and creates an airport scene. ANNE remains under the table because she is in a different place. CHAIRMAN enters the airport. He speaks into a handheld voice recorder.)

CHAIRMAN: Saturday, August eighth.[*] Eighteen hundred hours. Heathrow Airport. The Chairman has arrived. The story begins.

(ENSEMBLE erupts into stream-of-consciousness riffs.[†] CHAIRMAN cuts them off.)

CHAIRMAN: The story begins with a chance encounter in Greenwich, Connecticut when the child of a bourgeois wallpaper salesman escapes schoolyard bullies by ducking into the janitor's closet. The janitor was a custodian. A custodian of Communism.

(A MEMBER OF THE ENSEMBLE steals CASSIE's bag. CHAIRMAN sees.)

CHAIRMAN: Dude! That lady just stole your bag!

STEWARDESS: *(To BRIAN.)* Omigod. Ashton Kutcher? Please your autograph!

BRIAN: No, I'm Brian Kavanagh.

(BRIAN and CASSIE back into each other. BRIAN turns to her, but does not see her face.)

BRIAN: I'm sorry.

(STEWARDESS pushes CASSIE and BRIAN apart. The airport scene falls apart with rapid exits by EVERYONE except CASSIE. She is left onstage, confused and overwhelmed. Blackout.)

SCENE TWO

Many places simultaneously. CLAIRE enters. She sits at the table with the favors

---

[*]We've always inserted the actual date here, changing it for every performance.
[†]We've always made an effort to break into different languages to establish the international feel of Heathrow.

on it. She is on the phone. ANNE is still under the other table.

CLAIRE: Nicole. Listen to me. You need to have favors. The old people expect favors. They want favors. They'll be unhappy if there's nothing to take home with them. They'll defame you and curse your marriage. This is a happy day, and you don't want that. Trust me, you don't want that. And the old people. They're mean and staunch. They will curse your skinny ass…well, it's too late isn't it? Because I'm sitting here with Anne and a case of Jordan Almonds working a wonder of joy to help you avoid ignominy and disaster…I don't care if you don't like almonds, they're not for you.

(HAL enters, speaking on phone.)

HAL: Hi Larry, this is Hal Smith…yeah, I'm all right. I was wondering if you saw my wife come in. Cause if she's still there, I was hoping you could tell her we need some milk, too…No, you haven't see her yet, huh? Oh. Well, thanks, Larry. Listen, if you see her will you tell her about the cereal?…Right. Milk, Larry. That's right. Tell her to pick up some milk? Thanks, Larry. Much appreciated.

(JACK enters with luggage and the umbrella.)

ANNE: *(A memory.)* Favors? Are you kidding me? What do I need favors for? Who remembers favors? They get squished under car seats and put in pocket books that get used only every other year. We're not handing out favors. I'm not spending good money on favors.

JACK: *(The same memory as ANNE.)* We have to have favors.

ANNE: Please be joking.

JACK: It's tradition. We can be as irreverent as we want, but we can't mess with tradition. Brings nothing but bad luck. *(Exits.)*

(CASSIE enters, sits in a vacant chair, and starts a letter. She is stuck in London, at a friend's or in a hotel room. BRIAN enters, sits in a vacant chair. He is at his flat in London. He goes through his mail.)

CASSIE: This is the thirty-seventh time I have tried to start this letter today. Writing to you suddenly seems imperative. Well, not suddenly. Maybe *perpetually* is a better word. Habitually. *(Beat.)* In the interest of full disclosure, I habitually don't send you unfinished letters I perpetually begin writing, but never quite get right. Does that make sense? You probably appreciate not having to figure out what to do with the stubs of stunted letters, so it's better I don't send them. But I like to think you'd enjoy receiving a complete one. A whole letter. This one.

(SARA enters, panicked. She is at the side of a road in Vermont.)

SARA: Oh god. Oh my god. Oh god. Did I hit it? I think I hit it.

(ROB enters.)

ROB: Don't look. Sara, don't look.

HAL: *(Dials another number.)* Hi there, Cindy. This is Hal Smith again. I'm afraid I have to call out all together today. *(Lying.)* My car's, uh, just busted. Talk about inconvenient. Um…sure, I'll tell Lotte you said hello. She's not feeling so well. So, when she wakes up. Thank you for the casserole, by the way. I think I forgot to say that…No, it tasted great. It reheated just fine. We're so tired, to be honest I wolfed it…Much appreciated. *(He hangs up. Exits.)*

SARA: Is it dead? Please tell me it's not dead.

ROB: He's dead.

SARA: We have to get it to a vet.

ROB: He's dead.

SARA: It just ran out. What was it doing there, what was it thinking? I have to pay a fine right? I have to report this? If I don't it's illegal.

ROB: Get out of the road.

SARA: Is there a collar? Does it have a collar on? The poor thing. The sound it made. Please tell me there's no collar.

ROB: Get out of the road, Sara.

SARA: I can't stand telling an owner. Will you go with me? You'll go with me, right? You won't make me do it alone. Please say I won't have to do this alone.

ROB: Get out of the fucking road, Sara! You're going to get yourself killed. *(Beat.)* What do you think you hit?

SARA: A dog, right? It was a dog.

ROB: No. A deer. A little guy. A fawn.

(ROB and SARA slowly exit. JACK enters, sits in a vacant chair. He is on a plane.)

CLAIRE: *(From the table with the favors.)* Anne. Anne, are you under the table again?

ANNE: *(From under the other table.)* No.

CLAIRE: Yes, you are.

ANNE: No, I'm not.

CLAIRE: I would appreciate some help in here. Can you at least bring me the trash can?

(ANNE slowly gets up and goes to a trash can. JACK gets up from his seat on the plane.)

ANNE: *(To herself.)* I feel like I've been here before. I've never been here before. I have. I have been here. *(Begins to throw up into the trash can.)* Piss.

JACK: *(Entering ANNE's space, a shared memory happening simultaneously.)* Annie?

ANNE: *(Still retching.)* Leave me alone.

JACK: What is it?

ANNE: Don't. Don't come near me. Back off! Septic. God. *(Retches.)* You smell.

JACK: It's soap. Annie, it's only soap.

ANNE: It's disgusting. Get away.

JACK: Babe, let's go to the doctor. Let me call the doctor.

ANNE: I don't need a doctor.

JACK: I'm calling the doctor.

ANNE: I'm late.

JACK: For what? You're not going anywhere like this.

ANNE: I am late. As in late. L. A. T. E.

(HAL reenters.)

HAL: *(On phone, lying a little bit.)* Mom. Sorry, didn't mean to wake you. Good, great, everything's great…tired. Real tired. I'm—ah—staying home today so Lotte can get some rest, but we're out of milk. I can't make the baby's formula…I know, Ma, but now's not the time to go on about the breast feeding. Okay? She's exhausted. Point is I need someone to pick up some milk so I can feed Evie…You don't? You use water? Are you sure?…No I didn't read the directions. I just used milk. She liked it…Constipated? No. Well. I just fed her. She's not going to be constipated yet, is she?...Please tell me other people do these things to their children...Um. Okay. I guess I don't need you to bring over milk. Thanks, Mom. *(Hangs up, exits.)*

JACK: How late is late?

ANNE: Five weeks.

JACK: That's late. This is good. This is a very good thing.

ANNE: How is this good?

JACK: Anne.

ANNE: It is. It is good. But it's surprising.

(JACK rises, returns to his seat on the plane. ANNE rises, brings the trash can to CLAIRE.)

CASSIE: Should I start with formalities? I should. After all, the last time we were in touch was a flurry of emails three years ago. How are you? Where are you? Off on some adventure or other, I'm sure. I'm still in Nairobi. Not actually at the moment. At the moment, I'm in London. Before that home. I was home. In Chicago. That looks so strange on the paper. Nairobi's home these days. My unfinished attempts to write to you *feel* more like home than the house on Lake Drive. But then that's neither here nor there. What does that mean? Neither here nor there?

(Blackout.)

Scene Three

Heathrow Airport and the BYRNES's house in Vermont. ANNE and CLAIRE sit assembling favors. Music. Same music as previous airport scene. STEWARDESS enters.

STEWARDESS: Flight 735 to Belgrade now boarding upper class passengers.

(BRIAN enters, holding a sign that reads, "Jack Kavanagh." JACK enters, sees BRIAN.)

JACK: You didn't have to pick me up. I could have taken the train.

BRIAN: Of course I needed to pick you up.

JACK: How did you...?

BRIAN: I have my ways. Missed connections have never stopped me before. How was the flight?

JACK: A lot of turbulence. Guy next to me barfed.

BRIAN: So, what's all this about?

JACK: Meet with some contacts. A few editors. Some friends. See what's out there. Who's where. What's going on. What's about to be going on. It's easier to do here than in New York. At least for me. Right now the intention is to get to Africa. Start in Chad and take it from there.

BRIAN: Right. But what's it about?

JACK: Oh. Well, a little pressure from the University. From the department. I work with some prolific people, and I haven't quite been keeping up.

BRIAN: I meant your wife.

JACK: Oh, that. It wasn't working. Happens to marriages all the time. Can you do me a favor—hold this for me?

ANNE: I didn't have favors.

CLAIRE: You should have had favors.

ANNE: Favors are stupid.

CLAIRE: Not having favors brings nothing but bad luck.

ANNE: Obviously. That's why my marriage broke up. We didn't have fucking favors. You're so right, Claire.

CLAIRE: Per usual.

BRIAN: What?

JACK: Nothing. Stupid. Sorry.

STEWARDESS: Flight 735 to Belgrade now boarding regular people. All regular people now, please board for Belgrade.*

BRIAN: What are you looking at?

JACK: What are you doing this weekend?

BRIAN: Showing you London.

JACK: I don't have any appointments until Tuesday.

BRIAN: Good. Then we can relax. I only just got back in town myself.

JACK: Actually.

BRIAN: What?

JACK: Do you have your passport on you?

BRIAN: Yeah. My only ID.

JACK: What say we go to Belgrade for the weekend?

BRIAN: You just got here.

JACK: I know.

BRIAN: Belgrade's cold.

JACK: Let's go, let's do it. On me. I'll pay.

BRIAN: Seriously. I just got back here three days ago.

JACK: I'd like to see how things have changed.

BRIAN: Things are constantly changing, man, you can't catch it all.

JACK: That's exactly my point. Let's see what's changed.

BRIAN: Right on. Yeah, okay. Right on.

JACK: Eastern Europe, man. You ever been?

BRIAN: Never. What the hell? Sure. Let's go. Let's do it. Kavanagh squared.

JACK: Yeah?

BRIAN: Yeah.

JACK: You're easy.

BRIAN: That's what the ladies say. Let me buy some underwear in the duty free, then I'm good to go.

(JACK, BRIAN, and STEWARDESS exit.)

Scene Four

BYRNES's house only, Vermont. ANNE and CLAIRE continue working on wedding favors. ROB and SARA enter.

ROB: It happens all the time.

SARA: No, it doesn't. If it happened all the time everyone would be driving around town with dead deer on their bumpers.

ROB: I was trying to make you feel better. *(Exits.)*

CLAIRE: Don't touch anything. There's a very intricate system—

ROB: *(Offstage.)* Anne! Where are my shoes?

---

*In performance, we've translated the Stewardess's line into a different language.

CLAIRE: Try your feet, Rob.

ROB: *(Offstage.)* I was asking Anne.

SARA: Nicole said she didn't want favors.

CLAIRE: Nicole doesn't know what she wants.

(ROB reenters with a shovel.)

ROB: Come on. Back in the car.

CLAIRE: Should I ask or will it bite?

SARA: That's not funny. You're not funny.

CLAIRE: Oh yeah? Guy with a shovel walks into a bar and says, "Do ya dig?"

ROB: Claire. Really. Sara hit a deer.

SARA: You said you wouldn't tell. Why did you tell?

ROB: It looks a little weird.

SARA: When did you start caring about what looks weird? You said you wouldn't tell anyone.

ANNE: Bambi.

SARA: See? She hasn't said anything all day and that's what she says. That's why you don't tell. Right there. You people are heartless. *(SARA huffs offstage.)*

CLAIRE: She's not quite spunky, is she?

ANNE: Petulant.

CLAIRE: Takes the pressure off you, Anne. You should write her a thank you note.

ROB: I'll be back in an hour. Go bury the deer. Maybe grab a beer. You might want to apologize.

CLAIRE: So might you, dumb ass. She's not my girlfriend.

(ROB exits.)

ACT TWO
SCENE ONE

Music. ANNE and CLAIRE remain at the table with the favors. LOTTE enters. She wanders around. ICE CREAM MAN enters. He hands LOTTE an ice cream cone and exits. She sits for a long while, eating her ice cream cone. HAL enters on the phone.

HAL: Stan. This is Hal Smith. Listen, Lotte went out to pick up some cereal, I mean milk, early this morning and uh, she's still not back...not really a fight, no. No. Not a fight at all. We were talking about softball. We were just out of milk, but you know, she had one of her bad nights with the dreams and the headaches and the nausea and with the baby on top of it, we're going through a rough spot...I think she took my wallet. Yeah, actually, I know she took my wallet...But, we got to do something. At what point does she become a missing person?

(ANNE leaves the table with the favors and wanders to the other table. She examines her wedding ring. CHARLIE enters and sits in a vacant chair eating a sandwich. ANNE is pulled into a recent memory of CHARLIE. She moves toward his chair.)

CHARLIE: *(Seeing ANNE.)* I didn't know you were in town, Annie. I mean, I had no idea.

ANNE: I am. I mean, obviously. I am. In town.

CHARLIE: It's good. Good to see you. It's nice. And good.

ANNE: Right. Good and nice.

CHARLIE: Nice and good to see you.

(ICE CREAM MAN reenters and wanders past them and waves to ANNE. She moves back to the table and examines her wedding ring, then wanders back to the table with the favors. CHARLIE resumes eating his sandwich. Enter ROB and SARA. ROB carries a shovel.)

ROB: —that there are two! I'm not crazy.

SARA: Two what?

ROB: Two people who look exactly alike.

SARA: How does it matter?

ROB: *(Puts shovel down.)* If Platonic love is the cleaving of souls and their never-ending search for each other, hence, soul mates, those two souls keep cleaving into more and more souls…well, then, we're operating on partial souls. Which makes me a little uncomfortable. But then, I see no reason why the same principle can't apply to our genetic makeup and the manifestation of that makeup.

SARA: Two people who don't know each other could look exactly alike?

ROB: Yes.

SARA: That's not good logic. If we're splitting, we just keep splitting. It would only be the semblance and not the substance of similarity.

ROB: Yes! But we're recombinant! As in recombining parts of the whole. I don't think I'm too off here, Sara. I believe with my heart and intuition that I have a Doppler-radar.

ANNE: Doppelgänger.

ROB: Yes. That.

SARA: You're paranoid. I'm going to bed. *(Exits.)*

ROB: We couldn't find the deer.

CLAIRE: Did you retrace your steps?

ROB: No. I wasn't driving. They weren't my steps.

CLAIRE: Well, it's not like you can bury anything out there. It's the dead of winter. What made you think you could bury it? No one buries deer. That's why you see them on the side of the road.

ROB: Apparently, I don't have enough of a brain left to think critically when my girlfriend's hysterical. She killed the shit out of that poor thing.

(ANNE exits with shovel.)

CLAIRE: Don't turn this into some thing about your "condition."

ROB: I will, too. You try learning to tie your shoes when you're thirty.

CLAIRE: Don't be melodramatic.

ROB: It's only slightly melodramatic. I. Have. A. Condition.

CLAIRE: What you have is an artful excuse to keep you from growing up like the rest of us.

ROB: It's not an excuse.

CLAIRE: Enough. Let's go back out, drive around a little bit, we'll come back and say we found it and gave it a good Christian burial.

ROB: No. I'm done. My ass is tired. I've already been sitting in the car for two hours. Where'd Anne go?

CLAIRE: Anne, get out from under the table.

ROB: *(Crosses to the other table.)* She's not under the table.

CLAIRE: Anne?

(ROB and CLAIRE look at each other. Lights down.)

Scene Two

A street in Belgrade and Buckingham Palace, London. Music. JACK wanders down a street in a daze, disoriented and dreamlike. BRIAN follows him, a little too closely.

BRIAN: So what happened with your woman, bro?

JACK: I'm trying to figure things out, Brian. Give me a little space. Let me carry my own bag.

BRIAN: Why are you walking ten feet ahead of me?

JACK: Sorry.

BRIAN: I don't know where the hell I am, man. Don't go trucking ahead of me.

JACK: Sorry. I know this place. This place is familiar.

BRIAN: Is it a shop?

JACK: Well.

BRIAN: A whorehouse?

JACK: No. No. God. Well. No. No, it's not.

BRIAN: You going in?

JACK: Yeah.

(JACK and BRIAN exit. CHAIRMAN stands facing out, he addresses an imaginary Beefeater.)

CHAIRMAN: You ever thought of regicide? I have. Does that make you nervous? Good. Cause listen, man, monarchy denies the people. Like you and me, man. We are the people. You. You go home every night to your wife and the tea kettle with the tea cozy and your digestive biscuits and you think it's all good because once more you made it through a day of protecting the bitch. But what are you doing? Nothing, man. Protecting the vagina. I mean, Regina. Right. You eat beef, man? You know if we turned all the grazing land we give to cattle to vegetable and grain we could feed continents of starving children. Not that I believe in intervention, but tell me, how's that feel, Mr. Beef Eater? *(Throws a fake punch.)* Flinch much? No? Sucker. That's American for "you suck."

(KATARINA enters, sits on the floor holding her breath. CHAIRMAN exits. KATARINA'S SISTER enters and flips aimlessly through a magazine. She absently times KATARINA holding her breath. A knock on the door. KATARINA'S SISTER opens the door.)

BRIAN: What is this place?

JACK: Hand the girl your money.

KATARINA'S SISTER:[*] <Welcome to the House of Katarina. Katarina has been in the *Guinness Book of World Records* in 2001, 2002, and 2003. You may view the certificates on the wall. She has the

_____

[*] When lines are bracketed (< >), this means the characters are speaking Serbian. Though they never actually do speak a different language, directors should take note to make clear what each character is able to understand when. One nifty trick we used was to alter Jack's syntax to imply that while he could speak Serbian, he couldn't speak it well. For example, "Why does she do this?" would be changed to "Why doing this she is?"

lung capacity of a great blue whale! Please do not take flash photography or try to touch Katarina—you will regret such moves. We have a very large dog in the hallway. If you have questions you must direct them to me.>

JACK: *(To BRIAN.)* You have any questions?

BRIAN: What is she doing? Why is she holding her breath?

JACK: *(To KATARINA'S SISTER.)* <Why does she do this?>

KATARINA'S SISTER: <Oooooooh, American.>

(She moves to KATARINA and whispers into her ear.)

JACK: <My brother would like to know why she does this?>

KATARINA'S SISTER: <Why not?>

JACK: *(To BRIAN.)* You get that?

KATARINA'S SISTER: <What did he say?>

JACK: <He doesn't speak Serbian.>

KATARINA'S SISTER: <Obviously. But what does he say?>

BRIAN: That can't be good for her brain.

JACK: <Nothing important. I met you a long time ago. Do you remember?>

KATARINA'S SISTER: <No. I meet many people.>

JACK: <You told me about your sister and how she almost drowned. I told you about my sister. Do you remember?>

KATARINA'S SISTER: <You are American?>

JACK: <Yes. You do remember?>

KATARINA'S SISTER: <I don't remember. I'm sorry.>

BRIAN: She still hasn't breathed. Is she going to explode or something?

JACK: <You told me how your sister was pushed into the water by...)

KATARINA'S SISTER: <—Nothing happened to Katarina. She is fine. She does this because she enjoys it.>

JACK: <Do you remember the girl who found your sister, who took her out of the water. Her name was Eva?

(KATARINA loses her breath; she begins to breath frantically. BRIAN sympathetically begins to panic a bit.)

JACK: <Eva. She was a friend of mine. Do you remember?>

(Freeze. KATARINA chases BRIAN around the table. Music. KATARINA'S SISTER chases JACK to the door where they begin a surreal dance. And then, stillness.)

BRIAN: You remind me of someone.

KATARINA: You remind me of someone.

BRIAN: Who do I remind you of?

KATARINA: Who do I remind you of?

BRIAN: I asked you first.

KATARINA: I can't tell you. I'm holding my breath.

BRIAN: What language are we speaking?

KATARINA: I don't know, what language are you speaking?

BRIAN: Whatever language you're speaking. Weird.

KATARINA: Yes. You're weird.

BRIAN: I'm not weird. You're the one holding your breath.

KATARINA: Who do I remind you of?

BRIAN: You look so much like her.

KATARINA: Who?

BRIAN: An old friend. She was a friend of my sister's, but my sister, she, never mind. Then she became my friend. I haven't talked to her in years. You look so much like her.

KATARINA: Your sister?

BRIAN: No. My sister's friend. Who do I remind you of?

KATARINA: I'm sorry. I'm holding my breath now.

BRIAN: But—

(Music. The chasing and dancing resume until ALL return to initial freeze. Music stops. The scene becomes normal again.)

KATARINA'S SISTER: <Please leave. You are distracting my sister. She is in training.>

JACK: <I know you know who I'm talking about.>

KATARINA'S SISTER: <Please. Go. Go now. >

JACK: <Have you seen Eva? Do you know where she is?>

BRIAN: Eva?

KATARINA'S SISTER: <Why are you looking for Eva? Who is this man? Leave. You must leave.>

(KATARINA loses her breath again.)

JACK: <Did something happen to Eva?>

BRIAN: Did something happen to Eva?

JACK: <What happened to Eva?>

BRIAN: Who's Eva?

KATARINA'S SISTER: <Please. Please leave. I cannot speak with you. I cannot.>

JACK: <Please.>

KATARINA'S SISTER: <I cannot. I cannot. I am sorry. I do remember you. But, I cannot.>

(JACK and BRIAN exit, leaving the SISTERS alone, KATARINA still breathing as if she is terrified.)

Scene Three

Vermont and Belgrade. ROB is looking at notebooks. LOTTE wanders. JACK sits at a bus stop with BRIAN.

ROB: Two lines. Coming together. For example, you have two eyes. They each take in different information. But when you're looking at one thing, one point, there's a focal intersection. A convergence. But, it's more than that. It's metaphorical. You, from your perspective, see one thing. If we agree we see the same thing, our vision has intersected. Another convergence. But, it doesn't need to be an object we have converged upon. It can be an idea. A memory. Maybe a dream.

(SARA enters.)

SARA: Who are you talking to?

ROB: My shadow.

SARA: What are these?

ROB: Notebooks. From college.

SARA: It's because of Koko.

ROB: Who? What is?

SARA: Koko. The gorilla. Everyone knows Koko.

ROB: I don't know Koko.

SARA: *(Petulantly.)* She's the gorilla who knows sign language.

ROB: What's the matter with you?

SARA: What's the matter with you?

(JACK pulls out his wallet. ANNE enters with the shovel. JACK jolts upright. He stands. ANNE walks to him, takes his wallet. He steps out of his space and into a shared memory.)

ANNE: Wait. Who are these girls with you and Brian?

JACK: That's Kate. And that's her best friend Cassie.

ANNE: Who's Kate?

JACK: Let's go. We're going to be late.

ANNE: Ex-girlfriend?

JACK: No.

ANNE: Kate. She looks like you.

JACK: Let's go.

ANNE: The more you don't answer, the more trouble I have to cause. It's human nature.

JACK: It's obnoxious.

ANNE: Who is this? Who's Kate?

JACK: My sister.

ANNE: Your sister? You don't have a sister.

JACK: Let's go.

ANNE: Jack?

JACK: Now's not the time.

ANNE: John. What is the matter with you?

(JACK returns to the bus stop. ANNE exits.)

ROB: What's the matter with you?

SARA: What's the matter with you?

ROB: What's the matter with you?

SARA: Stop. Stop it. Stop asking me things. Stop stop stop.

ROB: Did I miss something?

SARA: Koko saw a hurt horse and told her trainer the horse was sad. She made the sign for crying. Inside. Gorillas have and recognize emotions. Horses feel pain. I killed an animal who knew it was afraid.

ROB: I killed a squirrel once.

SARA: I never killed anything before. *(Beat.)* Did you bury it?

ROB: It's being taken care of.

SARA: Why did it run out? Why then?

(ROB and SARA exit slowly as the next scene begins.)

SCENE FOUR

A bus, Belgrade. JACK and BRIAN are still seated at a bus stop.

BRIAN: That was surreal.

JACK: What did you expect?

BRIAN: I have no expectations. It's what keeps me happy. But. That was strange. Stranger than I expected. I mean. Not that I was expecting...you know what I mean.

JACK: No.

BRIAN: There's something cruel and dreamy about those people.

JACK: Everyone has the right to make a dime.

BRIAN: What are you being so defensive about?

JACK: Because the second there's a language barrier, we make it into some quaintness of the natives. It's an imperialist mentality. There's weirder shit half a block from home in Chicago.

BRIAN: She holds her breath for a living. On a scale of one to weird that's setting off the red lights with all the bells and whistles. What's this with Eva?

JACK: We lost touch.

BRIAN: Is that why we're here? Is that why you brought me here?

JACK: Eva? No. But, I'm here. I should ask. I should look her up.

BRIAN: Of course, you should. Anything else would be rude. Easy as finding a phone book. But, if this is why we came, then be straight with me. It's too cold to mess around.

JACK: No. You piss me off. You think there's no sense of irony outside of America? No eccentricity? You don't think the Serbians find her weird, too? It's not like she's their national mascot.

BRIAN: What's your point? I thought it was weird. I think you're weird for bringing me there. It's a weird way to introduce someone to a new culture. No coffee. No tea. No pastries or vodka. Just the chipmunk cheeks and the red face.

JACK: People have their reasons.

BRIAN: Get off it already, Johnny. What are we standing here for?

JACK: You have something against public transportation? Those girls were forcibly expelled from their house after watching both their parents get shot point blank in the living room. They had to walk fifteen miles to a UN safe zone in the middle of January. The little one, the one who holds her breath—she was tired from all the walking and fell into a ditch full of rainwater or wash-off from the thaw in the spring. She nearly drowned. In the million and one oddities of war, it just so happened she was particularly skilled at holding her breath.

BRIAN: Okay. Fair enough. Kind of low of you. A bit emotionally manipulative. But fair enough.

JACK: Fair enough? Fair enough! Glib. That is so glib.

BRIAN: Enough with the bleeding heart! We all have sad stories. You want to start quantifying them? Let's start polling people. We can create a social litmus test of fear, woe, dread, and anxiety. Probably best if we start with perfect strangers so we can maximize their discomfort and our own. Cause I'm sure that's what everyone here wants to be thinking about. The freaking past. What the hell kind of vacation is this?

JACK: I hope nothing happened to her. That's all. If something happened to her…

BRIAN: Who? That girl? Of course something happened to her. You just told me. It's a miserable story.

JACK: No. Eva.

BRIAN: Oh. What would have happened to Eva? Someone would have called you.

JACK: I suppose.

BRIAN: Sent you an email. Or something.

JACK: Sure.

BRIAN: Then what are you worried about?

JACK: I didn't leave under very good circumstances. How was Nepal?

BRIAN: It was good. It was cold. Lots of yaks. Don't change the subject.

JACK: What do you think about humanitarian work?

BRIAN: I don't. Where we gonna stay?

JACK: You should think about aid work. You'd be good at it.

BRIAN: Then why aren't you doing it? What does this have to do with anything?

JACK: Nothing. Never mind. Sheraton. Sheraton's easy.

BRIAN: Good, when we check in we'll look Eva up in the phone book.

JACK: Not going to be listed.

BRIAN: Negative. Why so negative?

JACK: Cause there's no way she still lives here. Who do you miss most from home?

BRIAN: Mom.

JACK: Other than Mom.

BRIAN: I don't think about it much. Maybe Father Quinn.

JACK: Other than old people.

BRIAN: I don't think about it much. Were you lovers? You and Eva?

JACK: Lovers. What a pretentious word. No offense. It sounds ridiculous.

BRIAN: Then come up with a better one.

JACK: It's okay. You don't have to tell me.

BRIAN: Tell you what? I asked the question.

JACK: About home. Who you miss from home? I miss Brad the most. For the record. What about Africa? What did you think about Africa?

BRIAN: Is this whole trip going to be like this? I thought we were here to spend some time together. You're making me feel like I'm a nice excuse for looking up your old girlfriend.

JACK: She was never my girlfriend.

BRIAN: That's beside the point.

JACK: Of course it's not. It's exactly the point. *(Beat.)* I ran into Cassie in New York.

BRIAN: You what?

JACK: I ran into Cassie. In New York.

BRIAN: Really.

JACK: She was passing through town.

BRIAN: How was she?

JACK: Good. We had dinner.

BRIAN: Where'd you take her?

JACK: Vietnamese.

BRIAN: French?

JACK: Viet-nah-mese. How do you get French from that?

BRIAN: Oh. I get French from that. *(Beat.)* How did she look?

JACK: Good. Thin. She looked thin. A little too thin.

BRIAN: What was she doing in town? Visiting? Visiting you?

JACK: She had a layover.

BRIAN: Right. A *lay*-over.

JACK: What is the matter with you?

BRIAN: See. See? You. It's like peeling an onion dealing with you.

JACK: You think something happened? Nothing happened.

BRIAN: Except for you leaving your wife.

JACK: They're not even related subjects.

BRIAN: Now we have to do a parade of all your ex-lovers? You had to bring me to the heart of Eastern European darkness for this? A few stiff drinks at Heathrow would have been a lot cheaper.

JACK: All my ex-lovers?

BRIAN: Now that you're single.

JACK: I'm not single. And Cassie and I never nothing, for the record. She lives in Africa.

BRIAN: And?

JACK: It's Africa.

BRIAN: You're going to Africa. I'm alive with admiration.

JACK: Up yours. I'm trying to give you a little friendly advice about what you should do with your life, in not so many terms, and you won't remove your head from your ass long enough to hear any of it. *(JACK leaves.)*

BRIAN: You can't leave me. I don't speak Serbo-Bonsai-Croatian—whatever the hell they speak here. You'll break the guest-host relation and the gods will rein fury on you.

(JACK stops.)

BRIAN: See. I know you think that's funny. Let's go find Cassie.

JACK: You mean Eva?

BRIAN: Right. Who's Cassie? Who's on second? What is this all about? I'm having culture shock. Let's go get a drink. *(Beat.)* Let's go get a Coke. Let's go check into the hotel and get a Coke. They do have Coke in the Eastern bloc, don't they? See. I know you think that's funny, too.

Scene Five

Many places simultaneously. HAL enters. Sits. ROB is in his bathrobe, poring over his notebooks.

HAL: *(In a half-reverie, a wished-for conversation.)* I think a lot about the past these days. About chance. About how a second or two can mean nothing, or how it can change everything. How holding a stare can be the most terrifying split-second decision you might ever make. I felt both so nervous and brave the first time I looked at you. There's nothing much poetic about me, about my life. But that one moment. *(Nods off in his chair.)*

(ANNE enters. She is at the side of the road looking at the deer.)

ANNE: Oh, god. Poor thing. Where's your mommy? *(Starts crying and slides into a memory of hers.)*

(JACK enters. ANNE sees him and looks weary, nauseated.)

JACK: I'm going for a walk.

ANNE: Okay.

JACK: *(Turns and sees her.)* What's the matter? What is it? What's the matter?

ANNE: I think I'm pregnant again.

JACK: Are these good tears or bad tears?

ANNE: Both. I'm scared. I'm excited. I'm scared of being excited.

JACK: This is a good thing. Annie. This is a wonderful thing.

(JACK fades offstage. ANNE begins to shovel dirt.)

ROB: I talk too much. It's the by-product of being horribly inarticulate. Everything's tangential. A web of neurons firing like mad, my tongue trying to make sense of it all before something gets lost. Right now I'm thinking of the second theory of thermodynamics, how it smells like lemons in this general vicinity, how I feel warm, how I may be blushing or feverish, but that every second we're spinning slower and slower and one day we may come to a dead standstill in our rotation around the sun. How cold it will be if we're on the wrong side of the earth, how horrible the perpetual light would be if we're stuck on the sunny side. I'm also thinking about Coke bottles. Not cans. Not the plastic two-liter bottles. But the old-fashioned ten-ounce glass bottles, the blue-green of the glass, how the bottles remind me of summer, how I get nostalgic for the desire to share a vanilla Coke with someone at a diner. Which is weird, cause I don't think I've ever done that. *(Continues to pore over his notebooks until the end of the scene.)*

(CHARLIE enters.)

CHARLIE: You always hang out by the side of the road in the middle of the night?

ANNE: You scared the crap out of me.

CHARLIE: Sorry. I saw you and pulled over.

ANNE: Rob's dipshit girlfriend hit a deer. Just a fawn. He came back to the house for a shovel, then couldn't remember where they hit it. I don't know what I'm gonna do with that kid.

CHARLIE: *(Pulling a can from his coat.)* Wanna beer?

ANNE: Please.

CHARLIE: Com'ere. You got some dirt smudged on your face.

ANNE: For crying out loud.

CHARLIE: Rob's okay. He's an okay guy.

ANNE: People laugh at him. He's doomed to become an eccentric.

(ANNE and CHARLIE look up at the sky.)

CHARLIE: You see it yet?

ANNE: No.

CHARLIE: Keep looking. Don't blink.

ANNE: I'm not blinking.

CHARLIE: You can't blink. Or it won't happen.

ANNE: Stop telling me what to do. I know how to do this.

CHARLIE: Then stop blinking.

ANNE: I'm not. *(Gasp.)*

CHARLIE: Yeah?

ANNE: Three dimensional.

CHARLIE: Best feeling in the world. You can feel the universe wrapping around you in every direction.

ANNE: God, I miss it here.

CHARLIE: I wish you hadn't left like you did.

ANNE: You had a little something to do with that, Charlie.

CHARLIE: I know. I don't know what the hell I was thinking.

ANNE: The hell you don't. Worth it?

CHARLIE: Sleeping with her?

ANNE: Yeah.

CHARLIE: No. Not the sleeping with her part. That was just sex. I didn't know anything else was out there.

ANNE: Me neither.

CHARLIE: So in a way it was really good. It was a good thing.

ANNE: As far as ass-kicking life-altering events go.

CHARLIE: This way you didn't get stuck here letting your armpit hair grow and making your own soap from scratch.

ANNE: How long did you travel with her?

CHARLIE: Three years, all told. But only a few months with Gretchen. She was a total pain in the ass. You know, all told.

ANNE: I'm afraid to leave the apartment these days.

CHARLIE: Afraid? That doesn't sound right.

ANNE: Why'd you come back? Here. Why back here?

CHARLIE: My dad. He was sick.

ANNE: I didn't know that.

CHARLIE: Yeah. I didn't make it back in time.

ANNE: That's horrible.

CHARLIE: Yeah. It's pretty horrible. All told.

ANNE: Rob puked on me at my mom's funeral. If that makes you fell any better.

CHARLIE: No, that doesn't make me feel any better. That makes me feel bad. Jesus, Anne.

ANNE: Wanna adopt a kid with me?

CHARLIE: I don't know, I was thinking maybe we should go on a date first. Or something.

ANNE: I was trying to be funny.

CHARLIE: I know. I wasn't.

ACT THREE
SCENE ONE

A café, Belgrade. BYRNES's living room, simultaneously.

JACK: I wanted to be a pilot. When I was a kid.

BRIAN: What?

JACK: When I was a kid. You asked earlier.

BRIAN: I didn't ask you. You asked me.

JACK: I wanted to be an astronaut. Chuck Yeager. Yeager was never an astronaut. I don't think I knew that when I was a kid. Maybe I did. I wasn't stupid. Maybe the outer space part wasn't what appealed to me. Maybe it was Yeager. The Yeagerness of Yeager. The respect without all the attention. The under the radar admiration. The skill. The daring. The dedication. He broke the sound barrier for Cripesake. Annie hates flying. A plane crashed in her backyard when she was a kid. A Cessna. Two people died, and her family's dog caught fire. They had to put it to sleep.

BRIAN: That's a horrible story. Don't you have any good stories at all?

JACK: By good, you mean happy?

BRIAN: I mean good. I mean stories that make you feel good. Listen. Stuff you never dream could happen, happens. I'm hiking with a team. Seven of us. Been in the rainforest about nine days, and it's strange because the light—your perception of the light—is completely altered by that point. You've been absent the higher frequencies and get tuned into this very, very vivid scheme that exists only in the near dark. Our guide was in tune with the light just like we were, but he had a far more sophisticated ability, no, um, *adeptness* with sound and vibrations. He could hear things at impossibly low frequencies. Thunder from miles away when we couldn't hear anything at all. Movement. Trees. Sliding. Chirping. Calls. Everything.

(SARA enters in sleeping clothes.)

SARA: Wassumatter? What're you doing up?

ROB: Unsettled. Skeebed out. I can't flick off this dream. I'm standing there naked and these shrunken women—

SARA: Like Pygmies?

ROB: Like, but not. I don't believe there are any Pygmies in the Amazon, though there are many explicably and inexplicably short people. These women were indigenous. And they were painting me.

SARA: You were being painted by short women?

ROB: Not short. Miniature. Waist high. They're painting me in different shades of red and brown and green. Wait. In the light it all looked brown. But when they made me drink their tea—

SARA: They made you? Like forced you?

ROB: No, they offered. But in that way that made me feel, like, god they're so poor, this is all they have, it would be rude to not take their tea.

SARA: You drank it?

ROB: And I felt supple. And they seemed even smaller than before. And they had this high-pitched giggle cackle. But had jingling bells at the end of every laugh.

SARA: You're not supposed to take candy from strangers. Any five-year-old knows that.

ROB: Then they painted me! Well. They ripped off my clothes, and then they painted me.

SARA: Did they paint your (ahem)...?

ROB: Oh yes.

BRIAN: So nine days in, you've let go of your Western proprieties. It's easier to cop a squat, if you catch my drift. You start to relax into the moisture, cause you're constantly wet. We were trucking along rhythmically, quietly—

JACK: Copping squats.

BRIAN: Copping squats when necessary. Seriously, that much walking is meditative. Suddenly our guide stops dead in his tracks, every muscle taut and slowly a look of horror washes over him. He starts this incantation, and the prick anthropologist traveling with us starts translating, "the bells the bells the bells." And it's freaking out the Southern girl who'd never been in the field before, she starts crying, she's apparently a bell-o-phobe. And the guide stops the incantation and shimmies up a tree. I'm standing there like a fool wondering what the hell's the matter.

ROB: But when we were in the forest I wasn't brown. I was green and red and orange and okra.

SARA: Like a shag carpet.

(ANNE enters with the shovel.)

ROB: They made me march for three days. Occasionally pricking me with small needles or stabbing me with very small daggers in the back of my calves.

(ANNE hands the shovel to ROB.)

ANNE: All done. *(Exits.)*

SARA: What were the little women going to do to you?

ROB: Eat me. Naturally.

SARA: That's unenlightened of you to presume that.

ROB: They filed their teeth, Sara.

BRIAN: Then I started to hear it, this very creepy fairy-tale kind of laugh. And the brush in front of us shook.

ROB: We hit a clearing.

BRIAN: Out of the brush, comes this group of Pygmies.

JACK: There aren't any Pygmies in South America.

BRIAN: They were short, and they had me with them.

ROB: In the middle of the clearing, I'm standing there looking at myself.

BRIAN: Only I was naked and painted brown.

ROB: Only I had on teevas and cammo shorts.

JACK: What did you do?

BRIAN: I freaked out and climbed up the tree with the guide.

ROB: This very nice girl from Tupelo took my hand and the miniature women ran away.

SARA: Tupelo?

JACK: You had to get out of that tree eventually?

BRIAN: Turns out the guy I saw just looked a lot like me. Some geologist who'd gotten lost. He was all drugged up from this tea he'd been drinking. Charlotte helped him out. Brilliant guy, little too brilliant. They took off together when we hit civilization. Went to Bolivia. Or Ecuador. Can't remember.

SARA: Why Tupelo?

JACK: Charlotte?

BRIAN: The girl from Tupelo. The Southern one afraid of bells. Beside the point. Point is I thought I saw myself. In the jungle. I ran into a man who looked exactly like me. In the jungle. Where there are no white men. Okay? What are the chances?

(SARA exits.)

JACK: You ever met Rob? Anne's brother Rob?

BRIAN: Nah. He wasn't at your wedding.

JACK: Right. You know, I do. I do have one of those stories. I met my wife in a dream. How about that?

(JACK sees DRAGO reading a paper. JACK goes over to him.)

JACK: <Excuse me. Is your name Drago? You're Drago. Do you remember me? We met a long time ago. During the war. I met you through a friend of mine. Eva? Eva Obrovnich? You lived near her. Do you not remember who I'm talking about? Do you remember me? No? I know you. You have three cats. A fat one. A skinny one. One with a lazy eye.>

DRAGO: <I have no cat. Not since...>

JACK: <You see, you do remember.> *(Beat.)* Omigod. I just remembered something.

(Blackout.)

Scene Two

BYRNES's house, Vermont.

ROB: You're getting home late.

ANNE: I had trouble finding the deer.

ROB: Nicole called. She saw your car and Charlie's truck pulled over off West Hill Road. Claire went ballistic.

ANNE: For crying out loud. I can't talk to an old friend?

ROB: He's not an old friend.

ANNE: You're remarkably lucid.

ROB: You don't have to be mean to me, just because I'm right. Charlie's a jerk.

ANNE: You all are so freaking nosy.

ROB: You're playing with fire.

(ANNE listens, then exits, only to reenter seconds later.)

ANNE: I'm angry at you. Do you know that?

ROB: Because you had to bury my girlfriend's dead deer? Or because I chastened you?

ANNE: Chastened? That is the most offensive word you could have chosen.

ROB: Good. Then it was effective.

ANNE: You think I'm selfish.

ROB: You are. You're a brat.

ANNE: Who buried your girlfriend's dead deer?

ROB: Generosity doesn't negate selfishness.

ANNE: Have you been reading your notebooks again?

ROB: What notebooks?

ANNE: Never mind. No notebooks. We had a phone conversation. Do you remember?

ROB: We've had several phone conversations.

ANNE: About adopting. The one about me adopting a child from China.

ROB: I remember.

ANNE: Jack and I have tried and tried and tried and I cannot try anymore. My body can't handle all this *trying*. Do you understand that?

ROB: I stand by what I said. There are kids here. In the States.

ANNE: There are also mothers here in the States. And if they want their babies back they can have them. Anytime. Jack and I—well, you know all about what's going on between Jack and me. But it doesn't change how much I want…

ROB: Say it.

ANNE: How much I want a baby.

ROB: How are you going to get China to pick a baby up? You'll have to swim.

ANNE: Fly.

ROB: That's what I said.

ANNE: Of course I'll have to fly. As much as I don't want to.

ROB: I don't think that's selfish. For the record. But I don't think it's totally right, either.

ANNE: Of course, it's not totally right.

SCENE THREE

A street, Belgrade. JACK enters and begins feverishly knocking on doors and screaming up at windows.

BRIAN: What the hell are you doing? Bro. What is this? You can't go banging on people's doors. It's late. Stop. Stop this. It reeks of desperation.

JACK: What did you want? When you were ten what did you want to be when you grew up?

BRIAN: Dad.

JACK: I shouldn't have brought you here.

BRIAN: I wanted to come.

JACK: This is not what I wanted it to be like.

BRIAN: What? Normal?

JACK: Yeah. Normal.

BRIAN: Seems to me you're going to be seeing all sorts of un-normal shit in about a week. When you hit Niger—

JACK: That's the problem, Brian. It is normal. For the people who live it, it's normal. I need to find Eva.

BRIAN: Why?

JACK: Haven't you ever just *needed* something? I can't tell you why. She. I thought it was incomprehensible. She. When Katie died, who did you talk to? Who was the first person?

BRIAN: Cassandra. Cassie. Immediately. Within the hour.

JACK: What did you tell her?

BRIAN: Nothing. And then everything. All at once. Even the ugly shit. The bloating and the missing teeth and her left eye. Everything. What does this have to do with Kate?

JACK: I never told Anne. I'm sure Mom did. But. It's not the same. Obviously.

BRIAN: That was stupid of you.

JACK: I mean. I told her. Eventually. When she asked. But. It's melodramatic and cheap after a certain point. It's not like I could just bring it up over breakfast could I?

BRIAN: You could have tried.

JACK: Cassie, huh. You don't think you told her just as an excuse?

BRIAN: An excuse?

JACK: To be close to her. To have her comfort you.

BRIAN: Fuck you.

JACK: It was only a question. Let's go. Let's get out here.

BRIAN: What are you, some kind of martyr? You think you're the only one making three two was tough for? What's the matter with you?

JACK: Cassie's in Africa.

BRIAN: You already told me that. Several times. Don't try to change the subject.

JACK: How are they separate? None of it's separate, you tool.

BRIAN: Tool? You're banging on people's doors, shouting in a foreign language in the dead of night, and I'm the idiot? You raving lunatic. All you're missing is froth in the corners of your mouth.

JACK: Aw. That's witty. You're a regular Larry David.

(BRIAN punches him.)

JACK: What the fuck? What the fuck was that? You jealous? Jealous I know where Cassie is? Look at you. Only person stupider than me for coming here is you for following me. You always gotta follow me? Can't think for yourself? Always got to follow your older brother around?

(Ugly brother fight. BRIAN prevails.)

BRIAN: You can't change the past to make it some vision of who you think you are. Bang on as many doors as you want.

JACK: You through?

BRIAN: No. I looked up to you. I look up to you. What's the problem with that?

JACK: There's no problem.

(They sit.)

BRIAN: Tell me about Cassie. Tell me about you and Cassie.

(CASSIE enters.)

JACK: I never pressed her back up against a tree. I never took her down to the lake. I never stayed up talking to her 'til morning. Man. That was you. Fools.

BRIAN: She told you about that?

JACK: Listen, I got my own problems, I don't need to make shit up.

BRIAN: How did she look?

JACK: I told you. Thin. Tired. Beautiful. But tired. It's not an easy thing she's doing. Aid work is hard. It's thankless.

BRIAN: Where in Africa is she?

JACK: Nairobi.

BRIAN: Shit. I don't speak Nairobian.

JACK: Brian.

BRIAN: Joke. Joking. How's the nose?

JACK: I do. Brian. I do have good stories, too. They're not all miserable.

(JACK exits. BRIAN lingers for a moment in half light.)

CASSIE: The point is, I have to finish this letter. Because this time I bought the stamps. Also in the interest of full disclosure, I should tell you I had something odd happen to me. I wasn't only home. I was in New York before I came to London. I had a layover. Strangely, incongruously, I walked past a bench in the park your brother was sitting on. Stupidly, I thought he was still in the Balkans though that was years ago. I had to walk by him three times and watch him for ten minutes from fifteen feet away before I decided it was, in fact, him. For some reason, I thought time had stopped and only I was moving forward, away from childhood. But there he was, living proof life goes on. He looked old. His voice was nothing like I remember it.

(BRIAN and CASSIE exit separately.)

SCENE FOUR

BYRNES's house.

ANNE: Hey. Missy. I have a bone to pick with you.

SARA: Why don't you like me?

ANNE: No. Wait. This is my bone to pick. Do you know that leaving the sponge in the sink does nothing but help the fungus and bacteria multiply? Like filth?

SARA: We didn't learn us about the cleaning in the trailer park.

ANNE: That would be funny if it didn't ring painfully true.

SARA: What is your problem? Why don't you like me?

ANNE: First, my default is not set to "like." By nature, I don't "like" many things. Second, I'm not obligated to like you. Or be nice to you. Or treat you with any sort of special behavior. Girlfriends come and go, Sara. You're a temporary fixture. And I was raised in a town with stone walls.

SARA: Have you been rehearsing that?

ANNE: No.

SARA: Because it sounded rehearsed.

ANNE: Sara, what are you hiding?

SARA: I'm not hiding anything.

ANNE: I'm bigger and meaner than you. What are you hiding?

SARA: Nothing. It's a notebook.

ANNE: Are you a scientist?

SARA: No.

ANNE: Then I can't imagine why Rob's notebooks would be of any interest to you.

SARA: You're not a journalist. You've never read your husband's articles?

ANNE: That's not the same. Jack is my husband. I can't just throw him away when I'm done being interested in him.

SARA: I'm not doing that. I'm not gonna do that.

ANNE: We'll see.

SARA: Listen, I know you're Rob's sister and everything, and I can be civil to you if it makes him happy. But I sure don't need your good opinion. Okay? *(Under her breath.)* Hypocrite.

ANNE: What?

SARA: You're a hypocrite. Pulled over by the side of the road with Charlie.

ANNE: Charlie's an old friend.

SARA: Please. Even I know who Charlie is.

ANNE: Parking with Charlie. Now that would have been a nice evening. *(Beat.)* I was burying your dead deer.

SARA: Oh.

ANNE: The ground was frozen.

SARA: Was it?

ANNE: Yes.

SARA: I'm sorry you had to do that. Thank you. *(Starts to recede, moving to exit.)*

ANNE: Do you understand any of what you're reading?

SARA: No.

ANNE: Rob was very smart. And very talented.

SARA: He still is.

ANNE: Why Rob? And why Vermont? Why not Maine or Ontario or Pennsylvania?

SARA: Because this is where my car broke down.

(ROB enters.)

SARA: Whattaya got there?

ROB: Fossils.

SARA: Fossils? From where?

ROB: Backyard.

SARA: How do you know they're fossils?

ROB: Instinct.

(BRIAN and JACK enter. They are in their hotel room. LOTTE enters.)

BRIAN: You want to find Eva? *(Picks up the phone.)* Hi, this is Room 427. I'm looking for a local number for a woman named Eva Obrovnik. *(To JACK.)* How do you spell her last name?

JACK: O-brov-with a v-N.I.K.

BRIAN: *(Into the phone, overlapping JACK.)* O-brov-nik. Will you be so kind as to connect me? Thank you. *(To JACK.)* Did you not even bother to ask anyone?

JACK: I asked.

BRIAN: Did not.

JACK: You're right. I didn't.

BRIAN: And I'm the tool?…Hi, this is Brian Kavanagh. May I speak with Eva, please? Eva! Hi, this is Brian, I'm sorry you don't know me from Adam. I'm Jack Kavanagh's little brother. You remember Jack, I hope.

ROB: I found them. In the backyard.

ANNE: They're fossils, eh?

ROB: Yes. Fossils.

ANNE: Of?

ROB: Dinosaurs. Little ones.

BRIAN: No, no. Jack is fine. Completely healthy, a bit jet-lagged and passed out at the moment…I was calling because we're in Belgrade, and I know he was hoping to see you while we're here.

ANNE: Have you been reading your journals again?

ROB: I have journals?

ANNE: Yes. In the attic.

ROB: I didn't know that. I found some notebooks.

ANNE: They're the same thing.

ROB: Don't speak to me like I'm stupid. I'm not stupid. I have a condition.

ANNE: How do you know they're dinosaurs?

ROB: They're not, actually. They're caryophyllids. They're very rare. I'm surprised we had them in the backyard.

ANNE: Did you bury them there?

ROB: No. Stop talking to me like I'm stupid.

ANNE: Did you take them from your boxes upstairs and bury them so you could find them? Is that what you did?

ROB: Why would I do that?

BRIAN: Wonderful. I can't wait to meet you. Jack is going to be thrilled. Goodbye, Eva. *(BRIAN hangs up.)* Tomorrow, eleven. Tea for three.

ANNE: Rob. You found fossils the last time I was visiting. We put them in a box. Upstairs.

ROB: We should check the box.

ANNE: No. Rob. Just enjoy your fossils. Look. You found caryflids.

ROB: Caryophyllids. They're prehistoric carnations. See.

(ANNE, BRIAN, and JACK exit. LOTTE stands in front of ROB. He does not see her.)

ACT FOUR
SCENE ONE

HAL: *(On phone.)* Mom? I don't know what I'm doing here. Charlotte left me this morning. And the baby's crying…No she left. She up and left. We didn't have a fight or anything. She took the keys and my wallet and walked right out the door…No! We did not fight. I really don't think I did anything…Please. I feel like I got hit by a truck right in my chest…Can you please, please can you, can you please come over and watch Evie? Can I please borrow your car?…Thank you Mom. Thank you…I love you, too.

ANNE: I don't want to. I don't want to fly.

(JACK enters.)

JACK: But it's Prague.

ANNE: I know. I can't fly.

JACK: Paris. Amsterdam. Rome. Venice. Berlin. Vienna. Zagreb. Athens. Edinburgh. We could go the other way, too. Honk Kong. Beijing. Tokyo. Djakarta. Singapore. Mumbai.

ANNE: It terrifies me. A plane crashed. A Cessna. In my backyard. I was eleven, Danny was a little older, but we were the only two home. It was horrendous. Please. Let's drive. I've never been to the Rockies or Newfoundland or Mexico—

JACK: Or New Zealand. Or New Guinea. Or Argentina. Zimbabwe. Morocco. There's so much I want to show you.

ANNE: I'm sorry.

JACK: You could take some Valium.

ANNE: The pilot was impaled on my swing set. The one my dad built.

JACK: Of the Cessna?

ANNE: Yes.

JACK: Fair enough.

ANNE: Please don't make me feel guilty about this.

JACK: No. Fair enough. Let's at least drive in style. *(Exits.)*

(ROB reenters with an empty shoebox. ANNE is still onstage.)

ROB: It's empty.

ANNE: Maybe you should read your notebooks? Claire! Get in here.

ROB: I already read them. I want to know why it's empty.

ANNE: I don't know. Maybe so you won't forget again. Or so you won't forget forever.

ROB: I'm confused.

ANNE: It's confusing.

(CLAIRE enters.)

CLAIRE: What is it?

ANNE: He found fossils in the backyard again.

ROB: Again?

CLAIRE: Okay, do you want me to explain it to you or do you want to figure it out yourself?

ROB: Both.

CLAIRE: One or the other.

ROB: Tell me.

ANNE: You don't remember everything. And what you do remember changes.

ROB: That's the same for everyone.

CLAIRE: But for you it's more extreme.

ROB: I have Alzheimer's?

ANNE: No. You have a little brain damage. That's all.

ROB: I'm brain damaged?

ANNE: Only a little.

ROB: Don't laugh.

CLAIRE: Don't laugh, Anne. It takes longer if you laugh.

ROB: Longer? How many times have I done this?

ANNE: I'm sorry. It's only that you're always very surprised to hear this.

ROB: You've told me this before? Why should I trust your memory? What if you're brain damaged, too?

CLAIRE: I guess that's a risk you've got to take. Listen. Those are your fossils. You did find them. But you found them when you were in South America on an archeological dig between your junior and senior year of college.

ROB: I was in South America. I drank tea.

ANNE: I don't know about the tea, but yes, you spent some time down there.

ROB: I was an archeologist. Like Harrison Ford.

CLAIRE: Indiana Jones. No. You weren't. You did, like, an internship.

ANNE: You studied geology.

CLAIRE: Weather patterns.

ANNE: And storm systems.

CLAIRE: Rob. You wanted to be a weatherman.

ROB: No, I didn't.

ANNE: Well, not on television. Not like that. A cool weatherman.

ROB: I was a storm chaser.

CLAIRE: Yes. Are you happy? With what you do now? With Sara? With the cars and the car shop and everything?

ROB: I sure am.

ANNE: Then do you really need to know all this?

ROB: Please.

CLAIRE: You had an accident. Do you remember?

ROB: Is this the first time you told me this part? Cause I know I had an accident. I fell in a volcano.

ANNE: No, you didn't. You were struck by lightning.

ROB: I was struck by lightning?

ANNE: It's not funny.

ROB: How would you know? You ever been struck by lightning?

ANNE: No, I haven't. You're right. It was not funny for *us*. For me and Dan and Claire and Mom. And especially not for your poor—well, never mind.

ROB: My poor what?

CLAIRE: Anne.

ANNE: No one. Nothing.

ROB: I had a No One?

ANNE: Never mind. It's irrelevant.

ROB: I remember being struck by lightning. I was going to the jeep.

CLAIRE: Yes.

ROB: Did you tell me this before?

CLAIRE: Yes.

ROB: Did you tell me the part about the jeep?

CLAIRE: Yes.

ROB: The jeep was yellow.

CLAIRE: It was.

ROB: Did you tell me that too? Or do I remember that part?

CLAIRE: I don't know.

ANNE: Maybe you remember a memory.

ROB: I was at a volcano, though, too, when it erupted.

ANNE: No. That was on television.

ROB: Mount Pinatubo.

CLAIRE: No. You saw it on television.

ROB: Why do I remember it?

ANNE: I don't know.

ROB: I had a girlfriend. Her name was Charlotte.

CLAIRE: No.

ANNE: Yes.

CLAIRE: Anne.

ROB: Why don't you want me to know that part?

CLAIRE: It's complicated, Rob. She never got it.

ROB: What didn't she get?

CLAIRE: Nothing, Rob. Nothing.

ROB: Sara knows a Charlotte.

CLAIRE: So do I. The point is maybe you buried these fossils so that you would find them. So you would remember them.

ROB: And I did. I did remember them.

ANNE: But you're only remembering a story you were told, Rob.

CLAIRE: You can't just make stuff up and believe it's the truth.

ROB: Of course, I can. Everyone else does.

SCENE TWO

EVA's flat, Belgrade. EVA is showing JACK and BRIAN a picture.

EVA: This is my daughter. This is Katya.

BRIAN: Eva, I'm sorry to interrupt. Can I use your bathroom?

EVA: Yes, of course. The toilet is through there.

(BRIAN exits.)

JACK: She looks very much like you. Very beautiful.

EVA: Thank you. I think she favors Pieter.

JACK: Her father?

EVA: Yes.

JACK: Did I know him?

EVA: No. We met in Macedonia after I left Pristina.

JACK: He's Macedonian?

EVA: No. Of course not. He's Danish. He was an aid worker. He was helping with the refugees. You and your brother—

JACK: Yeah?

EVA: You don't look very much alike.

JACK: I know. *(Beat.)* This is where you live?

EVA: This is where I live. And work.

JACK: It's quiet.

EVA: Yes.

JACK: What is it you do now?

EVA: Same as always. I translate.

JACK: Are you enjoying translating?

EVA: Of course. It appeals to my sense of order.

JACK: How frequently are you at the Hague?

EVA: The Hague? In Holland? Never. I don't, I don't do political work. Not anymore.

JACK: I thought you'd want to be there. During the trials.

EVA: No. The trials? Milosevic is a madman, verdict in, trial over. I don't have to travel to the Hague to know that. No. I translate for science and technology firms. Freelance. The pay is far superior. And teaching? You teach? School is over?

JACK: No. Sabbatical.

EVA: Sabbata? What? Like Shabbat?

JACK: No. Well, actually, a little. It's a sabbatical. A rest. Like a leave of absence. But they pay you.

EVA: For what reason?

JACK: Field work. Reuters. Africa.

EVA: Africa. To where? Congo? South Africa? Niger? Liberia? Rwanda? War or famine or AIDS?

JACK: Chad. Sudan.

EVA: Oh. Sudan. Yes. Don't get yourself killed. You know. I only just read this week about private donations in Malawi—

JACK: —right. Saving the country from a famine.

EVA: Makes you think. *(Beat.)* You like teaching?

JACK: Too much talking.

EVA: But you love to talk. You must be a fine instructor. The girls must find you very sexy. Debonair.

JACK: Some of the boys, too. You're happy?

EVA: Yes, very. *(Beat.)* Sorry. Do you mean in general or to see you?

JACK: Both.

EVA: Yes, both. I'm happy for both.

JACK: I didn't expect you to be.

EVA: That's silly.

JACK: It's a habit.

EVA: A bad one. When, really, was I ever unhappy?

JACK: The entire time I knew you.

EVA: Is that what you think? That's ridiculous.

JACK: You weren't happy.

EVA: Of course I was.

JACK: You cried—

EVA: —myself to sleep. Every night. Yes, of course I did. But I don't think about that. It was a war, John, let it be. And what is happiness that we should pursue it to insane lengths when it is out of reach? It would have been absurd for me to have been joyful or satisfied or content or anything of the sort during that time.

JACK: I came here to apologize, Eva. I am deeply sorry for everything I did.

EVA: For what? For behaving like everyone else? For not being able to control forces no one has any power over? It was war, John. It was war.

JACK: No one quite wants to remember.

EVA: I don't think that to be true.

JACK: No?

EVA: Of course, people want to remember. But memory is imperfect. It's driven by what we don't even know we want.

JACK: I suppose it is.

EVA: And who cares to remember feeling miserable?

JACK: You're right.

EVA: This is a surprise?

JACK: It...

EVA: What?

JACK: It makes what I do redundant.

EVA: No. It makes what you do necessary. You write it down. Sometimes you are obnoxious, and you remind people what they actually said.

JACK: Obnoxious?

EVA: Yes. It can be obnoxious.

(BRIAN reenters.)

BRIAN: And self-righteous.

EVA: You see? This is your, what is it called? Your track record. You will stay for lunch? Katya is coming with Pieter.

BRIAN: Depends on your cooking, Eva.

EVA: My cooking? What about your cooking, Brian?

BRIAN: I'm an excellent cook. I'd be happy to cook for you.

JACK: I'm sorry, Eva. *(Lying.)* We have a train. At noon.

EVA: You have a train!

BRIAN: At noon?

EVA: Take another one.

JACK: I can't. I have a meeting. In Pristina. It was very difficult to schedule.

EVA: In Pristina?

JACK: It's very late already.

EVA: Let me call you a car. *(Exits to get a phone.)*

BRIAN: A train?

JACK: I can't meet the kid. The husband maybe, but not—

BRIAN: Meet them. That's what you do. You meet them.

JACK: No. I can't. Whatever I needed to be here for is over.

BRIAN: You're an asshole.

JACK: Maybe. Yeah. Maybe I am. But, this is enough.

(EVA reenters.)

EVA: Please come back after your meeting. It is impossible for my head to believe you and Pieter don't know each other.

JACK: I fly directly to Africa.

EVA: Then, we are doomed this visit. But, we will look forward to the next. Yes? Please take this. *(She offers him an umbrella.)* It might rain.

JACK: It might.

EVA: Yes.

JACK: I can't take your umbrella.

EVA: Please. The very least I can do for you.

JACK: In that case, thank you.

(He takes the umbrella.)

EVA: You're married? You didn't say. Why not? This is wonderful.

JACK: Yes, it is. Anne is. My wife is. Anne. My wife, Anne. Anne is my wife. She hates to fly. There was of course her dad. But that's neither here nor there.

EVA: No? You have children?

JACK: No. Not yet.

EVA: Someday.

(Blackout.)

Scene Three

The doorway of CHARLIE's apartment.

ANNE: Are you really…

CHARLIE: Really what?

ANNE: Sorry?

CHARLIE: For?

ANNE: What happened?

CHARLIE: The way it happened, yes.

ANNE: But not that it happened?

CHARLIE: No. You had to get out of here. I was dead weight.

ANNE: Is that what you thought then? Or, is it something you started telling yourself along the way?

CHARLIE: It's kinda obvious, Anne.

ANNE: I never thought you were dead weight.

CHARLIE: Exactly. But just because you don't think something doesn't mean it's not true. Un-bite your lip. You have nothing to wallow in.

ANNE: I'm not wallowing.

CHARLIE: You're wallowing.

ANNE: I have some serious gripes.

CHARLIE: I told you I regret the way it happened.

ANNE: But not that it happened. What the hell kind of an apology is that?

CHARLIE: A forced one. Things needed to be this way, Anne.

ANNE: No. How is my life better? It's not. It's in shambles.

CHARLIE: And whose fault is that?

ANNE: That's not fair. What I'm trying to say is that…Never mind. It's embarrassing even being here.

CHARLIE: See? I embarrass you.

ANNE: No. No you don't!

CHARLIE: Of course I do.

ANNE: No, it's because you forced my hand.

CHARLIE: Maybe I did.

ANNE: Maybe I would have left on my own, maybe we could have left together. But you made the choice, Charlie. Not me. And you didn't choose me. Okay? I'm not exactly a gracious loser. That's why I'm embarrassed. So get over yourself and your insecurities.

(Beat.)

CHARLIE: You never would have left if I didn't—

ANNE: Why is leaving home such a good thing?

CHARLIE: Look at your life. New York is good for you. It's right for you. It's the right place.

ANNE: I hate New York.

CHARLIE: The guy you married. He's an important guy.

ANNE: Only if you think those kinds of things are important.

CHARLIE: And you don't?

ANNE: No. I don't know. Maybe. But—

CHARLIE: The people you met, that you know, they're important people.

ANNE: So? You make houses light up. Rob he makes cars go. Danny, he—

CHARLIE: Your brothers are good guys. But come on. We're, none of us, overachievers.

ANNE: Don't trick yourself into thinking you did something good.

CHARLIE: I know what I know. Are you coming in or are you going to stand there like a refugee all day?

ANNE: I don't know. I didn't know you knew I was married.

CHARLIE: Of course I did.

ANNE: Why did you say that? Why did you say that if you knew I was married?

CHARLIE: Say what? Come into the house out of the cold? Cause it's freaking cold. Oil's not cheap—

ANNE: No, last night. Why would you say that?

CHARLIE: Say what?

ANNE: That you weren't kidding. About the date. That you weren't kidding.

CHARLIE: Cause I wasn't. In or out, Anne.

(ANNE steps into CHARLIE's apartment.)

Scene Four

HAL's living room, a train station in Belgrade, CASSIE's friend's flat in London, simultaneously. JACK and BRIAN are at the train station.

HAL: I worry about all sorts of things I don't tell you every day. I worry about my socks not smelling when I put them on in the morning. I worry that my deodorant is leaving toxic metals in my armpit. I worry about the tires on the car, exactly how weatherproof they are and if they've got the right amount of air in them. I worry about the water in the oil heater. If there's not enough water, no heat. If there's too much I'll flood the house. I worry that the storm windows I bought don't keep the heat in, that they won't do much of anything if there's a real storm, that Evie will just go flying out the window. I guess that's irrational. But. I worry that you haven't got a new winter coat the whole time I've known you. That you might be cold, and you're not telling me. Not a very eclectic set of worries, but there you go.

CASSIE: I wonder what has become of you. I wonder how my memory would stand up alongside the living version of you. I wonder how long it would take you to recognize me. I wonder if we would pass by each other and never know it. I wonder if we already have. These unfinished letters are a way to cut through the loneliness. To overcome Kibera which is not at all a lonely place. Is it not dissonant to feel the most alone when you are surrounded by nothing but people? This all, all of it, sounds so formal. I hate to think about you, of all people, formally. Which is to say even the thought of you makes me feel safe. We can, both of us, pinpoint the moment when it stopped being safe, when life informed us we weren't the only ones on the planet. But the time before. That was lovely. So perhaps it's not you but a confident, happy, innocent version of myself that I miss. Perhaps that's who

you are to me. Perhaps that is what this perpetual, habitual letter is all about? Perhaps.

BRIAN: Belgrade rocks. Belgrade's rocking. Absolutely the most anticlimactic experience of my young life.

JACK: I'm sorry. I don't know what I was expecting.

BRIAN: What do you think? You and me, we go to Africa together?

JACK: I don't know.

BRIAN: You're right. It's too—

JACK: Too what?

BRIAN: Corny.

JACK: How is it corny?

BRIAN: How is it not corny? We're not in our twenties anymore. I can't pick up and travel around the world with my passport and a few spare undies.

JACK: Heck no. Need your credit card, too. Let me minimize the corniness. You go. You go ahead.

BRIAN: You're the one with a real reason for going.

JACK: I have to go to Pristina.

BRIAN: I could go with—

JACK: I have to go alone. But I'll meet you in Nairobi. How about that?

BRIAN: I'd like that.

JACK: Cassie's going to like seeing you.

BRIAN: You think? Even after all this time?

JACK: I don't think. I know.

BRIAN: What—? Never mind.

JACK: Say it.

BRIAN: What's your story? The good one?

JACK: Save it for another day. Hey. You had your shots?

BRIAN: Shots?

JACK: You have to have shots. You didn't get 'em when you went to Nepal?

BRIAN: No.

JACK: It's okay. You just—

BRIAN: Nah. Never mind. Shit.

JACK: Get yourself back to London. Get the shots. And then get to Africa.

BRIAN: It's too late. I can email her or call her or something.

JACK: I'm sorry, man. I thought it was a really good idea, too.

CASSIE: I may, in fact, fold this letter neatly into the envelope, press the seal shut, and affix the smart British stamps I bought onto the right-hand corner. I could say I love you, which is probably true or maybe just an idea of what love once was. It's closer to the truth to tell you simply that I miss you, Brian, and I think about you frequently. Cassie.

SCENE FIVE

CHARLIE's apartment.

CHARLIE: How did you two meet?

ANNE: Why do you want to know?

CHARLIE: I'm curious.

ANNE: Technically, we met on a subway platform. Nothing special. I didn't come in to talk about Jack.

CHARLIE: Special enough to make you stop.

ANNE: That's beside the point. The point is that John—

CHARLIE: John?

ANNE: Jack. John. His name is John. He likes to be called Jack. And Jack is never satisfied. Not with movement. Not with stillness. Not with war. Not with peace. He's constantly looking to the next thing, as if what he has isn't enough.

CHARLIE: What is wrong with that?

ANNE: Because. His whole psychosis is motivated by the development of his own posterity. He's archiving himself for the future. Everything he says is deliberate, as if he's worried someone might quote him or worse, quote him incorrectly. He misses the present. Entirely. He believes what he's doing, this reportage bullshit, is for the greater good. Ah, the greater good. How many hearts have been broken for the greater good?

CHARLIE: But what is he doing?

ANNE: I'm not here to talk about him. How are you? How are your parents?

CHARLIE: I told you.

ANNE: Tell me again.

CHARLIE: You wanna beer?

ANNE: It's not even noon yet.

CHARLIE: And?

ANNE: I know what you're doing.

CHARLIE: What am I doing?

ANNE: I don't know.

CHARLIE: Why say you know what I'm doing if you don't? I'm not doing anything. You knocked on my door.

ANNE: I know.

CHARLIE: Please don't me tell you know what I'm doing when I'm not doing anything. Where is this guy Jack? Where is he?

ANNE: I don't know. Somewhere.

CHARLIE: I read his book. It was a good book.

ANNE: He's a hypocrite.

CHARLIE: It was a good book. I liked it.

ANNE: Stop. How is your mother?

CHARLIE: Had a stroke about a year ago. In a nursing home.

ANNE: She's awful young—

CHARLIE: Not really. I'm the youngest. You gonna have a beer?

ANNE: No.

CHARLIE: How's work?

ANNE: I don't. I don't work. Not anymore.

CHARLIE: You don't paint anymore?

ANNE: I don't want to. I don't enjoy it. It makes me miserable. I'd rather spin wool. Really. Just because you can do something doesn't mean you should. And it doesn't mean you have to.

CHARLIE: But. You—

ANNE: What? Have a gift? Is that what you were going to say?

CHARLIE: Yeah.

ANNE: See, now that's ugly. Do you know how many times I've heard that? You of all people could at least come up with something original. Gifts? Let me tell you about gifts, Charlie. People don't like gifts they're given all the time.

They return them, exchange them, leave them unused in the basement. Why am I obligated to be any different?

CHARLIE: Un-bite your lip.

ANNE: I didn't come here to argue with you.

CHARLIE: Then why did you come?

ANNE: I don't know.

CHARLIE: You pissed he left you?

ANNE: Why do you assume he left me?

CHARLIE: Because.

ANNE: Because what? Because that's what happens to me? Why do you keep bringing him up?

CHARLIE: Who? Your husband?

ANNE: What makes you think I came here to talk about him? What are you, out of your mind?

CHARLIE: I could be.

ANNE: Don't we have anything else we can talk about?

CHARLIE: Okay, but let me ask you something. I swear I'm only a little obsessed here. *(Beat.)* I want nothing more than for one person to remember me when I'm gone. Someone to validate my being here.

ANNE: Are you afraid someone won't?

CHARLIE: Yes. Some of us don't have it as easy as you, Annie. You're hardwired for making beautiful mementos of your time on earth. If, at the end of the day, someone is healthier or happier or safer, because this Jack guy you married got them help, why does it matter if he wants to be remembered for it? Un-bite your lip.

ANNE: You read the book.

CHARLIE: I'm curious.

ANNE: You're jealous.

CHARLIE: I am.

ANNE: What are you trying to prove?

CHARLIE: You were gone way before I ever left.

ANNE: I never betrayed you, not the way—

CHARLIE: What is ambivalence but betrayal? You're a mess of contradictions. You know that?

ANNE: It's mass of contradictions. For the record.

CHARLIE: You can't expect people to pity you and believe you capable in the same breath. Which is apparently what you want.

ANNE: Good point. It is. It's a good point. *(Beat.)* Did you love her?

CHARLIE: Gretchen? Yeah. But I loved you too. It wasn't easy, Anne.

(A strange humming noise.)

CHARLIE: What the hell is that?

ANNE: I don't know.

CHARLIE: It's coming from your bag.

ANNE: God. It's my phone. I forgot I even had one.

CHARLIE: Let me see. *(He opens it.)* Hello?

JACK: Hello?

CHARLIE: Hello.

JACK: Yes, hello. I think I dialed wrong.

CHARLIE: No, no. Wait.

(He hands ANNE the phone.)

ANNE: Hello?

JACK: Anne?

ANNE: Yes?

JACK: Who was that?

ANNE: Who?

JACK: The guy who answered the phone?

ANNE: Charlie. That was Charlie.

JACK: I don't know who that is.

ANNE: I do. What do you want?

JACK: The dream. Describe it to me exactly.

ANNE: You sound like you're in a tunnel.

JACK: Describe the dream to me.

ANNE: I don't remember. I can't remember anymore. It was just a dream. Okay?

JACK: I'm having an existential crisis here.

ANNE: You're breaking up. Jack? I can't hear you.

JACK: Anne? Anne you're breaking up. I can't hear you.

ANNE: Keep talking. I'll keep talking. Can you hear me? Now? Now do you hear me?

JACK: Anne?

ANNE: Yes. I can hear you. Are you moving?

JACK: I'm on a train.

ANNE: Where are you?

JACK: On a train.

ANNE: But where?

JACK: I'm going to Kosovo.

ANNE: But, where are you?

JACK: Belgrade. I was in Belgrade. Now I'm on a train.

ANNE: I thought you were in London. Or Africa. Why are you in Belgrade?

JACK: I'm not. I'm on a train. Brian—

ANNE: Brian? You're talking to Brian? Since when are you talking to Brian?

JACK: Describe the dream to me.

ANNE: Who apologized, you or him?

JACK: I did. I apologized. Please, Anne. Describe the dream.

ANNE: What does it matter? It was only a dream.

JACK: It matters. Please.

ANNE: You're breaking up. Why are you going to Kosovo?

JACK: I can't hear you. Anne. I can't hear you.

CHARLIE: Anne.

ANNE: What?

JACK: Annie? I can't hear you.

CHARLIE: If you had everything to do over, would you do it differently?

ANNE: Maybe. But. No. I wouldn't. This isn't where…

CHARLIE: Where you want to be?

ANNE: No. No, it isn't.

CHARLIE: You love him?

ANNE: Yes.

CHARLIE: Give me the phone.

(ANNE hands him the phone.)

JACK: Anne?

CHARLIE: Hey there, Jack. This is Charlie. Can you hear me?

JACK: Charlie? Yeah. I can hear you. Charlie. And who are you, Charlie?

CHARLIE: I'm the electrician. I grew up with Annie.

JACK: Charlie Owen?

CHARLIE: Same. I'm sure you've heard all about me.

JACK: You sunovabitch. Put my wife back on the phone.

(CHARLIE hangs up on JACK.)

ANNE: Did you hang up on him? Why did you hang up him? He'll think—

CHARLIE: Yes, he will.

ANNE: Where are you going?

CHARLIE: I'm gonna go take a shower.

ANNE: And?

CHARLIE: And when I get out, you'll either be here, or you won't.

ACT FIVE
SCENE ONE

BYRNES's house. Late night. SARA is pacing.

ROB: Hey. Hey, what is it?

SARA: A dream. Just a dream. A dream I have all the time. Tornadoes.

ROB: What? Sit down.

SARA: I can't sit down. No. I can't. I can't sit down.

ROB: Then tell me.

SARA: They came from opposite directions, one from the east and one from the west. Gramma covered my face with both her hands and wrapped me tight into her, so that all I could hear was the sound of the things as they went by. We were picking beans. I had picked thirty-seven, and they were pressed between me and my grandmother the entire time. Such noise. Such renting. When it was all over, a wave of warm mud swept up to us, covering our legs and swallowing the beans I'd picked. When we opened our eyes, nothing was as it had been. We didn't move for the longest time. No sound. None at all. Then crying. A baby's cry, then crying from every direction. The baby, though, the baby was only a few feet from us, lying in the warm mud, in a place where only minutes before there had been no baby and no mud.

ROB: Just a dream, Sara. Just a dream.

SARA: It's not. Not when it's always there. Not when that's what happened. It happened. That's how it happened.

ROB: How what happened, baby?

SARA: Everything. Me. All of it.

ROB: What scares you more, beetles or bees?

SARA: Bees.

ROB: What do you like better, honey or molasses?

SARA: Honey.

ROB: Me, too. Hm. Tornadoes. Eh? I was studying tornadoes. By the looks of it.

SARA: Were you?

ROB: I was. I must have chased them around and found you instead.

SARA: I read your journals.

ROB: That's okay.

SARA: I read your letters, too.

ROB: They're from Charlotte.

SARA: I know.

ROB: You knew a Charlotte.

SARA: Yes. She was my cousin. I told you this. Charlotte was my cousin.

ROB: *Was.* Do you know where she is?

SARA: Does it matter?

ROB: No. *(Beat.)* Yes. If you know where she is and aren't telling me, then you're hiding something from me. Something from my past. And that doesn't feel quite right.

SARA: I don't know where she is.

ROB: Neither do I.

SARA: I guess we're even.

ROB: I love you.

(ANNE enters.)

ANNE: I'm sorry. I'm sorry, I didn't mean to interrupt. I'm going home tomorrow. I've got to go home tomorrow.

ROB: Anne?

ANNE: I'm sorry. I really am.

ROB: Annie?

ANNE: Why is it the best and worst things happen all together at the same time or the wrong time? Or coincidentally? Or today? Why is it always that way? There has to be a reason, right? There must be a reason?

ROB: Getting struck by lightning actually increases the probability you will be struck again. I mean. Statistically, what we like to think are radically spiritual coincidences of portent are nothing but a numbers game. Everything happens for a reason? Yes? Not really.

SARA: That's pessimistic.

ROB: It's not. We assign meaning because we need to, we need to believe we are important. And in doing so, we create meaning. And in creating meaning, we become meaningful. But, it is not predicated by meaning or design or intention. Significance is an after-effect of mathematics. But the end product is the same: we're meaningful.

ANNE: What are the chances of two people having the same dream on the same night?

ROB: You and Jack?

ANNE: Yes. Me and Jack. Have you told her? Does she know?

SARA: Know what?

ANNE: How I met Jack?

ROB: You didn't have the same dream. You had inversions of the same dream. There's a difference, and it's statistically a very important one.

(The phone rings.)

ANNE: It's Jack. *(Answers.)* Jack?

JACK: Anne?

ANNE: Yes.

JACK: Hello.

ANNE: Hello. Where are you? Are you okay?

JACK: I'm in Pristina. In Kosovo.

ANNE: Why?

JACK: Are you alone?

ANNE: No.

JACK: Is he with you?

ANNE: No.

JACK: I've been thinking a lot about family—that really precious period of time when you're all together, safe—how are you wearing your hair?

ANNE: It's pulled up, pinned up. What are you doing in Pristina?

JACK: Which clip?

ANNE: A plain brown one. It's plain. Why are you in Pristina?

JACK: I keep thinking about those car rides—once, Kate was eight, belted into the middle backseat of the station wagon, picking a scab on her knee, wiping the blood off with her own spit. Brian was asleep on her other side—his face pressed up against the glass, drooling probably. And Katie said to me in this little, tiny voice, "John, we'll never know what someone else is thinking, will we?"

ANNE: Did she call you John?

JACK: She did. I didn't do well. Not when she died. I could have done better, I could have been better. I know I knew there were things that were unfair in this world. Undeserved. Maybe god had something to do with it, maybe it was punishment, maybe it was that we didn't pay enough attention. I don't know. I was certain I could pay attention. That I could stop things by paying attention. But, I can't. No matter what I do, I can't change that. I wanted to be a pilot when I was a kid. It made sense then. Even though it makes no sense now. It's laughable.

ANNE: It's not laughable. Where are you?

JACK: I'm looking at a lot that used to be a building. My friend Bosko lived here. I fell on his floor. Ages ago. Chipped my tooth. Nothing I had seen or done in my life had remotely prepared me for just how ugly it would be here. People just fucking killing each other. The whole six years. Just fucking at it. So mean. Cruel. Simple. I thought I knew. I thought I knew what it would be. That's the power of being young. But, I didn't. I didn't know what it would do to me. War is the most fascinating and terrible force, there's a mesmerizing beauty to it—

ANNE: Please. Honey. Tell me why you're there.

JACK: This is where I had the dream, Annie. On Bosko's floor. After I chipped my tooth. But, it's not here anymore. The building's gone. It's just an empty lot.

(HAL enters.)

HAL: I guess it's a horrible question. Not one I want to ask. Not one I want to know the answer to, but it's better for us both if I do. Is this because I'm simple? I know you're smarter, I know your mind travels and has its own, I don't know what to call it—topography? Pulling out the big words for ya. I only understand a fraction of your mind, and I know that's all I'll ever understand. But, the fraction I know, I love dearly. But, if I'm too simple then…

(ANNE and JACK are not on the phone, they have stepped into a shared memory.)

ANNE: I have to tell you something.

JACK: What?

ANNE: Don't look at me like that.

JACK: Like?

ANNE: Like I'm going to hit you.

JACK: Is that what I look like?

ANNE: You have to stop looking like that every time I have something I want to talk about. You look like I'm gonna deal you a vicious blow with a blunt object.

JACK: I wasn't aware I was—

ANNE: I'm gonna have to tell you all sorts of things for the rest of our lives. I can't have you looking at me like that every time—

JACK: I know. I know. What is it?

ANNE: I had a dream.

JACK: Okay?

ANNE: A long time ago. Sit down. I had a dream and you were in it.

JACK: Okay?

ANNE: I didn't know you yet.

JACK: What are you talking about?

ANNE: I know. It's weird. Early last summer. Pablo had just died and I was coming home from the hospital. I was walking to the train and this crazy chick palmed me into the stairwell.

JACK: What?

ANNE: This woman jumped me. She attacked me. And palmed my face. I guess I fell and wound up in the same hospital where Pablo died. I missed his funeral. It was ridiculous.

JACK: Someone jumped you?

ANNE: She palmed me. My face. It was crazy—

JACK: She palmed you?

ANNE: My face. She looked totally crazy and hellbent on kicking my ass. But, then so do most crazy people. I just didn't think anything would actually happen. She palmed my face and cracked my head.

JACK: Okay?

ANNE: When I was passed out, I had a dream. And you were in it.

JACK: Last summer?

ANNE: Last June.

JACK: June *sixth*.

ANNE: Crazy, I know. Maybe it wasn't even you. Wait. How did you know that? How did you know June *sixth*?

JACK: You had a dream about me?

ANNE: Did I tell you this before?

JACK: No. No, I had a dream that night.

ANNE: People have dreams most nights, babe.

JACK: It was a strange one.

ANNE: Okay?

JACK: I was in a church. It was like a church. People were waiting. Amicably. There were people from all different time periods. Druids and smithies and soldiers wearing WWI gas masks. It wasn't a church. It was a cathedral. But, there were divans and swans—

ANNE: Are you bullshitting me? Did I tell you this already?

JACK: No. No. I swear to god as my witness, no.

ANNE: What were you wearing?

JACK: A suit.

ANNE: What color was it?

JACK: What were you wearing?

ANNE: I don't know. I don't see myself when I dream. What color was it?

JACK: Sand colored.

ANNE: It was linen.

JACK: Holy shit. Write down what you said. Do you remember?

ANNE: Of course, I remember. Do you remember what you said?

JACK: I only said one thing.

ANNE: Write it down.

(*They write. Fold. Exchange the folded papers.*)

JACK: Are you ready?

ANNE: Jack. It doesn't matter. We don't need to do this.

JACK: Sure we do.

ANNE: No. No, we don't. This is crazy.

JACK: It's not going to change anything.

ANNE: Okay, but—

JACK: But, if we had the same dream. These things don't happen. Anne. These things don't happen. How did you know I said that?

ANNE: I told you this before. Is this a joke? Are you joking?

JACK: June sixth I was in Kosovo. Where were you?

ANNE: The woman palmed my face.

JACK: In New York?

ANNE: This doesn't make any sense.

JACK: Annie. Look at me. Look right here. It doesn't have to.

HAL: Forget that. My goals haven't changed. I've never really had goals. At least nothing other than exactly this. Boring shit like the quality of a recliner and the durability of a car engine and the variety of the seeding on the lawn. Ambition is a completely bizarre itch—I wouldn't know it if I felt it. I want things to be safe. I like quiet. What is there I can offer you other than that? I can't. I can only do what I can do. I can't pretend to be what I'm not. I'm not that type of guy.

ANNE: What made you leave Kosovo?

JACK: I crossed the line.

ANNE: What does that mean?

JACK: I means I didn't know who I was anymore. I hurt my friend Eva badly.

ANNE: Who was Eva?

JACK: I was in love with her. For years. We worked together. She translated for me.

ANNE: What did you do to her?

JACK: I'd rather not say. Is that okay?

ANNE: No.

JACK: I hurt her. I was in a bad place. I got in a fight. Broke my hand. Destroyed my knee. She was…I hurt her. Do you remember what you said to me? In the dream?

ANNE: That I would be back.

JACK: You kissed me.

ANNE: I did.

JACK: Where were you going? The day you stopped to hand me my umbrella?

ANNE: I was riding the train to ride the train. I'd found twelve umbrellas. I thought—I don't know what I thought.

JACK: Yes, you do.

ANNE: I thought they meant something. Where were you going?

JACK: To the dentist. To fix my tooth.

ANNE: I was so angry at the umbrellas. They were everywhere. I kept finding them everywhere.

JACK: What made you stop me?

ANNE: I don't know. I was ready. I looked up in time. I recognized you.

HAL: Actually, you know what, Charlotte? You want to know what? Stuff it. That's right. Stuff. It. I don't need you. Your brainy neurotic crap. Who needs it? Not me. Stupid long silences. Science teacher. Please. Only people who teach are people who can't do. Who don't have any ambition. How are we any different? Huh? You tell me that. How are we different? Aw, who says "stuff it"? No wonder she took off. Fuck.

JACK: What happened? What happened with Charlie?

ANNE: Different life. Man, um. We were young. Engaged. I hadthebiggestcrushonhimwhenwewereinmiddleschool finallyheaskedmeoutinhighschoolwedatedthroughsenioryear—

JACK: Anne. I meant what happened tonight?

ANNE: Nothing. We talked. That's all. We talked.

JACK: You never told me you were engaged to him.

ANNE: There are all sorts of things people don't tell each other. Maybe we made the mistake of thinking the way we met was the end of the story.

JACK: Nope. Only the beginning.

(Blackout.)

Scene Two

BYRNES's house, Hyde Park, HAL's house. ROB and SARA dance in dim light. A light and sound shift. CHAIRMAN and LIME LADY enter and stand on soapboxes and begin improvising diatribes. BRIAN and CASSIE enter, unaware of each other and listen to the ranting.

CHAIRMAN: *(To CASSIE.)* Hey! I'm talking to you.

LIME LADY: *(To BRIAN.)* Pay attention, will ya?

(BRIAN, CASSIE, CHAIRMAN, and LIME LADY freeze. LOTTE enters carrying a gallon of milk.)

HAL: Charlotte? God, oh my god. Where have you been? I've been wor-

ried. I've been sick with worry. Where have you been?

LOTTE: We needed milk.

(Hyde Park scene resumes.)

CHAIRMAN: Hey! I'm talking to you.

LIME LADY: Pay attention, will ya?

(BRIAN and CASSIE turn and see each other.)

LIME LADY: *(Pulling out a lime and showing it to CHAIRMAN.)* I've always found limes to be sensuous, soothing.

(CHAIRMAN sees her, grabs the fruit, and kisses her madly. ANNE and JACK have wandered onstage. They are on the subway platform; JACK has his umbrella in hand. They wait and wait. JACK suffers a sharp pain in his knee, and his umbrella pops open. He drops it on the ground. He moves to exit. ANNE turns and sees the umbrella. She picks it up.)

ANNE: Excuse me, sir. Your umbrella.

(JACK turns and sees ANNE. She offers him the umbrella. He takes it.)

(END OF PLAY.)

A WORD ABOUT THE *FORCE TRILOGY*

The particular challenge of writing this play was to satisfyingly complete the trilogy while also creating a singular play capable of standing independently as its own significant piece of theatre. While what you are about to read below is not crucial to understanding *Convergence*, I do hope it elucidates two of the characters in the play and offers some context to the significance of some scenes/monologues that may seem mystifying.

In 2003, after a string of recurring nightmares about tornadoes, I sat down to write a series of monologues spoken by a woman named Sara who had seen seven twisters by the time she was fourteen. Sara was a restless, solitary, wry figure who told her story over and over again in increasingly poetic language. The telling and retelling turned Sara's story into a *tale*, an epic and horrifying compilation of words, meant to ask one simple question: what if something entirely out of your control destroyed everything you knew and loved instantaneously?

At the same time I was writing through Sara's crisis, Aisling Arts was becoming and more focused as a theatre company with an exacting set of artistic preoccupations. All of our work dealt with fate, causality, and individual accountability in the context of visions, dreams, and memory. Are events destined to be? Does the answer to that question affect morality, integrity, and self-actualization? Because people have different answers to all these questions and ideas, we found ourselves searching for theatre pieces that probed these issues in depth and with ambiguity. We know (and knew) there are no answers to these questions and were uninterested in pieces that asserted to know what is impossible to know. What we craved was the discussion.

When sharing Sara's monologues with my creative partner and co-founder of Aisling Arts, Wendy Remington, we both became resolved there was more to explore. Any question we asked about Sara provoked more questions. Our ambition was to create new work, and ambitiously, to create a monster piece, an epic play comprised of intricate, meditative, intimate pieces inviting audiences to congregate around a set of ideas. Having never done it before, we didn't know where precisely to start. But inspired by the works of Robert LePage and Simon McBurney, we knew it was possible, and a story about a girl haunted by tornadoes seemed as good a place to start as any.

As so frequently happens when one's awareness is turned to a particular set of desires or ideas, everywhere I turned I saw evidence of what I knew was the beginning of a thesis. I became obsessed with images of natural destruction (the Tsunami of 2004 and Katrina had not yet happened). Digging through a closet at my parents' house for a stray mitten, I instead found a 1981 issue of *National Geographic* about the eruption of Mt. St. Helens. Several of the images of ash-covered streets in Washington State were indistinguishable from images of Lower Manhattan in autumn 2001. The same week, I became captivated by a documentary on war photographer James Nachtwey.* To me, the images he captured were no different than the images of natural destruction I had been poring over for weeks. Also, there was something undeniably gripping about Nachtwey himself. Something I could not shake off. Something I didn't *want* to shake off.

Inspired by Mr. Nachtwey's captivating, stoic, reserved persona, I created the character of Jack Kavanagh. Jack is a former war journalist who finds himself living a horribly quotidian life. Jack is as haunted by war as Sara is by the weather. While they both are horrified by the power of destruction, neither can deny the thrill and awe such power excites. Man is as capable as nature of creating awesome force.

From this simple juxtaposition of characters, the *Force* trilogy was created.

Wanderlust is simply about how Sara's car fortuitously breaks down directly in front of a mechanic's house in rural Vermont. Not so simply, it is about the secretive longings and quiet compulsions people have to be anywhere but where they should be, and the interconnectedness of, well, everything.

Threshold is simply about how Jack decides to go back to journalism. Not so simply, it is about the sum of breakable moments that push relationships to a point of no return. The relationship in this case is between Jack and his eccentric (and somewhat misanthropic) wife, Anne.

A WORD ABOUT THE STAGING

The three plays can be performed independently of each other or as one very long play. Aisling Arts has a long history of performing sparsely designed plays with tiny budgets. *Convergence* was written with the budget constraints of small, independent theatre companies in mind. We have never mounted any of the *Force* plays with anything more than a few chairs and a table or two.

---

*The film is *War Photographer* by Christian Frei with James Nachtwey.

As a matter of fact, the sheer velocity of overlapping locales prevents significant set changes. Directors should instead focus on the bare minimum of what it takes to clue an audience in: a hand-held photo, a music cue, a coat, a suitcase. The ultimate goal is not for the performers to relive a memory with a gush of emotion and accuracy, but to create for the audience a sense of time that is slippery, of a world where memory and sensation permeate every new experience we have. We have found creating an environment that immediately stretches our audience's imagination is a very effective way to get to that goal.

A WORD ABOUT INTIMACY AND ACTING STYLE

People speak very plainly and earnestly with each other during *Convergence*. But theatre cannot sustain so much direct honesty; the space is too vast and unrelenting. Verisimilitude dictates that people are most honest when they are not staring each other in the face. In order to pull this play off without it being painfully naked and just plain embarrassing, it is crucial that every scene is performed indirectly. Characters talk through phones, through notebooks, while they are doing the dishes or waiting for a bus or assembling wedding favors or looking at the stars.

RED TIDE BLOOMING

Taylor Mac

TAYLOR MAC is a theatre artist who works in the genre of pastiche. He was born in 1973 in Laguna Beach, California, and grew up in Stockton, California. His works as both a writer and performer include *The Be(A)st of Taylor Mac* (the Sydney Opera House, The Public Theatre's Newman Theater and Joe's Pub, La MaMa, Soho Theatre, Edinburgh Festival), *The Young Ladies Of* (The Battersea Arts Center), *Cardiac Arrest or Venus on a Half-Clam*, *The Face of Liberalism*, and *Okay* (all at HERE Arts Center). Other acting credits include the Sci-Fi Channel original movie *Crimson Force*, Steve Silver's *Beach Blanket Babylon* (Club Fugazi and The San Francisco Opera House), and the premieres of Elizabeth Swados's *Jabu*, Kristin Marting's *Orpheus*, and Karen Finley's *Make Love*. He is the recipient of the Ensemble Studio Theatre's New Voices Fellowship (2000), a HERE Arts Center Resident Artist Fellowship (2004–07), an Edward Albee Foundation Fellowship (2005), Performance Space 122's first-ever Ethyl Eichelberger Award for Artistic Excellence (2005), and the Herald Angel Award (2006). Mac is currently working on Part Two of his Armageddon coupling, *The Lily's Revenge*, as well as a new work with Elizabeth Swados, *The Spider's Opera*. He lives in Manhattan with his boyfriend, Patt.

Red Tide Blooming was first presented by Performance Space 122 (Vallejo Gantner, Artistic Director) on April 13, 2006, at P.S. 122, New York City, with the following cast and credits:

Todd D'Amour ....Citizen, Collin, The Collective Conscious, Blue-Haired Lady, Himself
Bridget Everett ....Lynnne Cheney, Herself
James Tigger! Ferguson..........Citizen, The Blowfish, Surfer, Gift Shop Guru, Cloud, White/Red Hippo, Ethyl Crisp, Himself
Laryssa Husiak .. Allana, Cool-Kid, Christian, Blue-Haired Lady, Herself
Stacie Karpen .... Citizen, Aquata, Cool-Kid, Eleazar, Regina Carlson, Herself
Bianca Leigh.....Constance Faubourg, The Collective Conscious, Blue-Haired Lady, Herself
Taylor Mac.........................Himself, Olokun, White/Red Hippo
Linda "Dirty" Martini.............Citizen, Atina, Cool-Kid, Sabrina Rustin, Yemanja (cut from this script), Cannibal, Herself
Steven Menendez ....Saddam Hussein, Cabbie, Jesus, Himself
Ruby Lynn Reyner ....Slavaskia, Slavaskia's Breasts, Herself
Suzi Takahashi....Citizen, Beep, The Collective Conscious, Herself
Layard Thompson ......Citizen, Arista, Truck Driver, Surfer, False Jesus, Blue-Haired Lady, Himself

Directed by: Taylor Mac
Puppets: Basil Twist
Choreography: Julie Atlas Muz
Dramaturgy: Nina Mankin
Costumes: Steven Menendez
Scenic design: Derrick Little
Lights: Garin Marschall

www.taylormac.net

The initial production of *Red Tide Blooming* was a result of the first-ever Ethyl Eichelberger Award, a commissioning award given by Performance Space 122 to honor Ethyl's memory and to recognize artistic virtuosity and adventurousness. The Ethyl Eichelberger Award is grateful to the Gesso Foundation for its generous support.

This play is dedicated to the creators of the Coney Island Mermaid Parade and the memory of Ethyl Eichelberger.

Special thanks goes to Patterson Scarlett.

ABOUT THE CAST

Although you should feel free to add or subtract the cast numbers with your own inventiveness, the original production of *Red Tide Blooming* was performed with a cast of twelve. They were pulled from a community of "outsider" artists working in New York City. I used burlesque performers, performance artists, a transsexual, a couple of drag queens, radical fairies, a self-proclaimed slut, naked bodies of all shapes and sizes, four generations, all different kinds of sexual persuasions, and even a former Playhouse of the Ridiculous and Andy Warhol superstar (Ruby Lynn Reyner). The intent was to have this musical about the divine freaks having disappeared, performed by an entire cast of performers who have chosen to be divine freaks. Because the end of the story has the performers stepping away from their characters and becoming themselves, creating the cast out of a group of people who have chosen, in their daily lives, to fight homogeny, helped emphasize the over-arching point of the tale: if the world is bland and boring and you want it to be interesting then you have to be interesting. The cast I chose are artists who embrace variance. They are brave, no-holds-barred, attempt-anything-you-ask-of-them artists. If you are lucky enough to have these types of performers in your world—use them.

ABOUT THE SETTING

The original production of *Red Tide Blooming* was set in a phantas-magorical underwater world. We used the homemade arts and crafts aesthetic of the Coney Island Mermaid Parade to have (beautifully painted) cardboard fish hanging from the grid and jellyfish made out of hairnets and sparkles dangling over the action; giant freak show and aquatic cartooned banners formed the backdrops. I was lucky enough to have one of the most inventive minds in the business, Derrick Little, create the entire set—if you are not lucky enough to have your own Derrick Little, find out how to hire him and do so. Rather than changing the scenery for each location, I took a page from the Greeks, concentrated on a general atmosphere, and allowed the dialogue to let us know where we were at any given time. Having said all that, make it your own.

ABOUT LOCATION

This musical was inspired by the revitalization of Coney Island and the antics of the Coney Island Mermaid Parade (an annual event where hundreds of subversives dress up like sea creatures and act the fool). If you've never been to the parade, it is a unique New York experience and I highly recommend it (before it gets turned into one big commercial). My goal in creating *Red Tide Blooming* was to directly address the community of people I live and work with. I'm a grassroots activist and believe the best way to effect change in the world is to effect change in your neighbor. Having writ all this, it does not mean *Red Tide* cannot be played in other places. The play may be about the suburbanization of New York and that may seem like a topic that is unsuited for people living in Salina, Kansas, but the funny thing about globalization is: it is a global problem. The eradication of variance is something we are all dealing with. If you have chain stores and khaki pants where you live, then your audience will understand this play.

A NOTE ON POP CULTURE REFERENCES

Do not use them. I have censored them all out of my text for a reason. Although I encourage you to allow your performers to improvise here and there—if they fall into the trap of using pop culture references to get an easy laugh, I will sue. Pop culture references are the death of the intellect, a scourge against inventiveness, and the plague of beautiful specificity.

LIST OF MUSICAL NUMBERS

"Suburbia" – Constance Faubourg and the Citizens
"Imploding World" – Olokun
"The Palace of the End" – Lynne, Olokun, Saddam, and Atina
"Surfing in a Red Sea" – Slavaskia and Slavaskia's Breasts
"The Collective Conscious" – The Collective Conscious, Collin
    Clement, Beep, Constance Faubourg, Gift Shop Guru, False
    Jesus, and Cool-Kids
"Collin Clement" – Collin Clement and Cool-Kids
"Beep" – Beep and Cool-Kids
"Red Tide Blooming, Part 1" – Collin Clement and Ensemble
"Bearing the Sorrow" – Constance Faubourg and Collin Clement
"The Weather Report" – Collin Clement and Ensemble
"Red Tide Blooming, Part 2" – Collin Clement, Beep, Constance
    Faubourg, and Ensemble
"The Hippo and the Heifer" – White Hippo, Olokun, Christian,
    Eleazar, Gift Shop Guru, Collin Clement, and Beep
"I Came Before You" – Slavaskia, Blue-Haired Lady Regina, Sa-
    brina, Ethyl, and Blue-Haired Ladies Ensemble
"The Boob Chase" – Mermaid Atina, Gift Shop Guru, Constance
    Faubourg, and Kazoo Band
"Little One" – Olokun and The Red Hippo
"The Seven Stages of the Apocalypse" – Olokun and Ensemble
"Safe" – Actor Playing Olokun

PROLOGUE

The overture plays and continues to do so during the following. Thunderous applause. An announcement is made over the speakers.

VOICE: Welcome one and all to the Coney Island Mermaid Parade. Let the Aquatic festivities begin!

(Thunderous applause. Pictures of generic Little Mermaid drawings are projected. The following starts slow and works itself into a frenzy until the halt.)

VOICE: Here comes our first entry. Contestant Number 1: The Little Mermaid.

(A generically pretty Little Mermaid with shells for breasts is projected.)

VOICE: Isn't she darling! Let's give a round of applause for The Little Mermaid. Up next: The Little Mermaid.

(Another generic mermaid comes on—perhaps the exact same one as before.)

VOICE: Ahhhhhh. That's what I call adorable. Isn't she adorable. The Little Mermaid. And here comes our next entry: The Little Mermaid.

(Yet another mermaid who looks the same.)

VOICE: Give it up for the Little Mermaid. And our next contestant: Ariel, the Little Mermaid.

(Little Mermaids descend one after another.)

VOICE: And now—the underwater world of The Little Mermaid. The Little Mermaid. The Little Mermaid. The Little Mermaid. The Little Mermaid, The Little Mermaid, The Littlest Mermaid, The Little Mermaid, The Little

Mermaid, The Little Mermaid, The Little Mermaid, The Little Mermaid, The Little Mermaid, The Little Mermaid. THE LITTLE MERMAID.

(OLOKUN, a hermaphrodite sea creature, runs onstage. It is naked with deranged genitalia. The actor playing OLOKUN has tucked his penis [taping the penis to his butt cheeks], and his testicles hang loosely. This is funny, awkward, disturbing, and sweet all at the same time. The overture comes to a halt. A screech of wheels. Silence.)

VOICE: Olokun: Hermaphrodite creature of the sea. FREEEEEEAK!

(Lights shift to direct address special.)

ACTOR PLAYING OLOKUN: *(To audience.)* This is not a true story. But like all stories it has truth in it. You take snippets of truth and piece them together. That's how you make a story. For example: While at the Coney Island Mermaid Parade, no one ever called me a freak. Someone did call a friend of mine "Aqua Faggot," but that was more funny than anything else. And I got a couple dirty looks for being—not the same. Dirty looks for not being the same when I was at a parade originally designed for freaks to well—show off what makes them freaky. *(With circus showmanship.)* The truth of what you are about to see: When I was a child, harassed on the playground for my feminine walk, I would often stay home where it was safe and make adventures with my toys.

SCENE I

A desert island is rolled on. It is made of discarded toys and stuffed animals. Mermaid ALLANA wiggles onstage.

ALLANA: Stockton, California. Not the California of the sea but the land of tract housing—of blending into nothing.

Here, in the middle of a man-made lake, on a desert island, sits the hermaphrodite sea creature Olokun.

(ALLANA wiggles off. CONSTANCE FAUBOURG enters. She is a typical fifties housewife, with an edge. She poses in the light as if she were about to sing her big production number, which in fact she is.)

"SUBURBIA"

CONSTANCE FAUBOURG: HERE IN
    SUBURBIA

(CITIZENS enter. They are suburban clones in swimwear.)

CITIZENS: HERE IN SUBURBIA
HERE IN SUBURBIA
HERE IN SUBURBIA

(CITIZENS see OLOKUN, who covers its genitalia with a HIPPO puppet.)

CITIZEN #1: Hey look at that thing.

CITIZEN #2: Quick kill it!

CONSTANCE FAUBOURG: First make it go to church. Then kill it.

CITIZENS: Ah Ha Ha Ha Ha
HERE IN SUBURBIA
ON A PADDLE BOAT
PADDLING IN A MAN-MADE LAKE
MADE OF DUCK FECES
AND PIPED-IN WATER
TO GIVE A SENSE OF A MAKESHIFT FAKE
SAFE
OASIS
HERE IN SUBURBIA
THE WINNERS

CITIZEN #1: That's me!

CITIZEN #2: No me!

CITIZEN #3: No me!

CONSTANCE FAUBOURG: No me!

CITIZENS: THE WINNERS
ALL HAVE BACKYARD ACCESS
TO THE FAKE SAFE LAKE
THEY HAVE LAWNS AND CAR WASHES
SOAPY SPONGES
RED TRUCKS GLEAMING
ON FLAT ASPHALT BUBBLING ROADS
TAKING YOU TO DRIVE-INS
TAKING YOU WAXY PAPER CUPS
FULL OF HYPER, HYPER, HYPER, HYPER
HYPERACTIVITY
AND MOOD SWINGS

CONSTANCE FAUBOURG: BUT HERE
    IN SUBURBIA

CITIZENS: WE HAVE
SAFETY IN NUMBERS
SAFETY, SAFETY *(Becoming frantic.)*
SAFETY IN NUMBERS
SAFETY IN NUMBERS
SAFETY IN NUMBERS
SAFETY IN NUMBERS
SAFETY IN NUMBERS
SAFETY IN NUMBERS
SAFETY IN NUMBERS
SAFETY IN NUMBERS

CONSTANCE FAUBOURG: *(As if to say—"whoa horsey.")* Wooooooooo.

CITIZENS: HERE IN SUBURBIA
EVERY SUNDAY WE TAKE THE FAMILY TO
    CHURCH
WE LEARN THAT WE HAVE DOMINION
WE LEARN CONTRADICTIONS
TO PUT OUR FAITH IN MALEDICTIONS
AND THAT
THE END OF THE WORLD IS COMING
HERE IN SUBURBIA...

(CITIZENS become the Four Horses of the Apocalypse carrying CONSTANCE in her chariot. They chase after OLOKUN, singing "Here in Suburbia." OLOKUN, scared, covers its eyes with HIPPO, exposing the obscure genitalia.)

CITIZENS: AHHHHHHHHHH.

(All CITIZENS, except CONSTANCE, run off in a panic due to seeing OLOKUN's nether region.)

CONSTANCE FAUBOURG: Nice hippo. *(Exits calmly.)*

"IMPLODING WORLD"

OLOKUN: PINK PUFFY HEART SHAPED
BOUNCE UPPY UP UP
SAND EXFOLIATING FEET SUNSHINE SURF
    MUSIC BUBBLES
ZOOM ZIMMY ZAM ZAM
ZAM ZOOMMY ZOOM ZOOM
SKIP DIP FLIP INTREPID
CARICATURES ANIMATED STUFFED IN AND
    OUT OF JOYFUL TROUBLE
I'M HAPPY HAPPY HAPPY HAPPY
HAPPY HAPPY HAPPY HAPPY
HAPPY HAPPY HAPPY HAPPY
HAPPY HAPPY HAPPY HAPPY
HERE I'M HAPPY HAPPY HAPPY HAPPY
HAPPY HAPPY HAPPY HAPPY
HAPPY HAPPY HAPPY HAPPY
HAPPY HAPPY HAPPY HAPPY

(Starts to cry but pulls itself together.)

Introducing my faithful band of play-mates. A community of divine freaks: Lolly, Pop, they're twins, Hugh and Buffet, my sea cows, and my best friend—the Hippo. The desert island is a giant hot air balloon. Or a raft. Things with buoyancy. Peacefully floating. Racing conspicuous robust sea mammals. Breaching high into the air. Lilting above the surface to breathe, we never see the ocean floor and we never reach the coast. No walls so no concept of boundaries. We just go. And I know it's silly—

OLOKUN AS HUGH: Yeah baby, it sure is.

OLOKUN: But I just can't seem to find anyone other than manufactured-super-powered-mythical-costumed-action-stuffed-fantasy-animated-endangered-figure-species like you.

YOU WANNA STOP A WAR?
YOU WANNA PLAY SOME CARDS?
YOU WANNA START SOME LORE?
KEEP SECRETS OF WHO YOU ARE?
YOU WANNA BUILD A CRAFT
TO OUTER SPACE AND BACK?
YOU WANNA LIGHT THE SKY
WITH ALL THEIR DOS OR DIES?
YOU WANNA BREAK THE BINDS
OF COMPETITION CLIMBS?
YOU WANNA TAKE ME UP
TO MULTIFACETED LOVE?
YOU WANNA END THE DRAIN
SENDING US TO SAME?
OH BABY COME ON
BUT YOU'RE JUST PLASTIC
PLASTIC AND PAINT
STORIES TOLD THAT
CAN'T TAKE AWAY
ALL THE FADE
THE DWINDLE DOWN TO SAME
SO HERE ALL ALONE
I SIT ALL ALONE
I LOVE ALL ALONE
I AM ALL ALONE
WITH NO ONE
NO ONE
NO ONE

(Mermaids AQUATA, ALLANA, ARISTA, and ATINA wiggle on.)

AQUATA and ALLANA: Information you need to know, regarding the logic of this story.

ATINA: We will redefine what a curse word is. Instead of a censored beep for words like fuck, fuck, fuck, and fuck—*corporations* and *pop culture references* will be eradicated.

ARISTA: For example:

ALLANA: Hey Aquata who's your favorite pop star?

AQUATA: Beep.

ALLANA: And now introducing the current darling of cache, he of infantile longings and fifteen-minute fame: The Blowfish.

(The MERMAIDS wiggle off as THE BLOWFISH swims on [his outfit is made of balloons], carrying a man-bag and doing lines of coke in between giving orders to his personal assistant [LYNNE]. LYNNE follows him, floating in a blowup preserver, wearing a one-piece bathing suit, turning pages of his magazine, dialing his cell phone, setting up lines of coke for him, and taking notes and photos of him.)

THE BLOWFISH: (Regarding the magazine, coke, and phone.) Turn! Line! Dial! Take a note! Take a photo. Let me see! Ah ha ha ha ha ha ha ha ha. (Snorts.)

OLOKUN: Oh Mr. Blowfish. Mr. Blowfish.

THE BLOWFISH: (Turning around as if to greet a fan but then seeing OLOKUN's genitalia.) Ah!

OLOKUN: Oh Mr. Blowfish do hang out and play.

THE BLOWFISH: Sorry babe, but I'm in a hurry. Finally the Blowfish craze has arrived. I've got a luncheon with beep. Then a meeting with the folks over at beep. And a date with the peeps at the top of beep. We're thinking feature. We're thinking merch. I guess it takes a couple canoodling sessions with beep for people to start appreciating what's been there all along.

OLOKUN: Yes it does seem the freaks aren't appreciated.

THE BLOWFISH: Freak! Are you calling me a freak?

OLOKUN: You're a blowfish.

THE BLOWFISH: What's that supposed to mean?

OLOKUN: You're a freak like me.

THE BLOWFISH: I, like you? Just because I don't have genitalia flapping about everywhere doesn't mean I lack a discernible gender. Turn! Line! Dial! Take a note! (Regarding OLOKUN's genitalia.) Take a picture! Let me see it! (Pointing at the picture of OLOKUN's genitalia.) Ah ha ha ha ha ha ha.

(ARISTA and ALLANA wiggle on.)

ALLANA: The truth of Olokun's genitalia.

(ALLANA begins to tie a scarf around OLOKUN's waist, covering its genitalia.)

AQUATA: About fifty to ninety percent of the audience is having a hard time listening to anything that is being said right now because they're too discomforted by Olokun's mangina.

(The MERMAIDS wiggle off.)

THE BLOWFISH: I, like you? No! You are the last of the freaks.

OLOKUN: That can't possibly be true.

THE BLOWFISH: They've all disappeared.

OLOKUN: All the freaks? Disappeared? They can't have disappeared. Maybe they've gotten sad and have hidden away for a time.

THE BLOWFISH: No.

OLOKUN: Or perhaps they come out when you have gone to bed.

THE BLOWFISH: Nuh-hu.

OLOKUN: They can't have simply disappeared. There must be more like me somewhere.

(The lights shift to a spot on THE BLOWFISH.)

THE BLOWFISH: Once crinkled in an aged yellow snapshot. A whole show of freaks. On a floating landfill. An amusement park of oddities.

OLOKUN: *(Entering THE BLOW-FISH's light.)* What?

THE BLOWFISH: Seeking to eradicate discomfort begot from the freaks, The Collective Conscious forced them onto the floating landfill long ago. But now The Collective has infiltrated the landfill and the freaks are even disappearing from it.

OLOKUN: A show of freaks! Did you say a whole show of them?

(Lights return to normal.)

THE BLOWFISH: Turn!

OLOKUN: But what is The Collective Conscious?

THE BLOWFISH: Line!

OLOKUN: Hey, what is The Collective Conscious?

THE BLOWFISH: Dial!

OLOKUN: The Collective Conscious?

THE BLOWFISH: Take a note!

OLOKUN: Collective Conscious!

THE BLOWFISH: Take a photo!

OLOKUN: Collective!

THE BLOWFISH: Let me see!

OLOKUN: Conscious!

LYNNE: Ahhhhhhhhhh.

(LYNNE pops one of THE BLOWFISH's balloons, which is the equivalent of stabbing him.)

THE BLOWFISH: *(Dying.)* You are so fired.

LYNNE: And you are so fucked.

(LYNNE pops another balloon. THE BLOWFISH screams at each pop.)

LYNNE: *(Popping another balloon.)* Dial! *(Popping another.)* Take a line! *(Another.)* Take a photo!

(LYNNE pushes THE BLOWFISH down and straddles his face with her crotch.)

LYNNE: Take your last breath bitch.

(LYNNE pops one last balloon. THE BLOWFISH is now dead. The actor playing THE BLOWFISH is butt naked. LYNNE picks up THE BLOWFISH and carries him offstage, slapping his ass as she goes. She reenters. Starts to pick up her stuff. ALLANA begins to wiggle on.)

LYNNE: *(Seeing ALLANA and going in for the attack.)* Ahhhhhhh!

(ALLANA hops off in fear. THE BAND starts to play THE BLOWFISH underscore.)

LYNNE: *(Threatening the band.)* Ahhhhhh!

(THE BAND goes silent. LYNNE takes out a bump of coke. OLOKUN stares at her with fear.)

LYNNE: *(Referring to the coke.)* You want some?

(OLOKUN stares. LYNNE snorts.)

LYNNE: Lynne. Cheney.

(OLOKUN stares.)

LYNNE: You should know better than to try and speak to a blowfish. They only talk about themselves.

OLOKUN: That's no reason to kill it.

LYNNE: You always this sensitive?

OLOKUN: I'm all right, it's just if you're still sleeping with your stuffed animals when you're thirty…I don't care about The Blowfish but he was going to tell me more about The Collective Conscious.

LYNNE: I wouldn't interfere with The Collective Conscious if I were you.

OLOKUN: You know about them?

LYNNE: Did you catch my name? You know who I am? I helped make The Collective Conscious. And now look at me. Thrown out of the upper echelons, now I've been left to wallow in infantilism.

OLOKUN: Me too.

LYNNE: Shut it. Take my purse. *(Motioning for OLOKUN to sit in the audience.)* Take a seat.

(A spot comes up on LYNNE.)

LYNNE: The Second Lady sings an epic song of self-destruction.

"THE PALACE OF THE END"

LYNNE: THERE'S A LESBIAN
ROMANCE NOVEL
BY LYNNE CHENEY
WIFE OF V.P.
DICK CHENEY

Just checking

IN HER LESBIAN
ROMANCE NOVEL
LYNNE CALLS *SISTERS*
SHE WRITES THE FOLLOWING

OLOKUN: Why are you talking about yourself as if you were in the third person?

LYNNE: I quote from my novel

"LET US GO,
AWAY FROM ANGER
AND THE IMPERATIVES OF MEN
WE SHALL FIND,
A SECLUDED BOWER
WHERE THEY DARE NOT VENTURE
THERE WILL BE ONLY THE TWO OF US
AND WE SHALL LINGER THROUGH LONG
    AFTERNOONS
IN THE EVENINGS I SHALL READ TO YOU
WHILE YOU DO YOUR CROSS-STITCH
IN THE FIRELIGHT
THEN WE SHALL GO TO BED
OUR BED
MY DEAREST GIRL"

OLOKUN: And that's why they kicked you out? 'Cause you wrote a lesbian pulp fiction novel?

LYNNE: I've only just started.

THERE'S A ROMANCE
ROMANCE NOVEL
BY SADDAM HUSSEIN
CALLED "ZABIBAH-
ZABIBAH AND THE KING"
ALL ABOUT A KING WHO SAVES A POOR
    WASHERWOMAN NAMED ZABIBAH FROM
    THE NINETEEN-YEAR-OLD IMPERIALIST
    WESTERN SOLDIER WHO WANTED TO
    RAPE HER
ZABIBAH WAS RESCUED ON A WHITE
    HORSE
BY A DARK STRANGER

WHO LATER SHE DISCOVERED WAS VERY
 RICH
BUT ONLY AFTER ZABIBAH
HAD DECLARED HER LOVE TO THE STRANG-
 ER
WHO REALLY WAS THE KING
WHO REALLY IS A METAPHOR FOR SADDAM
 HUSSEIN
SO THAT SADDAM, HE KNEW THAT ZABIBAH'S
 LOVE WAS TRULY GENUINE, NOT CLOUD-
 ED BY MATERIAL POSSESSIONS OR FEAR
 LIKE ALL OF HIS PREVIOUS LOVERS
 BEFORE HER

OLOKUN: What does this have to do
with you?

LYNNE: My story!

THERE'S A ROMANCE
ROMANCE EPIC SONG
BY THE GODS AND ME
ALL ABOUT LYNNE CHENEY
WIFE OF V.P. AND HOW SHE GOES TO SEE
THE EXECUTION OF SADDAM HUSSEIN
IT IS HELD IN A CASTLE IN IRAQ
A CASTLE WHERE SADDAM WOULD TORTURE
 AND KILL HIS VICTIMS
A CASTLE SADDAM CALLED
THE PALACE OF THE END

LYNNE HAS GONE THERE FOR A PHOTO OP
FOR A SYMBOLIC GESTURE OF AMERICA BE-
 ING ON TOP
SHE EXPECTS TO BE PLEASED WHEN SHE SEES
 SADDAM DIE
SO VIOLENTLY
BUT AS SHE SITS DOWN ACROSS
FROM THE PROTECTIVE GLASS
SADDAM AND LYNNE MAKE
EYE CONTACT
AND LYNNE CAUGHT OFF GUARD
ALLOWS HER EYES TO TELL A STORY
ALL ABOUT HER HUSBAND DICK CHENEY
 WHO IS AWAY IN HIS UNDISCLOSED
 LOCATION
LYNNE IS LEFT ALONE

TO RAISE HER LESBIAN DAUGHTER
TEACH HER ALL ABOUT JESUS
GO ON TALK SHOWS, CAMPAIGNS
SPEAK OF FAMILY VALUES EVERY DAY
SHE WEARS HER POWER SUITS
NOT TOO FLASHY, NOT TOO FEMININE
BUT NOT MANLY
POWERFULLY SUITABLE
AND SHE WORKS HARD, SHE GIVES IMPERA-
 TIVES
OH SHE SPEWS ANGER
YA YA YA YA YA YA YA YA YA
SO THAT SHE CAN FIND HER HUSBAND IN
 HIS UNDISCLOSED LOCATION
SO THAT SHE CAN BE AN EQUAL IN THE EYES
 OF HER LOVE

*(A man dressed as SADDAM HUSSEIN
appears. He stands still as LYNNE continues to tell their story.)*

LYNNE: AND WHEN SADDAM SEES LYNNE:
 HE TOO IS CAUGHT OFF GUARD
AND HIS EYES TELL A STORY OF HOW
WHEN HE WAS JUST A WEE LAD HIS FATHER
 DIED OR LEFT HIM
AND HIS MOTHER SHE REMARRIED IBRAHIM
IBRAHIM WAS A SHEPHERD
WHO WOULD OFTEN BEAT SADDAM BLACK
 AND BLUE
AND SADDAM WOULD STEAL CHICKENS
 AND SHEEP
TO PLEASE IBRAHIM, PLEASE, PLEASE IBRA-
 HIM
PLEASE, PLEASE IBRAHIM, PLEASE PLEASE
 IBRAHIM
PLEASE, PLEASE, PLEASE, PLEASE, PLEASE,
 PLEASE IBRAHIM
BUT SADDAM NEVER COULD PLEASE, PLEASE
 IBRAHIM, NEVER COULD PLEASE, PLEASE,
 PLEASE, PLEASE IBRAHIM
AND HE GOT HIMSELF INTO A VICIOUS SUB-
 CONSCIOUS CIRCLE WHERE HE SOUGHT
 ACCUMULATION OF TREASURES AND
 POWER TO
GET LOVE

BUT SADDAM NEVER COULD GET LOVE
    'CAUSE SADDAM NEVER COULD GIVE
    LOVE, NO
SADDAM NEVER COULD GIVE LOVE 'CAUSE
    SADDAM NEVER COULD GET LOVE, NO
LYNNE CHENEY NEVER COULD GET LOVE
    'CAUSE LYNNE CHENEY NEVER COULD
    GIVE LOVE, NO
LYNNE CHENEY NEVER COULD GIVE LOVE
    'CAUSE LYNNE CHENEY NEVER COULD
    GET LOVE, NO
LYNNE CHENEY NEVER COULD GET SADDAM
    AND SADDAM NEVER COULD GET LYNNE
    CHENEY AND

OLOKUN: ENOUGH ALREADY!

LYNNE: I told you it was epic.

OLOKUN: Sorry.

LYNNE: AND WHEN LYNNE SAW SADDAM
AND SADDAM SAW LYNNE
AS HE BREATHED THE POISON GAS IN

Poetic license.

LYNNE BREATHED IN AND OUT WITH HIM
THROUGH THE PROTECTIVE GLASS
SHE BREATHED IN AND OUT WITH HIM
THEY BREATHED IN AND OUT

SADDAM AND LYNNE: TOGETHER
    IN AND OUT
IN AND OUT
IN AND OUT

(ATINA wiggles on.)

ATINA: Last night I laid in bed with
my lover, belly to belly. Our inhales and
exhales in sync. The inhales pushing us
apart. Exhales pulling us away. I switched
my breathing to go in when his went out.
Out when his went in. But at the same
time he switched his breath to do the
same. Once again, our bellies collided
and separated. An awkward attempt at
forced perfection.

(ATINA takes SADDAM off.)

LYNNE: IN AND OUT
IN AND OUT
IN THE PALACE OF THE END

OLOKUN: You're a freak.

LYNNE: What?

OLOKUN: You're a freak like me.

LYNNE: I am not.

OLOKUN: You're in love with Saddam
Hussein. You're a freak.

LYNNE: Falling in love with diabolic
dictators is hardly obscure.

OLOKUN: But you ended up here?

LYNNE: Dick thought if I spent time as-
sisting The Blowfish in suburbia I might
learn how to collect ceramic kittens and
come back to the fold. But it's no good.
I am drawn to the under and over-bel-
lies. The middle is markedly bromidic.
I've popped The Blowfish and blew any
chance I had. The only way I can save
myself now is to make my way back into
the spotlight.

OLOKUN: Why?

LYNNE: I'm impenetrable in the
spotlight.

OLOKUN: How you gonna do that?

LYNNE: I don't know?

OLOKUN: They always say, "Do what
you're good at."

LYNNE: I always loved writing.

OLOKUN: Well okay.

LYNNE: Oh no, I couldn't.

OLOKUN: Sure you can, just pick a
topic.

LYNNE: It would have to be a story so subversive that the general population wouldn't understand it was subversive.

OLOKUN: You need the story of a freak.

LYNNE: Yes.

OLOKUN: A tragic hero.

LYNNE: Yes.

OLOKUN: But you heard The Blowfish, The Collective Conscious has captured all the freaks and now I'm the only one left.

(A ding from THE BAND.)

LYNNE: I'll take you to it.

OLOKUN: What?

LYNNE: The Collective Conscious. I'll take you to it.

OLOKUN: I thought you said I shouldn't interfere with them.

LYNNE: Oh fuck that. We will venture to the floating landfill where you will defeat The Collective Conscious and free the freaks.

OLOKUN: Me?

LYNNE: You will be my muse. I can start writing again. Yours is the story for me.

OLOKUN: It is?

LYNNE: A poor lonely hermaphrodite sea creature on the road to revolution.

OLOKUN: Revolution?

LYNNE: Companionship.

OLOKUN: Companionship!

LYNNE: Safety.

OLOKUN: Yes.

LYNNE: We will find Slavaskia.

OLOKUN: Who?

LYNNE: Queen of the Floating Landfill. She will know where to find the other freaks—if any remain.

OLOKUN: How will we get there?

LYNNE: With a thumb and a lack of self-respect.

(A TRUCK DRIVER comes on. Sexual acts are had as they ride across the stage, get off, and THE TRUCK DRIVER exits.)

OLOKUN: Thanks for the ride.

SCENE II

SLAVASKIA (sixty-five, Russian immigrant) enters. She has enormous breasts and is so tan her skin is charcoal.

SLAVASKIA: Home of Slavaskia. Floating Landfill, East Village apartment. *(To OLOKUN.)* Hey Floating Landfill newbie you want rent room?

OLOKUN: Rent room?

LYNNE: *(Writing in her pad.)* The scum lord looked Olokun over—a gleam of saliva glistening in her greedy calculations.

SLAVASKIA: Did she just call me scum lord?

LYNNE: Her irate eyes bloodshot from years of plots run dry.

SLAVASKIA: I not slum lord.

OLOKUN: She's just writing a book.

SLAVASKIA: I have rent-controlled apartment—I pay little, charge you lots. You live in bathtub. I have costume jewelry to acquire. Do I know you?

LYNNE: We've never met but I know all about you from when I used to censor history. Of course I don't remember you being so…

SLAVASKIA: *(Indicating her breasts.)* Present?

LYNNE: Well—

SLAVASKIA: I was Floating Landfill Queen of Freakies. They see me and say, "You are emotionally bold iconoclastic intellectually dynamic artist. You are one for leading freaks."

OLOKUN: Wow.

SLAVASKIA: But now they want revitalize, want young, want big breast things. Now they drown old in sea. So I fool Collective Conscious. *(Takes her top off to reveal her naked puppet breasts.)* I get enlargement. I do tap number. I keep title.

LYNNE: *(Getting her notes straight.)* A tap number?

SLAVASKIA: Now they have talent competition for title of queen—they want like TV—they want like everything everywhere. I'm not great but I make up for with sass. We forgive multitude of sins for sass and smile.

SLAVASKIA'S BREASTS: God is in the distraction.

OLOKUN: I don't understand that.

SLAVASKIA: Exactly.

"SURFING IN A RED SEA"

SLAVASKIA: I'M SURFING IN A RED SEA
ON A WAVE OF BLUE-HAIRED LADIES

SLAVASKIA'S BREASTS: THAT'S ME

SLAVASKIA: SURFING IN A RED SEA

ON A WAVE OF BLUE-HAIRED LADIES

SLAVASKIA'S BREASTS: TEE HEE

SLAVASKIA: I GOT STYLE
I GOT SASS

SLAVASKIA'S BREASTS: I GOT BIBBITY
    BOBBING PANACHE

SLAVASKIA: I'M YOUNG
I'M YOUNG
I'M YOUNG
SO YOUNG

I have this awake dream I'm young again. No ex-husband, no baby, no past. Just young. And I'm surfing in a Red Sea. The boys in their wet suits ride next to me—

(TWO SURFERS come out and surf.)

SLAVASKIA: —jaunty blond hair sea lions. I'm a champion with the salt water—they are impressed. I've been so happy gliding down the waves, I haven't realized that the foam rolling under my board is really the hair from the heads of all the blue-haired ladies. Too much coloring.

(THE SURFERS fall and roll off.)

SLAVASKIA: They've been trapped inside the ocean by The Collective Conscious. Forever doomed to create the waves. At least I'm safe I think. Safe in my disguise.

WITH MY BOUNCING TCHOTCHKES
SHINING IN THE SUNLIGHT
MY SKIN BRONZING
PULLED BACK SO TIGHT
I'M YOUNG I'M YOUNG
I'M YOUNG SO YOUNG
UNTIL THE TITS BEGIN TO DRIP
INTO THE FRAZZLED HAIR

SLAVASKIA'S BREASTS: DRIP DRIP DRIP

SLAVASKIA: OH DEAR
I DON'T
I DON'T
I DON'T
WANNA GO.

OLOKUN: Go where?

SLAVASKIA: To the sea with other blue-haired ladies. I keep hair dyed. I win title.

LYNNE: *(Taking notes.)* You're very tan.

SLAVASKIA: I am tanorexic—I look in mirror, I don't see tan person.

OLOKUN: You're a freak.

SLAVASKIA: No! I am former freak. They see me now, with improvements. They say, "Ah you must be queen of Cool-Kids." I have gotten special invite to "Cool-Kid" freak-cleansing party.

OLOKUN: What's a "Cool-Kid"?

SLAVASKIA's BREASTS: Drag queen in park is freak. Drag queen in park goes to TV—no longer freak—now "Cool-Kid."

OLOKUN: Is that good?

SLAVASKIA: Good/not good—boils down to: not-so-Cool-Kids come to city with goal to get even at suburban cool-kids by being Cool-Kids in bigger place. Now—too many Cool-Kids, not so many freaks. What freaks have remained have locked themselves in Freak Show.

OLOKUN: Can you take me there?

SLAVASKIA: What?

LYNNE: He's on a quest to defeat The Collective Conscious and free the freaks.

OLOKUN: Right.

SLAVASKIA: You no go there. Tonight is final freak-cleansing ceremony. Tonight Collective will flood Freak Show with army of blue hairs eliminating freakies once and for all.

OLOKUN: Maybe you could go ask them not to?

SLAVASKIA: I go with this request, they throw me to sea. There is no helping you little freakie. All must concede to same or must be eliminated.

LYNNE: *(Writing in her pad.)* The former queen, like all, was too consumed with fear to help the poor lonely hermaphrodite sea creature.

SLAVASKIA: Hey what you write there, I am no victim of fear-based culture.

LYNNE: Her years of revolution dried up like a dehydrated apple doll.

SLAVASKIA: You cannot be writing these things, I have reputation.

LYNNE: A moldy dehydrated apple doll.

SLAVASKIA: I no mold.

LYNNE: M.

SLAVASKIA: No!

LYNNE: O.

SLAVASKIA: No.

LYNNE: L.

SLAVASKIA: NO.

LYNNE: D.

SLAVASKIA: NO.

{ LYNNE: Y. Moldy, Moldy, Moldy, Moldy, Moldy, MOOOOOOOOOOOOOOOLDY.

SLAVASKIA: No. No. No. No. No. No. No.

SLAVASKIA: Okay. I take you.

OLOKUN: All right.

SLAVASKIA: But that is all. I am not becoming blue-haired lady trapped in ocean for you.

OLOKUN: Okay.

SLAVASKIA: Ooooo. I have idea. We give newbie freakie, what you say, makeover. You have appearance of Cool-Kid, then you come with me to pre-party.

OLOKUN: I don't know.

SLAVASKIA: It only way to get close enough to Collective Conscious to defeat it.

OLOKUN: I'm not so good at passing.

LYNNE: Olie, it's the only way to be with the other freaks.

OLOKUN: Okay, I'll do it.

SLAVASKIA: Come we do makeover in taxi. *(Hailing a taxi.)* Take us to Clubland.

(A CAB DRIVER appears. The three of them get behind CABBIE and conga offstage.)

LYNNE: Olokun put his pre-lubricated androgenous sea hand on the throbbing man-nipples.

(OLOKUN tweaks CABBIE's nipples.)

LYNNE: As the newly renovated road took them smoothly to their destination.

SCENE III

A disco ball is lowered, indicating that we are now in Clubland. FALSE JESUS, the cocktail wench, comes out in a loincloth and serves drinks to the audience. GIFT SHOP GURU enters.

FALSE JESUS: Who ordered the Floating Landfill? *(Etc.)*

GIFT SHOP GURU: Get your deity artifacts here. I got the thorn of Christ. The tooth of Buddha. Mohammed's turban. Lott's table salt…

(THREE WOMEN enter wearing the exact same sweater. They, along with GIFT SHOP GURU and FALSE JESUS, are the COOL-KIDS.)

COOL-KIDS: Hmzebazacabubu-flood. Hmzebazacabubu-mass destruction. Hzmebazacabubu-bird flu. Hmzebazacabubu-flood. Hmzebazacabubu-mass destruction. Hzmebazacabubu-bird flu.

(LYNNE, SLAVASKIA, and OLOKUN enter. OLOKUN, disguised as a COOL-KID, wears a conglomerate sweater and sunglasses. COOL-KIDS continue their chanting.)

SLAVASKIA: We made it.

OLOKUN: This is the freak-cleansing pre-party?

FALSE JESUS: *(Offering a drink.)* Floating Landfill?

OLOKUN: No thanks.

(COLLIN CLEMENT, a TV weatherman, enters.)

COLLIN: Slavaskia, welcome. Thank you for coming.

SLAVASKIA: Pleasure. This is—errrr—VJ Olokun and *(Regarding LYNNE.)* personal assistant.

LYNNE: Biographer.

COLLIN: Honor. Care to join in on the chanting?

OLOKUN: We just came to watch.

COLLIN: Oh, I'm a fan of observation, which lacks participation but I think you'll find by chanting you can use traditional metaphysical techniques and passive aggressively bring about the Armageddon with untraceable participation.

COOL-KIDS: Hemzababubu-horsemen.

COLLIN: Mind over matter.

OLOKUN: *(To LYNNE.)* Maybe this wasn't such a good idea?

FALSE JESUS: The Collective Conscious is about to make an appearance.

LYNNE: *(To OLOKUN.)* Now's your chance. You can kill the Collective and free the freaks hauled up in the Freak Show.

OLOKUN: Kill?

(There is a drum roll.)

FALSE JESUS: And now ladies and gentlemen I present to you: The Collective Conscious.

(THE COLLECTIVE CONSCIOUS comes out. It is a sweater manipulated by COLLIN CLEMENT, CONSTANCE FABOURG, and BEEP, a bearded lady dressed as a male corporate cliché.)

OLOKUN: It's a sweater.

LYNNE: *(Aroused.)* Oh.

"THE COLLECTIVE CONSCIOUS"

THE COLLECTIVE CONSCIOUS:
OH BABY, WHAT YOU LIVING FOR
OH BABY, YOUR HEART IS WRECKED AND TORN
THE WORLD IS CRUMBLING ALL AROUND YOU
ONLY UGLINESS IS ABOUND TO

BRING YOUR SADNESS TO THE FOLD
OH BABY WHAT ARE YOU WAITING FOR
JOIN

ENSEMBLE: THE COLLECTIVE CONSCIOUS CREATIVE VISUALIZATION
OF THE ARMAGEDDON IT'S FOR YOU AND ME

(The sweater is held in front of BEEP as if he were wearing it.)

BEEP: Some call me "The Evil Them." An old white man sitting in a boardroom with a protruding belly and a secretary to sharpen my pencil.

(The sweater is held in front of CONSTANCE.)

CONSTANCE FAUBOURG: Or I'm called a fearful housewife, killing germs, consuming packaged fat-free food and daytime telly.

(The sweater is held in front of COLLIN.)

COLLIN: Or even a media spokesman—bringing terror addiction and mental oblivion into your home.

THE COLLECTIVE CONSCIOUS:
BUT REALLY I'M JUST A SIMPLE SWEATER.
I GO WITH EVERYTHING FROM SUITS TO JEANS.
I MAKE A PERFECT HOLIDAY, BIRTHDAY, OR "JUST BECAUSE" GIFT.
I'M MADE OF FINE YARN.
I'M MADE OF COMFORT.

COOL-KIDS: Hemzababubu-comfort.

THE COLLECTIVE CONSCIOUS: I'm made of safety.

COOL-KIDS: Hemzababubu-safety.

THE COLLECTIVE CONSCIOUS: I'm made of everyday.

(The sweater is held in front of CONSTANCE.)

CONSTANCE FAUBOURG: I will take the uncomfortable seat you're sitting in at this very moment and turn it into a lounge chair.

(The sweater is held in front of BEEP.)

BEEP: Why would I do such a thing? Because I am committed to the eradication of discomfort.

(The sweater is held in front of COLLIN.)

COLLIN: And how can I do it, you may ask? Simply because:

THE COLLECTIVE CONSCIOUS:
I AM MADE OF SMALL ITALIAN FARMS AND ESPRESSO
I'M MADE OF WATCHING SUNSETS SHINE ON GOLDEN FIELDS
PASTA DISHES, LOG CABIN WISHES, KISSES IN THE BARN
I'M MADE OF WORKING HARD SO NO WORK CAN BE DONE LATER
I'M MADE OF LATER
(To SLAVASKIA.) OH DARLING, YOU'RE LOST OUT ON THE SEA
STOP YOUR WAITING AND COME AWAY WITH ME
YOUR HEALTH IS WANING

COOL-KIDS: WHAT YOU WAITING FOR

THE COLLECTIVE CONSCIOUS:
YOUR YOUTH IS FADING

COOL-KIDS: WHAT YOU WAITING FOR

THE COLLECTIVE CONSCIOUS:
Try me. You'll like me.

COOL-KIDS: TRY ME YOU'LL LIKE ME YOU'LL LIKE ME, YOU'LL LIKE ME

THE COLLECTIVE CONSCIOUS:
What, you've already tried me and you like me? You're probably wearing me right now. And deep down inside you know I'm not "The Evil Them."

I'M ITALIAN MERINO

THE COLLECTIVE CONSCIOUS and COOL-KIDS: *(Chanting during the following dialogue.)* The Collective Conscious creative visualization of the Armageddon is for you and me.

OLOKUN: *(To LYNNE.)* It's evil.

LYNNE: But kinda cute.

OLOKUN: You're a freak.

LYNNE: I am not!

OLOKUN: You're in love with the evil sweater.

LYNNE: I like its form.

OLOKUN: Admit it. You're a freak.

LYNNE: There is nothing freaky about wanting a little comfort.

OLOKUN: Well sure but—

LYNNE: *(Pointing at THE COLLECTIVE CONSCIOUS.)* Look. Now's your chance.

(LYNNE hands OLOKUN a lipstick to ruin the sweater with.)

LYNNE: Kill it while it's chanting.

(During the following OLOKUN attempts to mark up the sweater, but every time OLIE gets close enough, THE COLLECTIVE sees OLOKUN, who then acts like its putting lipstick on.)

THE COLLECTIVE CONSCIOUS AND COOL-KIDS: THE COLLECTIVE CONSCIOUS CREATIVE VISUALIZATIONOF THE ARMAGEDDON I'M (IT'S) FOR YOU AND

THE COLLECTIVE CONSCIOUS: Is there testimony someone would like to share this evening?

(COLLIN CLEMENT separates himself from the sweater and jumps up and down with hand-in-the-air exuberance.)

COLLIN: Me. Oh me, me, me, me, me.

BEEP: Ladies and gentlemen, the Floating Landfill's weatherman himself and our prophet: Mr. Collin Clement.

COOL-KIDS: Welcome Collin.

COLLIN: Thank you, Collective, Cool-Kids, *(To SLAVASKIA, OLOKUN, and LYNNE.)* honored and invited guests, and thank you, our viewing public.

"COLLIN CLEMENT"

COLLIN: I HAVE EVERYTHING ANYONE
    COULD EVER WANT
FAME AND FORTUNE, BEAUTIFUL GOLDEN
    LOCKS
I AM THE WEATHERMAN FOR THE LOCAL
    ISLAND NEWS
I HAVE MUSCLES, I HAVE SMOOTH SKIN
I CAN AFFORD THE VEGETABLE TANNING
    SPRAY
I'M THE STATE HERO, I PROVIDE THE PEOPLE
    WITH THE OBVIOUS

You can't imagine how grateful people feel when you present them with the obvious.

AND FOR A WHILE IT MAKES ME FEEL IM-
    PORTANT
ONLY I BEGIN TO REALIZE
THE ONLY THING ANYONE TALKS TO ME
    ABOUT IS
THE WEATHER
EVERYWHERE I GO

COOL-KIDS: COLLIN, WHAT'S THE
    WEATHER GONNA BE LIKE TODAY,
    COLLIN
IS IT GONNA RAIN COLLIN?
IS IT GONNA RAIN COLLIN
IS IT, IS IT, IS IT, IS IT, IS IT IS IT IS IT

COLLIN: MY LIFE HAS BECOME ONE
    SMALL-TALK SESSION
DAY AFTER DAY AT WORK I REPORT, SMILE,
    MAKE DUMB JOKES THAT I START TO
    FIND FUNNY, WORRY ABOUT MY HAIR
WHETHER I'VE MATCHED MY CLOTHING
EVERY DAY I WAKE UP, GOTTA GO TO
    MAKEUP
EVERY DAY I WAKE UP, GOTTA GO TO
    MAKEUP
EVERY DAY, EVERY DAY, EVERY DAY, EVERY
    DAY, EVERY DAY, EVERY DAY
BUT THEN SOMETHING HAPPENS, SOME-
    THING MIRACULOUS

CONSTANCE FAUBOURG: Ladies and gentlemen, may I introduce you to our church and corporate sponsor Beep.

COOL-KIDS: Welcome Beep.

CONSTANCE FAUBOURG: In this issue Beep comes to our Weatherman and says:

"BEEP"

BEEP: COLLIN CLEMENT
MY COMPANY MAKES PLASTIC TOYS
THAT GO INTO THIN COLORFUL CARDBOARD
    LUNCH BOXES
MARKETING BOXES OF JOY
WE MAKE PEOPLE
HAPPY, HAPPY, HAPPY,
HAPPY, HAPPY, HAPPY,
HAPPY, HAPPY, HAPPY,
HAPPY, HAPPY, HAPPY,
HAPPY, HAPPY, HAPPY,
HAPPY, HAPPY, HAPPY,
HAP HAPPY
THESE TOYS ARE MADE TO FRITTER
THESE TOYS ARE MADE TO BE REPLACED SO
WE CAN MAKE MORE OF THEM
SO THEY CAN MAKE YOU
HAPPY, HAPPY, HAPPY,
HAPPY, HAPPY, HAPPY,

HAPPY, HAPPY, HAPPY,
HAPPY, HAPPY, HAPPY,
HAPPY, HAPPY, HAPPY,
HAPPY, HAPPY, HAPPY,
HAP HAPPY
NOW IMAGINE IF YOU WILL A GROWN MAN
ONCE A CHILD BORN WITH ALL THE COM-
FORT ONE COULD MUSTER
TAUGHT THAT WINNING IS THE ANSWER
RAISED REHEARSING STRENGTH AND CAN-
DOR
AND STILL HIS SADNESS OVERWHELMS HIM
BOILS FORTH, OH HOW IT SCORNS HIM
TEARS TO SHREDS AND IT EMPLOYS HIM
TO FIND A PLACE WHERE HE'LL BE
HAPPY, HAPPY, HAPPY,
HAPPY, HAPPY, HAPPY,
HAPPY, HAPPY, HAPPY,
HAPPY, HAPPY, HAPPY,
HAPPY, HAPPY, HAPPY,
HAPPY, HAPPY, HAPPY,
HAP HAPPY

How can we fix my, this man's dilemma you may ask? My company, we purchase the network. We will use our combined resources to manipulate the sky. While we work to fill the landfill, adding toxicity, providing fodder for your disaster reports, you will promote:

(In rhythm.) THE COLLECTIVE CONSCIOUS CREATIVE VISUALIZATION OF THE AR-MAGEDDON

COOL-KIDS: HEMZABABUB-MASS DE-STRUCTION. HEMZABABUBBU-MASS DESTRUCTION

BEEP: YES! COLLIN CLEMENT WE NEED YOU TO SENSATIONALIZE THE SKY
TO USE THE PROPHECY MYTHS PASSED ON TO US FROM THE HOLY OF HOLIES

COOL-KIDS: THE HOLY OF HOLIES

BEEP: THE SCRIPTURE SAYS THE

ENSEMBLE: END OF THE WORLD IS COMING

BEEP: AND THE PEOPLE DISTRAUGHT WITH FEAR
WILL CLING TO THINGS THAT MAKE THEM HAPPY
THEY WILL BUY MORE TOYS, FILL THE LANDFILL
SEND US TO ETERNAL JOY AND MAKE US HAPPY
THEY'LL MAKE US HAPPY
HAPPY MOMMY, HAPPY

OLOKUN: That's horrible.

FALSE JESUS: Someone judges. Someone judges.

CONSTANCE FAUBOURG: Shut up False Jesus.

OLOKUN: He wants to use consumerism as a way to pollute the world, destroying the planet so he can go to heaven and be happy.

BEEP: I am not a monster. I am not part of the problem. My daughter is a lesbian.

LYNNE: Mine too.

THE COLLECTIVE CONSCIOUS: Enough.

COOL-KID #1: Collin Clement continue.

COLLIN: Where were we? Right. I'm stuck in a rut and the network comes to me to make a change for the good of mankind and an increased paycheck, in the process I begin to report on a disturbing phenomenon. Red Tide Blooming.

"RED TIDE BLOOMING, PART 1"

COLLIN: RED TIDE DISCOLORATION CAUSED BY A DENSE CONCENTRATION

OF MICROSCOPIC PLANTS OF THE SEA

So called phytoplankton known as dino-flagellates. *(To audience.)* Say it with me: Dinoflagellates. Very good. Occasionally, these algae grow very fast or bloom and accumulate into dense, visible patches near the surface of the water changing the pigment of the sea to:

RED, RED TIDE BLOOMS

Some of these species produce potent neurotoxins that can be transferred through the food web.

THE FIRST SYMPTOMS ARE A TINGLING, PRICKLING, STINGING, OR BURNING SENSATION OF THE LIPS, TONGUE, AND FINGERTIPS
NUMBNESS OF THE ARMS
LEGS AND NECK
OTHER SYMPTOMS DEVELOP LATER AND INCLUDE:

Dizziness, general muscle incoordination, headaches, vomiting, impaired respiration, blah blah blah blah…and death. Scientists have concluded that red tides are occurring with increasing intensity and frequency over a wider global distribution, and that this may be a result of human activities. *(Going to BEEP.)* Pollution such as trash piled high in the landfill is thought to have influenced the intensity and frequency of red

RED TIDE BLOOM

And along with the Red Tide I speak of hurricanes, earthquakes, tornadoes, skin cancer, images of tidal waves engulfing skyscrapers—suffocating the sinful,

(COLLIN brings OLOKUN center.)

COLLIN: sending the expendable extras cluttering our central character peripheral visions to sea.

(OLOKUN is pushed out of the spotlight.)

COLLIN: Suddenly my fan mail, well it triples.

BEEP: Now is time to introduce the nurturer of nature. Concerned citizen, she of the perpetual diet and warm breath on wounds. Ladies and gentlemen our congregation and protectress—Constance Faubourg.

CONSTANCE FAUBOURG: Hey.

OLOKUN: That's the lady who wanted to kill me in suburbia. What's she doing here?

LYNNE: I feared this.

OLOKUN: What?

LYNNE: The suburbanites are on the rise.

SLAVASKIA: They spread like mold.

LYNNE: They hate suburbia.

SLAVASKIA: But they afraid to go anyplace that is not suburbia.

LYNNE: So they make everyplace suburbia.

SLAVASKIA: So they can escape suburbia.

COOL-KIDS: Welcome Constance.

THE COLLECTIVE CONSCIOUS: Constance Faubourg sits down at her sturdy factory-farmed table. She pulls out her writing pen, absentmindedly stolen from the local bank, drug store, checkout stand. Her trusty book of Gospel at her side, instructing her every move, she writes a fan letter.

CONSTANCE FAUBOURG: Dear Collin Clement, each morning I wake. I pour my children glasses of orange juice. Jenny gets No Pulp. Susie likes some. Billy—Calcium Enriched, 'cause he won't drink dairy. I worry about his bones. I have argued with him: Billy you must drink the milk of a cow. If not:

"Bearing the Sorrow"

CONSTANCE FAUBOURG: YOU AS HUMPTY BEFORE YOU
WILL SCATTER TO
DERISION, SPIRITUAL MALNUTRITION
BROUGHT FROM FAULTY DECISIONS
LEAVING LOVED ONES, ALL ALONE
TURNING TO DUST, AND GOING FAR AWAY FROM HOME
I CANNOT BEAR THE SORROW
OF WATCHING YOU GROW

But Billy holds to his stubborn ways. And sometimes all a mother can do is impart information. It is not the mother's fault if none choose to listen. Collin, you and I are so similar. We give warnings of what is to come. I to my children—you to the congregation. Collin Clement, I see you each morning, so beautiful to behold. You are my Saint John the Divine. You eat the book of knowledge and report the grand conclusion. You are the prophet.

COLLIN: Yes.

CONSTANCE FAUBOURG: Know Collin Clement—I am listening. I am listening.

RECEIVING MESSES
RECEIVING MESSAGES
FROM AN ANGEL
CLOTHED IN A CLOUD
WITH A RAINBOW
SURROUNDING HIS HEAD
HIS FEET PILLARS OF FIRE

COLLIN: Encouraged by the millions of letters and an increased paycheck I can see a way out of the monotony and fear. The Grand Conclusion. I can make it happen while I'm on the air. Even on the pretty days I can make it happen. Looks like it's clear skies for the rest of the week but on the horizon. Every drizzle of rain becomes a biblical onslaught. It goes something like this.

(GIFT SHOP GURU, now dressed as a cloud, does an interpretive dance, representing an Armageddon weather report, with FALSE JESUS.)

"The Weather Report"

COLLIN: TODAY THE CLOUDS WILL BE A TUMULTUOUS PANACEA
TO ALL OUR UNREQUITED HEARTLESS FRIENDS
AND LOVED ONES
TODAY THE CLOUDS WILL BRING US
TO THE LOVE OF JESUS
TO THE LOVE OF GOD AH MEN

(BEEP conducts ENSEMBLE.)

ENSEMBLE: TODAY THE CLOUDS WILL COMMENCE
TUMBLING FORTH WITH VENGEANCE
DIVVYING ALL THE MANY PUNISHMENTS
TODAY THE CLOUDS WILL TORTURE
DESTROY EXTOL AND SCORCHER
TEARING UP THIS MORTAL FIRMAMENT

CONSTANCE FAUBOURG: And the prophecy! The prophecy says.

COLLIN: What does it say? What does it say?

CONSTANCE FAUBOURG: The Seven Last Plagues of Revelation 16 are:

BEEP: Number 1!

(COOL-KIDS, FALSE JESUS, and GIFT SHOP GURU represent the various plagues.)

CONSTANCE FAUBOURG: Sores.

COLLIN: The AIDS epidemic.

ENSEMBLE: Hemzababubu-sores.

BEEP: Number two!

CONSTANCE FAUBOURG: Heat!

COLLIN: Global warming!

ENSEMBLE: Hemzababub-heat.

BEEP: Plague number three.

CONSTANCE FAUBOURG: Darkness on the throne of the beast.

COLLIN: The 2003 Eastern North American Blackout.

ENSEMBLE: Hemzababub-darkness.

BEEP: Number four!

CONSTANCE FAUBOURG: Euphrates dries up. What does that mean?

BEEP: A great military loss.

CONSTANCE FAUBOURG: And the sign of this?

COLLIN: Death toll in Iraq!

ENSEMBLE: Hemzababubu-Iraq.

BEEP: Plague number five!

CONSTANCE FAUBOURG: Disaster from the air and earth!

COLLIN: Hurricane Katrina and the Pakistani quake.

ENSEMBLE: Hemzababubu-disaster.

CONSTANCE FAUBOURG: And our final two plagues of Revelations?

FALSE JESUS: Oooooooo I know. I know.

CONSTANCE FAUBOURG: Shut it!

BEEP: Numbers six and seven.

(CONSTANCE drags OLOKUN and HIPPO forward to represent the final two plagues.)

"RED TIDE BLOOMING, PART 2"

CONSTANCE FAUBOURG: BLOOD IN THE RIVER
BLOOD IN THE SEA
RED TIDE BLOOM FOR
YOU AND ME

COLLIN and CONSTANCE FAUBOURG: BLOOD IN THE RIVER
BLOOD IN THE SEA
RED TIDE BLOOM FOR YOU AND ME

COLLIN, CONSTANCE, and BEEP: BLOOD IN THE RIVER
BLOOD IN THE SEA
RED TIDE BLOOM FOR YOU AND ME

COOL-KIDS: *(Spoken in rhythm.)* The Collective Conscious creative visualization of the Armageddon is for you and me

ENSEMBLE: RED
RED TIDE BLOOM

COLLIN: Tonight the final steps towards fulfillment will occur.

BEEP: Tonight we will cleanse the only remaining refuge of discomfort—the Freak Show.

COOL-KIDS: *(Shuddering.)* Ewwww.

CONSTANCE FAUBOURG: The Scriptures say a flood is needed to wash those few resisters out to sea.

COLLIN: And bring us to perpetual comfort.

CONSTANCE FAUBOURG: And only way to bring about a flood, so says Numbers—

COOL-KIDS: Hemzababubu-numbers.

(FALSE JESUS presents the triumvirate with the sweater, who then become it.)

THE COLLECTIVE CONSCIOUS: Is to cleanse the Freak Show with the ashes of a flawless red hippo.

COOL-KIDS: Hemzababubu-hippo.

OLOKUN: A hippo?

THE COLLECTIVE CONSCIOUS: And now children. I present to you…The Perfect Red Hippo.

(EVERYONE looks at OLOKUN's WHITE HIPPO.)

LYNNE: That's white.

ENSEMBLE: *(At LYNNE's audacity.)* Gasp.

LYNNE: Well it is.

COOL-KIDS: *(With sadness.)* Ahhhh.

THE COLLECTIVE CONSCIOUS: She speaks truth.

LYNNE: I told you.

THE COLLECTIVE CONSCIOUS: We have an invited guest this evening. One who holds the solution to turning the white hippo red.

(EVERYONE looks in the direction of SLAVASKIA, who is standing behind LYNNE.)

LYNNE: Me?

SLAVASKIA: I am special guest. I am queen.

COLLIN: A curious side note to the red tide phenomenon: Red Tide dinoflagellates have silicon in their cell walls.

THE COLLECTIVE CONSCIOUS: We need your boob juice.

LYNNE: That's disgusting.

BEEP: The old lady's breasts are the answer.

SLAVASKIA: I NOT OLD LADY.

CONSTANCE FAUBOURG: She will breast feed the white hippo with red tide blooming breast milk and make the perfect red hippo.

SLAVASKIA: I do no such thing.

CONSTANCE FAUBOURG: You want your title, bitch? Well, Beep is the title sponsor. Collin Clement is the judge. We can provide it for you. But first you have to breast feed the hippo.

SLAVASKIA: I not want title that much.

CONSTANCE FAUBOURG: You know what happens to the elderly Slavaskia.

SLAVASKIA: I not elderly.

CONSTANCE FAUBOURG and BEEP: They are thrown to the sea.

SLAVASKIA: No.

CONSTANCE FAUBOURG, BEEP, and COLLIN: Drowned in the ocean to make the waves with their blue hair.

SLAVASKIA: I no go!

THE COLLECTIVE CONSCIOUS: Forced to bring the flood.

SLAVASKIA: Okay. I do it. I do it.

OLOKUN: Slavaskia you can't. They want to kill it and reduce all the freaks to nothing.

LYNNE: Besides it's disgusting.

SLAVASKIA: They crazy, they think reduction is simple as volume control. Let them think so. I get title, world keep going, freaks keep popping up.

OLOKUN: But they want to kill it.

SLAVASKIA: What do I care for hippo? What do you know? I am queen you are just hermaphrodite sea creature in conglomerate sweater.

(Angry with OLOKUN, SLAVASKIA pulls its waist scarf off—revealing the obscure genitalia.)

ENSEMBLE: *(A collective gasp of disgust.)* Ah!

THE COLLECTIVE CONSCIOUS: *(Seeing OLOKUN and turning truly horrifying.)* FREEEEEEAK.

LYNNE: Run.

(FALSE JESUS threatens them with the thorn of Christ.)

LYNNE: This way!

(GIFT SHOP GURU is on the other side with the tooth of Buddha. LYNNE and OLOKUN are captured.)

THE COLLECTIVE CONSCIOUS: Tie them up—we will lobotomize them into submission.

LYNNE: God damn it.

(ATINA wiggles on.)

ATINA: Wait!

(EVERYONE stops to wait for ATINA to wiggle center.)

ATINA: The truth of the hippo and the heifer.

(Suddenly EVERYONE breaks character and sets up a blue sheet that both represents

the ocean and is the masking for a puppet show theatre.)

ATINA: In keeping with our aquatic theme we have changed the actual bible prophecy of the Red Heifer into the Red Hippo. For those of you confused as to who or what the Red Heifer is…listen carefully as we all break character to sing the actual truth of the Red Heifer.

(The ACTOR PLAYING OLOKUN animates HIPPO.)

"The Hippo and the Heifer"

WHITE HIPPO: THIS IS THE TRUTH OF THE HIPPO AND THE HEIFER
AND THE HEIFER AND THE HIPPO AND THE HIPPO AND THE HEIFER
THE PERFECT SPOTLESS EFFERVESCENT RED HIPPO HEIFER
THE HIPPO IS A METAPHOR FOR THE RED HEIFER
THE HEIFER IS A PROPHECY WRITTEN IN THE SCRIPTURE
THE SCRIPTURES TELL THE WAY TO GET PASSAGE TO THE TEMPLE
WITH THE ASHES OF THE FLAWLESS EFFERVESCENT RED HEIFER
THE TEMPLE IS A HOLY SPOT UPON WHICH WHEN ENTERED
A PRIEST CAN BRING THE END OF ALL CREATION
WITH THE ASHES OF A FLAWLESS EFFERVESCENT RED HEIFER
NOT FLORESCENT, EFFERVESCENT PERFECT RED HEIFER

COLLIN: There sure are a lot of details to keep track of.

BEEP: It's an old trick of the trade. The more details they throw at you, the more you get frustrated and let 'em do whatever they want.

WHITE HIPPO: IN 1996, THANKS IN PART TO CATTLE BREEDERS

(A CHRISTIAN appears.)

CHRISTIAN: WHO ARE FUNDAMENTALIST CHRISTIAN TEXAN OIL RANCHERS

WHITE HIPPO: WHO ARE WORKING WITH A RABBI NAMED ELEAZAR.

(A RABBI appears.)

ELEAZAR: DNA EFFORTS MADE A PERFECT RED HEIFER

WHITE HIPPO: THE PERFECT RED HEIFER WAS BROUGHT TO THE ALTAR
BUT THEN IT WAS DISCOVERED THAT THE DNA FALTERED
THE PERFECT RED HEIFER HAD WHITE HAIRS ON HER NOZZLE
IT WAS BACK TO THE DRAWING BOARD TO PURIFY THE HEIFER APOSTLE
AND THIS IS WHY THE CHRISTIANS DO THE JEWS THIS FAVOR
SO THAT THEY CAN HAVE THEIR HOLY SAVIOR
THE SCRIPTURES SAY THEY'LL GET THEIR SECOND COMIN'

ELEAZAR: ONLY IF THEY GET THE JEWS TO TEMPLE HUMMIN'

CHRISTIAN: THE CHRISTIANS THINK THE JEWS WILL BURN IN HELL FOREVER

ELEAZAR: THE JEWS THINK THE CHRISTIANS WILL ALL BE SEVERED

WHITE HIPPO: FROM THE HOLY LAND, YES THEY'LL ALL FINALLY TRIUMPH

GIFT SHOP GURU: OVER ALL THE MUSLIMS AND THEIR SUICIDE RELIANCE

ALL FOUR: YOU CAN LAUGH 'CAUSE IT'S ALL KINDA FUNNY
BUT THE FACTS ARE THE MUSLIMS WON'T BE SUNNY

WHEN THE JEWS ENTER THE MUSLIMS' HOLY MOSQUE
WHICH MEANS THE MUSLIMS WILL DESTROY
THE JEWS WILL TEAR TO SHREDS, EMPLOY THE CHRISTIANS TO REJOICE THE END OF ALL CREATION OH YES AND
IT COULD ALL BE BROUGHT ABOUT
DUE TO A NEW PERFECT RED HEIFER SNOUT
THOUGHT TO BRING THE RESURRECTION
DEATH AND DESTRUCTION FROM FORCED PERFECTION
OH THIS IS THE TRUTH OF THE HIPPO AND THE HEIFER
AND THE HEIFER AND THE HIPPO AND THE HIPPO AND THE HEIFER AND THE PERFECT SPOTLESS EFFERVESCENT RED HIPPO HEIFER

WHITE HIPPO: NOT FLORESCENT, EFFERVESCENT, PERFECT RED HEIFER.

(GIFT SHOP GURU grabs HIPPO.)

GIFT SHOP GURU: I got the hippo!

OLOKUN: Hey gimme back my hippo!

GIFT SHOP GURU: *(Diabolic laughter.)* Wa ha ha ha ha ha!

(OLOKUN chases GIFT SHOP GURU, but gets tangled up in a hanging jellyfish.)

CONSTANCE FAUBOURG: *(To SLAVASKIA.)* Now suckle.

SLAVASKIA: Come little one, I turn you red.

WHITE HIPPO: Mooooo—baby.

(SLAVASKIA begins to breast feed WHITE HIPPO. She and HIPPO disappear behind the ocean/sheet. We hear suckling sounds and exclamations from SLAVASKIA. When she pops up again, her breasts have been suckled to sags.)

SLAVASKIA: AHHHHHHHHHH-HHH! My precious tchotchkes.

(A drum roll.)

CONSTANCE FAUBOURG: Behold! The Red Hippo!

(RED HIPPO pops up from behind the water/sheet.)

RED HIPPO: Hi everybody!

CONSTANCE FAUBOURG: And now...

RED HIPPO: Drown the hag!

(THE COLLECTIVE CONSCIOUS and GIFT SHOP GURU begin to drown SLAVASKIA.)

SLAVASKIA: You said I get title.

THE COLLECTIVE CONSCIOUS: You. You're an old lady.

SLAVASKIA: Noooooooo!

LYNNE: My God that sweater is forceful.

SLAVASKIA: I am victim of youth-based culture.

OLOKUN: We have to stop them.

LYNNE: Help me get free so I can keep writing.

OLOKUN: You can't write now, we have to save Slavaskia.

LYNNE: Olie, this is how it has to be.

OLOKUN: What?

LYNNE: There is no saving the old lady, there is no freeing of the freaks.

OLOKUN: But you said—

LYNNE: I said, I said.

OLOKUN: You lied.

LYNNE: Of course I lied, I'm telling the story of transcendence—it's all one big perpetual lie.

OLOKUN: It looks real.

LYNNE: Because there's truth in it. You take snippets and squish them together. That's how you come up with a story. How you make it believable and convince yourself of its merit. That's what this story is really about. About the convincing.

OLOKUN: No.

LYNNE: And there are parts of the story of transcendence that must be told. There's a sacrifice. An abandonment. Many deaths. Maybe millions. A crusade. Vast amounts of marbles lost. An eradication of the odd, old, ugly, different. There is a plot to end the world, a media frenzy, mythic beings, a microscopic titan, and finally a metamorphosis into perpetual comfort.

OLOKUN: But perpetual comfort means everyone being the same, you want that?

LYNNE: It doesn't matter what I want. We've reached the moment when you can't reverse the trajectory.

(SLAVASKIA breathes her final breath and dies—the actor has changed wigs and now has blue hair.)

CONSTANCE FAUBOURG: Now on to the freak-cleansing ceremony where we can bring about the Armageddon in peace and quiet.

(EVERYONE exits with diabolic laughter [if you think it's diabolical enough—it's not].)

ENSEMBLE: Wa ha ha ha ha ha ha ha ha ha.

SCENE IV

ATINA enters doing a dance. She makes her way to a microphone and begins singing on the mouth trumpet. ARISTA enters doing a dance. Lights change. We are now underwater.

ARISTA: It is a noble occupation communing with something as temperamental as water on the move. On the bad days I fight her thrashing and end up bruised and fucked up. On the good days, when she's decided my piggybacking is enough, I let her twist and bend my body as she will. A win and a defeat. Bliss and fright. All at the same time.

(The MERMAIDS dance off. SLAVASKIA enters. She explores her new environment. One by one, ENSEMBLE enters, carrying puppets who are THE BLUE-HAIRED LADIES that make the ocean waves.)

"I CAME BEFORE YOU"

SLAVASKIA: I CAME BEFORE YOU
PRIOR TO ALL YOUR JOYS
AHEAD OF YOUR THOUGHTS AND CARES
I CAME BEFORE YOU
WE DANCED THESE STREETS TO GROUND
WE SWAM THIS OCEAN BROWN
WE TRANCED THE PEOPLE WITH TRADITIONS
    TURNED 'ROUND
BROKE THROUGH THE BARRICADES
WE MADE THE PEOPLE LAUGH
JIGGLING VITAL ORGANS
WE CRACKED THE WORLD IN HALF
TURNED THOUGHTS INSIDE OUT
GAVE NEW PERSPECTIVES
VANQUISHED SELF-CONSCIOUS DOUBT
WHEN WE CAME BEFORE YOU
I WAS THE RAGING STAR

SOON A DEAD DISCOVERY
NAMED AFTER A COMPANY
SELLING SELLING
BUT I CAME BEFORE YOU
YOU'RE JUST A COPY
A WATERED-DOWN PIECE OF ME
MY DEAD MEMORIES

BLUE-HAIRED LADIES: BENEATH THE
    SURFACE OF MY DRINK I'M SWIMMING
DWINDLING DOWN TO, DWINDLING DOWN
    TO NOTHING
BENEATH THE SURFACE OF MY DRINK I'M
    FLOATING
DWINDLING DOWN, DWINDLING DOWN
    TO I AGREES

BLUE-HAIRED LADY REGINA: Regina Carlson. I moved to the floating landfill in 1952. Sprawled out in a cold-water flat on the Lower East Side, each Sunday we held great big macrobiotic potluck diners. Every week, dozens of people from all walks of life would show up full of ideas and flirtations. Regina Carlson.

BLUE-HAIRED LADY SABRINA: Sabrina Rustin. It seems nowadays it is a revolutionary act to leave your house when you're old or ugly. This does not surprise me, as in my youth acts of bravery were simple gestures as well: a black man holding a white woman's hand on the street, or two men kissing in a parked car. Sabrina Rustin.

BLUE-HAIRED LADY ETHYL: Ethyl Crisp. Many of my generation look back on our youth and claim, "We changed the world!" I wouldn't say we changed it so much, but to the chagrin of every downtown theatre institution, we did invent glitter. Sprinkling a little glamour and beauty into the wrinkles of our floorboards and ourselves. When you think about it, the invention of glitter is not too shabby an accomplishment. Ethyl Crisp.

(THE BLUE-HAIRED LADIES begin to fade away.)

SLAVASKIA: BUT HERE STILL I FADE AWAY
INTO SOLICITOUS WANDERING
ALL THAT WE HAD TO SAY
TURNED BARGAINING CHIPS OF LET ME STAY
AND BROKEN STATUS NEON SIGNS BLINKING REMEMBER
PLEASE REMEMBER MMMMMM-E-MMMMMM-E-MMMMMMM-E-MMMMMMMMM.

(SLAVASKIA is pulled off by the LAST OF THE BLUE-HAIRED LADIES.)

SCENE V

CONSTANCE enters with ELEAZAR, who carries a giant bible, large enough for the audience to read the actual verses, opened to Numbers, chapter 19, verses 2–5. The bible looks like a Holy Scripture Cookbook. GIFT SHOP GURU carries RED HIPPO and ushers the tied-up LYNNE and OLOKUN to the opposite side of the stage.

CONSTANCE FAUBOURG: Welcome one and all to the final freak-cleansing ceremony. Tonight we will cut the throat of the Red Hippo and finalize the cleansing process.

(ARISTA enters, carrying cans of tuna.)

ARISTA: Get your tuna here. Tuna.

CONSTANCE FAUBOURG: And now do we have the ingredients to finish the dwindling process? According to the Holy Scriptures we need one spotless "Red Hippo."

(Wherever it says "Heifer" in the bible, it should be crossed out and "Hippo" should be written above it.)

ELEAZAR: Check.

ARISTA: *(To OLOKUN.)* Pssssst.

OLOKUN: *(To ARISTA.)* Get away from me, sell-out.

CONSTANCE FAUBOURG: One priest Eleazar.

ELEAZAR: Check.

CONSTANCE FAUBOURG: That he may "bring the Red Hippo forth without camp."

GIFT SHOP GURU: Whatever you say Mary.

(The THREE laugh silently and continue an exaggerated silent conversation.)

ARISTA: Listen I don't have long. Me and some of the other Little Mermaids, we're incognito.

(AQUATA and ALLANA come to untie their rope.)

ALLANA: Really we're a bunch of freaks like you.

AQUATA: Forced to conceal our boobies behind shells.

CONSTANCE FAUBOURG: *(To ELEAZAR.)* Now Eleazar has to cut the Red Hippo's throat and stick his finger in her bloody slot and then sprinkle the blood in front of the paparazzi.

(In the bible, the word "congregation" should be crossed out and "paparazzi" written in its place. BEEP and COLLIN enter with the sweater, which has a camera tied around its neck.)

THE COLLECTIVE CONSCIOUS: One paparazzo.

ELEAZAR: Check.

ARISTA: We're fed up with this story of revitalization and reduction.

ALLANA: We're shedding light on truth.

AQUATA: And we've got a few surprises.

BEEP: It says here you sprinkle her blood seven times, then burn her flesh, her blood, and her dung.

CONSTANCE FAUBOURG: One piece of dung.

(ELEAZAR pulls a piece of dung out of RED HIPPO.)

RED HIPPO: Mooooo.

ELEAZAR: Check.

ARISTA: When the time is right—grab the hippo and run.

OLOKUN: But what if they see me?

ALLANA: Mermaid Atina's about to make the ultimate sacrifice to ensure they don't.

ARISTA: You know what to do girls.

ALLANA and ATINA: The Gods are in the distractions.

(ALLANA unties OLOKUN and LYNNE.)

CONSTANCE FAUBOURG: Are you ready?

ELEAZAR: Ready.

THE COLLECTIVE CONSCIOUS, ELEAZAR, and GIFT SHOP GURU: KILL THE HIPPO!

ATINA: WAAAAAAIT!

(EVERYONE stops and waits for ATINA to wiggle center.)

ATINA: *(Taking her shells off.)* I'm a freak!

(GIFT SHOP GURU, in horror, throws HIPPO up in the air. OLOKUN catches it and sneaks off.)

THE COLLECTIVE CONSCIOUS: COVER THOSE BREASTS!

"THE BOOB CHASE"

(The Boob Chase is done to kazoo accompaniment. During the Boob Chase, GIFT SHOP GURU chases after ATINA, trying to cover her breasts with his hands. She eludes. He tries again and is knocked back by them.)

CONSTANCE FAUBOURG: She nearly knocked you out.

(GIFT SHOP GURU tries again and is knocked down once more.)

GIFT SHOP GURU: Why do you think they call 'em knockers?

(GIFT SHOP GURU tries one more time and is successful. Speaks with his hands on her breasts.)

GIFT SHOP GURU: Got 'em.

ELEAZAR: Now finally we can kill the hippo.

BEEP: Hey. Where'd it go?

ELEAZAR: *(Holding a piece of dung.)* Shit.

(EVERYONE runs off in search of RED HIPPO. LYNNE acts like she's with them.)

ENSEMBLE: Here little hippo. Here hippo... *(Etc.)*

SCENE VI

OLOKUN enters with HIPPO.

OLOKUN: The Freak Show. We made it. We're safe now. Lynne was wrong. It doesn't have to end badly.

RED HIPPO: Moooo.

OLOKUN: I found us a sanctuary where all the others like us live. We'll have so many friends to play with now. Look. "The Bearded Lady."

(A sign says "The Bearded Lady." OLOKUN looks for her, but all that's left is an electric razor and some beard clippings.)

OLOKUN: Oh. Well maybe this one. "The World's Tiniest Man." *(Looks. Nothing.)* Maybe he's just too small to see? Well maybe this one then. Our last hope. "The Sword-Swallowing Gagless Geek." *(Sees a note where the Sword Swallower should be standing.)* "Left to get a job with benefits."

RED HIPPO: Mooo.

OLOKUN: Oh, don't cry little hippo. Two freaks are better than one.

"LITTLE ONE"

OLOKUN: LITTLE ONE DON'T BE AFRAID
I HAVE FOUND A PLACE
WHERE WE CAN HIDE AWAY
FROM THE MADNESS TURNED RIGHT
FROM THE SADNESS TURNED TO FRIGHT
FAR FROM THE PEOPLE
WHO WANT TO BE OH SO YOUNG
OH LITTLE ONE

(HIPPO begins to vomit violently.)

RED HIPPO: Blackkkkackkkk…

OLOKUN: Red Hippo what's wrong? What's…

(HIPPO shits ferociously.)

RED HIPPO: Pheppurbpheppurb…

OLOKUN: No. Don't die little hippo. Don't die.

(HIPPO dies a horrible death. OLOKUN runs away from it. COLLIN, BEEP, CONSTANCE [with sweater], and LYNNE enter.)

COLLIN: *(To OLOKUN.)* Now look what you've done.

OLOKUN: You can't come in here. It's the Freak Show.

BEEP: Well now that the freaks are all gone, who's gonna stop us?

LYNNE: *(Writing in her pad.)* The little red hippo lies asphyxiated on dreams of interminable beauty.

OLOKUN: What are *you* doing with them?

LYNNE: I'm trying to get all sides of the story.

CONSTANCE FAUBOURG: You killed it.

OLOKUN: I didn't do anything. You're the ones who—

COLLIN: It was going to die anyway. Hippo was not meant to eat silicone.

BEEP: You could have at least let us use it for the good of the end.

OLOKUN: It was going to die because you poisoned it.

CONSTANCE FAUBOURG: Yes well…now we'll need a replacement.

OLOKUN: What?

COLLIN: We convinced the masses we needed a Red Hippo—

BEEP: Why not now that we really need the sacrifice of a green hermaphrodite sea creature?

OLOKUN: You are a mean… sweater.

THE COLLECTIVE CONSCIOUS:
Yes.

OLOKUN: *(To LYNNE.)* You were
right. I can't reverse the trajectory of
oddities being classified, revitalized,
appropriated, and turned to salesmen
of shit.

CONSTANCE FAUBOURG: Well.

OLOKUN: You are all just a bunch
of flies hovering the airstreams, wings,
clear as nothing, palpitating dysfunction,
"Please let the shit hit the fan. Please
gimme the shit. Gimme the shit." And
maybe, you think, if you're an obedient
fated god-given special fly, maybe a speck
of brown hope will de-cling itself from
the fan, propel through the airstreams
and smack you right in the 303rd eye.

CONSTANCE FAUBOURG: Are you
finished?

OLOKUN: You're all just a bunch of
lonely people!

BEEP: That's the point.

OLOKUN: And you can obliterate
yourself to same all you want; you will
never not feel lonely.

THE COLLECTIVE CONSCIOUS:
Don't you burst my bubble!

OLOKUN: This story. *(To LYNNE.)*
Your story sucks.

LYNNE: Olie!

OLOKUN: I want to tell a story where
people celebrate discomfort.

BEEP: Oh!

OLOKUN: Where the hero is a soggy
sock.

COLLIN: Ew.

OLOKUN: Or a hermaphrodite sea
creature.

LYNNE: Yes!

OLOKUN: *(A revelation.)* Oh!

CONSTANCE FAUBOURG: Bullshit!
Bullshit you want a soggy hermaphrodite
hero. I know you! You're not special. You
just want safety like me.

COLLIN: You just want approval like
me.

BEEP: You just want to be so young;
nothing's your fault. Like me.

OLOKUN: Oh yeah. *(Pulls the scarf
away to reveal its esoteric genitalia.)*

THE COLLECTIVE CONSCIOUS:
Oh!

(OLOKUN wiggles the genitalia.)

COLLIN: Ewww.

BEEP: Mommy!

CONSTANCE FAUBOURG: Stop
that!

(OLOKUN wiggles.)

CONSTANCE FAUBOURG: *(To
the audience and OTHERS.)* Don't let
him fool you. He's not special. He's
not different. He's not even a real hermaphrodite.

BEEP: What?

CONSTANCE FAUBOURG: He just
taped his dick to his ass so he could look
like one.

COLLIN: I knew it!

OLOKUN: Yes I did! *(Rips the duct tape
off his genitalia.)* I'm a freak *because* I

did that! And what's more, I'm not the only freak. *(Pointing to BEEP.)* That's a bearded lady. And it's not even a real beard. And you. Collin Clement. You. Come here. *(Slapping COLLIN's sixpack stomach.)* That's not normal. *(To CONSTANCE.)* And you. You're a freak too. You're from the Bronx.

CONSTANCE FAUBOURG: *(With a heavy Bronx accent.)* Oh no he din't!

OLOKUN: I'm not the only freak. You're all freaks. *(Pointing to an audience member.)* You're a freak too. I slept with him. He's a freak. And you, look at you! I'm not the only freak. We're all—

(CONSTANCE grabs the GIFT SHOP GURU's sword, THE COLLECTIVE CONSCIOUS holds OLOKUN's arms down, and Constance stabs OLOKUN.)

OLOKUN: Ackkkk!

(OLOKUN begins to bleed to death. The lights shift. Storm music plays.)

BEEP: What's happening?

CONSTANCE FAUBOURG: We sacrificed it.

COLLIN: Does that mean?

CONSTANCE FAUBOURG: We've brought about the Apocalypse.

BEEP: Oh goodie.

(While bleeding to death, OLOKUN makes his way to a microphone.)

"THE SEVEN STAGES OF THE APOCALYPSE"

OLOKUN: And now ladies and gentlemen, having been sacrificed, it is my duty to present to you the seven stages of the Apocalypse. Number one. *(Sprinkles blood for each stage.)* The Flood.

(THE BLUE-HAIRED LADIES enter in flood formation and scatter, attacking everything in their wake.)

OLOKUN: Number two. The Tornado.

(A hula-hooping JESUS comes in. BEEP, CONSTANCE, and COLLIN are blown around.)

COLLIN: It's a tornado.

CONSTANCE FAUBOURG: No shit!

(They are blown off.)

OLOKUN: Stage number three. Love in the Time of Collar.

(LYNNE comes on with THE COLLECTIVE CONSCIOUS sweater [without the OTHERS]. She makes love to it.)

LYNNE: Green on pink baby. Pink on green.

OLOKUN: Number four. The Kick Line.

(ENSEMBLE enters and does a kick line.)

OLOKUN: Number five. Blood Lust.

(CANNIBALS circle CONSTANCE at the stake.)

OLOKUN: And now, the final two stages of the Apocalypse. Numbers six and seven, Chaos and the Rapture.

(A CANNIBAL breaks the cannibal circle screaming…)

CANNIBAL: Fuck me now!

(The COMPANY MEMBERS fuck each other. A triple threat all-in-one JESUS/ MOHAMMED/BUDDHA enters and stands center. BLUE-HAIRED LADIES flood the stage, attacking their PUPPE-

*TEERS. GIFT SHOP GURU and FALSE
JESUS enter screaming, rip each other's
tear-away clothes off, and exit naked and
screaming. OLOKUN, barely alive, pulls
his wig off and puts it in a bucket, shits in
the bucket, and burns the contents while
still singing. LYNNE enters with a giant
"Connect-the-Dots Mohammed." She is
about to connect her first dot when…)*

OLOKUN: WAIT!

*(EVERYONE stops what they're doing
and wiggles offstage, as if they were mermaids.)*

ACTOR PLAYING OLOKUN (TAY-
LOR): The Actor Playing Olokun, that's
me…I sing the final song.

"Safe"

TAYLOR: *(Picking up a ukulele.)* I'M SAFE.
I'M NOT SAFE.
I'M AN OUTSIDER.
WHAT AM I TALKING ABOUT
I'M A PRIVILEGED WHITE MALE AMERICAN.
I'M A HOMOSEXUAL
AND SO I'M NOT SAFE *(As if to say, "you can't
use that excuse anymore.)*
HOMOSEXUALS ARE ON TV
AND THAT MEANS I'M SAFE?
I'M NOT SAFE
I'M A TRANSSEXUAL.
NO, I'M A DRAG QUEEN. NO, I'M AN ARTIST
OR MAYBE I'M NOT

Maybe you can see that I just like to dress
up in funny costumes. And besides Jackie
Curtis is the only original, 'cause he did it
all before me. Wait are you trying to say
that the Greeks never dressed feminine
and went on the stage? Shit Taylor, this
is in my DNA.

AND IF I KEEP EXPECTING THE PARTY TO
    PROVIDE ME WITH THE FUN INSTEAD OF
    ME PROVIDING THE FUN TO THE PARTY,

THEN I'LL NEVER BE SAFE FROM THE
    DWINDLING AWAY INTO HOMOGENY.
SO I'M SAFE, AND I'M NOT SAFE
I'M A NEW YORKER, I CAME FROM CALIFOR-
    NIA TO ESCAPE SUBURBIA WHERE I WAS
    NOT SAFE, AND STILL I'M NOT SAFE I WILL
    NEVER BE SAFE BECAUSE SUBURBIA HAS
    MOVED TO NEW YORK AND SAN FRAN-
    CISCO, AND EVERY BASTION OF ESCAPE
    FROM NORMALCY AND MADE IT MUCH
    TOO SAFE AND SO I'M NOT SAFE,

Wait, are you trying to tell me you'd
prefer New York to be full of violence
like in the old days? But all the freaks
have gone away and we have become
much too safe, I mean, things aren't the
way the used to be *(Freakier and freakier
with each "used to be.")*

USED TO BE
USED TO BE
USED TO BE
USED TO BE

You're right. *(With sweet sarcasm.)* All the
freaks have gone away and things aren't
the way they used to be. I didn't used
to be freak. I used to go out at night
and grow foliage up against the wall.
And what's worse, I would do it wearing khakis. And then one day I said to
myself, "Taylor!

IF YOU KEEP EXPECTING THE PARTY TO PRO-
    VIDE YOU WITH THE FUN INSTEAD OF
    YOU PROVIDING THE FUN TO THE PARTY,
    THEN YOU'LL NEVER BE SAFE FROM THE
    DWINDLING AWAY INTO HOMOGENY."

(A light shifts.)

TAYLOR: And so the hermaphrodite sea
creature named Olokun was sacrificed
and the great Apocalypse came. And
the truth of the story is…among those
washed to sea and among those few who
remained, none went to eternal comfort

and none went to eternal pain. They merely floated, until dissipation turned them to stories.

(COLLIN enters wearing a torn-up sweater that was once THE COLLECTIVE CONSCIOUS.)

COLLIN: Whether the weather is cold, or whether the weather is hot, we'll be together, whatever the weather, whether we like it or not.

TAYLOR: And the actual truth of the story is...

ACTOR PLAYING LYNNE (BRIDGET): *(Calling out the name of the actor playing OLOKUN.)* Taylor!

(From here to the end, substitute the names of the actors playing these characters in your production.)

TAYLOR: Bridget!

BRIDGET: You have fun at the parade?

TAYLOR: It was fantastic. Too few people dressed up and too many people taking pictures but all in all it was a great parade. Someone called Tigger "Aqua Faggot" but that was more funny than anything else.

ACTOR PLAYING THE BLOWFISH (TIGGER): Taylor.

(Members of ENSEMBLE come on half-dressed as if at the Mermaid Parade. They lie about.)

TAYLOR: Tigger. We were just talking about your Aqua Faggot moment.

TIGGER: Oh that was more funny than anything else. *(To BRIDGET.)* Hey, you know Steven.

BRIDGET: Of course. You have fun today?

STEVEN: It was full-tilt boogie.

DIRTY MARTINI: *(Calling to them from the mermaid encampment.)* Hey. You guys were gorgeous out there.

STEVEN: You too.

(LAYARD runs up.)

LAYARD: You see Ruby?

(THE ACTOR PLAYING SLAVASKIA comes walking by, looking as spectacular as can be.)

ENSEMBLE: Work bitch.

TAYLOR: *(To the audience.)* This is my favorite part of the Coney Island Mermaid Parade. After the parade, when everyone hangs out on the beach, tired from frolic. Half-costumed. One big messy mass of divergence. A community of divine freaks.

TIGGER: How much longer you think before everything becomes a mall?

TAYLOR: *(As if to say pleasantly— "Whenever...I'm gonna keep doing what I do.")* A year or two.

(End of Play.)

THE ADVENTURES OF NERVOUS-BOY

A Penny Dreadful

James Comtois

JAMES COMTOIS was born in Cold Springs, New York, in 1977 and raised in Candia, New Hampshire. He graduated from Boston University with a bachelor's in English literature. He is one of the founding members of the Boston-based sketch comedy group *Slow Children at Play*. He is also the co-founder of and resident playwright for the New York-based theatre company Nosedive Productions. Since 1999, Nosedive has produced twelve of Comtois's plays, including *Monkeys* (2000), *The Awaited Visit* (2001), *Ruins* (2002), *Evil Hellcat and the Liquid Lunch* (2003), *Mayonnaise Sandwiches* (2004), and *A Very Nosedive Christmas Carol* (2004 and 2005). Two of his plays, *The Awaited Visit* and *Mayonnaise Sandwiches*, won OOBR Awards for Overall Excellence from the online theatre magazine *The Off-Off-Broadway Review*. Nosedive Productions is currently working on Comtois's next play, the comedy *Suburban Peepshow*. He lives in Brooklyn.

The Adventures of Nervous-Boy (A Penny Dreadful) was first presented by Nosedive Productions (Pete Boisvert and James Comtois, Artistic Directors) on June 8, 2006, at the Gene Frankel Underground, New York City, with the following cast and credits:

Nervous-Boy .... Mac Rogers
Emily ....Rebecca Comtois
The Skank, Ensemble..Anna Kull
The Client, Ensemble... Marc Landers
The Grog, Ensemble .... Patrick Shearer
The Patron, Ensemble ....Ben Trawick-Smith
The Stripper, Ensemble .... Tai Verley
The Gentleman, Ensemble.............................Scot Lee Williams
Asmodeus.. James Comtois
Understudies for Mr. Comtois....Pete Boisvert, Christopher Yustin
Understudy for Ms. Kull .... Shay Gines

Directed by: Pete Boisvert
Stage Manager: Stephanie Williams
Fight Choreographer: Qui Nguyen
Set Designer: Rose AC Howard
Lighting Designer: Sarah Watson
Sound Designer: Patrick Shearer
Makeup Designer: Cat Johnson
Costume Designer: Stephanie Williams
Producers: Pete Boisvert, James Comtois, Patrick Shearer, Stephanie
    Williams
Associate Producers: Rebecca Comtois, Chris Daly, Christopher
    Yustin

www.nosediveproductions.com

AUTHOR'S FOREWORD

"Poor Grendel has had an accident…So may you all."—John Gardner

"At least I hate myself as much as I hate anybody else."—R. Crumb

This was my attempt at writing a horror show, and for lack of a better category, we're labeling it as a "horror" (although I think Pete Boisvert, the director, and I will both contend that we hope people also find it funny, which isn't surprising, considering the line between comedy and horror is a pretty damn thin one).

We're living in very sad and alienating times. Very few of us deal with real tragedy on a day-by-day basis (with some exceptions; I'm not indifferent to family illness or things of that ilk). Living in the wealthiest country in the world—and for us New Yorkers, in one of the wealthiest and most expensive cities in the country—very few (if any) in this theatre right now are toiling or befallen with catastrophe. This is, I suspect, a rule of the game when everything is automated and everything is provided for us.

Yet still…a number of people I know have this free-floating dread and anxiety, that feeling that Something Is Wrong. We can't put our finger on it, but we feel it: that feeling that we're obsolete, that we don't matter, never have mattered, and never will matter to anyone or anything.

So, sometimes people create drama for themselves: make their lives more chaotic and problematic than they really are, thereby giving themselves and their situations a (false) depth of meaning.

I really don't know what the solution to this is. Maybe there isn't one. Maybe we just need to sing "Que Sera Sera" and acknowledge how small we are in the world. Yeah, I know: easier said than done.

The Adventures of Nervous-Boy is a play for anyone who has felt a constant and steady fear of dread, who's felt that the water is up to his or her eyeballs and rising. A play for anyone who's felt at times that they're always in the wrong place doing the wrong thing; who's felt alienated and isolated despite being surrounded by people all the time. A play for people who have had their heart broken and have never been able to mend it properly and move on; who have wanted to go on a rampage after a week from hell.

This is a play for anyone who has wondered if we are indeed in hell.

Always nervous,

James "Native Alien" Comtois
New York, 2006

NERVOUS-BOY enters. He speaks his thoughts throughout, but they're not to the audience per se. The characters throughout aren't hearing his asides and internal monologues, but he makes eye contact more often to the person opposite him or to no one. In other words, he should avoid looking/talking directly to the audience as much as possible. Also, until the end, he shows no real emotion. He never "acts" nervous, despite the cruel nickname the playwright has given him. It's not boredom, and it's not sadness; the cadence of his speech should be vague, detached, and candid. He also doesn't react to the weird things he sees throughout the play. Again, he shouldn't look bored, exasperated, or surprised; he's just seen these sorts of things so many times they don't even register. This should not be confused with speaking monotonously. You'll see what I mean.

NERVOUS-BOY: Living in New York, I'm around a lot of people who are stressed out. Always stressed, always freaking out, always multi-tasking, and always living in a constant state of self-created panic. I don't really get these people. I mean, I get them, but I don't understand why they like living that way. I'm not really like that. I don't really stress out. At least, not in the way that people I know do. I'm always externally calm, I get eight hours of sleep at night, I don't work overtime. I don't feel stress. Well, stress is the wrong word. No. It's more of a constant feeling of steady dread. That vague feeling that I'm missing something, forgetting something, doing something wrong. This feeling never intensifies or diminishes, it stays at the same level every waking moment. That's why I can never really enjoy myself—if I'm feeling good or calm or happy, I have this worry that I'm doing something

wrong and the other shoe will drop at any second.

(He's now in line at a food stand manned by a SERVER. A GUY ON A CELL PHONE is in front of him.)

GUY ON CELL PHONE: *(To the person on the phone.)* Hold on. *(To SERVER.)* Uh…hold on. *(To the phone.)* Hold on a sec. *(To SERVER.)* Hold…hold on. *(To phone.)* Uhhhhhh…hold on. *(To SERVER.)* Hold on. *(Etc. Keeps going like that.)*

(Again, NERVOUS-BOY makes no indication of this—he's not mad, amused, impatient.)

NERVOUS-BOY: I don't have a cell phone, or Palm Pilot, or personal organizer. I have no access to voicemail outside of my apartment. I'm kind of tough to get in touch with if I ever go out, which is probably why I wander around so often. I think people who know me know this, which is why they've stopped trying to contact me. If someone has a personal self-made crisis, they know I'm probably not the best person to call to fix their drama.

(GUY ON CELL PHONE and SERVER exit.)

NERVOUS-BOY: I guess by "fix," I mean "get sucked into." Stress seems to be a contagious disease, and a disease that wants to be spread more than…well, anything, I guess. I don't get stress. It's more of a constant quiet dread.

(A BARTENDER and PATRON enter; BARTENDER hands NERVOUS-BOY a beer.)

NERVOUS-BOY: I don't hate people, and don't avoid interaction. But sometimes I just don't get people.

PATRON: *(To NERVOUS-BOY.)* You think Pentland's gonna make up for the 3-0 split in the fourth?

NERVOUS-BOY: What? Oh, I don't know. Let's hope so.

PATRON: FUCK YEAH!

(PATRON raises his glass. NERVOUS-BOY has no idea what he's talking about.)

NERVOUS-BOY: *(Directly to PATRON, but as if talking to the audience.)* I like going to bars, preferably with other people, but usually people I know are too busy. But I don't know what to say to strangers.

PATRON: I tell ya, brother. This country's never been so divided since the election!

NERVOUS-BOY: Sometimes I pretend to be involved…

PATRON: I don't think we saw this coming! Well, maybe things'll be looking up. I mean, the guy can't get reelected.

NERVOUS-BOY: Sometimes I tune out.

PATRON: Still, this war thing is bullshit.

NERVOUS-BOY: I vaguely wonder if I'm supposed to be somewhere else, and think I most likely am, but can't for the life of me figure out where I'm supposed to be and what I'm supposed to do.

(PATRON's cell phone rings.)

PATRON: Hang on. *(Answers. Talks on the phone, the bulk of his end of the conversation being stuff like "What?," "What's that?," "I can't hear you," and "You're where…?")*

NERVOUS-BOY: I'm freelancing as an art designer for magazines. I have a pretty decent client base; one magazine you've probably heard of, the rest are small trade magazines. I don't really like a lot of my clients but work's work. But it's nice that most of my clients allow me to work at home. You may be wondering how I can freelance without a cell phone. I can.

(A few more PATRONS enter the bar in staggered intervals throughout, and the PATRON on the cell phone drifts away to the background. Everyone in the bar is either on a cell phone or staring intently at their cell phones.)

NERVOUS-BOY: It's easy. I know my schedule by heart, and if my clients can't get in touch with me, they can't treat me like my boss. Plus, if I always do my job on time—which I do—they have no reason to nag me. *(Pause.)* I also have little ambition. I never ask for more money, more projects, my own office. I just want enough money to pay rent, eat, and get drunk.

PATRON: Getting drunk, fuck yeah!

(PATRON raises his glass. NERVOUS-BOY nods toward him politely. PATRON goes back to his phone conversation.)

NERVOUS-BOY: I really don't get why people are in such a tizzy over the smallest things of little consequence. Almost everyone I know is constantly exhausted, and it's not like they ran a marathon or climbed a mountain or anything. They just went to work and did some errands. Well, I guess that can be stressful, if you think about it. *(Pause.)* Maybe people need to occupy their minds with extraneous stuff that doesn't matter so they can avoid thinking about the real horrors of their lives. I don't know. I'm talking out loud.

(Walks over to a park bench. He passes by a MAN and a WOMAN: WOMAN has an iMac and cell phone.)

WOMAN: Okay, okay, I've got to stop doing this. No more work! Okay! No more work or I'll get a headache!

MAN: *(Milquetoast.)* Honey, you work too hard…try to take a break.

WOMAN: I know! I know!

MAN: Try to relax.

WOMAN: I know!

(Cell phone rings.)

WOMAN: I've got to take this! Sandy's ex-boyfriend.

MAN: You don't need to an—

WOMAN: *(Answers the phone.)* Hello? Hello? Omigod! You're SERIOUS?! OmiGOD! No. No! What are you doing calling him from his phone? YOU'RE WITH HIM?! No!

(They disappear. NERVOUS-BOY sits on the park bench, looking relaxed but still lost in thought. An OLDER GENTLE-MAN approaches him and sits down next to him.)

OLDER GENT: Hiya.

NERVOUS-BOY: Hey.

OLDER GENT: Beautiful day.

NERVOUS-BOY: Yeah.

OLDER GENT: I just need to take a break from my wife.

NERVOUS-BOY: Yeah?

OLDER GENT: I mean, she's complaining to me constantly about my drinking.

She doesn't want me to drink in the house. But she gets mad at me if I go out drinking. She says I always smell like a winery. And I tell her I can't deal with this anymore. I'm tired of being treated like a damn kid, y'know?

NERVOUS-BOY: Yeah.

OLDER GENT: So I tell her I don't need you getting on my case every five minutes. Just because you don't have any joy in your life doesn't mean you have to take it out on me, y'know?

NERVOUS-BOY: That sucks.

OLDER GENT: You really think that after all these years this shit gets easier but it's still always the same old shit.

NERVOUS-BOY: Sometimes I wish I had a full-time job with health benefits and a car and a house and a wife and kids so I could just feel normal but most of the time I see couples and I realize I'm not missing out on a whole lot.

OLDER GENT: Even my bitch of a sis-ter-in-law likes to harp on me whenever I have a small snifter of scotch. I swear, my wife just calls her up to make fun of me. I get so tired of this shit sometimes.

NERVOUS-BOY: Don't get me wrong, I've had relationships before, even long-term ones, but the last one was a few years ago, and I don't really date or go cruising so I don't see that situation changing anytime soon.

OLDER GENT: I feel bad yelling at my sister-in-law because then it gives my wife more of an excuse to harp on me about some stupid shit.

NERVOUS-BOY: I also don't see myself buying a house anytime soon. Or a car. I'm still too attached to New York.

OLDER GENT: I mean, there's only so much shit a guy can take, y'know?

NERVOUS-BOY: I hear ya. *(Pause.)* It's a beautiful day.

OLDER GENT: It really is.

(Silence.)

NERVOUS-BOY: *(To no one in particular.)* Monday was my meeting with Emily. She was an actress, and had just gotten an agent that was theoretically getting her some work.

(OLDER GENTLEMAN disappears; NERVOUS-BOY gets up off the park bench. Scene is changed to a coffee house.)

NERVOUS-BOY: She just got a small role in some movie by a well-known indie filmmaker. I guess she's "made it," which I suppose is why I haven't seen her recently. But, I had called her, and she left a message with me a few days later, and we agreed to meet. When I sit down, I have a nagging feeling that I'm supposed to be somewhere else, or worse, if I have fun talking to her (which I don't think I will, to tell you the truth), I'm going to go home super-depressed. I'm just weird that way, I guess.

(EMILY enters, all dolled up, with a wire earpiece to a cell phone in her ear. Her over-the-top demeanor is more cartoony than most cartoons. She should have a huge fake smile that doesn't go away until indicated and her eyes should be bulging out of her head, ready to pop out of her skull.)

EMILY: OMIGOD HELLO! IT'S GREAT TO SEE YOU!

NERVOUS-BOY: Hi, Emily.

EMILY: HOW HAVE YOU BEEN IT'S BEEN SO LONG OMIGOD YOU LOOK GREAT!

NERVOUS-BOY: Thanks, you, too.

EMILY: I MEAN I HAVE TO BE MEETING UP WITH THIS ASS-HOLE PRODUCER DON'T GET ME WRONG HE REALLY KNOWS WHAT HE'S DOING BUT HE'S JUST ALWAYS

(Phone rings.)

EMILY: HOLD ON A SECOND HELLO? *(On the phone.)* HI, HOW ARE YOU LONG TIME NO HEAR LISTEN THAT SOUNDS GREAT BUT YOU KNOW WHAT I'M KIND OF IN THE MIDDLE OF SOME-THING SO IF YOU COULD CALL ME BACK IN LIKE FIVE MINUTES THAT WOULD BE SUPER WE RE-ALLY NEED TO CATCH UP AND BY THE WAY CONGRATULATIONS I KNOW I KNOW OKAY BYE. *(Hangs up.)* SO HOW HAVE YOU BEEN?

NERVOUS-BOY: Good. How's the movie business?

EMILY: IT'S GOING REALLY WELL I MEAN I'M LEARNING SO MUCH I MEAN I NEVER GET TO SLEEP AND I HAVEN'T HAD ANY TIME FOR MYSELF WHICH IS A DRAG BUT CRAIG IS SUCH AN AMAZ-ING DIRECTOR I'VE SERIOUSLY LEARNED SO MUCH JUST BY BE-ING ON THE SET WITH HIM AND I'M THINKING ABOUT GOING BACK TO DO SOME STAGE WORK BECAUSE THEATRE REALLY IS WHERE THE ART IS YOU KNOW BECAUSE LET'S FACE IT AS MUCH AS I LOVE THE MOVIES SO MANY OF THEM ARE SUCH COMPRO-MISED HACK WORK AND HAVE YOU EVER THOUGHT OF GOING INTO PRODUCTION?

NERVOUS-BOY: Me? Oh, uh…I don't know. Don't think so. Maybe.

EMILY: WELL LET ME TELL YOU IT'S NOT FOR EVERYONE BUT I LOVE IT I DEFINITELY LOVE IT I MEAN IT'S EXHAUSTING BUT WHEN PUSH COMES TO SHOVE IT FEEDS MY SOUL.

NERVOUS-BOY: Wow. That's…gee, that's…great. Wow. Yeah.

EMILY: OH SAME OLE YOU I MEAN IT DARLING DON'T EVER CHANGE YOU'RE JUST THE BEST IT'S WONDERFUL TO SEE YOU.

NERVOUS-BOY: Oh. Thanks. *(Pause.)* So…how's the movie business?

EMILY: OH IT CAN BE SO EX-HAUSTING I MEAN DON'T GET ME WRONG IT'S GREAT I'M LIVING THE DREAM AND I'M LEARNING SO MUCH BUT SOME-TIMES IT CAN BE A REAL PAIN LIKE THIS ONE TIME MY AGENT SENT ME TO THIS AUDITION BUT WOULDN'T TELL ME WHAT IT WAS FOR BUT IT WAS FOR SOMETHING ON TV AND IT WAS SUPPOSED TO PAY WELL SO I FIGURED WHY NOT AND ANYWAY I GET THERE AND IT'S A CATTLE-CALL AUDITION FOR A NEW REALITY SHOW AND THERE WERE QUITE POSSIBLY OVER A THOUSAND PEOPLE IN LINE.

NERVOUS-BOY: Really?

EMILY: OH YEAH IT WAS AWFUL I WAS SO EMBARRASSED ABOUT IT AND I REALIZED I'M GOING TO HAVE TO GO TO A TON OF THESE THINGS AND THE THING IS IS THAT ACTORS ARE TREATED LIKE SHIT IT'S REALLY AWFUL WE'RE LOOKED DOWN UPON BY EVERYONE ELSE IN THE BUSI-NESS.

NERVOUS-BOY: That's awful.

EMILY: BUT DON'T GET ME WRONG IT'S GREAT I'M SO HAP-PY ABOUT THIS AND I'M SO EX-CITED FOR THE FUTURE AND IT'S SO MUCH BETTER THAN HAVING TO DEAL WITH MY FATHER'S WHINING FOR HIS MEDICINE BUT AT LEAST I'LL BE MAKING ENOUGH MONEY TO HELP HIM OUT AND IT'S WON-DERFUL AND IT'S SO GREAT TO SEE YOU!

NERVOUS-BOY: Same here.

EMILY: *(Dropping the cartoony voice and demeanor and talking to/at NERVOUS-BOY, but only the audience can hear her.)* I really worry about you sometimes. You don't really seem particularly happy ever. I can tell you have nothing but contempt for me, but I can't tell if it's jealousy. It's not just that. I disgust you. I mean, you're polite enough but part of me disgusts you. And that…really hurts. I know, I'm not what you'd call a success, but…I'm really happy with what I'm doing. Are you at all happy for me? *(Pause.)* I mean…you used to be so nice and funny to me, and…I miss you. I…do want you to like me, but I think…I think you think I'm beneath you or something. I guess I just miss my friend. *(Now talking to NERVOUS-BOY, and although she's still frenetic in her speech, it's not as cartoony. She's still smiling and wide-eyed, but just not as grotesque.)* So I was thinking that we wanted to go see this piece that a friend of mine is in I got two tickets would you like to go?

NERVOUS-BOY: What is it?

EMILY: It's by this great director and I don't remember what it's called but it's over in Chelsea and I've heard some really good things about it I don't know if it's your cup of tea or anything but maybe it could be fun.

NERVOUS-BOY: When is it?

EMILY: It starts in about an hour so whadda ya say?

NERVOUS-BOY: *(Thinks about it. Smiles.)* Sure. Why not? Sure.

EMILY: Okay let's go then.

(They get up and walk. The stage is struck.)

EMILY: So are you still freelancing or what are you doing for work nowadays?

NERVOUS-BOY: *(To her.)* I told her about my freelancing gigs and she seemed politely interested. That is, she nodded and smiled and said "uh-huh" assuredly at all the right points. As we were talking I was feeling much better about meeting her. Despite some of the annoying affectations she put on, she was nice and seemed relatively happy to see me. I was able to loosen up, too. And I was glad to get over seeing her as this caricature. We talked a bit about her father, who apparently isn't doing so hot healthwise. To be honest, I did kind of feel bad about that, other people's drama and all. *(Pause.)* We took the train over to West 25th and saw this piece. I don't know if it was a play or what but it had some funky title that was long and incoherent and I couldn't remember it.

(They sit down in front of a stage and watch a pantomime play/performance art piece. You really can make this whatever

you like. I'm assuming it's avant-garde, but it can really be whatever, as long as it doesn't interrupt NERVOUS-BOY's speech.)

NERVOUS-BOY: I really can't tell if I like it or get it. Some parts I like, but sometimes I just wonder if I'm fooling myself into thinking it's not bad in order not to feel like I'm wasting my time. But what else am I going to do? I don't really feel cultured, or entertained. But maybe it's because I'm not very smart. I don't really know. I wish I liked this more. I wanted to talk to Emily more, but panicked that she'd be tired and wouldn't want to go out afterwards. Maybe she would, and I wouldn't know what to say, where to go, or what to do. Do I want to have sex with her? Maybe. Does she want to have sex with me? Probably not. I'd rather not think about it. *(Watches show. Laughs.)*

EMILY: *(Whispering.)* Terrible choices they're making.

NERVOUS-BOY: Oh…?

EMILY: I don't know why they would want to do that. It makes no sense. Can't they see that he's *clearly* only interested in his work rather than his family?

NERVOUS-BOY: I…uh…I guess so. Yeah. You're right.

EMILY: And there's no reason that this character is being played by a man. No reason at all. So wrong. So wrong.

NERVOUS-BOY: Yeah.

(They watch for a while.)

EMILY: That's good.

NERVOUS-BOY: Is it?

EMILY: Yeah, yeah.

NERVOUS-BOY: I really don't know what she's talking about, but okay. I guess some of the moves are good, and some are bad. I really can't tell the difference. It's all right, I guess. But I guess this really isn't my thing.

(They watch for a bit.)

NERVOUS-BOY: There got to be some point near the end where I was pretty sick of watching it. I was ready for it to be over so we could get on with the next awkward part of the evening. My legs were falling asleep and my back was hurting.

(It ends. They applaud. The PERFORM-ERS in the piece exit. EMILY and NER-VOUS-BOY stand.)

NERVOUS-BOY: So…

EMILY: Yeah.

NERVOUS-BOY: Uh…you want…you want to go around the corner? There's a pretty good bar that…

EMILY: Actually, I've been invited to this party that the director is holding. So…

NERVOUS-BOY: Oh, okay. So I guess I'll—

EMILY: —Would you like to come?

NERVOUS-BOY: What? Oh. Yeah. Sure.

EMILY: And if it's bad, we can use each other as an excuse to bail out early.

NERVOUS-BOY: Works for me.

EMILY: It's just a couple blocks from here.

NERVOUS-BOY: Okay.

(They walk.)

NERVOUS-BOY: I don't particularly like parties, especially if I don't know anybody there. I just feel too self-con-scious and out of place, and a lot of times I go out of my way trying to become invisible. The problem with that is that since I'm always moving away from people and trying to position myself in an empty corner of the room, I feel like I'm standing out even more. I'm the stranger all by himself watching people. It really isn't fun. But hey, they'll have free alcohol and I can at least say I'm with someone there so nobody will accuse me of crashing.

(A number of PEOPLE show up and are posturing with drinks in their hands, not unlike characters in a New Yorker *cartoon. EMILY mingles elsewhere; NER-VOUS-BOY sits down and listens in on a conversation.)*

LADY 1: I think it's simply dreadful the way the public schools are treating our children. After all, I am philosophically against taking my children to private school because that would be giving such a horrible message but they treat the youth like interchangeable cogs in a giant machine.

LADY 2: Well, I believe things are going to be getting worse if the presidential administration keeps committing such atrocities on the middle class.

LADY 1: Oh, don't I know it! It will only be a matter of time before all social services dry up.

LADY 2: It's just awful how the lower classes are treated.

LADY 1: And so perverse! After all, we have adopted more of a diamond-shaped caste system than a pyramid, where there is no real need for oppression.

LADY 2: *(To NERVOUS-BOY.)* Do you have children?

NERVOUS-BOY: What? Me? Oh, uh…no…I mean, uh…no. I don't.

LADY 2: I tell you. Having children does put things in perspective for you.

NERVOUS-BOY: I guess so.

LADY 1: Well, the election has put things in perspective for everyone, I believe.

NERVOUS-BOY: Yeah. I guess…yeah. It's…sad. I mean…yeah.

GENTLEMAN: The problem with the state of things as I see it is that people don't want to be happy and therefore they keep electing people who deliberately manipulate them. Ah, well, yes, you do know that television is the opiate of the masses.

NERVOUS-BOY: I uh…I don't watch that much television. But, uh…uh…I've seen some really good shows on HBO recently.

GENTLEMAN: Oh, well I must admit, I do enjoy watching anything by Al Franken, I think he's simply wonderful.

LADY 2: Oh, indeed! He's simply mad for him.

GENTLEMAN: I confess!

NERVOUS-BOY: Yeah…I haven't seen his show.

LADY 1: It is nice to see that there's someone out in the media world who isn't a complete idiot!

LADY 2: Indeed. I mean, I had thought that at this point in civilization we had evolved past the need for war.

GENTLEMAN: I agree.

NERVOUS-BOY: I really don't understand these people. I mean, I do, but I don't relate to them. Even though I share the same political views, I suppose, I don't feel any affinity with them.

LADY 1: Why is that?

NERVOUS-BOY: Well, it just seems so stuck-up.

LADY 1: So we're not allowed to converse?

NERVOUS-BOY: No, I didn't say that, it's just…

LADY 2: Just what?

NERVOUS-BOY: These opinions are so lazy and clichéd and…

GENTLEMAN: Do you not agree with what we're saying?

NERVOUS-BOY: Well, I…

GENTLEMAN: Because you can feel free to voice your opinion.

NERVOUS-BOY: That's not the problem! I think the conversation is so shallow and you people are such lazy intellects who want to pretend that you're smart and caring and worrying about How the Other Half Lives and it's such bullshit!

LADY 1: So you're saying you're not caring?

NERVOUS-BOY: No. I mean, I care, sure, but I don't like wearing my fake sympathy for the poor and oppressed on my sleeve. I've got my own problems.

LADY 2: Well, if we had a socialist economic structure none of these problems would be happening…

NERVOUS-BOY: That's not true! This is just such a simple way of looking at these problems and it's so arrogant! You're actually making things worse with this attitude.

GENTLEMAN: How are we making it worse?

NERVOUS-BOY: Because if people don't agree with your worldview you accuse them of being right-wing redneck fascist bigots. And you would never in a million years want a socialist society because you're living pretty extravagant lives and you're not about to give any of that up. We're addicted to our morning coffee brewed from beans picked by fourteen-year-olds for fifteen cents an hour. And we can act sympathetic and concerned all we want but we bitch enough as it is that a large coffee costs $2.50. And you can afford to choose between private and public schools for your kids, and it doesn't really matter where they go because you've established trust funds, CDs, and stock plans for them. The real truth is that you love to complain about the status quo but you're all in hog heaven and would rather slit your throats than incorporate any real changes. And I'm not even saying I'm blaming you. I work as little as possible and I still make enough money to live in one of the most expensive cities in the world and go cavorting and gallivanting around. I'm not the biggest fan of our current political leaders but I don't hear a lot of realistic alternatives from you people.

GENTLEMAN: (To EVERYONE ELSE, dismissing NERVOUS-BOY.) So hey, you know I got a new car!

LADY 1: You did?

LADY 2: Wow!

GENTLEMAN: Oh yes, it's great!

NERVOUS-BOY: I looked around to see where Emily was. She seemed entrenched in conversation with someone…probably the director…she'd probably end up ditching me to go home with him. Lousy simple-minded whore. I wanted to get her attention but she wasn't noticing me. I felt bad about cutting into her talk and I didn't want her to get the feeling that I was being possessive. Plus, if she was having fun I didn't want to worry her with letting her know I wanted to go. I never do good at these things. (Pause.) After what seemed to take forever to get her attention, I finally went over to her. (To EMILY.) Hi.

EMILY: Hey…you…

NERVOUS-BOY: How are you doing?

EMILY: How's it going with you?

NERVOUS-BOY: She wasn't getting the hint. In fairness, that was about as cryptic and passive-aggressive a hint as one could make without seeming pushy or offensive. But fortunately, she whispered to me…

EMILY: (Whispering.) We'll get out of here in a second.

NERVOUS-BOY: Okay. (Pause.) I finished my drink, used the bathroom, then put my coat on, waiting by the door. Despite her saying that we'd be leaving soon, like all chicks, she took her sweet-ass time making long-winded goodbyes to everyone. And everyone did the obligatory feigning of shock and sorrow that she was leaving. No, I really don't do well at these things. No matter how much alcohol you get at these things, your self-consciousness burns the booze up too fast and you're always sober. *(Pause.)* Finally...

EMILY: Let's go.

NERVOUS-BOY: Okay. *(Pause.)* Do, uh...do you wanna go get a drink?

EMILY: Well...

NERVOUS-BOY: There's a place nearby that's pretty good.

EMILY: Maybe. I have to get up for a photo shoot in the morning...

NERVOUS-BOY: It'll be on me.

EMILY: Oh, okay. Sure. Why not?

NERVOUS-BOY: I guess you feel mildly guilty that we haven't seen each other in a while and we hadn't talked much since the show started.

EMILY: I can't stay out too late, though.

NERVOUS-BOY: Or maybe you just feel sorry for me.

EMILY: But yeah, let's go.

NERVOUS-BOY: At any rate, I'm glad I convinced you. I think.

(GUESTS disappear, they sit down at a bar. Other PATRONS are milling about.)

NERVOUS-BOY: *(To EMILY.)* So.

EMILY: So.

NERVOUS-BOY: The show was good.

EMILY: It was okay, yeah. The party was kind of lame.

NERVOUS-BOY: Yeah.

EMILY: I saw you talking with some people.

NERVOUS-BOY: Yeah. A little bit.

EMILY: I'm impressed.

NERVOUS-BOY: What do you mean?

EMILY: Well, you usually don't initiate conversation with new people.

NERVOUS-BOY: No?

EMILY: Not really.

NERVOUS-BOY: Huh.

EMILY: I'm glad you've loosened up a bit. You seemed pretty wound up when we first met up.

NERVOUS-BOY: Oh? Well, I had some...things on my mind.

EMILY: Like what?

NERVOUS-BOY: Oh, nothing important. I've forgotten them now.

EMILY: Okay.

NERVOUS-BOY: You seem a little less nervous now, too.

EMILY: Yeah, well. You can have a calming effect on me from time to time.

NERVOUS-BOY: I've heard that before.

EMILY: Yeah?

NERVOUS-BOY: Yeah.

(Silence.)

EMILY: Sorry for taking you to that stupid party.

NERVOUS-BOY: Oh, don't worry about it. It's fine.

EMILY: I just had to make an appearance. You know. Say hi.

NERVOUS-BOY: That's fine.

EMILY: Did you have any fun at that thing?

NERVOUS-BOY: Not really, no.

EMILY: Me, neither.

NERVOUS-BOY: I was going to ask her why we had to stay so long, but decided against it. I wasn't drunk enough to yell at her. Not that I really wanted to.

EMILY: So…what do you want to do…?

ANNOUNCER: *(Off.)* WHAT WILL OUR FEARLESS NERVOUS-BOY DO? WILL HE…TELL HER THAT THEY SHOULD GO BACK UP TO HIS PLACE TO "CHECK OUT HIS CD COLLECTION?" *(Pause.)* CALL IT AN EARLY NIGHT AND SUGGEST THEY DO THIS AGAIN SOME-TIME? *(Pause.)* TELL THE BITCH WHAT A SHALLOW, BORING, SELF-ABSORBED CUNT SHE'S BECOME AND THAT HE NEVER REALLY LIKED HER IN THE FIRST PLACE AND THROW HIS DRINK IN HER FACE? *(Pause.)* OR…

NERVOUS-BOY: I've been…look…I'm sorry for being like this.

EMILY: Like what?

NERVOUS-BOY: I've…I mean…I just think you're so funny, and…smart, and…interesting…and beautiful. I just feel like I'm throwing myself at you, and…I'm sorry. I just…think you're wonderful. I've had feelings for you since we first met, and…I've been trying to snap out of it for the longest time, but…no. I love you. That is…I'm falling in love with you. I care about you. And I worry about you. I worry about your career and whether or not you're being exploited. I worry about your father. I care about what you want in life and I care about you getting it. It's just so many

times we talk and I'm listening but part of me is terrified that you see the hearts in my eyes and…I just…think you're wonderful. And I love you. And…I'm sorry. *(Pause.)* I haven't been able to find a full-time job since I got laid off two years ago. I really don't know what I'm doing with my life and I'm kind of freaking out about it but I think I'm too lazy to really fix that problem and I get so sick of being lost in my thoughts and being by myself and I'm tired of being too scared to look at anyone in the eye anymore and I just love seeing you, Emily, and talking to you, because when I do I forget about all my anxieties for a short while and it feels like a giant weight has been lifted for a brief time and I'm not filled with guilt or self-loathing…I just like…being with you. I feel like a real person. You know? And…I'm sorry. I just…I haven't felt like that in a while and I'm sorry and I'm rambling.

(Silence.)

NERVOUS-BOY: You must have known all this.

EMILY: I'm actually pretty oblivious to that sort of thing.

NERVOUS-BOY: Wow. *(Pause.)* Uh…huh. *(Pause.)* Yeah. *(Embarrassed chuckle.)* I wish I hadn't told you all that.

EMILY: Oh, don't worry about it. I won't hold it against you.

NERVOUS-BOY: Thanks.

EMILY: It'll be our little secret.

NERVOUS-BOY: Sure. *(Laughs. Pause.)* So…we taking off or do we want an-other?

EMILY: Yeah, we should go. I have to do some things.

NERVOUS-BOY: Okay.

(They get up to leave. NERVOUS-BOY thinks about it.)

NERVOUS-BOY: I actually…I'm gonna stay.

EMILY: You sure?

NERVOUS-BOY: Yeah. I need one more. To collect my thoughts.

EMILY: And watch people.

NERVOUS-BOY: Yeah. *(Laughs.)*

EMILY: You're a sick, sick man.

NERVOUS-BOY: It's part of my charm.

EMILY: Well, I had a wonderful time.

(They hug and kiss each other on the cheek.)

EMILY: And hang in there.

NERVOUS-BOY: Yeah.

EMILY: I'll see you later.

NERVOUS-BOY: 'Bye.

(She exits.)

NERVOUS-BOY: *(Sighs.)* That was the wrong decision. *(Pause.)* I try to convince myself that I was really only after getting laid, and I guess that's partly true, although to tell the truth, I never really wanted sex from her. I mean, I wouldn't mind it, but I guess I just wanted to stave off a bit of loneliness. The weird thing is, is when I'm by myself for long stretches at a time, I don't feel at all lonely. It's only when I'm around someone and they leave, I feel that weird emptiness. Like I know I'm going to miss them before they leave. After all, I did spend a good chunk of time with this very annoying and pretentious woman who I didn't

have much to talk about with, but I now wish I had a cell phone so I could call her. It's weird, yeah, I know, but…yeah. Also, I wasn't exactly lying to her. She did make me feel like a real person. Don't real people have weird inexplicable emotions and feelings toward others? Don't real people make fools of themselves? Don't real people act stupid and selfish and want to take chicks out to some show or movie or bar or restaurant to get laid? I don't…I don't know. *(Pause.)* That was the wrong decision.

GIRL AT BAR: *(Drinks. Pause. Looks nervous.)* What…what did you do?

GUY AT BAR: You like it? I made it special for you.

GIRL AT BAR: *(Horrified.)* Michael! Why did you… *(Drops the glass. Gags and grabs her throat as she clings to GUY's shirt and falls toward the floor.)*

GUY AT BAR: You'll be dead in a minute, don't worry.

(She throws up on GUY's shirt.)

GUY AT BAR: Shouldn't have blown that guy.

(She collapses. GUY makes noise of dismissive disgust and exits. She's dead. As NERVOUS-BOY talks, two…vampires? Demons? Whatever the fuck they are, they slither to GIRL's body and slide her offstage as they drink her blood. NERVOUS-BOY either doesn't notice or just doesn't acknowledge. He addresses the following to a nearby BARFLY.)

NERVOUS-BOY: One of my problems is that I'm at the point in my life where I actually have so many options, I don't even know where to begin. If I make even one choice, no matter how small or banal, I feel like I've made the wrong one, and all of my options will dry up. It's stupid, I know, and I tell myself that it's only in my head, but I can't really help it; it's just who I am. What Emily said at the show really hit me. Some choices are wrong. Actually, "terrible." You can make terrible choices. And other people can notice them, even if you can't. That just bothers me. *(Pause. To BARTENDER.)* There was one day when I was in a state of near paralysis, it was awful. I would lie down on my bed, and my thoughts would keep me wide awake. My brain going a million miles a minute. Thinking awful thoughts. Anxieties, fears, that stupid stuff that only creeps up on you when you're trying to sleep. So, I would get up out of bed, and the second I stood up, I'd be dead tired and so sleepy I couldn't keep my eyes up. My mind would be a complete blank. So I would lie back down and—boom—I'd be wide awake, fraught with fear.

(Bar scene gets struck. While this happens, NERVOUS-BOY actively addresses the audience.)

NERVOUS-BOY: It was weird. This went on for hours. I'd stand, and be ready to pass out. Lie down, be wide awake. I just kept bobbing up and down. Couldn't sleep, couldn't stay awake. It was awful. I never want that to happen again, but I'm sure it will. But there's no point in worrying about it now. Not that I really ever worry per se, but I think you know what I mean.

(Walks across stage. He passes by TWO GUYS on the street. NERVOUS-BOY is only vaguely aware of them.)

GUY ON CORNER: You know it's the end of the world, man.

GUY 2: Naw, man. Naw…ya jus paranoid. Jus paranoid…

GUY ON CORNER: No, man. I'm tellin ya. Nostradamus predicted it. You may not believe him, man, but I'm tellin ya…he got some things wrong but I'm tellin ya…he predicted Hitler, he predicted World War Two, he predicted September 11…

GUY 2: Thas bullshit. Wussa hoax.

GUY ON CORNER: No it wasn't, man! You read that prediction?

GUY 2: Wussa fuckin hoax, man! They released that t'scare everybody!

GUY ON CORNER: No, man. Ya dunno.

GUY 2: Whateva.

GUY ON CORNER: This fuckin guy in the White House? He's gonna kill us all.

GUY 2: Naw, man. Naw…ya jus paranoid. Jus paranoid…

GUY ON CORNER: Fine, fine. Just don't say I didn't warn you when it rains fuckin cats and dogs…

GUY 2: Tha's rainin frogs, ya fucknut.

GUY ON CORNER: Whatever, man. Whatever.

(GUYS disappear. NERVOUS-BOY goes back to his apartment and checks his answering machine.)

ROBOT VOICE: Message One.

GUY'S VOICE: Hey man it's me. Where you at? You are one tough nigga to find. Anyway, me and the crew are going over to blah blah blah—

(NERVOUS-BOY hits the button.)

ROBOT VOICE: Message Two.

WOMAN'S VOICE: Hello, yes, we're looking for a Mr.... *(Unintelligible.)* Please give us a call at your earliest convenience at 800-236-4900. It's very important that you give us a call so we can discuss your account etc., etc...

(NERVOUS-BOY hits the button.)

ROBOT VOICE: Message Three.

(The sound of the street. Obviously someone's phone has turned on accidentally in their pocket. NERVOUS-BOY realizes this, then hits the button.)

ROBOT VOICE: Message Four.

VOICE: Hello, this is Donovan. Look, I've got some bad news and...and I've been trying to get in touch with you for the past few days now, but...I hate to do this on a machine but I don't know how else to get in touch with you. There have been some budget cuts in the art department, and from now on we're going to be only using internal people for the designing. I'm really sorry about this, I hope there are no hard feelings. If you get the chance, call my office and we can—

(NERVOUS-BOY pushes the button.)

ROBOT VOICE: Message Five.

VOICE: Hey it's me I just wanted to jibba-jabba jibba-jabba yak yak yak and blah blah blah stupid bullshit stupid bullshit... *(Continues quietly in this fashion.)*

NERVOUS-BOY: *(Looks upset but not freaked out.)* Great. That's just what I need. I lost a client. I didn't particularly like the job and this was a long time coming but it really bums me out that a portion of my income has been wiped out. I mean I guess this means more free time,

and it's nothing personal, it's just budget cuts. This shit happens. But still, now this is going to be a dark cloud over my head for the rest of the day. This is just what I need. Damn. *(To the audience.)* I really wish you hadn't heard that.

(The blathering voice goes on for a little while, saying nothing, then NERVOUS-BOY presses the button.)

ROBOT VOICE: Message Six.

CLIENT'S VOICE: Hi there, great job on the spread last week by the way. Anyway, I wanted to let you know that I have your check here at the office. I didn't know if you wanted to get it right away or not, so I didn't mail it to you. Last time you got a bit cranky about me mailing your checks, so come by anytime today or tomorrow to pick it up. I should be in the office for the most part. And if I don't hear from you by Thursday, I'll just go ahead and mail it. Take care. *(Beep!)*

ROBOT VOICE: End Of Messages. *(Beep! Beep! Beep!)*

NERVOUS-BOY: I don't know if I like stuff like that or not. Instantly I'm bummed out and made to feel miserable, then the next second I'm elated with good news, as if a huge weight just put on my shoulders has been immediately lifted. I'm not really one for roller coaster emotional states, so I'm not sure if I dig that so much. Then again, this paycheck will be just the thing to lift my spirits about losing the account. *(To the audience.)* There was this one dream I had a couple of nights ago where I was vomiting shards of glass. It didn't hurt or anything, but it was really disturbing. I couldn't stop. I'd be talking to somebody, I couldn't remember who (maybe I didn't know them) and shards of glass mixed with some muddy water poured out my mouth. I decided to just let it go and think it was just "one of those things." I guess when you're dreaming you let some weird shit just slide. But it kept happening, like, every few seconds. Well, it's kind of hard to tell time in dreams. It felt like every few minutes but it was probably just every few seconds. I left the friend…or he disappeared…and I'd be walking down the street and BLEAUGH! Shards of glass mixed with muddy water would spray from my mouth all over the street. Nobody seemed to notice or care, so at least my embarrassment was kept to a minimum. After the fourth or fifth purge I swept my finger around my mouth to make sure I hadn't cut anything. There was no blood, no cuts of any kind. But after I swept my mouth clean (or as clean as clean could be) three teeth fell out into my hand. I had read somewhere that the dreams where your teeth fall out represent the worst kind of emotional state. I don't know if that's true or not, but I never like those kinds of dreams. I felt my front teeth with my tongue and there were no teeth there anymore. I vomited up some more shards of glass and the rest of my teeth. This wasn't fun anymore. I needed to go to the dentist. So I remember walking in Manhattan—it looked like the East Village—and the next thing I know I'm somewhere in the countryside, holding a fistful of enlarged teeth that were crumbling.

(Out on the street, a COUPLE is arguing loudly.)

MAN: GET THE FUCK BACK IN THIS HOUSE BITCH!

WOMAN: DON'T TELL ME WHAT TO DO!

MAN: NO, YOU GET BACK—

WOMAN: —DON'T TELL ME WHAT TO DO YOU USELESS MOTHERFUCKER!

MAN: KEEP YOUR FUCKING VOICE DOWN!

WOMAN: WHO WAS THAT BITCH YOU WERE TALKING TO?

MAN: NONE OF YOUR—

WOMAN: —WHO WAS SHE?

MAN: JUST A FUCKIN—

WOMAN: —WHO WAS SHE?

MAN: GET THE FUCK BACK IN THIS HOUSE!

WOMAN: IF I FIND OUT THAT'S THE BITCH YOU'VE BEEN TALKING DIRTY TO ON THE PHONE THIS WEEK I'M GONNA—

MAN: —THERE'S BEEN NOBODY I'VE BEEN TALKING TO!

WOMAN: BULLSHIT!

MAN: YOU'RE SUCH—

WOMAN: BULLSHIT!

MAN: A FUCKING BITCH SOMETIMES—

WOMAN: BULLSHIT!

MAN: YOU KNOW THAT?

WOMAN: BULLSHIT!

MAN: GET THE FUCK BACK IN THE HOUSE AND STOP FUCKIN SCREAMIN!

(They disappear.)

NERVOUS-BOY: When I woke up I was relieved to see that I still had my teeth, and my throat was intact. A very troubling dream. Not very original, but still it bothered me. *(Pause.)* That morning I started brushing my teeth, and my gums were bleeding. This wasn't a dream. They were bleeding pretty hard upon contact with the toothbrush's bristles. Was my body trying to tell me something through my dreams? I don't know. Maybe. I don't know. But I didn't know what to do. Since I freelance, I don't have health or dental insurance, so it wasn't like I could afford to get my teeth or gums looked at. So I just quietly fretted. Laid low. If it persisted then I would bite the bullet, get some cheap-ass insurance and go to some cheap-ass dentist. *(Pause.)* After a couple of days my gums stopped bleeding, and I stopped worrying. *(Pause.)* There's no punch line to this story or anything, it's just something that happened and I thought about. *(Pause.)* After a lot of weird anxiety and dread, I decided on Thursday that enough was enough and it was time to go have a night out where I relax and blow off a little steam. I like those nights off. If you don't blow off a little steam you really start to lose perspective. Especially in this city. You get locked up in your own head. Anyway, it was time for a night off. But I needed to get that paycheck from one of my clients. So, I went to his office…

(NERVOUS-BOY enters an office. Sits down at a desk in front of a CLIENT. The lights should be those awful stark halogen overhead lights like at the office in Joe Versus the Volcano. *CLIENT looks something like a zombie.)*

NERVOUS-BOY: *(To CLIENT.)* Hello.

CLIENT: Oh. Hello.

NERVOUS-BOY: How are things?

CLIENT: The RTX branch is being bought by B307 for $12.35 a share.

NERVOUS-BOY: Wow. What does that mean for you?

CLIENT: If the voting power remains in the hands of Ericsson and Reilly, we may end up having our MDDL-compliant base go back to FpML.

NERVOUS-BOY: Are you worried about your job?

CLIENT: XTR4 is putting an embargo on all proxy statements regarding our options, so I don't know.

NERVOUS-BOY: *(Not to CLIENT.)* This reminds me why I don't work full time. I don't understand these people. But the real problem is that I feel like I'm missing something. It's weird but I'm jealous of this client. I wish I could talk about this and know what I'm saying. I'd like to be aware of the implications of all this. So I feel a bit like a jerk when I say, *(To CLIENT.)* I saw this really good movie last night called "Treason." Have you seen it? *(Back to himself.)* And I feel bad when he says…

CLIENT: *(Sad.)* No. I don't have any time to go out anymore. I really envy you. You're really smart to not go corporate. *(Pause.)* I know…in my soul of souls…that if I stuck with tenor sax, I'd be successful. *(Pause.)* You came here for your check.

NERVOUS-BOY: Yes.

CLIENT: Okay, hold on. *(Rifles through a desk drawer, pulls out an envelope, hands it to NERVOUS-BOY.)*

NERVOUS-BOY: Thanks.

CLIENT: You gonna be back for October?

NERVOUS-BOY: Yeah, should be.

CLIENT: They laid off the entire accounting department last week.

NERVOUS-BOY: That sucks.

CLIENT: Rules of the game. Times are tough.

NERVOUS-BOY: Don't I know it.

(CLIENT and office disappear; lights go back to normal. NERVOUS-BOY looks at his check.)

NERVOUS-BOY: You may be thinking that I would feel more at ease if I found myself a permanent full-time job, one with a salary and health benefits. Well, I used to have those here and there, but they never really suited me. I like having the independence that freelancing offers me, if only so I can say I don't have a boss. Still, steady work and steady paychecks do mitigate anxieties. One time, when the anxieties got particularly bad (because my checks were coming in late), I tried interviewing for a more steady position. A recruiting agency helped set up the meeting.

(He sits down in front of an INTERVIEWER, who is glancing over NERVOUS-BOY's resume.)

INTERVIEWER: So…hmm…tell me about your last job.

NERVOUS-BOY: Well, I…I was pretty much at one point responsible for the entire art department.

INTERVIEWER: Really?

NERVOUS-BOY: Oh, yeah. There was pretty much this mass exodus from the department and I was the only one who stayed, with the exception of this new freelancer, so it was just the two of us

completely responsible for getting the magazine shipped out.

INTERVIEWER: Huh.

NERVOUS-BOY: Yeah, well, it was stressful, but in a lot of ways it was a lot of fun. A rush, you know?

INTERVIEWER: So…ah…what's your…ah….Dream. Job…?

NERVOUS-BOY: Well, I don't have a dream job anymore, to tell the truth. And I guess that's because I don't dream that much. Except…I do have dreams about vomiting glass and bleeding at the gums. Although that's really not a job I wanna take. *(Pause.)* Truth is, I landed some shitty job that made me get up at five in the morning, and it was boring, mind-numbing work. They laid me off immediately. That actually was my dream job. It was perfect. I worked with sad people, and I interacted over email with frauds, but I didn't work with zombies. There's a huge difference. But they got rid of me like a hot potato. *(Pause.)* I like to kid myself by saying that I was too edgy for them, too personable, too interesting, but the fact is, I was a bad worker. And I didn't fit in. I have a tough time fitting in. But I was actually interested in fitting in. That is, I started to feel good about fitting in. *(Pause.)* My last few jobs, I never fit in, and I didn't want to. And my freelance jobs, they…they give me a lot of free time. A lot of free time to think about how I don't fit in anywhere. And that's not fun. It's just…lonely is too much of a "buzz" word nowadays. "Useless" is more like it. "A Complete Mistake" is more like it. "Your Dad Was Too Drunk To Pull Out And Roe V. Wade Wasn't Implemented And Here You Are For Everyone To Deal With" is more apt. *(Pause.)* I don't dream anymore. Except bad dreams. And it sucks. I guess...I guess I'm looking for a job that doesn't give me bad dreams anymore. Does that make sense?

(Silence.)

NERVOUS-BOY: Uh...uh...

(Silence.)

NERVOUS-BOY: I have some references if you need them, they should say...Huh...they should say nice things about me.

INTERVIEWER: *(Stares blankly. Blinks.)* Well.

(Silence.)

INTERVIEWER: Okay then.

NERVOUS-BOY: *(Excuses himself.)* Yeah.

(INTERVIEWER disappears.)

NERVOUS-BOY: I got a call later that day from the recruiting agency, telling me in a very apologetic voice that they just wanted to let me know that the company decided to go for someone else, but they'd Get Right Crackin' on getting something else for me. That pretty much burnt out my energy for finding full-time work. *(Pause.)* I wanted this money to burn tonight. I sort of need to relax and blow off some steam. And to celebrate. Celebrate what? Well, getting paid. A bit of circular logic, I know, but the real truth of it is I just want to have a night out. *(Pause.)* Usually when I go out to relax I like to do it alone. *(Puts check away.)* But a small part of me feels guilty for not at least inviting people, which is weird, considering it's pulling teeth to get my friends to go out—even for a beer—without at least two weeks' notice. Getting in contact with a bunch of

people is tough, not having a cell phone. So, after cashing my check, I went to a friend's apartment. I knew he'd say no (he never comes out), but at least I can relieve myself of the guilt for alienating him. Plus, he has a cell phone.

(NERVOUS-BOY goes over to his friend's apartment, where he meets said friend, ASMODEUS, a demon from the under-world. He has horns, red face, glowing yellow eyes, and deep voice. He's holding a crack pipe.)

ASMODEUS: Hey man, what's up?

NERVOUS-BOY: Hey, Asmodeus, how's it going?

ASMODEUS: It's good to see you.

NERVOUS-BOY: Same here, man.

ASMODEUS: What's been going on?

NERVOUS-BOY: Not much.

ASMODEUS: Come on in, come on in. *(Holds out the crack pipe.)* Want...?

NERVOUS-BOY: *(Thinks about it.)* I'll just have a beer for now.

ASMODEUS: Fair enough. In the fridge.

(NERVOUS-BOY exits to get himself a beer as ASMODEUS smokes the crack.)

ASMODEUS: Gonna be having some hot bitches over tonight.

NERVOUS-BOY: *(Off.)* Yeah...?

ASMODEUS: Gonna be some fun.

(NERVOUS-BOY reenters with beer.)

NERVOUS-BOY: That's cool.

ASMODEUS: Hey, you know Shirley's gonna be in town next week.

NERVOUS-BOY: Really?

ASMODEUS: Yeah.

NERVOUS-BOY: Oh, cool. That'd be cool to see her again. We should meet up.

ASMODEUS: Yeah. She gave me her new number, so I'll give you a call when she gets into town.

NERVOUS-BOY: Sweet. So what have you been up to?

ASMODEUS: Oh…been working on some new songs, man.

NERVOUS-BOY: Really?

ASMODEUS: Yeah. It's tough. I mean, I'm exhausted every time I come back home. I really hate my job.

NERVOUS-BOY: That's too bad.

ASMODEUS: I really admire you for not working full time. That must be really nice.

NERVOUS-BOY: Yeah, well, it has its drawbacks, too.

ASMODEUS: If I can finish these songs by next month, I can have a new album.

NERVOUS-BOY: Oh, that's cool, man!

ASMODEUS: Yeah.

NERVOUS-BOY: You playing anywhere anytime soon?

ASMODEUS: Not sure. Like to.

NERVOUS-BOY: Well, let me know.

ASMODEUS: Sure, sure. *(Sighs.)* I'm so sick of my job.

NERVOUS-BOY: You should quit.

ASMODEUS: I should. *(Pause.)* Hey, I got the new PlayStation. Wanna play?

NERVOUS-BOY: What games you got?

ASMODEUS: "Exiled Angel," "Maximum Intensity," and "Operation Insider."

NERVOUS-BOY: You have any *Star Wars* games?

ASMODEUS: No, man. I wish. I hear the new one is supposed to be pretty hot.

NERVOUS-BOY: Yeah. No, I'm okay. Maybe later.

ASMODEUS: *(Pause.)* You okay, dude?

NERVOUS-BOY: I'm fine, why?

ASMODEUS: I don't know. You've been…strange, lately.

NERVOUS-BOY: *(Shrugs.)* I don't know.

ASMODEUS: I worry about you, man. You know?

NERVOUS-BOY: Thanks. You shouldn't have to.

ASMODEUS: I hope not.

NERVOUS-BOY: Yeah, well…I should get going.

ASMODEUS: Yeah?

NERVOUS-BOY: Yeah. Sure you don't want to come out?

ASMODEUS: Yeah, I think I'm in for the night.

NERVOUS-BOY: Okay, no problem.

ASMODEUS: Okay. Well, I'll see you later?

NERVOUS-BOY: Yeah. Maybe we'll see each other this weekend.

ASMODEUS: Okay, I'll give you a call. Want one for the road? (*Indicating crack pipe.*)

NERVOUS-BOY: (*Thinks about it.*) Ah, why not? (*Smokes.*) Thanks, man.

ASMODEUS: Sure thing. Take care of yourself, dude.

NERVOUS-BOY: Thanks. You, too, Asmodeus.

ASMODEUS: Later.

(*NERVOUS-BOY leaves ASMODEUS's place; ASMODEUS disappears.*)

NERVOUS-BOY: I don't know if Asmodeus is my best friend, but he's definitely one of the people I hang out with the most. He listens, and he doesn't give me shit. That is, he doesn't give me as much shit as most people. He's cool, although I think he has a bit of a drug problem. But who am I to judge? I've got my own vices. (*Pause.*) So I wanted to try this bar down in the Lower East Side. I considered calling Emily, but then came to my senses and thought better of it. I was thinking of inviting this one friend I haven't spoken to in a while, but chickened out. We went out a while back and I said some really mean things to her because I drank too much. I don't think she's forgiven me. Maybe she has, but I've been too scared to call her and find out. It's really a shame because we've been pretty close for years and now it's all over because I was mean. I don't really like talking about it. (*Pause.*) I found a pay phone and called up someone to see if they wanted to go out. I really didn't want him to come or anything, but he's one of those people that would be kind

of a dick about it if he heard I was going out and he wasn't invited. I knew it was a bad idea, just knew it, but I'm just stupid that way, I guess. (*Calls on pay phone.*) Hello? Hey, man, how's it going? Good, good. Yeah, well, listen…what's that? Uh-huh? Yeah. Well…okay. Uh…okay. (*Pause.*) Okay. (*Pause.*) Okay. (*Makes some spastic gesture of frustration.*) Sounds good! Well…uh…then… I'mmmmmmonmywaythen. (*Hangs up.*) Shit. (*Pause.*) Here I am feeling guilty about not inviting this guy out with me and he's insisted I tag along with his group of useless friends who are out at a bar in SoHo. He didn't even invite me. It didn't even occur to him to call me. But of course, before I can let him know what's what, I'm being pressured to meet up with his group. (*Starts walking.*) Maybe I'll just make a quick stop and then go on my way (I'm not going to like this).

(*Scene is set up to be a pool hall.*)

NERVOUS-BOY: When I got there I realized it wasn't one of those chichi SoHo bars but a divey pool hall in SoHo. They would be playing pool all night. Great. I hate pool. I didn't want to be spending any time here with these people.

(*The GROUP in question is at a table at the pool hall having some drinks. They mostly resemble apes. The alpha of the group, GROG, beckons NERVOUS-BOY over.*)

GROG: Dude! Come on over, come on over!

HRMPH: Waasaaapbuuudyyyyy?

PHHT: Huuuuh!

GROG: What's going on?

NERVOUS-BOY: How ya doing?

GROG: What's happening?

NERVOUS-BOY: What have you been up to?

GROG: What's up, man?

NERVOUS-BOY: Good to see you guys.

GROG: What's going on?

NERVOUS-BOY: How long have you been here?

GROG: What's happening?

NERVOUS-BOY: I'm in hell.

GROG: What's up, man?

NERVOUS-BOY: My soul seems to be rotting faster and faster.

GROG: What's going on?

NERVOUS-BOY: I really don't know how much longer I can endure these horrible interactions with you fucking zombies and vampires but then again what choice do I really have in the matter?

GROG: What's happening?

NERVOUS-BOY: Then again, since I do live in such a crowded city like New York it's not like I have any real reason to complain I mean I could always just move to the country.

GROG: What's up, man?

NERVOUS-BOY: But then again I get really lonely and I'd have to spend money on a house and car and that wouldn't be any good, either.

GROG: What's going on?

NERVOUS-BOY: I have no earthly idea what I stand to gain by interacting with you this evening.

GROG: What's happening?

NERVOUS-BOY: Eep.

GROG: What's up, man?

NERVOUS-BOY: Hmm.

GROG: What's going on?

NERVOUS-BOY:...

GROG: What's happening?

NERVOUS-BOY:...

GROG: What's up, man?

NERVOUS-BOY:...

GROG: What's going on?

NERVOUS-BOY:...

GROG: What's happening?

NERVOUS-BOY:...

GROG: What's up, man?

NERVOUS-BOY:...

HRMPH: Yyyyyyyeeeeaaaahhh-buuudyyyyy...

PHHT: WHOOOOOOOOOOO!

GROG: Wanna play some pool, man?

NERVOUS-BOY: Lemme get a drink. You guys go first.

HRMPH: I'll playyagrog...

GROG: Awright, man.

PHHT: Ahhhplaywinner.

GROG: Awright.

(NERVOUS-BOY gets a beer. GROG and HRMPH play pool. NERVOUS-BOY watches and drinks.)

PHHT: (To NERVOUS-BOY.) Soyou-wannabeatumarts?

NERVOUS-BOY: *(???)* Uh…no thanks.

PHHT: Haffenuvian.

NERVOUS-BOY: Mmn.

(Some DUMB DRUNK SKANK goes over to NERVOUS-BOY.)

SKANK: Hey, wanna play pool?

NERVOUS-BOY: Excuse me?

SKANK: I wanna play some pool. Wanna?

NERVOUS-BOY: Well, I didn't really know. I mean, she was fuckable and all, but she seemed really aggressive and annoying. Too much of an ordeal to have fun with.

SKANK: What's that supposed to mean?

NERVOUS-BOY: I mean, my guess is you're going to be nattering in my fucking ear all night and insist I buy you drinks and you'll most likely be really rude and hostile about it. You'll be very clingy and possessive but be standoffish and annoyed if I try to kiss you. You'll most likely be swearing at me and pissed at me for not giving you enough attention yet not give a fuck about what's going on with me. Still, I'll be buying you drink after drink even after you start a fight with the bouncer. Eventually, you'll be falling down and throwing up or even worse, get sidetracked and find some other guy in this place to take home and fuck. And the real problem is that it's pretty much a lose-lose situation for me, since I'll feel really disgusted with myself for hooking up with such a clearly dumb drunk skank and I'll feel really bad about myself if I fail in this endeavor. Plus, I hate to say it but you're really not all that cute. I'm under

the impression that even if you were stone-cold sober you'd have something in the way of a double-digit IQ but now that you're really this drunk it's dropped significantly. Not to mention that even if you were stone-cold sober and didn't have that repellent "eyes-at-half-mast" thing going on or that drunken, bloated cheek thing going on or that kind of perpetually nauseous expression going on you'd still not be that particularly attractive. So my guess is that this is too much of an ordeal for what's basically a lose-lose situation for me.

SKANK: So no?

NERVOUS-BOY: I don't know. Maybe later.

SKANK: That a no?

NERVOUS-BOY: Yeah. Yeah, that's a no.

SKANK: Whatever. Faggot. *(Leaves to go scam some free drinks from someone else.)*

("I Want You Back" by the Jackson Five plays overhead.)

HRMPH: Thissa gooplace.

(GROG laughs jocularly with HRMPH. Then the laughter is a bit more maniacal. Then without warning GROG hits HRMPH with the pool cue. The APE-MEN start a brawl in the pool hall—"I Want You Back" by the Jackson Five still of course playing—while NERVOUS-BOY watches from the seat. This goes on for a little bit.)

NERVOUS-BOY: I left the bar without saying goodbye. I don't think they'll miss me or notice that I'm gone. Well, I'll get a call from the asshole tomorrow I'm sure, but I'm in no mood to placate him right now.

(GROG and the BOYS disappear, as does the pool hall.)

NERVOUS-BOY: In fact, I'm in no mood for dealing with bottomless black holes of need. Which is really what people are. Or, to be fair, people I interact with on a regular basis. Like that old man on the park bench who felt the need to vomit his boring problems about his wife to me as if I cared. And it's not as if he wanted to listen to anything I said. Sometimes people bug me.

(Walks across the stage to a counter of a liquor store. To CLERK and pointing to the wall behind him.)

NERVOUS-BOY: The bottle of rum? The fifteen-dollar bottle?

(CLERK hands him the bottle in a brown paper bag. NERVOUS-BOY pays him.)

NERVOUS-BOY: Thanks.

(CLERK and liquor store disappear.)

NERVOUS-BOY: I bought a bottle of rum and realized I was through dealing with other people. I didn't need these others to have a fun night out. So, I went to the place where I like to relax. *(Enters a gentlemen's club.)* This is where I go to relax. It's kind of expensive, and I do know some people who go to strip clubs way too much and get addicted to them, but I don't think I'm like that. *(Pays the admission.)* Drinks are too expensive, so I usually sneak in a bottle of something. *(Sits down, pulls out a bottle of rum, and waits to be entertained.)* I know I'm supposed to feel guilty going into a place like this but I don't. I find women attractive and when they're good-looking, naked, and pretending to like me, I like that. Besides, this is my night off and I'm not going to feel guilty about how I like to have fun.

(A STRIPPER enters. She is very pretty, but has pale blue zombie-like skin. She gives NERVOUS-BOY a lap dance. NERVOUS-BOY hands her dollar bills throughout.)

STRIPPER: What's your name, big-boy?

NERVOUS-BOY: Tom.

STRIPPER: My name's Perry.

NERVOUS-BOY: Yeah?

STRIPPER: Yeah. Perry Chopcicle.

NERVOUS-BOY: Okay.

STRIPPER: So where you from?

NERVOUS-BOY: Here.

STRIPPER: Oh.

(He breathes in her scent.)

STRIPPER: So, Tom. How come I haven't seen you here before?

NERVOUS-BOY: I've been around. It's been a while.

STRIPPER: Guess we've just missed shifts.

NERVOUS-BOY: *(Starting to get into it.)* Guess so.

STRIPPER: Well, we're here together now, Tom.

NERVOUS-BOY: Well, it's not really Tom but I guess your name isn't Perry Chopcicle, either, so what difference does it make?

STRIPPER: You like this?

NERVOUS-BOY: Interestingly enough, I do. You're the first person in a while who's actually been nice to me and actively concerned about making me feel happy.

STRIPPER: Well, it is my job.

NERVOUS-BOY: Yeah, but you're actually good at it. It's the kid who works at Starbucks' job to be friendly to me as I buy my coffee, but he can't be bothered. You're actually seeming like you like me. Which is more than I can say about most people I interact with.

STRIPPER: *(Indicating her nipples.)* Squeeze them.

(He does. He's starting to show emotion.)

STRIPPER: Yyyyyeeeeaaahh…

NERVOUS-BOY: You don't have to pretend around me.

STRIPPER: I'm not pretending.

NERVOUS-BOY: Okay, fine.

STRIPPER: You bein' a naughty boy?

NERVOUS-BOY: Sure.

STRIPPER: You sure?

NERVOUS-BOY: I'm VERY sure. I mean, fuck. I haven't been "naughty" since I don't remember when. Hell, I can barely afford to be "naughty." I'm just bending over backwards to accommodate fuckwits who look down on me.

STRIPPER: That's awful.

NERVOUS-BOY: It gets really tiresome.

STRIPPER: You need someone to put you out of your misery? You need to be released.

NERVOUS-BOY: Oh please yes.

STRIPPER: So how would you like to go to the back room?

NERVOUS-BOY: *(Into it.)* Oh, yeah.

STRIPPER: Yeah? You can handle that?

NERVOUS-BOY: *(Pulling out fistfuls of money.)* I got paid today. And I had a bad week. Yeah, I can handle it.

STRIPPER: Okay.

(Lights change to indicate that they're in the back room. She rips off his dress shirt.)

STRIPPER: Don't mind it rough?

NERVOUS-BOY: I like it rough. I'm sick of all this pussy-footing around with people. I'm sick of euphemisms.

STRIPPER: *(Getting rough.)* You're from here, you say?

NERVOUS-BOY: *(Now hands on, grabbing her.)* Yeah.

STRIPPER: Well, if you're from here how come you're so polite?

NERVOUS-BOY: I don't know.

STRIPPER: Wanna stop being polite?

NERVOUS-BOY: *(Pulls out the rum.)* Yes.

STRIPPER: *(She grabs the bottle and chugs it.)* Stop being so polite.

NERVOUS-BOY: Okay. *(Takes a swig of the rum.)*

STRIPPER: *(Pulls out a knife.)* Wanna be really dirty?

NERVOUS-BOY: I do.

STRIPPER: *(Slices her arm with the knife.)* Yeah…?

NERVOUS-BOY: Yeah.

STRIPPER: *(Slices the side of his face.)* You sure?

NERVOUS-BOY: I'm sure.

STRIPPER: *(Slicing her arms with the knife.)* Fuck me.

NERVOUS-BOY: *(Another swig.)* Okay.

STRIPPER: Don't be nervous.

NERVOUS-BOY: Trust me, I'm not.

(He fucks her, grabbing her by the throat. She hands him the knife. He wields it, smiling with glee like a kid in a candy store, and cuts her with it. Then he stabs her repeatedly. She screams in ecstasy as blood splatters all over him. She smiles as she spits blood in his face. He, too, is making loud moans of delight as he keeps stabbing her. She's thrashing around. Throughout this, he's occasionally saying, "Yeah? Yeah? Like that, you cunt?" or something of that ilk. She occasionally says stuff like, "Fuck me, you useless piece of shit." He then bites her in the neck and tears off her flesh with his teeth. He stabs her in the throat, and she finally stops thrashing. She lies still, unmoving. He comes. He stares at her. He's covered in blood. He screams with joy and takes a big gulp from the bottle of rum.)

NERVOUS-BOY: YES! YES!! *(Spits rum all over the place and trashes the room.)* THAT'S what I needed, THAT! Oh, YES!! THIS is how I can relax. I may not always be stressed but I need this release from the BULLSHIT I have to put up with in this SHIThole! This is WHAT I've been MISSING! Let's fucking DO THIS!! WHOOOOOOOOOOOOOO! I'm SO fucking SICK of being surrounded by LITTLE STUPID LEMMINGS that have no idea how to have FUN! FUCK ALL THOSE STUPID MOTHERFUCKERS I WILL EAT THEM ALL ALIVE THOSE STUPID SPINELESS CLOSE-MINDED FUCKING MAGGOTS! YES!!

(BOUNCER enters and sees the mess.)

BOUNCER: Whoa whoa whoa what the fuck is oh my God.

(NERVOUS-BOY turns and glares at BOUNCER, smiling. BOUNCER looks at him, terrified.)

BOUNCER: You!

(NERVOUS-BOY darts at him, and guts him with the knife. Blood sprays everywhere. BOUNCER drops dead. NERVOUS-BOY looks possessed, pleased with his work.)

NERVOUS-BOY: *(Catches his breath.)* Where are we going next, huh? What the fuck, where we going? We gotta go somewhere else this place is boring.

(Exits. Police arrive at the scene. The two DETECTIVES on the case are stereotypical plainclothesmen. Their exchange should be quick and heavy with that clichéd "cop talk" feel.)

SERGEANT CROWLEY: What a mess.

DETECTIVE CRUMP: Thass right.

SERGEANT CROWLEY: What a shame.

DETECTIVE CRUMP: Prolly-prolly.

SERGEANT CROWLEY: Let's go through the files.

DETECTIVE CRUMP: Le's do dat.

SERGEANT CROWLEY: Strange case.

DETECTIVE CRUMP: Sure is.

SERGEANT CROWLEY: Strange world.

DETECTIVE CRUMP: Diff'rent strokes.

SERGEANT CROWLEY: Sick world.

DETECTIVE CRUMP: Sad world.

SERGEANT CROWLEY: Sick people.

THE ADVENTURES OF NERVOUS-BOY   277

DETECTIVE CRUMP: Chammy-choo.

SERGEANT CROWLEY: Don't get this town no more.

DETECTIVE CRUMP: Jabba doodoo.

SERGEANT CROWLEY: Maybe I'm gettin too old.

DETECTIVE CRUMP: Chumba-grog-grog.

SERGEANT CROWLEY: Okay. Let's go through the files.

DETECTIVE CRUMP: Jibba-jab.

(They leave the scene, taking the CORPSES away. As part of the stage is being set up to be NERVOUS-BOY's bedroom, EMILY is at a bar and on her cell phone.)

EMILY: Hi, it's me. Uh…look. I just wanted to say that I had a really fun time the other night, and…well, to tell you the truth, I'm kind of surprised I haven't heard from you since. I really figured you would have called. Well, I'm out in the East Village, I…I'm not sure what the name of this place is. It's on…somewhere on East Sixth between 1st and A. I don't know if you'll get this in time or not, but…I think it'd be really nice to see you. I realized just how long it's been and…also, I wanted to apologize for the way I acted before. I've just been thinking about it and I feel I was really rude to you. And I feel that's why you haven't called me. Look, uh, yeah, I mean, anyway…it's just, just…give me a call whenever you can. I may be up for a little while, just needed to blow off some steam.

(Bedroom is now made, but not lit. At one point in her message, NERVOUS-BOY crawls into bed.)

EMILY: Anyway, heh, uh…I really don't know. Gimme a call when you can. Or…or…maybe you don't really want to talk to me right now I don't know. *(Pause.)* I'm sorry…sorry for leaving such a long rambling message. We'll talk. Yeah. We'll talk. Okay. Talk to you later. Bye. *(She hangs up and disappears.)*

(Lights come up on his bedroom. NERVOUS-BOY gets up out of bed, looking hung-over and mildly guilty in that way you look after a night of "tying one on." There's no blood on his clothes.)

NERVOUS-BOY: I wake up feeling mildly embarrassed but I can't remember why. I think I hurt some people's feelings last night. And I remember I shouldn't drink so much. Hmm…yikes. Don't have that much money to last me for the rest of the month. One of the downsides of freelancing. Maybe I can get another client to advance me for the project I'm working on now. Yeah, I feel vaguely guilty and bad, but at the very least I didn't have any trouble sleeping. And didn't have any bad dreams. At least, none that I can remember. I really need to stop drinking. I just have this vague feeling that I did something wrong. I do remember meeting up with someone. I figured I should call him just to double check that things were cool. *(Picks up the phone and dials.)*

(GROG enters on the opposite side of the stage, obviously somewhere in the city. He picks up his cell phone.)

GROG: Hey, man.

NERVOUS-BOY: Hey man, how's it going?

GROG: Cool, man. Good.

NERVOUS-BOY: Cool.

GROG: What are you up to?

NERVOUS-BOY: Oh, have to go into the office. Look, I'm sorry about last night if I was way out of line—

GROG: Oh, no, dude. No worries, you were fine.

NERVOUS-BOY: Okay.

GROG: You were funny.

NERVOUS-BOY: Oh. Cool.

GROG: We should hang out again, dude. *(Exits.)*

NERVOUS-BOY: Yeah. *(Hangs up.)* Living in New York, I'm around a lot of people who are stressed out. Always stressed, always freaking out, always multi-tasking, and always living in a state of constant self-created panic. I don't really stress out. At least, not in the way that people I know do. My heart rate remains at forty-eight beats per minute, I remember appointments, I have all my teeth. I don't feel stress. What I feel is a feeling of steady dread. That constant feeling that I've missed something, forgot something, did something wrong.

(He's now in line at a food stand. A GIRL ON A CELL PHONE is in front of him.)

CELL PHONE GIRL: *(On phone.)* Yeah…? Yeah…! Yeah! Yeah? Yeah. Yeah, well…yeah. Yeah yeah yeah. Yeah. Yeah. Yeah. *(Continues until curtain.)*

NERVOUS-BOY: I would like for this feeling to pass. If only for a short while.

(END OF PLAY.)

ANOTHER BRIEF ENCOUNTER

Stan Richardson

STAN RICHARDSON is a playwright, actor, and director from St. Louis, Missouri. He has lived in New York City since 1995. His plays include *wHormone, Columbus, Play Without Gravity, Mr. T & Sympathy, The 52nd Annual Davenports Clan Yearly Family X-mas Spectacular* (Ars Nova Theater, December 2003 and 2004), and *Ma Vie En Rosewood* (with composer Hal Goldberg). *And/Or*, an evening of his short plays, ran throughout August 2006 as part of the HOT! Festival at Dixon Place; *The Children* (also with Hal Goldberg) was presented in the New York Musical Theatre Festival in September of 2006. As an actor, Richardson has appeared in *Johnny McGovern's Dirty Stuff* (Westbeth Theatre, 2000) and as the title role in John Moran's *The Little Retarded Boy* (Ace of Clubs, 2005). A graduate of NYU/Tisch School of the Arts, the Upright Citizens Brigade, and Edward Albee's Playwrights' Workshop, and a former resident of Albee's "Barn," Richardson is presently a staff reviewer for nytheatre.com and a proud member of the Writer's Room and the Dramatists Guild of America.

Another Brief Encounter was first presented as part of a larger evening of Stan Richardson's work entitled *And/Or* by Dixon Place (Ellie Covan, Executive Director) and KEITRIK Productions (Dwayne Mann and Denis Guerin, Executive Producers) on August 3, 2006, at Dixon Place, New York City, with the following cast and credits:

1	Matt Steiner
2 & 6	Nick Dothee
3	Jim Bray
4	Harris Doran
5	Caleb Damschroder
1's & 6's Thoughts	Megan Reinking

Director: Ben Rimalower
Stage Manager: Zac Chandler
Original Music: Hal Goldberg
Set Designer: Lex Liang
Costume Designer: Michael Woll
Lighting Designer: Shane Mongar
Sound Designer: Travis Sawyer

ACKNOWLEDGMENTS

Thanks to Dwayne & Denis for their fervent confidence in this play, and to the original cast, especially our fine understudy Adam Rihacek. Special thanks to Sarah & Yuval for their clear-eyed and comprehensive dramaturgy, and to Hal, my favorite collaborator, for *Rach The Beat!* This play would not have been conceived were it not for Dan Callahan, who introduced me to one of his favorite films, and Liz Scharffenberger, whose adventurous erudition forever changed my appreciation of parody. I am indebted to Richard Steuer for his emplawyerly understanding, and Jeff Richards for his inestimable guidance and friendship. I am astounded by the tireless support and enthusiasm of Martin & Rochelle Denton and Michael Criscuolo of nytheatre.com. (Huge thanks to Mom & Dad, natch.) Finally, thanks to Jilly D. for the daily check-ins and all the compelling reasons to enjoy life outside of the theatre.

Another Brief Encounter is dedicated to the inimitable Maria de Cesare, my muse and confessor, whose laughter is the best absolution.

longing so hard to make
inclusions that the longing
has become in memory
an inclusion
—Thom Gunn, "Autobiography"

CHARACTERS

1, 2, 3, 4, 5 & 6: gay men in their mid-twenties (2 & 6 are played by the same actor)

1's Thoughts: voice of a middle-aged British woman, underscored by Rachmaninov's 2nd piano concerto

6's Thoughts: the same

A NOTE ON THE SETTINGS

Most scenes take place in a vibrant gay coffee shop with a large rainbow banner that reads "Gay Pride Week"; the remainder are set in 1 and 6's apartment: cramped and subdued, barely able to accommodate a love seat, an easy chair, and a table with a stereo.

TIME AND PLACE

Gay Pride Week; New York City, now.

[ONE]

Friday night. 1 and 2 are seated, forlorn, in a coffee shop; both are young men in their mid-twenties.

1: The tea is cold.

2: Quite.

1: Why did you say you had to go to Africa?

(Suddenly the door swings open: 3 enters on rollerblades.)

3: AND STAY OUT! *(Sees 1.)* OH, 1, 1, 1, you must be wondering who I was talking to just then! *(Sees 2.)* Who are you?

2: *(A tad wearily.)* Forgive me, I'm—

1: He's—

3: Wait: don't tell me yet. Won't you get me some coffee first? My rollerblades. No—wait—tell me first—NO—get the coffee—yes, the coffee first—the coffee and then the talk.

(2 goes.)

3: *(Poking 1.)* Oh, 1, 1, 1—I wonder what's going on with you two. I just wonder—No! Let me just wonder...*(Wonders a bit, then.)* Gosh, I just don't know...Hmm...Golly...*I. DON'T. KNOW. (Laughs.)* I just passed your hubby on the way home from the restaurant—isn't that sweet? I mean, of course, that *he* was on his way back home from the restaurant, and not me. Not I. Isn't that odd? I mean, wasn't that clear? Sweet, odd, clear? I mean, do you think I used a misplaced modifier just then?—Hello?! Where did that phrase come from? I can't remember the last time I...

(3's voice fades out. 1's thoughts become audible, spoken by a quiet middle-aged British woman, underscored by Rachmaninov's 2nd piano concerto.)

1'S THOUGHTS: I wish I could trust you. I wish you were a wise, kind friend, instead of a gossiping acquaintance I've known casually for years and never particularly cared for. I wish you would shut up. No, I don't mean that. That was silly and unkind. Oh, what an awful thing to / think…*

3: *(Fading back in.)* "Predicates" sounds like "impregnates" and "past participle" sounds like "octopus." *(Spots 2 approaching with the coffee.)* Three coffees—all for me! All for 3! *(Drinks from one cup.)* I think we're all schizophrenic, don't you? In this day and age? Age…Age worries me. As a gay man. Watching my brothers go to seed: each roll and wrinkle radically reduces the rikelyhood they'll be rescued. Sometimes it's just *hell* in here. Let me OUT! Switching personalities…Switched! *(Drinks from another cup.)* Do you think I should get exorcized? I think that kids today are schizophrenic—I think I am, too—but what does it mean? So many people incorrectly believe that schizophrenia means multiple personalities—I do, too. Whose jet is that?

2: *(Glances out the window, solemnly.)* It's mine. I'm afraid I must go. *(Looking at 1.)* How very nice to meet you…3.

3: I do very well, thank you.

(There's a honk from outside. 1 nods. 2 nods. 2 exits. Pause.)

3: I wonder, is it alright for me to begin talking again? The experience of silence has become too intense—a great chasm of loneliness is threatening to open up inside me…

---

*When one character starts speaking before the other has finished, the point of interruption is marked /, and the first character continues talking regardless.

1'S THOUGHTS: I wish you'd stop talking. I wish you'd stop prying and trying to find things out. I wish you were dead—No, that's awful. What an awful thing to say. Oh, I am a sister of Satan!

3: *(Skating over to the bar.)* I must get another cup of coffee, and quick! I can feel another personality coming on! *(Ordering at the bar.)* Bon monsieur, quel est votre parfum du jour? Yesh lecha hamlatsa al rabi tov? Ani chadash ba-ezor. Il suo caffè me fa sente come Sophia Loren sullo schermo di film grande. Nein! Ich lese Manuskripte nicht momentan! Gracias.

(During the above, 1 stares after 2, then impulsively runs outside. 4 enters; he sees 3 and he runs to the bathroom in tears. After a beat, 1 reenters, distraught and missing an eye. He resumes his seat.)

3: *(Returns to table with coffee.)* 1, 1, 1…I just wonder—Can you tell between my personalities? I can't. Was I a slut just then? Was that the slutty personality? Can I name her Sadie? Sexy Sadie the Sample Sale…But 1, you seem to suffer somehow. Sitting there, crying your eye out.

1: I'm fine. Really, I am. Just feeling a bit dizzy is all. I should go home now.

3: I'll roll you there.

1: No really…It's only twenty blocks…

3: Tsk tsk tsk.

(3 takes 1 by the arm and leads him out of the coffee bar as 4 enters from the bathroom.)

4: *(Screaming to 3.)* You're killing me!

1: 3, I think someone / is…

3: That was me. I throw my voice. But which "me" was it?

(4 collapses in tears. 3 leads 1 out. 5 enters, and sees 4 on the ground. 4 immediately recovers.)

5: Ff–4?

4: *(Aloof.)* Hello. Nice to see you.

5: If I were him…I would love you / so much…

4: What are you talking about? God, you're so desperate! Why can't you just be normal?!

5: I'm—I'm—I'm—

[TWO]

1: I'm home.

(Friday night. 1 and 6's apartment. 6 is curled up in the chair with a manuscript. TAFFY, a long fat laconic cat, is sprawled across his lap.)

6: *(Gasps, to the cat.)* Taffy, is someone home? Look who's home. Tell 6 who's home.

(1 leans down to kiss 6, but ends up kissing TAFFY. 1 tries again, finally managing to kiss 6 as well as TAFFY.)

6: Did 1 have a nice day?

1: Yes. Did you?

6: Laundry, grocery shopping, and a whole lotta reading—what? What's that, Taffy? Taffy wants to know if you saw any other kitties today.

1: N-no, Taffy. What are you reading?

6: Just a friend's screenplay. I brought you the lasagna you like from the restaurant.

1: *(Moved.)* Oh, 6…

6: It's on the stove. Maybe we'll take a walk down by the pier in a little bit, watch the fireworks for Pride.

1: Yes. I'd…love that.

6: *(Re: the manuscript.)* I'm almost done with—

1: *(Sinks down into the love seat.)* Of course. Keep reading. I'll just… *(Realizes he's sitting on something: it is knitting. He looks at it, unfamiliarly, then begins to knit.)*

1'S THOUGHTS: 6, dear 6. You're the only one in the world with enough wisdom and gentleness to understand what has happened to me. As it is, you're the only one in the world that I can never tell. You see, I'm a happily married woman—or I was, rather, until a few days ago. This is my whole world, and it's enough, or rather, it was until a few days ago. But, oh, 6, I've been so foolish. I've fallen in love. I'm an ordinary woman. I didn't think such violent things could happen to ordinary people. It wouldn't have happened if I hadn't gotten that bit of grit in my eye from the subway explosion last Monday by some terrorist group or other…

[THREE]

Monday night. The coffee bar; several days earlier. 2 approaches the coffee bar.

2: Hello, yes, I'd asked for some artificial sweetener in my—Oh, how silly of me, it's in the spoon, of course.

(A loud explosion from without. 1 enters with a piece of subway grit in his eye.)

1: *Shit!*

2: *(Rushes over to him.)* Here, may I help you?

1: *(Quite distressed but…)* Uh, yeah, could I have a Chamomile tea with honey and—

2: Your eye—

1: *(Not fine.)* It's fine, I'm / fine.

2: I in / sist.

1: It's only a piece of subway grit—

2: Please! Some inevitable intangible intuitive force heretofore unbeknownst to me except in the verse of great poets and singer-songwriters compels me to help—

1: Okay!

2: *(Extracts the grit from 1's eye with his handkerchief.)* There.

1: *(Blinking at 2.)* Wow. Thanks.

(They stare at each other. An enormous honk outside.)

2: *(Steps toward the door.)* That's / me.

1: *(Desperately.)* Don't go— *(Embarrassed.)* I'm sorry. Ha! Sometimes when I cough it sounds like a...plea. *(Coughs a bit to demonstrate, then.)* Thank you for the...

2: The pleasure was entirely mine.

(2 exits. 1 remains, shrugs it off with a laugh and crosses to order his tea. 4 enters coolly, followed by a smitten 5.)

5: *(The end of an anecdote.)* So, I told him to fuck off.

(4, distracted, sort of laughs.)

5: I love your laugh. It sounds like you're snoring. So...how are you?

4: *(Getting coffee; sort of laughs again.)* I'm fine. How are you?

5: I love your smile. It always looks like it takes so much energy to prop it up—like it's—like it's five times the size of a nor-

mal smile and there are a million hands behind it, waiting for it to collapse.

4: My mouth looks big?

5: I love our dynamic. It always feels like a blind date. Is one of those for me?

4: You always buy *me* coffee so I felt obligated / to—

5: That means I'm buying next time. *(A moment.)* That means there will be a next time.

(Suddenly the door swings open: it is 3 on rollerblades.)

3: Don't move him! I'll call for help! *(Spots 1.)* Oh, 1,1,1! Don't you just wonder what's happening anymore to the outer world? What are you drinking?

1: *(Seating himself, picking up a gay magazine.)* Chamomile with honey and lemon. I never caffeinate before I go home. It scares 6 when I'm passionate.

(4 and 3 lock eyes.)

5: *(Fishing in his bag.)* Oh, hey, I brought those movies I was talking about. *(Hands 4 some videotapes.)* They're some of my faves.

4: *(Barely looks at them.)* Yeah, black-and-white romantic tearjerkers. My mom likes these.

3: *(Staring longingly at 4.)* Oh, 1,1,1, I just wonder when I will have a hubby like yours, whose face will be emblazoned on mine like Our Lord's on Veronica's handtowel.

5: Well, they're classic love stories. You know, very earn / est.

3: I'm so tired of talking to new people in sexual situations.

5: Everything is so dripping with irony these days. Parody, satire, spoof. We can't invent anything new so we reuse old forms because we're too addicted to their com / fort.

3: How thin, the ice of shared language upon which we perforce must skate.

4: *(Staring longingly at 3.)* Uh-huh.

5: *(Watching 3 and 4 staring longingly at each other.)* That's why I'm a novelist. I mean—*Screenwriter.* I *used* to be a novel / ist.

4: Neat. You should cast me.

5: Don't you wanna know what my screenplay's about?

4: *(Reluctantly wresting his gaze from 3.)* It's not another gay love story, is it?

5: It…well…

4: I'm kinda done with that. I'm interested in the more political stuff. Like this show I'm doing for Pride. Okay: the main cause of gay men getting sick is because they infect each other while whacked out on drugs, right? The main reason they take drugs is because of poor body image—you know, to make themselves feel better? So we're doing this show where a whole bunch of us get naked onstage and have sex with one another to show that it's okay if you're ugly or fat or if you're getting old because even though we will wait for you to leave the steam room at the gym before we get each other off, once a year you can come see hot young guys who'll let anyone watch them do it onstage AND all the donations go to fighting the disease.

3: But you'll excuse me, 1, I am great with urine. *(Exits to the bathroom, indicating for 4 to follow him.)*

4: *(Hastily hands the videos back to 5.)* I can't watch tapes on my computer.

5: I have a VCR. Do you want to / come—

4: *(Exiting into the bathroom; winks.)* Bring me your screenplay!

(5 tries to make eye contact with 1 as if to say "Can you believe that?"; 1 does his best to appear engrossed in his magazine.)

[FOUR]

1'S THOUGHTS: The next day was, of course, Tuesday and I had stopped off at the bookstore because the new novel had just arrived for my Repressed Romantics reading series. I was engrossed, and wasn't even thinking of the man who'd extricated the bit of subway grit from my eye.

(Tuesday night. The coffee bar. 1 sits at the table, sipping tea and looking around, barely glancing at his book, which he holds upside down. 3 enters from the bathroom.)

3: OH, 1! *(Skates over to 1's table.)* 1, 1, 1! I was just headed uptown but I decided to peek in and see if you were here. And you are! Uh-oh. That guy who just entered. He's one of my exes. I do have an excess of them, you know.

1: *(Looks to the door.)* Who— ?

(Then 4 enters, spots 3, and approaches him cheerfully.)

4: Hey! What's up? *(To 1.)* Hi, I'm sorry, I'm–

3: *(Quick introductions, eyes averted.)* 4, 1, 1, 3.

4: *(Awkwardly.)* Sooo…Can we talk?

3: *(To 1.)* Ask him "about what?"—NO, I'll ask him. No, you ask him. No, I'll—

4: I just wanted to see if you wanted to grab a—

1: I have to go.

3: *(To 1.)* I have to go too. Where are *you* going?

4: *(To 3.)* Come on now.

1: I'm—um— / home…

3: I'll roll you—

4: *(To 3.)* Hey, what's your problem?!

(5 enters.)

5: Hey—4! I brought you my—

4: *(To 5, looking at 3.)* Hijustasec!

3: TOO MUCH! TOO MUCH! SWITCHING PERSONALITIES! *(Switching—a slot-machine-like motion.)* Tchk! Tchk! / Tchk! Tchk!

1: *(To 4.)* I'm just going to put him outside. He's—It's not a good idea…

4: Wait, are you his…

1: *(Pushing 3 out the door.)* NO. No.

(As 1 starts to exit, he bumps into 2.)

2: Hello.

1: Hello. OH, Hi. You were the one who / extricated that bit of subway grit from my eye.

2: Extricated that bit of subway grit from your eye. I'm 2.

1: Too what? Oh, DUH. I'm 1.

2: Am I keeping you from your—

1: Oh, no. *(Opens door, calls after 3.)* Right behind ya! *(Back to 2.)* No, my

friends and I mean the world to one another, so naturally we totally understand whenever we completely blow one another off.

2: Would you care to join me then? Let me buy you some coffee or tea—

1: Oh, no, *I* should be buying *you*—

2: I must insist—

1: I couldn't possibly—

2: My parents are quite wealthy—

1: Chamomile, please.

(2 purchases the tea while 1 waits.)

5: *(Approaching 4 again, arms open.)* Can I…give you a hug?

4: *(Brief hug—two pats is sufficient.)* Oh. Sure. Fine. Mmhm. Okay.

5: I love the way you hug. It's like hugging a pigeon.

4: Whatever. I guess I'm a fucking stalker.

5: A hundred years ago, you'd've just been sick with love. Sit down. I'll buy us coffee.

4: Triple lat—

5: No, really. It's on me this time. You've had a rough day and so…

4: *(Waits, then.)* Triple latte with an extra shot.

5: Triple latte with an extra shot.

(5 goes to purchase coffee, passing 2, who retrieves their tea from the counter and sits down across from 1.)

1: So…where in the city do you live?

2: I don't, exactly.

1: Oh, I'm not a snob about boroughs—

2: No, I live on a jet, actually. You may have heard it—

1: Oh, how…nice. So you're just—So you're visiting.

2: *(Here goes.)* My parents, as I've said, are astonishingly wealthy and so naturally I've grown up with an utterly unrealistic sense of the world, even though I've seen most of it. You see, they've insisted that I see the world, become well rounded, missing out on *nothing* before ever committing to *anything*, so I don't settle for *something* less than I deserve, which is, for them, *everything.*

1: Jeez, well, you'll find me pretty…Ha! I haven't been anywhere. My boyfriend—

2: Oh, you have a—

1: Yes. What? Yes. What? Were you going to ask if I had a—

2: As well you should.

1: You have one, too, of course. Come on, I'm sure guys throw themselves at you like like…I don't know, Italian women at funerals—Jeez, I'm—

2: *(Laughs.)* You must have a wonderful inner life.

1: Me? *No*, I—Well, thank you, but no I really don't have an inner life at all. Or if I do, I don't know about it / so…

(5 hands 4 the latte and an envelope.)

5: Here's my screenplay.

4: Oh, right, I forgot. Neato.

2: Tell me about your boyfriend.

1: We're so happy.

2: What does he do?

1: Who? 6? Oh, well, his name is 6, and he owns a restaurant in the neighborhood. It keeps us from ever traveling or taking vacations, but it gives us the lifestyle we want. It's important with all that's going on in the world to build a fortress around whatever you think makes you happy to keep out everything that would want to harm it, what with all the danger in the I'm rambling so is this your new favorite place in the city?

2: Now it is.

(4 flips through 5's manuscript.)

5: I did another revision. I was sitting right over there actually, because there's an outlet.

1: *(Averting his eyes.)* I think it's important to be a faithful consumer to businesses run by whichever minority group you belong to. Plus it's twenty-four hours, so I always come here and sometimes I even spend the night. Not sleeping. Reading, or people- / watching.

5: I love this place. I love writing here, because it always helps me not to get too focused on what I'm actually writing.

2: And your boyfriend is okay with this?

1: It keeps things fresh. The longer I'm gone, the happier he is to see me. For 6's last birthday, I staged a kidnapping of myself and went missing for two weeks. He loved that. It's a great gift…absence.

5: Marx said "Religion is the opium of the people," but *I* say, "Coffee shops are the opium of my ability to introspect."

1'S THOUGHTS: He looked so young. His eyes were clear blue, like a swimming pool—no sea creatures, not even a jellyfish. Just children with toy boats and floaties and an occasional Band-Aid with some hair attached—

1: *(Taps his head.)* Shh.

2: Sorry?

1: And *your* boyfriend. What does *he* do?

2: I can't quite say. My parents have picked him out, but I won't know until the wedding.

1: *Really.* How progressive…ly traditional. I guess the whole world's getting more enlightened, isn't it? Safer? Every day I feel like there's less hate, less disease, more tolerance, more…disease…less…ness. Pretty soon we'll be just like ordinary people and we won't have to even *think* about identity, because even if we all *hate* each other, at least we'll all be the same.

(4 hands 5 back his manuscript.)

4: It's great. I like it.

5: Did you read it?

4: *(Packing up his bookbag.)* I counted how many lines the lead guy has and it looks pretty / good.

1: Anyhoo, what a fun surprise. I'm *sure* they'll pick someone as…handsome as you. Are.

1'S THOUGHTS: His lips would fit so perfectly in between mine. His hair looked so soft and well cared for. *(Sound of sniffing.)* God, it smells like…*(Sound of sniffing.)* Shampoo. And his tongue—digging in to each word like a soft pink trowel—

1: *(Smacks his head.)* Shut up! Not you—I'm sorry. Please continue.

2: I wasn't saying anything.

5: I—I really want you to *read it.* I was thinking of you when I / revised it—

1: Oh. Well. So you've toured the world and now…

4: Don't say things like that.

5: What—

4: Just…*come on.* You don't even *know* me.

2: There's still Africa.

1: Africa? You mean, *Africa* Africa? When do you…

2: Friday.

1: Oh. That's…three days from—How…exciting…for you.

5: I know. You like mean or careless people. / I know.

2: *(Touches 1's leg.)* Is everything…

4: *(Taking the script.)* OH, HERE—I'll read it and we'll / talk!

1: *(Scooting away a bit.)* Oh, me, no I'm fine. I'm happy.

(4 exits. There is a honk from outside.)

2: That's me.

1'S THOUGHTS: His cheekbones, his eyelids, his cuticles—

1: *(Viciously beating his head.)* Stop it! Shut up! Shut off!! SHUT—

2: *(Arresting 1's hands.)* Please! Have a little…mercy on yourself.

1: Well…goodbye.

2: Goodbye. *(Starts to go, then turns back.)* Meet—

1: *Yes.*

(Short pause.)

2: Tomor—

1: *Okay.*

(1 smiles cautiously, 2 beams and exits. 5, also beaming, turns to 1.)

5: Sometimes it all works out so perfectly.

[FIVE]

1'S THOUGHTS: But, oh, 6, by the time I'd returned home later that night, the whole conversation felt quite foolish, and I was relieved to see you there in your favorite chair. My life made sense again.

(Tuesday night. 1 and 6's apartment. 1 enters. 6 is in his chair watching a television program with the cat.)

1: I'm home.

6: *(To the TV.)* Yea!

(1 smiles broadly, goes to kiss 6, who jumps in surprise.)

6: Taffy, is someone home? Is 1 home?

(1 leans down to kiss 6 again, but kisses TAFFY, and has to struggle to kiss 6, which he finally does.)

6: I brought home the lasagna you like from the restaurant.

1: I had the most bizarre conversation at the coffee shop this afternoon. *(Putting down his bookbag.)* It may not sound strange to anyone else, but I—

6: *(To the TV.)* What?!

1: 6, you don't feel trapped in a passionless and banal union, do you?

6: *(To the TV.)* No!

1: *(Exiting into the other room; from off.)* Neither do I. Someone had asked me if I felt that way and of course I said "no."

6: *(To the TV.)* BOO!

(1 reenters with lasagna.)

1: Oh, just some handsome world-traveler guy who bought me—

6: *(Turns around to 1; not alarmed.)* Hunh?

1: I thought you asked—Can we turn this off for a minute, please. *(Switches off the TV.)* I'm sorry if that was too aggressive. I just miss you. I think we should go away somewhere very soon, just the two of us, without Taffy. I mean, I'm totally content, but you seem a little—

6: My father had a heart attack this morning.

1: Oh, 6, I'm so sorry!

6: *(Shrugs, heading off to the bathroom.)* He'll be out of the hospital within forty-eight hours, they said. I might stop in and see him tomorrow.

1: You should have called me or—

6: *(From off.)* Silly rabbit. He didn't die or anything.

(6 returns.)

6: Your forehead is twitching.

(1 sits them both down.)

1: It…gets that way when I'm feeling guilty or upset. 6…6, are you sure you're alright?

6: *(Holding it in, eyes averted.)* He's getting so old. *(Begins to cry silently, then becomes hysterical.)*

1: *(Cradling 6.)* Oh, 6, I feel like it's—it's somehow all my fault. I know I shouldn't. I know it doesn't make sense, but oh 6. I feel like I've been so selfish so…inattentive…so…uhh…

(6, still sobbing, points shakily toward the TV. After a beat, 1 turns on the TV, and 6 stops crying instantly.)

6: *(To the TV.)* YES!

[SIX]

1'S THOUGHTS: The next night was Wednesday and I showed up at the appointed time, more out of obligation than anything else. I sat people-watching for a while.

(Wednesday night. The coffee bar. 1 sits alone at a table. 4 enters. A beat. 5 enters.)

5: Hey, 4, did you get a chance to read—

1'S THOUGHTS: Seconds seemed like hours.

(The following is in very slow motion.)

4: *(Turns around to see 5.)* No.

5: *(Pulling another script out of his bag.)* Good, cuz I did a rewrite.

3: *(Enters on rollerblades.)* 1,1,1! I just wonder—

[SEVEN]

1'S THOUGHTS: He never arrived. You must have noticed how out of sorts I was when I returned home.

(Later Wednesday night. 1 and 6's apartment. The following is in very fast motion. 6 is watching TV with the cat. 1 enters.)

1: I'm home.

6: Taffy, is someone home? Did 1 have a nice day?

1: No.

6: There's lasagna on the stove.

1: I'm nauseated.

6: My dad's fine. He says hi. I wanna buy a bigger TV.

1: I wanna jump off the roof.

[EIGHT]

1'S THOUGHTS: The following evening, I went to the coffee shop as usual. I ordered my tea as usual.

(Thursday night. The coffee bar. 1 enters and orders as 4 and 5 cross to sit down with their coffee. 4 hands script back to 5.)

4: It's great. I like it.

1'S THOUGHTS: I felt like a ghost.

5: *(Forces a chuckle.)* How can it be "great" if you only "like" / it?

1'S THOUGHTS: I tried to pinch myself to see if I'd feel it.

(1 does so.)

4: Some of it went over my head.

1'S THOUGHTS: I even tried to walk through a wall.

(1 tries this, and bruises himself slightly.)

5: Like what?

4: Umm uhh…like the "math" speech.

5: Oh! Well, the writer—he's likening—he's saying that—Okay, *Everyone* claims to be "single" and "available" and "looking for someone," but if that's true, then why are there so few "additions"?

4: Auditions?

5: No, uh—combinations. Couplings. Like—Here, the writer says: "We begin each day trying to make additions—" or couplings, if you will—"but each *unsuccessful* addition feels like a subtraction," so, blahblahblah, in essence, by the *end* of the day, the writer seems to say, you feel *less* of a person than you did—

4: Aren't *you* the writer?

1'S THOUGHTS: And then I realized: all of this had been a dream.

(1 laughs a bit.)

1'S THOUGHTS: Yes, it was just that old dream I'd have where I met my soulmate and it was someone I'd known all along, but I'd wake up and couldn't remember the face or the name—only the feeling.

(1 laughs more, laughs harder.)

1'S THOUGHTS: What a relief to know it was not some awful illicit longing, but pure unadulterated dementia that had made for such an unpleasant four / days—

(2 dashes in, spots 1 laughing madly.)

2: *(Breathless.)* 1! Our jet was grounded because of the explosion last night! I'm so sor / ry—

1: Explosion…Oh, right. I didn't see the news this morning—

2: I had no way of finding you. I didn't know where you lived. But you're here now.

1: *(Retrieving his tea from the counter.)* Oh, I'm always here. I think it's so important to be a faithful consumer—

1'S THOUGHTS: His eyes, his lips, his cheeks, his neck, his chin—

1: Shut up! Well, I should probably get going—

2: *(Forces 1 down into a chair.)* Please! If you do, I'll never see you again.

1: That's okay. I mean, for you. You'll meet another 1. There are so many 1s. It's the most common name on—

2: *(To hell with whomever hears him.)* I've met *countless* 1s in every damned city on this earth! So much variety and so many combinations, yet *no one* has *ever* unlocked me. I never knew what, *if anything*, I had inside to save, cherish, or protect. Until you. Now I look inside and I see the best thing anyone can see in themselves: the future!

1: *(Backs away from him.)* We can't. We can't let ourselves imagine— We'll become so *greedy and and and cruel,* we'll turn into—*We can't* think of a future for us. We have to be sensible. *I* have to be sensible. I'm not as *ff…free…* as you. *(Tearing up.)* No! No! This isn't REAL. We're *not* archetypes or or or heroes, we're just underdeveloped and everything we're feeling at this moment is is is fake and unsubstantiated and and and wrong! I don't even *know* me— I mean, *you.* WE'RE NOT REAL. And these are *not* real tears! They have *nothing* to do with us. *Genuine feeling does NOT occur between two people who've only just met!* *(Slaps himself.)* It can't! *(Slaps himself.)* It can't!

2: *(Intercepting 1's hand.)* I / Love—

1: *(Slapping 2.)* I love you too!

(They kiss. 4 has been reading a gay magazine; 5 dejectedly flips through his script. 1 and 2 break the embrace.)

5: I guess it IS just another gay love story.

1: We should go someplace. We should go someplace else.

5: A fairy tale.

2: To your place?

1: No, we can't go there. What about your jet?

2: The pilot might try to watch.

1: Let's—Where have you not been that you want to go? In the city?

2: I've seen everything. But nothing with *you*—

5: I know it's not very political, but I think that for people to actually *be* political, they have to determine first how or *IF* they want to interact in the world.

1: I can't think of anything.

5: Politics are about what we fight for, right? But if you feel unlovable, why bother fighting?

2: Where do you dream we'll go? What do you fantasize we'll do?

1: I Can't Fantasize. I—…

5: People who feel unlovable don't need newspapers. We need *fairy tales.*

1'S THOUGHTS: Central Park.

1: Uhhh…Central Park? I don't know. I'm so boring—

2: Take me there.

5: Because the people who *understand* newspapers—who can *comprehend* politics—at one point or another felt safe in this terrifying world.

1'S THOUGHTS: In a boat on the lake.

1: We're renting a boat or—or a gondola, or whatever they're called.

5: Other people—the ones who *get* politics—were at one time allowed—*encouraged*—to believe in fantasy…

1'S THOUGHTS: Running our fingers / through the water.

1: Run your hands—fingers through the water. It's warm.

2: I'm running them through your hair—it's thick and soft.

5: *Encouraged* to believe in fairy godmothers and prince charmings and fathers who really loved them and stepmothers who deserved to die, so that they would *believe*…

1'S THOUGHTS: The creek behind our house.

1: Okay—Now—*Now* we're in a creek I used to go to when I was a kid. Catching turtles and snakes and lizards— I've always wanted to take someone here.

2: I want to take *you* here!

5: They could *believe* that while they were lost in the woods, or languishing in the cinders of pubescence, that they were the subject of some gorgeous and epic story…

1'S THOUGHTS: Driving.

5: And that all of this unbearable…

1: Yes!

5: …*life* would actually be worth fighting *for.*

1: We're in a motor car in the country—

5: So I know this is a fantasy—a dream, but for most of my life I haven't even felt safe enough to fall / asleep, so

1: And there's no roof and the wind is blowing through our hair / and there's music—perfect music—the kind we've never heard and yet—

2: I LOVE your hair! I love the music! / I love how you taste—So so so…

1: Miles and miles and / miles miles miles Ahhhhhh

5: So for me to even dream, / that's—

2: Ahhhhhh

5: Amazing. Do you know

1 & 2: I love you!

5: what I'm saying, that's—

1 & 2 & 1'S THOUGHTS: I love you!

(3 skates through, headed toward the bathroom, indicating 4 should follow him. 4, frantically collecting his stuff, accidentally spills his coffee on 5's script.)

4: *CRAP.* Sorry. I hope that wasn't an only copy.

5: It / was.

1 & 2: *AHHHHHH*

4: Let me know when you get money behind it. *(Exits after 3.)*

5: Why is everybody so out of their minds, except for me?!

1 & 2: *AHHHHHH*

5: *(As if channeling someone.)* "No, *you* are out of your mind; everyone else is trapped in theirs."

1: Don't leave.

5: *(Himself again.)* Okay. But. Have I wrecked it with him? Have I been too persistent?

2: I won't.

5: *(Channeling.)* "A bit." *(Himself again.)* Okay. But. If I hadn't behaved the way I did, would that…have made a difference?

1: Don't *ever* leave.

5: *(Tries channeling; static, perhaps?)* "………………………………" *(Himself again.)* Hello? How can I keep this from happening again?

2: I…won't…tonight I won't…

5: *(Ibid.)* "………………………" *(Himself again.)* What can I do? Hello? *(Ibid.)* "……"

[NINE]

Friday night. The same. 1 and 2 have not moved.

1: The tea is cold.

2: Quite.

1: Please don't go to Africa—Please!—

(Suddenly the door swings open: 3 enters, yelling behind him.)

3: AND STAY OUT! OH, 1, 1, you must be wondering who I was talking to just then! *(Sees 2.)* Who are you?

2: I'm–

1: He's–

3: Oh, wait—don't tell me yet. *(Continues to speak, muted.)*

2: *(To 1.)* I don't want to. I really really don't. Maybe I could come back to visit in a few months—stay for a while—if you'd have me—

1: You couldn't stay with me—my boyfriend—

3: —just passed your hubby on the way home from the restaurant—

2: Why don't you leave him?

1: Why don't you stay, then?!

2: Why won't you come with me?

3: Sweet, odd, clear? I mean,

1: Just miss the plane—

2: It's *my* plane—or my parents'—

3: Octopus. Where's my coffee?

1: Don't be spineless!

3: Three coffees—all for me! All for 3!

1: I thought you wanted to jump into my world—or or—

2: Why won't you jump into mine?

3: LET ME OUT!

2: Come with me! Now! We can have *everything!*

1: *I…*

3: Whose jet is that?

1: Can't.

2: It's mine. I'm afraid I must go.

3: I do very well, thank you.

(1 is silent. A honk from outside. 2 exits. 1 suddenly runs outside after him.)

3: I wonder—is it alright for me to begin talking again—

[TEN]

Outside. 1 stands below, as the jet takes off.

2: *(Distantly, from above.)* I'm Sorry!

1: *(To himself, to the plane?)* It's just not real! If I knew for sure it was real—

(Suddenly, a piece of the plane's engine drops from above, and gets lodged in 1's eye.)

1: OW! FUCK!

(5, passing by, sees this.)

5: Here—let me help—

1: *(Turns on him, madly.)* NO! Don't touch it! Leave it alone!

5: I'm not trying to come on to you, I just want to help.

1: DON'T TOUCH MY EYE.

5: Listen: I actually fell in love tonight. For real. I met this guy at this restaurant and we talked for hours and I gave him my script to read and we're gonna meet there for brunch / tomorrow.

1: OW FUCK MY EYE FUCK MY FUCKING EYE!

5: From the minute we looked into one another's eyes, we knew. We *knew*. He has a boyfriend, but—

1: GODDAMMIT!

5: Let me help. I want to give something back. I've been so selfish. And it's Gay Pride. *(Reaches for 1's eye.)* I'm karmically obligated to—

1: *NO! (Tears out the bit of engine, taking his eye in the process. Cries in agony.)* NEVER AGAIN! Please…never again… *(Goes back into the coffee shop.)*

[ELEVEN]

Friday night. Split scene: the coffee shop, and 1 and 6's apartment. Action in the coffee shop continues as in first scene, without 1 present. 1 and 6 are seated as they were in previous scenes.

3: Oh, 1, 1, 1…I wonder—Can you tell between my personalities? I can't.

(1 begins to cry, with abandon.)

3: Oh, but 1, you seem…to suffer somehow…inexplicably, given what a life you've had. How kind the hand of fate has been to you.

6: *(Looks up from his manuscript.)* Is something the matter? 1?

1: I'm fine, really. Just feeling a bit dizzy is all.

(6 goes over to 1 and awkwardly holds him. 1 cries harder.)

1: I should go home now.

3: I'll / roll you there.

6: You…*are* home.

1: No. I insist…I…

(6's thoughts are heard; a voice remarkably similar to 1's. During the following, 6 stacks up the screenplay, revealing the cover page which has a huge coffee stain.)

6'S THOUGHTS: Oh, 1, dear 1. You're the only one in the world with enough wisdom and gentleness to understand what's happened to me. And you're the only one I can never tell. I've fallen in love. I didn't know such violent things could happen to ordinary people. We only met today at my restaurant where we talked for hours, and he gave me his screenplay to read and it's…dense. 1, oh, 1, I'm so frightened of hurting you and the children. But can I allow myself to let this slip away? What if this is Fate? What if it's Real? What if—

(The fireworks begin outside the window to 1 and 6's apartment.)

4: *(Enters, sees 3.)* YOU'RE KILLING ME!

(3 exits, as 5 enters. 4 immediately recovers.)

5: If I were him…I would love you so much…

6: You wanna go watch the fireworks? *(Gently trying to pull 1 off the couch.)* Let's go see the fireworks.

4: What are you talking about? God, you're so desperate! Why can't you just be normal?!

5: I'm—

1: scared.

5: I'm—

1: scared.

5: I'm—

1: scared.

(End.)

AUTHOR'S NOTE

Brief Encounter, the 1945 Coward-Lean film, chronicles the ill-fated affair of a married man and woman, whose chance meeting at a train station leads to a series of less accidental encounters, culminating in the bittersweet realization that they have fallen in love. An abrupt ending to this romance comes, however, when the man is given the opportunity to realize a lifelong dream: to open a practice in Africa. Beginning with his departure, the film depicts their relationship entirely in flashback, as the woman silently confesses this folly to her sweetly oblivious husband—"the only one in the world with enough wisdom and gentleness to understand... [and] the only one in the world that I can never tell."

Another Brief Encounter is also saturated with my reaction to Frederic Jameson's essay, "Postmodernism and Consumer Society," in which he purports that parody is no longer possible for us, because we do not have any sort of shared context. Rather, he suggests, we are an infinite number of linguistic islands—united in our nostalgia (the blanket of familiarity that comforts us from "the failure of the new, the imprisonment of the past"), but fragmented in our schizophrenia (the utter incognizance of history and inconsideration for the future). For Jameson, as for certain of these dream-drunk characters, reality has become, in essence, a constant deadening exposure.

CORPS VALUES

Brendon Bates

BRENDON BATES is an actor, playwright, and producer. He was born in Boston, on July 27, 1975, and grew up in New England. He holds a BA in theatre from Allegheny College and an MA in acting from the New Actors Workshop and Antioch University, where he studied with George Morrison, Mike Nichols, and Paul Sills. His plays include *The Savior of Fenway* (New York International Fringe Festival, 2003), *Trent Galley's Dying Wish* (Full Circle Theatre Company, 2005), and *The Assassination* (the Second City Training Center, New York, 2005). As an actor, Bates has appeared on stage in *Stories of Red Hanrahan* (directed by Paul Sills), *Jeffrey* (Full Circle Theatre Company), *The Savior of Fenway*, and *Generation F'd* (the Second City Training Center, New York). His film and television credits include *The Departed, 16 Blocks, The Sopranos, Law & Order, Third Watch, All My Children*, and *Guiding Light*. He is the co-founder of Full Circle Theatre Company and BC Productions, LLC. Bates has also written the screenplay adaptations of his plays *The Assassination* (which will be released in spring 2007) and *Corps Values* (which will begin shooting in November 2007). His play, *The Savior of Fenway*, won a 2003 FringeNYC Excellence in Playwriting Award. He has worked for William Ivey Long Studios and is currently a faculty member at the New Actors Workshop, as well as a middle school drama and creative writing teacher at the Carroll School in Lincoln, Massachusetts. Bates lives in Massachusetts during the school year and spends his summers in New York City.

Corps Values was created and written by Brendon Bates in 2005. It was then developed by BC Productions and Michael D. Laibson through a workshop production at the New Actors Workshop in Manhattan. *Corps Values* was first presented by Winsor Productions in association with BC Productions as part of the New York International Fringe Festival (Elena K. Holy, Producing Artistic Director) on August 12, 2006, at Classic Stage Company, New York City, with the following cast and credits:

Col. Kyle Adamson .... Christopher McHale
Wade Taylor .... Tom Stechschulte
Casey Taylor... Joe Curnutte
Capt. Samko ....Aaron Mathias
Agent Dunn... Brett Andres
Sgt. Wilson .... Marc Bovino
Agent Conner... Todd Estrin
Agent Galley ....Andrew Jessop

Directed by: Susan W. Lovell
Set Design: Josh Zangen
Lighting Design: Jennifer Schriever
Sound Design: Matt Kraus
Costume Design: Sarah Sophia Turner
Fight Choreography: Randy Spence
Makeup Design: Erin Andréa
Prop Master: Elsama Colón
Production Stage Manager: Ritchard Druther

Corps Values was subsequently presented by Pittsburgh Playwright's Theatre Company (Mark Clayton Southers, Artistic Director):

Col. Kyle Adamson ....Marcus Muzopappa
Wade Taylor ....Wali Jamal
Casey Taylor..Joshua Elijah Reese
Capt. Samko .... Joseph Martinez
Agent Dunn... Ezra Smith
Sgt. Wilson .... Leo Beatty
Agent Conner..David Conley
Agent Galley .... Tom Chun

Directed by: John Gresh
Set Design: Mark Clayton Southers
Lighting Design/Prop Master: Eric Smith
Sound Design: Brendon Elder
Costume Design: Derek Tines
Fight Choreography: Randy Kovitz
Makeup Design: Cheryl El-Walker
Production Stage Manager: Eric Smith

SCENE 1

Lights up. Late November 2004. The small rustic kitchen of the TAYLORS' nineteenth century farmhouse. The farmhouse sits on a big piece of land in Lower Tyrone, Pennsylvania, about a half hour south of Pittsburgh. The kitchen is heated by an old wood-burning stove. The temperature outside is freezing. A breeze dances with the wind chimes. The outside bottom half of the window above the sink is covered with frost. The trash can near the sink is overflowing with garbage. The top half of a picture frame peeks above the mountain of garbage. COLONEL KYLE ADAMSON (fifty-nine years old) enters the kitchen through a door that leads to a bedroom. KYLE is tall, well built for his age, and very good-looking. He wears the uniform of the U.S. Marine Corps. His chest is covered with ribbons, telling us he has fought in both Vietnam and Desert Storm. He's been awarded two Purple Hearts and a Bronze Star. He holds the rank of a Full Bird Colonel. A cell phone is attached to his belt. KYLE carefully observes the surroundings. He notices that the stove is burning a fresh log. He notices the dirty dishes in the sink with fresh crumbs on the top plate. He crosses to the coat rack and notices a few uncovered hooks. He looks at the trash can and crosses to it. He kneels down and pulls the framed picture out of the trash. He peels a piece of tissue off the front of the picture. The picture frame displays a recent photograph of a young Marine wearing his dress blues. He looks at the picture for a moment and then returns it to the trash can. He stands. He turns his head toward the window. He squints as he looks out the window and quickly crosses to it. He sees something. He pulls out his cell phone and presses "Send."

KYLE: *(Into phone.)* Here comes the father, out of the woods. He's alone and

seems unarmed…Affirmative. Do not move in without my order.

(KYLE hangs up. He returns his cell phone to its belt holster and quickly moves away from the window. He takes a few deep breaths and composes himself as WADE TAYLOR, sixty years old, walks onto the front porch. WADE is a large man with broad shoulders. He stands over six feet. He has a neatly groomed beard that covers a scar on his left cheek. He is wearing a bright orange vest with a hunting license attached to the back of it. He also wears a bright orange wool cap. His nose and cheekbones are red and so are his knuckles—he's been outside in the cold all morning. WADE walks with a limp from an injury that is still fresh and tender. The premature wrinkles under his eyes and his faded complexion are the byproduct of his heavy drinking over the past few decades. Before entering the kitchen through the front door, WADE stands cautiously on the porch. He turns his head and observes something offstage. He seems like a deer in the woods that has picked up a disturbing scent. WADE kicks the snow off his boots and walks through the front door. He sees KYLE.)

WADE: *(Surprised)* Kyle…

KYLE: Morning, old friend.

WADE: Good to see you.

KYLE: Good to see *you*.

(They take a long look at each other.)

WADE: It's been a long time, Colonel.

KYLE: Yes it has, Lieutenant…I let myself in, hope you don't mind.

WADE: Of course not.

KYLE: The door was unlocked and it's freezing out there.

WADE: Yeah, it's a cold one all right.

KYLE: Good thing the wood burner's still going strong.

WADE: Oh yeah. Winter decided to come early this year…

KYLE: I would've brewed some coffee, but I couldn't find any beans.

WADE: We don't need any beans to warm the blood. *(Crosses to the cabinet, opens it, and reaches inside. He pulls out a bottle of Maker's Mark. There are only a few drinks remaining in the bottle. He holds the bottle up to KYLE.)* Shall we?

KYLE: I could really go for some coffee.

WADE: Well, I ain't got any. Ran out a few days ago. And I haven't been able to drive into town all week 'cause of the snow. Tires can't handle the icy roads.

KYLE: Ah… Well… I'll just pass then…

(Awkward silence.)

WADE: Please don't tell me Casey's been killed.

KYLE: What? Oh, NO! No, no, no, no.

(WADE releases a huge sigh. Laughs. He sits down to untie his boots, which he leaves by the door.)

WADE: Whoo! My heart dropped down to my feet when I saw the black car with them government plates sitting in my driveway.

KYLE: Yeah. Sorry. I tried calling but—

WADE: Yeah. The storm knocked down the phone lines.

KYLE: Well, I didn't mean to scare you.

WADE: No, no, no. It's just—the last thing I want to do right now is bury my only son.

KYLE: I imagine.

WADE: The boy's made it this far. Only six more months of combat left and he gets to come home for good. Counting the days. My nerves freeze up every time that phone rings. *(Laughs.)* For a second, I thought maybe they sent *you* over here to tell me… I'd be eating Christmas dinner alone for the rest of my life.

KYLE: Hmm.

(Pause.)

WADE: *(Stands.)* How 'bout that drink?

KYLE: It's a bit early for me.

WADE: It's five o'clock somewhere.

KYLE: Aw, hell, why not.

(WADE grabs two small glasses from the sink. KYLE looks at his watch. WADE limps over to the kitchen table. He pours the drinks. His hands tremble slightly.)

KYLE: What happened to your leg?

WADE: Pardon?

KYLE: What's with the limp?

WADE: …The accident.

KYLE: Oh. *(Embarrassed)* Right.

WADE: The air bag saved my ass, but it bruised some of my ribs and slammed the hell outta my bad knee. Doc says I got bit of a concussion too.

KYLE: Well, knock on wood you're still breathin'.

WADE: Yeah.

(WADE hands the drink to KYLE.)

WADE: Sorry 'bout the dirty glass.

KYLE: Ah, that's okay.

WADE: I forgot to pick up dishwashing soap.

KYLE: No problem. *(Takes drink.)*

WADE: *(Raises his glass.)* To Semper Fi.

KYLE: *(Raises his glass.)* To the only surviving Marines of Bravo Company.

(They drink.)

KYLE: Listen...I'm real sorry about Allison.

WADE: Thank you.

KYLE: She was a good woman.

WADE: Yes. She was.

KYLE: And I'm sorry I didn't make the funeral last week.

WADE: We got your flowers.

KYLE: I just couldn't get away.

WADE: We're at war. You're a busy man.

KYLE: Well, I should have been there.

WADE: *(Nods.)* Ya missed a nice service.

KYLE: She was something special.

WADE: Sure was...No matter how much of a jackass I was—and I can be a *real* jackass.

KYLE: Oh yeah.

WADE: She just kept on loving me.

KYLE: You're a lucky man.

WADE: How's Kelly doing?

KYLE: We separated two years ago.

WADE: Oh...Shit.

KYLE: Filed for divorce last June.

WADE: I'm sorry to hear that.

KYLE: Yeah...

WADE: *(Finishes his drink.)* How the girls doing?

KYLE: Pissed off. Amy seems to be on my side, but Joan won't talk to me.

WADE: Hmm...Kids.

KYLE: Yeah...

(Pause.)

KYLE: I'm glad we were able to fly Casey back for the service.

WADE: Yes. Me too.

KYLE: How's he holding up?

WADE: Who? Casey?

KYLE: Yeah.

WADE: He's hanging in there.

KYLE: Did he seem...Okay?

WADE: Well, you know, war changes a man.

KYLE: Yeah.

WADE: And the funeral wasn't easy for him. Him and his mother...They were close.

KYLE: Did he seem stable?

WADE: *(Looking at him.)* Yeah...Considering...

KYLE: Mm...Is he still dating that Miss Know-It-All, whatever her name is—the little hippie brunette?

WADE: *(Laughs.)* Yeah. *Katie.* I swear to God—that girl is the spitting image of Allison.

KYLE: How so?

WADE: Has an opinion on everything!

KYLE: *(Laughs.)* Yes she does. I remember.

WADE: She ain't afraid of a good argument. The two of us bark back and forth about the war every time we're together.

KYLE: Ohh, she's being one of *those*, huh?

WADE: Well, you know. She's getting straight A's over at Carnegie Mellon—International Development something—so she thinks she knows everything about everything.

KYLE: How does she feel 'bout her boyfriend being a Marine?

WADE: Hates it.

KYLE: Does she make him feel guilty 'bout what he's doing over there?

WADE: No, no, no. She knows better.

KYLE: Good.

WADE: She just wants him to come home alive, that's all.

KYLE: We all do.

WADE: Yeah…Well, like I said: six more months…He survived *Fallujah*.

KYLE: That was a nasty invasion.

WADE: Yeah.

KYLE: You survive a battle like that…

WADE: Yeah. He received a Bronze Star. You hear?

KYLE: I did.

WADE: And a Purple Heart.

KYLE: Yup. I read a report from his C.O. that he was a victim of a car bomb explosion.

WADE:…Yup.

KYLE: Suffered second-degree burns along the upper body.

WADE: *(Nods.)* And still went on fighting…until he was brought back here for the funeral.

KYLE: He's a good Marine.

WADE: Yup. Sure is.

KYLE: Apple doesn't fall far from the tree.

WADE: Mmm. *(Grabs bottle.)* 'Nother?

KYLE:…One more.

(WADE pours them another drink. He struggles to take the cap off with his injured right hand, which is wrapped in torn cotton. Fresh blood seeps through the cotton.)

KYLE: What's an old geezer like you doin' trekking 'round the woods on a day like today, middle of winter?

WADE: Oh, you know…Keeping track of what's moving where. Three days 'til Opening.

KYLE: Buck season?

WADE: Yup.

KYLE: Were you in a knife fight?

WADE: Pardon?

KYLE: *(Pointing at hand.)* Your hand.

WADE: Oh! I cut it on some barbed wire.

KYLE: That's a nasty wound.

WADE: Yeah. I came across this beautiful twelve-point bout half mile southeast of here. He was dead. Got his back leg tangled in this old, rusty barbed wire fence that used to mark the property line between me and Jeff Reardon's land. The fence collapsed years ago and it was covered by snow. He stepped right into it. The wire was deep into his bone, weighing him down like a ball and chain. Looked like he was trying to pull himself free but the spurs kept digging deeper and deeper into his bone…

KYLE: That's a damn shame.

WADE: Yeah. Most beautiful creature I ever laid eyes on. I mean, you should see this *rack*. And his coat looked like untouched gold. *(Sighs.)* That's no way for a fine animal to go: leg tangled in a fence…

KYLE: Nope sure isn't. You gonna take his *rack?*

WADE: No! No, no, no.

KYLE: Why not?

WADE: I thought about it, but…It's too nice.

KYLE: That's the whole point, ain't it?

WADE: Yeah, but…This creature: he's built like a king. And he was smart enough to move under my radar all these years. I have no right stealing his crown.

KYLE: Well, then…*(Raises his glass.)* To the death of a great king.

WADE*: (Raises glass.)* Finest king to ever walk them woods.

(They drink. KYLE turns his glass upside down and places it on the table.)

KYLE: Aren't you gonna ask me what I'm doing here, Lieutenant?

WADE: *(Chuckles.)* You can call me Wade.

KYLE: Pardon?

WADE: I've been outta the service for thirty-five years.

KYLE: Once a Marine, always a Marine.

WADE: Well, this ain't the jungle now, is it?

KYLE: You'll always be a Lieutenant in my eyes.

(WADE nods.)

KYLE: Do you know why I'm here?

WADE: *(Interrupting on "you.")* How come they haven't made you General yet?

KYLE: What? Uh…

WADE: How many times they pass you over? Two, three?

KYLE:…Four.

WADE: Christ All Mighty. Bullshit if you ask me…

KYLE: Mmm.

WADE:…All the shit you've done, you should've been made General three years ago.

KYLE: Maybe.

WADE: *(Pointing to the medals on KYLE.)* I mean, look at that chest. More fruit salad than *I've* ever seen. Who they making General these days?

KYLE: *(Interrupting on "making.")* Come on, Wade! Cut the shit. You know why I'm here.

(They look at each other.)

KYLE: Where's he at?

WADE: Who?

KYLE: Your son.

WADE: He returned to duty Thursday. After the funeral.

(KYLE looks at WADE.)

WADE: Why?

KYLE: Casey never reported to Lejeune.

WADE: What?

KYLE: He was scheduled to attend his mother's funeral here in Dawson County on Wednesday and report to Camp Lejeune on Thursday, eighteen hundred.

WADE: Right.

KYLE: The N.C.I.S. tells me he flew into Pittsburgh on Tuesday evening...

WADE: The N.C.I.S.?!

KYLE: ...And he was scheduled to take Flight 261 Delta Airlines the following Thursday and report to Camp Le—

WADE: Whoa, whoa, whoa...He left for Charlotte early Thursday morning.

KYLE: Well, he never showed up.

WADE: What do you mean, he never showed up?

KYLE: We haven't seen him. He's missing.

WADE: That's impossible.

KYLE: Then why is his graduation picture sitting in the garbage can?

(WADE is speechless. Fade up: A prerecorded version of a resonant Native American lullaby. An older woman is singing the lullaby. Lights down.)

SCENE 2

Lights up. The same kitchen. A few days earlier. Late night. CASEY TAYLOR (twenty-four years old) sits at the kitchen table. He is drinking the final gulps of a tall glass of ice water. There is a pen in his right hand. After a couple more gulps, he sets the empty glass on the table and returns to a piece of paper that lies on the table in front of him. He begins to write a letter. A handful of sealed envelopes lie on the table, with addresses written on each of them. CASEY sports a closely cropped crew cut. He has an athletic build that's been fine tuned by military training. He is dressed in a long-sleeved T-shirt and thermal underwear. The small CD player on the kitchen counter continues to bellow the Native American lullaby. WADE enters. He is dressed in his pajamas. WADE towers over CASEY, who stands no taller then six feet. CASEY's framed picture of him in his dress blues now sits proudly on the kitchen counter.

WADE: I said turn that music down, boy. It's nearly midnight.

CASEY: Oh...Sorry.

WADE: Christ All Mighty. God Damn Pow-Wow...(He turns to CD player.) What is this?

CASEY: Just a collection of old Native American...whatever.

WADE: Your mother use to play it.

CASEY: I know.

WADE: (Looking at CD case, he reads the cover of the CD.) "North American Lullabies." (Chuckles.) She used to buy these at gas stations.

CASEY: This song right here, she sang it to me as I laid in the hospital bed after getting my appendix removed.

WADE: Really?

CASEY: Yeah.

WADE: *(Smiles.)* Hmm. She was always humming, singing to herself.

CASEY: Or to anybody who would listen.

WADE: *(Laughs.)* Yyyup. When you were a kid, she loved singing you to sleep every night. Remember?

CASEY: Yeah. She said it would scare away the darkness.

WADE: You turned twelve, I told her you were getting too old for her to sing you to sleep. She snarled at me and slammed the bathroom door in my face.

(CASEY laughs. WADE smiles.)

WADE: I actually remember her...humming *this* song.

CASEY: We should've played it at the service today.

WADE: Yeah. Why didn't I think of that?

CASEY: Ahhh, the "Amazing Grace" was perfect.

WADE: Yeah?

CASEY: It was a beautiful service.

WADE: Thanks...

CASEY: You see the flowers the Colonel sent us?

WADE: Yup. Biggest arrangement at the cemetery.

CASEY: Sure was...You talk to Kelly?

WADE: Briefly. We spoke at the church, but we didn't have time to catch up.

CASEY: You talk to Amy, Joan?

WADE: *(Shakes his head.)* Same thing.

CASEY: I did.

WADE: Oh yeah?

CASEY: Yeah...I think the Colonel and Aunt Kelly got divorced.

WADE:...Nah.

CASEY: I think so. Amy was telling me—

WADE: *(Interrupting.)* He would've told me.

CASEY: *(Shrugs.)* Amy said something 'bout her mom's new house and Joan said something 'bout Uncle Kyle's new girlfriend.

WADE: Nah. I would've heard about it.

CASEY: When was the last time you heard from the Colonel?

(Pause.)

WADE: *(Pointing to empty glass.)* How 'bout a refill?

CASEY: Sure.

(WADE picks up the glass, crosses to the sink, and fills the glass with cold water.)

WADE: You've been drinking like a camel ever since ya stepped off the bus.

CASEY: I'm used to drinking two gallons a day out in the desert.

WADE: Right, right.

CASEY: Plus this new medication: makes my mouth dry up.

WADE: Mmm. I overheard you talking to your Cousin Delmar about it.

(He returns the glass to CASEY, filled to the brim. CASEY accepts it.)

WADE: Drink up.

(CASEY gulps down the drink until it's half full. Sets it down on the table.)

WADE: Did Katie go home?

CASEY: 'Bout an hour ago.

WADE: The two of you have a nice time together?

CASEY: *(Smiling.)* Yeah.

WADE: *(Smiles.)* Good. She's a good reason to make it back here alive.

CASEY: Yup. Sure is.

WADE: I never got the chance to thank her—for all she's done the past few days.

CASEY: Ahhh…

WADE: The service, driving me around, talking to guests, all the cooking…I woulda fell apart if it wasn't for her.

(CASEY nods.)

WADE: We didn't argue once. Not even about Iraq.

CASEY: *(Chuckles.)* You can write her a nice card or somethin'.

WADE: I will…She could've stayed the night, ya know.

CASEY: I know.

WADE: I wouldn't of minded.

CASEY: Yeah…Well…I was hopin' you and I could…

WADE: *(Smiles.)* Sure thing. *(Pulls out chair.)* Would ya like a nightcap?

CASEY: Nah…

WADE: Since when have you turned down a free drink?

CASEY: It'll dehydrate me.

WADE: I got Maker's Mark, the good stuff.

CASEY: Maker's Mark?! You know, if you took all the money you've spent on whiskey over the past fifteen years and put it into a mutual fund, you'd be the wealthiest man in Dawson County.

WADE: What are you? My accountant now?

CASEY: No. I'm just saying.

WADE: When you're a family man, putting food on the table every night, then you can talk to me about money, all right?

CASEY: All right.

WADE: You still take it on the rocks?

CASEY: Not tonight, Dad.

WADE: Oh, come on!

(He slaps his son hard across the back of his shoulders. CASEY winces in pain and crumbles onto the surface of the table.)

CASEY: *(In pain.)* Ahhhh!

WADE: Oh! I forgot. Sorry 'bout that.

CASEY: *(Wincing. Under his breath.)* Damn it.

WADE: They okay? Want me to take a look at 'em?

CASEY: *(Stands.)* No.

WADE: You want some lotion?

CASEY: *(Moving away from his father.)* I got some. Just…

WADE: What kind of lotion is it?

CASEY: Huh?

WADE: Don't you need something special for a magnesium burn?

CASEY: Of course. The doctors gave it to me.

WADE: What?

CASEY: A special lotion—medication.

WADE: Good. You're using it, right?

CASEY: Yes!!

WADE: Okay, okay…

(Pause. CASEY is still in pain.)

WADE: Was that the first car bomb you encountered?

CASEY: No. They go off all the time over there. And they gave us a demonstration at Basic.

WADE: Did it take any of your men?

CASEY: What?

WADE: The car bomb.

CASEY: My best friend, Benjamin Ba—Private First Class Benjamin Badger from Peabody, Massachusetts. Sergeant John Wilson from Erie. And Private Santana Ruiz from Miami.

WADE: Well…Let's drink to their memory?

(CASEY nods. WADE crosses to the cabinet. He grabs the bottle of Maker's Mark and two small glasses out of the cabinet. He crosses to the table and pours both of them a drink.)

WADE: I read about them car bombs in *National Geographic*. They are bad news. If all you got is a few burns and a Purple Heart…

CASEY: Yup.

WADE: Too bad that mug of yours didn't get burned. Would've made an improvement.

CASEY: Just pour them drinks, would ya old man…Christ All Mighty.

(WADE chuckles. CASEY is comforting his shoulders.)

CASEY: Seriously though: don't do that again.

WADE: Okay, okay…Here: I'll make ya a double. That'll ease them burns.

(CASEY looks at him as he pours the drink.)

CASEY: I saw your ghost tonight.

WADE: Pardon?

CASEY: I saw the creature been leaving them tracks over at the southeast ridge.

WADE: Oh yeah?

CASEY: Biggest twelve-point you ever seen.

WADE: No!

CASEY: Yeah. I saw him standing 'bout thirty yards from the porch, rubbing against the oak.

WADE: *(Pointing.)* This oak tree?

CASEY: Yeah.

WADE: When was this?

CASEY: 'Bout an hour ago. I went outside to start Katie's car. I turn the ignition, headlights turn on, and there he was: big as a four-legged giant. Huge neck, enormous rack—perfect symmetry. Looked like a painting or something. He stared right into the headlights and I gazed right back at him.

WADE: I've been tracking him for months, never seen 'im.

CASEY: *(Laughs.)* I know. Katie keeps a disposable camera in the glove compartment. I thought, "I should take a picture of this thing, show Dad." So, I looked down for—like—two seconds, open the glove compartment, grabbed the camera, I look up, and he's gone. Vanished like a ghost.

WADE: Oh…Son of a…I'm gonna get him this year. You watch. I'm gonna mount that rack right above the—a twelve-point? Really?

CASEY: *(Nodding.)* Perfect symmetry. Thick as hell. Reached about *(Shows with hands.)*…to the stars, it seemed like. Biggest crown I ever seen.

WADE: God Damn. Everyone 'round here's seen this creature 'cept me.

CASEY: He's playin' with ya, Dad, messin' with your head.

WADE: Yeah, well…We'll see come Opening Day.

CASEY: *(Takes drink.)* That's right.

(WADE raises his glass. They look at each other for a moment.)

WADE: To your fallen brothers.

CASEY: *(Raises glass.)* May they find whatever it is they were fighting for.

(WADE nods. They clink glasses and drink. There's a long moment of silence.)

CASEY: You know, ever since the first day of Basic, all I could think about was sitting in my tree stand, overlooking Johnson Creek, on a brisk autumn morning, first day of Buck Season.

WADE: *(Smiles, chuckles.)* Mmm…

CASEY: Waking up before dawn after a good night sleep, sitting at this table, eating a big breakfast—bacon and eggs—scraping the ash off Mom's burnt toast.

WADE: *(Laughs.)* Best cook in the world that woman was, always burnt the toast.

CASEY: Yeah, yeah, *every* time…Then we'd grab our rifles and head into them woods together, sun peeking up over the hills.

WADE: *(Smiling.)* Mmm.

CASEY: By noon one of us would take down a big ten-point. We'd gut it together, allowing his blood to warm our cold hands, and we'd drag him back here together, swearing the whole way, bitchin' 'bout how heavy he is.

WADE: *You're* the one that bitches.

CASEY: *(Laughing.)* Yeah, right!

(WADE chuckles.)

CASEY: And then we'd string him up over the oak and sit on the porch together, eating ham sandwiches and drinking Mom's hot cocoa, laughing about this and that.

WADE: *(Nods.)* Always the best day of the year.

CASEY: Yeah…And we never drank the entire day. Not a drop.

WADE: Nope. First day of Buck is a Holy day. A sacred day.

CASEY: Every day's a sacred day.

WADE: Yeah, well…I'm gonna miss ya come Opening Day next week.

(CASEY nods.)

WADE: *Next year*, right?

(CASEY doesn't answer.)

WADE: So, did they finally toughen you up in Basic?

CASEY: (*Looking at him, nodding.*) I must've learned about five hundred different ways to kick your ass.

WADE: Is that a fact?

CASEY: No. More like *six* hundred.

WADE: I don't care if you're a God Damn Navy Seal. You'll never be able to lick your old man.

CASEY: Careful, don't get too excited now. My CPR ain't too good.

WADE: (*Laughs.*) You're right. I'm getting old. Old and bitter. That's why I need you here: to keep me laughing.

(*CASEY nods.*)

WADE: I should get back to bed. Been a long day.

CASEY: Yes it has.

WADE: You should do the same. We got to wake up real early.

CASEY: I will in a bit.

WADE: The Weather Channel says a blizzard is rolling in from the northwest tomorrow, noon time.

CASEY: I know. I'm almost finished.

WADE: Who you writing to?

CASEY: The other two surviving members of my squad.

WADE: You're going to see them in a couple days, aren't ya?

CASEY: I want them to know I think about 'em every day.

(*WADE rubs CASEY on the top of the head.*)

WADE: You're a good Marine, Private Taylor—P.F.C. Taylor, sorry 'bout that.

(*CASEY makes a gesture that says "no worry."*)

WADE: Just make sure you get enough sleep tonight. We gotta catch the six forty-five a.m. out of Uniontown. The Ford won't make it to Pittsburgh.

(*CASEY doesn't answer.*)

WADE: You hear me? Hey? You hear what I said?

CASEY: Yeah. I heard ya.

WADE: Good. Get your stuff together and throw it in the truck before hitting the hay.

CASEY: Okay.

WADE: (*Stands. Exits into bedroom, carrying the bottle of bourbon with him. Yawning.*) Good night.

CASEY: Dad…

WADE: (*Reentering.*) Yeah?

CASEY:…I'm not going back.

WADE: Pardon?

CASEY: I'm not returning to duty.

(*Pause. WADE laughs.*)

WADE: You have to go back. You got six months left.

CASEY: I know.

WADE: You got an entire Company counting on you.

CASEY: Half my Company has been wiped out.

WADE: Well, the *other half* is counting on you.

CASEY: I'm writing a letter to each member of my platoon, explaining myself, asking for their forgiveness…

WADE: What?

CASEY: Encouraging them to do the same.

WADE: Encouraging them to do what?

CASEY: To walk away from the war.

WADE: Have you lost your mind?

CASEY: I'd rather rot in jail than…

WADE: *(Interrupting him.)* What are you saying?

CASEY: I'm saying I'm done with this war.

WADE: Listen…Go get some much-needed rest. You've had a rough couple of months. And we just buried your mother. It's hard for you to…think straight.

CASEY: I'm thinking perfectly clear.

WADE: Listen…War is messed up. Believe me, I know. But, right or wrong, you made a *commitment*. A commitment to those men who fight beside you. Think about your squad members. Your *brothers*. Look at me, God Dammit!!

(CASEY looks at him.)

WADE: Remember when you told me you wanted to enlist? I sat right here; you sat right there. I looked you in the eye and I told you, in full detail, the horrors I faced as a Marine, the horrors *you* would face as a Marine, what would be expected of you wearing that uniform. Remember all that?

CASEY: Yes.

WADE: And you *still* enlisted. You *still* made that commitment. So, be a man and face the consequences. *(Turns his back on CASEY and heads for the bedroom.)*

CASEY: I killed a young boy.

(WADE stops.)

CASEY: A young Iraqi boy. In Fallujah. Couldn't of been fifteen years old. Shot him right through the throat. He was firing at me from an elevated position. Bullet nicked my helmet. I got down, took aim. He stood up for some stupid reason. And I fired. He fell three stories.

WADE: You did what you had to do.

CASEY: I heard a woman scream as soon as he hit the ground. I couldn't tell where the scream came from, but I knew it was his mother.

WADE: Listen, we're going to get you some help. You can see a doctor.

CASEY: *(Ferociously.)* I DON'T NEED A DOCTOR!!!

(WADE seems shocked.)

CASEY: I need to walk away from this war. That's what I need. And I am prepared to face the consequences.

WADE: Are you?

CASEY: Yes.

WADE: When I was in Nam, a kid by the name Justin Shear, Private First Class Rifleman, went over the hill and disappeared. They found him a month later in a place called The Dog Patch outside of Da Nang. He got busted. They sent him back to our company. The C.O. made him walk *point*, day after day, until…I don't need to tell you what often happens to the Point Man.

CASEY: I'll just tell them I refuse to fight.

WADE: *(Laughs.)* Oh…Okay!

CASEY: I'll just flat out refuse.

WADE: You think they're going to grace you with mercy? This is the military. Not Little League.

CASEY: I know that.

WADE: They will work…you…over… Do yourself a favor: Finish the six months, get out, and protest when you *get back*. No shame in that.

CASEY: Yes there is.

WADE: Marines did it all the time during Vietnam.

CASEY: There's no way in hell I can spend another day contributing to this war.

WADE: What the hell you gonna do then? Go run, hide in the woods? Escape to Montreal? What?

CASEY: I'm going to Washington.

WADE: D.C.?

CASEY: Yeah. Katie is Vice President of a grassroots organization that's connected to Charlie Waltz, the editor of the *Pittsburgh Post-Gazette*. Mr. Waltz is a board member for the organization Vietnam Veterans Against the War.

WADE: Oh, for crying out loud!

CASEY: *(Continuing.)* He's going to print my letter— *(Holds up letter.)* this letter—in the Sunday edition and, then, drive me down to a huge rally at the Capitol.

(CASEY pulls out a purple flyer from his back pocket. He unfolds it. He hands it to his father, who looks at it.)

CASEY: He says I can *speak* at the rally.

WADE: Speak at the rally?

CASEY: Yeah.

WADE: What do you mean, *speak at the rally?*

CASEY: You know…Tell my story…Inspire others to stand against this war…

WADE: Jesus Christ. Is this Katie's idea?

CASEY: No! It's mine.

WADE: Bullshit.

CASEY: She tried to talk me out of it.

WADE: I find that hard to believe.

CASEY: *(Shrugs.)* All she's doing is introducing me to Mr. Waltz.

WADE: Pph…So—okay, fine—you speak at this thing, get people hootin' and hollerin', and then…What?

CASEY: And then…We…*rally*.

WADE: And *after* the rally? The rally *ends*, everyone goes *home*. What happens *after* the rally?

(CASEY shrugs.)

WADE: Oh, for crying out loud! You're going back. And I'm taking ya. *(Rises.)* Get your stuff, throw it in the truck, we're leaving at dawn. *(Points at him.)* If I wake up and you're missing, I will hunt you down. You hear me?

CASEY: So be it.

(They stare at each other. Lights down.)

SCENE 3

The same kitchen. We are back to Scene 1, a few moments later. WADE sits at the table. KYLE stands, observing both WADE and his notes from a small notebook. CASEY's photograph is now in the trash can, just as it was throughout Scene 1.

WADE: That was the first time I ever heard him raise his voice in this house. Twenty-four years he never showed me his teeth like that.

KYLE: Did he seem out of control, *dangerous*?

WADE: No, no. Just...*Resistant*. We argued back and forth all night, but come Thursday morning he started thinking clearly.

KYLE: Was this before or after you called the Pittsburgh Recruitment Center?

WADE: *(Looks at him.)* Uh...After.

KYLE: You sure about that?

WADE: Yeah.

KYLE: *(Looking at notes.)* The phone records at the P.R.C. indicate that Captain Samko received your phone call at eleven hundred on Thursday.

WADE: *(Looking at KYLE on "Samko.")* Yeah. I had trouble helping Casey think clearly. So, I called the P.R.C., hoping to get *Sergeant O'Brien* who recruited him, got a hold of *Captain Samko* instead—don't ask me how—and I asked him to talk to Casey.

KYLE: Did the Captain talk with Casey?

WADE: Yes.

KYLE: And Casey told him he made up his mind—he wasn't going back?

WADE: Yeah.

KYLE: And then what?

WADE: *(Sighs.)* Casey hung up on him.

KYLE: Hung up on the *Captain*?

WADE: *(Sighs.)* Yes.

KYLE: And then what?

WADE: The Captain *called back*. Casey refused to speak to him. And the Captain told me he was on his way over here.

CASEY: Uh-huh. And then what happened?

WADE: I told him—Casey, that is—if he went AWOL, he would be dead to me. I told him to never come back if he welched on his commitment to the Corps.

KYLE: How'd he respond?

WADE: He said *fine* and stormed out the door. Thirty minutes later, he comes back in here with a clear look in his eye and told me he was ready to go back.

KYLE: And then what?

WADE: Christ All Mighty!!! What is this? Third degree?

KYLE: I just wanna know what happened.

WADE: I'm *tellin'* ya what happened!

KYLE: Better *me* then the pit bulls from Shore Patrol...

(WADE mumbles.)

KYLE: Captain Samko told you he was on his way over, you hung up, and then...

WADE: He showed up forty minutes later.

KYLE: Samko?

WADE: Yes.

KYLE: ...And?

(Pause.)

WADE: Casey told him he was sorry for hanging up on him. Told him he was ready to return to duty. And the Captain offered to give him a ride all the way to Lejeune because Casey missed his flight to Charlotte.

KYLE: Awfully nice of him.

WADE: Yeah. And Casey accepted. So, we threw his uniform and duffle bag into the truck and Samko drove away with him.

KYLE: Really?

WADE: Yup.

KYLE: *(Looks at him for a moment.)* What? Did the Captain bring backup with him?

WADE: Pardon?

KYLE: Did Captain Samko come over here with *backup?* Or did he come alone?

WADE:...He had two friends with him.

KYLE: Friends?

WADE: Yeah.

KYLE: You met the two of them?

WADE: Yes I did.

KYLE: Get along with them?

WADE: Yeah.

KYLE: *(Looks at him for a moment.)* Did anything happen that I should know about?

WADE: Like what?

KYLE: Wade...*(Stepping closer.)* Captain Samko never reported back to the P.R.C. He's missing. And the last we heard of him he was on his way over here.

WADE: Yeah?

KYLE: And his father is *General* Raymond Samko of the U.S. Marine Corps—three-star General. Those two *friends* with the Captain, they work for the N.C.I.S. They're also missing.

(WADE looks at him.)

KYLE: Where's Casey?

(WADE doesn't answer.)

KYLE: Where's Captain Samko?

(WADE doesn't answer. KYLE steps forward.)

KYLE: I don't have to tell you how serious this is.

WADE: No you don't.

KYLE: The only reason I'm standing in your kitchen right now instead of every Brig Unit on the East Coast is because you and I are old friends...

WADE: That's what you call us?

KYLE: *(Sighs.)* I am pulling more strings right now than you could possibly imagine. And the General is asking *me* where his God Damn son is...Now, I will do *whatever* it takes to help you out, but there's only so much I can do for you in a situation like this. Understand?

(WADE nods.)

KYLE: And there won't be *shit* I can do for you if you don't tell me the *truth*.

(Pause.)

KYLE: Wade...There are two units from the N.C.I.S. parked halfway down this valley. They are going to move in here if they don't hear from me *real* soon.

WADE: *(Sits on the bench next to the front door. Pulls out the purple flyer for the rally from his back pocket. It's wrinkled.*

He looks at it.) He and I were so excited
the day he enlisted…We got drunk that
night. Drank Maker's Mark until dawn,
toasting each other back and forth. I
couldn't wait to see him in a uniform.
I was worried about him, of course, but
I knew he would make a fine Marine:
brave, loyal, strong. I knew he would be
a leader, respected. A hero. Because it's
in his blood. We talked all night about
what it means to be a Marine. How
much of an honor and a privilege it is to
be one of those few men who wear the
uniform. He smiled so brightly. I never
felt so close to him in my entire life. His
mother stayed in the bedroom all night,
crying. She didn't talk to me the next
day. All she said was, Casey doesn't need
a uniform to be *my* hero.

*(KYLE looks at watch again. WADE hangs
his head.)*

KYLE: Wade…We don't have much
time. Tell me where he is.

*(WADE looks at KYLE, purple flyer in his
hand. Lights down.)*

SCENE 4

*Lights up. The same kitchen. Ten or
twelve hours after the ending of Scene 2.
It's morning. CASEY stands in the middle
of the kitchen. He is wearing his jacket,
jeans, and a hat—he is ready to go out. He
holds a dozen sealed envelopes with stamps
on each of them. WADE blocks CASEY's
exit. He sits in a kitchen chair which he
has positioned in front of the door. He
holds a twelve-gage shotgun. They both
look tired—they have been up all night
arguing. There is a tall glass of ice water
on the counter. It sits next to the framed
picture of CASEY wearing his dress blues,
which still stands proudly on the kitchen
counter—instead of the trash can.*

CASEY: This is ridiculous, Dad. Move
out of the way. Please.

WADE: Call back the Captain right now.
Apologize for hanging up on him.

CASEY: *You* call him back. Tell 'im he's
wasting his time, driving all the way
down here.

WADE: He wants to help you.

CASEY: I'm not listening to anybody
who hasn't set foot in Iraq.

WADE: I wouldn't say that to him if I
were you.

CASEY: You gonna sit there until he
arrives?

WADE: Yup. And I wouldn't try runnin'
if I were you.

CASEY: Why?

WADE: I'll blast you with rock salt—
right in the ass.

CASEY: *(Laughs.)* No you wouldn't.

WADE: Try me.

CASEY: You'd shoot your own son?

WADE: If you ran, you wouldn't be
my son. You'd be a deserter. *(Pause.)*
You know what? I should call your
Godfather.

CASEY: Pph. The Colonel don't give a
God Damn 'bout us.

WADE: He'll be standing on the front
porch by noontime if I call him right
now.

CASEY: Oh yeah?

WADE: Yeah.

CASEY: Well, I didn't see 'im at the
funeral—did you?

WADE: …He's a busy man.

CASEY: *Busy?!*

WADE: He's trying to win a war and save his marriage at the same time.

CASEY: He hasn't even returned your phone call in—what?—three, four years?

(Pause.)

WADE: That man would lay his life down for you.

CASEY: *(Laughs.)* I wrote to him five times during my service—*five times*—he never wrote back.

WADE: *(Surprised.)* What?

CASEY: Not once.

WADE: Well…

CASEY: He doesn't give a shit.

WADE: He's your *Godfather*, you're like a *son* to him.

CASEY: He wants nothin' to do with us, Dad. He thinks we're trash.

WADE: *(Stands.)* You don't know nothin' 'bout friendship, boy.

CASEY: Whatever…Move outta the way, Dad.

(WADE doesn't move.)

CASEY: Come on, it's gonna start snowin' soon.

(He still doesn't move.)

CASEY: If you move out the way, I will help you track down that twelve-point when I return from New York.

WADE: I don't need *your* help tracking that thing down.

CASEY: Yeah you do.

WADE: Everything you know 'bout them woods you learned from me.

CASEY: *(Sighs.)* Is that right?

WADE: Oh yeah…Plus, you'll probably run off to Canada.

CASEY: *(Laughs.)* Canada?

WADE: Or you'll climb up the side of the barn, jump off the roof.

CASEY: Why the hell would I do that?

WADE: Break your leg or something.

(CASEY looks at him.)

WADE: You could say it was an accident. By the time your bones healed, your service would be up.

CASEY: I'm not one of those punks.

WADE: Then get in the truck and return to duty.

CASEY: That's not gonna happen.

WADE: *(Sighs.)* Remember when you almost quit football your senior year? You lost the starting job to Eric Winslow and you were alllll ready to turn in your helmet. But your mom and I didn't let ya. We made you stick it out, finish the season. And ya *did*. And after your final game, you didn't want to take off that uniform. You were crying, telling us how proud you felt. Ya thanked me for making ya stick it out. Remember?

CASEY: This ain't football, Dad.

WADE: No shit! But imagine if you *did* quit…If you go AWOL, you'll regret it for the rest of your life.

CASEY: That'll be my problem. Not yours.

WADE: *(Bites lip.)* Fine…Fine…But whatever happened to all that Patriotism you were barking when you decided to drop out of college and enlist? Huh? What happened to that sense of duty you felt after graduating from Basic? All that talk 'bout freeing the world from terror and oppression? About Semper Fi? What happened to all that fire, all that pride, all that love, all that loyalty. Did it just wash away? Did ya forget about it? Misplace it? WHERE THE HELL DID IT GO?!

CASEY: Something changed inside of me when I saw a fifty-year-old woman burning alive—right in front of me —somebody's *mother.*

WADE: *(Sighs.)* Son…It's not easy makin' sense of all this, but—

CASEY: It makes perfect sense!!!

(Pause.)

WADE: Those burns you got, you caught on fire when that car bomb exploded. Right?

CASEY: *(Uncomfortable.)*…Yes.

WADE: And someone put the flames out, right?

CASEY: *(Picking up the glass of water from the counter.)* Private Brady and Sammy Rado extinguished the flames and transported me to safety. *(Finishes the last few gulps of ice water and places the glass in the sink.)*

WADE: They saved your life.

CASEY: Yes. They did.

WADE: And now you're going to let those two men be shot at for the next six months while you sit on your ass over here and do nothing.

CASEY: *(Biting his lip.)* God Damn it, Dad…*(Big sigh. Looks at his watch.)*

WADE: You late for something?

CASEY: Yes. I'm meeting Charlie Waltz in two hours.

WADE: Are you now?

CASEY: And I need to stop by the post office on the way to Pittsburgh.

WADE: What for?

CASEY: To mail these letters.

WADE: You mail them letters, this world is going to come down on you like an eagle on its prey.

CASEY: So be it.

WADE: You will be Court Marshaled. Discharged. *Dishonorable* discharge. Thrown in a Federal Penitentiary.

CASEY: Yup.

WADE: *Prison,* boy. That's worse than war. If you're lucky to make it out alive, there won't be a soul on this planet who will give you work. Nobody wants to associate themselves with a deserter, an ex-con. Your reputation will be tarnished forever. It will follow you everywhere you go.

CASEY: I'm willing to pay that price.

WADE: The *family's* reputation will be tarnished. Your grandfather fought in Iwajima and Okinawa. I fought in Kay Sahn, the first Tet Offensive. You've got a Bronze Star, a Purple Heart. This family has EARNED this country's RESPECT!!! And now you want to *shit on it*? Shit on the family's name? Bring shame to it? After all we done?

(WADE grabs CASEY where the shoulder meets the neck.)

WADE: Huh?

CASEY: *(In pain.)* Ahhh!

WADE: You'll be a God Damn embarrassment!

(CASEY slaps his father's hand away.)

CASEY: Don't touch my shoulders!!!

WADE: *(Patronizing.)* Ohhh, booo-hoo... You want me to feel sorry for you, is that it? Mom's not here to nurse you back to health, treat you like a baby, so don't expect any more pity under this roof!!! How do you think your mother would feel right now, after finding out her son's a...

CASEY: A what?

WADE: *(Disgusted.)* Pph. *(Steps aside.)* Go on. Get on outta here. Mail your letters. Meet up with Charlie Waltz. *(Turns his back on CASEY and crosses to the counter.)* Go make your statement. Prove whatever the hell it is you want to prove. Spit on everything we stand for. *(Picks up the framed picture of CASEY in his dress blues and drops it into the trash can.)* Go, you self-righteous...

(CASEY stares at his picture that now sits in the trash can. WADE opens the cabinet and pulls out the bottle of bourbon. He pours himself a drink. CASEY crosses to the door and opens it. Before crossing the threshold, CASEY turns to his father.)

CASEY: I need the keys to the truck.

(WADE reaches into his pocket and pulls out a set of keys. He tosses CASEY the keys without looking at him. CASEY catches them and exits. He closes the door behind him. WADE collapses. His knees hit the floor and he grabs onto the counter for support. He breathes heavily. There is a noise of a car in the distance—a car roll-ing along the long dirt driveway. After a moment, CASEY reenters onto the front porch. After hearing footsteps on the porch, WADE quickly stands and composes himself. CASEY opens the front door and enters the kitchen. WADE turns and looks at him. The sound of the car grows louder, closer. CASEY drops the keys on the kitchen table.)

CASEY: You might wanna put that twelve-gage away... Captain Samko is here.

(Lights down.)

SCENE 5

The same kitchen. Moments after the end of Scene 3. WADE sits on the bench. KYLE is on the phone. He is holding the purple flyer. The framed picture sits in the trash can.

KYLE: *(On phone.)* Yes. That's right, Major. There's a big anti-war rally being held in Constitutional Gardens, Washington D.C. P.F.C. Taylor spoke at the rally this morning. He's being escorted by the organization, Vietnam Veterans Against the War. Apprehend Private Taylor with caution... Transfer me to General Samko. Thank you, Major. *(To WADE.)* You did the right thing, Wade. *(Into phone.)* Good morning, Sir, Colonel Adamson. No, Sir... You may send them in now. Thank you, Sir. *(Hangs up. To WADE.)* We're going to have to take a look around. It's just procedure.

WADE: What you need to look around for?

KYLE: We still need to find Captain Samko.

WADE: Samko ain't *here.*

KYLE: Then you got nothing to worry about.

WADE: What? You think I pumped 'im full of lead, did away with 'im?

KYLE: I've seen you sacrifice Marines before.

WADE: *(Points at him.)* Fuck you! You wouldn't even be breathing right now if it wasn't for me!

KYLE: LISTEN!!! This ain't about *you and me!* We need to show everyone that Casey had nothing to do with Samko's...*Disappearance.* Understand that? Put your bullshit aside for one day, you arrogant prick, ONE DAY! For Casey. For my *Godson.* Please!

(Pause. The sound of a distant motor. A parade of trucks is heard rolling down the long dirt driveway.)

KYLE: Tell me where Samko is.

WADE: *(After a moment.)* The stupid son-of-a-bitch shoulda stayed put, but he tried to be a hero.

(The sound of the trucks grow louder, closer. KYLE crosses over to him and looks him in the eye. The trucks grow louder, closer.)

KYLE: Tell me what happened, Wade...

(The sound of the tires rolling over the dirt comes to a halt. The sound of doors opening and closing. Voices. A large group of men moving about. WADE looks at KYLE. Lights down.)

SCENE 6

Lights up. CAPTAIN SAMKO (late twenties) sits at the kitchen table with a glass of bourbon in front of him. WADE sits across from him, also sipping on a glass of bourbon. CASEY stands, leaning back against the kitchen counter, sipping on a glass of ice water. SAMKO is a tall, well-built Marine. He is very clean cut, very good looking, and has a radiant glow about him. He appears untouched, yet he seems like a guy that most people would enjoy being around. The framed picture still sits in the trash can.

WADE: Wait a minute, wait a minute, *(Pointing.)* this junction, over here?

SAMKO: Yes, Sir. About five, six hundred yards down the road. I pulled up to the stop sign, looked down at my map, looked up, and there is this ENORMOUS ten- or twelve-point buck, standing right in the middle of the road, looking straight at me. Had a rack the size of...Taller then my *truck.* He just stood there, looking straight at me. I keep a rifle in the back cabin. I was tempted to grab it, take him down, he was such a prize, but I didn't want to get a call from the hunting and game commission.

WADE: Yeah. Season doesn't start until Monday.

SAMKO: Right, right. So, I just sat there looking at him, wishing it was buck season already. And then, few minutes later, he sniffed the air and bounded off.

WADE: Which way?

SAMKO: Toward you guys, into the woods.

WADE: *(Looking out window.)* God Damn.

SAMKO: I wouldn't mind mounting a rack like that right above my fireplace.

WADE: If you were to be so lucky.

SAMKO: That's enough meat for two winters.

WADE: Mm-hm.

SAMKO: You better bag him before he sheds that rack of his.

WADE: Well, he's an elusive creature this one.

SAMKO: I thought deer sleep during the day?

WADE: Sometimes they get restless.

SAMKO: Huh…

WADE: There's a storm brewin'. He could be nervous 'bout that.

SAMKO: Right, right…

(CASEY laughs. SAMKO turns, looks at him, and smiles.)

SAMKO: What's so funny, Private?

CASEY: You grow up 'round here, Sir?

SAMKO: No. Germany, France, North Carolina, boarding school in Connecticut…My family moved around a lot.

CASEY: Did the P.R.C. give you a crash course on Buck hunting?

WADE: Boy…

CASEY: *(To WADE.)* I'm just curious.

SAMKO: My father's a big outdoorsman.

CASEY: Ah.

SAMKO: I understand you just lost your mother.

CASEY: Yes, Sir.

SAMKO: My condolences. To the both of you.

WADE: Thank you, Captain.

SAMKO: *(To CASEY.)* You know, I lost my mum when I was your age. Breast cancer.

WADE: I'm sorry.

SAMKO: The world becomes a different place after ya lose your mother. Am I right, Private?

CASEY: Mm-hm.

WADE: Answer him, boy.

CASEY: I said *Yes.*

SAMKO: It was scary at first: the world without my mum. I couldn't live and breathe without her. I was grieving. And grieving is a *bitch*—pardon my French—and there is this great psychiatrist at Lejeune—Doctor O'Malley is his name—who helped me through it all. He's helped a lot of Marines deal with grief and trauma. And he's ready to sit down with *you*…

CASEY: Captain…

SAMKO: He's a *specialist* who can help you get your head straight.

CASEY: With all due respect, Sir, I'm not returning to duty. And there's nothing you can do or say to change that, Sir.

(Pause. WADE stands.)

WADE: Captain, I'm going to introduce myself to your men, see if they need anything.

SAMKO: *(Stands.)* That's awfully nice of you, Sir.

WADE: *(Pulls on his jacket and hat.)* I'll offer 'em something to eat, a little coffee. Maybe a drink.

SAMKO: Very thoughtful, Sir. Your son and I will continue our conversation.

WADE: All right then.

SAMKO: *(Pointing to car.)* Sergeant Wilson is from Butler County.

WADE: Is he now?

SAMKO: Yes, Sir. I'm sure the two of you will have plenty to talk about.

WADE: (Exiting.) Well, I'll be damned.

(WADE exits. SAMKO turns to CASEY. They look at each other for a moment.)

SAMKO: Take a look out the window right there, Private.

(CASEY crosses to the window and looks outside.)

SAMKO: See those two federal agents sitting in my truck, talking to your father?

CASEY: Yes, Sir.

SAMKO: They're from the N.C.I.S. You know what that is?

CASEY: Yes, Sir.

SAMKO: You're going back today. And you're going to report to Lejeune *on time*. Now you can do that by your own free will or you can do it kicking and screaming.

CASEY: What's it matter to you, Sir?

SAMKO: Your Godfather called me as soon as he heard about your mother.

CASEY: (Looks at him.) Uncle Kyle?

SAMKO: The *Colonel*, Private!

CASEY: You don't work for the Pittsburgh Recruitment Center. Do you, Sir?

SAMKO: (Laughs.) No. I'm currently stationed at Lejeune with the Colonel.

CASEY: And he sent you here to babysit me?

SAMKO: He gave me a direct order: *Make sure P.F.C. Taylor returns to duty on*

time. If he tries to run, bring him back by any means necessary and make sure nobody hears about it.

(CASEY is speechless.)

SAMKO: The Colonel is pulling a llllllllllot of strings for you right now, Private. If you were any other punk, those men out there would have barged in here, taken you down, dragged you to Lejeune, and thrown you in the Brig. But you have friends in high places, count your lucky stars.

CASEY: Just like you, Sir.

SAMKO: Pardon.

CASEY: Captain *Samko*. That's an unusual name, Sir.

SAMKO: Yes it is.

CASEY: I assume you're related to *General* Samko.

SAMKO: I am…

CASEY: Four Star General, received the Medal of Honor in Vietnam?

SAMKO: That's right.

CASEY: I heard some amazing stories about him, Sir.

SAMKO: I'm sure you have.

CASEY: He addressed my company before we moved into Fallujah. Fired everyone up.

(SAMKO chuckles. CASEY smiles.)

CASEY: My father was up for that same award. (Looking out the window.) That old bag of bones out there planted C-4, hand over hand, along the Sun Lou bridge, Red River, North Vietnam. Under enemy fire. The Vietnamese needed that bridge to transfer tanks. My father's entire company would've been wiped out if my dad didn't blow up that bridge.

SAMKO: This country is in debt to him.

CASEY: Yeah. Don't tell *him* that.

SAMKO: Why not?

CASEY: Because he had to sacrifice four of his men in order to complete the mission. There were Marines laying wounded underneath that bridge and the tanks were rolling in fast. He only had time to save one: Lance Corporal Kyle Adamson. The other Marines called for him, pleading for his aid, but the tanks grew closer and closer. He was forced to choose between the mission and his men. He chose the mission. He blew up that bridge and watched it fall onto his brothers.

SAMKO: Mmm.

CASEY: Have you ever sacrificed your men in order to complete a mission, Captain?

SAMKO: Yes. I have, Private...

(CASEY turns and looks at SAMKO.)

CASEY: I see you did a campaign in Desert Storm.

SAMKO: Yes. I did.

CASEY: And Afghanistan.

SAMKO: No.

CASEY: Don't I see an Afghan ribbon on your uniform?

SAMKO: Nope.

CASEY: Huh. Thought I saw one.

SAMKO: Nope.

CASEY: No campaign in Iraq either?

(SAMKO does not answer.)

CASEY: You have any idea what's going on over there...Sir?

SAMKO: 'Course I do.

CASEY: After seeing what I've seen, I don't appreciate the General's son telling me to go back to the front.

SAMKO: You think I'm some *Fortunate Son*, hiding behind my daddy's Four Gold Stars? *(Shows his badge.)* 2nd Force Recon...I've led missions that you will never hear about. I've taken a thirty-eight in the shoulder, shrapnel in the knee. I've injected my best friend with morphine after his legs were blown off. And I shot two young African boys, no older than twelve, right in the chest, because they had a drop on one of my men. I *have* seen all that, Private, just like you. Eight years of therapy, I still have all the nightmares, the cold sweats. And every morning when I wake up I hear those young black kids gasping for air. It's a terrible thing, war, I know, but this one *neeeeeds* to be fought...

(CASEY shakes his head and sighs.)

SAMKO: I got ten years on you, Private, and I've been all around this planet. You probably never set foot outta Western P.A. before Iraq. Am I right?

(CASEY doesn't respond.)

SAMKO: I was sent over to New York City after those 747s flew into the Towers. While you watched it all happen on CNN, I stood at Ground Zero and laid my eyes upon that mountain of twisted steel, smoking like a coal oven, knowing three of my best friends lay trapped underneath—dead, burned to ash. One mother and two fathers, along with three thousand other innocent people. Do you know what it's like to see something like that on American soil, your *home*land? It is the *worst* heartache you could ever imagine, Private. And I'll be *damned* if something like that happens again! Not on my watch. I don't care how many nightmares I must sleep through...Pour me another drink.

(After a moment, CASEY crosses to the bottle, picks it up, crosses back to the table, and pours SAMKO a drink.)

CASEY: I can't kill anymore, Sir. I just don't have it in me. If I had a clear shot at the enemy who had a clear shot at my Captain, I couldn't take it, Sir.

SAMKO: You'll feel differently when you reunite with your brothers.

CASEY: Those men mean the world to me, Sir. I want them to make it home alive. And they have a better chance of doing that without me fighting next to them.

SAMKO: You honestly believe that?

CASEY: Yes, I do, Sir.

(SAMKO looks him in the eye. He gulps down his drink.)

SAMKO: I find that hard to believe, Private...I read your S.R.B.

CASEY: What's it say about me, Sir?

SAMKO: Your S.R.B?

CASEY: Yes, Sir.

SAMKO: *(Pause.)* It says you're a damn good Marine.

CASEY: Does it?

SAMKO: Sure does...I also had a chat with your C.O.

CASEY: You did?

SAMKO: I sure did.

CASEY: What'd *he* have to say about me, Sir?

SAMKO: He said...Your company needs you so your brothers can make it home alive.

CASEY: Well, I'll pray for them, Sir. Every day for the rest of my life.

SAMKO: He also said you're suffering from second- and third-degree burns. *(Pause.)* From a *car bomb*.

(CASEY avoids eye contact.)

SAMKO: Those bombs are nasty items, aren't they?

CASEY: *(Quietly. Can hardly hear him.)* Yes, Sir.

SAMKO: Look at me, Private.

(CASEY struggles with eye contact.)

SAMKO: You're not the first person to lose his head in battle.

CASEY: Huh?

SAMKO: I know what happened in Fallujah.

(CASEY backs away, almost tripping over his own feet. SAMKO remains grounded.)

SAMKO: That kind of shit happens all the time, Casey. Don't go beating yourself up over it.

(CASEY begins to hyperventilate.)

SAMKO: Listen to me: nobody is going to find out. It's going to remain between you and the Corps. Me and every Marine that knows about it will take it to their fucking grave. And nobody will ever think ill of you because it happens all...the...time. To good Marines. It's a part of war.

CASEY: *(Panic.)* Get outta my house.

SAMKO: Casey, if you go AWOL, some piece of shit reporter will want to make a story out of you and he will somehow manipulate you into telling him about what happened over there and then he'll print the story and you'll be in a world of shit. So will Private Brady.

CASEY: *(Turns and looks SAMKO in the eye on "Brady." Ferocious anger.)* You stay away from Brady!!!

SAMKO: Casey...

CASEY: Get the fuck off my land!

(WADE enters with an empty glass of bourbon. He begins to say something, but SAMKO stops him.)

CASEY: You deaf, Captain? I said get on outta here!

SAMKO: I'm here to help, Private!

CASEY: Take yer men and move on outta here before I bury yins down at the crick!!!

(Dead silence. Pause. A gust of wind dances with the chimes on the front porch.)

SAMKO: I'll give you fifteen minutes. Get your stuff ready. Get in my truck. We're driving to Lejeune. That's a direct order, Private. *(Exits.)*

WADE: God Dammit, boy! What the hell's gotten into you?

(CASEY seems dizzy.)

WADE: Get your stuff together and get in that truck.

CASEY: No. I'm going to the rally.

WADE: Those two agents say you're going to Lejeune.

CASEY: I have an appointment with Mr. Waltz.

WADE: They will drag you out and throw you in the trunk if they have to.

CASEY: Well, they're gonna *have to*.

WADE: Christ All Mighty...

(WADE crosses toward CASEY's bedroom. CASEY stops him.)

CASEY: Dad...

WADE: These men are here to protect you and you're ready to *bite*.

CASEY: *(On "bite.")* Dad, LISTEN! Keep the Captain and his little...*posse* preoccupied. I'll sneak out the back, run into the woods, make my way over to Reardon's farm, borrow his truck, and drive to my meeting. If they lean on you hard, ask you where I gone, tell them they can apprehend me tomorrow at the rally in D.C.

WADE: Have you lost your God Damn mind?!!!

CASEY: Dad, all I need is a head start. Once I'm in the woods, they won't be able to find me.

WADE: I'm not helping you go AWOL.

CASEY: I'm not going A—I will turn myself in after the rally. Promise. If I'm gonna do time, I want people to know why...

(WADE looks out the window. CASEY pulls out the twelve-gage. He opens the chamber and sees that it is loaded.)

WADE: *(Looking out window.)* Those agents are carrying Berettas.

CASEY: Well...If they go to draw, blast 'im in the leg with rock salt.

WADE: *What?!*

CASEY: Or just *hold it on them* until I make it to the ridge.

WADE: And then what?

CASEY: I don't know. Play it by ear.

WADE: Christ Allllllll Mighty!

(WADE mumbles and crosses into the bedroom. CASEY crosses to the edge of the window and carefully peeks through the curtain. Moments later, WADE reenters with CASEY's duffle bag, which is already packed, and a garment bag. CASEY blocks the doorway.)

CASEY: What do I gotta do to get you on my side?

WADE: I *used* to be on your side. Before you…*(Bites his tongue.)*

CASEY: Before what?

(WADE tries to move around CASEY. CASEY stops him.)

CASEY: If those men try to put me in that truck, I'm going to resist.

WADE: And you will not see the light of day for twenty years.

CASEY: Nothing is stopping me from seeing Charlie Waltz this afternoon…*Nothing.*

WADE: Son…You got to choose your battles in life. And the key is knowing the difference between the battles you can *win* from the ones you can't. And you can't win this one. And, if you continue fighting it, you'll destroy everything good in your life. I won't sit back and watch that happen. Your mother wouldn't want that either…I'll meet you outside.

(WADE crosses past his son and opens the front door.)

CASEY: Katie's pregnant.

WADE: *(Stops.)* Come again.

CASEY: Katie's pregnant. Four and a half months. It's a boy. We're gonna name him *Benjamin.*

WADE: Pregnant?

CASEY: Yeah.

WADE: *How*—When?

CASEY: Remember last August: they shipped us back to Lejeune for five days to remodify our Urban Combat Training?

WADE: Yeah.

CASEY: *(Shrugs.)* She's due in May.

WADE: *(Heavy sigh.)* Welllll…

CASEY: We're getting married.

WADE: That's what yins decided?

CASEY: *(Smiles and nods.)* Last night.

WADE: Listen, I'll take care of everything while you're gone.

(CASEY laughs.)

WADE: I will. I will sit down with Mr. and Mrs. Keenan, work out all the financial matters. I'll find the best doctors, drive Katie around, everything. We'll figure this out…together. All you gotta do is make it home alive. That's all you gotta do.

CASEY: I am home. And I'm *staying* home.

WADE: You won't be any good to your son, sitting in some jail cell. Make it home *alive*, and you'll be a free man with a G.I. Bill and a whole lot of respect. What more can a son ask for?

CASEY: A father who doesn't burden him and his mother.

WADE: What?

CASEY: I am not going to let Katie and my son bear the same burden me and mom did, even if that means losing the respect of every drunk halfwit in this county.

WADE: Pardon me?

(WADE moves in, towering over his son, looking him in the eye. CASEY stands his ground.)

CASEY: Stand down, Dad. If you don't have the courage to back me up right now, then get out of the way.

WADE: Or else what?

CASEY: Go stick your head in that bottle—same place you've been hiding it for the past thirty years.

WADE: I ain't hiding from no one.

CASEY: Mom use to say this stuff was your *medicine*. She said that the two of us had to be strong until you found the strength to forgive yourself. But you never did. You just kept *tipping it back*, forcing me and Mom to carry a load that nearly suffocated us. You're a heavy burden, Dad! And I shouldn't of left home, 'cause Mom had to bear that burden all alone. And it finally BROKE HER.

(WADE explodes forward. He grabs his son where the shoulder meets the neck and squeezes hard. CASEY cries in pain.)

CASEY: Ahhh!

WADE: You ungrateful, son-of-a—What gives you the right to judge me after all I done for you. (Yanks the shirt.) Huh?

(CASEY grabs hold of his father's wrist. He twists it, which spins WADE around. WADE grunts in pain, and CASEY shoves

his father. His father flies into the refrigerator. WADE turns around and charges his son like an angry bull. CASEY executes a quick move that brings WADE down to the floor. CASEY is on top of WADE.)

CASEY: You killed her!!! That truck needed new brakes for the past two years, but you were too busy spending everything on your medicine! You drunk piece of shit! And my mother flew through the windshield because of it—MY MOTHER!!!

(CASEY hits him. A surge of energy explodes through WADE's body as he wiggles out from underneath his son just enough so he can maneuver himself in a position that allows him to grab the bottom of CASEY's shirt and pull it up over his son's head, NHL-style. WADE rips the shirt off his son and then shoves his son, who sails across the room and slams against the wall. CASEY yelps in pain as his back hits the wall. He forces himself to stay standing. CASEY's upper body is revealed. His chest, shoulders, and right arm are covered with second-degree burns that will soon turn into scars. WADE looks at his son's burned upper body.)

CASEY: GO ON! You wanted to take a look, take a look. (He turns around. His back is covered with scars.) These are not magnesium burns. There never was a car bomb. My C.O. claimed it to be so I wouldn't be... (Chokes up.)

WADE: Huh?

CASEY: I was having a smoke with my best friend, Badger. In Fallujah. We finally secured the area. The city was in ruin, quiet, motionless. We fought for three days straight. We hadn't slept in four. We were leaning up against a truck, happy to be alive. It was early morning and we just finished eating a can of peaches. He was telling me about his grandmother's Swedish pancakes and then, BANG, his skull exploded and my face was covered in his blood. I couldn't see anything for a few seconds. I heard two more shots. I heard my squad members taking cover. I quickly wiped the blood from my eyes and I saw this old woman charging at me, holding an AK-47. I don't know where she came from or how she got a hold of that rifle, but she looked like an angry grizzly bear dressed in rags. She pointed the rifle at me. I froze. She had the drop on me. I thought, *this is it.* And then I heard a few clicks. It was empty. So, I grabbed my rifle and charged at her. I cross-checked her to the ground. Knocked the wind out of her. I grabbed her weapon and threw it behind me. I pointed my rifle at her and told her not to move. Then I heard someone say, *Badger is dead.* And something came over me—I don't know what. I didn't care who this woman was; she killed Badger—my best friend, my *brother.* So, I walked over to the truck while she laid on the ground, gasping for air. I grabbed a five-gallon jerry-can out of the back, opened it, walked back over to her, and dumped the whole thing on her head, covering her in gas. Everyone watched me do it. I told Private Brady to hand me his book of matches. He did. Without hesitation. I took it from him, opened it, struck a match, and threw it on her. She went up so quick. Like a brush fire in a high wind. She let out this *scream* that pierced my ears; it shook my whole body. That scream...It was the same scream I heard when I killed that young boy. It was his mother. Her scream awoke something inside of me and, all of a sudden, I was seeing this fifty-year-old woman burning alive right in front of

me, rolling around on the ground. And I realized what I had done. And I wanted to save her. I wanted to ease her pain. I should've just shot her, put her out of her misery, but—for some reason—I thought I could put out the flames and save her. So I hurled myself onto her, hoping to smother the flames. That's when I caught on fire. My men saved me before any serious damage was done, but not before the flames left their mark.

(Pause. WADE looks at the burns.)

CASEY: Don't look at me like you've never seen shit like this before. You've seen it. You lived through Vietnam—Vietnam—and you still let this *stupid fucking war happen*...Again! Why didn't you take a *stand?* How could you just *let it happen?* Did you learn nothing? What does it take to get this fucking world to do what is right?!?!? We just keep passing down our sins. From one generation to the next. *(Points to himself.)* Well, it stops *here!* I will not pass these scars down to my son. I don't care WHAT IT TAKES! I will bear these burns all the way to my fucking grave and they will decay into the fucking dirt...*(Grabs his shirt off the floor. He struggles to slide it over his burns.)*

WADE: Need some help?

(CASEY nods. WADE crosses to him. He takes the shirt out of CASEY's grasp and gently embraces his son. CASEY sobs, collapsing into his father's soft embrace. WADE holds him. He cradles his son as he slowly sways back and forth, softly humming the Native American lullaby we heard in Scene 2. CASEY continues to sob. After a while...The front door swings open. SAMKO enters.)

SAMKO: Private Taylor? *(Turns and signals toward the car.)* Everything okay in here?

(Footsteps on the front porch. Enter TWO FEDERAL AGENTS.)

SAMKO: Private? It's time to go.

WADE: We need a few minutes.

SAMKO: I'm afraid we have to leave now, Sir. It's starting to snow.

WADE: One minute, Captain, please.

SAMKO: I don't like the thought of driving up and down these hills during a snowstorm, Sir. *(To CASEY.)* Private Taylor? You ready?

(CASEY doesn't move.)

SAMKO: Don't turn this into something you'll regret.

(CASEY still doesn't move. WADE moves around the table.)

SAMKO: Come on now. Let's go…

(CASEY still doesn't move.)

SAMKO: *(To the NCIS AGENT.)* Agent Dunn…

(AGENT DUNN moves forward.)

DUNN: Private First Class Taylor, turn around please. Hands on the wall and spread 'em.

(CASEY still doesn't move. SECOND AGENT places his hand on his sidearm.)

DUNN: I said turn around, place your hands on the wall, and spread 'em.

(CASEY still doesn't move. DUNN pulls a zip cord.)

DUNN: That's an order, Private Taylor…

(CASEY slowly turns his back to DUNN and walks toward the back room.)

DUNN: PRIVATE!

(SECOND AGENT draws his firearm. So does DUNN.)

DUNN: I'm warning you!

(DUNN advances toward CASEY as the SECOND AGENT covers him. Suddenly, the pump of the twelve-gage echoes throughout the kitchen. DUNN freezes, turns his head. WADE holds the fully loaded shotgun. He points it at the MEN.)

WADE: My son isn't going anywhere.

(Lights down.)

SCENE 7

Lights up. WADE sits in a chair. KYLE stands over WADE. AGENT GALLEY stands near the counter with a forbidding look in his eyes. He eyeballs WADE the entire time as KYLE interrogates him. CASEY's framed picture remains in the trash can.

WADE: I thought those Agents were gonna to take me down, but Samko didn't let 'em. Casey threw on his coat and ran out the door. I lowered the shotgun. Samko and his men chased after Casey. I yelled at those boys to *stay put*, because the sun was going down, but they followed his footprints right into the woods…and never came out.

KYLE: What do you mean, they never came out?

WADE: This morning I followed their tracks south, all the way down to Sheep's Pond. The pond is frozen, but the ice ain't thick enough yet to hold a grown man. I found Casey's tracks along the bank, leading around the pond, toward Jeff's house. Then I saw three sets of tracks that led across the ice, toward a huge hole in the center of the pond…I believe them boys fell through the ice and drowned...It was probably dark when it happened.

(KYLE releases a huge sigh. He stands. He pulls WADE's coat off the rack and tosses it to WADE. WADE catches it.)

KYLE: Lead us to Sheep Pond.

(Enter AGENT CONNER from the NCIS.)

CONNER: Colonel...

KYLE: Yes, Conner.

CONNER: We just received word from Shore Patrol. They've got Private Taylor. They're transporting him down to Lejeune.

KYLE: Did everything go smoothly?

CONNER: No, Sir. We arrived after the Private delivered his speech. He fired everyone up. A huge fight broke out as we apprehended him. Veterans verse soldiers, protesters yellin' and screaming, police, firemen, people trying to protect the Private. There were several arrests. And, apparently, there were cameras everywhere.

KYLE: *(Sighs.)* Thank you, Conner.

CONNER: Thank you, Sir. *(Exits.)*

KYLE: Agent Galley...

GALLEY: Colonel.

KYLE: Inform your unit that Mr. Taylor is going to lead us to Sheep's Pond. Prepare to rake the lake.

GALLEY: Yes, Sir.

(GALLEY exits. WADE pulls on his coat, crosses to the coat rack, and pulls on his orange hunting vest, hat, and gloves. KYLE sits in his chair and composes himself.)

WADE: Do my son a favor. When General Samko speaks ill of him, when every other Marine starts calling him yellow, stand up for him.

KYLE: I'm done doing Casey favors.

WADE: He's your Godson!

KYLE: He's a deserter.

WADE: Yeah. Well...You had no right ignoring all those letters he wrote to you during his service.

KYLE: You wanna know why I never wrote him back? Because every letter was the same. He'd ask me to come over here and make sure you and his mother were okay. He'd ask me to help you...financially. And I didn't have the heart to tell him that you're beyond help, Wade. I've been *trying* to help you for the past *thirty-five years!* I can barely look at you because *(Pointing to WADE.)* there stands a man who saved my life, who I owe *everything* to, and I can't return the favor because he won't fucking let me. He won't let *anyone.* Just like his son...

WADE: Just write him back. Reply to every letter he sent you during his service.

KYLE: *(Sighs.)* You have my word.

WADE: *(Nods.)* It'll be dark soon. We better get movin'. *(Pulls on his jacket.)*

KYLE: Why did you pull me out of Red River?

(WADE stops.)

KYLE: A piece of myself drowned in that river that day. I don't know what, but—whatever it was—I never got it back...You should've saved Rinaldi, Hacker, Sludge, or the *Captain.* They all outranked me. And they were better men than I. Why the hell did you choose *me?*

WADE: *(Shrugs.)*...All I remember is dropping behind that ledge. And the sound of those fifty calibers were making my bones tremble...I was about to ignite the C-4 and you told me to wait because Rinaldi was trying to save Hacker...You begged me to wait for them. Maybe I *could've* waited one more minute. Just one more minute, but...I didn't. I made eye contact with Rinaldi just as I set off the C-4. He gave me this look from across the river that said...*(Hangs his head.)* His eyes follow me wherever I go...

(KYLE places his hand on WADE's shoulder. WADE cries. KYLE embraces WADE. There is a ruckus outside, voices. Footsteps on the front porch. Laughter from the front porch. The two MEN quickly separate.)

CONNER: *(Offstage.)* God Damn, that's a beauty, Galley! Stop it, stop it, be careful with it.

(CONNER enters.)

CONNER: Colonel, Sir. Check this out. *(Calling out the door.)* Agent Galley, bring that on in here, show the Colonel. *(To KYLE.)* We found this big-ass deer *(Pointing.)* 'bout five hundred yards that way along the ridge. It was caught in some wire, dead frozen...

(AGENT GALLEY enters, carrying something. He hands it to CONNER, who receives it carefully, then holds it up to the COLONEL triumphantly. It's a twelve-point rack of a large buck, which has been carelessly severed from the head with a large, sharp knife. Some of the blood is still on the antlers. The only thing binding the antlers together is the roof of the skull at the base along with some flimsy

flesh. WADE explodes out of his chair. He advances toward CONNER. KYLE restrains WADE.)

WADE: *(Standing.)* You sons-of-bitches...

CONNER: Whoa!!!

KYLE: Easy, easy.

WADE: What gives you the right to touch that creature?

KYLE: *(Settling him.)* Wade...Wade.

WADE: I will break your God Damn neck!!! You hear me? I will rip it clear off your shoulders. You're a dead man!

KYLE: Calm down.

WADE: Bring me the son-of-bitch who did that—BRING HIM TO ME!!!!

(KYLE throws him against the wall and leans into him, looks him in the eye.)

KYLE: Take it easy! They're just kids. Take...It...Easy...Wade!!!

(WADE settles down. Whispering.)

KYLE: Easy...Easy...*(While holding WADE, looking him in the eye.)* Agent Conner, step out of here, please.

(CONNER's hand is on his firearm. He looks at the COLONEL before drawing it.)

KYLE: Galley...Go make sure your unit is ready to move into the woods.

CONNER:...Yes, Sir.

(CONNER and GALLEY turn to exit.)

WADE: Leave that rack...Set it on the table. Carefully.

(CONNER looks at KYLE.)

KYLE: Leave it on the table, Conner.

CONNER: Yes, Sir.

(CONNER leaves the rack on the table. A few last drops of blood drip off the flesh. CONNER and GALLEY exit. CONNER closes the door behind him. KYLE releases WADE. WADE collapses onto the floor.)

KYLE: I'm sorry…They're just kids, tryin' to impress me. *(Crosses to the rack.)*

WADE: Don't touch it.

KYLE: I'm not, I'm not. Just looking…

WADE: They stole it from him. Like a bunch of degenerate thieves.

KYLE: *(Grabbing his jacket.)* Let's go. We only have a few more hours of daylight…

WADE: I'll be out in a minute…I want to be alone for a while.

KYLE: I'll be on the porch.

(KYLE slowly turns and crosses to the front door. He exits, closing the door behind him. WADE crosses to the CD player. He presses the play button. The Native American tune from the beginning of Scene 2 fades up. He crosses to the trash can. He pulls the framed picture of his son out of the garbage. He sits in the kitchen chair and begins to clean the picture very gently with his hand and sleeve, looking at his son. We hear voices of the SOLDIERS outside. After carefully cleaning the picture he places it on the table, next to the antlers. He looks at the picture of his son next to the rack. He gently removes a small piece of garbage that covers the image of his son's face. We hear SOLDIERS barking orders from offstage. The music grows louder as the lights slowly fade down.)[*]

(End of play.)

---

[*]The director may also end the play using the following:

WADE turns on the music. He pulls the photograph out of the trash can, cleans it, and sets it on the table beside the antlers. Then he crosses to the counter, grabs the bottle of bourbon, opens it, and empties it into the sink. As the bourbon pours down the drain, the lights slowly fade down.

DIVING NORMAL

Ashlin Halfnight

ASHLIN HALFNIGHT was born in London and raised in Toronto. He has a BA in English and American literature from Harvard University and an MFA in playwriting from Columbia University. His plays include *Playtherapistplay* (Montreal and Toronto Fringe Festivals, 2001), *Fat Kid in a Freezer* (American Theatre of Actors, 2003), *The Way to Begin* (Alternate Theatre Company, 2004), *Arms, Legs, and Hand Sanitizer* (Sam French Festival, 2004), *Garotting* (Kraine Theatre, 2004), *God and Hockey* (Focus Theatre Festival, Toronto, 2005), *God's Waiting Room* (New York International Fringe Festival, 2005), *A Hush Hush Hidden Thing* (Merlin Theatre, Budapest, Hungary, 2006), and *Nevermind the Baby* (Hungarian National Theatre, Budapest, 2006). *God's Waiting Room* won the Best Play Award at the 2005 New York International Fringe Festival. His play, *Bird Bones*, received staged readings at New York Theatre Workshop and Cherry Lane Theatre. In 2006–07, *The Stars Above Balaton* was in development at the Lark Play Development Center; a commission, *Dis*, was in rehearsal at St. Andrews College; and *Mud Blossom*, was being workshopped at the Emergency Theater Project in preparation for its premiere at SoHo Rep's Walkerspace. Halfnight is the recipient of a Ford Grant (1997), a Ludwig Vogelstein Artist Grant (2003), a Howard Stein Playwriting Fellowship (2005, Columbia University), and a Fulbright Fellowship (2005–06, National Theatre of Hungary). He spent time on two Canadian National Hockey teams and two U.S. World Junior National teams. He was the captain of the Harvard Varsity Hockey team, and played two seasons of professional hockey after being drafted by the Hartford Whalers (now the Carolina Hurricanes) of the NHL in 1994. He works mostly in education, and lives in New York City.

Diving Normal was first presented by Electric Pear Productions (Melanie Sylvan, Executive Producer) as part of the New York International Fringe Festival (Elena K. Holy, Producing Artistic Director) on August 13, 2006, at the Access Theatre, New York City, with the following cast and credits:

Dana .... Eliza Baldi
Fulton .... Josh Heine
Gordon .... Jayd McCarty

Directed by: Mary Catherine Burke
Lighting Design: K.J. Hardy
Sound Design: Jake Hall
Costume and Makeup Design: Sarah Maiorino
Scenic Design: Jesse Poleshuck
Stage Manager: Andrew Michaelson
Technical Assistant: Felicia Cutrone
Assistant Producer: Colleen Katana

www.electricpear.org

First and foremost—to everyone who worked so hard to put it up the first time—Melanie, Mary Kate, Jayd, Josh, and Eliza. To Jesse, Kevin, Sarah, Jake…to Andrew and Felicia. And to Colleen…thank you. I owe you a deep, deep debt of gratitude. It was a long haul, but well worth every minute. And a special thanks to anyone who dealt with the door—building it, stabilizing it, opening it, closing it…and eventually, destroying it. Thanks. To Andrea Wales for running the remix version on 14th, and Denise Mauroney for doing makeup. To Eduardo Machado and Megan Smith, for space and support. To Rebecca Frank, Nancy Heller, Reed Ridgely, Amy Nederlander, and Marc Routh for sound advice. To the Epsteins for storage, flexibility and generosity. To Emily Long, Michael Nachbar, Erin Callaghan, Erin Viola, and Erin Halfnight for passing out programs. To Charles Socarides, Gretchen Hall, Derrick Thadani, Matt Pilieci, and Keenan Henson for invaluable help with early versions. To Lisa Rothe, Aran Cravey, Brian Sacca, and Glenn Fleshler, for the reading of *Bird Bones* at NYTW and Cherry Lane. To Christian Parker for valuable thoughts, Adam Moore and Matt Morrow for arrangements and assistance with the readings. To Martin and Rochelle Denton, Michael Criscuolo, and Seth Solloway for championing new work and a dedication to downtown theatre. To Theresa Rebeck, for analysis and encouragement. To MJ and Frank Johnson, for friendship and support. To Judy and Brian Famigletti for being there at the start, in so many ways. To my friends and family, especially my dad, for reinforcement in uncertain times. And, of course, to everyone who came to see the play…Thank you.

CHARACTERS

FULTON: Late twenties. Smart but unsure.
DANA: Late twenties. Rough and pretty.
GORDON: Early thirties. Kind and awkward.

SETTING

A post-college, East Village apartment in New York City.

SCENE I

Sounds of rain. The lights come up on DANA, drenched and bleeding from her eyebrow. She stands in the middle of the room, looking around. From the back of the apartment, FULTON yells.

FULTON: *(Offstage.)* You sure? You might need stitches.

DANA: I don't need stitches.

FULTON: *(Offstage.)* Fuck...I've got some first-aid stuff around here some-where...I—if you'd mentioned some-thing on the phone I could have had all this shit ready—I've...Why didn't you say something?

DANA: Sorry.

FULTON: *(Offstage.)* No—it's fine—

(He enters carrying a towel and some first-aid junk.)

FULTON: It's totally fine. Don't apolo-gize. *(He wraps the towel around her.)* Here—sit down.

(He leads her to the couch and goes at her eye.)

FULTON: So what happened?

DANA: Nothing—I don't know—this guy just / like rammed—*

FULTON: Wait—this was at Canal? After I saw you?

DANA: Yeah. Anyway he—ow.

FULTON: Sorry. Rubbing alcohol.

DANA: No—it's okay.

FULTON: So...

DANA: So, she was a crazy bag lady, you know? And she just started screaming and yelling and pushing everyone—and she smacked my head into the door of the train. *(Winces.)*

FULTON: Sorry. If you want to do it yourself—I'm not very good at this kind of thing.

DANA: No. / You're doing great. Thank you.

FULTON: I'm not really a nurse. Or a male nurse. Or whatever.

DANA: It's fine.

(He cleans a bit more, blows on the spot to dry it. She looks at him.)

FULTON: What? Does my breath smell?

DANA: No.

---

*When one character starts speaking before the other has finished, the point of inter-ruption is marked /, and the first character continues talking regardless.

FULTON: I was eating pickles when you called. *(He applies the Band-Aid.)* What?

DANA: Nothing. You've gotten cuter. Sort of.

FULTON: Thanks...since when—

DANA: I don't know—whenever I saw you last...

FULTON: Like this afternoon?

DANA: No—high school, or whatever...

FULTON: Oh. Yeah. Thanks. You look cute, too—you were cute then—really cute—Ahm, now, you kind of look *gangsta-hot*. With the Band-Aid and all. Maybe not. *(Beat.)* You cold?

DANA: No. No. It's warm in here.

FULTON: Too warm? I can open a window.

DANA: No.

(He collects the stuff. He holds out a T-shirt.)

FULTON: Okay—well here's a T-shirt. It's dry. You can put it on. I'll go in the other room.

DANA: Thanks.

FULTON: I'll...I'm just going to put this stuff away. You can change.

(He leaves the room. She pulls her shirt up, revealing several welts on her back. She puts the T-shirt on.)

FULTON: *(Offstage.)* So, you took the train in?

DANA: Yeah.

FULTON: *(Offstage.)* Gotta love Metro North.

DANA: Yeah...gotta love Metro North. What?

FULTON: *(Offstage.)* Nothing.

DANA: *(Takes a pill bottle out of her purse and pops a pill.)* It's...um...yeah...I don't drive...so it's the only way to...get in.

FULTON: *(Offstage.)* Yeah. Of course. Are you decent?

DANA: I guess so.

(He reenters.)

FULTON: So—I think there's still a 12:10 train—but...by the time you get to the subway...

DANA: Yeah I can probably catch it if...um...

FULTON: You're welcome to stay. On the couch.

DANA: No. I wouldn't want to impose.

FULTON: No really. It's fine. I got the couch. I ordered Chinese.

DANA: Okay...

FULTON: Double rice.

DANA: Okay then.

FULTON: Okay then. Stay.

DANA: Thanks. That's nice of you. This is nice. Better than...well, better than Brewster any day of the week.

FULTON: Yeah?

DANA: Yeah. You know...there's nothing to do. Work. Sleep. The mall.

FULTON: You working?

DANA: Yeah. Greenhill. Assisted living.

(Beat.)

FULTON: Oh. Yeah. How's your mom doing?

DANA: Fine.

FULTON: She's still…?

DANA: Um…

FULTON: Umm, you know…

DANA: Paralyzed. Yeah. You can say it.

FULTON: Yeah. Sorry. But Greenhill—that's good, though. You get to spend time together.

DANA: No—she lives at home. With me. I mean, I do. Spend time with her. In the evenings. At night. *(Beat.)* But, ahm, I heard you got one of your novels published.

FULTON: It was a graphic novel, actually.

DANA: I haven't read it—or looked at the pictures—or whatever you do with a graphic novel—but, yeah, congratulations.

FULTON: Thanks.

DANA: Yeah—little Fulton Ditmer, yearbook editor, makes good. It was in the paper.

FULTON: Yeah. *(Beat.)* Who was that guy? That your boyfriend?

DANA: Him? No. Just a guy…we went to the Gap.

FULTON: Yeah. I saw the bag. Okay. You want a drink?

DANA: I'm not—yeah—you got something to eat actually? I'm kinda hungry.

FULTON: Sure. The Chinese should be here any minute…but ah, I've got melba toast…

DANA: Melba *what?*

FULTON: Toast. It's like this thin… never mind. I'll just get it. *(Goes to the cupboard.)* So, ah, Jimmy Dobbs is a karate champion in New Mexico. Cheryl Hood is making a movie about dingoes. You know, like *the dingo ate my baby…*

DANA: What?

FULTON: So—I just, you know, it's interesting how people turn out—nine years…long time, you know? *(Beat.)* So what's up with you?

DANA: I've done a bunch of things. Little of this—the Sears catalogue—

FULTON: I did hear about that. With like a barbecue or something?

(He hands her a cracker.)

DANA: A kiddie pool, actually. And another one with a lawn mower—me and my fake husband, doing the gardening. Fucking ridiculous. And you probably heard that I was doing some—table dancing.

FULTON: No, actually.

DANA: Yeah. Did that. *(Chews. Stops.)* This tastes like ass.

FULTON: Really? *(Smells the box.)*

DANA: Ugh—seriously—you eat this shit?

FULTON: You want pickles?

DANA: No. Thanks. *(Beat. She shivers. Fades.)* Ugh…

FULTON: Hey. I know it's not my place, but, are you okay?

DANA: Yeah.

FULTON: Really? *(Beat.)* I mean, if you don't want to tell me what happened, it's okay, but if you're in / trouble maybe we should call someone.

DANA: I told you what happened.

FULTON: Yeah. Sort of.

DANA: What's that supposed to mean?

FULTON: Nothing—just when you were telling the story the *guy* changed to a *girl*.

DANA: What?

FULTON: Well first it was a guy who pushed you. You said *guy*—and then it was a woman.

DANA: So? No. I started to say that there was a guy who was next to me and she pushed him first—then me.

FULTON: Okay. I'm just saying that— when you first came in—when you started to tell the story—and I mean, maybe I'm way out of line here—

DANA: What?

FULTON: No. But, if that guy I saw you with is, you know, beating you or something—you know what—never mind. Forget I said anything. It's okay. I'll get you some blankets. My neighbor has extras.

(He goes to the door. She stands, putting on her coat.)

DANA: Hey…you know what? The last thing I want to do is make trouble. I'm gonna go.

FULTON: Make trouble? What the hell are you talking about?

DANA: Nothing. Thank you for the Band-Aid.

FULTON: What?

DANA: It was good to see you.

(She exits. He follows her.)

FULTON: *(Offstage.)* Dana! It's fucking pouring outside! *(Beat.)* Dana!

(He reenters and shuts the door, shaking his head. He stands a moment, thinking about going after her. No. He exits to the bedroom. There is a knock on the door. He reenters quickly and opens it.)

FULTON: Oh.

VOICE: *(Offstage.)* 2D?

FULTON: Hey—yeah—thanks. Keep the change. *(Hands over some cash, closes the door, and reenters with a bag of Chinese food.)* Fuck. *(Sets the food down and reaches for an umbrella.)* Fuck fuck fuck.

(He hesitates. Opens the door. DANA is standing there.)

FULTON: Oh…

(There is a long beat of silence during which they look at each other.)

DANA: Sorry.

FULTON: It's okay. I'm sorry, too.

DANA: No. I just…don't call me a liar.

FULTON: I wasn't.

DANA: Yes you were.

FULTON: Okay—no. I was asking for a clarification.

DANA: You were calling me a liar.

FULTON: I didn't mean anything…I really didn't mean to make it sound like that. I'm sorry. I just wanted to help.

DANA: Yeah, well, I don't need your help.

FULTON: Okay. *(Beat.)* Do you need my kung pow chicken?

DANA: What?

FULTON: Are you hungry? You said you were hungry.

DANA: Maybe.

FULTON: I'm on kung pow overload in here...

DANA: Yeah?

FULTON: Yeah...we could eat and, um, stare at each other like in eleventh grade bio.

DANA: What?

FULTON: Oh come on...I stared at you—you stared at me...bio class... Bunsen burners...

DANA: Um, I hate to be the one to tell you this, but I was pretty much baked out of my mind in bio...so I don't think I was / staring at you...

FULTON: We can just eat then. No staring. Just eat. And look at the floor. If you'll come back in.

(She does. Lights fade.)

SCENE II

The lights come up to reveal DANA, sleeping on the couch, eye bandaged as before, in FULTON's sweats and T-shirt. GORDON stands over her, eating Raisin Bran.

DANA: Jesus! What the fuck / are you doing?

GORDON: Don't be scared. / Good morning.

DANA: Fulton!

GORDON: Shh...Don't wake him up.

DANA: You woke *me* up.

GORDON: False. I waited patiently for you to come out of your sleep naturally.

DANA: Uhuh. Whatever. Can you back up?

GORDON: I live next door. *(Moves.)*

DANA: Uhuh—is it Gerald?

GORDON: False. It is Gordon. Those are my blankets.

DANA: Okay—yeah—sorry—Gordon—you're kind of creeping me out.

(He pushes the box toward her.)

DANA: No. Thanks. *(Stands, wrapping the blanket around her.)*

GORDON: The apartment smells nice. Like you.

DANA: Fulton!

FULTON: *(Offstage.)* Coming! Hang on.

GORDON: Good morning, Fulton! *(To DANA.)* I could make you some eggs and coffee. Don't be scared.

DANA: I'm not / scared.

GORDON: An omelet? I make a very good Western omelet. A five-star Western omelet.

DANA: A Western omelet.

GORDON: Yes.

DANA: Like with eggs and...whatever...

GORDON: Yes. I was famous for it at my summer camp.

DANA: Hmm...

GORDON: What were you famous for at your summer camp?

DANA: Ha.

(FULTON enters.)

FULTON: Gord—not before eleven. *(To her.)* Sorry.

GORDON: You needed blankets. I just came to collect my blankets.

FULTON: I have a guest.

GORDON: I know. She's very nice.

FULTON: So—it's ten o'clock in the morning Gordon—and she's tired—and she had an accident last night and the last thing she needs is some total stranger waking her up first thing in the—just, Christ!

GORDON: Oh.

FULTON: No. No…it's fine. Gord. Seriously. It's not a big deal. Just, maybe give us an hour. I'll come over and we can go down and grab a coffee. Cool?

GORDON: Yes.

(FULTON opens the door. GORDON leaves, sadly.)

GORDON: Okay. Sorry. Goodbye.

DANA: Bye, Gordon.

FULTON: Later.

GORDON: I am sorry for my intrusion.

(FULTON shuts the door.)

FULTON: Sorry. He's harmless. Pain in the ass sometimes, but he's—

GORDON: *(Offstage.)* I heard that!

FULTON: Well, you *are*! *(Comes closer to DANA.)*

FULTON: He's on the board of the building—takes the rules very seriously. Like that kid Marvin whatever…had Asperger's…he was always the referee in gym class…

DANA: Huh. He was kind of cute. Gordon, I mean.

FULTON: Uhuh…?

DANA: He was going to make me an omelet.

FULTON: So?

DANA: So…I'm hungry. *(Beat.)* And he is famous / for his—

FULTON: He's famous for his fucking Western omelet. I know. He won't shut up about it.

DANA: So. Go get him.

FULTON: Go get him?

DANA: Yeah—why not? He obviously wants to be here.

FULTON: Go get him…you sure.

(She nods.)

FULTON: Okay…fine.

(FULTON opens the door. GORDON is standing right there.)

GORDON: Hello.

FULTON: Uhuh. Hello. *(Beat.)* Just don't burn the apartment down.

(FULTON motions him in.)

GORDON: You don't trust me?

FULTON: I trust you. *(Heads back to the bedroom.)*

GORDON: I'm famous for my omelet.

FULTON: *(Offstage.)* We know, Gord.

GORDON: *(Crosses to the kitchen area and makes a show of getting ready.)* Ham, cheese, and mushrooms. Is that good?

DANA: Sure.

GORDON: That's *the regular.* Fulton and I sometimes go to the diner on Saturdays. We walk in and he says *the regular* and then I say *the regular. Please.* And they know. It means ham, cheese, and mushrooms. *The regular. (Beat.)* You should always ask about allergies to certain foods before preparing a meal for a guest.

DANA: That seems sensible.

GORDON: I like to take care of people.

DANA: That's nice.

GORDON: Especially when they are in trouble.

DANA: What?

GORDON: Okay—Do you have allergies?

DANA: What? No.

GORDON: Rhonda was allergic to shellfish. That / was not good.

DANA: Oh…

GORDON: Would you mind if I put the radio on?

DANA: Knock yourself out.

GORDON: We don't get to listen to the radio at work. I am employed by the City of New York, as a library information technician.

DANA: Cool.

GORDON: No. It's not very cool.

DANA: Okay.

GORDON: No. Libraries are not cool.

DANA: I like them. I think they're pretty cool.

GORDON: *(Looks at her.)* You don't actually think that. You're just saying that to be nice.

(Beat.)

DANA: Okay. Fine. Yes. I was.

GORDON: That's okay. People are nice to me like that all the time.

DANA: Oh. *(Beat.)* That must be okay.

GORDON: No. I hate it.

DANA: Oh. Sorry. Well…it's better than people being mean to you all the—

GORDON: *(Looks in the fridge.)* Ahmm. There are no eggs. It is completely physically impossible to make *the regular* with no eggs. Out of the question. *(Beat.)* Fulton! There are no eggs!

FULTON: *(Offstage.)* What do I look like, a fucking chicken?

(There is a beat of silence. Nobody says anything. GORDON stares, lost in thought.)

DANA: It's okay. We could just have toast.

GORDON: *(Walks out.)* Goodbye.

(She looks after him. FULTON reenters.)

DANA: Wait—what? That—What's up with that? He just, like, took off. *(Laughs a little.)*

FULTON: Yeah. He does that. *(Beat.)* I know—I've got a strange little existence going here.

DANA: I like it.

FULTON: Well…stay as long as you want.

DANA: I have to get home. My mom's got…I need to be back by seven to relieve the nurse.

FULTON: Okay. I mean…there is a five o'clock train—you'd be home by six.

DANA: I don't want to put you out.

FULTON: Put me out? Please. We've got leftovers… *(Pulls out the Chinese food.)*

DANA: No. If I'm staying—I want an omelet. I liked the idea of an omelet. It's Sunday morning. Omelets. The *regular*.

FULTON: / Uhuh.

DANA: Golf shirts, mocha lattes, walking the dog in the park with your girlfriend.

FULTON: I'm lactose intolerant and I don't have a dog or a girlfriend. What are you talking about?

DANA: Isn't that what you people do?

FULTON: What do you mean *us* people?

DANA: I don't know…like normal people.

FULTON: Normal people.

DANA: Brunch people.

FULTON: I'm not brunch people. That's ridiculous.

DANA: / No?

FULTON: I don't even like brunch. I hate brunch. And brunch people. I'm so far—

DANA: Hey, maybe *Brunch-Man* could be a character in your next book. He has like this razor-sharp popped collar and he shoots deviled eggs out the tailpipe of his Audi. And he's got a gay teenage sidekick named *Quiche-Boy*—or

FULTON: Shut it. First of all, that doesn't even make sense. Second, if

it did, it would be the worst idea I've ever heard. Third, I am not *brunch people*—I'm, like, kung pow people. Clearly…much more *kung* and *pow* going on over here than, you know, *brunch*. *(Beat.)* I'm very well kung…

DANA: Okay. Right…

FULTON: Yeah…

(Beat.)

DANA: Do you mind if I take a shower?

FULTON: No. Not at all. Of course.

DANA: Okay. Can I borrow a towel?

FULTON: *(Smiles.)* Yeah. Sure.

(Beat.)

DANA: Okay…you want to show me where they are?

FULTON: Yeah… *(Really smiling.)*

DANA: What.

FULTON: You want company?

DANA: Finding the towel?

FULTON: No. Like, in the shower…

DANA: No.

FULTON: No?

DANA: No.

FULTON: Oh. Sorry. I thought you were…

DANA: No. I wasn't.

FULTON: Oops. My bad.

DANA: I'm—

FULTON: No. Never mind. Forget it. Forget I said anything. Towels are on the shelf in the bathroom. Right there. Left of the sink.

DANA: Thanks. *(Exits. She peeks her head back.)* Quiche-Boy...seriously, think about it.

FULTON: Yeah. I'll think about it.

(She leaves. He shakes his head and puts the Chinese food away. Lights fade.)

SCENE III

GORDON and FULTON sit on the couch. FULTON is sketching.

GORDON: So.

FULTON: Mmhmm...

GORDON: It is almost eight o'clock.

FULTON: Mmhmm...

GORDON: Perhaps my watch is fast.

FULTON: Maybe.

GORDON: She told you seven forty-five.

FULTON: Yes she did.

GORDON: I'm very nervous.

FULTON: What? Why?

GORDON: Maybe she was hit by a bus.

FULTON: She wasn't hit by a bus. Just calm down.

GORDON: I am not the only person who needs to calm down.

FULTON: Who? Me? *(Beat.)* I'm fine.

GORDON: That is a terrible drawing.

FULTON: It's rough.

GORDON: It's rough. And terrible. Your leg is shaking.

FULTON: *(Tosses the sketchbook.)* Yeah, well, I'm a little nervous. So what.

GORDON: This is your first date.

FULTON: Not really.

GORDON: Does last week count?

FULTON: I don't know.

GORDON: Maybe she isn't coming.

FULTON: So what? If she doesn't come, I'll call somebody else.

(The phone rings.)

FULTON: See? There she is. No bus. No accident. *(Picks it up.)* Hey. Come on up.

GORDON: She's coming up.

FULTON: I know.

GORDON: Did you put on clean underwear?

FULTON: What are you, my dad?

GORDON: No. Your dad lives in Los Angeles. You have never seen him or met him.

FULTON: Shut up.

GORDON: It would be funny if I were / your dad. *(Laughs.)*

FULTON: Just...Gord...focus. Remember...like five minutes. Just a quick hello and what we talked about—then make up an excuse, and beat it.

GORDON: Shh. She's coming.

(She enters.)

GORDON: Hi Dana.

FULTON: Hey...

DANA: Hey guys.

GORDON: I bought fresh eggs for Sunday. For *the regular.*

DANA: Great. Can't wait. *(Looks around, holding her bag.)* Um—where should I put this?

FULTON: I'll take it.

DANA: That's okay.

FULTON: No, come on…

DANA: I can carry my own shit.

FULTON: Okay. Then…why don't you put it in the back. By the bedroom? Or wherever.

DANA: Okay. *(She begins to exit.)* That shirt looks nice.

GORDON and FULTON: Thanks.

DANA: No, I meant Gordon.

FULTON: Oh.

GORDON: Thank you.

(She walks off toward the bedroom.)

GORDON: She is definitely nicer than Rhon—

FULTON: Shhh.

GORDON: Oh yes. Sorry. *(Beat.)* But she is.

FULTON: I know.

GORDON: And prettier.

FULTON: I know.

GORDON: You like her.

FULTON: Yeah—and I don't want to fuck this up. So, just be your regular self and help me out a bit here.

GORDON: I remember exactly what to say.

(She reenters.)

DANA: So…What's the big surprise?

FULTON: I can't tell you yet.

GORDON: It is very good.

DANA: Oh yeah?

GORDON: Yes. Almost as good as the other big surprise—which is the fact that Fulton sold the film rights to his book.

DANA: No shit. Really?

GORDON: Yes. For a large sum of money—well—I think it is a large sum of money, but Fulton says it's peanuts.

FULTON: It's not exactly peanuts, but it's not what other—

GORDON: It's more than fifty thousand dollars.

DANA: Wow—cool. Congratulations. That's great.

GORDON: They think Patrick Swayze, the *dirty dancer*, is going to play Puck.

FULTON: They don't know for sure, but he's interested.

DANA: Patrick Swayze…as the main character, the guy who can predict the future?

FULTON: Yeah—you read it?

DANA: Of course.

GORDON: Puck can *tune*. It's / called *tuning*.

FULTON: It's called *tuning* in the book.

DANA: I know. I read the first twenty pages before I fell asleep on the train.

FULTON: My book put you to sleep.

DANA: No. It's really good.

GORDON: I like it.

DANA: It's smart. And funny.

GORDON: Like Fulton.

DANA: What are you, his mother?

GORDON: No. I work at the library.

DANA: Right.

(Beat.)

GORDON: Well, I am glad that you were not hit by a bus.

DANA: What?

GORDON: Nothing. *(To DANA.)* You were several minutes late. Fulton was nervous.

FULTON: I was not. Dick.

GORDON: He was.

FULTON: Okay...well...Gordon...

GORDON: Oh yes. I have asparagus on the stove.

FULTON: *(Mimed.) Asparagus?*

DANA: Asparagus?

GORDON: Yes...asparagus—and it might be done. So I should go.

DANA: You left asparagus on the stove?

FULTON: *(Mimed, again.) Asparagus?*

GORDON: Perhaps not. In any case, I had better go home and find out. Good night.

DANA: 'Night.

FULTON: See ya. Thanks, Gord.

(Beat.)

DANA: So...um, you tell him to say all that?

FULTON: Me?

DANA: Yeah you.

FULTON: Never.

DANA: *Asparagus?*

FULTON: *(Shrugs.)* You want to change?

DANA: Do I need to change?

FULTON: Nope.

DANA: Okay...maybe I'll just wash my face and then we can take off.

FULTON: Huh...*take off*...

DANA: What?

FULTON: Nothing...

DANA: What?

FULTON: Let's just say that I hope you're not afraid of heights.

DANA: Yeah?

FULTON: Yeah.

DANA: I've already been up the Empire State Building.

FULTON: Oh please, this is so much cooler than that. The Empire State Building? Who do I look like, Tom Hanks?

DANA: Well...

FULTON: Careful... *(Gets a little closer.)*

DANA: Okay. So what are we doing?

FULTON: Hey...You'll just have to be patient. You'll just have to wait...

DANA: Just tell me.

FULTON: I'm not telling you. You need to wait.

DANA: I'm kind of impatient.

FULTON: Yeah?

DANA: Yeah.

FULTON: Well, let's just say that from where I'm taking you, you'll be able to *spit* on the Empire State Building.

DANA: Nice. I've kind of always wanted to do that…

(They get a little closer.)

FULTON: Somehow that doesn't surprise me.

DANA: No?

FULTON: No.

DANA: I'm predictable, huh?

FULTON: No. Not so much predictable…more unavoidable…and…hot… and…

(They're very close for a considerable beat.)

DANA: Are you going to kiss me, or are we going to stand here like idiots / (for the rest of the night.)

FULTON: I'm going to kiss you.

DANA: Okay. Hurry up. Fuck.

FULTON: It's okay?

DANA: I'm not sure. I'll let you know when we're finished.

(He leans in for the kiss. Lights fade.)

SCENE IV

The lights come up as DANA walks in, wearing FULTON's shirt, just waking up. GORDON sits on the couch.

GORDON: Good morning

DANA: Oh…Jesus…hey Gordon.

GORDON: Hello to you too, Dana.

DANA: What time is it?

GORDON: Eleven oh-nine.

DANA: Right. After eleven.

GORDON: *Well* after eleven.

DANA: Okay. *(Sits down.)* How are you?

GORDON: Fine, thank you for asking.

DANA: No problem.

GORDON: Did you sleep well?

DANA: Yeah. Fine.

GORDON: How was the helicopter ride?

DANA: It was…pretty fucking cool, actually.

(Long pause.)

GORDON: I've decided to start reading all of the writers with the initials C.B.

DANA: Uhuh.

GORDON: I've started with Charles Baudelaire. Next will be Charlotte Brontë.

DANA: Why?

GORDON: There are lots of books in the New York Public Library system, and without a premeditated objective, it can be quite overwhelming.

DANA: Sounds right.

GORDON: I'll finish with Charles Brockden Brown. That's C.B.B. I'm developing an affinity for initials. Don't you like initials?

DANA: Sure. I've never really thought about it, but I guess initials are pretty cool.

GORDON: Do you want some Raisin Bran?

DANA: Not just now, thanks.

GORDON: I am a member of the board of directors for the building. I am in charge of the laundry facilities and the yearly holiday party. I'm an excellent planner. My initials are G.H.C. For Gordon Henry Coburn. What are yours?

DANA: D.M.H.. Dana Michelle Henry.

GORDON: *Henry*...Those are nice initials. *(Beat.)* Yes. *(Beat.)* Do you know other initials?

DANA: What do you mean?

GORDON: Like—F.P.D., for Fulton Peter Ditmer or N.Y.C. for New York City. That one's easy.

DANA: Yep—knew that one.

GORDON: Or Y.M.C.A. for Young Men's Christian Association.

DANA: Huh.

GORDON: I go every Sunday to the YMCA to take my diving lessons. I used to go to church, but now I go to the pool. *(Beat.)* Today is Sunday.

DANA: Yes. It is.

GORDON: Yes. I go *every* Sunday, except in April when the pool is closed for cleaning.

DANA: You—um—what kind of dives do you do?

GORDON: Head first. *(Beat.)* And other kinds. *(Beat.)* I have green swimming trunks.

DANA: Right. Cool.

GORDON: I'm working very hard at diving normal. Normal dives. Because most of the time my body goes crooked and it makes a big splash.

DANA: Yeah—you want to keep the splash to a minimum.

GORDON: Yes. And I'm going today at two o'clock.

DANA: That must be fun. Do you have some—um—like—diving buddies?

GORDON: No.

DANA: Oh.

GORDON: Would you—because today is Sunday is why I mention it—and I have an appointment at two o'clock—would you like to come—maybe not today—but some time—on a Sunday—to the YMCA—to watch me dive?

DANA: Sure.

GORDON: Really?

DANA: Sure. Why not?

GORDON: Okay. *(Beat.)* Would you like to come today?

DANA: Today?

GORDON: Yes today. It is Sunday.

DANA: Right. *(Beat.)* Well...umm... hmm...I don't really have any plans. Fulton is supposed to—

GORDON: Fulton can come too.

DANA: No he's got his brainstorm meeting thing—

GORDON: Thrash session.

DANA: Right—the *thrash session*—so... hey...let's go. Sunday at the Y. Why fucking not...

GORDON: Y-*MCA*.

DANA: Yeah. YMCA.

GORDON: Great. I'll go get my swimming trunks. We can leave in one hour.

DANA: Okay.

(He gets up and exits. She looks at the door and then starts to giggle. Lights fade.)

SCENE V

FULTON enters with a manuscript in hand.

GORDON: Eight thirty-three. She's very late.

FULTON: I know, Gord. There's not much I can do about it. She's not picking up her cell.

GORDON: Okay. *(Beat.)* What are these? *(Picks up a brochure.)*

FULTON: Brochures. I picked them up.

GORDON: For Teachers' College. For Dana.

FULTON: Yeah.

GORDON: Hmm. *(Beat.)* What's this?

FULTON: It's the wedding invitation—for LA.

GORDON: Oh. *(Points to FULTON's lap.)* And that?

FULTON: It's a draft.

GORDON: A draft of what?

FULTON: A graphic novel.

GORDON: Whose graphic novel? *(Beat.)* Oh. Rhonda.

(Beat.)

FULTON: It's work. Okay? I'm editing it for her. If we're going to sit here and wait, I'm going to get some work done.

GORDON: Okay. *(Beat.)* She has a scar. On her forehead. In her hairline. It looks very bad.

FULTON: She was in a car accident.

GORDON: Oh. *(Beat.)* Is she okay?

FULTON: Yeah.

GORDON: Does it still hurt?

FULTON: I don't know. Probably not. It was a few years ago.

GORDON: She takes pills.

FULTON: Huh?

GORDON: I saw her.

FULTON: When?

GORDON: Last week at the pool. Not the first time she came, but last week, I did see her take pills.

FULTON: What kind of pills?

GORDON: White pills.

FULTON: What kind of *white pills?*

GORDON: Small white pills.

FULTON: Did you ask her about them?

GORDON: No.

FULTON: So, how do you even know they were *pills?* How do you know they weren't vitamins? Or aspirin? Or birth control?

GORDON: That is possible.

FULTON: Yeah, it's possible, so just give her some space, okay? Just because she came to watch you dive doesn't mean that you can start, you know, interfering in her life.

GORDON: I did not interfere.

FULTON: Okay. Good.

GORDON: Okay.

FULTON: So just drop it.

GORDON: Okay.

FULTON: Okay…

(The phone rings. FULTON picks it up.)

FULTON: Yeah. Come on up.

GORDON: Okay. It is Dana.

FULTON: Yeah.

GORDON: Okay…finally.

(DANA knocks and enters, wobbly.)

FULTON: Hey.

DANA: Sorry. I'm really sorry.

GORDON: Hello Dana.

DANA: I just…I'm late. I know. I'm sorry.

FULTON: Are you okay?

DANA: Yeah. Just—I'm sorry. *(She kisses him.)*

GORDON: Perhaps I should go.

FULTON: Yeah…thanks.

(GORDON leaves.)

DANA: Sorry… *(Collapses onto the couch.)*

FULTON: Are you okay?

DANA: Will you just come here please? I'm… *(Beat.)* Please…

(He sits next to her. She lies down in his lap and he strokes her head. Lights fade.)

SCENE VI

ALL THREE enter.

GORDON: So…thank you for coming.

FULTON: No problem.

GORDON: It is not very exciting, I know.

FULTON: Come on—

DANA: It's cool to see, you know, how you do things…where all the books go…

GORDON: The books go back on the shelf—it's not very exciting.

DANA: No, but the sheer number that come through there. It's a shitload of books.

GORDON: It is a lot.

FULTON: Your boss, though—what's her name?

GORDON: Rebecca.

FULTON: Yeah, Rebecca's a bit, um, stiff.

GORDON: She smells like mothballs.

FULTON: She kinda does.

GORDON: And she's a *squirrely bitch.*

FULTON: Um…?

GORDON: That's what Dana called her.

FULTON: Okay.

DANA: She is. She kept giving me this dirty look.

FULTON: Maybe because you kept asking her for books on kama sutra.

GORDON: No, she gives everyone that look.

(GORDON does the pirate eye. DANA does it back.)

DANA: Yeah—seriously—what's that about?

GORDON: I suspect she's incontinent. She changes her pants twice a day.

FULTON: Maybe she just needs glasses.

GORDON: Or diapers.

DANA: Or maybe she's just a squirrely bitch.

(Beat.)

GORDON: Yes, well, in any case I enjoyed giving you the tour.

FULTON: We enjoyed getting it.

GORDON: Saturdays are very busy. If you come back on a weekday, I can help you to get a library card and take out books. Seven is the limit.

FULTON: Cool…

GORDON: And especially if you are thinking about going back to school for teaching, Dana, you will need to borrow books. *(Beat.)* So, just let me know if you need any assistance.

DANA: Okay. *(Starts off.)*

GORDON: Where are you going?

DANA: Um…I have to use the bathroom.

GORDON: Oh. Okay.

DANA: Okay?

GORDON: Yes. Okay.

(She exits.)

FULTON: I haven't asked her. You think I should ask her?

GORDON: About Los Angeles?

FULTON: Yeah.

GORDON: I don't know.

FULTON: It's a little soon.

GORDON: Yes. And you were thinking of Rhonda as your date.

FULTON: No—I just needed a date—I don't really want to take Rhonda, okay? I want to take Dana; I just don't know how to bring it up…

GORDON: Do you want me to bring it up?

FULTON: I don't know…it's a lot to dump on her—a wedding and a family thing…

GORDON: Well…she seems to like you…a lot.

FULTON: Yeah…?

GORDON: Definitely. And she *does* enjoy my diving. She said so.

FULTON: Yeah. But, Gord, focus, Los Angeles.

GORDON: Travel can put considerable strain on a relationship.

FULTON: I know.

GORDON: I could get those books on kama sutra.

FULTON: No, I'm just—

(DANA reenters.)

GORDON: Yes, well, Los Angeles is really very nice. I'm sure you will enjoy it. Perhaps you should rent a *convertible*…

(Beat.)

DANA: You going to LA?

FULTON: / Yeah.

GORDON: Okay—I'm going to take a shower. The movie starts at eight, so we should leave here by seven fifteen.

FULTON: Okay…seven fifteen it is…

GORDON: See you in a bit… *(Exits.)*

DANA: What's up in LA?

FULTON: Nothing. I just have a wedding…and…yeah…a buddy from college.

DANA: Cool. When?

FULTON: Few weeks.

DANA: Cool.

FULTON: Yeah. Cool. *(Beat.)* I'm also meeting my dad for the first time.

DANA: Wow.

FULTON: Yeah…he's finally agreed to see me. In the airport.

DANA: Jees. You okay?

FULTON: Yeah. It'll be good. You know, get some things off my chest.

DANA: You sure?

FULTON: Yeah.

DANA: Huh. You okay?

FULTON: Yeah well, it's like suddenly I've got a lot of shit, you know? My dad finally writes me back, the book sells… and plus you, showing up all fucked up the other night—I'm trying to—

DANA: I wasn't fucked up.

FULTON: No?

DANA: No.

FULTON: What were you?

DANA: I was upset and tired…and I wanted to go to sleep…you know… *(Beat.)* …it's hard, what I do. It's not easy, and some days I just…I don't know, I shut down.

FULTON: Okay.

DANA: I didn't mean to complicate things.

FULTON: It's fine. I'm just—I've got a lot going on. Sorry. My head is…you know, this whole thing with my dad is just stressing me out. Never mind.

(Beat.)

DANA: Do you need me to come with you?

FULTON: To LA? To the wedding?

DANA: Well—to the wedding or to meet with your dad, whatever—I want to help, if there's anything I can do.

FULTON: Okay. Um—yeah…that's cool—It's the seventeenth. I leave the morning before…

DANA: Oh.

FULTON: What…

DANA: My mom's got surgery on the fifteenth.

FULTON: Okay. Big week. *(Beat.)* That's also my birthday.

DANA: The fifteenth?

FULTON: Yeah.

DANA: Shit. Shit. You should have told me—fuck—

FULTON: It's okay—forget it. Your mom needs you. Don't even think about it.

DANA: No, no. Shit. I'll get you a present.

FULTON: A *big* present.

DANA: Fuckin' supersize. *(Beat.)* That sucks…

FULTON: No—really—don't worry about it. *(Beat.)* Oh—speaking of presents…I almost forgot…I got you this.

(He grabs a train pass from somewhere... and then hands it over.) You can use it whenever. Just hand it to the conductor and...voilà... free ride to...me. It's good for a month.

DANA: Oh. A month. Is that the shelf-life on this whole thing?

FULTON: This is a *thing?*

(Beat. She's caught.)

FULTON: I think she said it was a *thing.*

DANA: Shut it.

FULTON: Is it a *thing?* I think it's a *thing.* She called it a *thing.* She did. I think we can go ahead and call it a *thing.*

DANA: Shut it. Maybe it's a thing. With a small *t.*

FULTON: Okay. I like small *t*'s.

DANA: Good.

FULTON: Yeah, good. So then you can be here every Friday, at eight p.m. Standing invitation. For a *small t* thing.

DANA: I'll be here at seven forty-five.

FULTON: I'll be here at seven forty-four.

DANA: Okay. Weirdo.

FULTON: Okay. Gimme a kiss.

DANA: Small *k* kiss?

FULTON: Small *k* kiss.

(They kiss—small k. Lights fade.)

SCENE VII

Sounds of shower. GORDON enters, a carbon monoxide detector and screwdriver in hand.

GORDON: Hello? Helllloooo? *(Beat.)* Fulton?

(He walks out and toward the bedroom. DANA screams from offstage. GORDON comes running back on.)

GORDON: Sorry! Sorry! I was—Sorry! *(Beat.)* I need to install the carbon monoxide detector. Sorry.

(DANA enters pulling on a shirt.)

GORDON: Sorry. I did *not* mean to see anything.

DANA: It's okay. I'm sure you've seen it before. / You just—you scared me.

GORDON: I am very sorry. *Thank you.* I am only here to install the carbon monoxide detector. I did not mean to intrude.

DANA: Okay.

GORDON: Every apartment is required to have one.

DANA: Okay.

GORDON: It's the law. I am only here because of the building codes.

DANA: Gord, you practically live here / it's cool.

GORDON: I need to be here to install it.

DANA: Okay...Gordon...it's okay. Calm down.

GORDON: Yes... Yes...Okay. Where should I install it?

DANA: *(Looks around.)* Ask Fulton—or—

GORDON: Nice flowers. Whose flowers are those?

DANA: Mine.

GORDON: Oh. *(Looks at them.)* Is there a toothbrush among them?

DANA: A what?

GORDON: A toothbrush.

DANA: Gordon—what the hell are you—

GORDON: A toothbrush.

DANA: I have no idea.

GORDON: *(Goes over to the flowers.)* Yes. Yes there is. An *Oral-B Advantage Control Grip.* Purple.

DANA: *(Follows.)* What the hell? *(Beat. She plucks it out.)*

GORDON: It is purple.

DANA: Yes it is.

GORDON: Like the bruise you had on your back. *(Beat.)* I did not mean to see it...

DANA: / Ughm...

GORDON:...Were you in a fight?

DANA: Sort of. Someone pushed me on the subway.

GORDON: Oh. That was many weeks ago.

DANA: Yeah. I...um... *(She holds up the toothbrush and nudges him.)*

DANA: What the hell is this all about?

GORDON: Well. It was in the flowers, pointing straight up. And the chances are *very* small that a toothbrush would land in a flower arrangement in just such a way. *(Beat.)* The evidence points to a premeditated act.

DANA: Uhuh.

GORDON: And, as Fulton is the one who gave you the flowers...

DANA: Uhuh.

GORDON: And as he did the same thing for Rhonda...

DANA: Uh...huh...Rhonda...

GORDON: Yes. I would suggest that he is our number one suspect.

DANA: Right. Huh. *(Beat.)* So—tell me about this Rhonda.

GORDON: Rhonda Sparelli. She is a graphic novelist...I have to install the carbon monoxide detector.

DANA: Wait a second—

GORDON: Every apartment is required to have one.

DANA: Okay, but—

GORDON: Hello Fulton!

(Nothing.)

GORDON: FULTON! I am installing your carbon monoxide detector!

FULTON: *(Offstage.)* Okay! Whatever!

(GORDON goes back in the hall somewhere. DANA pulls out salad fixings.)

GORDON: Perhaps here.

DANA: Isn't the super supposed to do that?

GORDON: *(Offstage.)* Well...I am the volunteer repairman for the building.

DANA: Oh. That's nice of you.

GORDON: *(Offstage.)* I am handy with my tools.

DANA: I'll bet you are.

GORDON: *(Offstage.)* Pardon?

DANA: Nothing. Nothing. Really. Nothing. Just, you know, blah blah blah...

GORDON: *(Approaches.)* Pardon?

DANA: No...really...just talking to myself.

GORDON: Oh. *(Beat.)* I do that, too.

DANA: Yeah. Crazy, huh?

GORDON: No. Just lonely.

(FULTON enters.)

FULTON: Hey, Gord. What's up?

GORDON: I am only here to install the carbon monoxide detector.

DANA: Just *dropped* in...

FULTON: Oh, okay—you know what, actually? Don't sweat it...I'll take care of it tomorrow morning. No worries.

GORDON: Okay. But I must come back to inspect it before you leave for Los Angeles. I have a list.

FULTON: No problem. We've got a couple of weeks.

GORDON: Yes. True. Nice flowers.

FULTON: Thanks. *(Looks at DANA.)* So...

GORDON: So...

DANA: Okay, so we're going to have some dinner, I think...

GORDON: What are you having?

FULTON: Salad.

GORDON: Salad. Are you a vegetarian, Dana?

DANA: No.

GORDON: Protein is important.

DANA: The salad has chicken in it.

GORDON: Oh. *(Beat.)* Bird flu.

FULTON: What?

GORDON: Regular citizens must be vigilant. I watch the pigeons in the park.

FULTON: For what?

GORDON: Signs of flu.

FULTON: Like puking?

GORDON: No.

DANA: Well, I'm going to cook the shit out of it, so I think we'll be okay.

GORDON: The supermarket is becoming a terribly risky place. Mad cow, fish-farm salmon, bird flu, salmonella, trichinosis, mercury tuna, *E. coli*—

DANA: We'll be okay. Hey—we're going to be okay.

GORDON: I am only trying to help.

FULTON: It's cool. But...ah... *(Takes a moment with him.)* We kind of planned to do the whole romantic thing tonight... table for two. We rented *Titanic*.

GORDON: Oh. Well—of course. Why didn't you say something? I...Titanic... *(To DANA.)* Well—the ravioli was excellent last night, Dana. I must say. Truly delicious. And I certainly don't need to eat here two nights in a row. That would be a little much. So, I'm going to leave you two to your chicken and salad...No spinach in there, I hope?

DANA: No spinach.

GORDON: Okay. That's good, then. *(Turns to go.)* Yes, and I have diving again this weekend. And if you enjoyed yourself previously, and you always say you do, you may certainly consider coming again this weekend.

DANA: I'll be there Gord. Two o'clock.

GORDON: Okay. Good. Right. *(Beat.)* Well, then, good night all.

FULTON: 'Night man.

DANA: 'Night Gordon.

GORDON: 'Night Dana. Brush your teeth. *(Exits.)*

FULTON: Seriously, sometimes I swear he's C-3PO's love child or something.

DANA: He's a sweet guy. And you should see him at the pool. Everyone loves him.

FULTON: Of course they do. Guy's got a heart of gold.

DANA: And he's kind of hot.

FULTON: What? Are you kidding me? Gordon?

DANA: Not like that…I mean, he's nice. He looks out for me. He's always making sure I'm paying attention when he does his dives and whatever.

FULTON: He's right next door…you know, if you're jonesing for his company.

DANA: I'm good right here.

FULTON: You sure about that?

DANA: Yeah. I got a brand-new toothbrush and everything.

FULTON: Oh, you finally noticed it.

DANA: Who's Rhonda?

FULTON: Ha. Nobody.

DANA: Nobody?

FULTON: No. Just a chick I used to date.

DANA: Used to?

FULTON: Yeah.

DANA: You sure?

FULTON: Yeah.

DANA: She go to the thrash sessions?

FULTON: Yeah…

DANA: Yeah?

FULTON: Yeah.

DANA: You give *her* a toothbrush?

FULTON: Sure.

DANA: Hmm.

FULTON: But it was a Duane Reade toothbrush. Totally ghetto. I mean, I don't know if you noticed, but I went all out on this little bad boy here… *(He shows her.)*…purple…with a bendy neck…and the bristles are soft…so…so…soft…it's like brushing your teeth with a baby's bum.

DANA: What's the story?

FULTON: Nothing. You just take the baby, turn him over, and open your mouth…no…there's no story…it's like an invitation.

DANA: To do what?

FULTON: I don't know—stay.

DANA: You want me to stay? Like stay stay?

FULTON: Yeah. Why…is that weird?

DANA: No. But…it's only weird if this is the seventeenth time you've pulled this cutesy-bullshit routine with the flowers and the toothbrush.

FULTON: This isn't about a toothbrush, Dane.

DANA: What's it about?

FULTON: You moving in.

DANA: I can't move in. In case you've forgotten, I have a mother in a fucking wheelchair in Brewster.

FULTON: I know. God, calm down.

DANA: No. It's just, I can't up and move because you give me a fucking toothbrush.

FULTON: Fine. Sorry. I'll take it back.

DANA: Fulton—it's, like, Jesus—I don't have a lot of options—I wake up, okay, every morning—without exception—and sponge down a pair of scrawny legs that don't fucking work—that's how I wake up. *(Beat.)* Okay…so leaving her is not an option. *(Beat.)* What?

FULTON: This isn't about your mother.

DANA: This is about my mother, okay—fuck you—you don't know what you're talking about.

FULTON: This isn't about your mother—it's about the secretive bullshit with the pills.

DANA: What secret / ive bullshit?

FULTON: The morphine, Dana, and whatever else you don't want me to see—I read the label okay? And it fucking pisses me off that for weeks and weeks I've been going out of my head here, falling in love with you, and all you've been doing is getting high and feeling sorry for yourself, behind my back.

DANA: You don't know / what it's like.

FULTON: You're right—I don't. I don't have a fucking clue what it's like to have an accident like that—but don't twist

this around—I'm not asking you to abandon your mother, okay? / I'm not.

DANA: No? / Because it sounds—

FULTON: No. You need to take care of her. I get it. I totally understand that. What I'm asking you to do—I, fuck, I just want you to wake up and recognize that what we have here—whatever this is—is more valuable than a handful of pills that put you to sleep and make you act like a goddamned child—okay?

DANA: I do / Okay—I recog—

FULTON: Because I feel like the most important thing to you right now is hiding from me—and hiding this drug shit from me—and that sucks—because I'm in love with you, okay.

DANA: I'm sorry. / I know.

FULTON: So, move in—don't move in—but don't go back home and pin this on your mother. It's the drugs and the bullshit that's keeping you from taking that toothbrush—not her.

DANA: I know. I'm sorry. I'm trying to stop. Okay. I am. I'm sorry I didn't tell you—I should have told you. But I'm stopping, so—please, Fulton. *(Beat.)* And I recognize what this is—I do—I just…I wanted to…fuck, I got scared or something—I don't know. *(Breaks down.)*

FULTON: I'm not going anywhere… you know…hey…look at me…okay?

(Beat.)

DANA: Okay. I'm…um…it was stupid…I'm sorry.

FULTON: No it's okay. *(Beat.)* Yeah… and um…sorry to spring the whole *love* thing on you…

DANA: No. It's good.

FULTON: Yeah. Sort of.

DANA: *(Gets up.)* 'Cause I feel the same way.

FULTON: Wait—what?

DANA: Whoa...I need to finish the salad.

FULTON: No—no—fuck the salad. Fuck the salad. You come back here.

DANA: No. I have—

(He catches her.)

FULTON: What did you say?

DANA: You heard me.

FULTON: No—no—I think I didn't. You'd better repeat it. Like right now.

(She whispers something in his ear.)

FULTON: I'm sorry. It's going to have to be louder.

DANA: *(Whispered.)* I love you.

FULTON: Say it. Say it again, loud.

DANA: You say it.

FULTON: I already did. I love you. Say it again—

DANA: I love you.

FULTON: I love you for—hoo...No shit...you love me...

(He kisses her.)

DANA: Yeah.

FULTON: ...holy shit!...hoo... *(Stands up on the couch and starts...)*

DANA: Oh no...what are you doing?

FULTON: *(...singing "Be With You," by Mr. Big.)* I'm the one who wants to...

DANA: Please stop...

FULTON: ... be with you...

DANA: Oh...my...god.

FULTON: Deep inside I hope you feel it, too...

DANA: Please stop.

FULTON: Feel it, too...

DANA: Stop singing—STOP SING-ING!

(They kiss. Lights fade to black.)

SCENE VIII

The lights come up on GORDON, sitting on the couch, tea in hand. A paper bag is at his feet. DANA enters.

GORDON: If you do not want to come today, you do not have to. You could take a rain check.

DANA: What?

GORDON: If you are too tired or if you have other plans with Fulton, you may take a rain check.

DANA: What? I want to. Okay? I want to come. I totally like it.

GORDON: You like it. Even if my dives are crooked.

DANA: I love your crooked dives.

GORDON: You have already come a lot. A lot, a lot. The most of anyone.

DANA: Well, see, there. I'm the record-holder. I'm like the number one freaking fan of Sunday morning diving at the Y.

GORDON: Afternoon.

DANA: Right—whatever. I'm the fuck-ing record-holder.

GORDON: You are the reigning champion. *(Drinks.)* This is good tea. Thank you.

DANA: Don't thank me—you brought it.

GORDON: I know. I brought good tea.

DANA: *(Sips, dissatisfied.)* Yeah. Umm... I need coffee.

GORDON: *(Pulls out a large coffee.)* Will this do?

DANA: What is that—is that coffee?

GORDON: True.

DANA: You're a nut—what did you do—get both?

GORDON: True. *(Pulls out four more cups.)* Caffe latte. Americano. Chai. Moccacino.

DANA: *(Laughs.)* Thanks, Gord. *(Kisses him on the cheek quickly.)* You're a doll.

GORDON: False.

DANA: What?

GORDON: I am not a doll.

DANA: I know—not really—it's a figure of speech.

GORDON: It's a manner of talking that dehumanizes the subject in question.

DANA: / Uhuh?

GORDON: With people who are different than ourselves, we must resist the temptation to dehumanize them. We must have tolerance. That's what Martin Luther King was trying to tell us. By us, I mean the white people. Black, Jewish, and Japanese people already knew about this kind of tolerance from

having been chained to trees, showered with gas, and bombed by nuclear bombs. Respectively.

DANA: Huh. I never...um...I never thought of it that way.

GORDON: It is a drastic oversimplification...but I am an original thinker.

DANA: Yes you are. *(Beat.)* I like it.

GORDON: Did I already tell you the story of when I fell off / the horse at—

DANA: Fell off the horse at camp—yes. But you can tell it again. I don't mind.

GORDON: Well...it is a sad story. My parents did not come to visit me. I was only ten.

DANA: I know.

GORDON: I don't like to repeat myself.

DANA: It's okay.

GORDON: Thank you. That's a nice thing to say. I feel it would be selfish to talk about horses when you are in a mood about Fulton.

DANA: In a—what are you talking about?

GORDON: There was a great deal of singing and shouting and shenanigans last night.

DANA: Oh...mmm...yeah. Sorry. We're...um...we were having a good time.

(Pause.)

GORDON: The story about the horse is not terribly exciting. And you already know the end.

DANA: Yeah. You spend a week in the infirmary. Your parents call once, but you're asleep. The nurse was named Dorothy, like in—

GORDON: *Wizard of Oz.* Yes. Are you going to get married?

DANA: I don't know.

GORDON: And babies?

DANA: Well…

GORDON: I used to go to church, but not anymore. Now I go diving. I am pro-choice, and pro-contraception, just so that you don't feel ill at ease.

DANA: Uhuh. *(Starts to laugh.)*

GORDON: I'm going to put you in my speed dial.

DANA: Good. Do that.

GORDON: Yes. I will. *(Beat.)* Not now. Later.

DANA: Okay. *(Beat.)* Hey Fulton— what's the deal? Gordon's here—we're waiting…

(FULTON enters, coming from the bedroom.)

FULTON: Hey—sorry. I was looking for my notes.

GORDON: I brought some tea. And other assorted beverages.

FULTON: Nice. Thanks. *(Picks one up.)* Okay…so, ideas?

GORDON: *(Stands.)* Well…He may be nervous. Therefore I think you should let him speak first.

FULTON: Okay.

GORDON: And you should be non-threatening in your body language.

FULTON: What's that mean?

GORDON: Maintain an open stance. Use appropriate eye contact, don't stare, and respect his personal space. That's important. Two to three feet is culturally appropriate.

FULTON: Okay.

GORDON: And I think you should be patient.

FULTON: / Cool.

DANA: Wait—I…um…I think you should at least ask him some questions— I mean, what about all that stuff your mom said? You should see if it's true.

FULTON: Yeah.

DANA: And all these notes and pages of stuff…I think it's great/ but I think—

FULTON: But you think I'm overdoing it.

GORDON: Preparation is important.

DANA: Yeah, but I mean, what's the point of being all worked up about it—you've made it this far without him—just show up and talk.

FULTON: Yeah. Okay…but I need to plan it out a little. I've written him like three hundred and sixty-eight letters asking to meet him—I'm going to look kind of stupid if I don't have something, you know, substantial to say.

DANA: Okay…yeah. But just, I mean, be cool about it.

GORDON: Yeah. Be cool about it. Cool and *nonthreatening.*

DANA: But don't wimp out…I mean— he wants to meet you in an *airport* for Christ's sake. He might be an asshole.

GORDON: Perhaps he's a pilot.

FULTON: Maybe he's an asshole *and* a pilot. *(Tosses the pad away with a smile.)* Okay—whatever. It's fine. Dane—you're right. I'll be cool. We'll just talk like two grown men and then I'll shake his hand and get on the plane.

DANA: Right.

FULTON: So what's up? You going to the Y this afternoon?

DANA: Yep.

GORDON: You could come too, Fulton.

FULTON: I've got my session, but maybe we could meet up after.

GORDON: We could meet you at Willie's.

FULTON: The burger joint?

GORDON: Yes. They have big baskets of fries.

FULTON: Okay.

GORDON: And while we are talking about meetings, I have another invitation that I would like to extend.

(Beat. GORDON waits for the go-ahead. They stare at him.)

DANA: What is it?

GORDON: Thank you. It is a classical music concert. One of my fellow employees at the library is playing the violin in a church concert next weekend. Saturday the eighteenth of May.

FULTON: Sounds good, Gord, but I'm going to be in LA.

GORDON: Of course. Sorry. I forgot. And Dana is going?

DANA: My mom's got another surgery on Wednesday, so I'm going to need to be at home for a few days.

GORDON: You will miss Fulton's birthday dinner.

DANA: I know.

GORDON: I see…but will you be available on Saturday night? Post-concert refreshments will be provided. Wine and cheese.

DANA: Um, yeah. Probably. I could take off in the late afternoon. *(To FULTON.)* Is that cool?

FULTON: Totally. Come in. Hang out. I'll be back Sunday morning.

DANA: We can do *brunch*.

FULTON: I'm not brunch people, okay?

DANA: Okay. *(Beat.)* Brunch-Man…

FULTON: Okay, shut up. Would a brunch person have a poster of eight different types of shit hanging over his toilet? Huh? Does that seem very *brunchy* to you?

DANA: Yeah. Actually, I've been meaning to talk to you about that poster.

FULTON: What's wrong with my poster…

DANA: I'm just saying…don't look at me if it mysteriously disappears while you're gone…

FULTON: I've had that poster since college.

GORDON: It is a gross poster.

FULTON: Hey—nobody asked you.

GORDON: You have poop on your wall.

(Beat.)

FULTON: Okay…maybe it should come down. You want to take it down?

GORDON: Yes.

DANA: Uhuh.

FULTON: Okay—fine. The poop comes down. We'll take the poster down…

(Lights fade.)

SCENE IX

Darkness. After a beat, GORDON enters, carrying DANA, who is in rough shape. He sets her down on the couch and then goes off. Sounds of toilet.

DANA: Uhn.

(He reenters and turns on a light. She is bleeding from the mouth a little.)

DANA: Fuckin' shit. *(Sits, waking up.)*

GORDON: Would you like some tea?

DANA: No. *(Beat.)* Yes.

(He goes to the stove.)

DANA: What the fuck is going on?

GORDON: You were sleeping on the stairs.

DANA: Oh.

(Beat.)

GORDON: There are several substances which are on the list of—well they are against the law and are therefore against building codes of conduct.

DANA: What?

GORDON: The pills. There are several substances—

DANA: Oh fuck Gordon—I don't need a lecture, okay? My head hurts.

GORDON: I am just informing—

DANA: Yeah well, shut up.

(Long beat. The water is put on the stove.)

DANA: Sorry.

GORDON: You are bleeding.

DANA: I know.

GORDON: And you have some—marks on your…Bruises.

DANA: I know.

GORDON: Are you okay?

DANA: No. No, I'm not.

GORDON: I can help you.

DANA: No you can't.

(Beat.)

GORDON: Perhaps if you just talked for—

DANA: There's nothing to talk about Gordon.

GORDON: Perhaps we could find the men who did this and—

DANA: Ha!

GORDON: I could go to the—

DANA: And what would you tell them, Gordon?

GORDON: I—I…

DANA: Where are my pills?

GORDON: I put them in the toilet.

DANA: What?

GORDON: I like to help people.

DANA: Oh—Gordon—fuck—this is *so* out of your league. Seriously. I appreciate the gesture, but this is beyond you—

GORDON: People just need company, Dana. It can be easier with someone who shares—

(DANA has picked up a card.)

DANA: Company? Fuck company— how is company going to fix this shit?

GORDON: What is that?

DANA: It's a birthday card with a Polaroid of Fulton's cock in Rhonda's mouth—how does company fix that? Huh? It can't, okay.

GORDON: I'm sorry you found that. *(Beat.)* I will make some tea and we can just talk. And then tomorrow we will go to the YMCA. *(Beat.)* Sundays are my favorite day of the week.

DANA: I fucking hate Sundays.

(Beat. He brings over a warm cloth and gently offers to clean her mouth—she pushes him away.)

GORDON: The concert was very good tonight.

(She realizes she has missed the date.)

GORDON: I waited for you until the very last minute.

DANA: Well, fuck me, I forgot.

GORDON: I had to sit at the back because all the seats were taken.

DANA: Well Gordon—that's just too bad.

GORDON: It was nice. I listened. And thought about you.

(She lets him wipe her mouth.)

GORDON: Just about you.

(Beat. He leans in and kisses her. Awkward moment. She stares straight ahead.)

GORDON: And the marks on your back? Where were you tonight?

(Long beat.)

DANA: Gordon. Look. I'm not a normal person. Okay?

GORDON: I am not a normal person either.

DANA: Yeah, but you're good. You've got a good heart—and you fit in with people. People like you.

GORDON: I eat my lunch by myself every day.

DANA: That's not what I mean—

GORDON: I eat my dinner alone in front of the television.

DANA: I'm not talking about being lonely—

GORDON: I have had sexual inter- course with eight prostitutes. It's my birthday present each year.

DANA: Oh.

GORDON: Where were you tonight?

DANA: I—Gordon—it's like…

GORDON: I love you Dana.

DANA: Don't say that.

GORDON: I do. I do love you. So I can say it.

DANA: Just don't.

GORDON: Where were you tonight?

DANA: Why?

GORDON: I want to know.

DANA: You want—what? Why?

GORDON: I am in love with you. When you love somebody, you want to know everything.

DANA: Don't say that.

(Long beat.)

GORDON: I will wait all night.

DANA: You don't want—

(He kisses her again.)

DANA: Oh fuck, Gordon…there's this guy—this, whatever—and he lives downtown and he ties me up and he puts his hands around my neck and he whips me and he fucks my ass—and that's not the half of it—but the point is, I like it and I can't stop thinking about it. I thought I could, but it turns out I can't, okay? Which…sucks. And I take pills—the hundred bucks you just flushed down the toilet—I take them because I don't feel—whatever—decent—normal. Okay. There. Now you know. That's the whole fucking story, okay? You satisfied? Now leave.

GORDON: Is he your boyfriend?

DANA: No. Fulton's my boyfriend. Or was. I don't know.

GORDON: Oh.

DANA: It's complicated—like an old boyfriend or an extra boyfriend.

GORDON: I could be your extra boyfriend.

DANA: No. Gordon, you do diving lessons and you work at the library, and you're sweet and—and fuck, I don't know—you're a good person.

GORDON: I am not sweet.

DANA: Yes you are.

GORDON: I go to prostitu—

DANA: So what? So what? Once a year! Who cares? *(Beat.)* Fuck.

GORDON: I'm sorry.

DANA: Oh fuck Gordon, shut up.

GORDON: Okay. We can just sit here together.

DANA: No we can't—okay? That's not going to work for me—you need to / leave

GORDON: Together we can—

DANA: There is no *together*. We're always by ourselves—we're always alone, and the sooner you fucking realize that, the better.

GORDON: I know.

DANA: You don't know. You have no fucking idea. Please leave.

GORDON: I do not think that would be a good idea.

DANA: I want to be alone. I just want to be alone.

GORDON: No. You are—

DANA: Please. Just go away.

GORDON: No.

DANA: Yes. Get the fuck out. I'm going home.

GORDON: No.

(He tries to clean her mouth again.)

GORDON: I can help you—

DANA: GORDON—FUCK OFF!

GORDON: NO!

DANA: FUCK OFF, YOU FUCKING RETARD—GET OUT!

(He grabs her throat. There is a long beat of silence. She looks at him.)

GORDON: Is this what he does?

(She nods.)

GORDON: You like it.

(She looks down.)

GORDON: Yes. *(Beat.)* You are the most beautiful woman. I think about you.

(He lets go.)

GORDON: Sorry.

(She grabs him.)

DANA: Put it back.

GORDON: No.

DANA: Do it again. Gordon—you want to.

(She kisses him, brings his hand to her throat. He grabs. Lights fade.)

SCENE X

Morning light. FULTON sits, a travel bag beside him. DANA's and GORDON's clothes are strewn about. After a beat GORDON enters, nervously, boxers on. He quietly picks up his things.

FULTON: Those are my boxers.

(Beat.)

FULTON: I said: those are my boxers.

GORDON: Yes.

FULTON: Take them off.

GORDON: No.

FULTON: I said, take them off.

GORDON: I do not have anything—

FULTON: THOSE ARE MY FUCKING CLOTHES! TAKE OFF MY FUCKING CLOTHES!

(GORDON hides himself and pulls off the boxers and then puts his own on. A door shuts offstage.)

FULTON: Gord, what the fuck is going on?

GORDON: I don't know. I am very confused.

FULTON: That's not going to cut it.

GORDON: I love Dana.

FULTON: Uhuh.

GORDON: And she loves—

FULTON: Okay. Sit down.

GORDON: But Fulton—I underst—

FULTON: Just sit the fuck down.

GORDON: I think I should go home.

FULTON: You fucked up really bad— just sit down.

GORDON: Okay.

FULTON: It's not okay. *(Beat.)* Dana. Dana. I know you're back there.

DANA: *(Offstage.)* I'm sorry.

FULTON: Come out here.

DANA: *(Offstage.)* Can we—

FULTON: Come out here.

GORDON: Perhaps—

FULTON: Perhaps nothing. Shut your mouth.

(*DANA appears in the doorway, wearing FULTON's shirt.*)

DANA: Yeah?

FULTON: Come in here.

DANA: Gordon—you should go home.

FULTON: No. He stays.

DANA: Can we talk alone—

FULTON: No. Gordon and I are sharing a lot these days…

DANA: Nothing / happened.

GORDON: Today is Sunday. I would be very moved / if you both came to the YMCA.

DANA: / Gordon…

FULTON: I don't really give a shit about the fucking YMCA! I want to know what the hell is going on here!

DANA: Please, Fulton…can we talk somewhere.

FULTON: No. We're talking here. Say what you have to say. Explain this. Please.

DANA: (*Points to the picture.*) What's that?

FULTON: Yeah. I wondered how that got out here. You go through my drawers?

DANA: I was looking for something—who cares—what is it?

FULTON: That's a picture.

DANA: Of you.

FULTON: Of me.

DANA: And Rhonda/

FULTON: Yeah. And Rhonda. In Buffalo. Eight months ago. And I have three more—just like it—you find those?

DANA: No.

FULTON: What's going to happen when you find them? Huh?

DANA: Nothing.

FULTON: Every time you get upset you're going to revenge-fuck one of my friends? That's really / fucked up!

DANA: I'm not / going to—

FULTON: No—don't! Because, you know, nine hours ago I was sitting across from this guy—my dad—thinking—this guy's got it all wrong. He made a stupid choice. He could have held onto something worthwhile. He could have built something with his life—something beyond a stack of dollar bills—but instead he pissed all the important things away.

DANA: I'm not—

FULTON: Shut up—see, he's lonely and sad and angry because he's got a fucking Rolex, but he hasn't got much of anything else. And so I came back from LA with big ideas—good ideas—about you and me and a family and vacations and all sorts of mundane beautiful stuff. (*Beat.*) But you know, maybe he's right—maybe a fancy watch is better than coming home to this. (*Picks up her underwear.*) I want you both to leave. And take all your shit with you—I don't /

DANA: Fulton—

FULTON: No—get out. I don't want these reminders that this fuckfest went on in my apartment—in my own *bed*, for Christ's sake.

GORDON: That is not what happened. Fulton.

FULTON: I don't really—

GORDON: Fulton! You should know that some intimacies transpired last night, but no sexual acts of any kind. I only took care of her.

FULTON: You took care of her? What the hell does that mean?

GORDON: She was very sick from the pills. She was very upset and falling asleep and… (Beat.) And I took off her clothes.

DANA: Gordon—

GORDON: No Dana. He should know the truth. Everyone needs to know the truth. (Beat.) I took off my clothes. And I took her into the bedroom. (Beat.) And we slept in the bed. I touched her. I did touch her. On the head. On her body in a gentle way. Her eyes were closed and she said your name…And then she fell asleep and I stopped. I did stop. (Beat.) I only went to sleep. Next to her.

DANA: Gord—

GORDON: And I am very sorry for everything. I wish I had not done the things that I did. I wish I had stayed in my apartment and watched television. (Beat.) I deserve to be punished.

(Beat.)

FULTON: Is that true?

GORDON: Yes.

FULTON: Dana?

(Beat.)

FULTON: Dana?

DANA: No.

GORDON: Yes.

DANA: No. Gordon, it's not.

FULTON: Holy shit—will somebody please tell me what the *fuck* is going on here!

DANA: We had sex.

FULTON: You had sex.

DANA: Yeah.

FULTON: You and him…

DANA: Yes.

GORDON: We made love.

DANA: We fucked.

FULTON: You fucked. So what's all this bullshit about the touching and taking care of people?

DANA: He was trying to protect me—Fulton / leave him alone.

FULTON: No, I want to hear it from him. Gordon? What's all this stuff about taking care of her?

GORDON: I…I am sorry. I lied.

FULTON: You lied? So you fucked my girlfriend and then lied to my face / about it.

DANA: Fulton / stop it!

GORDON: / Yes. But—

FULTON: You looked me right in the eye / and told me—

GORDON: / Sorry.

DANA: Fulton / it's not his—

FULTON: Get out.

GORDON: But I want—

FULTON: Get the fuck out! Take your shit and get out!

DANA: Fulton!

(GORDON gathers his things and leaves.)

GORDON: I'm / sorry. *(He's gone.)*

DANA: You've got the wrong person. You're yelling and screaming at the wrong person, Fulton. You want to yell at someone, yell at me! Huh? Here I am—let's / have it out—

FULTON: Stop—

DANA: No! You want to blame somebody, blame me—you know, because I'm the one who fucked this whole thing up—

FULTON: I want / you gone, too. *(Beat.)* Leave!

DANA: Gordon's not the only person I slept with last night, okay? Just so you know—I need to—shit—COME BACK HERE!

FULTON: I—I can't talk to you right now.

DANA: I'm sorry—I just need to tell you that I love you—okay?—I love you, but I made a mistake / and I want you—

FULTON: You're / fucking insane—

DANA: I want you to know—that I slept with—since—the night we met… the guy…I saw him a lot, before—and again last night—and Gordon—and I'm sorry.

FULTON: You're sick—I can't—You fucked two guys?

DANA: There—

FULTON: In one night?

DANA: Yeah—I'm sorry—it's what I do, okay? I—god—I got all messed up and

did something stupid and then I got all messed up again and I came back here and I—I grabbed Gordon and… I'm not…um…I'm not a good person, okay? *(Beat.)* I need help.

FULTON: I—I want you out.

DANA: Please—just let me explain.

(FULTON leaves. She goes to the door.)

DANA: Fulton! *(Beat.)* Fuck. Fuck. Fuck. *(Stops speaking, steels herself, and begins picking up her clothes.)*

(Lights fade.)

SCENE XI

Lights come up on FULTON, seated, drawing. There is a rustling by the door, then nothing, then more rustling. A knock.

GORDON: *(Offstage.)* Fulton?

(No answer.)

GORDON: *(Offstage.)* Fulton. I have left three of your compact discs and two of your books, including *The DaVinci Code* here. *(Beat.)* I know you are very angry and you do not want to see me, so I am returning your belongings.

(Beat. Knock.)

GORDON: *(Offstage.)* Please open the door. *(Beat.)* I want to make sure that you got my note of apology.

(Knock.)

GORDON: *(Offstage.)* I know you are angry about everything that happened and I know that you are upset with me and think that I am a bad friend—I am a bad friend—friends do not lie to each other. They do not…betray each other…and there are more things that we need to talk about. Because I…

(Knock.)

GORDON: *(Offstage.)* Please open the door. I know you can hear me. *(Beat.)* Ahm, I did not go to diving on Sunday. And I did not go to work today. Or yesterday. *(Beat.)* Nobody called to find out where I was. *(Beat.)* Which is to be expected because nobody ever used to call me, except you. *(Beat.)* And Greenpeace.

(Beat. Nothing. A rustling at the door and then a photograph slides under.)

GORDON: *(Offstage.)* I am sliding a photograph under the door. It is from Willie's. It is a good one. Of you, me, and Dana. And a big basket of fries. *(Beat.)* You are both very photogenic. *(Beat.)* I love Dana. That is true. *(Beat.)* But, Fulton, I also love you. *(Beat.)* Dana said…she told me that we are always all by ourselves…that nobody is ever…she said we are all alone, and I would very much like to believe that this is not true. *(Beat.)* I would like to believe that we are not alone.

(Long beat.)

GORDON: *(Offstage.)* Okay. I will leave your belongings here. Thank you for letting me use them. *(Beat.)* I will be in my apartment.

(Long beat. FULTON goes over to the door and picks up the picture. He looks at it.)

GORDON: *(Offstage.)* Ahm, when I said that I loved you, I did not mean that I love you in a homosexual way.

(FULTON laughs to himself.)

GORDON: *(Offstage.)* I just wanted to clarify that. *(Beat.)* More like a brother. Like the kind of love between friends and brothers and people who take care of each other. *(Beat.)* You know what I mean.

(Long beat.)

GORDON: *(Offstage.)* Okay. I bought fresh eggs and I am making *the regular*, in case you are hungry. *(Beat.)* I do not want to eat alone again today. *(Beat.)* Please come join me.

(Long beat. FULTON opens the door, picks up the stuff, and sets it down inside his apartment and then walks out. The lights come down as the music comes up. Blackout.)

'NAMI

Chad Beckim

CHAD BECKIM is a playwright, actor, and co-founder and co-artistic director of Partial Comfort Productions, a New York-based theatre company. He was born on July 21, 1973, and grew up in Monmouth, Maine. He has a BFA in theatre from Utica College of Syracuse University, where he studied with Scott Macdonald and Jerry Weiss. As an actor, he trained with Maggie Flanigan. Beckim's plays include ...*a matter of choice*, directed by John Gould Rubin (Partial Comfort Productions, 2005). His acting credits include the OBIE Award-winning *Benton Kozo*, directed by Jim Simpson (The Flea Theater, 1999), *Craft* by Sam Marks (Partial Comfort Productions, 2002), and *American Ma(u)l* (Reverie Productions, 2003) and *Booty Candy* (Partial Comfort Productions, 2003), both written and directed by Robert O'Hara. Beckim is also a teaching artist at both the New Victory Theater and Stella Adler Conservatory. He is currently working on a new play, *Lights Rise on Grace*, and a collection of short stories. Beckim lives on the Lower East Side of Manhattan.

'nami was first presented by Partial Comfort Productions (Chad Beckim and Molly Pearson, Co-Artistic Directors) on September 14, 2006, at the Kirk Theatre, New York City, with the following cast and credits:

Keesha..Quincy Tyler Bernstine
Donovan .... Michael Gladis
Lil .... Eva Kaminsky
Roachie .... Alfredo Narciso
Harry .... Marc Rosenthal

Directed by: John Gould Rubin
Set Design: Heather Wolensky
Costume Design: Lex Liang
Lighting Design: Jason Jeunnette
Sound Design: Zach Williamson
Casting: Judy Bowman
Fight Choreographer: Qui Nguyen
Stage Manager: Caitlin McAndrews
Assistant Stage Manager: Jamie Thoma
Assistant Director: Jamie Klassel
Production Manager: Zac Chandler
Graphic Design: Robin Hendrickson
Photographer: Ryan Jensen
Publicity: Spin Cycle LLC

www.partialcomfort.org

For Molly

na•mi 1. (nä-mE) n. (*abbrev.* Tsunami): a large destructive wave caused by an underwater earthquake or another movement of the Earth's surface: tidal wave **2.** ACRONYM: National Alliance for the Mentally Ill

THE NATURE OF 'NAMI

In January 2005, two weeks after the 2004 tsunami that ravaged much of the coastal land of the Indian Ocean, my partner and I were at a cocktail party when I told her of my latest idea: a woman suffering from hysterical pregnancy, so desperate to have a child that she fully believed she was pregnant with each intimate relation she shared with her husband. The image of this woman so haunted me that I'd been unable to get her out of my mind; she literally lurked in the darkness of my dreams. My partner paused, shrugged, then casually said "write it."

A week later a major weekly magazine published an article on the devastating affects of the tsunami. The article claimed that after disease and famine, child sex slavery was the number one epidemic in that area of the world. With no formal system of tracking (many of the ravaged areas lack the formal conventions we take for granted: social security numbers and/or fingerprinting), tsunami orphans were swept off the streets and sold in record numbers, fetching high prices for young, untouched children, who were then used accordingly and disposed of.

The following week a major human trafficking ring was busted in Corona, Queens (the location of our play). Dozens of women were held hostage in a residential home, forced into prostitution by their captors to pay off their "immigration fees." Neighbors were amazed that this had been going on in the areas where they lived and worked, where their children attended school. (One woman tearfully remarked "This is a family neighborhood!")

What struck me most about this story was that in a city of millions most of us know nothing about our neighbors, aside from perhaps holding the door to help them in the building or a voiceless "hello" in the hallways. Most of us have absolutely no idea what's going on in the apartments next to us, above us, or below us…and quite honestly, most of us prefer it that way.

I often think that Baby 'nami was not written so much as she was born; I often wonder whether she wrote herself, as I honestly do not recall much of the process of writing this play. I'm honored and flattered to have my little labor of love included in this fantastic collection, and wish to thank not only Martin Denton and the good folks at nytheatre.com, but my co-conspirators Molly Pearson, Robert O'Hara, John Gould Rubin, and the Partial Comfort Productions' family, without whom this baby would have had no life.

Chad Beckim
October 5, 2006

THE CHARACTERS

LIL: White, mid-/late thirties.
HARRY: White, mid-forties.
KEESHA: Black, mid-/late twenties.
ROACHIE: Black/Latino mid-/late twenties.
DONOVAN: White, early thirties.

PROLOGUE: CONCEPTION

Darkness. The sounds of lovemaking are heard as lights slowly rise to reveal the bedroom of a rent-controlled shoebox apartment in Corona, Queens. The surroundings are meager, consisting of little more than a bed, a dresser, a halogen floor lamp, some carefully arranged shoes, a wall mirror, perhaps some clothes piled neatly on a chair. The lights rise just enough to make out the silhouette of a COUPLE under the covers of their bed—their lovemaking is quiet, routine, tame—married lovemaking. It continues for several minutes and should be the only sound on the stage. Orgasm. Silence marred only by heavy breathing, perhaps a kiss, the shuffling of some covers. A WOMAN rises from the bed and covers herself with a thin robe, walks to the halogen lamp, and turns the dial to flood the room with dim light, then crosses to the full-length mirror mounted on the wall. She stares into the mirror for several moments, transfixed by her own image—pretty but tired-looking—almost haggard—and painfully thin. Her hand wanders to her lower stomach as she examines her profile from either side, then stands square in the mirror. She turns to the FORM in the bed, excited, glowing, maternal, then:

LIL: I'm pregnant.

(Long beat. The MAN in the bed remains motionless, eyes closed, head against the pillow. A weary sigh cuts into the silence of the bedroom. Another beat, then:)

HARRY: *(Eyes closed, defeated.)* No, honey. You're not.

(Darkness.)

ACT 1: GESTATION
Scene I

Morning. The living room. The sofa. HARRY lies on his stomach and LIL is perched on top of him, rubbing his back.

HARRY: Any thought about what you'd like to do tonight?

LIL: I'd like to go out. Somewhere nice.

HARRY: We can do that.

LIL: And I also know what I'd like.

HARRY: Oh, you do, do you?

LIL: Yes. I've been thinking about it. And it would be something we could both use.

HARRY: Something for both of us?

LIL: It's fifteen years, Harry. Most people are lucky if they stay together fifteen months. Can you believe it's been fifteen years?

HARRY: No, I can't. The best fifteen years of my life, honey. *(Kisses her hand.)* But it's your day—

LIL: Our day—

HARRY: Our day. But I don't really need anything.

LIL: Yes, you do. When you hear what I'm thinking of—for both of us—you'll want it. It's…delicious.

HARRY: Delicious?

LIL: *(Seductive.)* Delicious.

(LIL stops, massages HARRY's shoulders, whispers in his ear.)

LIL: I would like a dog.

HARRY: *(Laughs.)* You would, huh?

LIL: Yes, a dog. I would like a dog.

HARRY: You would like a dog.

LIL: Or two. I would really like two dogs.

HARRY: Two dogs, huh?

LIL: Yes. A big dog and a little dog. Actually, two is better—that way the little dog, Rufus—

HARRY: You've already named him?

LIL: Yes. Rufus might get lonely when we're not here—

HARRY: Where will we be?

LIL: Well, you'll be at work, of course.

HARRY: Ugh…speaking of work… *(Props himself up on his elbows.)*

LIL: No! Not yet.

(LIL pushes him flat down.)

LIL: You're not leaving yet. This is my time.

HARRY: *(Settles back in.)* Sorry. You're right. Where will you be?

LIL: Huh?

HARRY: You just said that—Rufus? Rufus will need company when we're not here.

LIL: Well, if I get a job—

HARRY: A job?

LIL: *(Matter of fact.)* I can't stay home forever, Harry.

HARRY: I know.

LIL: Well, when the time comes and I'm working again—because I need to work, you know? I could easily get cabin fever home by myself all the time. But when I get a job, Rufus will need company. And that's why we'll have Beasley.

HARRY: Beasley?

LIL: The big dog. Beasley. He'll provide Rufus with company during the lonely times and serve as a low-cost home security device. No one messes with big dogs, Harry. And this building isn't exactly safe. You wouldn't have to check up nearly as much if we had a big dog. And if we had two dogs? You'd never have to leave your shift again.

HARRY: We'll see, Lil.

LIL: You always say that.

HARRY: And I always mean it.

LIL: No you don't. "We'll see" is your way of saying "No."

HARRY: That's not fair.

LIL: It's true, isn't it?

HARRY: No, it isn't true. And it isn't fair.

LIL: Why not come out and just say "No" directly, Harry? Instead of "handling" me all the time. I'm a big girl. I can take hearing the word "No." And I don't need you to handle me all the time.

HARRY: How am I "handling" you?

LIL: You treat me like a child / every second.*

HARRY: I do not—

LIL: Working all the time. Keeping me trapped in this place. / Alone.

HARRY: This "place" is your home—you're not "trapped" here—this is your home—

LIL: May as well be. Not like I can go out. Surrounded by drug dealers and hookers and dirty people. Even if I wanted to go out—

HARRY: I resent that, Lil.

LIL: Not to mention that you won't even let me get a dog—

HARRY: Dogs are expensive, honey, and—

LIL: They're not that expensive, Harry. You act like I want poodles or something. I don't. I want regular dogs. *Two* regular dogs.

HARRY: My point is that I'm not so sure it's smart to take on any extra expenses, not when we still have such a long way to go towards paying off everything—

LIL: Everything? You mean hospital bills.

HARRY: *(Beat.)* When we move.

(LIL rises off of HARRY's back.)

HARRY: Where are you going? Come back, Lil.

LIL: *(Infantile; a child working toward a tantrum—pouting, foot stomping, the*

works.) When we move? When are we going to move, Harry? We've been talking about moving forever. And you don't even know when! When are we going to move? Can you give me a time line? A date? Can we put a big calendar on the wall so we can "X" out the days until we move? *(Beat; waiting.)* I didn't think so. Always the same thing. When we move! When we move!

HARRY: *(Rising from the bed.)* Lillian, please—

LIL: *(Mocking.)* "Lillian, please." You're not my father.

HARRY: No, I'm not. I'm your husband. Who loves you. Very much. But we cannot continue this conversation until you calm down—

LIL: I am calm!

HARRY: No, you're shouting. We cannot have a discussion until you calm down—

LIL: Stop handling me!

HARRY: I'm not handling you, Lil. Please, honey—we've been through this. We don't have the money right now. We're trying to save to move, right? We agreed—

LIL: You agreed.

HARRY: No, we agreed. We were almost there. And we had…a…we're starting over.

LIL: *(Beat; soft.)* What did we have, Harry?

HARRY: What—

LIL: What did we have? Why are we starting over?

HARRY: Lil, please, let's not let it get there—

---

*When one character starts speaking before the other has finished, the point of interruption is marked /, and the first character continues talking regardless.

LIL: We're not going to let anything get anywhere. I just want you to say it. What happened to—

HARRY: Lil? Please? Don't.

LIL: I want to hear you say it.

HARRY: I—Lil—I'm asking—

LIL: You can't say it. Six months and you can't even say it. But I have to live with it, right? Pretend like nothing happened?

HARRY: No. I don't know.

LIL: And the whole time, being alone, being trapped here—

HARRY: You're not trapped.

LIL: I haven't barely even left this apartment since then. Since that. *(Tearfully.)* I'm like…I'm like…Rapunzel. With short hair. Because you like it short. So I can't even let it down. So I'm worse than Rapunzel. I'm like Gretel. Without Hansel. Trapped in the gingerbread prison. With no friends. No dogs. No life. *(Beat.)* I feel trapped, Harry. When you're not here I'm all alone.

HARRY: I…I realize that. You don't think I realize that? This situation fucking sucks, Lil.

LIL: I have no one here, Harry. Nothing.

HARRY: You have me.

LIL: No family, no friends. Nothing, Harry. I don't go anywhere. I don't do anything. You never let me do anything! You never let me have anything!

HARRY: I have to go to work.

LIL: Of course you do. Anything to be away from your crazy wife, right? What does that say about me when you'd rather spend time with strangers than with your wife? So go ahead. Leave. Like always. *(Throws herself face down on the sofa.)*

HARRY: *(Quiet.)* I'm trying, Lillian. You know that. You have to know that. I'm working. Saving. I'm doing everything I can. I know this is hard. But I'm trying. And hopefully? Not much longer. But please, Lil. Please. I have to go to work now, honey. *(Turns to exit.)*

LIL: Harry? Wait! Come here. *(Runs toward the door, waving him back to her.)* I'm sorry, Harry. I didn't mean that—I don't want to ruin our day. I'm sorry, okay? Just hurry home tonight. Come home to me as soon as you can. *(Kisses him.)* Oh! And Happy Anniversary.

HARRY: Happy Anniversary, honey.

SCENE II

Next door. Late evening, the same day. KEESHA sleeps on a tattered sofa, fully clad in a McDonald's uniform. ROACHIE enters, holding a large Styrofoam cup. He sees KEESHA in the chair and attempts to pass through the room unnoticed.

KEESHA: *(Stirring.)* Hi baby. You juss gettin home?

ROACHIE: Yeah. My bad. I ain't mean ta wake you.

KEESHA: You dint. Iss late. *(Beat.)* Where you been?

ROACHIE: Tha roof.

KEESHA: Whachoo on tha roof for?

ROACHIE: I was juss lookin at tha moon.

KEESHA: You tol' me you was gonna be home a hour ago.

ROACHIE: I woulda been heah like on time, cept I couldn't stop lookin at tha moon. Yo, you shoulda seen it, baby. That shit was fuckin amazin! I was walkin towards tha buildin an juss looked up and, boom! It was so ill. I had ta go up ta tha roof ta look at it. It was like, like tha kinda moon you see in them movies bout California or tha Wild West? Juss fuckin, huge an orange an so, so bright! An I'm sittin there, all like, hypnotized an shit, juss starin at it. An I started thinkin of you—funniest shit, me lookin at tha moon an thinkin of you, knowin you prolly waitin for me in tha apartment, prolly heated at me—but I couldn't make myself leave. An then, like, boom, I remembered—tha only other time I evah seen tha moon look like that was tha night when we was at that club in Ozone? Member? Like, one of tha first times we evah went out-out, like on a date out? An that Dominican niggah came out his face at you, an I gave that niggah tha beat-down of his life for disrespectin you, an afterwards we was sittin on some park bench, lookin at tha moon an talkin? You member that night? How tha moon was? I was up there, on tha roof, lookin at tha moon an thinkin of you, thinkin how I should get you ta see it, an then, before I knew it, it like, went away or whutevah. Got all, normal an shit. I'm sorry you ain't see it, baby. That shit was hot. So thass where I been. *(Beat.)* Whah? Whah you lookin at me like that for?

KEESHA: I ain't lookin at you like nuthin.

ROACHIE: Oh. Anyways, go back ta sleep, baby. I ain't mean ta wake you.

KEESHA: You hungry?

ROACHIE: Nah, I'm cool.

KEESHA: *(Nods at the cup.)* You already ate?

ROACHIE: Naw. Juss sumthin ta drink.

KEESHA: Well, you still need ta eat. I shoulda been had dinner ready. I dint even realize I fell asleep. I sat down for a minnit an fell out. Long day. *(Beat.)* Where you been at? Besides tha roof?

ROACHIE: Out. With Caesar.

KEESHA: Doin what?

ROACHIE: Same shit. You know. Juss talkin an shit.

KEESHA: You take care of everythin today?

ROACHIE: Yeah. Everythin all done. Good ta go. Doan worry bout dinner, baby. I'm fine. Juss relax for lil while. *(Crosses toward the bedroom.)*

KEESHA: Richie? C'mere a second, baby.

ROACHIE: Hol' up. Gimme a minnit, baby.

KEESHA: I ain't seen you all day.

ROACHIE: One minnit, I be right back.

KEESHA: *(Soft.)* Richie? Come over heah, please?

ROACHIE: I gotta take a piss.

KEESHA: Look at me.

ROACHIE: C'mon, Keesh—

KEESHA: Look at me. Richie? Damn, baby. Can you at least talk ta me for a few seconds? You juss got heah, you already runnin off.

(He pauses; KEESHA studies him.)

KEESHA: Whachoo did today, baby?

ROACHIE: *(Shrugs.)* Chilled with Caesar.

KEESHA: You tired, huh?

ROACHIE: What?

KEESHA: Your eyes are all red.

ROACHIE: Long day, baby. Yo, I gotta take a piss, else Ima burst. *(Crosses to exit.)*

KEESHA: You smoke today?

ROACHIE: A coupla Newports.

KEESHA: Thass it?

ROACHIE: Yeah.

KEESHA: Hey, lemme get a sip of your drink? My mouth is dry.

ROACHIE: It's almost dead.

KEESHA: I just need a sip.

ROACHIE: It's all watery an shit. I'm bout ta throw it out.

KEESHA: That a milkshake, Richie?

ROACHIE: What?

KEESHA: There. In your hand. Tha white cup? Is. That. A. Milkshake?

ROACHIE: Yeah. I mean, it was, yeah.

KEESHA: *(Beat.)* You smoke today, Richie? With Caesar?

ROACHIE: Why you automatically assume I smoked juss cause I got a milkshake?

KEESHA: I'm not assumin anythin. I'm axin you a question.

ROACHIE: Naw, you tryin ta draw conclusions about me, thinkin you all detective like or sumthin, like you, fuckin, Jerry Orbach in this muhfuckah.

KEESHA: I'm not drawin anything, Richie.

ROACHIE: You interrogatin me like I'm a suspect or some shit, an I doan preciate it.

KEESHA: I doan appreciate bein lied to. So Ima axe again. Did you smoke today, Richie?

ROACHIE: Why you all up in my shit, Keesha?

KEESHA: I'm in your shit because usually, when your eyes are all red like that, iss cause you smoked. Usually, when you hang out with Caesar, you smoke. An' when you drinkin a milkshake after you hung out with Caesar, it means you smoked cheap rock an your throat is all irritated an dried out.

ROACHIE: *(Beat, sighs.)* Yeah, we split a lil sumpin-sumpin. Nothin heavy, baby. Yo, I'm sorry I lied ta you. I fucked up. I know I shouldn'ta done it, but I did. I hate lettin you down, baby. I'm sorry. F'real. *(Beat.)* I gotta take a piss now, Keesha, else Ima burst.

(ROACHIE exits, closing the bathroom door behind him. Eyeing the door, KEESHA reaches her hand between the cushions of the sofa, finds what she's looking for, and withdraws her hand. After a moment she sits up, sighs, stretches, and moves to the bathroom door.)

KEESHA: *(Through door.)* I ran into Nora today. She came in ta get some Happy Meals for those three fat-ass fuckin kids—all them damn kids over three hundred pounds an her lazy ass still force feedin em Happy Meals. Anyways, Nora said she seen you an Caesar over on Crescent today.

ROACHIE: *(Offstage, over the sound of running water.)* Yeah, we were over there earlier. Caesar had some shit he had ta take care of.

KEESHA: Yeah, she said she seen you—bof a you. But she dint think you seen her. She said Big Moe was there, too.

ROACHIE: *(Offstage.)* Course he was. He live over there.

KEESHA: She said she seen you an a bunch of fellas playin dice over there.

ROACHIE: *(Offstage.)* Nora talk too much.

KEESHA: She damn sure does. Talk outta bof sides a her mouf. Oh well. I tol' her ta min' her bizness, anyways. *(Beat.)* I saw Donovan when I was comin up.

ROACHIE: *(Offstage.)* Oh yeah?

KEESHA: Yeah. Downstairs. In tha hallway. He axed if I seen you, but I tol' him I hadn't.

ROACHIE: *(Offstage.)* Oh yeah?

KEESHA: Yeah. Funny, cause I tol' him I was juss bout ta axe him tha same thing.

(Silence. The water stops.)

ROACHIE: *(Offstage.)* Why you gonna do that? I tol' you I would handle it.

KEESHA: You right, you did tell me that. So you did see him today, then?

ROACHIE: Well, naw, I dint see him, see him.

KEESHA: Oh. I musta got confused or sumthin. So what, you juss slid tha envelope under his door?

ROACHIE: …Yeah.

KEESHA: What time did you do that? I'm juss axin cause Donovan, he must

not a been home ta find it or nothin, cause after axin me bout you, he axed me bout tha rent. So what I'm thinkin is that you musta juss missed each other, right?

(Silence.)

KEESHA: Richie? Am I right?

ROACHIE: *(Entering.)* Whachoo gettin at, Keesha?

KEESHA: I ain't gettin at nothin. Juss tryin ta make sense a everythin.

ROACHIE: Cause if I dint know better, I might think you accusin me of sumthin.

KEESHA: Why would you think that, baby? What I gotta accuse you of, Richie? You tol' me you slid tha money under Donovan's door, I'm inclined ta believe you, right? Cause you wouldn't lie bout nothin like that. Right baby? My husband would not look in my face an lie bout that, would he? My husband would do tha one thing I axed him ta do early this mornin before I bust my ass workin a double, servin Mayor Mc-Cheese specials an Super Sizes ta these ghetto mothafuckahs around heah. An my husband would certainly not embarrass me by pissing away our rent money—*my* rent money—on dice games an dime bags of rock, then lie in my face bout it! My husband would not do that, would he?!?

ROACHIE: Careful, Keesha.

KEESHA: No. You be careful, you grimy, lyin mothafuckah! How dare you!

(KEESHA launches herself at ROACHIE, clawing and slapping at him. He takes the hits for several seconds, then grabs her by the wrists and pushes her backwards. KEESHA

rushes to the sofa and reaches between the cushions, but before she can grab what she's looking for, ROACHIE pins her down, pushing his knee into her neck. He reaches between the cushions, withdraws a hammer and holds it in KEESHA's face.)

ROACHIE: You reachin for this? You gonna hit me wit a hammer? Damn, baby, you fierce! *(Tosses the hammer across the room.)* I can't believe my baby was bout ta hit me wit a hammer! You like hittin things, Keesha? You like hittin things? *(Puts his clenched fist to her face.)* Why you do this ta yourself, woman? Huh? You bring this shit on ya'self, practicly forcin me ta do this ta you! All up in my grill from tha minnit I come up in heah, barkin an naggin at me like Ima fuckin child or sumthin.

(Keys in the door. DONOVAN enters.)

ROACHIE: Why you gotta get all up in my face like that? You throw gas on tha fire, you know you gonna feel tha heat!

DONOVAN: That's enough, Roachie! Let her up. I need her to do something for me.

(ROACHIE climbs off KEESHA and backs away. KEESHA lies motionless on the sofa.)

DONOVAN: *(Holds out a twenty.)* Go to the corner for me. I need a bottle of red wine. Something nice. And take your time. Me and your hubby need to talk.

(KEESHA walks to DONOVAN, takes the bill from his hands, and exits.)

DONOVAN: Trouble in paradise? I'm glad I came up when I did.

ROACHIE: Damn, man! She love ta test me, man! Love ta get on my lass nerve!

DONOVAN: She seemed upset earlier when I saw her in the hall. Why was she so upset, Roachie? Any idea?

ROACHIE: I dunno.

DONOVAN: You have something to tell me?

ROACHIE: No.

DONOVAN: Nothing? At all?

ROACHIE: *(Beat.)* Why you gonna make me say it?

DONOVAN: You want to play Mr. and Mrs. Homemaker, I'm going to treat you as such. That means that each month, the rent is due, just like all the other happy families in the building. Does that not make sense?

ROACHIE: I'll get it, Donovan—

DONOVAN: Don't. Do not do that to me or to yourself.

ROACHIE: F'real, Donovan—

DONOVAN: Shut up. Shut the fuck up. So help me God, Roachie, do not test my patience again. *(Beat.)* I've trusted you. Befriended you. Given you a place to lay your dirty fucking head. Given you a job. Given you your wife—

ROACHIE: You ain't give me my wife.

DONOVAN: No? I didn't? Correct me if I'm wrong, but I believe your wife was mine before she was yours, no? She was quite an earner, that one, and I only granted her her freedom when you came to me, blathering, stuttering, snot-nosed and crying, begging me to release her to you. Which I did. Without hesitation. And since then, I've upheld my end of the deal, have I not? So it's disappointing, Roachie, that we're having this discussion because I've been quite proud of you as of late. You've handled your business like a pro. Earned my trust, almost earned some respect. But today…

ROACHIE: I'll get you tha money.

DONOVAN: Do not insult me again.

ROACHIE: What I said? I doan know—

DONOVAN: What happened today, Roachie?

ROACHIE: Tha truth? Me an Caesar was rollin dice…an I was hot, man…I was so fuckin hot! An then, next thing I knew, I…was not so hot. What Ima say? I fucked up. I'll get it back.

DONOVAN: Is that it?

ROACHIE: Yeah. Mostly.

DONOVAN: What else?

ROACHIE: Um, well, afta that, I was so heated I went out an bought a ten-pack and, you know…

DONOVAN: That's it? Nothing else happened today, Roachie? Let me re-phrase that. It actually sounds like a very eventful day—it seems a lot happened for you today. *(Beat.)* What happened to Linda, Roachie?

ROACHIE: Linda?

DONOVAN: Yes, Linda. Who is now laid up for the next few weeks nursing a split lip and some cracked ribs. What happened to her?

ROACHIE: She—

DONOVAN: Hold on. Come here, Roachie.

ROACHIE: I am heah.

DONOVAN: No. Over here. I want to look into those baby browns while we discuss this. Come here.

ROACHIE: Yo, D—

DONOVAN: I won't ask again. Come over here.

(ROACHIE moves to DONOVAN.)

DONOVAN: Closer.

(ROACHIE moves closer.)

DONOVAN: Kneel down, now.

(ROACHIE kneels.)

DONOVAN: Good. *(Quiet, calm.)* What happened to Linda, Roachie? And before you answer, I want you to take a moment and consider your words care-fully. Agreed? Good. What happened to Linda?

ROACHIE: Afta…I smoked…I went out an tried ta handle some bizness for you, you know? And, damn, Donovan, Linda, this bitch tried ta come out her face on me. Screamt on me, tried ta hold out on collection, all that. I can't have that—

(DONOVAN lands a vicious kick to the side of ROACHIE's face. ROACHIE falls to the ground in the fetal position, holding his head. DONOVAN rises and punctuates each sentence with a kick to ROACHIE's back and side.)

DONOVAN: Wrong answer.

(Kick.)

DONOVAN: How many times must I tell you?

(Kick.)

DONOVAN: Do. Not. Hit. My. Girls.

(Kick.)

DONOVAN: Ever.

(Kick.)

DONOVAN: Your job is to protect them. To collect from them when I can't, to offer them some modicum of comfort and safety, to look after them.

(Kick.)

DONOVAN: That's all. Look at me.

(No response.).

DONOVAN: Now, Roachie. Look at me.

(ROACHIE does.)

DONOVAN: Don't touch my girls again, Roachie.

(DONOVAN releases ROACHIE, who lies motionless on the floor. Beat.)

DONOVAN: You owe me now, you know.

ROACHIE: I know.

DONOVAN: I don't think you do. You realize you have to make up for Linda's absence. You do realize that, don't you? *(Turns to the bedroom.)* Now that I think about it, this isn't going to be so bad after all.

ROACHIE: No?

DONOVAN: No. There's actually an easy solution to this. The little lady should be back any moment, right Roachie?

ROACHIE: *(Scrambles up to his feet.)* Naw! C'mon, D! You can't do that!

DONOVAN: I what?

ROACHIE: I mean—please, D. I'll get it. I'll make it all up. Everythin.

DONOVAN: You already owe me the money you pissed away earlier today. Where are you going to come up with all of this—on top of that? I can't have you selling anymore—you smoke all the product. My girls won't trust you any longer—I can't trust you any longer—not after today—

ROACHIE: Course you can, Donovan! It was a mistake—a simple mistake— ain't gonna happen again. You can truss me. There must be sumthin. You always got sumthin, right? I'll do whatevah. Anythin.

(DONOVAN reaches into his jacket pocket, pulls out a bag of crack, and tosses it at ROACHIE's feet.)

DONOVAN: I'm sure we'll think of something.

SCENE III

HARRY and LIL's apartment. Early a.m, the next day. LIL is seated on the floor, heavily made up and in her wedding dress, ear pressed against the door, occasionally peering through the peephole.

HARRY: *(Offstage.)* Lil? Honey? Where are you?

(Beat; HARRY enters.)

HARRY: Lil, what are you—

LIL: I'm not talking to you right now.

HARRY: How long have you been back out here?

LIL: Long enough. We're not talking right now. We're not friends.

HARRY: Lil—

LIL: I'm mad at you.

HARRY: You're what? Why?

LIL: Why didn't you wake me?

HARRY: What?

LIL: When you came home. Why didn't you wake me? It's our anniversary, Harry. Why didn't you wake me?

HARRY: It was late.

LIL: You didn't even try?

HARRY: I…no, I didn't. It was late.

LIL: I wanted to surprise you. I fell asleep out here waiting for you, and you just carried me to bed and didn't even wake me up. You don't even care.

HARRY: Hey—that's not true. Baby…I came home, it was late, I was…embarrassed that I was so late. Of all nights. Got stuck with two late airport fares. I came home and you were sleeping on the floor. In your wedding dress. So I carried you to the bedroom to sleep. I'm sorry, Lil. I'm so sorry. You're right. I should have woken you up. *(Beat; remembers.)* Oh! Did you see what I brought you? *(Goes to table, grabs bouquet of cheap bodega flowers.)* See? *(Mock disgust.)* I don't even care. How could I not care? I was just…late.

LIL: They're pretty. Thank you. *(Appraises him, then:)* I had something for you…but I'm not sure you deserve it.

HARRY: I don't deserve it?

LIL: Maybe. Maybe not.

(She leans over and kisses his cheek, then fumbles in the bosom of her dress and withdraws a folded piece of paper, which she hands to him.)

LIL: Here.

HARRY: What is this? A love note?

LIL: Maybe.

HARRY: *(Reads.)* Are these…?

LIL: I rewrote my vows for you. I was going to surprise you in my dress and read them to you when you came home. Only, you didn't wake me up.

HARRY: This is really wonderful. I can't believe this—I love this, Lil. And you. Tomorrow, okay? We'll make up for it tomorrow?

LIL: We don't have to. It's okay.

HARRY: No, we'll make up for it. Tomorrow. *(Studies her.)* The dress looks great, Lil.

LIL: You think? It's a little loose.

HARRY: Not too many women can say that on their fifteenth anniversary. You look fantastic, my love. Tomorrow night. I promise. I'll work a regular shift and be out early. I know I was supposed to do that tonight, but…Okay? I mean, it's not exactly the same, but—

LIL: It's really okay, Harry. I'm not mad anymore. And I have something else to tell you. *(Long beat.)* Promise you won't be mad.

HARRY: What is it?

LIL: Promise!

HARRY: I promise.

LIL: *(Nervous.)* I called my mom today.

HARRY: *(Beat.)* You…what?

LIL: You can't be mad!

HARRY: What the fuck did you do that for?

LIL: Don't be mad—you can't be mad. I had to. I had to call her and tell her that they—she—was wrong. Fifteen years, Harry.

HARRY: You shouldn't have called her—

LIL: I had to. I had to tell her they were wrong. She was wrong. Everything she said…she was wrong. So I told her.

HARRY: When?

LIL: Earlier. I was writing my vows and I got so angry at her. She was so awful, Harry. And she was wrong. So I told her.

HARRY: I wish you wouldn't have.

LIL: Well I did. So there. *(Remembers.)* Oh! I have something else, too!

HARRY: You've been busy today, huh?

(LIL goes to the sofa, reaches under it, and withdraws a bottle of cheap wine and two coffee mugs.)

HARRY: Whoa! Where did this come from?

LIL: Donovan. And Keesha.

HARRY: Who is Keesha?

LIL: Keesha is our next-door neighbor.

HARRY:…?

LIL: The black lady? The loud people?

HARRY: Okay…wait—our landlord bought you a bottle of wine?

LIL: Yes. When he came over for the rent—

HARRY: Shit.

LIL: No, it's okay! I took care of everything. See, he came over for the rent and I told him you were at work, then told him it was our anniversary and

asked him to help me, because I know that you don't like when I leave the building. He's such a nice man. Serious, but very nice. Oh—and this is the best part—when I tried to give money, he wouldn't take it!

HARRY: Wait—how did you—where did you get money?

LIL: *(Matter of fact.)* I have money, Harry. I roll all of our pennies. And I tried to give it to him but he wouldn't take it.

HARRY: I'll pay him back tomorrow.

LIL: No you won't! It's a gift. He insisted. And then Keesha knocked on the door and gave it to me and said "Compliments of Donovan." I asked her to come in, but she said she couldn't.

HARRY: Lil, you have to be careful—

LIL: She's our neighbor, Harry. She was doing us a favor.

HARRY: I know. Sorry. I'm just…over-protective. *(Beat, he motions to the wine.)* Shall we?

(LIL unscrews the bottle of wine, holding it out for HARRY to read the label. Upon his nod of approval, she pours him a small amount, which he sips into his mouth à la a professional wine taster. After a moment, he gulps it down and gives her the go-ahead to finish the pour.)

LIL: A toast.

HARRY: A toast.

LIL: To fifteen years with my husband.

HARRY: To the love of my life.

(Silence. They drink. LIL stops, cocking her head as if listening to something.)

LIL: *(Intense; whispers.)* Do you hear that?

(She sets her glass down and presses her ear against the door. Silence.)

LIL: Do you hear it?

HARRY: *(Listens. Whispers.)* What are we supposed to be hearing?

LIL: Shhhh! *(Beat.)* That! Right there. Do you hear it?

HARRY: I don't, honey.

LIL: You have to listen over here! *(Presses her ear to the door.)* Like this.

HARRY: Lil—

LIL: Shhhhh! You won't hear if you're talking—

HARRY: It's late, honey, I'm tired.

LIL: *(Desperate.)* Please, Harry. Do you hear that? I need for you to listen and tell me if you can hear that or not. Please.

(HARRY relents, listens. Silence, then:)

HARRY: Someone's crying. Is that it? Someone's crying?

LIL: It's a little girl. All night long I've been hearing that. A little girl, crying.

HARRY: How do you know it's a little girl?

LIL: *(Shrugs.)* I just do. *(Beat.)* I'm glad you hear it, Harry. It started earlier tonight, while I was writing my vows.

HARRY: You've been listening out here all night?

LIL: Not all night. I fell asleep for a little while. And it stopped a couple of times. But while I was waiting for you I was listening to that. To her. I wish I knew where it was coming from.

HARRY: Somewhere on the floor, maybe.

LIL: There are no children on this floor, Harry.

HARRY: Maybe someone's babysitting.

LIL: But if someone is babysitting, why are they just letting her cry like that? She just keeps crying. All night. Why isn't anyone helping her? Children don't cry for no reason, right?

HARRY: Sometimes they do. Maybe she's visiting and in a strange place and she's scared. She's probably scared. Little kids cry when they're scared. *(Beat.)* We have to go to bed, Lil. Okay, honey? It's time for bed.

LIL: What if something's wrong? What if she's hungry? What if she's locked in a dark room all alone and no one is there to hear her cries?

HARRY: I'm sure she's not alone, Lil.

LIL: *(Listens. Quiet.)* You wanna know something? Something silly? *(Beat.)* It scared me. You don't know how scared I was.

HARRY: Scared you?

LIL: Well, not at first. At first—never mind.

HARRY: At first, what? Talk to me.

LIL: At first I liked it.

HARRY: You liked the crying?

LIL: Let's stop. I don't want you to be upset. It might make you upset.

HARRY: No, baby. It's okay. You can tell me.

LIL: I liked it because I pretended that it was coming from the bedroom.

HARRY: The bedroom?

LIL: Natalie.

HARRY: Natal—? Oh, Jesus, Lil. What are you doing?

LIL: Remember? "Nate" if it was a boy? But it was going to be a girl. Definitely. Natalie. But then it scared me. I was out here so long that I started to wonder if I was really hearing it, or if I wanted to hear it so badly that I made myself hear it. And I got scared.

HARRY: *(Gentle.)* This has to—we have to stop this. Now. This isn't… right. We have to go to bed. Now. Lil?

LIL: *(Ignoring him; a fugue.)* When I was sitting here, listening, pretending that I was laying in bed and she was in the other room, I missed her. *(Her hand drifts to her lower stomach.)* This wave of something washed over me. It was like, a wave of missing her. Remembering her in my stomach. Growing. Wondering what she would have looked like. Sounded like. How smart she would have been. Wondering if that's how she would have sounded when she cried. But I think she would have been a happy girl, mostly. Right? I would have been a good mother, I think. No, I know. And you would have been a great dad, Harry. *(Beat, she smiles.)* It's good to talk about these things.

(HARRY is silent; then:)

HARRY: I have to get out of here.

LIL: *(Startled out of it.)* What?

HARRY: I have to leave. Now.

LIL: What? Wait! Why? Harry, we were just talking—

HARRY: Don't "Harry" me, Lil! What the fuck? How am I supposed to react to this?

LIL: I'm sorry, Harry. I'll stop. I didn't mean—

HARRY: I come home on my fifteenth anniversary to find my wife asleep on the floor in her wedding dress? It's fucking creepy!

(HARRY crosses to exit. LIL tries to grab him, to cling to him. He shakes her off, backing away.)

LIL: *(Hurt.)* I thought you would like it. I'll change, Harry, please—

HARRY: Maybe if I had been home on time, it would have been cute. But coming home at two in the morning and finding you asleep like, like some fucking, ghost, talking about… *That*…Fucking A, Lil, what is wrong with you!

LIL: I didn't mean to—please, Harry—

(She grabs him. He pushes her away, violently.)

HARRY: Don't touch me! I have to go. I have to go. *(Exits.)*

LIL: No, Harry! Please don't leave, Harry! Please don't leave me here—

(He slams the door.)

LIL: Harry? Harry? Harry!

SCENE IV

Next door. Morning. ROACHIE sprawled out on the sofa. We hear a child's muffled cries leaking out behind the bedroom door.

ROACHIE: Damn, man! I wish this lil bitch would shutthafuckup! That shit is killin me!

(KEESHA enters from the bathroom, partially clad in her McDonald's uniform.)

ROACHIE: Ain't there sumthin you can do, baby? Go in there an talk ta her, sing her a lullaby or sumthin.

KEESHA: She doan speak English, Richie!

ROACHIE: Go in there an give her a hug, do some girl shit—whutevah. Just get her ta shut that damn cryin.

KEESHA: Nuh-uh. I ain't got shit ta do with this one. You in this all by ya damn self.

ROACHIE: How I'm in this by myself? You live heah too, right? Or do you not live heah any more?

KEESHA: Do I live heah, Richie? I would think that livin heah would mean that I have some say in what goes on heah, right? An since that obviously ain't tha case, well, then I guess that no, I doan live heah. I stay heah, try ta pay tha bills on time—

ROACHIE: Again with that—

KEESHA: You damn right, again with that. Thass tha whole reason we got a screamin Chinese girl in our bedroom.

ROACHIE: Indonesian.

KEESHA: Oh, now you wanna get specific? Like it matters?

ROACHIE: I done tol' you. She ain't Chinese. She Indonesian.

KEESHA: Whatevah. All tha same shit. An doan try ta change tha subject. Cause iss beyond me how you think you justifyin yourself, when you know you fucked up!

ROACHIE: Jesus, would you stop wit dat shit already? I done tol' you—

KEESHA: You tol' me? Whachoo tol' me, huh? You ain't tol' me nuthin! An I'd like ta see how you like comin home on ya break ta find some chil' in your house. Some illegal chil' no less. Cause I'm tellin you, Richie, tha cops come up in heah all gangbusters, axin questions, iss all on you!

ROACHIE: Who said anythin bout cops?

KEESHA: I'm juss sayin, I ain't got shit ta do with this!

ROACHIE: What, you doan think I know that? You think I like this? This tha only thing I could do ta try ta make this shit right, Keesh! An I know iss wack, I know iss inconsiderate an fucked up an all that. You think I don't? But what else was I supposed ta do, huh? I doan see no other way out…there ain't no other way out, Keesh…so whachoo want me ta do, huh?

KEESHA: I wanted you ta do whachoo was 'posed ta do yesterday.

ROACHIE: Doan keep beatin me ovah tha head with that, baby. C'mon! I'm embarrassed as hell right bout now.

KEESHA: You should be.

ROACHIE: I am. An you know what? I ain't axin shit of you. I would like it if you helped me with this, damn sure could use your help, but, whutevah, fuck it, I'll do it my damn self. It ain't like iss gonna be for long. Donovan said two, three days, tops! We basically babysittin. Two, three days work for tha equivalent of two months rent, an then some!

KEESHA: Yeah right.

ROACHIE: And you know we gonna get some, what, finder's fee or sumthin for babysittin! An she gonna end up somewhere nice, wit some white family or someplace. An we practicly humani-fuckin-tarians right bout now. We savin this kid's life!

KEESHA: Right.

ROACHIE: We are!

KEESHA: Whatevah.

ROACHIE: For all we know, this kid was gonna grow up on some Sally Struthers shit, walkin round wit flies all over her face like some human venus flytrap. We helpin ta give her a better life!

KEESHA: (Smiles, fake disgust.) What is wrong witchoo?

ROACHIE: Tell me I ain't right. She ain't heah, we'd see her on them commercials, belly all swole up an shit, lookin like she full, when she really juss fulla gas, like, mad farts waitin ta excape...

KEESHA: (Relents, bursting into laughter, then tries to recover.) You wrong.

ROACHIE: Yo, is my babygirl laughin? Thass my girl right there! My baby. (Beat, he studies her.) Why you doan laugh at me no more? You usta make me feel like tha funniest cat in tha world. I doan make you laugh no more, baby?

KEESHA: Yeah, you do.

ROACHIE: I miss you laughin.

KEESHA: I still laugh.

ROACHIE: Yeah...

KEESHA: I do.

ROACHIE: I member tha first time I heard you laugh...like fuckin, music. You member?

KEESHA: No. I don't.

ROACHIE: I was kickin it ta you, tryin ta keep calm, keep my game in check, tryin so hard ta stay cool. (Looks at her, holds her eyes.) You tha only one I had ta try ta stay cool around...never understood that, but always liked it. An I said sumthin silly an you laughed. Just...boom...like, music. Like one a them songs that juss make you feel nice. When you hear it, in tha supermarket or tha laundrymat or wherever, you stop whachoo doing... iss juss like—everything stops—you juss feel good...

KEESHA: (Softens.) Yeah. I like them songs.

ROACHIE: When you usta laugh at me, baby...I would leave you feelin like, like I could do anythin. Made me feel so good...Strong. Powerful. You always made me feel better than anythin. You were so fine. (Holds his hand out to her.) C'mere.

KEESHA: I'm a mess, Richie.

(ROACHIE rises, goes to her, takes her in his arms.)

ROACHIE: You a fine mess, then. (Beat.) Damn, baby, you so fine.

(He pulls her down to the sofa, onto his lap. They kiss. The kiss grows deeper, more passionate. Love. Her hands on the back of his head, his arm wraps tightly around her waist.)

ROACHIE: My girl. You always gonna be my girl.

(Keys in the door. DONOVAN enters.)

DONOVAN: I'm sorry. Am I interrupting?

KEESHA: (Rising.) I have ta finish gettin ready to go back to work. (Walks to bathroom, slamming the door behind her.)

DONOVAN: *(Locking door.)* Better?

ROACHIE: Uh. A little sumthin-sumthin.

DONOVAN: You're lucky she buys into your bullshit. She let you off easy.

ROACHIE: Say whah? Tha fuck you talkin bout?

DONOVAN: Personally? I would slit your throat. Imagine? Coming home from work to find a strange child in your home. Staying, in your home.

ROACHIE: Iss only for a coupla days, right?

DONOVAN: It's for however long it takes. *(Beat.)* So…how is our little orphan Tsunami?

ROACHIE: Fuckin kid won't stop cryin. Whachoo you gonna do bout that? F'real, man. That shit is straight up gettin ta me. Not ta mention that eventually someone's gonna hear that shit.

DONOVAN: That reminds me. *(Reaches into his inside coat pocket and withdraws a bottle of pills, which he sets in front of him on the table.)* I don't trust you with needles, so you're going to have to give her these, any time I'm not around.

ROACHIE: Tha fuck is that?

DONOVAN: Ketamine. It's a small dose, but I don't want to take any chances. Grind them up in her food. One half of one of those, any time she starts up. And don't even think about taking any of these—I'm keeping count.

ROACHIE: She ain't eatin much, man.

DONOVAN: She will. *(Beat.)* Did you debrief the little lady?

ROACHIE: No doubt. She gotta go ta work, though. Ima watch shortie.

DONOVAN: I'd feel much better if I knew Keesha was going to be around. This requires a woman's touch.

ROACHIE: Juss for a coupla hours, then she comin straight home. I got first shift.

DONOVAN: Perhaps I should speak with her directly? Discuss the general details, accountability, etcetera?

ROACHIE: C'mon, Donovan! You ack like I'm a fuckin retard or somethin. Keep tha kid in tha room, make sure she's okay, doan let no one else in tha apartment. Doan answer tha door under any circumstances, all that.

DONOVAN: I find myself in an unusual position, Roachie…a man without options. *(Beat.)* You're all I got.

ROACHIE: I can do this, D!

DONOVAN: I hope so. *(Beat.)* Look at me, Roachie. Do you see my face? The way I'm looking at you? Do you hear my voice?

ROACHIE: Yeah. Yes.

DONOVAN: Am I properly conveying to you the degree to which I am serious? Because I am speaking to you in this manner to ensure that you understand what might happen should you fuck this up, Roachie.

ROACHIE: I won't! Damn, man. I won't. You can truss me.

DONOVAN: *(Smiles; beat.)* I hope so. Because should you fuck this up—

ROACHIE: I won't!

DONOVAN: Let me finish. Should you fuck this up, do you know what will happen?

ROACHIE: I have an idea.

DONOVAN: I don't think you do. If you fuck this up, Roachie, I will kill you.

ROACHIE:...

DONOVAN: But before that? I will cut off your wife's fingers, one by one. Then her toes, then her breasts, then her tongue. While you watch. And then I will kill her. Accountability.

ROACHIE: I won't! I promise. *(Beat.)* Damn, man, c'mon, thass some foul shit.

(KEESHA enters from the bathroom. ROACHIE stares at her. A beat.)

KEESHA: What?

ROACHIE: *(Beat.)* Nuthin.

(A wail from the bedroom.)

ROACHIE: What tha fuck!

KEESHA: She gonna tire herself out eventually.

DONOVAN: Excuse me. *(Grabs pill bottle, exits to bedroom.)*

KEESHA: Where he goin? What he gonna do ta her?

ROACHIE: He ain't doin shit ta her. Give her a little sumthin-sumthin, help her calm down, stop cryin so much. She gonna disturb tha whole buildin.

KEESHA: Who she gonna disturb? Iss day-time. Anyways, ain't no one in this buildin give a shit bout what anyone else does.

ROACHIE: Tha crazy white lady next door.

KEESHA: She harmless. She doan bother nobody.

ROACHIE: That bitch always starin out in tha hall through tha peephole. All up in everyone's business like she Angela Lansbury or sumthin. Bitch think she slick, too. Every time I come up tha stairs I see tha shadow move away from tha peephole. Crazy bitch.

KEESHA: She ain't crazy. She juss a little off is all.

ROACHIE: That bitch is in-sane! An that lil weird-ass husband of hers. Lil meatball muhfuckah!

KEESHA: They good people, Richie. I doan see why you gotta be all negative. You always so negative bout everyone.

ROACHIE: I doan like crazies, plain an simple. An that bitch fuckin car-ray-zay. We livin next ta "Misery" an shit.

(KEESHA walks toward the door.)

ROACHIE: Where you goin? You ain't gotta be at work for another forty-five minnits.

KEESHA: I'm goin ta get that chil' sumthin ta eat. That chil' cryin cause she hungry.

ROACHIE: We got rice.

KEESHA: You been gave her rice! She need some food, Richie! Milk. Juice. Cereal. Fruit. Sumthin ta eat.

ROACHIE: Yeah, yeah. Bring me back sumthin.

KEESHA: Yeah, yeah. Fuck you.

ROACHIE: C'mon, Keesh! A beef patty, a slice, sumthin.

KEESHA: Not gonna happen.

ROACHIE: C'mon, baby. Please? I am mad hungry! My stomach is damn near eatin itself.

(DONOVAN enters.)

KEESHA: You want sumthin? Take yo ass ta tha store when I get back. Or axe Donovan ta get you sumthin. You on ya own. *(Exits.)*

DONOVAN: Ask Donovan what?

ROACHIE: To get me sumthin ta eat.

DONOVAN: I don't think so.

ROACHIE: Then lemme leave an come back.

DONOVAN: I've got to be somewhere. Sorry.

ROACHIE: C'mon, D! I'm starvin!

DONOVAN: Can't. And you heard the lady…

ROACHIE: Whachoo mean, I heard tha lady?

DONOVAN: You're on your own. *(Exits.)*

Scene V

Next door. Late morning. HARRY enters, bleary-eyed and silent. He closes the door behind him, then spots LIL, still clad in her wedding dress, sprawled out on the living room floor, sobbing into the silence of the apartment. She is covered in white, powdery dust, clutching two large pieces of sheetrock. HARRY drops his things and rushes over to her.

HARRY: *(Hysterically.)* Ohmigod! Lil! Lil! Are you alright? What happened? What happened, Lil?

(HARRY lifts LIL's arms as one would a child, and examines her for wounds and blood. LIL's arms remain extended out at her sides, still clutching the sheetrock. HARRY moves his face to hers and speaks directly to her.)

HARRY: Are you okay? Did the ceiling collapse? What's going on here? Who did this?

(LIL cries harder. HARRY looks up, scanning the walls and ceiling of the apartment. After a moment, he rises, walks to the bathroom, and stands in the doorway.)

HARRY: Jesus Christ, the wall is…what happened? Did the wall cave in? Lil? *(Beat.)* Did you do this?

(HARRY crosses, kneels beside her, gently lowers her arms, and attempts to remove the pieces of sheetrock from her hands, which she refuses to release. He smooths her hair, brushing the dust off her head and face, and cradles her in his arms. LIL cries.)

HARRY: Lil? Can you talk to me, honey? Calm down, baby. Shhhhh-hh…it's okay. Whatever it is, it's going to be okay.

(More crying. After a moment, HARRY releases her face, exasperated, and speaks very softly to her.)

HARRY: I'm going to get your pills now, Lil. *(Exits the room and reenters with a glass of water and a bottle of pills. He kneels down beside her.)*

HARRY: *(Softly.)* Honey? You have to take your medicine. Here you go, Lil.

(LIL cries. HARRY gently places the pill on her tongue.)

HARRY: Honey. Have some water, baby. Just a little bit.

(LIL spits the pill onto the floor. HARRY picks it up, dusts it off, and tries again. The same. HARRY tries again, this time putting the pill on her tongue and following with the glass of water. LIL knocks the water from his hands.)

HARRY: *(Resigned.)* I have to call the hospital now, honey. We have to call the hospital. *(Rises and turns to cross the room.)*

LIL: She wouldn't stop crying, Harry. She wouldn't…stop…crying. I could hear her crying, Harry. Even in the other room I could hear her crying. "Just stop crying," I kept saying. "Please, please stop crying." And she wouldn't stop, Harry. She. Wouldn't. Stop. Crying.

HARRY: *(Overwhelmed.)* I don't understand—you're not making any sense!

LIL: I could hear her, Harry. I could hear her crying. All night. She wouldn't stop. I could hear her through the wall. She was crying so hard, Harry. She wouldn't stop—

HARRY: I don't—Who—What—What happened—

LIL: But then she did stop! Like someone made her. She just stopped. But when I went to pee, I could hear them talking through the hole from where you hung the picture so I made it a little bigger—just a little bit—and it crumbled a little so I pulled at it a little more and it got bigger and bigger and before I knew it the whole wall was broken but I could hear them, perfectly, Harry! I could hear them talking—Oh God!

(LIL breaks down again, wracked with sobs. HARRY grabs her by the shoulders.)

HARRY: What are you talking about? Look at me! LIL! *Look at me! (Rises.)* I have to call the doctor.

LIL: *(Through her sobs.)* They're selling her, Harry. They're going to sell her!

HARRY: What? What the fuck are you talking about?

(Beat; LIL cries.)

HARRY: Listen to me, Lillian. Are you listening? *STOP CRYING AND LISTEN TO ME!*

(She stops, frightened.)

HARRY: I'm going to call the doctor now, order you a new prescription, and go to pick it up. While I am gone, understand that you have two options. One, you take your meds. Immediately. No complaints, no arguments. I know you don't like them, but I don't give a fuck, this is nonnegotiable. Or two…I call your parents and you go with them. Because I can't do this anymore, Lil. No more. I am not doing this—I cannot do this—I am not doing this anymore. I'm sorry…but I can't.

(Long beat, he watches her, she stares at the floor.)

HARRY: I'm going to call the doctor now.

ACT 2: LABOR
Scene I

Evening. LIL and HARRY's apartment. LIL sits on the sofa. She is eerily calm—it is almost like she is anchored in place, motionless. Throughout the scene, she remains fixated on KEESHA, her voice maintaining the same tone and pitch—even, still. KEESHA stands in front of LIL, nervous, wary, clearly uneasy in LIL's presence. She is clutching a plastic black bag, which a doll's head peeks out of.

KEESHA: So you doan need nuthin?

LIL: No.

KEESHA: Food?

LIL: No.

KEESHA: Sumthin ta drink?

LIL: No.

KEESHA: So why he had me come over heah?

LIL: Who?

KEESHA: Donovan. Why he had me come over heah?

LIL: I don't know. *(Noticing the bag.)* What's that?

KEESHA: Huh?

LIL: In the bag.

KEESHA: Nuthin.

LIL: It's pretty.

KEESHA: *(Hiding the bag behind her.)* It ain't nuthin.

LIL: I had a doll like that. When I was little. "Chatty Cathy." My favorite doll ever. I loved it until it fell apart. *(Long beat; she studies KEESHA's face.)* You have the sad black lady face.

KEESHA: What?

LIL: That face. The sad black lady face.

KEESHA: What tha fuck you talkin bout?

LIL: It's almost like you've seen all the pain and hurt of the world and it just shows on your face. There's just, something in your eyes. That's where it all starts—the eyes. The deepest pain. I used to see these women sometimes when I'd walk around. They look so sad, so horribly, painfully sad. I always want to hug them when I see them. But they're usually older black ladies. You're too young to have the sad black lady face.

KEESHA: *(Beat; stares at LIL.)* Whass wrong witchoo? Why you like that?

LIL: Like what?

KEESHA: Like that. Talkin all that crazy shit. You all slow, like. Like you bout ta drool on ya'self or sumthin.

LIL: Harry.

KEESHA: Harry what?

LIL: Harry made me. Take pills.

KEESHA: Why?

LIL: Because of the bathroom.

KEESHA: What?

LIL: Because I broke the wall in the bathroom.

KEESHA: *(Looks in the bathroom.)* You did that?

LIL: Yes.

KEESHA: How?

LIL: I just…pulled.

KEESHA: You did that witcha hands? That shit is destroyed. Look like someone took a hammer in there.

LIL: No. Just my hands.

KEESHA: Zat why ya husband axed Donovan ta check up on you?

LIL: I don't know.

KEESHA: He mad?

LIL: Who?

KEESHA: Your husband?

LIL: I don't know.

KEESHA: Cause I woulda snapped yo mothafuckin neck, you did that shit up in my house.

LIL: *(Shrugs.)* Well, I didn't do it in your house. I did it in my house.

KEESHA: Girl, you crazy.

LIL: I'm not crazy.

KEESHA: You damn near tore a hole clear through tha wall witcha bare hands, I'd say you pretty damn close.

LIL: Can you ever hear us?

KEESHA: Hear you what?

LIL: Through the walls. I can hear you, you know.

KEESHA: Good for you. But I got bettah things ta do than listen ta what go on in heah.

LIL: Because I can hear everything. You. And your husband. And Donovan. *(Whispers.)* And Natalie.

KEESHA: Who's Natalie?

LIL: The little girl.

KEESHA: Tha fuck you talkin about?

LIL: The little girl. In your apartment. Crying. *(Indicating bag.)* Is that for her?

KEESHA: *(Laughs it off.)* Lil girl? Crying?

LIL: I know what I heard.

KEESHA: Whachoo heard. Whachoo mean, whachoo heard?

LIL: Through the bathroom.

KEESHA: Through tha—? Well, whatevah, I dunno whachoo talkin bout.

LIL: Yes you do. You have a little girl. A little girl. In your house.

KEESHA: There ain't no lil girl.

LIL: Yes there is. A little girl. In your house. She was crying. But she stopped.

(A long beat. KEESHA is clearly rattled.)

KEESHA: So you doan need nuthin?

LIL: No.

KEESHA: Cause I'm supposed ta make sure you okay.

LIL: I'm fine.

KEESHA: You fine, I'm fine, I'm out. *(Turns to exit.)*

LIL: I heard her. All night last night. Her. Crying. You went to get food because you thought she was hungry and your husband was only feeding her rice. Then you gave her pills.

KEESHA: You crazy, you know that? Crazy-ass white woman.

LIL: You gave her pills to make her stop crying. Just like Harry does to me.

KEESHA: Ain't nobody gave no one nuthin.

LIL: And you're selling her. *(Beat.)* Why would you do that?

KEESHA: I'm tellin you—

LIL: Why would you do that to a little girl?

KEESHA: Look, I dunno whachoo think you heard—

LIL: I heard Donovan. Talking to your husband.

KEESHA: You ain't heard shit is whachoo heard.

LIL: I didn't hear you, though.

KEESHA: Thass cause there ain't shit ta hear.

LIL: You're selling her. To an older white man. Or some little Japanese man. To whoever gets there first. Like a race.

KEESHA: *(Quiet.)* Lady, I doan know what tha fuck you talkin bout, but you talkin bout some foul shit.

LIL: You're selling her. For a lot of money. For sex. Because she's so young. *(Beat.)* Why would you sell her?

KEESHA: I ain't doin nuthin like that.

LIL: Yes you are. Or they are. *(Indicating bag.)* That's for her, isn't it?

KEESHA: *(Long beat.)* Richie tol' me they waitin on a white family to adopt her.

LIL: Nope. They're selling her. For sex. Soon. *(Beat.)* Keesha? Can I ask you a question?

(No answer.)

LIL: Why don't you laugh at him anymore?

(Silence. KEESHA stares at LIL, who stares right back at KEESHA, unblinking. KEESHA backs toward the door, still staring, before turning and quickly exiting.)

SCENE II

Next door. ROACHIE sits on the sofa, nervously twirling the hammer in his hands. KEESHA enters.

ROACHIE: Damn, baby—where you been?

KEESHA: Work.

ROACHIE: You late. You shoulda been home fifteen minnits ago.

KEESHA: Donovan axed me ta stop next door.

ROACHIE: Where?

KEESHA: Where I said? Next door.

ROACHIE: Why he made you go over there for?

KEESHA: She sick. He axed me ta check on her.

ROACHIE: What tha fuck, we not only babysittin, we gotta play nurse, too? Ima say sumthin ta him.

KEESHA: No you ain't. It ain't no big deal, Richie.

ROACHIE: Whatevah. Ima still say sumthin ta him. He takin advantage of our situation. Shit ain't right.

KEESHA: Do whatevah you need ta do then, Richie. Whatevah you need ta do.

ROACHIE: You alright?

KEESHA: Tired.

ROACHIE: I'm glad you home. I been goin fuckin crazy in this muhfuckah all day. Shit is fuckin wack! Can't wait til shortie gone an shit back ta normal.

KEESHA: How much longer?

ROACHIE: Whah?

KEESHA: How much longer before she gone? When tha white people gonna get her?

ROACHIE: Soon, I imagine. Donovan said a coupla days, it ain't even been that yet.

KEESHA: We gonna get ta meet em?

ROACHIE: Who?

KEESHA: Whoevah she goin to? Tha white people. We gonna get ta meet whoevah she goin to?

ROACHIE: Naw, I doan think so. Why would we?

KEESHA: We been watchin her an all that. What if she end up someplace bad?

ROACHIE: Can't get much worse than where she was. This practicly paradise ta her.

KEESHA: Yeah.

ROACHIE: Anyways, that ain't our business. Our business is ta keep her heah until whoever gonna get her come ta get her. Thass it. Nuthin else. *(Indicating bag.)* Whass that?

KEESHA: Mrs. Montero was havin another yard sale, so I picked it up.

(He takes the bag from her and removes the doll.)

ROACHIE: Ugh. Shit is ugly. *(He raises and lowers it, making the eyes blink.)* I hate these dolls. They eyes are fuckin creepy. *(Beat.)* Hol' up—you ain't gettin attached, are you?

KEESHA: What? No. How would I? You been heah all day with her. I ain't barely seen her for ten minnits.

ROACHIE: Well, she can't have it. She gonna be leavin soon, an you can't get attached.

KEESHA: I'm not attached. *(Beat.)* She okay?

ROACHIE: Yeah, I guess.

KEESHA: She been eatin okay? Drinkin water an all that?

ROACHIE: Yeah, I guess. She ain't really leave tha corner all day.

KEESHA: What?

ROACHIE: She juss sittin in tha corner, starin an shit. She peed, though.

KEESHA: Where?

ROACHIE: Tha floor. I already cleaned it up. Them pills got her all fucked up.

Like, juss there. She ain't scared, ain't hungry, nuthin. Juss, like, a statue. Juss there.

(KEESHA crosses, opens the bedroom door, and sees the girl. Silence.)

KEESHA: It stink like pee in there.

ROACHIE: Cause she peed. But otherwise, she good ta go. See? I tol' you she okay. Juss sittin there. This babysittin shit easy as hell. Ain't nuthin to it, you know? Shit, you give me some a these pills, I'll be tha mastah fuckin babysitter.

KEESHA: She drugged, Richie. You ain't supposed ta drug a chil' like that.

ROACHIE: White people do it. Please, white people drug they kids like a muhfuckah.

KEESHA: They do not.

ROACHIE: They damn sure do. For every lil thing, they druggin they kids. Bad temper? Take a pill. Too tired? Take a pill. Bad day at school? Take a pill. Thass why black an Spanish folks havin so much trouble raisin they kids. No drugs. No legal drugs, anyways.

KEESHA: She got extra clothes?

ROACHIE: I dunno. Why?

KEESHA: Well, she peed herself, she gonna need ta take a bath, put on some clean clothes. Who gonna want her she all dirty an smell like pee? Think about it.

ROACHIE: I doan think they gonna care. They gonna be happy enough juss ta have her.

KEESHA: Well, I can't have no chil' in this house all sittin in they mess like some animal.

ROACHIE: Leave her be, Keesha. She fine.

KEESHA: How you figure she fine? She ain't fine. She like a fuckin zombie or sumthin. An she smell like pee.

ROACHIE: Leave her, Keesh. I'm tellin you. Doan make no difference. I doan want you getting attached ta her. Cause that's what happens.

KEESHA: Make a difference ta me. An I ain't gonna get attached. I juss doan like no lil girl smellin like pee is all.

ROACHIE: How you gonna come up in heah an juss try ta run shit? I been watchin her all day without a break. Juss me an her. So how you comin up in heah, talkin bout, "She smell like pee. She smell like pee." You damn well know she was smellin like shit back in tha motherland. What difference a lil pee make? Leave her be.

KEESHA: Richie—

ROACHIE: No more! What I tol' you? Where she goin, doan make one bit of difference.

KEESHA: Alright, Richie. You right.

ROACHIE: Thank you. Damn, man. I feel like I'm in jail or some shit. *(Beat.)* Whachoo fittin ta do?

KEESHA: I dunno. Juss walked in. No idea.

ROACHIE: You min' goin an gettin me sumthin ta eat? I'm starvin. Oh! An a Coke? I could sure as shit use a Coke.

KEESHA: We ain't got nuthin heah?

ROACHIE: Naw. Ain't shit up in heah.

KEESHA: I'm tired, Richie. My feet hurt, all that.

ROACHIE: C'mon, baby. Ain't gonna take you but a minnit.

KEESHA: All tha more reason you can do it yourself.

ROACHIE: I shouldn't leave.

KEESHA: Why not?

ROACHIE: Donovan—

KEESHA: Donovan don't give a shit who heah, so long as she ain't left alone. You said so yourself.

ROACHIE: I dunno if I should. Shit, I go out there, I might not come back for a while. On some escaped convict shit.

KEESHA: You need a break, take a break. Take two breaks. I ain't goin nowhere.

ROACHIE: I could damn sure use it.

KEESHA: Then take one. Cause I'm right heah.

ROACHIE: Yeah? *(Reconsiders, smiles.)* Hol' up. You think you slick, donchoo?

KEESHA: Whachoo talkin about?

ROACHIE: You think you slick.

KEESHA: I ain't think nuthin.

ROACHIE: You nevah want me ta go nowhere, an I'm tellin you that I got cabin fever like a muhfuckah, an you tellin me ta go ahead? Look at you.

KEESHA: Look at me what? You wanna go, go. You wanna stay, stay. Doan make me no difference.

ROACHIE: I know whachoo tryin ta do, Keesh. Doan think I don't.

KEESHA: What am I tryin ta do?

ROACHIE: You really think I'm so stupid? You juss wanna be alone with her, give her a bath, clean her up, play dolls with her cause I tol' you ta let her be.

KEESHA: *(Smiles.)* You got me, baby.

ROACHIE: I knew you was up ta sumthin. For real? You so crazy bout cleanin her up, clean her up.

(He hands her the doll.)

ROACHIE: An whutevah, you wanna give her tha doll, give her tha doll. Juss doan get attached. Cause we can't keep her. *(Beat.)* So you sure you doan mind?

KEESHA: You keep axin me, I'm gonna tell you no. Go on, get yourself something ta eat, take a break. I ain't goin nowhere notime soon.

ROACHIE: Say word! My baby! Look at my baby takin care of me! You need anythin while I'm out?

KEESHA: Nope.

ROACHIE: Ima prolly be back ina hour. Two, tops. Cool?

KEESHA: I'll be right heah.

ROACHIE: Cool an tha Gang! I'll be back in a lil while. Yeah?

KEESHA: Yeah.

(ROACHIE exits. KEESHA picks up the doll, crosses to the bedroom door, opens it, and stares inside. After an uncomfortably long beat, she crouches down.)

KEESHA: How you doin, little one? You good? Pee-yew! Stink like pee in heah. Can't have you smellin like pee, now, can we? You gonna let me clean you up? C'mere, baby, less get you cleaned up. No? *(Offers the doll.)* You lookin at this? Iss pretty, huh? You want it? No? You just gonna sit ovah there an stare at me? Thass okay, little girl. Thass okay. You

scared, honey? Prolly too tired ta be scared, too scared ta be tired. You miss your mother? Your father? *(Long beat.)* I usta wanna know my father—doan remember nuthin bout him cept his voice reminded me of smoke. Couldn't begin ta tell you what he look like, juss remember me lyin in bed an hearin him talk ta mama, voice like smoke. Fill up a room, then just as quick, be gone. *(Beat; slowly rises.)* I hope thass how my girls remember me. Cause I think if I evah woulda found my father, I woulda hated him for what he was. Instead, rememberin that voice…smoke…leaves me with one nice thing. Always good ta have one nice thing. I usta have a lil girl juss like you. Two lil girls. Juss like you. They bof with tha state now. Tha first child she got burned in tha bathtub. Tha second one born all sick an twisted from tha rock. Life over for both of those babies before it start. Cause of me. On account of me. I think about them, how they gonna hate me when they old enough ta realize what I did ta them. I have tha conversations in my mind, thinkin what Ima say when they find me, then hopin ta God that they have tha sense not ta look. *(Long beat.)* I ain't gonna let this happen ta you, lil girl. Ain't gonna let them do this ta you. My husband, he ain't a bad man, juss sorta—sick—or whatevah, but tha other one… *(Beat.)* I ain't gonna let these men hurt you…and even though I ain't doin it for this reason, I hope that maybe this will make up for what I done ta my own girls. Maybe not…but maybe so.

Scene III

The next morning. Both apartments grace the stage simultaneously, seemingly cut in half; KEESHA sits silently on one side of the sofa, LIL on the other. Their appearances are drastically different. LIL is calm, aware, maternal, while KEESHA appears disturbed, nervous, on edge. Silence. Doors open simultaneously on opposite sides of the stage, and HARRY and ROACHIE enter, equally tired and disheveled.

HARRY: *(Approaches LIL, kisses her cheek.)* Hi honey. How are you? Feeling better?

LIL: Much better. Long night, huh?

ROACHIE: *(Approaches KEESHA sheepishly, kisses her cheek.)* Yeah, baby. I ain't mean ta stay out so late. I was out, havin a bite, enjoyin my Coke, an next thing I knew, I broke night!

KEESHA: Iss all good. I tol' you ta stay out.

ROACHIE: Yeah, I know. But I dint mean ta abuse it an shit. Iss juss like, time flew, you know?

LIL: Yeah. I do.

HARRY: Those meds are really helping, huh? *(Appraises her.)* You look fantastic! This is the best I've seen you look in a long, long time.

LIL: Six months.

HARRY: *(Surprised.)* …yeah. Yeah, that's right. This coming from someone who just spent an entire night in a taxi. I imagine I'm looking like a bag of smashed assholes. *(Beat.)* You seem…I thought you were going to be mad at me.

KEESHA: Naw, I ain't mad atcha. Not at all.

ROACHIE: F'real? Cause I really ain't mean ta be out all night like that. An Keesh? Ima be straight up wit you cause I ain't tryin ta hide shit, but I met up with Caesar an'—

KEESHA: Iss okay.

ROACHIE: Yeah?

KEESHA: Yeah.

HARRY: Cause I feel like shit about everything. Absolute shit, honey.

LIL: I know.

HARRY: I don't think you do. Me, alone in the cab, driving all over the city, just thinking. About what I did, about what I said. It was wrong for me to leave you like that.

LIL: You were scared for me.

HARRY: Yes. Yes I was. But that doesn't justify—

KEESHA: You was cooped up all day, I half knew whachoo was gonna do. So whatevah, you home now.

ROACHIE: Anyone came by?

KEESHA: Nope.

ROACHIE: Donovan?

KEESHA: Nope.

HARRY: Because I promised him the rest of the rent. Thank God I had a good night.

LIL: No, Harry. It was actually a really quiet night. A wonderful night.

HARRY: Wonderful?

LIL: The best.

HARRY: Huh. I'm starting to feel a little jealous that I wasn't here.

LIL: There's nothing to be jealous about.

HARRY: So what was so wonderful about it?

KEESHA: It juss felt…good, you know? It juss felt good.

ROACHIE: Havin tha house ta ya'self?

KEESHA: Yeah. I guess.

ROACHIE: How is she?

KEESHA: Fine. She fine, Richie.

ROACHIE: You cleaned her up an all that?

KEESHA: Yeah. Gave her a bath, sumthin ta eat. I know you dint want me ta an all that, but—

ROACHIE: I knew you was gonna. Iss cool. An' tha pills?

LIL: Yeah. I took them.

HARRY: Lil? *(Beat.)* I'm sorry, honey. I'm so, so sorry.

LIL: I told you, Harry. I'm okay. I'm wonderful. *(Beat.)* Harry?

HARRY: Yeah?

LIL: We need to talk about everything. I think we should talk.

HARRY: Um, yeah. Okay. Let me just take a quick shower first, okay?

KEESHA: If thass whachoo need ta do.

ROACHIE: Where my towel?

KEESHA: Where you left it last?

ROACHIE: *(Smiles, snaps his fingers.)* Prolly in tha bedroom.

KEESHA: Then thass where it is.

(HARRY and ROACHIE exit simultaneously to their respective bedrooms. Silence.)

ROACHIE: *(Offstage.)* What tha fuck?!? Keesha!

HARRY: *(Offstage.)* Jesus Christ!

(The MEN race back onstage.)

ROACHIE: Where is she? Where tha fuck is she, Keesha?

HARRY: Lil—why is there a young Asian child in our bedroom?

{ ROACHIE: What did you do with her? Answer me!

HARRY: Where did you get her? Answer me!

{ LIL: She's ours.

KEESHA: She gone.

HARRY: What the fuck do you mean—

ROACHIE: —she gone?

KEESHA: Juss what I said. She—

LIL: Ours. She's ours.

HARRY: She's not ours, Lillian. This is not our child!

LIL: For now, she is. For now—

KEESHA: She safe.

ROACHIE: All I wanted was a fuckin Coke! Thass all I wanted, was a fuckin Coke! Jesus fuckin Christ—

{ HARRY: —Lil! What did you do? Answer me?

ROACHIE: —woman? What did you do? Answer me!

LIL: I'm babysitting. I'm watching her. She's with us, now—

KEESHA: She safe.

ROACHIE: She what? Bitch, where tha fuck is she?

(He grabs KEESHA by the hair and pulls his hand back as if to hit her. She does not flinch.)

ROACHIE: Where is she?

KEESHA: She gone, Richie. An thass all you need ta know.

(HARRY grabs LIL by the shoulders.)

HARRY: I need to know where you got this little girl from, Lil. Right now, you tell me—

ROACHIE: —where tha fuck is she, Keesha?!?

KEESHA: You can threaten me all you want, ain't gon' change tha fact that she gone.

LIL: And she's not going anywhere. Period.

(Both MEN stare at the WOMEN, incredulously. HARRY backs away from LIL in disbelief. ROACHIE pulls his hand back, releases KEESHA's hair, then launches an onslaught against the sofa cushions, hammering them repeatedly, then begins pacing frantically around the apartment.)

HARRY: Okay okay okay—

{ ROACHIE: —we can still save this.
  HARRY: —we can still save it.

HARRY: It's not too late.

ROACHIE: You have ta tell me, baby, now—

HARRY: —if you're ever going to tell me anything, ever again—

{ ROACHIE: —where she at, Keesha?
  HARRY: —where did you get her?

KEESHA: She gone.

LIL: Far away.

(ROACHIE rushes to KEESHA, grabs her head in his hands, and lowers his face to hers. HARRY maintains his stance, staring at LIL.)

HARRY: This is bad, Lil. This is very, very bad—

ROACHIE: Do you know what he gonna do ta us? Do you know—

HARRY: —how bad this is?

KEESHA: Doan matter, Richie. He gonna do what he gonna do. She—

LIL: —safe now. She's safe with us.

(ROACHIE grabs KEESHA into his arms and hugs her, rocking back and forth with her as he sobs. She does not reciprocate.)

HARRY: Awww, Lil! I don't understand—

ROACHIE:—all I wanted was a Coke, baby! All I wanted was a Coke...

(A knock at the door sounds through both apartments. Blackout.)

SCENE IV

HARRY and LIL's. HARRY paces the room. LIL remains seated on the sofa, perfectly still.

HARRY: There's still a way out of this. There has to be a way out of this. *(Kneels down to her, father to daughter.)* Okay—okay—okay—here's what we're going to do. Tell me what happened, Lil. You have to talk to me, honey. Tell me. Tell me what happened.

LIL: Nothing happened.

HARRY: *(Stares at LIL, incredulous. A beat, then, with forced calm:)* There's a child in our bedroom, honey.

LIL: I know.

HARRY: Do you? Because I don't think—

LIL: Of course I do. I put her there.

HARRY: Where did you get her?

LIL: I told you.

HARRY: Keesha from next door. Yes, you told me already.

LIL: I did.

HARRY: So this is Keesha's baby?

LIL: No. She's no one's. Donovan's.

HARRY: Our landlord?

LIL: Yes.

HARRY: That little Chinese girl—

LIL: Indonesian.

HARRY: That Indonesian girl is Donovan's.

LIL: Yes.

HARRY: And this is the same one you overheard him say he was going to sell.

LIL: For sex.

HARRY: Yes. That's right, for sex. To either a Japanese man or a white man.

LIL: Yes! That's why she's here. We're protecting her.

HARRY: You kidnapped a child, honey. You stole someone's child. Do you realize this?

LIL: No I didn't. They did.

HARRY: *(Soft.)* But that's what it looks like, yeah? Where did she come from? Can you tell me where she came from, then? Lil?

LIL: Stop it. I hate when you talk to me like that.

HARRY: *(Rises, turns away, then turns back.)* I'm trying—very, very hard—to make sense of this. To understand. To fix this. We can still fix this. But you can't lie to me.

LIL: I'm not lying to you. There's nothing to understand, Harry. There's nothing to fix. She has to stay here. Until it's safe.

HARRY: And she's safe here?

LIL: Yes.

HARRY: Safe from what?

LIL: You're not listening!

HARRY: I am listening, Lil. That's the problem.

LIL: I know what you're thinking—but you have to—

HARRY: *(Desperate.)* Lil, someone is looking for that child. Do you understand that? Someone is going to be looking for that child and, she can't—if she gets found here—

LIL: She's safe now, Harry. Safe here. With us.

HARRY: So if I go next door and ask Keesha and her husband—

LIL: You can't do that.

HARRY: Okay…so if I go downstairs to Donovan's—

LIL: You can't do that, either.

HARRY: Jesus Christ, Lil! What the fuck am I supposed to do?

LIL: You're not listening to me! I keep saying the same thing over and over, Harry!

HARRY: Then just tell me the truth! Tell me the fucking truth!

LIL: I am!

(HARRY grabs LIL by the shoulders.)

HARRY: You kidnapped her—do you realize that? You kidnapped a little girl and you're lying to me! Are you that broken that you don't realize that? Where the fuck did you get that little girl! Tell me!

LIL: I did, Harry! You're not listening!

HARRY: What is your defect—what are you thinking? *(Surrender.)* This is it. The end of it. Because I can't. I've spent the past six months taking care of you. Coddling you. Walking on eggshells so you wouldn't crumble into some pile of dust. Doing everything I could to make sure that you were getting better. Acting like a wet nurse for you, the same way your father does for your crazy fucking mother. For what? For nothing. It didn't make one bit of difference. Genetics finally caught up. And you. Sitting there. Wallowing in your own pity. Letting yourself waste away. Me thinking, "Tomorrow will be better. Tomorrow will be the day." And every single fucking day you slip further into oblivion. It hurts to look at you, Lil. You've become this horrible sideshow carnival version of yourself. I can't even look at you when I fuck you. And on those rare occasions we do fuck, you're so far gone you think you're knocked up. It's—you're…Sick. *(Beat.)* I'm going to the police now. Going to inform them that my crazy fucking wife, who has spent the past two days pressing her ear to the fucking door listening for voices, prancing around the house in her wedding dress, ripping our walls apart—has finally fucking cracked and abducted a little Chinese—sorry—Indonesian—girl. And I am going to watch as they strap your crazy fucking ass to a stretcher and cart you off to Bellevue. It ends. Now. Because this? You? Are worse than your

mother. She's just imbalanced. But you? You are absolutely fucking crazy.

LIL: I'm crazy, Harry? Why?

HARRY: What?

LIL: Why am I crazy, Harry? Do you know?

HARRY: I'm leaving.

LIL: For a long time it was a game. I pretended. Pretended to be worse than I was. For you. And then one day, one day I realized I wasn't pretending anymore. Because I couldn't find my way back. Did you know that?

HARRY: You're sick.

LIL: You made sure of that, didn't you, Harry? You stole me. Whisked me away, married me, brought me here, turned me into this. Do you like what you made, Harry? I hope so, because this is all you. Because I didn't start off this way, Harry. It took years. Fifteen years, one forced abortion, one hysterectomy. Do you remember? You never talk about it, but I imagine that you must… *(Beat.)* Did you watch them, Harry? Did you watch them rip my insides out? Strip me bare like some abandoned mine shaft, leave me like this, useless, hollow? Were you there when they were gutting me? Or were you hiding, because you knew what you did? That you ruined our child—Natalie—before she was even born.

HARRY: We didn't have a choice! You were—

LIL: No!

HARRY: The baby was—the doctors—

LIL: You blame everyone else. You blame Nature. Defects. The Doctors. A Mistake. But we both know. It was you. It had to be you. You polluted me, Harry. Poisoned me. You. Your defective cells—your vile, poisonous cells—did this to me. Took the best of me—the only thing that was mine—the woman—and made her rot from the inside out. And still, I could have almost forgiven you for that. Almost. But the fact that you polluted her…that she never had a chance, because of you…for that? For that I will *never* forgive you. I will never forget, and I will never forgive you. You killed two of us. And I can't figure out what's worse—you polluting me? Or me knowing…and still letting you?

(Silence. HARRY backs toward the door.)

LIL: Run away now. Go on, Harry. Run away…

(She turns her back to him. He exits. After a moment, LIL crosses to the bedroom door and opens it. She leans against the door frame, absolutely still, staring into the room. The silence is broken by a loud bang, followed immediately by a blood-curdling scream. LIL turns to the front door and stares at it for a moment, almost expectantly, then:)

LIL: It's starting.

Scene V

ROACHIE and KEESHA's. DONOVAN stands next to the table, holding a claw hammer menacingly. ROACHIE and KEESHA stand on the other side, KEESHA trying to comfort ROACHIE, who is obviously in shock. His hand is wrapped in a dirty T-shirt saturated with blood.

DONOVAN: We'll ask you now. *(To KEESHA.)* What happened today?

ROACHIE: I tol' you, man, she wasn't—

DONOVAN: I'm not talking to you right now. Keesha?

KEESHA: I dunno. I wasn't heah.

DONOVAN: Right, right. You were at work.

KEESHA: Yes.

DONOVAN: And you came home to find Roachie here, tearing through the building, looking for the child. Yes?

KEESHA: Yeah.

DONOVAN: *(To ROACHIE.)* So to recap, you walked to the store, came back, and found the child missing. You were here with the child the entire day, then left her alone—

ROACHIE: Juss for a minnit—

DONOVAN: You left her alone, came back, and poof. She was gone.

ROACHIE: Yeah.

DONOVAN: No sign of forced entry? No evidence of foul play? Nothing?

ROACHIE: No.

DONOVAN: And you went to the store, you say?

ROACHIE: Yes.

DONOVAN: Which store?

ROACHIE: Which—? Tha Korean joint on tha corner.

DONOVAN: When you came back, was the front door open or closed?

ROACHIE: *(Beat.)* Closed.

DONOVAN: So she let herself out and then closed the door behind her. Is that what you'll have me believe?

ROACHIE: Thass what happened.

DONOVAN: I realize that this must be boring for you, telling me the same thing over and over again, but humor me. I'm asking for this because I'm finding it harder and harder to believe that you took a quick jaunt to the store, leaving a drugged-up, four-year-old child alone, who then managed to let herself out of the apartment, taking the time to close the door behind her, before vanishing into thin air.

ROACHIE: Thass what happened. I'm telling you, Donovan, I doan know where—

DONOVAN: Again with that. You don't know? How the fuck do you not know anything? How the fuck—

(He rises; KEESHA moves in front of him.)

KEESHA: *(Shrieking.)* No!

DONOVAN: That's nice. Very sweet. "'Til Death Do Us Part" and all that. Okay. Let's try something else. *(To KEE-SHA.)* Take off your clothes.

ROACHIE: What?

KEESHA: Take off my clothes?

DONOVAN: You heard me. Take off your clothes.

KEESHA: Why you want—

DONOVAN: Do it.

ROACHIE: Donovan—

DONOVAN: You know what's coming, don't you? You remember what we talked about? What I said would happen to her if you fucked this up? Piece by piece, remember? Layer by layer, like an onion. *(To KEESHA.)* I'm waiting…

KEESHA: No.

DONOVAN: Excuse me?

KEESHA: No. I ain't doin it.

DONOVAN: You ain't doing it? You "ain't," huh?

KEESHA: No. I ain't. You can kill me, but I ain't gon' do this.

DONOVAN: I'm not going to kill you. But for every five seconds you take, I'm going to make a new puncture wound in his face. So if you don't get to taking it all off, I'm going to turn him into a human fucking bowling ball. You get me? Great. Here comes the pain.

(He rises; KEESHA pushes him back down.)

KEESHA: Stop it! I'll do it. I'll do it. *(To ROACHIE.)* I'm sorry baby.

(A beat. As DONOVAN speaks, she pulls the shirt over her head and tosses it on the sofa.)

DONOVAN: *(Appraising the hammer.)* I once beat a pit bull to death with one of these. A dog which I raised from the time it was a pup. Hold that thought. *(Noticing KEESHA.)* Not like that. Put it back on and start again. Like I'm a customer, baby. You know better.

(She puts the shirt back on, exhales, and during the following, slowly pulls it off, over her skin, over her head, allows it to dangle from her fingers, then drops it to the ground.)

DONOVAN: That's better. *(To ROACHIE.)* Where was I? Ah, yes. It was almost difficult for me to do, simply because I had so much time and money invested in it. The only way I was able to justify it was because the dog was a failure. A loser.

(KEESHA has begun to remove her pants, peeling them off of her, one leg, then the other, until she is clad only in a bra and panties.)

DONOVAN: Excuse me again, I'm finding it difficult to concentrate.

(He slaps her ass.)

DONOVAN: Does she still squeal when you fuck her in the ass?

KEESHA: Fuck you.

(DONOVAN slaps her.)

DONOVAN: What did we say about customer service? No more of that. *(Taps his lap.)* Come over here. *(Taps lap again.)* Come on.

(KEESHA slowly crosses to DONOVAN, turns her back to him and begins grinding against him.)

DONOVAN: Killing puppy was rough for me. I believe, however, that it would be quite easy for me to do to you, simply because, for one, I fucking hate you, and two, because, well, you know why.

(KEESHA grinds against him, a beat.)

DONOVAN: Ahhhh…the good ol' days. That's a girl. This is nice, huh? *(Beat.)* Roachie?

(ROACHIE has closed his eyes.)

DONOVAN: Open your eyes.

(No response.)

DONOVAN: Open your eyes and take a look at your girl before I come over there and cut off your fucking eyelids.

(ROACHIE does.)

DONOVAN: She's fine, huh? Now, imagine how she looked before you

ruined her. You know I used to fuck that whenever I wanted? I used to have that all the time. It was good, too. Real good. So me and you, we're practically family, all up in the same place. *(Beat.)* You know what my favorite part of Keesha is? When I'd be fucking her and her pussy would grip me. Does she still do that?

ROACHIE: Fuck you.

(DONOVAN pushes KEESHA to the floor and walks toward ROACHIE. She jumps on DONOVAN's back, who easily flips her onto the floor. He corners ROACHIE.)

DONOVAN: Give me your hand.

(He doesn't react. DONOVAN smashes him in the hip with the hammer. ROACHIE screams. DONOVAN grabs his hand and places it on the wall.)

DONOVAN: Keep still, please. And stay quiet. I need to concentrate.

(From next door, the wail of a child. DONOVAN backs away from ROACHIE. He turns to KEESHA, turns back to ROACHIE.)

DONOVAN: *(To KEESHA.)* This was all you, wasn't it? You did this. *(To ROACHIE.)* And you didn't even know. *(Back to KEESHA.)* You tricky, tricky little bitch. That's great. That's really fucking brilliant. Under my nose this entire time, huh? Wow—that's good stuff. I'm going to take care of a few things. I'll be back later, and we'll figure all of this out then, okay? Oh—and don't go anywhere—not that you could, but don't even think about it. If you make me look for you—well, you know.

(DONOVAN drops the hammer to the floor and exits. KEESHA cries quietly on the floor while ROACHIE stares in awe at her.)

Scene VI

HARRY and LIL's. A knock at the door. Silence. Another knock, harder. LIL stands at the door, pale and nervous.

DONOVAN: *(Offstage.)* Hello? Anyone home?

(Another round of knocks.)

DONOVAN: *(Offstage.)* Hello?

(The doorknob turns, but does not open. Locked. Keys. The door opens.)

LIL: You scared me.

DONOVAN: Didn't mean to do that.

LIL: I'm sorry it took me so long. I was sleeping.

DONOVAN: Forgive me. I didn't mean to wake you. Are you okay?

LIL: Yes. Tired. If you don't mind—

DONOVAN: Is Harry here?

LIL: He…stepped out. He'll be back any moment.

DONOVAN: Please excuse the interruption—I'm sorry for having entered like this, but, well, Harry asked me to check up on you if I thought anything was wrong. I was passing by and I thought I heard something—a cry of distress or something—and when you didn't answer the door, well, I let myself in to make sure everything was alright.

LIL: I'm fine. Thank you for your concern. I'll tell Harry you came by. If you don't mind—

DONOVAN: Did I hear crying from in here? I did, didn't I?

LIL: No. I don't think so.

DONOVAN: Are you sure? Because I'm quite certain—

LIL: Oh—you might have heard me. I was having a bad dream.

DONOVAN: Are you okay now?

LIL: Yes. Yes I am. Thank you. I'm sorry to be rude, but if you don't mind I'd really like to go back to sleep.

DONOVAN: Actually, if you don't mind I'd like to talk to you for a moment.

LIL: I'm sorry, I'm really not feeling very well—

DONOVAN: This will just take a few seconds. I promise. *(Motions to the table.)* Mind if I sit? *(Sits.)* Join me for a moment, would you?

LIL: I'm fine, thank you.

DONOVAN: Just for a moment. Join me. Please?

(She sits.)

DONOVAN: Thank you.

(He reaches into his jacket pocket and removes a crack pipe, a dime bag of crack, and a lighter. He opens the dime bag, removes a rock, and packs it into the pipe, then offers it to LIL. She remains perfectly still, watching him.)

LIL: No thank you.

DONOVAN: Please. I insist.

LIL: No.

DONOVAN: I won't take no for an answer.

LIL: I don't do that.

DONOVAN: You do now.

(He hands her the pipe, which she nervously fumbles with, rolling it over in her hands.)

DONOVAN: You see, I think we need to talk. In fact, I know we do. So let's talk, you and me. *(Beat, he leans in, lights the lighter.)* I believe you have something of mine.

(Blackout.)

SCENE VII

LIL at the kitchen table, perfectly rigid. Her arms are at her sides, palms down against the surface of the table, her back to the front door, staring down at the table. Keys in the door. HARRY enters, shuts the door behind him, then silently regards LIL. Neither of them move.

HARRY: *(Quiet.)* Every day, I stop at this coffee shop during my shift. Same time, every day. And every day there's this older man there, in the back by himself. Now, I have no clue what his story is, but I can clearly see that this man is alone far too much for his own good. He's…a reminder. He reminds me what I do not want to be. When I used to close my eyes, I used to see us. Me. You. Our family. Sitting somewhere nice. A house. Fresh air. Country. And then, "That." After "That," I would close my eyes and my dreams—my dreams were just the two of us. And I was okay—I made myself okay—with it. But now… I'm scared to sleep. I close my eyes and I don't see you anymore. Just me. I don't know where you've gone to. When I open my eyes, I realize how close I am to being that man. In that coffee shop. At that table. Alone. *(Long beat.)* Lil? Will you talk to me?

(HARRY walks to the table and sits across from LIL, who continues to stare at the table.)

HARRY: I'm sorry. *(Beat.)* We'll figure it out. We'll figure something out. *(Beat.)* Will you at least look at me? Please?

(Long beat. LIL looks up, still high. She is completely detached.)

LIL: He was here. *(Beat.)* He came here.

HARRY: What? Who was here?

LIL: He came here. From next door. He took her.

HARRY: What? Who from next door?

LIL: He took her.

HARRY: Who took who? The girl? I don't under—

LIL: He took her. He took her away.

HARRY: Where did he take her? Who? Next door? When?

LIL: I'm sorry, Harry. I didn't want to.

HARRY: *(Moving closer, examining her face.)* What happened? What's wrong with you?

LIL: I didn't want to.

HARRY: *(Spots the crack pipe.)* Whose is this, Lil? What the fuck is this?

LIL: He made me. Hemademehemade-mehemademe—

HARRY: Made you what? Who made you what?!?

LIL: He made me pregnant.

(Long beat. HARRY crosses to the kitchen, removes a knife from the butcher's block, and exits.)

SCENE VIII

Next door. ROACHIE is pale, sickly. His reactions are slow, labored—he is clearly in shock. KEESHA tends to his hand, which still bleeds freely.

ROACHIE: I think iss gettin bettah, yeah? Iss gettin bettah.

KEESHA: It won't stop, baby. I can't make it stop.

ROACHIE: You can.

KEESHA: We gotta get some help. I gotta get help.

ROACHIE: No. I doan want no one else touchin me. Only you.

KEESHA: Richie—

ROACHIE: No one else. Juss you. Only you.

(A beat. KEESHA stares at ROACHIE.)

KEESHA: Baby.

ROACHIE: Yeah, Keesh? Whassup?

(Silence, then:)

KEESHA: Nuthin.

ROACHIE: Iss okay, babygirl. Iss gonna be okay.

(A knock. Another knock. KEESHA grabs the hammer. The door swings open. HARRY.)

HARRY: You did this. All of this. You made this happen.

KEESHA: What tha fuck you think you doin? Get outta heah!

(She rushes toward HARRY, who thrusts the knife into her, pushing it completely through her chest. She drops the hammer and staggers backwards, eyes wide open and mouth moving frantically, silently. ROACHIE stands up in disbelief, then races to her, cradling her in his arms as he gently lowers her to the floor. He watches as the blood spreads across the front of her chest.)

ROACHIE: Keesha? Keesh! Ohmigod, baby! Ohmigod!

(Holds up his hand, which is slick with blood, then pulls her against him, rocking her against his chest as she slowly goes limp.)

ROACHIE: Jesus Christ! It ain't supposed ta be like this—you can't—no—no—no—no—no—aww, Keesha…I ain't mean ta do this ta you, baby—this wasn't supposed ta happen—I dint mean for none a this ta happen—I ain't mean ta fuck you up like this—I'm so sorry, baby! I'm so sorry! *(Lays her down on the floor, turning to HARRY, snarling.)* What did you do? What tha fuck did you do?!?

(HARRY stands motionless in the doorway, watching KEESHA on the floor, in full disbelief as to what he's done. ROACHIE scrambles toward the hammer, grabs it, rises, and races to HARRY. Blackout.)

EPILOGUE: BIRTH

Six months later. HARRY, in a wheelchair, completely incapacitated. LIL enters from the bedroom, holding a jar of baby food and a baby's bib.

LIL: Look what I found! *(Ties the bib around him.)* It's so good to have you back, baby. So good. I missed you so much. *(Stirs the baby food and has a quick taste, then begins feeding him as one would feed an infant, small spoonfuls, scooping the extra food back onto the spoon and in his mouth.)* Theeeeerrrrreeee you go. Good boy. Good, isn't it? Num num. I was so lonely without you here. *(Another spoonful, she wipes the side of his mouth with the bib.)* I didn't have anyone to talk to. And there's so much to talk about. I'm going to tell you all about it. *(Another spoonful.)* Everything is so much better since the last time you were home. So much better, baby. You're going to love it here. You're just going to love it here.

(The lights slowly dim as LIL continues to feed HARRY from the jar.)

LIL: That's good. That's a good boy. We're gonna get you all better, Harry. I'm going to take care of you until you're all better, the way you took care of me. I promise, baby boy. We're going to take care of you until you're all better. Just you and me. Isn't that right? Just you and me.

(Blackout. End of play.)

APPENDIX:
NEW AMERICAN PLAYS
IN NEW YORK

HELENA—RAISING THE BAR. *Written and performed by Helene Lantry. Directed by Padraic Lillis. Triad. Opened September 1, 2005. Closed September 22, 2005.* A rural American town attempts to become the next big tourist trap.

VIVIEN. *Written by Rick Foster. Directed by Peter Sander. American Theatre of Actors. Opened September 4, 2005. Closed September 23, 2005.* A solo play about the actress Vivien Leigh.

MIRACLE GROWN-UP. *Written and performed by Kelly Buttermore. Directed by Aaron Bergeron. Peoples Improv. Opened September 6, 2005. Closed September 27, 2005.* The author recounts her premature birth and traces her unusual journey toward adulthood.

THIS SPY SURFS. *Conceived, performed, and directed by T. Colburn and B. Klay. Where Eagles Dare. Opened September 6, 2005. Closed October 25, 2005.* A serialized mythic opera told instrumentally with surf and spy music, using computer-generated vocalizations and multidisciplinary image events.

FORGET ME NOT: THE NEW ECONOMY MASS. *Directed, handmade, and produced by Praxis. P.S. 122. Opened September 7, 2005. Closed September 13, 2005.* Performance duo Brainard Carey and Delia Bajo tell the unusual story of a loved one's death and burial.

THE AUDITION. *Created and directed by Betsy Head. Produced by Page 10 Productions, Inc. Wings Theater. Opened September 7, 2005. Closed October 1, 2005.* A reality-style theatre event in which ten actors (found in local ads and by word-of-mouth) and one lucky person chosen from the audience perform monologues for a panel of three entertainment industry professionals and the audience.

SCREEN PLAY. *Written by A.R. Gurney. Directed by Jim Simpson. Flea. Opened September 8, 2005. Closed September 30, 2005.* A political satire set in the year 2015 that envisions a future America ruled by a conservative religious majority.

ANATHEMAVILLE. *Written by Scott Venters. Directed by Jess McLeod. Produced by The Orphanage. Gene Frankel Theatre. Opened September 9, 2005. Closed September 18, 2005.* Citizens of a small town launch a battle against a giant, corporate superstore.

HALF LIFE. *Written by Robert Moulthrop. Directed by Teresa K. Pond. Produced by Seeking an Extended Run Company. Flea. Opened September 9, 2005. Closed September 24, 2005.* A family deals with the return home of a father who has just spent two years in prison for pedophilia.

HOLY CROSS SUCKS! *Written and performed by Rob Nash. Directed by Jeff Calhoun. Ars Nova. Opened September 9, 2005. Closed October 1, 2005.* A comedy about the tragedy of high school in the 1980s.

SAVING THE GREEKS. *Written by Jason Pizzarello. Directed by Michael Kimmel. Produced by Push Productions, Bay Bridge Productiions, The Grift. 14th Street Y. Opened September 9, 2005. Closed September 25, 2005.* Two ancient Greek characters create a new city where once-doomed tragic characters can start a better life.

COUCHWORKS. *Produced by Slant Theatre Project. The Tank at Chashama. Opened September 10, 2005. Closed October 4, 2005.* An evening of short plays by Rachel Axler, Evan Cabnet, Marcus Gardley, Adam Knight, Adam Rapp, Theresa Rebeck, and Mat Smart that all take place on a couch.

HI! *Written and performed by Amber Martin. Directed by Howie Baggadonutz. Greenwich Village Center Theater. Opened September 10, 2005. Closed September 24, 2005.* A solo show in which the author plays multiple characters.

PENNSYLTUCKY. *Written by Sloan MacRae. Directed by Amy Kalssar. Produced by Epiphany Theater Company. Phil Bosokowski Theatre. Opened September 10, 2005. Closed September 24, 2005.* A man tries to earn his grandfather's respect and prove his manhood by becoming a hunter.

THE TUTOR. *Book and lyrics by Maryrose Wood. Music by Andrew Gerle. Directed by Sarah Gurfield. Produced by Prospect Theater Company. 59E59. Opened September 10, 2005. Closed October 2, 2005.* A struggling young novelist's characters start coming to life while he tutors a sullen Manhattan girl for her SATs.

COMMEDIA DELL SMARTASS. *Written by Sonya Sobieski. Directed by Jean Randich. Produced by New Georges. Ohio Theatre. Opened September 12, 2005. Closed October 1, 2005.* A comedy about four students in "the treacherous ecosystem" called high school.

THE LIGHTNING FIELD. *Written by David Ozanich. Directed by Jared Coseglia. Produced by Vanner New York. Flea. Opened September 12, 2005. Closed September 28, 2005.* A New York couple makes a pilgrimage to a New Mexico art installation.

REVENGE OF A KING. *Written and directed by Herb Newsome. Produced by DAP Ensemble, Loaves and Fish Traveling Rep. Producers Club. Opened September 13, 2005. Closed September 18, 2005.* A hip-hop theatre adaptation of Shakespeare's *Hamlet*, transplanted to the gritty streets of New York.

THE BLOWIN OF BAILE GALL. *Written by Ronan Noone. Music by Haddon Kime. Directed by David Sullivan. Irish Arts Center. Opened September 13, 2005. Closed October 30, 2005.* On an Irish construction site, four workers struggle to build their futures in a changing world.

THEATRAINPLAYS, VOL. XX. *Neighborhood Playhouse. Opened September 13, 2005. Closed September 24, 2005.* A program of six fifteen-minute musicals, all created within a twenty-four-hour period, by Gaby Alter, Rick Hip-Flores, Brandon Patton, Jeremy Schonfeld, Kimberly Schwartz, Jordana Williams, amd Sean Williams (composer/lyricists) and P. Seth Bauer, Arlene Hutton, Michael Lazan, Stephen O'Rourke, Craig Pospisil, amd Erica Silberman (librettists).

LIMITLESS JOY. *Conceived and directed by Josh Fox. Produced by International WOW. CSV Cultural Center. Opened September 14, 2005. Closed October 1, 2005.* A play that examines the possibility that humanity's pursuit of joy could be the defining principle of human history.

GALAXY VIDEO 2. *Written and directed by Marc Morales. Produced by Edge of Insanity. The Red Room. Opened September 15, 2005. Closed October 8, 2005.* A sequel to *Galaxy Video*, in which the titular store re-opens under corporate ownership with plans to franchise.

GIANT-N-VARIATION. *Written by Francis Kuzler. Directed by Eric Amburg. Produced by Boomerang Theatre Company. Center Stage. Opened September 15, 2005. Closed October 1, 2005.* A linguist tours farms around the country researching her theory that some form of communication with cows is possible.

LUNCH AT ARMAGEDDON. *Written by Richard Lay. Directed by Sincha Borenstein. Produced by Sage Theatre Company. Blue Heron Arts Center. Opened September 15, 2005. Closed October 2, 2005.* An American, a Palestinian, and a former actress all cross paths at a northern Israel café.

STEALING HOME. *Written and performed by Raymond Alvin. Directed by Holli Harms. WorkShop Theatre. Opened September 15, 2005. Closed October 8, 2005.* A solo show set in 1957 Brooklyn amidst rumors that the Dodgers are leaving the borough.

STILL-LIFE WITH RUNNER. *Written by Steven Gridley. Directed by Steven Gridley and Jacob Titus. Spring Theatreworks. Opened September 15, 2005. Closed October 22, 2005.* An exploration of the wandering thoughts of a runner as he competes in a distance race.

THE ROOF. *Written by Suzanne Bradbeer. Directed by Maggie Low. Produced by Blue Collar Theater Company. Sanford Meisner Theatre. Opened September 15, 2005. Closed October 1, 2005.* A family drama set in New York during the inter-war years from 1919 to 1939.

THE ISRAELI-PALESTINIAN CONFLICT: A ROMANTIC COMEDY. *Written and performed by Negin Farsad and Alexander Zalben. Music by Gaby Alter. Directed by Bob Wittfong. Peoples Improv Theatre. Opened September 16, 2005. Closed October 14, 2005.* A sketch-based show that tracks the notorious Mid-East conflict back to a botched one-night stand at the Geneva Convention.

THE LAST BOHEMIANS. *Written and directed by Stelios Manolakakis. Produced by Princes' Kisses Theatre Group. Medicine Show. Opened September 16, 2005. Closed October 2, 2005.* A play about the final summer of poet Frank O'Hara and his friends as they inhabit a house in the Hamptons.

GOOD LIFE, GREAT PRICE. *Created and performed by Esteban Arboleda, J J Lind, Maki Takenouchi, and Liz Vacco. Produced by Immediate Medium. The Tank at Chashama. Opened September*

18, 2005. *Closed September 26, 2005.* A performance piece inspired by a trip to a Sears portrait studio, during which company members dressed in Sears clothing and posed together in six different family style portraits.

MIRACLE BROTHERS. *Written by Kirsten Childs. Directed by Tina Landau. Vineyard Theatre. Opened September 18, 2005. Closed October 16, 2005.* The story of two young Brazilian brothers during the 1600s—one black and one white, one a slave and the other free—divided by race but united in their determination to find a new way to live.

CONSTRUCTION. *Written by Victor Hawks. Directed by Bill Buell. Theatre 5. Opened September 19, 2005. Closed October 2, 2005.* The private lives of three construction workers who struggle with their identities at work and behind closed doors.

THE INTELLIGENT DESIGN OF JENNY CHOW. *Written by Rolin Jones. Music by Matthew Suttor. Directed by Jackson Gay. Atlantic Theatre. Opened September 19, 2005. Closed October 15, 2005.* An agoraphobic young woman builds an artificial version of herself to search for her birth mother.

KISSING FIDEL. *Written by Eduardo Machado. Directed by Michael John Garces. Produced by INTAR. Kirk Theatre. Opened September 20, 2005. Closed October 16, 2005.* A Cuban American novelist returns home on the eve of his mother's funeral to announce his plans to return to Cuba and kiss and fogive Fidel Castro.

THE PAVILION. *Written by Craig Wright. Directed by Lucie Tiberghein. Rattlestick Theatre. Opened September 20, 2005. Closed October 23, 2005.* Two old flames reunite at an old Minnesota dance hall for one last dance.

CHRISTINA OLSON: AMERICAN MODEL. *Conceived by Tamar Rogoff. Music by Rachel's. P.S. 122. Opened September 21, 2005. Closed October 2, 2005.* A solo dance piece about Christina Olsen, the woman in the pink dress depicted in Andrew Wyeth's painting, *Christina's World.*

DR. SEX. *Book by Larry Bortniker and Sally Deering. Signature at Peter Norton Space. Opened September 21, 2005. Closed October 9, 2005.* A musical about Alfred Kinsey, his wife, and their boyfriend.

GAY SLAVE HANDBOOK. *Written and directed by Blake Bradford. Producers Club. Opened September 21, 2005. Closed September 24, 2005.* A group of former high school friends try to cope with the love they used to share for one another during the New York City blackout of 2003.

MRS. WEINBERG'S PROFESSION. *Directed by Erin Smiley. Produced by Etcetera Theatre Company. Creative Place. Opened September 21, 2005. Closed September 28, 2005.* A new adaptation of George Bernard Shaw's *Mrs. Warren's Profession*, set in 1920s New York.

THE SAFETY NET. *Written by Christopher Kyle. Directed by Martha Banta. Produced by Broken Watch Theatre Company. Michael Weller Theatre. Opened September 22, 2005. Closed October 9, 2005.* A man returns to his Midwest home to uncover the secrets of his dead brother's past.

EINSTEIN'S SECRET LETTERS (A LOVE STORY). *Written by J.B. Edwards. Directed by G. Beaudin. Walkerspace. Opened September 23, 2005. Closed October 8, 2005.* Based on Albert Einstein's love letters to his close friend, Johanna Fantova.

GOOD CHRISTIAN. *Book by Brian Griffin. Music and lyrics by Ty Robinson. Directed by Ty Robinson. Theater Studio. Opened September 23, 2005. Closed September 24, 2005.* A contemporary musical love story about a man named Christian Johnson and what happens when he decides to "find himself."

POOR THEATER. *Directed by Elizabeth LeCompte. Produced by The Wooster Group. The Performing Garage. Opened September 23, 2005. Closed October 15, 2005.* An homage to the work of three seminal figures of twentieth century art: theatre director Jerzy Grotwoski, choreographer William Forsythe, and visual artist Max Ernst.

RAISINS NOT VIRGINS. *Written by Sharbari Ahmed. Directed by Thomas Cote. WorkShop Theatre. Opened September 23, 2005. Closed October 22, 2005.* A young American Muslim woman living in New York embarks on her own personal jihad after losing her boyfriend.

NOT ENOUGH PRINCESSES. *Adapted and directed by Shari Johnson. Looking Glass Theatre. Opened September 24, 2005. Closed November 6, 2005.* A play for children based on classic, though not well-known, Swedish fairy tales.

SUBWAY STORIES FROM WAYSIDE SCHOOL. *Adapted by John Olive. Directed by Laura Stevens. Produced by Manhattan Children's Theatre. 52 White Street. Opened September 24, 2005. Closed November 6, 2005.* A play for children adapted from Louis Sachar's *Wayside School* novels.

FRAN'S BED. *Written and directed by James Lapine. Playwrights Horizons Mainstage. Opened September 25, 2005. Closed October 9, 2005.* A middle-aged woman ruminates on her past while in a coma in a hospital bed.

GEORGE SAUNDERS'S PASTORALIA. *Adapted and directed by Yehuda Duenyas. P.S. 122. Opened September 25, 2005. Closed October 9, 2005.* Two employees at a historically themed amusement park face the possibility of getting laid off.

NO FOREIGNERS BEYOND THIS POINT. *Written by Warren Leight. Directed by Loy Arcenas. Produced by Ma-Yi Theater Company. 45 Below. Opened September 25, 2005. Closed October 16, 2005.* A play inspired by the author's experiences teaching English in China in 1980.

ASSISTED LOVING. *Written and performed by Bob Morris. Produced by MCC Theater. Lucille Lortel Theatre. Opened September 26, 2005. Closed October 17, 2005.* A solo play about a terminally single man and the efforts of his eighty-year-old father to help him find love again.

THE GREAT AMERICAN TRAILER PARK MUSICAL. *Book by Betsy Kelso. Music and lyrics by David Nehls. Directed by Betsy Kelso. Dodger Stages. Opened September 27, 2005. Closed December 4, 2005.* An on-the-run stripper moves into a trailer park and wreaks havoc on the other tenants.

IN THE WINGS. *Written by Stewart F. Lane. Directed by Jeremy Dobrish. Promenade Theatre. Opened September 28, 2005. Closed October 16, 2005.* Two struggling actors find their love put to the test when one of them gets their big break in a Broadway musical.

BUSH IS BAD. *Written by Joshua Rosenblum. Directed by Gary Slavin. Triad. Opened September 29, 2005. Closed December 30, 2006.* A musical revue that takes aim at President Bush and his advisors.

DESERT SUNRISE. *Written and directed by Misha Shulman. Theatre for the New City. Opened September 29, 2005. Closed October 23, 2005.* An Israeli soldier and a Palestinian man try to forge a bond based on something more than fear and hatred.

LA PLAYA (THE BEACH). *Written and directed by Roi "Bubi" Escudero. Produced by Environmental Theatre de Camara, ETdC Art Projects. Where Eagles Dare. Opened September 29, 2005. Closed November 12, 2005.* A multimedia theatre piece in which the main characters both have something to hide and a motive to kill.

LENZ. *Written by Stephen O'Connell and Sabrina Reeves. Produced by bluemouth inc. Ye Old Carlton Arms Hotel. Opened September 29, 2005. Closed October 8, 2005.* A site-specific performance installation that occurs in three separate hotel rooms simultaneously. **SEE PAGE 15.**

THE BUBBLE. *Written by Frank J. Avella. Music by Joe Morse. Produced by The New Cockpit Ensemble. Bank Street Theatre. Opened September 29, 2005. Closed October 16, 2005.* A playwright's characters come to life and stage a mutiny while he attempts to write the perfect play.

THE KARMA COOKIE. *Written by P. Seth Bauer. Directed by Eric Nightengale. 78th Street Theatre Lab. Opened September 29, 2005. Closed October 8, 2005.* Two brothers travel the world trying to follow the laws of the universe.

TO DIE FOUR. *Produced by Darknight. Next Stage. Opened September 29, 2005. Closed October 1, 2005.* A program of four one-act plays by Kevin Clancy, Thomas Patrick Clancy, Nick Leshi, and Danielle Nichole Tyler about being wanted, dead or alive.

BELLY. *Written and performed by Julie Tortorici. Directed by Alicia Arinella. Produced by On the Leesh Productions. Gene Frankel Theatre. Opened September 30, 2005. Closed October 28, 2005.* A solo play about a housebound, obsessive-compulsive housewife who is surprised to find an audience in her living room.

STILL LIFE GOES ON. *Written and directed by Christine Melton-Jordan. Music by Tyrone Brown. New Amsterdam Musical Association. Opened September 30, 2005. Closed November 6, 2005.* A reclusive nightclub owner and his headline singer cling to each other while trying to restore their shattered lives in 1968 Greenwich Village.

THE BEAST FESTIVAL. *Directed by Nancy Rogers. Triangle Theatre. Opened September 30, 2005. Closed October 15, 2005.* A program of plays exploring the relationships between humans and animals: **CALLING LUIS,** *by Leah Ryan*; **DOUGLAS,** *by Robert Fieldsteel*; **THE CAT,** *by Linda Thomas*; **DAILY BREAD FOR THE DOE,** *by Randy Moomaw*; **GORDY,** *by Don Carter*; **HEARING ELEPHANTS,** *by Frank Higgins*; **MAX,** *by Elise Robertson*; **PIGEONS IN THE PARK,** *by Alex Nicol*; and **THE WORLD'S FIRST VEGETARIANS BY MORAL CONVICTION,** *by Rich Amada*.

VENUS IN FURS. *Adapted and directed by Michael Scott-Price. Produced by Firebrand Theory Theatre Company. Collective Unconscious. Opened September 30, 2005. Closed October 16, 2005.* Based on the novel by Leopold von Sacher-Masoch, a wealthy dilettante falls in love with a woman who reluctantly agrees to role-play his desire to become a sex slave.

FATA MORGANA. *Directed by David Solomon Rodriguez. Produced by 2 Cities Productions. Triad. Opened October 1, 2005. Closed November 8, 2005.* A multimedia performance piece about a cabaret house whose family of performers has become trapped within a new and sinister reality.

LATE FRAGMENT. *Written by Francine Volpe. Directed by Michael Imperioli and Zetna Fuentes. Studio Dante. Opened October 1, 2005. Closed October 22, 2005.* A man flees the attack on the World Trade Center and returns home to face an impatient wife, their manipulative lawyer, and reporters desperate to spin his ordeal into a hero's story.

SLUT. *Music by Stephen Sislen. Directed by Gordon Greenberg. American Theatre of Actors. Opened October 1, 2005. Closed November 13, 2005.* The story of a charismatic and handsome man named Adam, his shy but brilliant friend Doctor Dan, and the sexy rocker named Delia who comes between them.

TOO CLOSE? *Directed by Mana Allen. Produced by Current Company. Duplex. Opened October 1, 2005. Closed October 15, 2005.* A cabaret musical about two girls and two guys seeking affection, distraction, and some room to stand.

A WOMAN OF WILL. *Written by Amanda McBroom and Joel Silberman. Music by Joel Silberman. Lyrics by Amanda McBroom. Directed by Joel Silberman. Daryl Roth Theatre. Opened October 2, 2005. Closed October 9, 2005.* The musical adventure of a writer in crisis—both personal and professional—who reaches out to Shakespeare's heroines for guidance as she tries to finish the lyrics for a Broadway musical version of *The Merchant of Venice.*

THE GREAT AMERICAN DESERT. *Book and lyrics by Joel Oppenheimer. Music by Joe Schlitz and Joe Jung. Directed by Garrett Ayers. Produced by Try Try Again Theatre Company. 78th Street Theatre Lab. Opened October 3, 2005. Closed October 16, 2005.* A musical about three cowboys on the run from the law after a bank robbery.

JULIA. *Music by Ken Mizak. Directed by Kathleen Torchia. Produced by Capitol Opera. Beckett Theatre. Opened October 4, 2005. Closed October 9, 2005.* Set in Virginia City, Nevada, in the early 1860s, a British courtesan becomes a prominent madam.

PLATINUM TRAVEL CLUB. *Written by Franca Miraglia. Directed by Anne Beaumont. Produced by New Perspectives Theatre. Pelican Studio/New Perspectives. Opened October 4, 2005. Closed October 22, 2005.* A successful businesswoman joins an exclusive business travelers' sex club while confronting the ghosts of her damaged childhood.

THE SEVEN DEADLY SINS: 2005. *Written by Dale Johnson. Directed by Dale Johnson and Jason Godbey. Kraine Theatre. Opened October 4, 2005. Closed October 26, 2005.* A satirical social commentary that covers job exportation, sexual mores, gun control, homelessness, and global warming.

...FOUR ONE-LEGGED MEN! *Written and performed by Gary Corbin. Directed by William Martin. Producers Club. Opened October 5, 2005. Closed October 23, 2005.* Four vignettes depicting four distinct amputees from different backgrounds, seasons, and eras.

TOUCH ME/ROSA RUGOSA. *Written by Charles Cissel. Directed by Terese Hayden. Center Stage. Opened October 5, 2005. Closed October 16, 2005.* A program of two plays by Charles Cissel.

A NAKED GIRL ON THE APPIAN WAY. *Written by Richard Greenberg. Directed by Doug Hughes. Produced by Roundabout Theatre Company. American Airlines Theatre. Opened October 6, 2005. Closed December 4, 2005.* The lives of a successful cookbook author and her husband, a distracted genius, are up-ended when two of their children return from a year of European travel and reveal surprising news.

REBEL WITHOUT A CAUSE. *Written by James Fuller. Directed by Brian Stites and Joshua Coleman. Produced by Barely Balancing Artists Group. Lion Theatre. Opened October 6, 2005. Closed October 30, 2005.* A stage adaptation of the classic James Dean film.

BURNING BUSH: A FAITH-BASED MUSICAL. *Written and directed by Noah Diamond and Amanda Sisk. Music by Death Mask. Produced by Nero Fiddled. HERE Arts Center. Opened October 7, 2005. Closed October 16, 2005.* A musical that features rubber frogs, a folk-singing First Lady, and the President's childhood envisioned as a parody of *The Who's Tommy.*

DEVIANT. *Written by A. Rey Pamatmat. Directed by Kara-Lynn Vaeni. Produced by Vortex Theater Company and TheatREX. Sanford Meisner Theatre. Opened October 7, 2005. Closed October 23, 2005.* Worlds collide when Sara and Valerie—a couple pursuing the American Dream—find out their new roommate James is a gay prostitute too jaded to believe that dreams still matter.

HAM AND CHEESE. *Written and directed by Jessica Arnold and Andrew Toutain. Produced by The Rapscallions of the Periphery. Under St. Marks. Opened October 7, 2005. Closed October 22, 2005.* A woman tries to get by working in the service industry by day and directing a play about her experience in the service industry by night.

MEMOIRS OF MY NERVOUS ILLNESS. *Adapted and directed by Michael Gardner. Brick Theatre. Opened October 7, 2005. Closed October 29, 2005.* A stage adaptation of the nineteenth century book by Daniel Paul Schreber, who wrote it, in part, to get himself out of the asylum in which he was incarcerated.

MOST HAPPY. *Written and directed by George Tynan Crowley. Bennigans. Opened October 7, 2005. Closed October 24, 2005.* The story of the political rise and fall of Anne Boleyn, second wife to England's King Henry VIII, and her quest to topple the wave of Catholic imperialism with the aid of her sister Mary and poet Thomas Wyatt.

SALLY AND TOM (THE AMERICAN WAY). *Book and lyrics by Fred Newman. Music by Annie Roboff. Directed by Fred Newman and Gabrielle L. Kurlander. Castillo Theatre. Opened October 7, 2005. Closed December 4, 2005.* An original musical about Sally Hemings, Thomas Jefferson's slave and (some say) the love of his life.

THE NANOLOVE REPORT. *Author/storyteller Jon Brunelle. Music by Mad EP. Produced by The Psychasthenia Society. Collective Unconscious. Opened October 7, 2005. Closed October 28, 2005.* Storytelling meets the sampling culture as live VJ and DJ action blends with satiric tales told through a stream of remixed movie stills.

THE CATERERS. *Written by Jonathan Leaf. Directed by Jose Zayas. Produced by Immediate Theater Company. Altered Stages. Opened October 10, 2005. Closed October 30, 2005.* A play that re-imagines the 1977 takeover of several buildings in Washington, D.C., by the radical Islamic group, Hanafi, in the present day.

MURDERING MARLOWE. *Written by Charles Marowitz. Directed by Jason King Jones. Produced by In Actu Theatre. Access Theatre. Opened October 11, 2005. Closed October 23, 2005.* A historical play about the theatrical and literary rivalry between William Shakespeare and Christopher Marlowe.

WAR IN PARAMUS. *Written by Barbara Dana. Directed by Austin Pendleton. Abingdon Theatre. Opened October 11, 2005. Closed November 6, 2005.* A New Jersey teenager wages war on the compromised values of her inadequate role models in 1970 Paramus.

THE WAR AT DAWN. *Written by Eric Alter. Directed by Rodney E. Reyes. Produced by Apricot Sky Productions. American Theatre of Actors. Opened October 12, 2005. Closed October 30, 2005.* In a fictitious 2010 America ravaged by nuclear attacks, two young soldiers stumble into a very private war on the eve of being shipped out for duty.

CONFERENCE ROOM A. *Written by Ben Cikanek. Directed by Mike Klar. The Red Room. Opened October 13, 2005. Closed November 5, 2005.* An office worker attempts to seduce her boss after hours while her former lover constantly tries to thwart her.

LA TEMPESTAD. *Written by Larry Loebell. Directed by Eric Parness. Produced by Resonance Ensemble. Ohio Theatre. Opened October 13, 2005. Closed October 30, 2005.* A contemporary retelling of Shakespeare's *The Tempest* set on the Puerto Rican island of Vieques.

LATINOLOGUES. *Written by Rick Najera. Directed by Cheech Marin. Helen Hayes Theatre. Opened October 13, 2005. Closed December 31, 2005.* A collection of comedic and poignant monologues revealing the Latino experience in America.

THE COLLECTION. *Written by Christina Masciotti. chashama. Opened October 13, 2005. Closed October 30, 2005.* An Austrian-born couturier embarks on a legal battle and finds the test of her will in the New York City subway system.

BLACK FOLKS GUIDE TO BLACK FOLKS. *Written and performed by Hanifah Walidah. Produced by Wabi Sabi Productions. Producers Club. Opened October 14, 2005. Closed October 30, 2005.* A solo show about homophobia in the African American community.

PENNY-4-EYES ROCK N' ROLL SHOW. *Written and directed by Jesse Cooper. Gibson Guitar Show Room. Opened October 14, 2005. Closed October 31, 2005.* A fourteen-year-old girl tries to break out of the dysfunctional cycles of her abusive parents.

THE ADVENTURES OF LOCK AND KAY. *Written and performed by Lennon Parham and Melle Powers. Directed by Julie Brister. Upright Citizens Brigade. Opened October 15, 2005. Closed December 12, 2005.* A fictional pop superstar duo grow from little pageant princesses to music royalty, struggle with their parents, and find their voices in one another.

THE GIRL IN THE FLAMMABLE SKIRT. *Written by Aimee Bender. Directed by Bridgette Dunlap. Produced by Ateh Theater Group. Walkerspace. Opened October 15, 2005. Closed October 29, 2005.* A play based on stories from the book by Aimee Bender.

BEOWULF. *Music and lyrics by Lenny Pickett. Directed by Charlotte Moore. Irish Repertory Theatre. Opened October 16, 2005. Closed November 27, 2005.* A ritualistic rock opera based on the old English epic poem.

FIVE COURSE LOVE. *Book, music, and lyrics by Gregg Coffin. Directed by Emma Griffin. Minetta Lane Theatre. Opened October 16, 2005. Closed December 31, 2005.* A musical that follows five dates in five restaurants as the characters search for love.

REBOUND & GAGGED. *Written by Aaron Ginsburg. Directed by Stephen Sunderlin. Produced by Vital Theatre Company. McGinn Cazale Theatre. Opened October 18, 2005. Closed November 6, 2005.* A heartbroken man nearing his thirtieth birthday goes through a quarterlife crisis while replaying scenes from his failed relationship with sock puppets.

HAIL, SATAN. *Written by Mac Rogers. Directed by Jordana Williams. Produced by Gideon Productions. Manhattan Theatre Source. Opened October 19, 2005. Closed October 29, 2005.* A man discovers all of his new coworkers are Satan worshippers.

POETICS: A BALLET BRUT. *Conceived and directed by Pavol Liska. Produced by Columbia Stages. Theatre of the Riverside Church. Opened October 19, 2005. Closed October 22, 2005.* A nonverbal performance piece.

THE DEVIL OF DELANCEY STREET. *Written and directed by Sharon Fogarty. Produced by Making Light. 78th Street Theatre Lab. Opened October 19, 2005. Closed November 5, 2005.* A kidnapped children's book author calls on the help of the local Devil in 1930s New York.

ASHLEY MONTANA GOES ASHORE IN THE CAICOS. *Written by Roger Rosenblatt. Directed by Jim Simpson. Flea. Opened October 20, 2005. Closed November 19, 2005.* A series of funny vignettes about aging, angst, missed opportunities, New York, new age, the next big thing, and the last hurrah.

IN MY LIFE. *Book, music, and lyrics by Joseph Brooks. Directed by Joseph Brooks. Music Box Theatre. Opened October 20, 2005. Closed December 11, 2005.* A musical by Joseph Brooks, who won an Oscar for the song "You Light Up My Life" back in 1977.

PAGANINI, SPEAK NO EVIL. *Written and directed by Samuel Harps. Music by Vracha Malkin. Produced by White Star Productions. Jan Hus Playhouse. Opened October 20, 2005. Closed October 22, 2005.* The life of seventeenth century Italian violinist Nicollo Paganini.

THE RETREAT. *Written and directed by Arthur Reel. Produced by Drama Committee Repertory Theatre. Theatre 54 @ Shetler. Opened October 20, 2005. Closed October 23, 2005.* A tragic farce, partly based on the short story "Enemies" by Anton Chekhov, about a tormented doctor who is bewildered by the sexual shenanigans of an eclectic group of people he encounters.

FLIRTING WITH REALITY. *Written by Suzanne Bachner. Directed by Trish Minskoff. Produced by John Montgomery Theatre Company. The Red Room. Opened October 21, 2005. Closed November 14, 2005.* This comedy goes behind the scenes at a reality dating TV show, and follows a producer and cameraman as they choose from hundreds of wannabe contestants.

FLYER. *Written by Kate Aspengren. Directed by Karen Sommers. Produced by 3Graces Theater Co. Bank Street Theatre. Opened October 23, 2005. Closed November 6, 2005.* A play based on the true account of the Mercury 13, the first U.S. female astronaut testing program in the early 1960s.

IN PRIVATE/IN PUBLIC. *Written by George Hunka. Directed by Isaac Butler. Manhattan Theatre Source. Opened October 23, 2005. Closed October 25, 2005.* A program of two short plays, one about a man and a woman trying to pin down the elusive nature of desire over time and distance, and the other about two married couples who play out their tensions and pleasures in a variety of Upper West Side locations.

INDIA AWAITING. *Written by Anne Marie Cummings. Music by Deep Singh. Directed by Tyler Marchant. Produced by Immediate Vision. Beckett Theatre. Opened October 23, 2005. Closed November 6, 2005.* A modern cross-cultural love story between a young Indian man and a Spanish American woman.

KARLA. *Written by Steve Earle. Directed by Bruce Kronenberg. 45 Below. Opened October 23, 2005. Closed November 13, 2005.* Based on the true story of Karla Faye Tucker, the first woman in Texas to receive the death penalty and have it carried it out since the Civil War.

THE TELLING. *Written by Crystal Skillman. Directed by Daniel Talbott. Produced by Rising Phoenix Repertory. Seventh Street Small Stage. Opened October 23, 2005. Closed October 31, 2005.* A one-act play about two estranged sisters who reunite on the night before the closing of their family's inn.

THIRD. *Written by Wendy Wasserstein. Music by Robert Waldman. Directed by Daniel Sullivan. Produced by Lincoln Center. Mitzi Newhouse Theater. Opened October 24, 2005. Closed December 18, 2005.* Wendy Wasserstein's final play, about a college professor whose life is thrown into disarray after she accuses a student of plagiarism.

MYSTIC TV. *Written by Mary Elizabeth Shanahan. Directed by Geeta Citygirl. Produced by Spotlight on Halloween Festival. The Monster. Opened October 25, 2005. Closed November 3, 2005.* The hosts and guests of a religious-themed TV show put their egos and personal agendas ahead of religion and tolerance.

RECONSTRUCTION. *Written by Clifford Lee Johnson III. Directed by Tom Coash. Produced by The Open Book. 78th Street Theatre Lab. Opened October 27, 2005. Closed November 19, 2005.* A married couple's love and sex life are tested when the wife is diagnosed with breast cancer.

SHORT STORIES 7. *Players Theatre. Produced by NativeAliens Theatre Collective. Opened October 27, 2005. Closed November 5, 2005.* A program of new short gay-themed plays:

- **THE VIGIL,** *by James J. Harker, directed by Jodi Smith.*
- **TRIPPING THE LIGHT FANTASTIC,** *by Sean Michael O'Donnell, directed by Nancy Rogers.*
- **(SNAP)SHOT,** *by Brian St. John Brooks, directed by Elizabeth A. Ramirez.*
- **FUN WITH JAY LENO: A SHAMELESS DOMESTIC DRAMA,** *by Julian Olf, directed by Jennie Contuzzi.*
- **SUBURBAN SOLDIER,** *by Erik Christian Hanson, directed by Elizabeth A. Ramirez.*
- **PENNY'S ONE DATE,** *by Lisa Ferber, directed by Scott Smith.*

THE INVISIBLE MAN. *Written by H.G. Wells. Music by Anthony Cochrane. Directed by Doug Varone. Produced by Aquila Theatre Company. Baruch Performing Arts Center. Opened October 27, 2005. Closed November 6, 2005.* A theatre and dance piece based on the classic H.G. Wells novel.

CATHAY: THREE TALES OF CHINA. *Written and directed by Ping Chong. Produced by Ping Chong & Company with the Shaanxi Folk Art Theatre. New Victory Theatre. Opened October 28, 2005. Closed November 13, 2005.* A puppet theatre piece that tells three different stories that span Chinese history.

TO NINEVEH. *Written by Bekah Brunstetter. Directed by Isaac Byrne. Produced by Working Man's Clothes Productions. American Place Theatre. Opened October 28, 2005. Closed November 13, 2005.* A Miracle Play about the fall of an American family and the birth of a new era.

RADIANT RUBY. *Book and lyrics by Dante Russo. Music by Rob Baumgartner Jr. Directed by Jason Summers. Produced by Vital Children's Theatre. McGinn Cazale Theatre. Opened October 29, 2005. Closed December 4, 2005.* A musical narrated by three goldfish about a seven-year-old girl's quest to become the most popular girl in school.

TOUGHING SLUMARIA. *Written by Janeen Stevens. Directed by Barry Gomolka. Produced by Original Intent Theater. Center Stage. Opened October 29, 2005. Closed November 13, 2005.* Four young single welfare mothers in the same apartment building form a bond to endure their sexually predatory landlord.

MANIC FLIGHT REACTION. *Written by Sarah Schulman. Directed by Trip Cullman. Playwrights Horizons Peter J Sharp. Opened October 30, 2005. Closed November 20, 2005.* A middle-aged professor must confront the demons of her idealistic past when her daughter learns that one of her past liaisons is the wife of a leading presidential candidate.

NORMAL. *Book by Yvonne Adrian. Music by Tom Kochan. Lyrics by Cheryl Stern. Directed by Jack Cummings III. Produced by Transport Group. Connelly Theatre. Opened October 30, 2005. Closed November 12, 2005.* A musical about a mother's determination to save her daughter, whose life is threatened by an eating disorder.

SEE WHAT I WANNA SEE. *Book, music, and lyrics by Michael John LaChiusa. Directed by Ted Sperling. Public Theater. Opened October 30, 2005. Closed December 4, 2005.* Two short musicals suggested by stories by Japanese writer Ryunosuke Akutagawa: the first is a retelling of the "Rashomon" story, set in Manhattan in 1951; the second is about a hoax gone badly astray, and takes place in Central Park in the present day.

THE MAN WHO LAUGHS. *Scenario and text by Kiran Rikhye. Music by Emily Otto. Directed by Jon Stancato. Produced by Stolen Chair Theatre Company. The Red Room. Opened October 31, 2005. Closed November 12, 2005.* A live silent film for stage, freely inspired by the novel by Victor Hugo.

A MOTHER, A DAUGHTER, AND A GUN. *Written by Barra Grant. Directed by Jonathan Lynn. Dodger Stages. Opened November 1, 2005. Closed November 20, 2005.* A dark comedy about mothers, daughters, and the emotional outbursts only they know how to trigger.

AN EVENING OF ONE ACTS. *Produced by Etcetera Theatre Company. Creative Place. Opened November 1, 2005. Closed November 3, 2005.* A program of short plays:

- ENOUGH, *by Kelly Barrett, directed by Wende O'Reilly.*
- MOTHER'S DAY, *written and directed by Debbie Feldman.*
- IN RETROSPECTIVE, *by Harman Ansevin, directed by Rob Aloi.*
- THE GUYS WATCH THE GAME, *by Eddie Dean, directed by Robert Sperling.*
- CATCHING FAIRIES, *by Le Wilhelm, directed by Sasha Kern.*
- MAN OF YOUR DREAMS, *by Le Wilhelm, directed by Irungu Mutu.*

EATFEST. *Produced by Emerging Artists Theatre Company. Theater Five. Opened November 1, 2005. Closed November 20, 2005.* New short works by emerging playwrights:

- WALLY AND JESUS, *by Christopher Heath, directed by Dylan McCullouogh.* A young man accuses Jesus of shooting his mother.
- LAUGHING ALL THE WAY, *by Carol Mullen, directed by Deb Guston.* A woman makes a life-altering confession to her lover.
- CLOUDY, *by Michael Griffo, directed by Derek Jamison.* A woman attempts to fit a piece into the puzzle of her life.
- ALL THE DETAILS, *by Cary Pepper, directed by Troy Miller.* An unidentified man sitting in a beach chair on a busy street gets some media attention.

- **REUNION,** *by William Borden, directed by Paul Adams.* Two former high school classmates, now elderly, come to terms with one another.
- **FINAL ANSWER,** *by Marc Castle, directed by Kevin Dodd.* An actress is a contestant on an absurdist game show.
- **CUPID'S BEAU,** *by Barbara Lindsay, directed by Ian Streicher.* A mild flirtation quickly develops into a deeper attraction.
- **A TOUCHING STORY,** *by Rich Orloff, directed by Jeffrey Lawhorn.* A swinging couple invites a man into their hotel room for a sexual adventure.
- **HOW CAN LOVE SURVIVE,** *by Kevin Brofsky, directed by S. Caden Hethorn.* A son visits his lonely mother at Christmas.
- **LEAN LOVE CITY,** *by Dan Blask, directed by Eric Chase.* Two lovelorn men plead their case to a friend.
- **PARK BENCH,** *by Kristyn Leigh Robinson, directed by Mahayana Landowne.* Differences in perspectives of two generations.
- **LARRY GETS THE CALL,** *by Matt Casarino, directed by Melissa Atteberry.* A moment in the afterlife gets an interesting twist.

ONE MAN'S WAR. *Written and directed by Sammy Dallas Bayes. Produced by New Century Productions, Steffles Productions. Triad. Opened November 2, 2005. Closed November 20, 2005.* The story of a 1960s New York gang member who is given a choice between going to jail and joining the Marines.

MAKING MAMA PROUD. *Written and performed by Alex Altomonte. Directed by Megan Staley. Under St. Marks. Opened November 3, 2005. Closed November 5, 2005.* A solo show about a fame-seeking, media-obsessed Cuban man and his like-minded mother.

OUT, OUT DAMNED CLOCK: FAUST MEETS MACBETH! *Written by Nathaniel Green. Produced by Footlight Players. Michael Weller Theatre. Opened November 3, 2005. Closed November 13, 2005.* A drama-comedy-fantasy about two brothers learning to value every moment of life.

SISTER AND MISS LEXIE. *Written by David Kaplan and Brenda Currin. Directed by David Kaplan. Flea. Opened November 3, 2005. Closed December 18, 2005.* A play with music adapted from the works of Mississippi author Eudora Welty.

SUICIDE, THE MUSICAL. *Written by Helen Stratford. P.S. 122. Opened November 3, 2005. Closed November 5, 2005.* A punk rock opera about a woman's struggle to survive in New York after leaving a comfortable but self-destructive relationship.

DANIELLA USES DIRTY WORDS. *Written by Matthew Moses. Music by Carlton DeWoody and Tyler Burba. Directed by Kim T. Sharp. Abingdon Theatre. Opened November 4, 2005. Closed November 20, 2005.* A Brooklyn teenager can't refrain from speaking her mind, much to the chagrin of her mother, boyfriend, high school principal, and classmates.

ESTRELLA. *Written by Kate Bell. Produced by Committed Theatre Company. Bernie West Theater. Opened November 4, 2005. Closed November 20, 2005.* Two women reunite many years after first meeting in a church.

JANE HO. *Written by John Pallotta. Music by Andy Cohen. Directed by Arian Blanco. Produced by Hudson Exploited Theater Company. Lion Theatre. Opened November 4, 2005. Closed November 19, 2005.* An exploration of the inner workings of the life of a high-priced call girl.

THAT'S NOT HOW MAHLER DIED. *Created and directed by Ryan Holsopple. Music by Tara Novak. Produced by 31 Down Radio Theater. Brick Theatre. Opened November 4, 2005. Closed November 19, 2005.* A multimedia theatre piece about a 1950s private investigator encountering the same loneliness and preoccupations with death that marked the last year of composer Gustave Mahler's life.

THE EVOLUTION OF A SEXY MUTHA FUKAH. *Written and performed by Sue Costello. Directed by John Gould Rubin. Zipper Theatre. Opened November 4, 2005. Closed November 12, 2005.* A solo show about the author's painful childhood and the liberating realization that her past did not have to be her future.

BARNSTORMER. *Book and lyrics by Cheryl L. Davis. Music by Douglas J. Cohen. Directed by Jerry Dixon. Lark Studio. Opened November 5, 2005. Closed November 16, 2005.* An African American girl from rural Texas yearns to be an airplane pilot.

SÉANCE ON WEST 36TH. *Written by Michael Kaimen. Directed by Shela Xoregos. Produced by Xoregos Performing Company. Where Eagles Dare. Opened November 5, 2005. Closed November 19, 2005.* A program of two one-act plays: one is a drama in four monologues about the seamy downside of an upscale corporate law firm; the other is a comedy about two phony spiritualists who inadvertently conjure up a very real spirit.

SIZE ATE. *Written and performed by Margaux Laskey. Directed by Steven McElroy. Produced by size ate productions. Theater Five. Opened November 5, 2005. Closed November 19, 2005.* A solo show about one woman's struggle with food, weight, and body image.

BARTLEBY, THE SCRIVENER. *Written by R.L. Lane. Directed by Alessandro Fabrizi. Blue Heron Arts Center. Opened November 6, 2005. Closed November 27, 2005.* A stage adaptation of Herman Melville's novella about the uproar caused by a young man's arrival in a mid-1800s law office.

JERSEY BOYS. *Book by Marshall Brickman and Rick Elice. Music by Bob Gaudio. Lyrics by Bob Crewe. Directed by Des McAnuff. August Wilson Theatre. Opened November 6, 2005.* A musical based on the life story of Frankie Valli and the Four Seasons.

BINGO. *Book by Michael Heitzman and Ilene Reid. Music and lyrics by Michael Heitzman, Ilene Reid, David Holcenberg. Directed by Thomas Caruso. Produced by Aruba Productions and Buddy & Sally Productions. Theatre at St. Luke's. Opened November 7, 2005. Closed February 12, 2006.* An environmental musical comedy, in which the audience gets to join in the bingo game at Hamerin County's church basement.

BHUTAN. *Written by Daisy Foote. Directed by Evan Yionoulis. Cherry Lane Theatre. Opened November 8, 2005. Closed November 19, 2005.* A play about a woman who dreams of a faraway land in order to escape the chaos of her everyday life.

COWBOY V. SAMURAI. *Written by Michael Golamco. Directed by Lloyd Suh. Produced by National Asian American Theatre Company. Rattlestick Theatre. Opened November 8, 2005. Closed November 27, 2005.* A contemporary retelling of Cyrano de Bergerac set in modern-day Wyoming.

SODOM: THE MUSICAL. *Book and lyrics by Kevin Laub. Music by Adam David Cohen. Directed by Ben Rimalower. Produced by Handwritten Theatre Company. Kraine Theatre. Opened November 8, 2005. Closed December 3, 2005.* A musical comedy about the last days of Sodom and Gomorrah.

ALMOST HEAVEN: SONGS OF JOHN DENVER. *Original concept by Harold Thau. Music and lyrics by John Denver. Directed by Randal Myler. Promenade Theatre. Opened November 9, 2005. Closed December 31, 2005.* A musical that weaves together the songs of John Denver to create a narrative that reflects upon the country during the years in which he wrote them.

SCREWUPS. *Written by Justin Warner. Directed by Courtney Birch, Michael D. Jackson, and Ari Laura Kreith. Produced by Buffalo Bridge Productions. Manhattan Theatre Source. Opened November 9, 2005. Closed November 19, 2005.* A program of six short comedies by Justin Warner: BUM STEER, HEAD GAMES, THE FACE OF GOD, FAT NAKED TRUCKERS, MICROCOSM, and PAGE-TURNER.

FULLY PACT. *Produced by Playwrights/Actors Contemporary Theater. Altered Stages. Opened November 10, 2005. Closed November 20, 2005.* Seven original short plays:

- THE EXCITING LIFE, *by Anthony Pennino, directed by Don Jordan.*
- THEORY OF HEAVEN, *by Patrick Kennedy, directed by Elizabeth London.*
- ISSUES, *by Danna Call, directed by Maryna Harrison.*
- TRAIN OF THOUGHT, *by Craig Pospisil, directed by Christopher Maring.*
- TRAGEDY (A COMEDY), *by Stuart D'Ver, directed by Jody O'Neil.*
- VERMOUTH AND CHICKEN, *by P. Seth Bauer.*
- OH, MR. CADHOLE!, *book and lyrics by Lisa Ferber, music by Robert Firpo-Cappiello, directed by Christopher Windom.*

LETTING GO OF GOD. *Written and performed by Julia Sweeney. Ars Nova. Opened November 10, 2005. Closed November 26, 2005.* A solo show about one woman's unexpected journey when two Mormon missionaries arrive on her doorstep and inadvertently challenge her way of thinking about religion, God, and the nature of self.

MEN. *Written and directed by Ken Wolf. Manhattan Repertory Theatre. Opened November 10, 2005. Closed February 18, 2006.* A comedy that illustrates the often bizarre, silly, and just plain ridiculous behaviors of the male creature.

MY JULLIARD. *Written by Gloria J. Browne. Directed by David Sheppard. Theatre for the New City. Opened November 10, 2005. Closed December 4, 2005.* A play about three generations of black women artists who are coping with the effects of Alzheimer's disease on the family matriarch.

HELP ME HELP MYSELF. *Written by Jenna Bans. Directed by Matthew G. Rashid. Produced by Off the Leesh Productions. Looking Glass Theatre. Opened November 11, 2005. Closed November 19, 2005.* A play about three young women coping with being single and slightly neurotic in New York City and trying to find (or avoid) love, fortune, and inner peace.

THE LOST BOY. *Written by Ronald Gabriel Paolillo. Music by David Wolfson. Directed by Kimberly Vaughn. Queens Theatre in the Park. Opened November 11, 2005. Closed November 20, 2005.* The story of the creation of Peter Pan by playwright James M. Barrie, as Pan's story mirrors the creator's own haunted memories.

ZARA SPOOK AND OTHER LURES. *Written by Joan Ackerman. Directed by Robert Combe and Ben Fabrizi. Produced by The Phoenix Players. Poppenhusen Institute. Opened November 11, 2005. Closed November 19, 2005.* A play about several women traveling to an annual women's fishing competition and facing their fears along the way.

BACH AT LEIPZIG. *Written by Itamar Moses. Directed by Pam MacKinnon. New York Theatre Workshop. Opened November 14, 2005. Closed December 18, 2005.* A historical play about seven rival organists angling for a much-coveted musical post in 1722 Leipzig, Germany.

CRESCENDO FALLS. *Written by Kevin Hammonds. Directed by Wes Grantom. Kraine Theatre. Opened November 14, 2005. Closed February 13, 2006.* A six-episode spoof of soap operas set in the fictional metropolis of Crescendo Falls, which thrives on the decadent affairs and backstabbing antics of its beautiful but deadly, double-crossing, bed-hopping, and always perfectly groomed residents.

THE ARK. *Book and lyrics by Michael McLean and Kevin Kelly. Music by Michael McLean. Directed by Ray Roderick. 37 Arts. Opened November 14, 2005. Closed November 20, 2005.* A contemporary musical look at the story of Noah's ark.

COMRADES AND WORMS. *Written by Rogelio Martinez. Directed by Debbie Salvetz. Produced by Baruch Fine and Performing Arts Department. Baruch Performing Arts Center. Opened November 15, 2005. Closed November 19, 2005.* Intrigue, lust, and black market shampoo inundate rehearsals of a modern Cuban theatre production.

RFK. *Written and performed by Jack Holmes. Directed by Larry Moss. Produced by The Culture Project. 45 Bleecker. Opened November 15, 2005. Closed February 26, 2006.* A solo show about Robert F. Kennedy, set in 1964, months after the assassination of his brother, John F. Kennedy.

THE RUBY SUNRISE. *Written by Rinne Groff. Directed by Oskar Eustis. Public Theater. Opened November 16, 2005. Closed December 4, 2005.* The dual story of a 1920s Midwestern woman who invents the first television, and her daughter who struggles to tell her mother's story twenty-five years later.

SIMPLY SELMA. *Written by Jonathan Joy. Where Eagles Dare. Opened November 17, 2005. Closed November 19, 2005.* A woman in her sixties tries to match her stripper daughter up with the man next door.

PENTECOSTAL WISCONSIN. *Written and performed by Ryan Paulson. Directed by Virginia Scott. Peoples Improv Theatre. Opened November 19, 2005. Closed December 15, 2005.* A solo show about the religious right and bashful Scandinavians.

BEYOND THE MIRROR. *Devised and written by Exile and Bond Street Ensembles. Music by Quraishi. Directed by Mahmoud Shah Salimi and Joanna Sherman. Produced by Exile Theatre (Kabul) and Bond Street Theatre (NYC). Theatre for the New City. Opened November 20, 2005. Closed December 4, 2005.* A journey through three decades of war and occupation in Afghanistan and a search for cultural identity.

MR. MARMALADE. *Written by Noah Haidle. Music by Michael Friedman. Directed by Michael Greif. Produced by Roundabout Theatre Company. Laura Pels Theatre. Opened November 20, 2005. Closed January 29, 2006.* A four-year-old's life revolves around her imaginary friend, an adult businessman named Mr. Marmalade.

MISS WITHERSPOON. *Written by Christopher Durang. Directed by Emily Mann. Playwrights Horizons Mainstage. Opened November 29, 2005. Closed January 1, 2006.* A woman is trapped in the netherworld with a Hindu spirit guide who continually sends her back to earth to live lives she refuses to lead.

SUPER VISION. *Written by Constance De Jong. Directed by Marianne Weems. Produced by The Builders Association and dbox. BAM Harvey Theatre. Opened November 29, 2005. Closed December 3, 2005.* A multimedia theatre piece about the data sphere and identity theft.

PAULSEN'S LONELY BANQUET. *Written and performed by John Paulsen. Directed by George L. Lewis. HERE Arts Center. Opened November 30, 2005. Closed December 17, 2005.* A program of two solo works by performance artist John Paulsen: **DOOLYMOOG,** an exploration of our isolated hearts, from prehistory to the post-apocalypse; and **THE TANGLE,** about a cross-country bus ride that turns into a classic Western shoot-out.

PROPHET. *Written and directed by Thomas Bradshaw. Music by Lois Dilivio. P.S. 122. Opened November 30, 2005. Closed December 17, 2005.* God personally tells a henpecked husband that he is a new prophet after the man's wife dies.

APT. 1A. *Written and directed by Stephanie Cardenas. Gene Frankel Theatre. Opened December 1, 2005. Closed December 3, 2005.* A young woman tries to manage both a sexually manipulative relationship with her female roommate and the unwanted affections of her male neighbor.

IN THE CONTINUUM. *Written and performed by Nikkole Salter and Danai Gurira. Directed by Robert O'Hara. Produced by Primary Stages. Perry Street Theatre. Opened December 1, 2005. Closed February 18, 2006.* A play dramatizing the problem of HIV/AIDS among African and African American women.

RACHEL. *Book and lyrics by Bernice Lee. Music by Lou Greene. Directed by Scott Pegg. Wings Theater. Opened December 1, 2005. Closed December 10, 2005.* A musical about Rachel Jackson, the wife of Andrew Jackson.

THE BABY JESUS ONE-ACT JUBILEE. *Curated by Hope Cartelli, Michael Gardner, and Jeff Lewonczyk. Brick Theatre. Opened December 1, 2005. Closed December 17, 2005.* A mini-festival of twelve holiday-themed fifteen-minute plays:

- **AN INTELLIGENT DESIGN,** *by Jeff Tabnick, directed by Anthony Luciano.*
- **WALKING SHADOW,** *by Danny Bowes, directed by Ivanna Cullinan.*
- **THE MOST WONDERFUL TIME OF THE YEAR,** *by John DeVore, directed by RJ Tolan.*
- **GRANDUNCLE TELLS THE CHILDREN A STORY OF KISSELRITE DURING THE WAR,** *by Jeff Lewonczyk, directed by Hope Cartelli.*
- **CHRISTMAS,** *by Young Jean Lee, directed by Yehuda Duenya.*
- **ICH LIEBE JESUS (A CHRISTMAS MUSICAL),** *by Robert Honeywell, directed by Jeff Lewonczyk.*
- **M*E*N*S*C*H,** *by Eric Winick, directed by Christian Parker.*
- **HUMBUGGERY,** *by Jon Marans, directed by Arnie Burto.*
- **EXECUTION OF A REINDEER,** *by Gary Winter.*
- **THE CHRISTMAS SUICIDES,** *by Peter S. Petralia, directed by Ian W. Hill.*
- **DAMN TEDDYBEARS,** *by Alexis Sottile, directed by Dominic d'Andrea.*
- **A CHRISTMAS FULL OF FAMILY LOVE,** *by Thomas Bradshaw, directed by Judson Kniffen.*

THE COLOR PURPLE. *Book by Marsha Norman. Directed by Gary Griffin. Broadway Theatre. Opened December 1, 2005.* A musical based on Alice Walker's Pulitzer Prize–winning novel.

THE DICKENS. *Written by Michael Scott-Price. Directed by Jaime Robert Carrillo. Produced by Firebrand Theory Theater Company. Altered Stages. Opened December 1, 2005. Closed December*

17, 2005. A holiday Western comedy about a priest, a pregnant whore, a greedy undertaker, and a gambler, who all spend Christmas Eve in a saloon together.

THE TRIAL OF MUMIA ABU JAMAL/VOICES. *Produced by Shades of Color Production. Producers Club. Opened December 1, 2005. Closed December 4, 2005.* A double bill of one-act plays: **THE TRIAL OF MUMIA ABU JAMAL,** about radio journalist and death row inmate Jamal; and **VOICES,** about a talk show host, a conservative politician, a liberal advocate, and a radical activist.

THREE DOLLAR BILL. *Written by Kirk Wood Bromley. Directed by Howard Thoresen. Produced by Inverse Theater. Center Stage. Opened December 1, 2005. Closed December 23, 2005.* A program of three short plays about being queer and conservative, all written by Kirk Wood Bromley: **WHAT ARE YOU THINKING, MARY CHENEY?,** about Vice President Dick Cheney's lesbian daughter; **CIVILI-ZATION AND ITS DISCO TENTS,** about a real-time gay conversion therapy session between an ex-gay therapist and a supposedly gay, but wanting to be a straight, patient; and **THE WELCOME MASK,** an off-kilter coming-out family drama.

VITAL SIGNS 10. *Curator/producer Linda Ames Key. Produced by Vital Theatre Company. McGinn Cazale Theatre. Opened December 1, 2005. Closed December 18, 2005.* New short plays:

- **RELATIONTRIP,** *by Sharyn Rothstein, directed by Catherine Ward.*
- **NORMAN!,** *by D. T. Arcieri, directed by Alexis Williams.*
- **PASSED HORDES,** *by Mark Harvey Levine, directed by Brad Caswell.*
- **SORRENTO,** *by Lucile Lichtblau, directed by Cynthia Thomas.*
- **ALL IN THE MIMING,** *by Qui Nguyen, directed by Alexandra Hastings.*
- **SANDLOT BALL,** *by Michael John Garces, directed by Mary Kate Burke.*
- **HARPER LEE'S HUSBAND,** *by Thomas H. Diggs, directed by S. Caden Hethorn.*
- **LAST STOP: NEVERLAND,** *by Jackie Maruschak, directed by Christopher Fessenden.*
- **AMERICAN SOIL,** *by Ellen Margolis, directed by Teresa K. Pond.*
- **THE PRISONER'S DILEMMA,** *by Michael Wolfson, directed by Mahayana Landowne.*
- **GIBLET: A NIGHTMARE,** *by Ian Finley, directed by David Hilder.*
- **RIDE,** *by Eric Lane, directed by Daisy Walker.*
- **SECOND KISS,** *by Andrea Lepcio, directed by Stephanie Gilman.*
- **PLEASE HAVE A SEAT AND SOMEONE WILL BE WITH YOU SHORTLY,** *by Garth Wingfield, directed by Laura Josepher.*
- **NOTES,** *by Kate Moira Ryan, directed by Marya Cohn.*
- **READING LIST,** *by Susan Miller, directed by Cynthia Croot.*

BEAST WITH TWO BACKS. *Written by Don Nigro. Directed by Ann Bowen. Produced by Specter Theatre Company. Walkerspace. Opened December 2, 2005. Closed December 17, 2005.* A young artist comes to Greenwich Village in 1927, and his life is changed by a madhouse full of bohemians.

ESCAPE FROM BELLEVUE AND OTHER STORIES. *Written and performed by Christopher John Campion. Music by Knockout Drops. Directed by Horton Foote Jr. Produced by Knockout Drops and Victoria DeRose. Paradise Factory Theatre. Opened December 2, 2005. Closed February 25, 2006.* Chris Campion, lead singer of the band Knockout Drops, tells the story of the band moving to New York City in 1993.

LETTERS FROM THE EARTH. *Created and performed by Brian Bickerstaff, Jim Dawson, Iver Findlay, Jim Findlay, Amy Huggans, and Tara Webb. Produced by Collapsible Giraffe. Collapsable*

Hole. Opened December 2, 2005. Closed January 22, 2006. A multimedia theatre piece inspired by Mark Twain's religious satire of the same name.

OFFICE SONATA. *Written by Andy Chmelko. Directed by Jason Zimbler. Produced by Impetuous Theater Group. Irish Arts Center. Opened December 2, 2005. Closed December 14, 2005.* Young employees just starting out in life get a crash course in the powerful and twisted methods of corporate America. **SEE PAGE 29.**

BALLETTO STILETTO. *Conceived and directed by Mary Fulham. Music by Benjamin Marcantoni. Lyrics by Paul Foglino. La MaMa. Opened December 3, 2005. Closed December 18, 2005.* A nondenominational holiday spectacular based on the Grimm fairy tale "The Twelve Dancing Princesses," and set at the height of the holiday shopping frenzy in New Jersey.

CORONADO. *Written by Dennis Lehane. Directed by David Epstein. Produced by Invisible City Theatre Company. Manhattan Theatre Source. Opened December 3, 2005. Closed December 17, 2005.* A thriller based on the author's own short story, "Until Gwen," about three seemingly disparate couples whose lives intersect in surprising ways.

UNDER A MONTANA MOON. *Written and performed by Bill Bowers. The Performance Factory. Opened December 3, 2005. Closed December 18, 2005.* A series of silent stories that portray three life-changing moments universal to all—losing one's innocence by coming of age, falling in love, and death—performed by the international mime Bowers.

APPARITION. *Written by Anne Washburn. Directed by Les Waters. Connelly Theatre. Opened December 4, 2005. Closed January 7, 2006.* A drama about a murder that may or may not have happened, and the feeling that something is coming to get you.

KLONSKY & SCHWARTZ. *Written by Romulus Linney. Directed by Jamie Richards. Ensemble Studio Theatre. Opened December 5, 2005. Closed December 23, 2005.* The mercurial and gifted poet Delmore Schwartz's lifelong partner and protégé, Milton Klonsky, fights to rescue his troubled mentor and friend in the turbulent 1960s.

Q&Y: A BRIEF COMEDY ABOUT DEATH. *Written and directed by Theresa Buchheister. Arthur Seelen Theatre. Opened December 5, 2005. Closed December 8, 2005.* A new play written and directed by Theresa Buchheister.

86 STREET. *Written and directed by Frank Terranova. Sanford Meisner Theatre. Opened December 6, 2005. Closed December 11, 2005.* A play set in the summer of 1985 in Bensonhurst, Broooklyn, where girls and guys search for love and lust.

FOLLOW ME. *Written by Melissa Collins, Clay Collins, and Michael Capecci. Directed by Melissa Collins, Michael Capecci. The Theatre @ GTT. Opened December 6, 2005. Closed December 18, 2005.* A musical that retells the story of Christmas.

THE RECKONING. *Written by M.Z. Ribalow. Directed by Tom Brangle and Suzanne DiDonna. Produced by IAAM Productions. Manhattan Repertory Theatre. Opened December 6, 2005. Closed December 10, 2005.* Three damaged souls fighting three separate and unique battles against a shared reality—a reality that seeks to wreck their lives, destroy their happiness, and break their spirits.

TIGHT EMBRACE. *Written by Jorge Ignacio Cortinas. Directed by Lisa Peterson. Produced by INTAR. Kirk Theatre. Opened December 6, 2005. Closed January 2, 2006.* The play is set in a safe-house where two kidnap victims—an elderly woman and a pregnant woman—try to survive with each other and the two men assigned to guard them.

EINSTEIN. *Written by Gabriel Emanuel. Directed by Howard Rypp. La MaMa. Opened December 7, 2005. Closed December 11, 2005.* A solo show that takes place on Einstein's seventieth birthday.

FIVE DAYS WITH DYLAN. *Written by Pamela Scott. Directed by Nye Heron. Producers Club II. Opened December 7, 2005. Closed December 18, 2005.* A woman's friends suspect she's having a baby because the father is a famous rock star.

REVENGE 2. *Produced by TheDrillingCompaNY. 78th Street Theatre Lab. Opened December 8, 2005. Closed December 17, 2005.* A program of short, thematically linked new plays:

- **SERVED COLD,** *by Katharine Clark Gray, directed by Adam Eisenstein.*
- **MEDEA UNHARNESSED,** *by Molly Rice, directed by Kara-Lynn Vaenie.*
- **THE DEAL,** *by Kate McCamy, directed by Richard Mover.*
- **STILL LIFE #2,** *by Tom Strelich, directed by Pedro Hernandez.*
- **BEE,** *by Stephen Bittrich, directed by Dan Teachout.*
- **THOR'S HAMMER,** *by Nicholas Gray, directed by Matt Cowart.*
- **STOP THE LAWNS,** *by P. Seth Bauer, directed by Gabriele Forster.*
- **BLUE CHRISTMAS,** *by Scott Baker, directed by James Davies.*

'TIS THE @#$%-ING SEASON. *Produced by kef productions and Rachel Neuberger. Lion Theatre. Opened December 9, 2005. Closed December 21, 2005.* A program of two original holiday stories for the stage: **THE FIRST ANNUAL ST. IGNATIUS CHANUKAH PAGEANT** and **WHY AM I ATTRACTED TO NARCISSISTS?—A CHRISTMAS STORY.**

IT GOES WITHOUT SAYING. *Written and performed by Bill Bowers. Directed by Martha Banta. Produced by Rattlestick Playwrights Theater. Rattlestick Theatre. Opened December 10, 2005. Closed December 12, 2005.* A solo show in which the author shares funny, heartbreaking, and unbelievable true stories from his career as an actor and mime.

CHITA RIVERA: THE DANCER'S LIFE. *Book Terrence McNally. Directed by Graciela Daniele. Schoenfeld Theatre. Opened December 11, 2005. Closed February 19, 2006.* A musical celebrating the life and career of Chita Rivera.

FEAR ITSELF (SECRETS OF THE WHITE HOUSE). *Written by Jean-Claude van Itallie. Directed by George Ferencz. Theatre for the New City. Opened December 11, 2005. Closed January 8, 2006.* A new farcical tragedy by Jean-Claude Van Italie.

HAYMARKET. *Written by Zayd Dohrn. Directed by Robert Saxner. Produced by Alchemy Theatre Company. Beckett Theatre. Opened December 12, 2005. Closed December 23, 2005.* A play about the Haymarket Riots that rocked the city of Chicago in the spring and summer of 1886.

A BROKEN CHRISTMAS CAROL. *Written by James Christy, J Holtham, and Kendra Levin. Directed by Drew DeCorleto. Produced by Broken Watch Theatre Company. Michael Weller Theatre. Opened December 15, 2005. Closed December 30, 2005.* A comedy by that examines the minor characters of the famous Dickens *Christmas Carol.*

'TWAS THE NIGHT BEFORE THE TWELVE DAYS... *Created by Ken Nintzel. P.S. 122. Opened December 15, 2005. Closed December 30, 2005.* A holiday spectacular that features the unabridged drama of Dickens's *A Christmas Carol* set to the complete score of Tchaikovsky's ballet *The Nutcracker* with a reading of "'Twas the Night Before Christmas" and the carol "The Twelve Days of Christmas."

YOUR TOWN. *Written by Walter Corwin. Directed by Jonathan Weber. Theatre for the New City. Opened December 15, 2005. Closed December 30, 2005.* In a small upstate New York town, where many of the citizens have been literally jumping off a bridge lately, the mayor fights to change the town's reputation.

FOUR ONE-ACT PLAYS. *Produced by Our Time Theatre Company. Theater Three. Opened December 16, 2005. Closed December 18, 2005.* New plays from this company that provides an artistic home for people who stutter; written and directed by teen members of the company:

- **SO YOU THINK YOU KNOW ME,** *by Angelina Bruno-Metzger.* The story of a perfect young woman with a secret.
- **IF YOU GOT IT…FLAUNT IT,** *by Naudia Vivienne Jones.* A high school freshman musters up the nerve to enter a singing competition.
- **BODY LANGUAGE,** *by Yoni Messing.* A young American meets a woman from Italy.
- **I, MAN ON STAGE,** *by Donny Sethi.* The story of a singular man, told through song and movement.

NEWSICAL 2006: THE NEXT EDITION. *Music and lyrics by Rick Crom. Directed by Donna Drake. Village Theatre. Opened December 17, 2005. Closed December 31, 2005.* The newest version of Rick Crom's musical revue satire of today's current events.

THE BULLY. *Book by David L. Williams. Music and lyrics by John Gregor. Directed by Suzu Mc-Connell-Wood. Produced by Vital Children's Theatre. McGinn Cazale Theatre. Opened December 17, 2005. Closed February 5, 2006.* A children's musical about the smartest kid in school and the school bully, who have to work together one day when they get stranded at the wrong school.

THROUGH A NAKED LENS. *Written by George Barthel. Directed by Richard Bacon and L.J. Kleeman. Wings Theater. Opened December 19, 2005. Closed January 21, 2006.* A play about the life of silent movie star Ramon Navarro and his involvement with *Photoplay* journalist Herbert Howe.

MANIGMA. *Created and performed by Michael Aronov. Directed by David Travis. 78th Street Theatre Lab. Opened December 22, 2005.* Closed January 28, 2006. A solo work about the six sides of one man's personality.

CHRISTINE JORGENSEN REVEALS. *Directed by Josh Hecht. Produced by Splinter Group Productions. Theatre Row Studio. Opened December 29, 2005. Closed April 1, 2006.* A lipsynched recreation of the only recorded interview given by Christine Jorgensen, the first American to undergo a sex change operation.

BRAVE IRENE. *Book, music, and lyrics by Joan Cushing. Directed by Bruce Merrill. Manhattan Children's Theatre. Opened December 31, 2005. Closed February 12, 2006.* A musical based on the book *Brave Irene* by William Steig, about a girl who has to deliver a dress to the Grand Duchess in order to help her sick mother make ends meet.

MOTHER TERESA GIRL. *Written and performed by Aviva Jane Carlin. Directed by Amy Feinberg. Produced by Hypothetical Theatre Company. 14th Street Y. Opened January 4, 2006. Closed January*

14, 2006. An autobiographical solo piece about a group of volunteers working with Mother Teresa as they search for a meaningful life.

KILLA DILLA. *Written by OyamO. Directed by Andre De Shields. Produced by The Working Theater. Players Theatre. Opened January 5, 2006. Closed January 15, 2006.* A play that uses a variety of performance styles such as blackface minstrelsy, rap, and evangelical preaching to tell the story of a woman whose own survival is threatened by her unresolved rage.

THE WHALES. *Written by M. Stefan Strozier. Produced by La Muse Venale Acting Troupe. Where Eagles Dare. Opened January 5, 2006. Closed January 29, 2006.* A new adaptation of the comedy by Aristophanes.

SUV: THE MUSICAL! *Book by Gregg Kuntzman. Music and lyrics by Marc Dinkin and Gersh Kuntzman. Produced by Neo-Shtick Theatre Company. Wings Theater. Opened January 6, 2006. Closed January 21, 2006.* A boy-meets-girl love story that includes car accidents, environmental activists, and crimes against humanity.

TABULA RASA. *Book and lyrics by Robert Lawson. Music by Henry Akona. Directed by Henry Akona. Produced by High Fidelity Theater. Theater Five. Opened January 6, 2006. Closed January 28, 2006.* An opera/theatre work of three interlocking stories about children lost in the woods.

THE BIRDS AND THE BEES OR THE BIRDS AND THE BIRDS. *Produced by Woman Seeking…a theater company. Center Stage. Opened January 6, 2006. Closed January 22, 2006.* A program of short plays that ask the question, "Did you learn it from your mother…or did she learn it from you?"—and everything that implies. The playwrights are: Barb Wolfe, Rich Orloff, Christine Mosere, Tara Meddaugh, Laurie Marvald, Kerri Kochanski, Judy Carlson Hulbert, Andy Davis, Ken Dashow, and Jordan Auslander. The directors are: Ken Dashow, Deb Guston, Kel Haney, Stephanie Hepburn, Andy Davis, Nancy Larsen, and Kate Place.

CJD. *Written and directed by James Jordan. Produced by The Boondogglers. Theater Five. Opened January 7, 2006. Closed January 28, 2006.* A multimedia one-man show about a neurologist and his experience with a patient with Creutzfeldt-Jakob Disease.

FISH BOWL. *Written by Simona Berman and Andrew Thomas Pitkin. Music by Stephen Pitkin. Directed by Chris Henry. Produced by I Ate What? Theatre Company. Michael Weller Theatre. Opened January 7, 2006. Closed January 22, 2006.* Six contestants who have been chosen at random to compete for $11 million on a new reality television show try each other's patience and reveal truths about themselves while waiting for the production team to arrive.

IMPOSTORS. *Written by Justin Warner. Directed by Ari Laura Kreith. Produced by Glass House Productions. Theater Five. Opened January 7, 2006. Closed January 29, 2006.* After surviving a brain injury, a son believes his parents have been replaced with exact duplicates of themselves, triggering a series of events that threaten to unravel the entire family.

NEUROSHORTS. *Theater Five. Opened January 7, 2006. Closed January 28, 2006.* A program of four short plays dealing with neurological disorders:

- **THE BOY WHO WANTED TO BE A ROBOT,** *by Edward Einhorn, directed by Barry Weil.* A fairy tale from a foreign culture—the culture of people with Asperger's Syndrome (a form of autism).

- **DOCTORS JANE AND ALEXANDER,** *by Edward Einhorn, directed by Ian W. Hill.* A portrait of the playwright's mother, who suffers from dementia, and other family members.
- **THE TASTE OF BLUE,** *by Alexandra Edwards, directed by Julia Martin.* About a woman with synesthesia, a condition in which every sense calls up another.
- **VESTIBULAR,** *by Kelly R. Haydon, directed by Jolie Tong.* As vertigo routinely attacks a former dancer stricken with Ménière's Disease, an informal conversation with his nurse turns into a revelation that challenges the idea of dependency as a passive force.

WELCOME TO TOURETTAVILLE! *Book by Jonathan Ospa, June Rachelson-Ospa, and Daniel Nelden. Music by Jody Gray, Doug Katsaros, and Daniel Nieden. Directed by Daniel Neiden. Produced by Bozomoon Productions. Theater Five. Opened January 7, 2006. Closed January 15, 2006.* A young boy's dreamworld contains three aliens—Tick, Blinky, and Screamer—who befriend and inspire the boy toward self-acceptance of his Tourette's.

CANDY & DOROTHY. *Written by David Johnston. Directed by Kevin Newbury. Theater Three. Opened January 9, 2006. Closed January 28, 2006.* A comic fantasy in which Dorothy Day (the activist who founded *The Catholic Worker*) is trapped in the bureaucracy of the afterlife with Candy Darling (the Andy Warhol discovery) as her caseworker.

OLSEN TERROR. *Created by Dave May and Chris Wells. Music by Jeremy Bass and Chris Wells. Dixon Place. Opened January 9, 2006. Closed March 13, 2006.* An exploration of America's obsession with celebrity, youth, addiction, and greed in which a man slowly turns into the Olsen twins.

WHAT THEN. *Written by Rinne Groff. Music by Joe Popp. Directed by Hal Brooks. Produced by Clubbed Thumb. Ohio Theatre. Opened January 9, 2006. Closed January 28, 2006.* A play about a struggling family and a struggling planet, set in the not-too-distant future.

BEAUTY OF THE FATHER. *Written by Nilo Cruz. Directed by Michael Greif. Manhattan Theatre Club. Opened January 10, 2006. Closed February 19, 2006.* A young woman who travels to Spain to visit her estranged father quickly becomes immersed in his vibrant, artistic world.

GIVE UP! START OVER! & HOWL. *Directed by Rachel Chavkin. Produced by TEAM. 59E59. Opened January 10, 2006. Closed January 15, 2006.* A double bill of short plays: **GIVE UP! START OVER!,** by Jessica Almasy, about a woman who has swallowed her television; and **HOWL,** adapted by Rachel Chavkin from Allen Ginsburg's famous poem, and combining the poem with excerpts from Kerouac's *On the Road.*

THE LITTLE DOG LAUGHED. *Written by Douglas Carter Beane. Directed by Scott Ellis. Second Stage. Opened January 10, 2006. Closed February 26, 2006.* An up-and-coming leading man and his overzealous agent become entangled with a sexy drifter and his naïve girlfriend.

THE MYTH CYCLE: AHRAIHSAK. *Written by Ruben Polendo. Music by Jef Evans. Directed by Ruben Polendo. Produced by Theater Mitu. CSV Cultural Center. Opened January 10, 2006. Closed January 28, 2006.* A pageant featuring puppetry, masks, movement, and music, telling the tale of a powerful leader driven to extreme violence to avenge his family's treachery.

ANTON. *Written and directed by Pierre Van Der Spuy. Greenwich Street Theatre. Opened January 11, 2006. Closed January 29, 2006.* A play about Anton Chekhov's search for love and happiness through his work and relationships.

FAIRY TALE MONOLOGUES: FABLES WITH ATTITUDE. *Written by Paul Weissman. Directed by Jeff Love. Produced by Point of You Productions. The Red Room. Opened January 11, 2006. Closed January 28, 2006.* A play that tells what REALLY happens after "happily ever after" for several familiar fairy tales.

LOSING TRACK. *Written and directed by Katie Letien. American Theatre of Actors. Opened January 11, 2006. Closed January 15, 2006.* A play reveals the truth behind trying to maintain a relationship as well as oneself.

ALMOST, MAINE. *Written by John Cariani. Music by Julian Fleisher. Directed by Gabriel Barre. Daryl Roth Theatre. Opened January 12, 2006. Closed February 12, 2006.* A romantic comedy about the residents of a small northern town, who are falling in and out of love at an alarming rate.

GUN PLAY. *Conceived and directed by Brian Rogers. Chocolate Factory. Opened January 12, 2006. Closed February 4, 2006.* A performance piece that celebrates firearms as they are represented in American popular culture by drawing parallels between real violence and imagined violence.

HAVANA BOURGEOIS. *Written by Carlos Lacamara. Directed by Jocelyn Sawyer. Produced by Reverie Productions. 59E59. Opened January 12, 2006. Closed February 5, 2006.* Set in a Havana advertising agency in 1958, this play is about a young talented commercial artist on the verge of getting the life he always wanted—until the Castro revolution comes.

THE ART OF LOVE. *Written by Robert Kornfeld. Directed by Tom Thornton. Theatre for the New City. Opened January 12, 2006. Closed February 5, 2006.* A biographical play about Ovid, the Roman poet who was silenced by Emperor Augustus.

THE END OF REALITY. *Written and directed by Richard Maxwell. Produced by New York City Players. The Kitchen. Opened January 12, 2006. Closed January 28, 2006.* A play that takes place in a "lobby-citadel," where guards attempt to secure a vulnerable area against unidentified intruders.

TROUBLE. *Written and directed by Michael Smith. Theatre for the New City. Opened January 12, 2006. Closed February 5, 2006.* A satirical fantasia on the real-life fall of former Miss America and New York City Commissioner of Cultural Affairs Bess Myerson.

CLEMSON COUNTY, SC. *Adapted and directed by Ryan Gilliam. Music and lyrics by Michael Hickey. Downtown Art. Opened January 13, 2006. Closed February 15, 2006.* A bluegrass musical comedy based on Jane Austen's *Pride and Prejudice*.

DELICIOUS RIVERS. *Written by Ellen Maddow. Music by Ellen Maddow. Directed by Paul Zimet. Produced by The Talking Band. La MaMa. Opened January 13, 2006. Closed February 5, 2006.* Set in a New York City post office, this play follows the lives of four postal workers and three neighborhood apartment dwellers whose lives are intertwined in a variety of ways.

HELP WANTED. *Written and performed by Josh Lefkowitz. Dixon Place. Opened January 13, 2006. Closed January 21, 2006.* A solo play that deals with growing up, leaving home, sexuality, racism, becoming an artist, becoming an adult—all in the shadow of Spalding Gray.

PING PONG DIPLOMACY. *Written by Joe Basque. Directed by David Hilder. Produced by Reverie Productions. 59E59. Opened January 13, 2006. Closed February 5, 2006.* A play about the 1971 U.S. Table Tennis Team's goodwill tour to China.

THE UNDERSTUDIES. *Written and directed by Jeff Bedillion. Produced by LMNO Theatre Company. Under St. Marks. Opened January 13, 2006. Closed January 29, 2006.* Two female understudies steeped in a brew of jealousy, conspiracy, and desperation several years into the run of a successful Broadway show.

WINTERKILL/THINGS YOU DON'T SAY OUTDOORS. *Produced by Wabi Sabi Productions. Producers Club. Opened January 13, 2006. Closed January 21, 2006.* A program of two one-woman plays: **WINTERKILL,** *by Denise B. Flemming,* and **THINGS YOU DON'T SAY OUTDOORS,** *by Dawn Winkler.*

PENINSULA. *Written and directed by Madelyn Kent. Soho Rep. Opened January 14, 2006. Closed February 4, 2006.* A play about what it means to live in a culture of contentment surrounded by raging violence.

THE BLACK BIRD RETURNS. *Written by Alexis Kozak and Barbara Panas. Music by Justin Kennedy-Grant. Directed by Alexis Kozak. Produced by KoPan/Roundtable Ensemble Productions. 45th Street Theatre. Opened January 15, 2006. Closed January 31, 2006.* After years apart, a man reunites with his true love, a woman he left years ago, who is torn between unresolved feelings for him and the commitment to her current relationship.

BAG FULLA MONEY. *Written by Scott Brooks. Directed by Sam Viverito. Clurman Theatre. Opened January 16, 2006. Closed January 29, 2006.* When a bag of stolen cash is left unattended in the kitchen of a fancy four-star hotel, a chef, his girl, and six others try to outwit, outcon, and outlast each other and make off with a million bucks.

POE-FEST. *Metropolitan Playhouse. Opened January 16, 2006. Closed January 29, 2006.* A mini-festival of thirteen new plays inspired by the work and life of Edgar Allan Poe.

- **ELEANORA,** *by Tara Bahna-James and Jonathan Portera.* A musical adaptation of one of Poe's less well-known (optimistic) stories.
- **101 WAYS…,** *by Stephen Peace.* A play about a book about murder.
- **QUOTH THE RAVEN,** *by Dan Evans.* Poe and a raven form a feisty, if productive, team.
- **POE,** *by Jack Aaronson.* A new musical in which Poe struggles to control the fates of those around him.
- **THE TELL-TALE HEART,** *by Danny Ashkenasi.* The famous story told and sung to the accompaniment of three demonic cellos.
- **CURSE OF THE NEKROPHENIAC,** *by Trav S.D.* An opium-crazed poet becomes obsessed with two women.
- **MASQUE OF THE RED DEATH,** *by Wandering Rom Players.* Tales and poems woven together through dance.
- **THE RAVEN PREPARES,** *by Patrick Blake.* The raven readies for his entrance in the famous poem.
- **MR. E.A. POE'S NEW YEAR'S BASH,** *by Jeremy Halpern.* Characters from Poe's work gather to celebrate his murder, scheduled for the stroke of midnight.
- **SOMEWHAT DAMAGED,** *by Alexander Poe.* Characters versus creator as Poe perfects his masterpiece.
- **THE PURLOINED DETECTIVE,** *by Laura Livingston.* Poe's detective Auguste DuPin meets Holmes and Watson.

- **BLACKHEART,** *by Dick St. George and Susan Hopkins.* "The Black Cat" and "The Tell-Tale Heart" told together.
- **RAVING,** *by Peter Lobdell and Charles Ditto.* A man is obsessed with the raven, and the raven depends on him.

THE FEAR PROJECT. *Music by David Herman. Barrow Group. Opened January 16, 2006. Closed February 13, 2006.* A program of seven short plays by Trish Alexandro, Joshua James, K. Lorrel Manning, Scott Organ, Eric Paeper, and Stefanie Zadravec, linked by original footage and compiled media images, that all deal with the question of finding balance between being informed and staying functional.

HUCK & HOLDEN. *Written by Rajiv Joseph. Directed by Giovanna Sardelli. Cherry Lane Theatre. Opened January 17, 2006. Closed February 25, 2006.* A romantic comedy is about a college student who comes to the U.S. from India to study engineering, but ends up getting a first-hand look at some of the other electives America has to offer, such as sex, porn, violence, and *The Catcher in the Rye.*

THINGS BEYOND OUR CONTROL. *Written by Jesse Kellerman. Directed by Justin Ball. Produced by The Grid Theater Company. Linhart Theater. Opened January 17, 2006. Closed January 28, 2006.* Guilt draws a Texas cab driver and his passenger together after they commit a hit-and-run, and seven lives change forever.

BY THE SEA. *Written by Craig Stewart. Directed by Barbara Pitcher. American Theatre of Actors. Opened January 18, 2006. Closed January 22, 2006.* Set on Cape Cod at the end of the summer, where three lovers come to terms with their relationships and confront their futures with the choices love has helped them make.

SAIL PAST MOLOKAI. *Written by Howard I. Laniado with Gregg Hauterbach. Produced by Artemis & the wild things. Theatre 54 @ Shetler. Opened January 18, 2006. Closed January 29, 2006.* A play that takes place at and off the leprosy settlement on Molokai.

ABSN: RJAB. *Produced by National Theater of the United States. P.S. 122. Opened January 19, 2006. Closed February 12, 2006.* A band of holy hellions traipse across the countryside with an ancient living relic they hold hostage and search for a fabled city of gold, while the devil himself walks among them in everyday clothes.

ANGRY YOUNG WOMEN IN LOW-RISE JEANS… *Written and directed by Matt Morillo. Produced by KADM Players. Duo Theatre. Opened January 19, 2006. Closed February 25, 2006.* A comedy comprised of two monologues and three short plays about the psychology of urban goddesses.

A BRILLIANT PLAY BY JOHN McENROE. *Written by Zachary Steel and Adam Carpenter. Directed by Maggie McBrien. Gene Frankel Theatre. Opened January 20, 2006. Closed February 5, 2006.* A play about tennis star John McEnroe's struggle to be understood by others, and himself.

THE GIFT OF WINTER. *Book by Michael Slade. Music by David Evans. Lyrics by Faye Greenberg. Directed by Janine Nina Trevens. TADA! Youth Theater. Opened January 20, 2006. Closed February 20, 2006.* A children's musical based on the book of the same name by John Leach and Jean Rankin, about a small town that revolts against winter.

SOUL SEARCHING. *Book by Matt Okin. Music and lyrics by Avi Kunstler. Directed by Matt Okin. Produced by Black Box Entertainment. Times Square Arts Center at The Laugh Factory. Opened January*

21, 2006. Closed June 29, 2006. A musical about a single Jewish woman in New York City who is struggling to find her match and her true spiritual place in the world.

BUSH WARS. *Created by Nancy Holson. Directed by Jay Falzone. Rattlestick Theatre. Opened January 22, 2006. Closed April 23, 2006.* A musical comedy revue that parodies everything from Dick Cheney literally in bed with the oil companies to George W. in a soft-shoe number with his bosom buddy Jesus.

LOVELY DAY. *Written by Leslie Ayvazian. Directed by Blair Brown. Produced by The Play Company. Beckett Theatre. Opened January 22, 2006. Closed February 12, 2006.* A couple celebrating their wedding anniversary learn of a military recruiter's visit to their only son's high school, and find themselves on opposite sides when faced with his possible enlistment.

APARTMENT 3A. *Written by Jeff Daniels. Directed by Valentina Fratti. Arclight Theatre. Opened January 23, 2006. Closed February 11, 2006.* After breaking up with her cheating boyfriend, a woman moves into shabby, but magical, new apartment.

I, CLAUDIUS LIVE. *Written by Tim Cusack and Jason Jacobs. Produced by Theater Askew. Ace of Clubs. Opened January 23, 2006. Closed February 27, 2006.* A free adaptation of the BBC miniseries *I, Claudius,* that relates the sexual intrigues and imperial ambitions of the Julio-Claudian family in first century Rome.

RELATIONSHIPS. *Book, music, and lyrics by Alastair King. Directed by Ron Schwinn. TADA! Youth Theater. Opened January 23, 2006. Closed February 7, 2006.* A musical revue about the different relationships we encounter on our journey through life.

THICKER THAN WATER 2006. *Ensemble Studio Theatre. Opened January 23, 2006. Closed February 18, 2006.* Nw plays by emerging playwrights:

- **HENRIETTA HERMALINE'S FALL FROM GREAT HEIGHTS,** *by Maggie Smith, directed by Abigail Zealey Bess.* A socially backward secretary is swept into a world of romance, heartbreak, and despair.
- **HUNGRY,** *by Amy Herzog, directed by Christine Farrell.* Three friends in New Jersey in the 1990s try to hold onto each other.
- **A BITTER TASTE,** *by Kevin Christopher Snipes, directed by R.J. Tolan.* The lifelong friendship between a mild-mannered college professor and a smooth-talking divorce attorney is knocked off balance by a prostitute.

THE ORPHAN SINGER. *Music by Antonio Vivaldi. Lyrics by Barbara Zinn. Directed by David Schechter. Produced by Making Books Sing. Opened January 24, 2006. Closed February 13, 2006.* A musical based on the children's book of the same name, about an orphan with an exceptional vocal talent who dreams of studying music with Maestro Antonio Vivaldi.

25 QUESTIONS FOR A JEWISH MOTHER. *Written by Kate Moira Ryan with Judy Gold. Directed by Karen Kohlhaas. Ars Nova. Opened January 25, 2006. Closed March 19, 2006.* A comedic portrait of what makes a Jewish mother a Jewish mother.

THE BAR PLAYS. *Written by Chuck Orsland. Directed by Lawrence Frank. Produced by Etcetera Theatre Company. American Theatre of Actors. Opened January 25, 2006. Closed January 29, 2006.* A program of four one-act plays, all set in a downtown bar, in which a cross-section of New Yorkers attempt to find their fortunes with varying degrees of success and legality.

ZOMBOID! *Written by Richard Foreman. Ontological Theatre. Opened January 25, 2006. Closed April 9, 2006.* A multimedia theatre piece featuring film components, five frequently blindfolded actors, and several metaphysical donkeys alternately mistreated and worshipped.

GOATS. *Written by Alan Berks. Directed by Mark Armstrong. The Production Company. Opened January 26, 2006. Closed February 12, 2006.* An urban, secular American Jewish boy finds himself living on a mountain outside Jerusalem, tending to the goats of a mysterious hermit.

HOME COOKED: A CAUTIONARY TALE. *Written by Greg Edwards. Music by Julia Meinwald and Zak Sandler. Directed by Lisa Siciliano. Seventh Street Small Stage at Jimmy's No. 43. Opened January 26, 2006.* Closed January 28, 2006. A program of two playlets and a cabaret featuring two twentysomething friends—Robbie the aerobics instructor, Joanna the professional violist, and Dora the newscaster—as they fight to preserve their Upper West Side environment.

THE BROOKLYN PLAYS. *Produced by Howling Moon Cab Company. Opened January 26, 2006. Closed February 4, 2006.* A festival of one-act plays about Brooklyn:

- **THE CATCHER IN BED-STUY,** *by David Dannenfelser, directed by Rebecca Reagan.*
- **PARACHUTE JUMP,** *by Meri Wallace, directed by Jonathan Wallace.*
- **THE LADY ELGIN,** *by Jerry McGee, directed by Elizabeth Bove.*
- **FUCKIN' WORK,** *by Ian Cohen, directed by Debra Henri.*
- **BRIAN FLOWERS,** *by Jonathan Wallace, directed by Janus Surratt.*
- **MIKE AND THE RABBI,** *by Heather Woodbury, directed by Zoe Moore.*
- **BALL CAPS,** *by J.J. Steinfeld, directed by Jonathan Wallace.*

BREUCKELEN. *Written by Chris Van Strander. Directed by Matthew Didner. Collective Unconscious. Opened January 27, 2006. Closed February 18, 2006.* A darkly comedic tale about the convergence of Brooklyn's gentrified present and its mostly forgotten past.

GIRL IN HEAT. *Written by Nelson Avidon. Directed by Robert Walden. Produced by August Productions. Michael Weller Theatre. Opened January 27, 2006. Closed February 19, 2006.* A lawyer and his secretary play sexual cat-and-mouse games after hours at the office.

KINGFISH, AMOS AND ANDY. *Written by Carl Clay. Directed by Bette Howard. Black Spectrum Theatre. Opened January 27, 2006. Closed April 30, 2006.* A play inspired by the famous and popular 1950s-era TV series *Amos and Andy*, which resets the action in Harlem.

MR. HOOVER'S TEA PARTY. *Written by Stanton Wood. Directed by Tamilla Woodard. Produced by Off World Theatre. Puffin Cultural Forum. Opened January 28, 2006. Closed February 12, 2006.* A play that explores the relationship between Martin Luther King Jr. and J. Edgar Hoover, during the time when Hoover kept King under surveillance.

SEPARATING THE MEN FROM THE BULL. *Written by Michael Heintzman and Neal Lerner. Directed by Becky London. Produced by Unofficial New York Yale Cabaret. Laurie Beechman Theater. Opened January 28, 2006. Closed February 19, 2006.* A comedy consisting of seven vignettes about the intricacies of male friendships.

WHAT WOMEN TALK ABOUT. *Directed by Hugh Sinclair and Wayne Parillo. Produced by Manatee on the Couch Productions and Dragonchase. Kraine Theatre. Opened January 31, 2006. Closed May 2, 2006.* An unscripted, improvised show that eavesdrops on the lives of four young women in New York City.

3 TO A SESSION. *Produced by Immediate Theater Company. Clurman Theatre. Opened February 1, 2006. Closed February 5, 2006.* An evening of three one-act plays:

- PLAY>, *written and directed by Paul Siemens.* A brother and sister play an imaginative game at bedtime.
- SEE THE WORLD, *written and directed by Jeremy McCarter.* A young couple and their daughter travel to an exotic foreign land, where their search for the real world leads them to fantastical adventures.
- 3 TO A SESSION: A MONSTER'S TALE, *by Desi Moreno-Penson, directed by Jose Zayas.* Sexual play-acting scenarios among three individuals.

DECEMBER FOOLS. *Written by Sherman Yellen. Directed by Donald Brenner. Abingdon Theatre. Opened February 1, 2006. Closed February 26, 2006.* A mother reunites with her estranged daughter amidst turmoil and the revelation of dark family secrets.

LENIN'S SHOE. *Written by Saviana Stanescu. Directed by Daniella Topol. Lark Studio. Opened February 1, 2006. Closed February 11, 2006.* A play that explores the effect of relocation, particularly on young immigrants who want to rid themselves of their pasts.

LENNY BRUCE…IN HIS OWN WORDS. *Written and directed by Joan Worth and Alan Sacks. Zipper Theatre. Opened February 1, 2006. Closed February 25, 2006.* A play created verbatim from the controversial satirist's most unforgettable routines.

THE RIDE. *Written by Crystal Skillman. Directed by Daniel Talbott. Produced by Rising Phoenix Repertory. Seventh Street Small Stage at Jimmy's No. 43. Opened February 1, 2006. Closed February 6, 2006.* The second in a series of ghost story one-acts (*The Telling* was the first), this play tells the story of an electrician hired to restore power to a country inn on a stormy winter night who encounters a mysterious woman in the dark.

BEYOND THE VEIL. *Written and directed by John Chatterton. Produced by La Muse Venale Acting Troupe. Where Eagles Dare. Opened February 2, 2006. Closed February 26, 2006.* A Victorian scientist engages in elaborate "experiments" with a medium under the guise of communicating with a dead lover.

C.COMMUTE. *Created by Ryan Colwell and Alexander Holt. Music by Daemon Hatfield. Directed by Ryan Colwell. Produced by The Narcissists. The Red Room. Opened February 2, 2006. Closed February 18, 2006.* A group of urbanites desperately try, yet often fail, to grow up.

FOLLIES OF GRANDEUR. *Written by Ross MacLean. Directed by Mark Finley. Theatre for the New City. Opened February 2, 2006. Closed February 19, 2006.* A inside look at life at the Ivar Theatre, an infamous Los Angeles burlesque house.

GREYHOUNDS. *Written by Daryl Lisa Fazio. Directed by Jesse Jou. Produced by Wickshaw Productions. Lion Theatre. Opened February 2, 2006. Closed February 19, 2006.* Two very different women—a provocative loner and a suppressed housewife—meet at a rural Oklahoma bus stop.

HAM & EGG. *Written and performed by Pam Wilterdink and Meg Schroeder. Produced by Brat Pak Productions. Under St. Marks. Opened February 2, 2006. Closed February 26, 2006.* A collection of sketches and playlets featuring ordinary women in strange and delicate situations.

LENNY & LOU. *Written by Ian Cohen. Directed by Sturgis Warner. 29th Street Rep. Opened February 2, 2006. Closed February 26, 2006.* A comedy about a middle-aged wannabe rock star, his younger brother, a lonely accountant, and their wildly inappropriate mom.

NO GREAT SOCIETY. *Directed by John Collins. Produced by Elevator Repair Service. P.S. 122. Opened February 2, 2006. Closed February 18, 2006.* A performance that conjures images of beat writer Jack Kerouac as both an enigmatically outsider poet and a tragically isolated alcoholic.

RABBIT HOLE. *Written by David Lindsay-Abaire. Directed by Daniel Sullivan. Produced by Manhattan Theatre Club. Biltmore Theatre. Opened February 2, 2006. Closed April 9, 2006.* A young husband and wife find themselves drifting apart after a life-altering accident.

THE ACCIDENTAL PERVERT. *Written and performed by Andrew Goffman. Directed by Charles Messina. Triad. Opened February 2, 2006. Closed February 24, 2006.* A solo show about how the author, as a boy, happened upon his father's collection of pornographic videotapes and then became addicted to porn.

BABIES WITH RABIES. *Written by Jonathan Calindas. Music by Mickey Zetts. Directed by Rodney E. Reyes. Produced by Cuchipinoy Productions. Looking Glass Theatre. Opened February 3, 2006. Closed February 26, 2006.* A comedy about a ragtag group of off-off-Broadway actors who write and put on a play about a group of inmates in an asylum who are putting on a play about a land plagued with rabid zombie babies.

LOVE ALWAYS. *Written and performed by Courtney Birch and Norman Crawford. Directed by Eric Morris. Ionica. Opened February 3, 2006. Closed February 12, 2006.* An epistolary play about a father and daughter who find they are unknown to one another when the matriarch who held them together suddenly dies.

SO SLOW THE BEAT OF MY HEART. *Written and directed by Michael J. Herron. St. John's University. Opened February 3, 2006. Closed February 4, 2006.* A young man in seminary prepschool shortly before Vatican II meets a young woman who causes him to question his vocation and to grapple with every aspect of modern life.

AVALON. *Directed by Glory Sims Bowen. Produced by FHB Productions. Looking Glass Theatre. Opened February 4, 2006. Closed February 25, 2006.* A retelling of the King Arthur legend, based on the women behind the throne.

ELLIOT, A SOLDIER'S FUGUE. *Written by Quiara Alegria Hudes. Music by Michael Friedman. Directed by Davis McCallum. Produced by Page 73 Productions. 45 Below. Opened February 4, 2006. Closed February 19, 2006.* A young man grapples with his recent return from active duty in Iraq, and discovers some startling similarities in the military experiences of his father and grandfather.

NORMAN & BEATRICE: A MARRIAGE IN TWO ACTS. *Written by Barbara Hammond. Directed by David Travis. Produced by Synapse Productions. Connelly Theatre. Opened February 4, 2006. Closed March 5, 2006.* A look at fifty years in the marriage of the title characters, one of whom eventually suffers from Alzheimer's disease.

THE BOOK OF THE DUN COW. *Book by Mark St. Germain. Music by Randy Courts. Lyrics by Randy Courts and Mark St. Germain. Directed by Cara Reichel. West End Theatre. Opened February 4, 2006. Closed February 26, 2006.* A musical adapted from Walter Wangerin Jr.'s novel of the same name, about an all-too-human rooster who battles evil forces for nothing less than the fate of the earth.

WINTER. *Written by A.J. Raath. Directed by W. Allen Wrede. Produced by 2B & Wrash Theatre Company. Looking Glass Theatre. Opened February 4, 2006. Closed February 26, 2006.* A play that mixes key scenes from Shakespeare's *The Winter's Tale* with a contemporary love story.

CONFESSIONS OF A MORMON BOY. *Written and performed by Steven Fales. Directed by Jack Hofsiss. Soho Playhouse. Opened February 5, 2006. Closed April 16, 2006.* A solo play about a young gay man's journey through excommunication from the Mormon Church, divorce, male prostitution, and drug abuse, as he struggles to reclaim himself.

FOUR WOMEN. *Written by Cheever Tyler. Directed by Christopher Carter Sanderson. Produced by One for my baby. Greenwich Street Theatre. Opened February 5, 2006. Closed February 28, 2006.* A play in four monologues about four very different women.

REAL BLACK MEN DON'T SIT CROSSLEGGED ON THE FLOOR. *Written by Malik. Directed by Passion. Produced by New Federal Theater. Henry Street Settlement. Opened February 5, 2006. Closed February 26, 2006.* A cohesion of poetry, prose, blues, rap, and rhythm that takes an unflinching look at being black and male in a hostile environment.

PARADISE. *Written by David Foley. Music by Margaret F. Heskin. Directed by Gary Shrader. Produced by Blue Coyote Theater Group. Access Theatre. Opened February 6, 2006. Closed February 26, 2006.* A play that follows three Manhattan couples and a dissolute priest who inadvertently set off a chain of events that leads to consequences none could have foreseen.

TRIPLE THREAT. *Produced by Emerging Artists Theatre. Theater Five. Opened February 7, 2006. Closed February 26, 2006.* Three new plays in repertory:

- **EDENVILLE,** *by Gregory Fletcher, directed by Tom Wojtunik.* A romantic comedy about one man's roller coaster ride toward life with Mr. Right.
- **THE KITCHEN TABLE,** *by Peter Levine, directed by Troy Miller.* A man's coming of age, from the 1950s through the present.
- **ROCK THE LINE,** *by Kathleen Warnock, directed by Steven McElroy.* Seven hard-core rock fans gather in a parking lot to await a show starring their favorite performer.

COMEDY EROTICUS: A LOVER'S FANTASY. *Written by Emmitt Thrower. Producers Club. Opened February 9, 2006. Closed February 19, 2006.* An erotic comedy that explores the passions and loves of ordinary people through the fantasies of a video store clerk.

LEMKIN'S HOUSE. *Written by Catherine Filloux. Directed by Jean Randich. 78th Street Theatre Lab. Opened February 9, 2006. Closed February 26, 2006.* A play set in the afterlife of Raphael Lemkin, the Polish American lawyer whose family died in the Holocaust and who invented the word "genocide."

RED LIGHT WINTER. *Written and directed by Adam Rapp. Barrow Street Theater. Opened February 9, 2006. Closed June 25, 2006.* Two college friends who spend a wild, unforgettable evening in Amsterdam's red light district with a beautiful young prostitute find that their lives have changed forever when their bizarre love triangle plays out in unexpected way a year later in the East Village.

THE RIGHT KIND OF PEOPLE. *Written by Charles Grodin. Directed by Chris Smith. Produced by Primary Stages. 59E59. Opened February 9, 2006. Closed March 5, 2006.* A send-up of a fashionable Fifth Avenue co-op board, where issues of race, gender, and social status glimmer just beneath the surface.

BOOM!: LOVE AT THE END OF THE WORLD. *Produced by Drove Theatre Co. Greenwich Street Theatre. Opened February 10, 2006. Closed February 11, 2006.* An evening of original short plays about love under the most inconvenient of circumstances: the end of the world; featuring works by Don Nigro, Mark St. Germain, Eric Walton, Dean Imperial, Rhett Rossi, Pat Swearingen, Mike Hampton, and Noah Barkley.

BACK OF THE THROAT. *Written by Yussef El Guindi. Directed by Jim Simpson. Flea. Opened February 11, 2006. Closed July 1, 2006.* Following a heinous terrorist attack, an Arab American writer is visited by two government officials, and what begins as a friendly inquiry soon devolves into a full-blown investigation of his presumed ties to terrorists.

THE SNOW HEN. *Written and performed by Hannah Bos and Paul Thureen. Directed by Oliver Butler. Produced by The Debate Society. Charlie Pineapple Theatre. Opened February 11, 2006. Closed February 25, 2006.* A play based on a fourteenth century Norwegian folk tale (Jostedal Grouse) inspired by the Black Death, in which a little girl has survived a deadly plague…and she is growing feathers.

JUMP/CUT. *Written by Neena Beber. Directed by Leigh Silverman. Julia Miles (WPP) Theatre. Opened February 12, 2006. Closed February 26, 2006.* Aspiring director Paul, his girlfriend Karen, and his lifelong buddy Dave embark on a filmmaking adventure that captures the complications of the human heart and the ethics of ambition.

KISS AND CRY. *Written by Tom Rowan. Directed by Kevin Newbury. Theater Ten Ten. Opened February 13, 2006. Closed March 12, 2006.* Stacy, a champion figure skater on his way to the Olympics, and Fiona, a hot young movie starlet, are the nation's favorite couple—as long as nobody finds out they're gay. **SEE PAGE 65.**

FANNY HILL. *Book, music, and lyrics by Ed Dixon. Directed by James Brennan. York Theatre. Opened February 14, 2006. Closed March 12, 2006.* A musical based on the eighteenth century novel *Fanny Hill*, which tells the story of a beautiful but poor country girl who travels to London to make her fortune, and ends up becoming the foremost practitioner of the so-called oldest profession.

I LOVE YOU BECAUSE. *Book by Ryan Cunningham. Music by Joshua Salzman. Directed by Daniel Kutner. Village Theatre. Opened February 14, 2006. Closed May 21, 2006.* A new musical about a young greeting card writer who is forced back onto the dating scene after he finds his long-term girlfriend in bed with another man.

NOW THAT YOU'VE SEEN ME NAKED. *Written and performed by Cleo's Comedy Players. Directed by Diana Blake. Sage Theater. Opened February 14, 2006. Closed July 1, 2006.* A musical comedy exploring the more ridiculous aspects of dating and relationships.

ALL THE BAD THINGS. *Written by Cusi Cram. Directed by Paula Pizzi. Produced by LAByrinth Theater Company. Public Theater. Opened February 15, 2006. Closed March 5, 2006.* A woman's life is thrown into disarray when she becomes a victim of rent destabilization.

CLEAN ALTERNATIVES. *Written by Brian Dykstra. Directed by Margarett Perry. Produced by Fresh Ice Productions. 59E59. Opened February 15, 2006. Closed March 12, 2006.* A play about how an environmentally friendly family business stays afloat in a sea of corporate sharks.

HARD LOVIN' EVER AFTER. *Written by Lucas Hnath. Music by Rika Lino. Directed by Jyana S. Gregory. Produced by Active Eye. Access Theatre. Opened February 15, 2006. Closed February 19, 2006.* Adapted from *Love Suicides at the Women's Temple* by eighteenth century Japanese dramatist Chikamatsu, this play tells the story of a pair of lovers pushed to the brink.

THE MONEY CONVERSATION. *Written and performed by Sara Juli. Directed by Chris Ajemian. P.S. 122. Opened February 15, 2006. Closed February 19, 2006.* A performance piece about the author's troubled relationship with money.

ACTS OF MERCY. *Written by Michael John Garces. Music by Matthew Suttor. Directed by Gia Forakis. Rattlestick Theatre. Opened February 16, 2006. Closed March 19, 2006.* During the course of one sweltering night, two sons must reconcile themselves to their dying father, hoping to gain redemption through small but life-giving acts of mercy.

GREENER. *Written and directed by Frank J. Avella. Music by Joe Morse. Produced by New Cockpit Ensemble. Bank Street Theatre. Opened February 16, 2006. Closed February 26, 2006.* Set in a cemetery, a play about a group of friends who gather together on the eve of their ten-year high school reunion after one of them has committed suicide.

HEDDATRON. *Written by Elizabeth Meriwether. Directed by Alex Timbers. Produced by Les Freres Corbusier. HERE Arts Center. Opened February 16, 2006. Closed February 25, 2006.* Ibsen is thwarted by August Strindberg and his kitchen slut throughout his fevered struggle to write the great feminist drama *Hedda Gabler*, while a contemporary housewife in Michigan is abducted by robots and forced to perform Ibsen's masterpiece over and over again...

THE LIBERATION OF LITTLE LULU. *Written by Eugenia Macer-Story. Directed by Eugenia Macer-Story and Michael-David Gordon. Theatre for the New City. Opened February 16, 2006. Closed March 5, 2006.* An expressionistic play about the assistance that can be provided to confused members of the middle class by those who have a mysterious link to spirits and angels.

THROAT. *Written by Mando Alvarado. Directed by Michael Ray Escamilla. 45th Street Theatre. Opened February 16, 2006. Closed March 4, 2006.* A play about a soldier fresh off the plane from Iraq, who must face the reality of living with the guilt of his mistakes and go to war with the demons of his past.

THE MAYOR OF BALTIMORE. *Written by Kristen Kosmas. Directed by Kip Fagan. Dixon Place. Opened February 17, 2006. Closed February 25, 2006.* A newly elected, low-level city government official in East Baltimore invites thirteen of her friends over for a victory party.

DEATH MIGHT BE YOUR SANTA CLAUS. *Conceived and directed by Lear deBessonet. Produced by Stillpoint Productions. 15 Nassau Street. Opened February 18, 2006. Closed February 21, 2006.* A sixty-eight-year-old man in Dallas leads a group of former homeless people and addicts in an undercover spy operation to expose televangelistic fraud.

OUT OF ORBIT—YOU CHOOSE THE ADVENTURE! *Book by Brianna Tyson and Ben Casey. Lyrics by Ben Casey. Directed by Catherine Ward. Produced by Vital Children's Theatre. McGinn Cazale*

Theatre. Opened February 18, 2006. Closed March 26, 2006. A stray comet knocks the moon off its orbit, sending it on a collision course with earth, and the audience must save the world.

THE LAST OF THE DRAGONS. *Adapted by Kristin Walter. Directed by Laura Stevens. Manhattan Children's Theatre. Opened February 18, 2006. Closed April 2, 2006.* A play based on the story by E. Nesbit, about a princess and a dragon, both determined to break from their traditional roles, but for very different reasons.

ENDINGS. *Written and directed by John Capo. Produced by Etcetera, a division of Love Creek Productions. Manhattan Repertory Theater. Opened February 21, 2006. Closed February 26, 2006.* A program of five plays, all of which chronicle various kinds of endings experienced in life.

I LOOK LIKE AN EGG, BUT I IDENTIFY AS A COOKIE. *Written and performed by Heather Gold. Ars Nova. Opened February 21, 2006. Closed February 22, 2006.* An interactive baking comedy, in which the author addresses questions with baking's simple truths, while she bakes cookies for her audience.

THE WOODEN BREEKS. *Written by Glen Berger. Directed by Trip Cullman. Produced by MCC Theater. Lucille Lortel Theatre. Opened February 21, 2006. Closed March 11, 2006.* Set in a fictitious and miserable land, a village tinker-turned-poet soothes his broken heart by creating a theatrical tale for the bastard child of the woman he lost.

THICK LIKE PIANO LEGS. *Written by Robert Attenweiler. Produced by Disgraced Productions. The Red Room. Opened February 21, 2006. Closed March 7, 2006.* A saloon singer prepares to leave the job he's held for years.

CHEPACHET. *Written and directed by James Crafford. American Theatre of Actors. Opened February 22, 2006. Closed February 26, 2006.* A play about the relationships among two middle-aged men and their mentally challenged maid.

INDOOR/OUTDOOR. *Written by Kenny Finkle. Directed by Daniel Goldstein. DR2. Opened February 22, 2006. Closed March 19, 2006.* A romantic comedy about the adventures of a pampered house cat.

INSIDEOUT. *Written by Jason Pizzarello. Directed by Aaron Rhyne. Produced by Live Project. HERE Arts Center. Opened February 23, 2006. Closed March 19, 2006.* A theatre/video hybrid performance piece where actors, cows, cameras, and video projections interact equally to challenge audience members to question identity, revenge, hell, and the role of beef in America.

PROMETHEUS PASSION. *Written by Andre Diniz. Directed by Eric Lesh. Produced by Sturm Und Drang Company. Kraine Theatre. Opened February 23, 2006. Closed February 25, 2006.* In Heaven, Prometheus is given the task of molding the human race, but only on one condition: he is forbidden from revealing himself to mankind.

REPUBLIC OF IQRA. *Written and directed by Bina Sharif. Theatre for the New City. Opened February 23, 2006. Closed March 19, 2006.* A drama with satirical and surrealistic elements about two fictional republics: one ancient, in a remote part of the world, called the Republic of Iqra; the other, a very powerful modern republic called the Republic of Make-Believe, which invades the Republic of Iqra under a false premise.

SOMEONE IN THE GHOST BOX TOLD ME IT WAS YOU. *Written and directed by Kenneth Collins. Music by Andrew Elsesser. Produced by Temporary Distortion. Chocolate Factory. Opened February 23, 2006. Closed February 25, 2006.* A theatrical meditation on the subjects of entrapment, surveillance, love, suicide, and psychosis.

TEMPLE. *Written by Tim Aumiller. Directed by Greg Foro. Produced by Bridge Club Productions. Manhattan Theatre Source. Opened February 23, 2006. Closed March 11, 2006.* A play that imagines an America in the near future where laws are being made and upheld in the courts that are borne out of religious ideology, dividing the country based on sexuality and freedom.

THOUSAND YEARS WAITING. *Written by Chiori Miyagawa. Music by Bruce Odland. Directed by Sonoko Kawahara. Produced by Crossing Jamaica Avenue. P.S. 122. Opened February 23, 2006. Closed March 12, 2006.* A play that contains three simultaneous realities—present-day New York City, Japan circa 1000, and inside *The Tale of the Genji*, the world's first novel—and tells the history of storytelling.

A PARSIFAL. *Written by Susan Sontag. Directed by John Jahnke. Produced by The Hotel Savant. P.S. 122. Opened February 25, 2006. Closed March 5, 2006.* A poetic deconstruction of Wagner's opera, in which the innocent knight is an Uzi-toting soldier wandering aimlessly through an anonymous landscape in search of arbitrary sex and violence.

BLACK MEN CRY TOO. *Written by Cilque Brown. Produced by Faith in God Theater. Producers Club. Opened February 25, 2006. Closed April 15, 2006.* A murder mystery about a love triangle involving African American GIs.

PARADISE LOST, THE MUSICAL. *Book and lyrics by Benjamin Birney and Rob Seitelman. Music by Benjamin Birney. Directed by Rob Seitelman. Produced by Niaterra Arts & Entertainment. Producers Club II. Opened February 25, 2006. Closed March 18, 2006.* A musical that tells the story of Adam and Eve, Lucifer and his minions, and the angelic host that opposes them.

[TITLE OF SHOW]. *Book by Hunter Bell. Music and lyrics by Jeff Bowen. Directed by Michael Berresse. Vineyard Theatre. Opened February 26, 2006. Closed April 30, 2006.* A musical about two struggling writers named Jeff and Hunter who try to write and submit a show to the New York Musical Theatre Festival, in hopes of getting discovered and optioned for a commercial run.

DEFIANCE. *Written by John Patrick Shanley. Directed by Doug Hughes. Manhattan Theatre Club. Opened February 28, 2006. Closed June 4, 2006.* A play set on a U.S. Marine Corps base in North Carolina in 1971, where two officers—one white, one black—are on a collision course over race, women, and the high cost of doing the right thing.

FROM ISRAEL TO SEX IN THE SITY. *Written and performed by Iris Zieber. American Theatre of Actors. Opened March 2, 2006. Closed March 19, 2006.* A chronicle of an Israeli woman coming to New York and going through the cultural clashes between Israeli and American mentalities.

SAKE WITH THE HAIKU GEISHA. *Written by Randall David Cook. Directed by Alex Lippard. Produced by Gotham Stage Company. Perry Street Theatre. Opened March 2, 2006. Closed April 8, 2006.* A play about a trio of foreign teachers who attend a party at a Japanese lodge hosted by a mysterious geisha who speaks only in haiku, in an evening that weaves together five interconnected tales of sexual mishaps, romance, and cross-cultural miscommunication.

THE PALOOKA. *Written by Brandon Ramos. Directed by Jeffery Lawhorn. Access Theatre. Opened March 2, 2006. Closed March 12, 2006.* A play about a career boxer, wanting to escape the punishment and monotony of the ring, who meets an old friend with a new and dangerous angle in 1950s Philadelphia.

FOUNTAIN OF YOUTH. *Written and performed by Noemi de la Puente. Directed by Mike Smith Rivera and Mateo Gomez. CSV Cultural Center. Opened March 3, 2006. Closed March 25, 2006.* A solo show about an assistant coroner who searches for the fountain of youth in the swamps of eastern Florida.

GOOD ENOUGH TO BE TRUE. *Written by Raphael Bob-Waksberg. Directed by Kielsen Baker. Produced by Theatre of Mass Destruction. American Theatre of Actors. Opened March 3, 2006. Closed March 19, 2006.* A play about four quarter-lifers, addicted to each other and trying to find themselves in a world that won't let them see clearly.

MY NAME IS HARRIET TUBMAN. *Written and performed by Connie Winston. Produced by Blackfriars Repertory Theatre. WorkShop Theatre. Opened March 3, 2006. Closed March 4, 2006.* A solo show about the life of Harriet Tubman, the former slave who became a conductor on the Underground Railroad.

RUE. *Written by August Schulenburg. Music by Michelle O'Connor. Directed by Kelly O'Donnell. Theatre for the New City. Opened March 3, 2006. Closed March 19, 2006.* A dark comedic farce about obsession, exploitation, and regret, set in a swank hotel on a mythical island.

THE FROG BRIDE. *Written and performed by David Gonzalez. Music by Daniel Kelly. Directed by Leonard Petit. Produced by RainArt Productions. New Victory Theatre. Opened March 3, 2006. Closed March 12, 2006.* A multimedia musical adaptation of the classic Russian fairy tale, "The Frog Princess," the tale of a prince who is forced to marry a frog when his arrow lands in her pond.

WRECKED. *Created and directed by Andrea Arden. Produced by Theatre Lila. American Theatre of Actors. Opened March 3, 2006. Closed March 18, 2006.* A play based on the *Oresteia* of Aeschylus.

BERNARDA ALBA. *Book, music, and lyrics by Michael John LaChiusa. Directed by Graciela Daniele. Produced by Lincoln Center Theater. Mitzi Newhouse Theater. Opened March 6, 2006. Closed April 9, 2006.* A musical based on *The House of Bernarda Alba* by Federico Garcia Lorca, about a widow who decrees that she and her daughters will not leave the house for seven years of mourning.

FATBOY. *Written and directed by John Clancy. Produced by Soho Think Tank. Ohio Theatre. Opened March 6, 2006. Closed March 25, 2006.* A modern adaptation of Alfred Jarry's *Ubu Roi*, about a brutish allegorical presence known as Fatboy who stands trial for war crimes.

PHENOMENON. *Written by Gordon Cox. Music by Lance Horne. Directed by Alyse Rothman. Produced by Nerve Ensemble. HERE Arts Center. Opened March 6, 2006. Closed March 25, 2006.* A multimedia theatre work about the 1980 eruption of Mt. St. Helens in Cougar, Washington.

QUENTIN AND I. *Book and lyrics by David Leddick. Music by Andrew Sargent. Directed by David Kingery. La MaMa. Opened March 6, 2006. Closed March 7, 2006.* A mini-musical about the author's twenty-year friendship with the late Quentin Crisp.

THE MUSIC TEACHER. *Written by Wallace Shawn. Music by Allen Shawn. Directed by Tom Cairns. Produced by The New Group. Minetta Lane Theatre. Opened March 6, 2006. Closed April*

9, 2006. A play/opera about a younger teacher and his brilliant female student who conceive and perform a new opera.

EATFEST—SPRING 2006. *Produced by Emerging Artists Theatre. Theater Five. Opened March 7, 2006. Closed March 26, 2006.* A festival of new short plays:

- MY SISTER THE COW, *by Gregory Fletcher, directed by Paul Adams.*
- BLACKOUT, *by Vladimir Maicovski, directed by Anthony Luciano.*
- STAR TRAIN, *by Susan Merson, directed by Melissa Atteberry.*
- PERFECTLY NORMAL FAMILY DINNER, *by Matthew J. Hanson, directed by Deb Guston.*
- THE SECRET OF OUR SUCCESS, *by Staci Swedeen, directed by Derek Jamison.*
- NAGASAKI, *by Kevin Brofsky, directed by Kel Haney.*
- MR. COMPANY, *by Marc Castle, directed by Max Montel.*
- WHAT WE TALK ABOUT, *by Emily Mitchell, directed by Ian Streicher.*
- THE TEST, *by Caitlin Mitchell, directed by Chris Marin.*
- MOM, STONED, *by Bekka Brunstetter, directed by Kevin Dodd.*

GREY GARDENS. *Book by Doug Wright. Music by Scott Frankel. Lyrics by Michael Korie. Directed by Michael Greif. Playwrights Horizons Mainstage. Opened March 7, 2006. Closed April 30, 2006.* A musical based on the 1975 documentary film of the same name, about the eccentric aunt and cousin of Jacqueline Kennedy Onassis, who live as notorious recluses in a run-down twenty-eight-room mansion.

33 TO NOTHING. *Written by Grant James Varjas. Music by Grant James Varjas. Directed by John B. Good. Produced by Argo Theater Company. Bottle Factory. Opened March 8, 2006. Closed April 29, 2006.* A slice-of-life look at a struggling New York rock band on the eve of their breakup.

MEASURE FOR PLEASURE. *Written by David Grimm. Music by Peter Golub. Directed by Peter DuBois. Public Theater. Opened March 8, 2006. Closed March 26, 2006.* A comedic love triangle between a man, a transvestite prostitute, and a handsome rake set in Restoration England.

NEVER AS HAPPY. *Adapted and directed by Javierantonio Gonzalez. Produced by Columbia Stages. Theatre of the Riverside Church. Opened March 8, 2006. Closed March 11, 2006.* A dramatization of the story of the House of Atreus, compiled and adapted from Aescyhlus's *Oresteia,* Sophocles's *Electra,* and Euripides's *Orestes, Iphigenia at Tauris,* and *Iphigenia at Aulis.*

SAVAGES. *Written by Anne Nelson. Directed by Chris Jorie. Produced by Back House Productions. Lion Theatre. Opened March 9, 2006. Closed April 1, 2006.* A play set in the midst of the Philippine-American conflict in 1902, as seen through the eyes of four different characters.

SEXTANGLE. *Written by Robert Leeds and Jacquelyn Poplar. Music by Ralph John. Directed by Jacquelyn Poplar. Produced by Queens Players. The Creek Theater. Opened March 9, 2006. Closed March 25, 2006.* A farce about love, sex, and marriage that tells the story of a rich old miser and his doddering old friend.

SPRING'S AWAKENING. *Adapted by Kenneth Nowell. Directed by Charmian Creagle. Looking Glass Theatre. Opened March 9, 2006. Closed April 2, 2006.* A new adaptation of the play by Frank Wedekind, about the onset of puberty within a group of children terrorized by adults.

TOTAL FAITH IN COSMIC LOVE. *Written by John DeVore. Directed by R.J. Tolan. Brick Theatre. Opened March 9, 2006. Closed April 1, 2006.* A dark romantic comedy that features revenge sex, angry coke dealers, and karaoke ambushes.

WHAT DO I KNOW ABOUT WAR? *Written and performed by Margo Lee Sherman. Theatre for the New City. Opened March 9, 2006. Closed March 26, 2006.* A solo performance piece based on the words of America's soldiers recently deployed, and some returned.

BLUFF. *Written by Jeffrey Sweet. Directed by Sandy Shinner. 78th Street Theatre Lab. Opened March 10, 2006. Closed March 26, 2006.* The story of a young couple in New York who are doing fine until her brash and vulgar stepfather comes to town for a convention, bringing with him all of the contradictions she has been trying to bury.

BULRUSHER. *Written by Eisa Davis. Music by Daniel Denver. Directed by Leah C. Gardiner. Urban Stages. Opened March 11, 2006. Closed April 9, 2006.* An abandoned multiracial girl grows up as an outcast in a mostly white town because of her clairvoyance.

SHORTLY AFTER TAKEOFF. *Written and directed by Stuart Warmflash. Produced by Harbor Theatre Company. Altered Stages. Opened March 11, 2006. Closed April 2, 2006.* Set in 1967, a fifteen-year-old boy who talks to frogs tries to find his place in the world.

BABY GIRL. *Written by Edith Freni. Directed by Padraic Lillis. Produced by Partial Comfort Productions. Center Stage. Opened March 12, 2006. Closed April 1, 2006.* A homeless and unemployed single mother tries to win back her ex-boyfriend and build a stable life for her baby.

HARD RIGHT. *Written and directed by David Barth. Players Theatre. Opened March 12, 2006. Closed April 1, 2006.* A slacker college student brings his girlfriend home for a visit with the folks.

RING OF FIRE. *Conceived by William Meade. Directed by Richard Maltby Jr. Ethel Barrymore Theatre. Opened March 12, 2006. Closed April 30, 2006.* A musical revue featuring the music of Johnny Cash.

THE TERRITORY. *Written by Tanya Krohn. Directed by Cris Buchner. Produced by Six Figures Theatre Company. West End Theatre. Opened March 13, 2006. Closed April 1, 2006.* Two surreal fables of suburbia examine how we search for safety and security in the face of chaos and senselessness.

FULL BLOOM. *Written by Suzanne Bradbeer. Directed by Linda Ames Key. Produced by Vital Theatre Company. McGinn Cazale Theatre. Opened March 14, 2006. Closed April 2, 2006.* A teenaged New Yorker trying to come to terms with a culture that seems to care more about how a woman looks than about what she thinks or can do.

BREATHE. *Written by Javon Johnson. Directed by Rajendra Ramoon Maharaj. Lark Studio. Opened March 15, 2006. Closed March 25, 2006.* A play about two teenagers—one white, one black—who are involved in separate acts of violence.

SIDD. *Book by Andrew Frank. Music by Doug Silver. Lyrics by Doug Silver and Andrew Frank. Directed by Andrew Frank. New World Stages. Opened March 15, 2006. Closed March 26, 2006.* A musical based on the novel *Siddhartha* by Herman Hesse, about the spiritual journey of one man, from his youthful wanderings to his adult enlightenment.

JUNTA HIGH. *Written by Clay McLeod Chapman. Music by Hungry March Band. P.S. 122. Opened March 16, 2006. Closed March 26, 2006.* A collection of stories for the stage that explores the what-if scenario of transposing the current political imbroglio of modern Iraq within an American public high school.

MRS. CALIFORNIA. *Written by Doris Baizley. Directed by Megan R. Wills. Produced by River Heights Productions. 78th Street Theatre Lab. Opened March 16, 2006. Closed April 1, 2006.* A female war veteran in the 1950s struggles to keep her dignity and self-respect while trying to win a contest for the best homemaker.

SODOM'S WIFE. *Conceived by Erin Brindley and Maximillian Davis. Directed by Erin Brindley. Produced by Ripple Productions. Phil Bosokowski Theatre. Opened March 16, 2006. Closed April 9, 2006.* A play that explores the biblical story of Sodom's destruction from the perspective of Lot's wife.

IPHIGENIA AND OTHER DAUGHTERS. *Written by Ellen McLaughlin. Directed by Michael Perlman. Produced by Temporary Theater Company. Actors Theatre Workshop. Opened March 17, 2006. Closed March 26, 2006.* A retelling of the classic Greek stories.

TWISTED HEAD. *Written and performed by Carl Capotorto. Studio Dante. Opened March 17, 2006. Closed April 7, 2006.* An autobiographical solo show about the author's childhood, growing up in the Bronx in the '60s and '70s.

CYCLONE. *Written by Ron Fitzgerald. Directed by Brian Mertes. Studio Dante. Opened March 18, 2006. Closed April 15, 2006.* A dark comedy about a young man searching for his life's worth after the death of his estranged father.

NOT CLOWN. *Written by Steve Moore. Directed by Carlos Trevino. Soho Rep. Opened March 18, 2006. Closed March 25, 2006.* In a world where circuses have been banned, a renegade troupe re-enacts the story of a girl who longs for their outlawed clown life.

POINTS OF DEPARTURE. *Written by Michael John Garcés. Music by Cristian Amigo. Directed by Ron Daniels. Produced by Intar. Kirk Theatre. Opened March 19, 2006. Closed April 16, 2006.* As one man tries to return to his village in Central America after years of being away and another woman tries to embark to the U.S., they find that if an immigrant's journey to the U.S. is difficult, the journey back home is almost impossible.

WALK THE MOUNTAIN. *Written and performed by Jude Narita. Directed by Darling Narita. 59E59. Opened March 19, 2006. Closed April 9, 2006.* A solo show that examines the lingering effects of the Vietnam War and the legacy of misinformation that exists in the U.S. about the war.

FAHRENHEIT 451. *Written by Ray Bradbury. Music by Andrew Recinos. Directed by Joe Tantalo. Produced by Godlight Theatre Company. 59E59. Opened March 21, 2006. Closed April 23, 2006.* The stage version of Ray Bradbury's novel of the same name, about a man who burns books in a future where freedom of thought is outlawed.

FEMALE BONDING. *Written by Susan Kaessinger. Directed by James Alexander Bond. Impact Theater. Opened March 22, 2006. Closed April 2, 2006.* A serio-comedy set at a bridal shower where seven diverse women experience failed marriages, struggles with sexual preference, motherhood, the quest for love, growing pains, and the loss of loved ones—all while maintaining close bonds with one another.

LIVING ROOM IN AFRICA. *Written by Bathsheba Doran. Music by Michael Friedman. Directed by Carolyn Cantor. Produced by Edge Theater Company. Beckett Theatre. Opened March 22, 2006. Closed April 15, 2006.* A British couple relocate to a remote African village, intent on opening an art museum, only to discover that the area has been ravaged by poverty and AIDS.

WHERE THERE'S NO WILL. *Written by Leon Kaye. Music by Brian McCallister. Directed by Dan Conrad. Produced by Random Coconuts. Medicine Show. Opened March 22, 2006. Closed March 26, 2006.* A comedy-farce-mystery set in 1930s Albany, where a group of zany relatives battle over a family member's unsigned will.

MERCY ON THE DOORSTEP. *Written by Gip Hoppe. Music by Rick Arnoldi. Directed by Jim Simpson. Flea. Opened March 23, 2006. Closed April 14, 2006.* An alcoholic widow and her born-again, right-wing stepdaughter must learn to coexist in the house that their husband/father left behind.

THE PROPERTY KNOWN AS GARLAND. *Written by Billy Van Zandt. Directed by Glenn Casale. Actors Playhouse. Opened March 23, 2006. Closed May 21, 2006.* A fictionalized backstage account of Judy Garland's final concert appearance.

TRAVELS, TOURS AND ONE-NIGHT STANDS. *Directed by Kim Ima. La MaMa. Opened March 23, 2006. Closed April 9, 2006.* A movement theater work inspired by the experience of travel: the first taste of a new food, the way a hot wind blows, and the sounds of a new city.

SHILOH RULES. *Written by Doris Baizley. Directed by Michaela Goldhaber. Produced by Flying Fig Theater. Gene Frankel Theatre. Opened March 24, 2006. Closed April 9, 2006.* A satire about hardcore Civil War buffs who set off the annual reenactment of the Battle of Shiloh prematurely.

THE LEDGE. *Written by Jack Hanley. Music by Alicia Mathewson. Directed by Christopher Eaves. Produced by eavesdrop. Dixon Place. Opened March 24, 2006. Closed April 8, 2006.* A play based on a short story by Lawrence Sargent Hall, about a fisherman stranded with his son and nephew on a small reef exposed at low tide in the North Atlantic.

LIMERICKS FROM UNDISCLOSED LOCATIONS/DÉJÀ VU PUNKED. *Written by Larry Myers. Produced by RWM Playwrights Lab. Theatre 54 @ Shetler. Opened March 25, 2006. Closed July 1, 2006.* Two monologue plays about Hurricane Katrina heroes and survivors, and contemporary cons, scams, and spam, respectively.

FRAGMENT. *Text assembled by Kelly Copper. Directed by Pavol Liska. Classic Stage. Opened March 26, 2006. Closed April 9, 2006.* A work drawn from remaining fragments of the lost plays of Sophocles and Euripides, which addresses issues of war abroad, fear at home, and a world divided between immediate gratification and the harsh realities that wait just around the corner.

RIDDLELIKELOVE (WITH A SIDE OF KETCHUP). *Written by Julie Fitzpatrick and Douglas Anderson. Directed by Douglas Anderson. Produced by Godlight Theater Company. 59E59. Opened March 26, 2006. Closed April 23, 2006.* The true story of coauthor Julie Fitzpatrick's irrepressible best friend, who had profound hearing loss.

TRIAL BY WATER. *Written by Qui Nguyen. Directed by John Gould Rubin. Produced by Ma-Yi Theater Company. 45 Below. Opened March 26, 2006. Closed April 9, 2006.* Two Vietnamese brothers confront their own mortality and morality when their boat breaks down during a journey to America.

TIGER BY THE TAIL. *Written by Frawley Becker. Directed by Jules Ochoa. Wings Theater. Opened March 27, 2006. Closed April 22, 2006.* Two men who meet via the personals—one is a middle-aged therapist in California, the other a young prisoner incarcerated in Florida—find their relationship challenged by the prison guards and some unexpected brutality.

THE GOD COMMITTEE. *Written by Mark St. Germain. Directed by Kevin Moriarty. Lamb's Theatre. Opened March 29, 2006. Closed April 16, 2006.* Medicine, money, and morality clash in the boardroom of an organ transplant committee as just one heart becomes suddenly available for one of three candidates.

THEY'RE JUST LIKE US. *Written by Boo Killebrew. Directed by Mike Doyle. Produced by Collaboration Town. The Red Room. Opened March 29, 2006. Closed April 15, 2006.* A play that explores a darkly satirical world in which the "wants" are superficial and the "needs" are delusional—much like the lives of some of our most beloved and berated celebrities. **SEE PAGE 125.**

ALICE'S ADVENTURES IN WONDERLAND. *Music and lyrics by John Dyer. HERE Arts Center. Opened March 30, 2006. Closed April 22, 2006.* The classic Lewis Carroll tale retold with puppets of the bunraku, shadow, and handheld styles.

CONVERGENCE. *Written and directed by Bryn Manion. Produced by Aisling Arts. NY Irish Center. Opened March 30, 2006. Closed April 14, 2006.* A play that spans three continents: a war journalist, two mechanics, one artist, one humanitarian aid worker, and a science teacher plunge into painfully normal and profoundly extreme moments in time when memory and identity are absolute. **SEE PAGE 165.**

HELL. *Music by Michael Webster. Lyrics by Eileen Myles. Directed by David Chambers. P.S. 122. Opened March 30, 2006. Closed April 9, 2006.* An opera inspired by the urgent and crucial need of vanguard artists to address the breaking events of their time.

THE MOTHER OF ALL ENEMIES. *Written and performed by Paul Zaloom. Directed by Randee Trabitz. Produced by apexart. Collective Unconscious. Opened March 30, 2006. Closed April 9, 2006.* A mutation of the traditional Middle Eastern Karagoz shadow puppet play about the consequences of being on the fringes of society…EVERY society.

THE LONG MARCH. *Written by Martin M. Maquire. Directed by Patrick Sutton. Greenwich Street Theatre. Opened March 31, 2006. Closed April 2, 2006.* A play that explores the roots of intolerance by telling the story of an oppressed people who, because of their differences from the prevailing temperament of the so-called hosts, are forced to continuously uproot and flee into exile.

MEN OF CLAY. *Written and directed by Jeff Cohen. Produced by The Theatre Outlet. Abingdon Theatre. Opened April 2, 2006. Closed April 23, 2006.* A semi-autobiographical comedy about the playwright's father set in early 1970s at Baltimore's Druid Hill Park clay tennis courts.

PEN. *Written by David Marshall Grant. Directed by Will Frears. Playwrights Horizons Peter J Sharp. Opened April 2, 2006. Closed April 16, 2006.* Confined to a wheelchair, a controlling mother holds tightly to her son by influencing his enrollment in a nearby college, while her ex-husband tries to spring the boy loose.

THE CATARACT. *Written by Lisa D'Amour. Music by The Broken Chord Collective. Directed by Katie Pearl. Produced by Women's Project. Julia Miles (WPP) Theatre. Opened April 2, 2006. Closed April 15, 2006.* A play fuses the natural elements of wind, water, wood, and stone to the interiors of its four characters, set against the backdrop of the Mississippi River.

IN DELIRIUM: AFTER THE SORROWS OF YOUNG WERTHER. *Adapted and created by Gisela Cardenas and Joshua Randall. Directed by Gisela Cardenas. Produced by Vortex Theater Com-*

pany. Sanford Meisner Theatre. Opened April 3, 2006. Closed April 23, 2006. A new adaptation of Goethe's novel *The Sorrows of Young Werther*.

THE ADVENTURES OF CHARCOAL BOY. *Music by Elyas Khan. Directed by Sarah Provost. HERE Arts Center. Opened April 3, 2006. Closed April 17, 2006.* A performance piece in which puppets constructed from organic and industrial objects are brought to life.

CHAMPION/THE STUTTERING PREACHER. *Produced by New Federal Theatre and Black Spectrum Theatre. Henry Street Settlement. Opened April 6, 2006. Closed April 30, 2006.* A double bill of short plays: **THE STUTTERING PREACHER,** about a handsome, speech-challenged ladies' man and a proud black woman tired of deceitful, game-playing men and bad relationships; and **CHAMPION,** about a man who struggles with major life-altering challenges, and another man whose own trials and tribulations are paramount to the play's plot.

DREAD AWAKENING. *Produced by Thursday Problem. 45th Street Theatre. Opened April 6, 2006. Closed April 23, 2006.* A program of four new short plays all with a common sensibility rooted in horror and the macabre: **BLOODY MARY,** *by Roberto Aguirre-Sacasa, directed by Pat Diamond*; **PEARLS,** *by Clay McLeod Chapman, directed by Arin Arbus*; **SLEEP MASK,** by Eric Sanders, directed by Amanda Charlton; and **TREESFALL,** *by Justin Swain, directed by Jessica Davis-Irons.*

MINE. *Written by David Epstein. Directed by Johanna Gruenhut. Theatre Row Studio. Opened April 6, 2006. Closed April 11, 2006.* A program of two one-act plays: **MINE,** in which four women, suddenly challenged by their greatest fear, bravely await the outcome of a mining disaster that will determine the course of their lives; and **THEY TOLD ME THAT YOU CAME THIS WAY,** in which two young men, prisoners of an unnamed war, come to grips with their personal demons, engaging one another in a desperate battle.

ONE GOOD MARRIAGE. *Written by Sean Reycraft. Directed by Diana Belshaw. Produced by D.I.Y. Theatre. Manhattan Repertory Theatre. Opened April 6, 2006. Closed April 23, 2006.* A young married couple celebrate their first anniversary under the cloud of a tragedy that occurred during their honeymoon.

SEVEN.11. CONVENIENCE THEATRE. *Directed by Darrow Carson. Produced by Desipina & Company. Kraine Theatre. Opened April 6, 2006. Closed April 23, 2006.* A program of seven eleven-minute plays, all set in convenience stores, and all created by Asian Americans:

- **BOMBAY SCREAMS,** *by Rehana Mirza.* An unemployed actor from Broadway's Bombay Dreams toils at the 7-11...until an up-and-coming female playwright comes in and sweeps him off his feet.
- **WHO KILLED MR. NAIDU FIRST?,** *by Samrat Chakrabarti and Sanjiv Jhaveri.* With three suspects and a heinous crime, a musical whodunnit that will send you singing and screaming from the convenience store!
- **HOMECOMING,** *by Celena Cipriaso.* A young woman stumbles into a convenience store to find her past.
- **THE OLD NEW WORLD,** *by J.P. Chan.* In the year 2106, superpowers fight for their right to claim the Jewel of Ancient America.
- **UNDONE,** *by Elizabeth Emmons.* Two girls stop for supplies on a runaway trip to Mexico to escape an arranged marriage.

- **JAFFNA MANGOES,** *by Vishakan Jeyakumar.* Race relations in a convenience store in Sunnyside, Queens, makes life juicier than the juiciest of mangos.
- **KUNG FU HUSTLE,** *by Jackson Loo.* A Chinese American teen, convinced that learning kung Fu should be easy for him since it's part of his heritage, struggles to master the art in a hurry to impress a pretty martial arts instructor.

SHOW PEOPLE. *Written by Paul Weitz. Directed by Peter Askin. Second Stage. Opened April 6, 2006. Closed April 30, 2006.* A pair of Broadway actors who haven't worked in years decide to take on a wildly unorthodox job for a rich, young New York banker.

TRYST. *Written by Karoline Leach. Directed by Joe Brancato. Promenade Theatre. Opened April 6, 2006. Closed June 11, 2006.* A handsome con man who woos loved-starved women hits a snag when he meets a desperate milliner.

COLD. *Written and developed by Present Tense Theatre Project. Produced by Present Tense Theatre Company. Bank Street Theatre. Opened April 7, 2006. Closed April 16, 2006.* A contemporary journey of Faith through Hans Christian Andersen's classic, "The Snow Queen."

PEAR COWBOY PLANET. *Written by Chris Yon and Justin Jones. La MaMa. Opened April 7, 2006. Closed April 9, 2006.* A modern vaudevillian, tragicomic triptych about the mysterious properties of addition and subtraction told through dance, theatre, and sketch comedy.

ADVENTURES OF CAVEMAN ROBOT. *Book by Jeff Lewonczyk. Music by Debby Schwartz. Lyrics by Jeff Lewonczyk and Debby Schwartz. Directed by Jeff Lewonczyk. Produced by Piper McKenzie Productions. Brick Theatre. Opened April 8, 2006. Closed May 13, 2006.* A musical based on Jason Robert Bell and Shoshanna Weinberger's cartoon character.

CINDERELLA'S MICE. *Book by Justin Warner. Music by Ben Morss. Lyrics by Justin Warner and Ben Morss. Directed by David Hilder. Produced by Vital Children's Theatre. McGinn Cazale Theatre. Opened April 8, 2006. Closed May 14, 2006.* A musical for kids and their families about a mouse who gets turned into one of Cinderella's horses.

IRON CURTAIN. *Book by Susan DiLallo. Music by Stephen Weiner. Lyrics by Peter Mills. Directed by Cara Reichel. Produced by Prospect Theater Company. West End Theatre. Opened April 8, 2006. Closed April 30, 2006.* A musical set in the 1950s about the adventures of an unsuccessful composer/lyricist team as they are kidnapped by the KGB and taken to the USSR to ghostwrite communist propaganda musicals.

JACK & THE BEANSTALK. *Book, music, and lyrics by Karl Greenberg and Dave Hall. Directed by Bruce Merrill. Manhattan Children's Theatre. Opened April 8, 2006. Closed May 21, 2006.* A new stage version of the classic fairy tale in which Jack is a forlorn, New York "artist-type" who is forced to actually work for a living.

THE DEBATE PLAYS. *Written by Mat Smart. Directed by Evan Cabnet, Wes Grantom, and Adam Knight. Produced by Slant Theatre Project. Phil Bosokowski Theatre. Opened April 8, 2006. Closed May 13, 2006.* Three interconnected comedies chronicling the history of a love triangle that's settled in a bar-room debate.

LOS BIG NAMES. *Written and performed by Marga Gomez. Directed by David Schweizer. Produced by Puerto Rican Traveling Theatre. 47th Street Theatre. Opened April 9, 2006. Closed May 14, 2006.*

An autobiographical solo show set in two eras—the New York Latin show business world of the '60s, and Hollywood in the '90s—follows the lives of an unconventional Latino family of three pursuing their dreams of fame and fortune

A JEW GROWS IN BROOKLYN. *Written and performed by Jake Ehrenreich. Directed by Jon Huberth. American Theatre of Actors. Opened April 10, 2006. Closed May 28, 2006.* A solo musical comedy that tells the story of the author's first-generation American journey, from his parents' survival of the Holocaust to his stickball recollections in Brooklyn to his Catskill Mountain memories.

CUPID AND PSYCHE. *Written by Joseph Fisher. Directed by Alex Lippard. Produced by Themantics Group. Altered Stages. Opened April 10, 2006. Closed April 30, 2006.* When the goddess Aphrodite has her mojo stolen by the most beautiful woman in the world, Psyche, she begins to age and decides to eliminate the problem.

LITTLE WILLY. *Written by Mark Kassen. Directed by John Gould Rubin. Produced by Like Minded Productions. Ohio Theatre. Opened April 10, 2006. Closed April 30, 2006.* A play about William Patrick Hitler, nephew of Adolf, who was a skirt-chaser, VW beetle car salesman, and U.S. naval soldier, and who used to bribe his notorious uncle.

BASED ON A TOTALLY TRUE STORY. *Written by Roberto Aguirre-Sacasa. Directed by Michael Bush. Manhattan Theatre Club. Opened April 11, 2006. Closed May 28, 2006.* A young playwright and comic book writer who's on the verge of breaking through experiences a frenzy of professional and personal drama when a veteran Hollywood producer decides she wants to turn one of his plays into a horror movie.

DAY. *Produced by Prospect Theater Company. West End Theatre. Opened April 11, 2006. Closed April 22, 2006.* A program of eight ten-minute plays by Kristoffer Diaz, Graeme Gillis, J. Holtham, Kyle Jarrow, Marisol Ling, Qui Nguyen, Sonya Sobieski, and Lloyd Suh, each of which takes place during a specified three-hour segment of the day.

ON THE LINE. *Written by Joe Roland. Directed by Peter Sampieri. Cherry Lane Theatre. Opened April 11, 2006. Closed April 23, 2006.* A play about three lifelong friends growing up in a world that has changed with a vengeance.

RED TIDE BLOOMING. *Written and directed by Taylor Mac. P.S. 122. Opened April 13, 2006. Closed April 23, 2006.* A musical extravaganza inspired by the gentrification of Coney Island and imagining the Last Mermaid Parade Ever. **SEE PAGE 213.**

THE TRAGEDY OF ABRAHAM LINCOLN. *Written by M. Stefan Strozier. Directed by Alan Kanevsky. Produced by LaMuse Venale. Where Eagles Dare. Opened April 13, 2006. Closed May 7, 2006.* A play that focuses on the last year of the life of Abraham Lincoln, up to his assassination by John Wilkes Booth.

NIGHTWATCHES. *Written by Victoria Stewart. Directed by Susanna L. Harris. Produced by Overlap Productions. Access Theatre. Opened April 14, 2006. Closed April 29, 2006.* A dark, erotic tale of sensuality, forbidden passion, and love in an early 1900s marriage of convenience based on the Cupid and Psyche myth.

SCREWMACHINE/EYECANDY. *Written by CJ Hopkins. Directed by John Clancy. Produced by Clancy Productions, Inc. 59E59. Opened April 16, 2006. Closed April 30, 2006.* A married couple is desperate to win on a TV game show where the host decides to play for keeps.

DEVIL LAND. *Written by Desi Moreno-Penson. Directed by José Zayas. Produced by Immediate Theater Company. Urban Stages. Opened April 17, 2006. Closed May 7, 2006.* A gothic tale about a couple in the Bronx who kidnap a twelve-year-old girl and keep her in their basement in a misguided attempt at creating a family.

61 DEAD MEN. *Developed by Janus Surratt. Produced by Beyond the Wall Productions. Producers Club. Opened April 19, 2006. Closed April 23, 2006.* The story of an artist who feels as if he cannot do enough simply by creating, so to instill change in a world gone wrong, he turns to destruction.

FLUKE. *Produced by Radiohole. P.S. 122. Opened April 21, 2006. Closed May 7, 2006.* An aquatic collage drawn from a variety of nautical sources, including Herman Melville's portrait of a sea captain obsessed with Esther Williams.

THEY CHOSE ME! *Book by Ned Paul Ginsburg and Michael Colby. Music by Ned Paul Ginsburg. Lyrics by Michael Colby. Directed by Janine Nina Trevens. TADA! Youth Theater. Opened April 21, 2006. Closed May 7, 2006.* A musical about a group of kids who all have one thing in common—being adopted!

TIME/UNSTUCK. *The Red Room. Opened April 21, 2006. Closed April 30, 2006.* A program of two original one-act plays: A TIME PIECE, *by Neal Bell*; and 2 SOLDIERS, *by Bathsheba Doran*.

GAUGUIN/SAVAGE LIGHT. *Music and lyrics by George Fischoff. Theatre Row Studio. Opened April 25, 2006. Closed May 21, 2006.* A musical about the life of artist Paul Gauguin.

LESTAT. *Book by Linda Woolverton. Music by Elton John. Lyrics by Bernie Taupin. Directed by Robert Jess Roth. Palace Theatre. Opened April 25, 2006. Closed May 28, 2006.* This musical inspired by Anne Rice's *Vampire Chronicles* tells the story of the journey of one man who escapes the tyranny of his oppressive family, only to have his life taken from him when he is thrust into the seductive and sensual world of an immortal vampire.

WELCOME HOME STEVE. *Written by Craig McNulty. Directed by Guilherme Parreiras. Produced by Madair Productions. American Theatre of Actors. Opened April 25, 2006. Closed May 7, 2006.* A black comedy about five friends involved in debauchery, delusions, drink, drugs, dealing, deception, and death on a hot Brooklyn night.

A FINE AND PRIVATE PLACE. *Book and lyrics by Erik Haagensen. Music by Richard Isen. Directed by Gabriel Barre. York Theatre. Opened April 27, 2006. Closed May 21, 2006.* A musical based on the 1960 novel by Peter S. Beagle, in which two couples (one living, and one of the spirit world) find that love and redemption can be found in the most unexpected places.

GHETTO CHRONICLES. *Written and directed by D. Whit. Produced by Wabi Sabi Production and Whit Pick Entertainment. Payan Theater. Opened April 27, 2006. Closed June 11, 2006.* A hip-hop musical comedy that blends an inner-city sensibility with political awareness.

HAM LAKE. *Written by Sam Rosen and Nat Bennett. Directed by Ian Morgan. Soho Playhouse. Opened April 27, 2006. Closed June 24, 2006.* A solo show about a guy who, upon running into an unstable old girlfriend at a party, quickly realizes that he has been the subject of a ruse and is stranded in the titular town in ice-cold weather without a jacket.

ONE BIG HAPPY FAMILY. *Written and directed by Joe Costanza. Produced by The Sackett Group. Brooklyn Music School Playhouse. Opened April 27, 2006. Closed May 21, 2006.* Set in Queens in

1979, a dysfunctional family of all talkers and no listeners zips along nicely until they are challenged with a life-changing event.

THE WEDDING SINGER. *Book by Chad Beguelin and Tim Herlihy. Music by Matthew Sklar. Lyrics by Chad Beguelin. Directed by John Rando. Al Hirschfeld Theatre. Opened April 27, 2006. Closed December 31, 2006.* A musical comedy based on the film of the same name, about a rock-star wannabe who makes his living as New Jersey's favorite wedding singer.

BLOODY MARY. *Written by Rachel Shukert. Directed by Stephen Brackett. Produced by Third Man Productions. CSV Cultural Center. Opened April 28, 2006. Closed May 13, 2006.* A play about Mary, Queen of Scots.

KNOWING BLISS. *Written by Arden Kass. Directed by Lorca Peress. Produced by MultiStages. CSV Cultural Center. Opened April 28, 2006. Closed May 13, 2006.* A serio-comedy about an adopted young African American woman and scholar whose confusion about her bigoted Southern family will not permit her to get on with her life.

LITTLE RED: LOST IN THE WOODS. *Written by Alex P. Baack. Music by Nate Farrar. Directed by David Michael Holmes. Produced by Toy Box Theatre Company. Morocco Studio. Opened April 28, 2006. Closed May 8, 2006.* A modern, multimedia adaptation of the classic fairy tale.

LOVE. *Music by Xavier Losada. Directed by Juan Souki. Schapiro Theatre. Opened April 28, 2006. Closed April 30, 2006.* A group of artists from Buffalo, Pittsburgh, Montreal, Caracas, Tel Aviv, Columbus, Kuala Lumpur, and New York get together in a room to stage a series of violent acts and bloody interludes related to love.

MORE FOR YOUR MONEY '06. *Produced by Working Man's Clothes. American Place Theatre. Opened April 28, 2006. Closed May 20, 2006.* Two double-bills of new one-act plays on the theme of love and loss:

- Program One—dealing with love and struggle, breaking away the false and unessential: **BOOP,** *by John Paul DeSena*; and **HILL,** *by Amy Sculz, directed by David Carr-Berry.*
- Program Two—separation and truth in a distorted, fickle world: **ARMS,** *by Bekah Brunstetter, directed by Will Neuman*; and **OCEAN SIDE PARKWAY,** *by Eric Sanders, directed by Steven Gillenwater.*

MUSTARD. *Written by Mitchell Polin. Music by Tungsten 74. Directed by Mitchell Polin. La MaMa. Opened April 28, 2006. Closed May 14, 2006.* A renegade adaptation of Ibsen's *A Doll's House* that combines live music, song, video, found texts, movement, and storytelling.

SUNDOWN. *Created and directed by Watoku Ueno. Music by Storm Garner. Produced by Yara Arts Group. La MaMa. Opened April 28, 2006. Closed May 14, 2006.* A play about the life and work of Hikoma Ueno, who is known as the father of Japanese photography.

TAILS. *Book and lyrics by Mark Masi. Music by Jess Platt. Directed by Christopher Scott. Produced by Vox Nova. Phil Bosokowski Theatre. Opened April 29, 2006. Closed May 14, 2006.* A musical that tells the story of five dogs in a dog pound awaiting adoption.

THE DEATH OF LITTLE IBSEN. *Conceived and produced by Wakka Wakka Productions. Music by Lars Petter Hagen and Wakka Wakka Productions. Sanford Meisner Theatre. Opened April 29,*

2006. Closed June 8, 2006. A dark comedy with puppets that maps playwright Henrik Ibsen's quest to find his true self,

THE HAMLET PLAYS. *Produced by Milk Can Theatre Company. Michael Weller Theatre. Opened April 29, 2006. Closed May 14, 2006.* Ten-minute plays inspired by characters from Shakespeare's *Hamlet*:

- **THE MATCH,** *by Sharon E. Cooper, directed by Pat Diamond.* Based on the character Laertes.
- **THE LAMP'S LIT,** *by Cheryl Davis, directed by Kate Marks.* Based on the character Gertrude.
- **BALONEY,** *written and directed by ML Kinney.* Based on the characters The Gravediggers.
- **MAYBE HE'S JUST NOT THAT INTO YOU...,** *by Bethany Larsen, directed by Tom Nondorf.* Based on the character Ophelia.
- **DECISIVE,** *music by Nick Moore, book and lyrics by Susannah Pearce, directed by Selda Sahin.* Based on the character Hamlet.
- **THE PLAYER KING MUSICAL,** *by Anne Phelan, music by Bill Tinsley, directed by Terry Berliner.* Based on the character The Player King.

CUL-DE-SAC. *Written by John Cariani. Music by Tom Kochan. Directed by Jack Cummings III. Produced by Transport Group. Connelly Theatre. Opened April 30, 2006. Closed May 13, 2006.* A dark comedy that explores the bizarre secrets of three couples on a suburban dead-end street who go to extreme measures to force their dreams, revealing long-suppressed agendas that threaten their survival.

HOT FEET. *Conceived and directed by Maurice Hines. Book by Heru Ptah. Music and lyrics by Maurice White. Hilton Theatre. Opened April 30, 2006. Closed July 23, 2006.* A musical featuring the songs of Earth, Wind & Fire about a beautiful young dancer whose fate is suddenly controlled by a magical pair of red shoes.

RELATIVITY. *Written by Cassandra Medley. Directed by Talvin Wilks. Ensemble Studio Theatre. Opened April 30, 2006. Closed May 14, 2006.* A mother and daughter, both rival scientists, put their relationship to the test when one tries to disprove the other's theories and research.

CASELOAD. *Written by Levy Lee Simon. Music and lyrics by Mark Bruckner. Directed by Mary Beth Easley. WorkShop Theatre. Opened May 1, 2006. Closed May 20, 2006.* Set in a treatment center somewhere outside New York City, this play follows eight patients from all walks of life who share one goal: to pull themselves out of their various addictions.

MORAL VALUE MEAL. *Written and directed by Noah Diamond and Amanda Sisk. Produced by Nero Fiddled. Urban Stages. Opened May 2, 2006. Closed May 3, 2006.* A musical comedy satire about the death of freedom in America.

J.A.P. CHRONICLES, THE MUSICAL. *Written and performed by Isabel Rose. Directed by Carl Andress. Perry Street Theatre. Opened May 3, 2006. Closed May 28, 2006.* A musical based on the author's novel *The J.A.P Chronicles*, in which a former ugly duckling turned self-made swan reunites with her old summer camp tormentors and hopes they have all grown into adult losers.

PAN ASIAN FESTIVAL OF NEW WORKS. *Produced by Pan Asian Repertory Company. West End Theatre. Opened May 3, 2006. Closed May 28, 2006.* New plays by emerging writers, presented in repertory:

- **ELEVATOR SEX,** *by Lan Tran.* About five strangers stuck together in an elevator on 9/11.
- **RECOLLECTIONS,** *by Kendra Ware.* A butoh movement meditation on the last day in the life of a homeless woman.
- **ABC (AMERICAN BORN CHINESE),** *by John Quincy Lee.* A comedy about the lack of Asian male role models in the popular culture.
- **38TH PARALLELS,** *by Terry Park.* A multimedia, autobiographical solo performance of divisions and reunifications.

STAGE KISS. *Written by Kiran Rikhye. Music by Emily Otto. Directed by Jon Stancato. Produced by Stolen Chair Theatre Company. The Red Room. Opened May 3, 2006. Closed May 27, 2006.* A gender farce in Elizabethan blank verse, freely inspired by John Lyly's *Gallathea* and also as an ode to the Ridiculous aesthetic of the late Charles Ludlam, in which two young women, each disguised as a man in order to escape their village's ritual sacrifice, fall in love with each other.

LIVING DEAD IN DENMARK. *Written by Qui Nguyen. Music by Dan Deming. Directed by Robert Ross Parker. Produced by Vampire Cowboys Theatre Company. Center Stage. Opened May 4, 2006. Closed May 21, 2006.* An action-adventure/horror sequel to William Shakespeare's *Hamlet*, in which Ophelia, Lady Macbeth, and Juliet are resurrected to fight an undead army set on taking over the world.

PENETRALIA. *Written by Randy Anderson, Stephenie Farnell-Wilson, Adam Hunault, and Joshua Tjaden. Directed by Nadine Friedman. Produced by Stone Soup Theatre Arts. Actors Theatre Workshop. Opened May 4, 2006. Closed May 20, 2006.* An examination of secret-keeping and the frightening consequences in a society that criminalizes it.

SUCK SALE AND OTHER INDULGENCES. *Written and directed by Evan Laurence. Theatre for the New City. Opened May 4, 2006. Closed May 21, 2006.* An evening of plays and improv featuring a 1950s housewife who brings vacuum cleaner salesmen together for a contest to win $1,000, alien life and spirit possession, and puppetry.

DOUBLE OCCUPANCY. *Directed by Virginia Scott. Barrow Group. Opened May 5, 2006. Closed May 22, 2006.* A program of two solo shows: **BODHICHITTA,** *by Sidse Ploug Soerensen*; and **FAULTY: HITCH,** *by Wendy Herlich.*

LOCOMOTIVE. *Written by Matthew Paul Olmos. Directed by Nicholas Cotz. Produced by woken'glacier theatre company. Gene Frankel Theatre. Opened May 5, 2006. Closed May 20, 2006.* The story of a mother, father, and daughter dealing with the disintegration of their family from alcoholism.

LYING. *Adapted by Jessica Burr and Matt Opatrny. Directed by Damen Scranton. Produced by Blessed Unrest. Interart Annex Theatre. Opened May 5, 2006. Closed May 8, 2006.* An adaptation of the memoir by Lauren Slater, about a precocious ten-year-old with a compulsion to lie, as she comes of age in a grown-up world.

PRIME TIME. *Written by Alex De Witt. Directed by Fern R Lopez. Produced by Cosmic Breeez Productions. Lion Theatre. Opened May 5, 2006. Closed May 27, 2006.* About a man who tries to decipher what all of the media's conflicting images of class, race, and pop culture mean, with a little help from the stagehands.

THE BALLAD OF JUNK AND MALFUNCTION. *Written and performed by Melaena Cadiz and Joseph Keckler. Music by Joseph Keckler. Directed by Erin Markey. Dixon Place. Opened May 5, 2006. Closed May 27, 2006.* A musical in which a pair of world-weary New York chanteurs chase their imagined glory days, trekking across a chaotic alternative reality to carve their comeback into the face of American history

A SPALDING GRAY MATTER. *Written and performed by Michael Brandt. Directed by Ian Morgan. Produced by The New Group (naked). Clurman Theatre. Opened May 6, 2006. Closed May 27, 2006.* A solo show that explores the curious story of Spalding Gray's illness, disappearance, and assumed suicide through the eerily parallel events of Brandt's own experience.

AMERICAN HWANGAP. *Written by Lloyd Suh. Lark Studio. Opened May 6, 2006. Closed May 13, 2006.* A play about a Korean man who returns to America for his sixtieth birthday (hwangap) to reclaim the wife and children he abandoned in the U.S. fifteen years earlier.

HAUNTED. *Written and directed by Alex Roe. Metropolitan Playhouse. Opened May 6, 2006. Closed May 28, 2006.* A family in the New Hampshire mountains is visited by ghosts of their own creation who force them to confront their own worst fears.

THE NECKLACE. *Written by Lisa D'Amour, Ellen Maddow, Lizzie Olesker, and Paul Zimet. Music by Peter Gordon. Directed by Anne Kauffman and Melissa Kievman. Produced by The Talking Band. Ohio Theatre. Opened May 6, 2006. Closed May 28, 2006.* A serial mystery in eight episodes set in a grand, decaying house on the edge of a moor, full of endless rooms, hidden passageways, and multiple realities.

TROIKA: GOD, TOLSTOY AND SOPHIA. *Written by Peter Levy. Directed by Karen Raphaeli. 13th Street Repertory. Opened May 6, 2006. Closed June 17, 2006.* A play about the final days in the life of Leo Tolstoy.

BONE PORTRAITS. *Written by Deborah Stein. Directed by Lear deBessonet. Produced by Stillpoint Productions. Walkerspace. Opened May 9, 2006. Closed May 20, 2006.* A play about the invention of the X-ray.

YOUNG PLAYWRIGHTS FESTIVAL XXIV. *Peter Jay Sharp Theatre. Opened May 9, 2006. Closed May 27, 2006.* Plays were selected from over 1,000 entries submitted to the Young Playwrights Festival National Playwriting Competition:

- FREEZEFRAME, by *Deborah Yarchun, directed by Richard Caliban.* An electrically charged techno-pop drama that focuses on how to freeze a man's soul and the apocalyptic reversal of the earth's magnetic poles.
- LOS ANGELES LULLABY, *by Kit Steinkellner, directed by Valentina Fratti.* A young woman struggling to mother her new baby girl finds herself becoming a little girl again when forced to confront her brilliant—yet emotionally absent—father.
- SUICIDE CLUB, *by Miriam Eichenbaum, directed by Valentina Fratti.* After an uncharacteristic attempt at suicide in the school bathroom, Brigitte—the witty "good girl"—ends up in the contradictory world of the so-called "bad girls" in a Catholic girls' school.

NO CHILD. *Written and performed by Nilaja Sun. Directed by Hal Brooks. Produced by Epic Theatre Center. Beckett Theatre. Opened May 10, 2006. Closed June 18, 2006.* A solo show about the New York City public education system.

TARZAN. *Book by David Henry Hwang. Music and lyrics by Phil Collins. Directed by Bob Crowley. Richard Rodgers Theatre. Opened May 10, 2006.* A musical based on the stories by Edgar Rice Burroughs and the 1999 Disney animated film.

I'D LEAVE YOU…BUT WE HAVE RESERVATIONS. *Produced by Living Image Arts. Linhart Theatre. Opened May 11, 2006. Closed May 28, 2006.* A program of four one-act plays by Jacqueline Christy, Stephanie Rabinowitz, Maria Gabrielle, and Robert Askins about public rejections in restaurants.

IN SIGHT 12. *Produced by Puerto Rican Traveling Theatre. Producers Club II. Opened May 11, 2006. Closed May 28, 2006.* New plays from the Professional Playwrights Unit of the Puerto Rican Traveling Theatre:

- **THE LAST OF BERNARDA,** *by Oscar A. Colón, directed by Sturgis Warner.* Cloistered daughters challenge a dominating matriarch in this post-Lorcan drama.
- **PHOMPH!!!,** *by Fred Crecca, directed by Mary Keefe.* A hustler of cheap hairpieces sets out to corner the men's market in 1962. Watch him tumble as his new assistant and girlfriend correct his "coarse."
- **THREE MEN ON A BASE,** *by Maria Elena Torres, directed by Shawn Rozsa.* The time is 1945 Brooklyn, and Branch Richey wants to bring the first black baseball player, Jackie Robinson, to Major League Baseball. Who's to stop him? Everybody.

ULTERIOR SIDE DISHES. *Written by Lori Payne. Directed by Kim Weston-Moran. The Nuyorican Poets Café. Opened May 11, 2006. Closed June 3, 2006.* A trilogy of one-act plays that explore the world of a man named Donovan Ray.

WOUNDED HOPES. *Directed by D.F. Ladd. Impact Theater. Opened May 11, 2006. Closed May 21, 2006.* A theatrical experience, based on the poetry of Gerald Zipper, about two brothers sent to war and the horrors they encounter abroad and at home.

A NIGHT NEAR THE SUN. *Written by Don Zolidis. Directed by James David Jackson. Produced by Impetuous Theater Group. 440 Studios. Opened May 12, 2006. Closed May 27, 2006.* A young girl disappears for three days before waking up along the side of the interstate, setting off a series of events that culminates in tragedy.

SUCKER FISH MESSIAH. *Written by Ryan Michael Teller. Directed by Taylor Brooks. Produced by Jean Cocteau Repertory. Bouwerie Lane Theatre. Opened May 12, 2006. Closed June 4, 2006.* Two brothers in modern-day New York have their relationship up-ended by revelations from the past.

ALL DOLLED UP. *Written by Bobby Spillane. Music by Alex Jost. Directed by Susan Campanaro. Acorn Theatre. Opened May 14, 2006. Closed June 11, 2006.* A comedy about a wiseguy from Bensonhurst who is trying to keep his newly discovered dressing fetish a secret from his associates.

ANULLA. *Written by Emily Mann. Directed by Pamela Hall. The Theatre at St. Luke's. Opened May 14, 2006. Closed June 11, 2006.* A play about the real life of Anulla Allen, who lived as a Jew but passed as Aryan during the Nazi regime in Germany.

AT SAID. *Written by Gary Winter. Directed by Tim Farrell. Produced by 13P. P.S. 122. Opened May 15, 2006. Closed June 4, 2006.* A mother writes out the experiences of her childhood spent under an oppressive regime, trying to convey her story to her daughter, as they negotiate the treacherous waters of memory, history, and family.

CAGELOVE. *Written by Christopher Denham. Directed by Adam Rapp. Rattlestick Theatre. Opened May 15, 2006. Closed June 18, 2006.* A man tries to salvage his fragile relationship with his fiancée after she is allegedly raped by her former lover.

I WILL COME LIKE A THIEF. *Written by Trish Harnetiaux. Directed by Jude Domski. Produced by Morning Line Productions. 78th Street Theatre Lab. Opened May 15, 2006. Closed June 4, 2006.* A play that investigates what happens when people are abruptly confronted with disaster and forced to make decisions about their own survival.

EXIT 13. *Written and directed by Frank Terranova. Produced by stir the sauce theater company. Greenwich Street Theatre. Opened May 17, 2006. Closed May 21, 2006.* A man is torn between his lifelong buddies in his mobbed-up Brooklyn neighborhood and a new life across the bridge in Manhattan with his long-suffering girlfriend.

NOT A GENUINE BLACK MAN. *Written and performed by Brian Copeland. Directed by Bob Balaban. DR2. Opened May 17, 2006. Closed July 16, 2006.* A solo show that tells the story of the author's African American family moving to one of the most exclusively white suburbs in America.

POGO & EVIE: A ZYDECO MUSICAL. *Written by Aaron Latham. Directed by Sergio Alvarado. Jacques-Imo's Cajun/Creole Restaurant and Theater. Opened May 17, 2006.* A story about forbidden love—the relationship between a young black man in a zydeco band and a young white woman in a Cajun band.

BACKSTAGE AT DA FONKY B. *Written and directed by Alycya K. Miller. Music by Darlyne Cain. Produced by Diversity Players of Harlem. Producers Club. Opened May 18, 2006. Closed May 27, 2006.* The story of a woman's rise to fame as she attempts to revive the black burlesque art form without revealing the secrets of her troubled past.

CLEANSING THE SENSES. *Created and performed by Peter Rose. P.S. 122. Opened May 18, 2006. Closed May 28, 2006.* A solo performance piece about the author's peripatetic wanderings in search of ecstasy, transcendence, and self-knowledge.

THE INVASION OF THE BODY SNATCHERS. *Written by Joe Giardina. Produced by OffWorld Theatre. The Puffin Cultural Forum. Opened May 18, 2006. Closed June 4, 2006.* A stage adaptation of the classic cult film.

A FAMILY'S PLAY. *Written and directed by Shawn Luckey. Music by Joseph Cornell. Produced by Diversity Players of Harlem. Producers Club. Opened May 19, 2006. Closed May 27, 2006.* A family embarks on a journey to seek the truth of family secrets.

HISTORICAL WOMEN IN LOVE AND POWER. *Written by Linda Cousins-Newton. Produced by Nia Productions. Michael Weller Theatre. Opened May 20, 2006. Closed June 11, 2006.* A program of two short history plays about women in slavery: **THE FIRST WIFE** and **THE SON BORN FROM JIM-LEE AND ME.**

HERAKLES VIA PHAEDRA. *Written and directed by Ellen Stewart. La MaMa. Opened May 21, 2006. Closed June 11, 2006.* A dance theatre epic that combines the myths of Herakles and Phaedra, placing them amongst the flappers, bootleggers, and jazz babies of the 1920s.

COLUMBINUS. *Written by Stephen Karam and PJ Paparelli. New York Theatre Workshop. Opened May 22, 2006. Closed June 11, 2006.* A play sparked by the April 1999 massacre at Columbine High

School in Colorado that weaves together excerpts from first-person interviews, diaries, and home video footage to examine the psychology underlying the catastrophe.

TROUT STANLEY. *Written by Claudia Dey. Music by Andrew Shapiro. Directed by Jen Wineman. Produced by Renaissant Arts. 45 Below. Opened May 22, 2006. Closed June 11, 2006.* A play about two female twins and the romance one of them starts with a man named after a fish.

MARATHON 2006. *Ensemble Studio Theatre. Opened May 23, 2006. Closed June 25, 2006.* The twenty-eighth annual presentation of the marathon, featuring one-act plays by a variety of noted writers:

- **BREAKFAST AND BED,** *by Amy Fox, directed by Abigail Zealey-Bess.*
- **THE OTHER WOMAN,** *by David Ives, directed by Walter Bobbie.*
- **DAVY AND STU,** *by Anton Dudley, directed by Jordan Young.*
- **NOT ALL KOREAN GIRLS CAN FLY,** *by Lloyd Suh, directed by RJ Tolan.*
- **BONE CHINA,** *by David Mamet, directed by Curt Dempster.*
- **100 MOST BEAUTIFUL NAMES OF TODD,** *by Julia Cho, directed by Jamie Richards.*
- **ON THE SPORADIC,** *by James Ryan, directed by Charles Richter.*
- **INTERMISSION,** *by Will Eno, directed by Michael Sexton.*
- **THE NIGHT THAT ROGER WENT TO VISIT THE PARENTS OF HIS OLD HIGH SCHOOL GIRL-FRIEND,** *by Ann Marie Healy, directed by Andrew McCarthy.*
- **THE BUS TO BUENOS AIRES (A MUSICAL),** *by Thomas Mizer and Curtis Moore, directed by Carlos Armesto.*
- **DETAIL,** *by Michael Louis Wells.*
- **LILA ON THE WALL,** *by Edward Allan Baker, directed by Kevin Confoy.*
- **THE SISSY LETTERS: NUMBERS 14, 29, AND 47,** *by Stephen Adly Guirgis, directed by Adam Rapp.*

ROLL WITH THE PUNCHES. *Written by Garet Scott. Music by Brian Cimmet. Directed by Kevin Thomsen. Produced by TightShip. Abingdon Theatre. Opened May 24, 2006. Closed June 3, 2006.* In 1950s San Francisco, a high-society family is brought low in this comedy about hysterical paralysis, murder, and chocolate soufflé.

CRUEL AND UNUSUAL. *Produced by Brooklyn Playwrights Collective. Siberia Bar. Opened May 26, 2006. Closed June 23, 2006.* A festival of one-act plays inspired by the work of French dramatist, thinker, and madman Antonin Artaud: **GERTRUDE STEIN'S PENIS,** *by Jeffrey Skinner;* **BREATH,** *by Al Lefcowitz;* **THE AUDIENCE,** *by Maria Micheles;* **DREAM PLAY,** *by Les Hunter;* **A LONG AND HAPPY MARRIAGE,** *by Will Cordeiro;* **COMMUNITY THEATER INTERVIEW WITH PERE UBU,** *by Cornelius Chapman;* and **STRAY,** *by Elizabeth Stapp.*

DARK YELLOW. *Written by Julia Jordan. Directed by Nick Sandow. Studio Dante. Opened May 27, 2006. Closed June 17, 2006.* In a rural place, a murder in a cornfield gradually becomes the focus of an unusual encounter between a local woman and a stranger she meets at the small-town bar.

THE IDIOT KING. *Written and directed by Susana Cook. Music by Julian Mesri. Dixon Place. Opened May 27, 2006. Closed June 3, 2006.* A political satire incorporating video, sound design, movement, and official and religious discourses that exposes the ridiculous arguments used by the ruling class.

THIS IS NOT A PIPE DREAM. *Written by Barry Kornhauser. Music by Gil Talmi. Directed by Tracy Bersley. Produced by Paddywack Players. Richmond Shepard Theatre. Opened May 27, 2006. Closed June 25, 2006.* A play about the early life and work of Rene Magritte.

BROKE HOTEL. *Written by Shanara Teumba McKeever. Directed by Rebecca A. Trent. Produced by The Ratutu Collaborative. Producers Club. Opened May 31, 2006. Closed June 10, 2006.* A play about the insane guests and frustrated employees at a busy hotel.

DEAD CITY. *Written by Sheila Callaghan. Directed by Daniella Topol. Produced by New Georges. 3LD Art and Technology Center. Opened June 1, 2006. Closed June 30, 2006.* A loose adaptation of James Joyce's *Ulysses,* in which the main character is now a middle-aged Manhattan woman.

THE ARCHITECT OF DESTINY. *Written by Michael Gianakos. Produced by Inch Mile Entertainment. Bank Street Theatre. Opened June 1, 2006. Closed June 10, 2006.* A play about a young man attempting to find meaning in his existence and take control of his life, despite his morally questionable psychiatrist, his overbearing mother, and codependent father.

DEATH BY JOINERY. *Written and directed by Mike Gorman. La MaMa. Opened June 2, 2006. Closed June 11, 2006.* A play about the timber-farming industry on the coast of Maine.

GUS & FRED SMASH THE TV. *Written and directed by Harold Lehmann. Produced by Dharma Road Productions, Inc. Center for Remembering and Sharing. Opened June 2, 2006. Closed June 17, 2006.* Two couch potatoes climb inside the mind of their TV in search of their true selves, only to find there's no place like home.

SELLOUT FESTIVAL. *Brick Theatre. Opened June 2, 2006. Closed July 2, 2006.*

- **BAD GIRLS GOOD WRITERS,** *by Sibyl Kempson, directed by Shoshona Currier.*
- **GIRLS! GIRLS! GIRLS!,** *directed by Jennifer Schmermund.*
- **BONBONS FOR BREAKFAST,** *written by Lisa Ferber, directed by Ivanna Cullinan.*
- **GREED: A MUSICAL LOVE STORY,** *written and directed by Robert Honeywell.*
- **THE IMPOTENT GENERAL,** *by Gary Winter, directed by Meredith McDonough.*
- **I.P.O.—FLIPPING REAL ESTATE,** *directed by Octavio Campos.*
- **THE KUNG FU IMPORTANCE OF BEING EARNEST,** *directed by Michael Gardner.*
- **MAGIC MONKEY DANCE COMPANY,** *directed by Yvan Greenberg.*
- **THE NIGERIAN SPAM SCAM SCAM,** *by Dean Cameron, directed by Paul Provenza.*
- **RED CARPET LIVE!,** *by Lisa Levy.*
- **SEXADELIC CEMETERY,** *directed by Jeff Lewonczyk.*
- **THE SOCCERGIRL SECOND,** *by Soccergirl and Ryan P. Murray.*
- **STARS IN HER EYES,** *by Clay McLeod Chapman, directed by Moritz von Stuelpnagel.*
- **THAT'S WHAT WE'RE HERE FOR,** *written and directed by Ian W. Hill.*
- **TRAV S.D.'S HEALTH AND WEALTH ELIXIR PROGRAM,** *by Trav S.D.*
- **THE TRUE LIFE STORY OF YOUR NAME HERE,** *directed by R.J. Tolan.*

THE PORCH. *Written by Kari Floren. Directed by Michael Berry. Produced by Right Down Broadway Productions. Altered Stages. Opened June 2, 2006. Closed June 25, 2006.* Four lost souls face off on the porch of a bed and breakfast on the brink of closure.

WHEN THE MOON HITS YOUR EYE. *Written and directed by Ryan Gilliam. Downtown Art. Opened June 2, 2006. Closed June 25, 2006.* The tale of an Italian American family and two feuding pizzerias.

CELEBRATE GOOD TIMES (MacBETH). *Created and directed by Yuval Sharon. Produced by Theater Faction. West End Theatre. Opened June 3, 2006. Closed June 11, 2006.* A deconstruction of Shakespeare's play, featuring flashbacks, pop ballads, and a Bollywood dance number, that confines the action to Macbeth's celebration banquet.

THE GOLD STANDARD. *Written by Daniel Roberts. Directed by Alex Lippard. Produced by Audax Theatre Group. Irish Arts Center. Opened June 3, 2006. Closed July 1, 2006.* Set in a fabled bar at an Ivy League university, the story concerns two college chums—a nervous businessman and his idol, an eccentric Korean poet—and what happens when, after years apart, they both fall in love with the same beautiful and driven woman.

MARK SMITH. *Written by Kate E. Ryan. Directed by Ken Rus Schmoll. Produced by 13P. Walkerspace. Opened June 5, 2006. Closed June 24, 2006.* A play that tells the story of an '80s American rock star who has fallen into obscurity, taking us behind the music to the people who knew him—his high school music teacher, his mother, his girlfriend, his dead father, and his hair stylist.

ELVIS AND JULIET. *Written by Mary Willard. Directed by Yvonne Conybeare. Abingdon Theatre. Opened June 7, 2006. Closed July 2, 2006.* College sweethearts Juliet Jones and Elvis Lesley's upcoming nuptials face the truest test of love—watching their two families come together for the first time.

HOW TO STAY BITTER THROUGH THE HAPPIEST TIMES... *Written and performed by Anita Liberty. Directed by Christopher Duva. HERE Arts Center. Opened June 7, 2006. Closed June 25, 2006.* A solo show that explains what it's like when an angry performance poet finds herself perilously close to true happiness and has to cling desperately to her artistic edge.

SAY HELLO CHILDREN. *Written by Nick Norman. Directed by Rachel Chavkin. Produced by Short Order Productions. The Red Room. Opened June 7, 2006. Closed June 10, 2006.* A dark comedy about the wanderings of a chaotic family and how they try to keep one of their own—a soldier soon to be sent to fight in a bloody conflict—safe at home at any cost.

SLOW NIGHT. *Written by Margot Leitman and Sarah Burns. Directed by Neil Casey. Upright Citizens Brigade. Opened June 7, 2006. Closed August 30, 2006.* Faced with the chance to leave their overnight shift waitress jobs, two women wonder if anyone ever truly gets out of Jersey.

STOPPING TRAFFIC. *Written and performed by Mary Pat Gleason. Directed by Lonny Price. Vineyard Theatre. Opened June 7, 2006. Closed July 2, 2006.* A solo show about the author's lifelong experiences with bipolar disorder.

SWOLLEN HEAD. *Written and performed by Rich Zeroth. Directed by Jon Friedman. Collective Unconscious. Opened June 7, 2006. Closed June 28, 2006.* A solo show in which the author comes clean about faking a rare brain disease in the fifth grade and missing 127 consecutive days of school.

BLACK BOX NEW PLAY FESTIVAL. *Produced by Gallery Players. Gallery Players. Opened June 8, 2006. Closed June 25, 2006.* New short plays:

BOX 1: Search & Destroy
- THE BIG GUY WITH THE THING, *by Olga Humphrey, directed by Tzipora Kaplan.*
- BOB DYLAN IN THE BATHROOM, *by Sarah Moon, directed by Michael Goldfried.*
- OFFICIAL LUNCH, *by Cristina Pippa, directed by James Shay.*
- THE TROPHY THIEVES: A HIGH SCHOOL LOVE STORY, *by Kristoffer Diaz, directed by Anthony Pound.*

BOX 2: War & Peace

- **COMPRESSION OF A CASUALTY,** *by Kevin Doyle, directed by David Henderson.*
- **LOCATION: HIGHWAY. TIME: NEAR DUSK.,** *by Michael Bettencourt, directed by Elfin Vogel.*
- **YEAR TEN,** *by Effy Redman, directed by James Shay.*
- **SIDELINES,** *by David Henderson, directed by Martin Miller.*
- **DEVILED SAUSAGE,** *by Larry Mudge, directed by Autumn Clark.*
- **GRIM,** *by Christopher Kloko, directed by Jayme Kilburn.*

BOX 3: Connect & Disconnect

- **NO GREAT LOSS,** *by Michael Bettencourt, directed by Elfin Vogel.*
- **CLICHÉ,** *by Meghan O'Neill, directed by Mary Ruth Goodley.*
- **SWING SET,** *by Richard Orloff, directed by Edward McKeaney.*
- **CLOSE ENOUGH FOR JAZZ,** *by Joe Lauinger, directed by Martin Miller.*
- **SINATRA SINGS,** *by Joe Lauinger, directed by Kevin Dodd.*
- **YES FEAR,** *by Daniel Kelley, directed by Autumn Clark.*
- **RICH ON SKINS,** *by Joe Lauinger, directed by Kevin Dodd.*

CARUSO—HIS MASTER'S VOICE. *Astoria Performing Arts Center. Opened June 8, 2006. Closed June 11, 2006.* A solo show exploring the life and music of Enrico Caruso.

SOME GIRL(S). *Written by Neil LaBute. Directed by Jo Bonney. Produced by MCC Theater. Lucille Lortel Theatre. Opened June 8, 2006. Closed July 8, 2006.* A man who is about to become engaged pays visits to four of his ex-girlfriends in four different cities.

THE ADVENTURES OF NERVOUS-BOY (A PENNY DREADFUL). *Written by James Comtois. Directed by Pete Boisvert. Gene Frankel Theatre. Opened June 8, 2006. Closed July 8, 2006.* A comedy-horror play in which the title character wanders around a grotesque nightmare version of the city and comes across New Yorkers of every kind. **SEE PAGE 249.**

THE LUNATICS' BALL. *Written by Claudia Menza. Directed by Harold Dean James. La MaMa. Opened June 8, 2006. Closed June 25, 2006.* A play about fourteen different New Yorkers as they reflect, confess, complain, posture, fight, and romance.

THE RELIGIOUS HOUR. *Written by Kevin Berry. Produced by Curan Repertory Company. Where Eagles Dare. Opened June 8, 2006. Closed June 11, 2006.* A play about five men who have joined a religious group designed to turn gay men straight.

THE TERRORIST. *Written by Howard Pflanzer. Directed by David Paul Willinger. Produced by Unofficial New York Yale Cabaret. Laurie Beechman Theater. Opened June 8, 2006. Closed June 24, 2006.* A dark comedy about a man who must outwit and outmaneuver a government agent bent on labeling him as a terrorist.

BOOGEYMAN AND THE WHITE CHICK. *Written by Lester Melvin. Directed by Darlene Gidney. Produced by Frank Silvera Writers' Workshop. Theatre for the New City. Opened June 9, 2006. Closed June 18, 2006.* The aftermath of the Rodney King verdict serves as the backdrop for a diverse cast of characters to explore their own perspective on race in 1992 Los Angeles.

CRAZY FOR THE DOG. *Written by Christopher Boal. Directed by Eric Parness. Bouwerie Lane Theatre. Opened June 9, 2006. Closed August 26, 2006.* A darkly comic tale of a brother and sister in New York entwined in a love/hate relationship that explodes when he decides to move across the country and leave her behind.

SECURITY. *Produced by TheDrillingCompaNY. 78th Street Theatre Lab. Opened June 9, 2006. Closed June 25, 2006.* Nine original short plays on the theme of security, in its many meanings. Playwrights include: Brian Dykstra, P. Seth Bauer, Stephen Bittrich, Neil Olson, C. Denby Swanson, Paul Siefkin, Kate McCamy, and Sheri Graubert. The directors are: Laura Strausfeld, Bradford Olson, Peter Bretz, Thomas Sherman, Shana Gold, and Richard Mover.

THE LEGEND OF PEARL HART. *Book and lyrics by Cathy Chamberlain. Music by Rich Look. Directed by Lea Orth. Produced by LCO Productions. Barrow Group. Opened June 9, 2006. Closed June 24, 2006.* A musical about a young Canadian woman who, in the 1890s, became famous when she robbed a stagecoach.

JESUS AND MANDY. *Written by Eric Bernat and Robin Carrigan. Directed by David Drake. Theatre for the New City. Opened June 10, 2006. Closed July 2, 2006.* A young boy's only hope for staving off depression lies with a recently deceased preteen girl determined to stay on earth.

THE FANTASY PARTY. *Written and directed by Larry Pellegrini. Edison Hotel. Opened June 10, 2006.* An interactive show that includes specialty drinks, dancing, adult games, pole-dancing lessons, and a variety of activities designed to keep female guests laughing all night long.

ALICE THE MAGNET. *Written by Erin Courtney. Directed by Pam MacKinnon. Produced by Clubbed Thumb. Ohio Theatre. Opened June 11, 2006. Closed June 17, 2006.* A play about an influential self-improvement guru who suddenly finds herself lost and the wayward student who may be her solution.

HER MAJESTY THE KING. *Written by Sarah Overman. Directed by Patrick McNulty. Produced by Dramahaus. HERE Arts Center. Opened June 12, 2006. Closed July 1, 2006.* A historical drama about Queen Margaret, who was the wife of England's King Henry VI.

THE MOST WONDERFUL LOVE. *Written by Matthew Freeman. Directed by Kyle Ancowitz. Access Theatre. Opened June 12, 2006. Closed July 1, 2006.* A satire of contemporary marriage and American fundamentalism in which a long-married couple plan an "unwedding" ceremony, much to the chagrin of their friends and relatives.

BURLEIGH GRIME$. *Written by Roger Kirby. Directed by David Warren. New World Stages. Opened June 13, 2006. Closed July 16, 2006.* A Wall Streeter is mentored by a man who may not be entirely sincere in appearance or agenda.

JAYSON WITH A Y. *Written by Darci Picoult. Directed by Sheryl Kaller. Produced by The New Group. Lion Theatre. Opened June 13, 2006. Closed June 24, 2006.* Two sisters in the midst of major changes in their lives are forced to decide who will care for their suddenly orphaned nephew, who has Asperger's Syndrome.

ACT ONE: ONE ACT. *Produced by The Queens Players. The Creek Theatre. Opened June 14, 2006. Closed June 24, 2006.* A program of six new plays by emerging writers: A DATE UNDER HIS OWN NAME, *by Paul Gibney, directed by Christa Savery;* GIRL TALK, *by Angela Lovell, directed by Tim Gore;* THIS JUST IN, *by Jay D Hanagan;* THAT DRESS, *by Steve Strangio, directed by Sean David Johnson;* FORWARD MOVEMENT, *by Danielle Abbatiello, directed by Rich Ferraioli;* and 13 STEPS, *by V.E. Kimberlin, directed by Richard Mazda.*

GETTING HOME. *Written by Anton Dudley. Directed by David Schweizer. Produced by Second Stage. McGinn Cazale Theatre. Opened June 14, 2006. Closed July 1, 2006.* Once upon a time on the enchanted isle of Manhattan, Tristan found himself a free ride home from a prince in a yellow chariot. Jan found herself the object of two rival princes' affections. And Nilesh realized that heartache and self-torment have a shelf life of about six years.

IT ISN'T THE MOON. *Written by Christina Fragola. Directed by Rosalyn Coleman Williams. Manhattan Theatre Source. Opened June 14, 2006. Closed June 29, 2006.* A play that pits two educated and otherwise beautiful women against each other in a heavyweight championship of the mind.

THE WATER'S EDGE. *Written by Theresa Rebeck. Directed by Will Frears. Second Stage. Opened June 14, 2006. Closed July 9, 2006.* A woman and her two children's lakeside home is visited by her long-estranged ex-husband and his girlfriend.

ARCTIC PROJECT X. *Produced by 2 Distinct Motions. Manhattan Theatre Club. Opened June 15, 2006. Closed June 18, 2006.* A satire that deals with issues of climate change, racial identity, pop celebrity, and the role of the corporation in human life.

BOX AMERICANA: A WAL-MART RETAIL FANTASIA. *Written by Jason Grote. Directed by Connie Grappo. Produced by The Working Theater. Bank Street Theatre. Opened June 15, 2006. Closed June 25, 2006.* A play in which the ghost of Sam Walton is resurrected with his own personal chorus of Chinese workers to sing the praises of consumer Utopia, and the world's largest employer is defending itself against the largest class-action lawsuit in American history for gender discrimination.

IN THE SPIRIT—FOR REAL. *Written and performed by Peggy Pettitt. Directed by Remy Tissier. P.S. 122. Opened June 15, 2006. Closed June 25, 2006.* A solo show about a feisty older woman left alone to raise her nephew, an urban youth.

JITTER. *Written by Richard Sheinmel. Directed by Clyde Baldo. Produced by Ladylike Productions. Arclight Theatre. Opened June 15, 2006. Closed July 1, 2006.* The story of four New York City kids, friends since high school and now in their twenties, whose lives are forever changed in the course of one night as limits are tested, boundaries broken, and secrets revealed.

LAST OF THE RED HOT DADAS. *Written by Kerry Reid. The Red Room. Opened June 15, 2006. Closed July 1, 2006.* A play that tells the true story of Baroness Elsa von Freytag Loringhoven, the so-called "Mama of the American Dadaist movement."

SPRING AWAKENING. *Book and lyrics by Steven Sater. Music by Duncan Sheik. Directed by Michael Mayer. Atlantic Theatre. Opened June 15, 2006. Closed August 6, 2006.* A rock musical based on Frank Wedekind's classic play, *Spring Awakening.*

THE AUSTRALIA PROJECT. *Produced by The Production Company. Kraine Theatre. Opened June 15, 2006. Closed July 2, 2006.* New plays that explore the relationship between the United States and Australia:

- **I AM NED KELLY,** *by Beau Willimon.*
- **ETHNIC CLEANSING DAY,** *by Brett Neveu.*
- **EASE,** *by Betty Shamieh.*
- **BOBO AN' SPYDER AN' A GIRL FROM DOWN UNDER,** *by Brett C. Leonard.*
- **MELBOURNE,** *by Stephen Belber.*

- **FAMISHED,** *by Frank Basloe.*
- **OUT OF NOTHING,** *by Kathryn Walat.*
- **TERRA AUSTRALIS INCOGNITO,** *by Trista Baldwin.*
- **THE FATAL SHORE,** *by Kate Moira Ryan.*
- **THE SOUND IN THE THROAT,** *by Elizabeth Meriwether.*
- **ADELAIDE,** *by Michael John Garces.*
- **MUSHROOM,** *by Ken Urban.*
- **NOT OUR LAST HURRAH,** *by Courtney Baron.*

TREASON. *Written by Sallie Bingham. Directed by Martin Platt. Perry Street Theatre. Opened June 15, 2006. Closed July 23, 2006.* A play about the life of Ezra Pound and five of the most important woman in his life.

UNDER THE SIGN OF THE HOURGLASS… *Text by Stephen Cedars. Directed by Anthony Cerrato. Ontological Theatre. Opened June 15, 2006. Closed June 24, 2006.* A new fantasy for the theatre inspired by the short stories of Bruno Schulz, about a young boy's memories and experiences, and his jumbled, confused, yet wondrous realizations of how he became who he is.

DRINKING THE KOOL-AID. *Written and performed by Fernando Maneca. Produced by MAN-OISECA. BAX/Brooklyn Arts Exchange. Opened June 16, 2006. Closed June 18, 2006.* A solo show in which visual/physical theatre, multichannel video projections, and good old-fashioned storytelling combine to create a world where mass marketing, religion, and politics intersect.

SINGLE BLACK FEMALE. *Written by Dr. Lisa Thompson. Directed by Colman Domingo. Produced by New Professional Theatre. Peter Jay Sharp Theatre. Opened June 17, 2006. Closed June 25, 2006.* A comedy about the pleasures and perils of being a single middle-class black woman who's got everything she wants and needs except more R-E-S-P-E-C-T…and a man.

THE FAIRY TALE ACADEMY. *Written by Jennifer Palumbo. Directed by Jonathan Valuckas. Produced by Brooklyn Family Theatre. Various locations in Brooklyn. Opened June 17, 2006. Closed June 24, 2006.* A play about three student storytellers—Aesop, Andersen, and Grimm—who have to pass the SATs (Storytelling Aptitude Tests) in order to graduate.

BROTHER, MINE. *Written and directed by Eric C. Dente and k.c.keene. Produced by The Watermark Ensemble. Manhattan Theatre Source. Opened June 18, 2006. Closed June 20, 2006.* A twenty-four-year-old African American man, adopted and raised by a middle-class Caucasian family, leaves his comfortable job to take what he has learned and put his talents to use in a community that he has never known—the community of his biological father, where the rules he's grown up believing in don't always apply.

QUAIL. *Written by Rachel Hoeffel. Directed by Kip Fagan. Produced by Clubbed Thumb. Ohio Theatre. Opened June 18, 2006. Closed June 24, 2006.* A play about a hapless legal secretary who must deal with her boss's incessant smoking, alluring and seductive clients, and her own search for purpose, all while trying to maintain the collapsing two-man firm.

SATELLITES. *Written by Diana Son. Directed by Michael Greif. Public Theater. Opened June 18, 2006. Closed July 2, 2006.* An interracial couple move into a transforming neighborhood in Brooklyn, with old friends and new strangers coming into their lives, and testing their instincts on who to trust and why.

CLEAN. *Written by Bob Epstein. Directed by Christopher Maring. Urban Stages. Opened June 19, 2006. Closed July 1, 2006.* A fantastical comedy about the spoiled daughter of a wealthy industrialist on an enlightening Long Island Railroad journey to the chic Hamptons.

THE HOUSE IN TOWN. *Written by Richard Greenberg. Directed by Doug Hughes. Produced by Lincoln Center Theater. Mitzi Newhouse Theater. Opened June 19, 2006. Closed July 30, 2006.* An intimate portrait of a marriage set in 1929 in a townhouse on New York's Millionaires' Row.

TROUBLE IN PARADISE. *Written by David Simpatico. Directed by Elyse Singer. Produced by Hourglass Group. Hudson Guild. Opened June 20, 2006. Closed July 22, 2006.* A stage adaptation of the 1932 Ernst Lubitsch film, about two grifters who attempt to swindle the heiress to a perfume empire.

BEER FOR BREAKFAST. *Written by Robert Scott Sullivan. Directed by Jenn Bornstein. Produced by Tailgate Productions. Producers Club II. Opened June 21, 2006. Closed July 23, 2006.* A play about four twentysomethings fresh out of school and pondering their next move.

BITE. *Written and directed by Suzanne Bachner. Produced by Dysfunctional Theatre and The John Montgomery Theatre Company. The Red Room. Opened June 21, 2006. Closed November 24, 2006.* An interactive comedy about two competing dentists, two dominatrixes, and a Southern belle.

PILGRIMAGE. *Written by Elinor Amlen. Directed by Deloss Brown. Produced by Medicine Show Theatre Ensemble. Medicine Show. Opened June 21, 2006. Closed June 25, 2006.* A group of four opera lovers from different cities gather each year to attend a performance of Wagner's *Parsifal* and catch up with each other.

EAST VILLAGE CHRONICLES, VOLUME 3. *Metropolitan Playhouse. Opened June 22, 2006. Closed July 2, 2006.* New short plays about the Lower East Side neighborhood where the theatre is located:

- **NONNIE,** *written and directed by Alberto Bonilla.*
- **LUCKY,** *by Anthony P. Pennino, directed by Sidney Fortner.*
- **FATHER'S NAME WAS DADDY,** *by Trav S.D., directed by Anthony P. Pennino.*
- **BINTEL BRIV,** *by Michael Bettencourt, directed by Anne Beaumont.*
- **FLIGHT,** *by Reneé Flemings, directed by Sidney Fortner.*
- **PETER STUYVESANT,** *by Stephen O'Rourke, directed by Anne Beaumont.*

GODOT HAS LEFT THE BUILDING. *Written by John Griffin. Directed by Will Pomerantz. Produced by FourScore Productions. 45 Below. Opened June 22, 2006. Closed July 9, 2006.* A play about the trials and tribulations of two men who seem to be the only people alive in a landscape of broken computers and the detritus of modern life.

I, SARAH. *Written by Robert W. Cabell. Music and lyrics by Robert W. Cabell. Directed by Joe Zingo. Where Eagles Dare. Opened June 22, 2006. Closed June 25, 2006.* A solo show about the life of the famous actress Sarah Bernhardt, as told by her from her deathbed.

HERETIC LOVE. *Written by Mike Dressel, Amanda Ifrah, and Julia Granacki. Directed by Sabrina Vajraca. Medicine Show. Opened June 23, 2006. Closed June 25, 2006.* As Armageddon looms, three unlikely heroes confront Masons, murderers, and a talking monkey in order to save themselves and all of humanity.

THE BUSY WORLD IS HUSHED. *Written by Keith Bunin. Directed by Mark Brokaw. Playwrights Horizons Mainstage. Opened June 25, 2006. Closed July 9, 2006.* A minister and bible scholar finds her faith at odds with that of her estranged wayward son.

LEVITTOWN. *Written by Marc Palmieri. Directed by George Demas. Axis Theater. Opened June 26, 2006. Closed July 16, 2006.* A young war veteran returns home on the eve of his troubled sister's wedding to reconcile with his family.

PIG FARM. *Written by Greg Kotis. Directed by John Rando. Produced by Roundabout Theatre Company. Laura Pels Theatre. Opened June 27, 2006. Closed September 3, 2006.* Life on a struggling pig farm explodes when an agent from the Environmental Protection Agency arrives to inspect the operation.

ALCIBIADES THE ATHENIAN. *Written by Gerald Kosloff. Directed by Samantha Tella. Producers Club. Opened June 28, 2006. Closed July 1, 2006.* A poetic drama about Alcibiades, a contemporary of Socrates, a general who never lost a war or a woman's heart.

SHAKESPEARE IS DEAD. *Written by Orran Farmer. Directed by Chris Chaberski. Produced by Eastcheap Rep. Paradise Factory. Opened June 28, 2006. Closed July 22, 2006.* A play about two young artists desperately trying to salvage their relationship after the accidental death of their small child.

HOT! *Dixon Place. Opened June 29, 2006. Closed August 26, 2006.*

- SKIN DEEP, *by Jeffrey Essmann.*
- PLEASE LET ME LOVE YOU, *by Dan Fishback, directed by Billy Rosen.*
- RIP ME OPEN, *by Michael Cyril Creighton and Desiree Burch, directed by Brian Mullin.*
- EMERALD CREST, *by Hank Hivnor.*
- AND/OR, *by Stan Richardson, directed by Ben Rimalower.* **SEE PAGE 279.**

MEN EAT MARS BARS WHILE TOUCHING THEIR PENIS. *Written by Jennifer Slack-Eaton. Directed by Jared Culverhouse. Produced by Working Man's Clothes Productions. Under St. Marks. Opened June 29, 2006. Closed July 15, 2006.* A play about the life and experiences of an exotic dancer in the modern world.

THE SEWERS. *Text by Jason Craig. Directed by Mallory Catlett. Produced by Banana Bag & Bodice. Ontological Theatre. Opened June 30, 2006. Closed July 22, 2006.* A theatrical extravaganza about a tiny village that mysteriously appears one night in a theater.

MILLICENT SCOWLWORTHY. *Written by Rob Handel. Directed by Ken Rus Schmoll. Produced by Summer Play Festival. Beckett Theatre. Opened July 5, 2006. Closed July 9, 2006.* A play that tells the story of some teenagers reenacting a murder that took place in their community.

RIVER DEEP. *Book by Gabrielle Lansner. Music and lyrics by Philip Hamilton. Directed by Gabrielle Lansner. Peter Jay Sharp Theatre. Opened July 5, 2006. Closed July 29, 2006.* An homage to singer/ entertainer Tina Turner, based on her autobiography, *I, Tina.*

SPLITTING INFINITY. *Written by Jamie Pachino. Directed by Matt Shakman. Produced by Summer Play Festival. Clurman Theatre. Opened July 5, 2006. Closed July 9, 2006.* A drama about a rabbi and his old friend, an astrophysicist who wants to prove that God does not exist.

THE SQUIRREL. *Written by Alex Moggridge. Directed by Patrick McNulty. Produced by Summer Play Festival. Kirk Theatre. Opened July 5, 2006. Closed July 9, 2006.* A black comedy that follows a woman and her oversensitive husband, overbearing sister, and a man she just hit with her car.

THE WANDERLUSTERS PRESENT "ACHTUNG GRIMM!" *Written and directed by Renee Philippi. Produced by Concrete Temple Theatre. Ohio Theatre. Opened July 5, 2006. Closed July 8, 2006.* A gothic and operatic retelling of two Brothers Grimm tales by an out-of-work traveling carnival troupe.

WEDDING BELLES. *Written and performed by Lally Ross. Directed by David Kester. Stage Left Studio. Opened July 5, 2006. Closed July 19, 2006.* A solo show about a bride fighting to be the center of attention at her own wedding.

ANGEL MOUNTAIN. *Written by John-Richard Thompson. Directed by Jessica Davis-Irons. Produced by ANDHOW! Theater Company. Connelly Theatre. Opened July 6, 2006. Closed July 29, 2006.* When a doctor comes home to investigate a reported death, she unearths a story hidden for over sixty years.

IDENTITY. *Written by Nicholas Linnehan. Directed by Ken Wolf. Manhattan Repertory Theatre. Opened July 6, 2006. Closed July 8, 2006.* An autobiographical tale of cerebral palsy, Catholicism, and homosexuality.

NEW YORK IS HERE! NEW YORK IS HERE! *Conceived and directed by Aaron Rosenblum. Produced by Sitelines. 32 Avenue of the Americas. Opened July 6, 2006. Closed July 15, 2006.* A performance installation that goes inside New York City's chaos to explore how individual tales form the legend of the mass.

SCHOOL OF THE AMERICAS. *Written by José Rivera. Directed by Mark Wing-Davey. Produced by LAByrinth Theatre Company and The Public Theater. Public Theater. Opened July 6, 2006. Closed July 23, 2006.* A young schoolteacher insists on speaking with Che Guevara two days after he is imprisoned in a one-room schoolhouse in the Bolivian jungle.

YORK. *Written by David Casteal and Bryan Harnetiaux. Directed by Susan Hardie. 78th Street Theatre Lab. Opened July 6, 2006. Closed July 9, 2006.* A play about the life of William Clark's manservant, who was the only black member of the Lewis and Clark Expedition.

A THOUSAND WORDS: SEVEN SHORT PLAYS ON PHOTOGRAPHY. *Produced by Shalimar Productions. Interart Annex. Opened July 7, 2006. Closed July 16, 2006.* An evening of new short plays inspired by Susan Sontag's book, *On Photography*:

- CLARISSE AND LARMON, *by Deb Margolin, directed by Patricia McGregor.*
- FOR ART, *written and directed by Nastaran Ahmadi.*
- LES CARABINIERS, *by Kirk Lynn, directed by Shoshona Currier.*
- OVEREXPOSED, *by Michael John Garces, directed by Mary Catherine Burke.*
- PATHETIQUE, *by Alex Dinelaris, directed by Rachel Wood.*
- PLEASE SEND PIC: STAGED EXPECTATIONS IN TEN MINUTES, *by Sharyn Rothstein, directed by Catherine Ward.*
- REDNECKS WITH FISH, *by Charles Forbes, directed by Camilo Fonticella.*

PRISCILLA. *Written by Jeff Love. Directed by Robert Zick Jr. Produced by New World Theatre. Stella Adler Theatre. Opened July 7, 2006. Closed July 29, 2006.* A play that puts Hamlet's premise of indecision into a more contemporary context—and with a woman as the protagonist.

FOOD FOR FISH. *Written by Adam Szymkowicz. Directed by Alexis Poledouris. Produced by Sanctuary Playwrights Theatre. Kraine Theatre. Opened July 8, 2006. Closed July 29, 2006.* A comedy, loosely inspired by Chekhov's *Three Sisters*, about three sisters: a stalker, an agoraphobe, and a scientist with a secret plan to isolate and eliminate the gene for love.

THE CALAMITY OF KAT KAT AND WILLIE. *Written by Emily Young. Directed by Heath Cullens. Produced by Babel Theatre Project. Medicine Show. Opened July 8, 2006. Closed July 29, 2006.* An English expatriate needs the help of her now-gone-straight sometime boyfriend to pull off one last heist.

THE INSOMNIA PLAY. *Written by Jessica Brickman. Directed by Geordie Broadwater. Produced by Babel Theatre Project. Medicine Show. Opened July 8, 2006. Closed July 29, 2006.* An absurdist examination of one woman's battle with the things that go bump in the night.

WHAT COMES NEXT. *Written by Pamela A. Popeson. Directed by Lorca Peress. Produced by Rebellion Dogs Productions. Access Theatre. Opened July 8, 2006. Closed July 29, 2006.* A modern American road story set on the wagon train trail in the latter days of the Westward Expansion.

ASKING FOR IT. *Written and performed by Joanna Rush. Directed by Lynne Taylor-Corbett. Peter Jay Sharp Theatre. Opened July 10, 2006. Closed July 24, 2006.* A solo comedy about a feisty dancer and former Outstanding Catholic Youth of the Year who takes on New York, where her convictions about religion bump up against the confusions of reality.

THREE SISTERS. *Written by Daniel Reitz. Directed by Daniel Talbott. Produced by Rising Phoenix Repertory. Seventh Street Small Stage at Jimmy's No. 43. Opened July 10, 2006. Closed July 19, 2006.* A one-act play, based on Chekhov's *Three Sisters*, in which Olga, Irina, and Masha gather in a downtown Manhattan restaurant to celebrate Irina's birthday and wonder whether they will ever be able to afford their beloved Upper West Side again.

FATHER JOY. *Written by Sheri Wilner. Directed by Pam MacKinnon. Produced by Summer Play Festival. Kirk Theatre. Opened July 11, 2006. Closed July 16, 2006.* A fantastical comedy about a girl whose father is actually disappearing before her very eyes.

FRESH FRUIT FESTIVAL. *Opened July 11, 2006. Closed July 23, 2006.*

- **LOVE IN THE WORLD OF FRUIT,** *by Jon Michael Spano and Robin Cloud, directed by Stephen Field and Kimmy Gatewood.*
- **COME BACK TO ME,** *by Jesse Alick, directed by Claudia Alick.*
- **WHY D'YA MAKE ME WEAR THAT, JOE?,** *by Vanda, directed by Melissa Attebery.*
- **TO WHOM IT MAY CONCERN,** *by Aurin Squire.*
- **MY MOTHER TOLD ME I WAS DIFFERENT,** *by Carol Polcovar, directed by David Gaard.*

GARDENING LEAVES. *Written by Joanna Pinto. Directed by Michael Goldfried. Produced by Summer Play Festival. Lion Theatre. Opened July 11, 2006. Closed July 16, 2006.* A British man's life is turned around when a pretty young Iranian woman comes to help with his rooftop garden.

HITTING THE WALL. *Written by Barbara Blumenthal-Ehrlich. Directed by Drew Barr. Produced by Summer Play Festival. Clurman Theatre. Opened July 11, 2006. Closed July 16, 2006.* A dark comedy about a pair of neighbors putting their lives back together after the death of one of their children.

LOOKING BACK. *Written and directed by Paul Eisman. Produced by Oxbridge Productions. Abingdon Theatre. Opened July 11, 2006. Closed July 15, 2006.* A play with music and dance that adapts works by F. Scott Fitzgerald, Oscar Wilde, and H.G. Wells into a reexamination of the Orpheus and Eurydice myth.

THE BUTCHERHOUSE CHRONICLES. *Written by Michael P. Hidalgo. Directed by Thomas Caruso. Produced by Summer Play Festival. Beckett Theatre. Opened July 11, 2006. Closed July 16, 2006.* A darkly comic horror show about four high school students in search of their missing history teacher.

ARUBA. *Written by Rob Evans. Produced by People Can Run. Ohio Theatre. Opened July 12, 2006. Closed July 15, 2006.* A darkly comic tour through the lives of three desperate young urbanites as their carefully constructed worlds begin to unravel.

DEAD CERTAIN. *Written by Marcus Lloyd. Directed by Andrey Esterlis. Produced by Expression Theatre of San Francisco. Gene Frankel Theatre. Opened July 12, 2006. Closed July 23, 2006.* A psychological thriller in which an out-of-work actor is hired by a reclusive, theatre-obsessed ex-dancer to privately act out a play she has written.

ORANGE LEMON EGG CANARY. *Written by Rinne Groff. Directed by Michael Sexton. Produced by Sammy Loves Emily Productions. P.S. 122. Opened July 12, 2006. Closed July 30, 2006.* A play about a magician with a dangerous past and a promising future, and his bright young assistant who looks for the truth behind the illusion.

PROOF BY DISPROOF. *Written by Christopher C. Beier. Directed by Bill Balzac. Sanford Meisner Theatre. Opened July 12, 2006. Closed July 15, 2006.* Having not talked for two weeks, a young married couple decides to meet in Central Park at midnight in an attempt to fix their marriage, but run into individual obstacles and intrigues on their way to meet.

MANHATTAN MADCAPS OF 1924. *Music by Richard Rodgers. Lyrics by Lorenz Hart. Book by Jerzy Turnpike (Isaiah Sheffer). Directed by Annette Jolles. Produced by Symphony Space. Leonard Nimoy Thalia at Symphony Space. Opened July 13, 2006. Closed July 23, 2006.* A new musical set to songs by Rodgers and Hart.

SECRETS. *Written by Gerald Zipper. Directed by Ted Mornel. The Theatre at St. Luke's. Opened July 13, 2006. Closed July 30, 2006.* Hidden relationships threaten friendship and love as this evening of wining and dining degenerates into a session of backbiting, snide comments, and a contest to see who can be the cruelest to their respective spouse.

FRANKENSTEIN THE MUSICAL. *Book, music, and lyrics by Robert Mitchell. Directed by John Henry Davis. Wings Theater. Opened July 14, 2006. Closed July 30, 2006.* A musical based on Mary Shelley's famous novel.

THE WOMAN'S ROOM. *Written and directed by Elizabeth Kerin. The Black Box Theatre at 440 Studios. Opened July 14, 2006. Closed July 15, 2006.* A play about a young woman from Saudi Arabia who is imprisoned and has visions from the outside world of women suffering just as she is.

MIDTOWN INTERNATIONAL THEATRE FESTIVAL. *Various venues in Midtown. Opened July 17, 2006. Closed August 6, 2006.*

- THE ANSWER IS HORSE, *by Julia Holleman, directed by Joya Scott, produced by Emergency Theater Project.*
- THE GIRLS OF SUMMER, *written and directed by Layon Gray, produced by Los Angeles African American Repertory Company.*
- THE MATERNAL INSTINCT, *by Monica Bauer, directed by Melissa J. Wentworth.*
- MOTION AND LOCATION, *by Lorna Littleway, directed by Sue Lawless, produced by Juneteenth Legacy Theatre.*
- THE SIBLINGS, *written and directed by Edward Elefterion, produced by Rabbit Hole Ensemble.*
- SURGERY, *by Karin Diann Williams, directed by Stuart Hynson Culpepper.*
- WHERE THREE ROADS MEET, *by John Carter, directed by Will Warren.*
- COUNTDOWN, *by Vincent Caruso, directed by Jerry Mond.*
- PIE OBSESSED DRUNKEN FATTIES, *by Julie Perkins and Marjorie Suvalle, directed by Michael Ormond, produced by Sox Productions.*
- PROPS, *by Michael Roderick, directed by Moira K. Costigan, produced by Small Pond Entertainment.*
- THE QUIET MODEL, *by L.A. Mitchell, directed by Chelsea Miller.*
- REMUDA, *by William Donnelly, directed by Tzipora Kaplan.*
- SHOOT THE DOG, *by Brittany Rostron, directed by Dennis X. Tseng.*
- STICKY GIRLS, THE ANTI-REALITY SHOW, *by Linda Evans, directed by Constance George.*
- THE TURTLE TATTOO, *by Jonathan Wallace, directed by Shannon Fillion, produced by Howling Moon Cab Company.*
- THE WASTES OF TIME, *by Duncan Pflaster, directed by David Gautschy, produced by Cross-Eyed Bear Productions.*
- DAS BRAT, *written and directed by Eric Bland, produced by Old Kent Road Theater.*
- FLEEING KATRINA, *by Rob Florence, directed by Mary Lee Kellerman, produced by Batture Productions.*
- IN A BUCKET OF BLOOD, *by John Kearns, directed by Michael Mellamphy, produced by Boann Books and Media.*
- IT IS WHAT IT IS, *by Cinda Lawrence, directed by Brandon Kalbaugh, produced by Two Spoons Theatre Productions.*
- JEWS DON'T JOIN THE CIRCUS, *by Beth Bongar, directed by Cheryl King.*
- JEWISH BY INJECTION ONLY, *written and directed by Michael Stockman.*
- LOVE, PUNKY, *by Robin Hopkins, directed by Billy Mitchell, produced by No Kneecap Productions.*
- THE SIT-DOWN SHOW, *by Desiree Burch, directed by Kate Pines.*
- TAXI STORIES, *by David O'Shea, directed by Lee Costello.*
- WAKE OF THE ESSEX, *by Lou Rodgers, directed by Robert Manzari and Lou Rodgers.*
- ABSENCE (A PLAY ABOUT LOSS), *written and directed by Kimberly Patterson, produced by Rake Theater.*

A WIVE'S TALE. *Written by Christina Ham. Directed by Rosemary Andress. Produced by Summer Play Festival. Beckett Theatre. Opened July 18, 2006. Closed July 23, 2006.* A futuristic drama about a group of barren women conspiring to create the perfect society.

MARGE. *Written by Peter Morris. Directed by Alex Timbers. Produced by Summer Play Festival. Lion Theatre. Opened July 18, 2006. Closed July 23, 2006.* A comedy about a man who hires a prostitute to help murder his wife.

SPAIN. *Written by Jim Knable. Directed by Jeremy Dobrish. Produced by Summer Play Festival. Kirk Theatre. Opened July 18, 2006. Closed July 23, 2006.* A comedy about a woman, whose husband has recently left her, who encounters a sixteenth century conquistador in her twenty-first century living room.

TRAINING WISTERIA. *Written by Molly Smith Metzler. Directed by Evan Cabnet. Produced by Summer Play Festival. Clurman Theatre. Opened July 18, 2006. Closed July 23, 2006.* A tragicomedy that combines a dysfunctional family with a dirty yard and home improvement on the evening of the son's graduation party.

WOMEN IN BOATS. *Produced by Developing Acts Company. Producers Club. Opened July 18, 2006. Closed July 23, 2006.* A collection of five new one-act plays:

- **FLIGHT,** *by Delanie Douglas, directed by Gregg David Shore.* A lake, a boat, a bird, and two women at a major crossroads in their relationship…what if anything will take flight?
- **THE SECRET IN THE LAKE,** *by David Gunderson, directed by Gregg David Shore.* Three generations of women embark one afternoon to discover the secret in the lake.
- **TOUGH TO SWALLOW,** *by Marcus Jones, directed by Gregg David Shore.* When old friends get together for a vacation, old truths become new revelations.
- **TRIANGULATION,** *by M. laBier Jones, directed by Marcus Jones.* Three longtime friends escape for an enchanting evening on the lake only to find they can't escape their own demons.
- **GETTING IN TOUCH WITH YOUR DARK SIDE,** *by Laura Rohrman, directed by Ian Streicher.* Three women take a rowboat trip to intervene in each other's lives. The discoveries they make are quirky and revealing—and hilarity ensues!

CONVERSATIONS WITH DOG. *Written and directed by Ken Wolf. Manhattan Repertory Theatre. Opened July 19, 2006. Closed July 22, 2006.* A play about a wise-cracking, sex-obsessed, three-hundred-pound dalmatian that is sent from Heaven to help a miserable young playwright get on with his life.

FLYING DREAMS. *Written and directed by Sharon Fogarty. Produced by Making Light! Manhattan Theatre Source. Opened July 19, 2006. Closed July 29, 2006.* A one-act fantasy about a man with Tourette's struggling to annihilate all memory of his abusive mother.

PARTICULARLY IN THE HEARTLAND. *Created by Rachel Chavkin with the Company. Produced by The Team. Ohio Theatre. Opened July 19, 2006. Closed July 22, 2006.* A theatre piece about six flawed, hysterical, and divine humans in a basement pageant of insomnia, cooking lessons, and birthday parties.

THE HUNCHBACK OF NOTRE DAME. *Adapted and directed by Ted Minos. Produced by Moose Hall Theatre Company. Inwood Hill Park Peninsula. Opened July 19, 2006.* Closed August 5, 2006. An outdoor adaptation of the novel by Victor Hugo, about a deformed bell-ringer's devotion to a beautiful gypsy girl.

IF YOU GIVE A MOUSE A COOKIE & OTHER STORY BOOKS. *Directed by Kevin Del Aguila. Produced by TheatreworksUSA. Lucille Lortel Theatre. Opened July 20, 2006. Closed August 18, 2006.* A musical revue based on eight popular children's books.

REVELATIONS. *Produced by Rising Sun Performance Company. Under St. Marks. Opened July 20, 2006. Closed July 22, 2006.* An evening of new one-act plays:

- **GOOD ENOUGH,** *written and directed by Kit Lavoie.* A Jewish college student has just met her fiancée's evangelical Christian family over Thanksgiving dinner.
- **WITHOUT,** *by Laura Rohrman, directed by Kuye Harris.* A young woman encounters and befriends a mysterious stranger, who happens to be the only witness to a brutal attack she survived while studying in Paris.
- **MUSIC TO TRAVEL BY,** *written and directed by Andi Stover.* Former best friends, a drifter and a housewife, reunite after many years and discover how much and how little has changed.
- **SOUTHERN WEREWOLF,** *by John Patrick Bray, directed by Rachel Klein.* A sweet young thing and an older gentleman take a midnight stroll on the bayou, where a sinister surprise awaits each of them.
- **COVER MAGNETS,** *by John Patrick Bray, directed by Rachel Klein.* Two aspiring punk rockers meet, reminisce, and mourn over their drummer's grave.

VANILLA MISTRESS. *Written and performed by Ophira Eisenberg. Directed by Eric Pliner. Daryl Roth Theatre. Opened July 20, 2006. Closed August 3, 2006.* A solo show about the author's experiences as a professional dominatrix.

A YELLOW BUTTERFLY CALLED SPHINX. *Written by Christian Palustran. Directed by Amanda Shank. 13th Street Repertory. Opened July 24, 2006. Closed July 26, 2006.* A play about a forbidden, secret relationship between a teacher and her student.

SCANDAL IN MANHATTAN. *Written and directed by Bobby Holder. Theatre 54 @ Shetler. Opened July 24, 2006. Closed July 25, 2006.* A one-act comedy about a sassy Southern belle who inherits a bunch of money and decides to go to Manhattan.

HARDBALL. *Written by Victoria Stewart. Directed by Lou Jacob. Produced by Summer Play Festival. Beckett Theatre. Opened July 25, 2006. Closed July 30, 2006.* A comedy about a rising female Republican political pundit.

SONIA FLEW. *Written by Melinda Lopez. Directed by Justin Waldman. Produced by Summer Play Festival. Clurman Theatre. Opened July 25, 2006. Closed July 30, 2006.* A Cuban exile is haunted by the memories of her past when her son announces his intention to join the Marines.

SWANSONG. *Written by Patrick Page. Directed by David Muse. Produced by Summer Play Festival. Lion Theatre. Opened July 25, 2006. Closed July 30, 2006.* A fictitious story about real-life playwright Ben Jonson putting together the first folio of William Shakespeare's work after his friend the Bard's death.

THE FEARLESS. *Written by Etan Frankel. Directed by Scott Schwartz. Produced by Summer Play Festival. Kirk Theatre. Opened July 25, 2006. Closed July 30, 2006.* A play about the decade-long journey of three friends who form a rock band in college and find out what it's like to live their dreams.

WHAT THE THUNDER SAID. *Created and produced by bluemouth Inc. 32 Avenue of the Americas. Opened July 25, 2006. Closed August 5, 2006.* A performance piece that explores the notion of ambivalence, utilizing the family as a model to examine the political and emotional contradictions that face today's society.

THE FLIGHT OF ICARUS. *Written by Aaron Mack Schloff. Based on the novel by Raymond Queneau, as translated by Barbara Wright. Directed by Samuel Buggeln. Produced by Soho Think Tank. Ohio*

Theatre. *Opened July 26, 2006. Closed July 29, 2006.* A stage adaptation of the novel by Raymond Queneau, in which Icarus flees from a novel and tries to build a life in 1890s Paris with a prostitute who herself escaped from a crossword puzzle.

A STONE CARVER. *Written by William Mastrosimone. Directed by Robert Kalfin. Soho Playhouse. Opened July 27, 2006. Closed August 27, 2006.* When a town wants to build a new highway off-ramp and issues eminent domain orders to clear the needed land, one elderly stone carver refuses to leave the home he built with his own hands.

ALL THIS INTIMACY. *Written by Rajiv Joseph. Directed by Giovanna Sardelli. Produced by Second Stage Theatre. McGinn Cazale Theatre. Opened July 27, 2006. Closed August 12, 2006.* A thirty-year-old poet learns that all three of his girlfriends are simultaneously pregnant.

GOING UP? *Written and directed by Scott E. Brown. Produced by Volunteer Creations. Soho Playhouse. Opened July 27, 2006. Closed July 31, 2006.* A darkly comic one-act about a young man and the mystery surrounding his death.

GROWING UP IS HARD TO DO. *Conceived and directed by Julie Bain and P. William Pinto. Produced by Rising Sun Performance Company. Under St. Marks. Opened July 27, 2006. Closed July 29, 2006.* A musical revue that revisits the horrors and wonders of growing up.

NEVER TELL. *Written by James Christy. Directed by Drew DeCorleto. Produced by Broken Watch Theatre Company. Michael Weller Theatre. Opened July 27, 2006. Closed August 13, 2006.* A play examines the fine line between trust and greed, repression and aggression, in today's virtual society.

TRIPLE THREATS. *Written by Alec Holland and Melissa Samuels. Directed by Ryan J. Davis. Produced by For Art's Sake Productions. Independent Theater. Opened July 30, 2006. Closed August 12, 2006.* A comedy about two deranged friends and roommates, convinced they are destined for stardom, who attempt to force their third roommate to cast them in his upcoming Hollywood action feature debut.

THE AMERIKAN TRIP, TIK. *Written and directed by johnmichael rossi. Produced by newFangled theatrer. Kraine Theatre. Opened July 31, 2006. Closed August 9, 2006.* A motley crew of actors in the tradition of carny America sweep into the Lower East Side to perform the AmerikAn trip, tik, a play about a fictional land called AmerikA.

FACES...VOICES. *Written by Doreen Perrine. Directed by Miriam Eusebio. Produced by Miriam Eusebio Projects. Women's One World Cafe Theater. Opened August 1, 2006. Closed August 26, 2006.* A dramatic work created to address hate crimes against the lesbian, gay, bisexual, and transgender community.

BETROTHED. *Directed by Rachel Dickstein. Produced by Ripe Time. Ohio Theatre. Opened August 2, 2006. Closed August 5, 2006.* A dance-infused adaptation of three stories exploring the dreams, expectations, and losses surrounding women's relationship to marriage and independence.

BARBARA'S BLUE KITCHEN. *Written by Lori Fischer. Directed by Marta Banta. Lamb's Theatre. Opened August 3, 2006. Closed September 2, 2006.* A comedy with music about a day in the life of the proprietor of the down-home coffee shop, her regular customers, and the lives that unfold over the blue plate special.

EVERYTHINGS TURNING INTO BEAUTIFUL. *Written by Seth Zvi Rosenfeld. Songs by Jimmie James. Directed by Carl Forsman. Produced by The New Group. Acorn Theatre. Opened August 3, 2006. Closed September 2, 2006.* A play that takes place on Christmas Eve in New York City and focuses on a pair of down-on-their-luck songwriting partners, both facing their forties, who come together for a night of composing and soul searching.

METRONOMA. *Written by Ryan Holsopple and Shannon Sindelar. Directed by Ryan Holsopple. Produced by 31 Down Radio Theater. Ontological Theatre. Opened August 3, 2006. Closed August 12, 2006.* A haunted sound portrait of evil and isolation that evokes the solace of a long walk with H.P. Lovecraft in a bitter New England forest of the 1930s.

WEASEL EROTICA. *Directed by Melissa Jo Talent. Produced by Baby Hippopotamus Productions. Looking Glass Theatre. Opened August 4, 2006. Closed August 27, 2006.* A wealthy widow suggests bringing the world's rarest animal to a zoo in dire need of revenue and funding.

ATLANTA'S DAUGHTERS. *Written and performed by Maggie Lauren and Amir Levi. Produced by Apple Girl Productions. Manhattan Theatre Source. Opened August 6, 2006. Closed August 8, 2006.* A program of two solo shows about people who were brought up in the same place yet turned out very differently.

THE HORTON FOOTE PROJECT. *Written by Horton Foote. Adapted by Wes Grantom, Amelia McClain, Stephen Plunkett, and Lori Wolter. Directed by Wes Grantom. Produced by Slant Theatre Project. 78th Street Theatre Lab. Opened August 6, 2006. Closed August 29, 2006.* A new work adapted from Horton Foote's nine-play *The Orphan's Home Cycle.*

DAMMIT, SHAKESPEARE! *Written by Seth Panitch. Produced by Poor Yorick Productions. Urban Stages. Opened August 8, 2006. Closed August 13, 2006.* A comedy about William Shakespeare and Richard Burbage collaborating for the first time.

INDIAN BLOOD. *Written by A.R. Gurney. Directed by Mark Lamos. Produced by Primary Stages. 59E59. Opened August 9, 2006. Closed September 2, 2006.* A play about a teen in 1946 Albany who uses his Indian ancestry as a cause and an excuse for his adolescent attacks on the genteel world around him.

THE JADED ASSASSIN. *Written by Michael Voyer. Conceived and directed by Timothy Haskell. Produced by Big Time Action Theater and Soho Think Tank. Ohio Theatre. Opened August 9, 2006. Closed August 12, 2006.* An original live-action drama about a mercenary who must end the curse and the misery that has plagued her land, even if that means killing everyone in her path to do it.

CREATION: A CLOWN SHOW. *Created by Orlando Pabotoy and Lucas Caleb Rooney. Directed by Orlando Pabotoy. Theater Five. Opened August 10, 2006. Closed September 10, 2006.* A solo clown show that offers a new view on the Book of Genesis.

AUTUMN MOON. *Book, music, and lyrics by David Velarde. Directed by Jonathan Stuart Cerullo. Wings Theater. Opened August 11, 2006. Closed September 2, 2006.* A rock musical about a twenty-something who discovers he's a werewolf, and travels backwards in time to one of his past lives in an attempt to break the curse.

EVENSONG. *Written by Mary Gage. Directed by Lewis Magruder. Produced by Broad Horizons Theatre Company and Jack W. Batman. TBG Arts Complex. Opened August 11, 2006. Closed August 27, 2006.* A play based on interviews with senior citizens over the age of eighty living in Michigan.

NEW YORK INTERNATIONAL FRINGE FESTIVAL. *Various venues in downtown Manhattan. Opened August 11, 2006. Closed August 27, 2006.*

- ...CATEGORIES (A SIMPLE PLAY), *by Melissa Osborne, directed by Kel Haney, produced by Alisa Sommer and Green Apple Entertainment.*
- 58!, *by Tony Mendoza. Directed by Pat McKenna. Produced by Common Theater Company/ Annoyance Productions.*
- A COLLAPSE, *written and directed by Vincent Marano, produced by teatro oscuro.*
- A SHOW OF FORCE, *by Donnie Mather, directed by Leon Ingulsrud.*
- A SMALL HOLE, *by Julia Jarcho, directed by Alice Reagan, produced by Performance Lab 115.*
- A TIME TO BE BORN, *by Tajlei Levis, music by John Mercurio, directed by Marlo Hunter, produced by Lemon Tree Productions.*
- ABSOLUTE FLIGHT: A REALITY SHOW WITH WINGS, *by Barbara Blumenthal-Ehrlich, directed by Rosemary Andress, produced by Don't Say Miami.*
- AIR GUITAR, *by Mac Rogers and Sean and Jordana Williams, directed by Stephen Wargo, produced by Gideon Productions.*
- AMERICAN MUSCLE, *by Richard Thompkins, directed by Christopher McElroen.*
- AMERICANBLACKOUT, *written and directed by Robb Leigh Davis, produced by Blakkaprikorn Productions.*
- AN AMERICAN GOSPEL, *by Ashley Christopher Leach, directed by Laura Klein.*
- AN OFF-WHITE AFTERNOON, *by Eric Meyer, directed by Jason A. Narvy, produced by Legitimate Theater Company.*
- ANIMA, *by Christiaan Greer, directed by Emily Meisler, produced by Wait Until May Productions.*
- BAND GEEKS: A HALFTIME MUSICAL, *by Becky Eldridge and Amy Petersen, directed by Andrew Eninger, produced by Single Box Turn Productions.*
- BEHIND THE STICKS, *by Adam Mervis, directed by Megan Marod, produced by The Moving Canvas Gang.*
- BIG DOOLIE, *by Richard Thompson, directed by Jenn Thompson, produced by River Rep Theatre Company.*
- BLACK STUFF, *by LeVan D. Hawkins and Alexander Thomas, directed by Kevin Vavasseur, produced by Eagle/Hawk Productions.*
- BLOODTIES, *by Ned Massey, directed by Catherine Miller Hardy, produced by Radmass Entertainment.*
- BLUE BALLS, *by Michael Tester, directed by Rye Mullis, produced by BroadwayClubhouse.com.*
- BREAKFAST FOR DINNER, *by Isaac Rathbone, directed by Joni Weisfeld, produced by Oracle Theatre, Inc.*
- BREATHE...OR YOU CAN DIE!, *written and directed by Anna Zastrow & Assocs, produced by Loka Loka/Loka Teater.*
- BREEZE OFF THE RIVER, *by Kyle Baxter, directed by DeLoss Brown, produced by The Collective Objective.*
- CHESS, *by Drew Brody, directed by Darrell Larson, produced by The Infinite Monkey Project.*
- CLARE'S ROOM, *by Lisa Del Rosso, directed by Colleen Brit, produced by Waving Not Drowning Productions.*
- CORLEONE: THE SHAKESPEAREAN GODFATHER, *written and directed by David Mann, produced by David Mann Productions.*

- CORPS VALUES, *by Brendon Bates, directed by Susan W. Lovell, produced by Winsor Productions.* **SEE PAGE 297.**
- DANNY BOY, *by Marc Goldsmith, directed by Christopher Goodrich, produced by DB Productions.*
- DEAR AMERICA, *by Michele Aldin, directed by Lauren Rosen, produced by Lucky Pelican, LLC.*
- DIVING NORMAL, *by Ashlin Halfnight, directed by Mary Catherine Burke, produced by Electric Pear Productions.* **SEE PAGE 331.**
- DON'T ASK, *by Bill Quigley, directed by Mark Steven Robinson, produced by QND Productions.*
- EENIE MEANIE, *by Teresa Willis, directed by Elizabeth Swenson, produced by Say Tiger Productions.*
- EVERY NIGGER IS A STAR, *by Mario Burrell, directed by Jemal McNeil.*
- FADED, *by Robert Dominguez, directed by Veronica Caicedo, produced by SloWriter Productions.*
- FALLEN ANGEL, *by Justin Murphy and Roger Butterley, directed by Josh Walden, produced by Fallen Angel Productions, LLC.*
- FANTASY, GIRL, *by LyaNisha Gonzalez, directed by Selena Ambush, produced by Two Little People Productions.*
- FATBOY ROMEO, *written and directed by Neal Freeman, produced by Engine 37.*
- FAY LINDSAY-JONES STORY, *by Greg Emetaz, directed by Desdemona Chiang, produced by MINORapocalypse.*
- FEAR UP: STORIES FROM GUANTANAMO AND BAGHDAD, *by Karen Bradley and Marietta Hedges, directed by Joe Brady, produced by The Democracy Cell Project.*
- FLYING ON THE WING, *by Michael Perlman, produced by GypsySoup.*
- FORNICATIONALLY CHALLENGED, *by Judi Lee Brandwein, directed by Mark Travis, produced by Papa Ball Productions.*
- FREE TO BE FRIENDS, *by Julie Klausner and Sue Galloway, directed by Dyna Moe, produced by Enchanted Patio Productions.*
- GARBAGE BOY, *by Christopher Millis, directed by Ashley Lieberman.*
- GIRL SCOUTS OF AMERICA, by Andrea Berloff and Mona Mansour, directed by James Saba, produced by elevenTWELVE/Ooh la la.
- GRACE, *by Shannon Thomason and Sara Thigpen, directed by Melanie Ashley, produced by Sweet Tea Creek.*
- GRACE FALLS, *by Daeil Cha, directed by Ryan Davis, produced by Mighty Myth Productions.*
- GRIOT: HE WHO SPEAKS THE SWEET WORD, *by Al Letson with Larry Knight Jr. and David Girard, directed by Barbara Colaciello, produced by Griot3/BarbWired Productions.*
- HA! HA! CLUB, *by Billie E. Hazelbaker, music by Patrick Barnes, directed by Frank A. Barnhart, produced by BEH Productions, LLC.*
- HAPPY SAUCE, *by Benjamin Lewis, directed by Matt Dickson, produced by Blue Cake.*
- HARRIET HOPPERDOODLE'S HAIR-BRAINED HISTORY TEST!, *written and directed by Jeanne Beechwood and Jon Copeland, produced by Martin City Melodrama Jr.*
- HENRY KISSINGER: A ROMANTIC COMEDY, *by John Attanas, directed by Melanie Moyer Williams, produced by Wood Frame Productions.*
- HERE.THIS.NOW., *by Tamilla Woodard and Sharahn LaRue McClung, directed by Tamilla Woodard, produced by Youth Communication.*

- **HERMANAS,** *by Monica Yudovich, directed by Claudia Zelevansky, produced by Changuitos Productions.*
- **HIGHER POWER,** *by Sam Ryan, directed by Chris Plante, produced by Little Red Square.*
- **HOT BLACK/ASIAN ACTION,** *by Quinn D. Eli, directed by Jessica Rotondi, produced by The Samira Company.*
- **HOUSE,** *by David Bromley, directed by Handan Ozbilgin, produced by Canta Entertainment.*
- **HOW 2 MEN GOT ON IN THE WORLD,** *written and directed by Emily Mendelsohn, produced by Saga Theater Company.*
- **HUGGING THE SHOULDER,** *written and directed by Jerrod Bogard, produced by Inky Thumbs Productions.*
- **I COULDA BEEN A KENNEDY,** *by Dennis Trainor Jr., directed by Ted Sluberski, produced by Rude Mechanicals Theater Company.*
- **I WANT TO BE MUSASHI: A CLOWN SAMURAI FANTASY,** *by Christopher Lueck, directed by Amanda Pekoe, produced by NOONTIME Theatre.*
- **I WAS TOM CRUISE,** *by Alexander Poe, directed by Alexander Poe and Joseph Varca, produced by Redux Productions.*
- **I, MARLENA,** *by Laylage Courie and Kenosha Kid, produced by Luminous Work.*
- **IF YOU SEE SOMETHING, SAY SOMETHING,** *by Elna Baker, directed by Joe Chiappa, produced by Elna Baker Productions.*
- **IMMINENT, INDEED,** *written and directed by Bryn Manion, produced by Aisling Arts, Inc.*
- **IN TRANSIT,** *by Matt Hoverman, directed by Padraic Lillis, produced by Thisbe Productions.*
- **IT'S A HIT: A KILLER NEW MUSICAL,** *by Beth Saulnier, Melissa Levis, and David Weinstein; directed by Julie Kramer; produced by Secret Soup LLC.*
- **LA FEMME EST MORTE,** *written and directed by Shoshona Currier, produced by Shalimar Productions.*
- **LETTER PURLOINED,** *by David Isaacson, produced by Theater Oobleck.*
- **LIGHT & LOVE,** *written and directed by S.P. Riordan, produced by Moving Faces.*
- **LIZARDSKIN,** *by Jen Silverman, directed by Katherine Kovner, produced by Altamont Productions.*
- **MELO-LLAMA: A MELODRAM,** *by Sarah Bagley, directed by Moritz von Stuelpnagel, produced by The Story Shop/Buxton Field Productions.*
- **MIKE'S INCREDIBLE INDIAN ADVENTURE,** *by Michael Schlitt, directed by Nancy Keystone, produced by Deus Ex Productions.*
- **MODERN MISSIONARY,** *by Julia Barnett, directed by Andrew Garman, produced by Barney Productions.*
- **MORAL VALUES: A GRAND FARCE,** *by Ian McWethy, directed by Jeffrey Glaser, produced by Sue Us Directly Productions.*
- **MOTHERS OF INVENTION,** *by Laura Poe, directed by Kimmy Gatewood, produced by po'house productions.*
- **MUSCLE-MAN VS. SKELETONMAN: A LOVE STORY...THE MUSICAL,** *written and directed by Richard J. Hinds and Ginamaria Trello, produced by Booty Slammin' Productions, LLC.*
- **NAUGHTY PREP SCHOOL STORIES,** *by Michael Quinones, directed by Malini Singh McDonald, produced by Black Henna Productions.*
- **NEON MIRAGE,** *directed by Wendy McClellan, produced by Apprentice Company, Actors Theatre of Louisville.*

- OBLIVIOUS TO EVERYONE, *by Jessica Lynn Johnson, directed by Chris Sorensen and Jessica Lynn Johnson, produced by Love Creek Productions.*
- ONLY A LAD, *by Andrew Loschert, music by Danny Elfman, directed by Rob Seitelman, produced by Westin Productions.*
- OPEN HOUSE, *by Ross Maxwell, directed by Josh Hecht, produced by Partial Comfort Productions.*
- OPHELIA, *by Ashley Minihan, directed by Ilo Orleans.*
- PARK-N-RIDE, *written and directed by Laura Park, produced by Amusement Park Productions.*
- PERFECT HARMONY, *by Andrew Grosso and The Essentials, directed by Andrew Grosso, produced by The Essentials.*
- PERMANENT WHOLE LIFE, *by Zayd Dohrn, directed by Wesley Savick, produced by Alchemy Theatre Company.*
- PICKING UP THE BABY, *by Ellen Margolis, directed by Teresa K. Pond, produced by magic portal productions.*
- PIECE OF MIND, *by Mary Crescenzo, directed by Richard Manichello, produced by Left Lane Productions.*
- PITCHED, *by S. Melinda Dunlap, directed by Luke Leonard, produced by DTX.*
- PLANET SAMOVAR, *by Harold Todd and Maura Kelley, directed by Maura Kelley, produced by The BoomCHet Theatre Company.*
- PLEADING INFINITY: THE BOB DONOVAN SAGA, *written and directed by T.J. Walsh, produced by infinity Company.*
- RAPUNZEL, *by Karen Rousso, Judy Duhlberg, and Kerry Wolf, directed by Karen Rousso; produced by Long Over 'Do Productions.*
- RED HERRING, *by Michael Albanese, directed by Jonathan Silverstein, produced by Zenith Film Group.*
- REQUIEM FOR NEW ORLEANS: A HIP HOP EULOGY, *by James Vesce, Donell Stines, and Jay Morong; directed by James Vesce; produced by Twilight Repertory Company.*
- RESERVOIR BITCHES, *by Laura McGhee, directed by Allan Guttman, produced by McManic Productions.*
- ROADSIDE, MARYLAND, *by Forrest Simmons, directed by David Thigpen, produced by Solemn Oath Productions.*
- RUM & COKE, *by Carmen Pelaez, directed by Carl Andress, produced by vibora productions.*
- SHELF LIFE, *by Camille M. Brown, directed by Matt Hoverman, produced by Camille M. Brown Productions.*
- SOLICITATION, *by Gib Wallis, directed by Nancy Hendrickson, produced by Discombobulatory Theatre.*
- SOME KIND OF PINK BREAKFAST, *by Chris Harcum, directed by Bricken Sparacino.*
- SOMETHING MORE PLEASANT, *by Joshua William Gelb, directed by Brittany O'Neill, produced by Alisa Sommer and Room5001 Theatre.*
- subURBAN STORIES, *written and directed by Tom Conklin, produced by What Exit Theater Company.*
- T.L.C., *by Robert Moulthrop, directed by Marc Silberschatz, produced by Twenty Feet Productions.*
- ROMANCING THE TERRORIST: TAJIKI NIGHTS, *written and directed by Mike Wallach and Negin Farsad, produced by Farrani Productions.*

- TAKE ON ME (ADOPTION, ADDICTION, AND A-HA), *by Christine Simpson, directed by Jesse Jou, produced by Happy Lade Productions.*
- TEA IN THE AFTERNOON, *by Vanessa Shealy, directed by Jon Michael Murphy, produced by Younger Child Productions.*
- THE ARMAGEDDON DANCE PARTY, *by David L. Williams, directed by Kara-Lynn Vaeni, produced by W & W Productions.*
- THE BIG PICTURE, *by Andrew Greer, directed by Lexie Pregosin, produced by The Troupe Theatre.*
- THE BLUE MARTINI, *by Michael Ferrell, directed by Jim Wren, produced by Kids with Guns.*
- THE BURNING CITIES PROJECT, *directed by Jennifer McGrath, produced by Dreamscape Theatre.*
- THE CHRYSALIS STAGE, *written and directed by Cobey Mandarino, produced by Different Light Theatre.*
- THE CITY THAT CRIED WOLF, *by Brooks Reeves, directed by Dan Barnes, produced by State of Play Theatre.*
- THE DAY THE UNIVERSE CAME CLOSER, *by Hiram Pines, directed by Jessica Porter, produced by Pair Theater.*
- THE DEEPEST PLAY EVER: THE CATHARSIS OF PATHOS, *by Geoffrey Decas, music by Michael Wells, directed by Ryan Purcell, produced by CollaborationTown.*
- THE DELICATE BUSINESS OF BOY AND MISS GIRL, *by Carly Mensch, directed by Marina McClure, produced by Odyssey Productions.*
- THE FAN TAN KING, A NEW MUSICAL, *by C.Y. Lee, music by Doug Lackey, directed by Tisa Chang, produced by Pan Asian Repertory Theatre.*
- THE FARTISTE, *by Charlie Schulman and Michael Roberts, directed by John Gould Rubin, produced by The Private Theater Corp.*
- THE FRENCH DEFENSE, *by Dmitri Raitzin, directed by Aleksey Burago, produced by Pp Productions.*
- THE HAPPINESS OF SCHIZOPHRENIA, *written and directed by Anthony Wills Jr.*
- THE INCONSTANT INFECTION, *by Ed Malin, directed by Kristina Leath, produced by Temerity Theatre.*
- THE INFLICTION OF CRUELTY, *by Andrew Unterberg and Sean McManus, directed by Joel Froomkin, produced by Tuesday Club Productions.*
- THE KITCHEN SINK, *written and directed by Meghan Gambling, produced by Teaspoon Productions.*
- THE LAST SPOKEN WORD, *by Frank Kuzler, directed by Philip Emeott, produced by Dedalus Productions.*
- THE ONION LOVERS, *by Robert J. Bonocore, directed by J. Julian Christopher, produced by Craigan Moon Productions.*
- THE PENGUIN TANGO, *written and directed by Stephen Svoboda, produced by Fresco Productions.*
- THE POOL WITH FIVE PORCHES, *by Peter Zablotsky, directed by John Ahlers, produced by Good Intentions Productions.*
- THE PROSTITUTE OF REVERIE VALLEY, *by Adam Klasfeld, directed by Sherri Kronfeld, produced by One Armed Man.*
- THE RABBI AND THE CHEERLEADER, *by Sandy Wolshin, produced by Hialeah Productions.*
- THE REVENANTS, *by Scott T. Barsotti, directed by Cara Scarmack, produced by Roundelay Theatre Company.*

- **THE SAINTS OF FESTUS,** *by Scott Hess, directed by David Drake, produced by ShowMe.*
- **THE SECRET RUTHS OF ISLAND HOUSE,** *by Claytie Mason and Alissa Mortenson, directed by Cecelia Frye, produced by Nebunele Theatre.*
- **THE TELL-TALE HEART—A MUSICABRE,** *by Danny Ashkenasi, directed by David L. Carson, produced by Fredrick Byers Productions.*
- **THE TRANSFORMATION OF DR. JEKYLL,** *directed by Edward Elefterion, produced by Rabbit Hole Ensemble.*
- **THE XXXOTIKA REVIEW,** *by Carmen Barika, directed by Aixa Kendrick, produced by SIR muMsila Media, Inc.*
- **THE YELLOW WALLPAPER,** *by Brian Madden, directed by Edward Warren, produced by Story 2 Productions.*
- **THEIR WINGS WERE BLUE,** *by Carmen Betancourt, directed by Jocelyn Sawyer, produced by Wings Were Blue Productions.*
- **THIS WON'T TAKE LONG,** *by David M. Korn, directed by Shango Amin, produced by A Shoestring Production.*
- **TRADITION!,** *by Alan Ostroff, directed by Jack Wann, produced by Cardinal Theatricals.*
- **TROUBLE IN SHAMELAND,** *written and directed by Bryan Putnam, produced by EMPYRE-productions LLC.*
- **TRUCE,** *by Marilee Talkington, directed by Justin Quinn Pelegano, produced by Vanguardian Productions.*
- **UNDERSTAND TO BE UNDERSTOOD,** *directed by Juliette Avila, produced by Find Your Light.*
- **UNEVENTFUL DEATHS FOR AGATHON,** *written and directed by Javierantonio Gonzalez, produced by theaterwagon.*
- **VICE GIRL CONFIDENTIAL,** *by Todd Michael, directed by Neal Sims.*
- **VILE AFFECTIONS,** *written by Vanda, directed by Franka Fiala, produced by Vanda Prods/ Emerging Artists Theatre.*
- **VOTE MCOWSKEY!,** *written and directed by Jeremiah Murphy, produced by Central Park West Studios.*
- **WALMARTOPIA,** *by Catherine Capellaro and Andrew Rohn, directed by Catherine Capellaro, produced by Outside the Big Box Productions, LLC.*
- **WE LOVE YOU, JOHNNY HERO,** *written and directed by Sara Cooper, music by Chris Shimojima, produced by The We Are Like So Morbid Theatre Company.*
- **WHIZ KID,** *by Michael Allen, directed by Helena Prezio, produced by Brilliant Mistake Productions.*
- **WOMEN AND THE TROJAN HORSE,** *by Sam Dowling and Nick Warren, produced by Praxis Theatre Laboratory.*
- **YOURPLACE…OR MINE?,** *directed by Kim Moore, produced by American Distractions/Firecracker Family.*

THE EQUALITY PLAYS FESTIVAL. *Produced by Diverse City Theater Company. Clurman Theatre. Opened August 11, 2006. Closed August 26, 2006.* A program of original one-act plays about gender identity issues of the twenty-first century:

- **CLEAN LIVING,** *by Robert Askins, directed by Steven Ditmyer.* An absurdist exploration of truth and men in the military where men can neither ask nor tell.

- **VEILS,** *by Joe Byers, directed by Gregory Simmons.* An American soldier in a war-torn Middle Eastern country and his first sexual encounter with a local woman.
- **ONNA FIELD,** *by Stuart Harris, directed by Carlos Armesto.* A play about a gay high school boy and his sports coach.
- **COLD FLESH,** *by Jorshinelle Taleon-Sonza, directed by Adam Fitzgerald.* Focuses on a recently outed gay Filipino doctor dealing with the arrival of his wife from the Phillipines.

MARCO MILLIONS (BASED ON LIES). *Created and produced by Waterwell. Adapted from the play by Eugene O'Neill. Directed by Tom Ridgely. Lion Theatre. Opened August 12, 2006. Closed August 26, 2006.* A play adapted from Eugene O'Neill's *Marco Millions,* about a Westerner encountering the East and the collision of cultures and economies that followed.

THE HYSTERY OF HEAT. *Created by The Performance Thanatology Research Society. Produced by Ontological Theatre. Ontological Theatre. Opened August 16, 2006. Closed August 19, 2006.* A performance-science experiment testing the effects of contemporary high anxiety global warming by measuring the amount of heat given off during moments of Great Fear.

BREAKING WALLS. *Written by Alexandria Beech. Directed by Christian Ely. Produced by Cherry Pit Late Nite. Cherry Lane Theatre. Opened August 17, 2006. Closed August 26, 2006.* An ambitious TV reporter gets a job offer at a firm on Wall Street—except the offer comes from a man who offers her much more.

MAGIC AND MAYHEM. *Produced by The Workshop Theater Company. WorkShop Theatre. Opened August 17, 2006. Closed August 26, 2006.* A program of one-act plays: **DECONSTRUCTING THE MAGICIAN,** by Nelson Lugo; and **THE DEVIL AND BILLY MARKHAM,** by Shel Silverstein.

MARTIN SHORT: FAME BECOMES ME. *Conceived by Martin Short and Scott Wittman. Music by Marc Shaiman. Lyrics by Scott Wittman and Marc Shaiman. Book by Martin Short and Daniel Goldfarb. Directed by Scott Wittman. Jacobs Theatre. Opened August 17, 2006.* A musical that starts out as a celebration of comedian Martin Short's life quickly turns into a faux-tabloid retelling of it, complete with the requisite struggle, pain, and psychobabble.

THE DEATH IN THE JUNIPER GROVE. *Written and directed by Le Wilhelm. Produced by Race Against Time in association with Love Creek Productions. 59E59. Opened August 19, 2006. Closed September 3, 2006.* Three friends return to the spot where a fourth friend disappeared thirty years earlier.

80S GIRL. *Written by Rachel Langley. Manhattan Theatre Source. Opened August 20, 2006. Closed August 21, 2006.* A solo show that revisits the pop culture glory days of the 1980s.

MR. DOOLEY'S AMERICA. *Written by Philip Dunne and Martin Blaine. Directed by Charlotte Moore. Irish Repertory Theatre. Opened August 20, 2006. Closed September 10, 2006.* A play about (and inspired by the writings of) Peter Finley Dunne, a turn-of-the-century newspaper columnist who wrote under the name Mr. Dooley.

TALL TALES OF THE LITTLE BLACK BOOK. *Written by Christopher Warre Smet. Directed by Jessica Dermody, Ari Kreith, Amy Neswald, and Steve Witting. Produced by Working Artists Theatre Project. Michael Weller Theatre. Opened August 20, 2006. Closed August 21, 2006.* A play that explores the stories of eight New Yorkers as they struggle to make a connection that will last a lifetime...or at least until tomorrow morning.

ANTICHRIST LAMENT. *Written and directed by Marcus Dargan. Produced by New Afrikan Theatre. Manhattan Theatre Source. Opened August 22, 2006. Closed September 9, 2006.* The story of a contemporary African American poet who is inadvertently arrested for conspiring to commit terrorist acts due to his connections with a radical reparations organization.

THE JACKIE SIMON SHOW. *Written by Sean Devney and Jerrod Bogard. Directed by Kristin Skye Hoffmann. Producers Club. Opened August 22, 2006. Closed August 24, 2006.* A satire of daytime television talk show culture that takes place at a live television studio taping.

FIRST DARK DRAMA. *Created by Daniel Givens and Baraka de Soleil. Produced by Ontological Theatre. Ontological Theatre. Opened August 23, 2006. Closed August 26, 2006.* An interdisciplinary theatre piece about a dystopic urban world where death is ever-present, yet survival is a must.

LOVE IS GOOD. *Written by Josh Drimmer. Directed by Erin Smiley. Producers Club. Opened August 23, 2006. Closed August 27, 2006.* A rock band with a robot drummer struggles with the price of fame.

THREE WAYS. *Written and directed by Matthew Barton. Produced by Alamo Theater. Altered Stages. Opened August 24, 2006. Closed September 2, 2006.* A comedic look at three people's distinct views of the same incident.

A ROCK AMIDST THE RUIN. *Written by Mark and Michelle Bruner. Directed by Mark Todd Bruner. Produced by Narrow Journey Productions. Michael Weller Theatre. Opened August 30, 2006. Closed September 3, 2006.* A play that examines five different lives in the aftermath of 9/11.

HURT SO GOOD. *Written by Johnny Blaze Leavitt. Directed by Johnny Blaze Leavitt and Suse Sternkopf. Produced by Point of You Productions. Medicine Show. Opened August 31, 2006. Closed September 16, 2006.* A romantic dramedy about the journey of one man exploring the world of BDSM (bondage/domination/sadism/masochism).

ABOUT THE EDITOR

MARTIN DENTON is the founder and executive director of The New York Theatre Experience, Inc., and the founder, editor, and chief reviewer for the popular Internet website nytheatre.com. He has edited all seven previous volumes of the *Plays and Playwrights* anthologies, which have featured the works of more than eight dozen emerging indie playwrights, as well as *Playing with Canons: Explosive New Works from Great Literature by America's Indie Playwrights*. Denton is also the creator of the *nytheatrecast*, New York's first regularly scheduled theatre podcast offering original content.

ABOUT THE PUBLISHER

THE NEW YORK THEATRE EXPERIENCE, INC. (NYTE), is a nonprofit corporation that uses new and traditional media to provide advocacy and support to the New York theatre community. In addition to its publishing program, NYTE operates the free website nytheatre.com and produces the weekly *nytheatrecast* programs. To learn more about NYTE's programs and about how you can support this organization, visit its website at www.nyte.org.

PLAYS AND PLAYWRIGHTS 2001
Edited by Martin Denton, Preface by Robert Simonson

ISBN 09670234-2-4   Retail $15.00

Washington Square Dreams by Gorilla Repertory Theatre
Fate by Elizabeth Horsburgh
Velvet Ropes by Joshua Scher
The Language of Kisses by Edmund De Santis
Word To Your Mama by Julia Lee Barclay
Cuban Operator Please... by Adrian Rodriguez
The Elephant Man —The Musical by Jeff Hylton & Tim Werenko
House of Trash by Trav S.D.
Straight-Jacket by Richard Day

PLAYS AND PLAYWRIGHTS 2002
Edited by Martin Denton, Foreword by Bill C. Davis

ISBN 09670234-3-2   Retail $15.00

The Death of King Arthur by Matthew Freeman
Match by Marc Chun
Woman Killer by Chiori Miyagawa
The Wild Ass's Skin by J. Scott Reynolds
Halo by Ken Urban
Shyness Is Nice by Marc Spitz
Reality by Curtiss I' Cook
The Resurrectionist by Kate Chell
Bunny's Last Night In Limbo by Peter S. Petralia
Summerland by Brian Thorstenson

PLAYS AND PLAYWRIGHTS 2003
Edited by Martin Denton, Foreword by Mario Fratti

ISBN 09670234-4-0   Retail $15.00

A Queer Carol by Joe Godfrey
Pumpkins For Smallpox by Catherine Gillet
Looking For The Pony by Andrea Lepcio
Black Thang by Ato Essandoh
The Ninth Circle by Edward Musto
The Doctor of Rome by Nat Colley
Galaxy Video by Marc Morales
The Last Carburetor by Leon Chase
Out To Lunch by Joseph Langham
Ascending Bodily by Maggie Cino
Last Call by Kelly McAllister

PLAYS AND PLAYWRIGHTS 2004
Edited by Martin Denton, Foreword by Kirk Wood Bromley

ISBN 09670234-5-9   Retail $16.00

Sugarbaby by Frank Cwiklik
WTC View by Brian Sloan
United States: Work and Progress by Christy Meyer, Jon Schumacher and Ellen Shanman
The Shady Maids of Haiti by John Jahnke
Cats Can See The Devil by Tom X. Chao
Survivor: Vietnam! by Rob Reese
Feed the Hole by Michael Stock
Auntie Mayhem by David Pumo
The Monster Tales by Mary Jett Parsley
Sun, Stand Thou Still by Steven Gridley

PLAYS AND PLAYWRIGHTS 2005
Edited by Martin Denton, Foreword by Steven Drukman

ISBN 09670234-6-7   Retail $16.00

Vampire Cowboy Trilogy by Qui Nguyen & Robert Ross Parker
second. by Neal Utterback
Bull Spears by Josh Chambers
Animal by Kevin Augustine
Odysseus Died from AIDS by Stephen Svoboda
Maggie May by Tom O'Brien
Elephant by Margie Stokley
Walking to America by Alberto Bonilla
The 29 Questions Project by Katie Bull & Hillary Rollins
Honor by TheDrillingCompaNY
Kalighat by Paul Knox
Platonov! Platonov! Platonov! or the case of a very Angry Duck by Eric Michael Kochmer

PLAYS AND PLAYWRIGHTS 2006
Edited by Martin Denton; Foreword by Trav S.D.

ISBN 09670234-7-5   Retail $17.00

The Top Ten People of the Millennium Sing Their Favorite Schubert Lieder by Alec Duffy
Burning the Old Man by Kelly McAllister
Self at Hand by Jack Hanley
The Expense of Spirit by Josh Fox
Paradise by Glyn O'Malley
Yit, Ngay (One, Two) by Michael Lew
Pulling the Lever by Rising Circle Theater Collective
The Position by Kevin Doyle
The Dirty Talk by Michael Puzzo
The First Time Out of Bounds by P. Seth Bauer
Aurolac Blues by Saviana Stanescu
The Whore of Sheridan Square by Michael Baron

Also from The New York Theatre Experience, Inc.:

PLAYING WITH CANONS: Explosive New Works from Great
Literature by America's Indie Playwrights
Edited by Martin Denton

ISBN 978-0-9670234-8-9   Retail $26.00

Want's Unwisht Work by Kirk Wood Bromley
La Tempestad by Larry Loebell
Titus X by Shawn Northrip
Genesis by Matthew Freeman
The Eumenides by David Johnston
Principia by Michael Maiello & Andrew Recinos
Uncle Jack by Jeff Cohen
Story of an Unknown Man by Anthony P. Pennino
The Brothers Karamazov Parts I and II by Alexander Harrington
Bel Canto by Reneé Flemings
Salem by Alex Roe
Bartleby the Scrivener by R. L. Lane
Frankenstein by Rob Reese
Northanger Abbey by Lynn Marie Macy
The Man Who Laughs by Kiran Rikhye
Bald Diva!: The Ionesco Parody Your Mother Warned You About by David Koteles
Fatboy by John Clancy
The Persians…a comedy about war with five songs by Waterwell

Additional information about the *Plays and Playwrights* series (ISSN
1546-1319) can be found at www.nyte.org/pep.htm.

Plays and Playwrights books are available in bookstores and online, or from
the publisher:

The New York Theatre Experience, Inc.
P.O. Box 1606, Murray Hill Station
New York, NY 10156